ALSO BY PETER G. BOURNE

Fidel: A Biography of Fidel Castro

Men, Stress, and Viet Nam

JIMMY CARTER

A Comprehensive Biography
from Plains to Postpresidency

PETER G. BOURNE

A LISA DREW BOOK

SCRIBNER

A LISA DREW BOOK/SCRIBNER
1230 Avenue of the Americas
New York, NY 10020

Copyright © 1997 by Peter G. Bourne

SCRIBNER and design are trademarks of Simon & Schuster Inc.

A LISA DREW BOOK is a trademark of Simon & Schuster Inc.

Set in Bitstream Transitional 511

DESIGNED BY ERICH HOBBING

Manufactured in the United States of America

1   3   5   7   9   10   8   6   4   2

Library of Congress Cataloging-in-Publication Data
Bourne, Peter G., date.
Jimmy Carter: a comprehensive biography from Plains to postpresidency / Peter G. Bourne.
p.   cm.
Includes bibliographical references (p.   ) and index.
1. Carter, Jimmy, 1924–   . 2. Presidents—United States—Biography. I. Title.
E873.B68   1997
973.926'092—dc21
[B]   96-48593
CIP

ISBN 0-684-19543-7

For Mary
who shared the joy
and the anguish

ACKNOWLEDGMENTS

I want to thank the numerous people who gave freely of their time and talents to make the writing of this book possible. I am deeply indebted to President and Mrs. Carter for the many hours of formal interviews and informal discussion they accorded me and for encouraging their friends and family members to collaborate with me. I want to thank Professor Kai Erickson, editor of the *Yale Review,* who strongly urged me to write about President Carter and published my initial article on this subject. I am grateful to the staff of the Carter Presidential Library, and in particular to Martin Elzy, James Yancey, and David Stanhope for their sustained interest and assistance in this undertaking for more than four years. Dr. Steve Hochman of President Carter's staff reviewed the manuscript making innumerable suggestions and corrections, shared his insights as a historian, and facilitated my work with the Carter Presidential Center. I also thank Dr. Robert Pastor for his review of the manuscript and helpful suggestions. I thank the staff of the Robert W. Woodruff Library of Emory University, and especially Linda Matthews, head of the special collections division. Thanks also to Bruce Martin of the Library of Congress, who has now provided me with invaluable help through two major book projects and has helped to make his institution feel like a second home to me. I am also grateful for the help I received at the Georgia State Archives.

I owe a lasting debt to my friend Charles Morgan, Jr., who over the years has helped me to understand the great tides and nuances of southern politics. His special insights contributed significantly to shaping my own perspectives. Ken Dean and Dr. James Dunn helped to educate me about the Baptist faith and its underpinning of the American ethos. I am grateful to Ken Thomas for sharing with me his extensive research and knowledge of the Carter family genealogy.

I am indebted to Ellen Metsky for her energetic research on the 1976 campaign and to Sara Seanor for her work on that portion of the manuscript. Caroline Wellons transcribed many hours of interviews and provided generously from her own wealth of experience in the Carter presidential race. I want to thank my friends Jack Nelson and Terry Adamson for reviewing portions of the manuscript and providing sage advice based on their intimate understanding of the South and its politics, and their own involvement with much of this story. I am grateful to Milton and Judith Viorst for allowing me to benefit from their seasoned literary experience and for their moral support. The generous hospitality of my stepmother Nelly, Golarz de Bourne, on my many extended visits to Atlanta, made this possible.

No one could have done more to sharpen the focus, remove the digressions, and improve the readability of my manuscript than my superb editor, Lisa Drew. Her knowledge of and interest in the subject as well as her painstaking labor in turning my sometimes protracted prose into clear, plainspoken English made this a vastly better product. I also wish to thank her assistant, Marysue Rucci, whose diligence and interest were vital to keeping me on schedule.

Finally, I would like to thank my agent, Gerry McCauley, whose sympathy and encouragement have sustained me in good times and bad.

JIMMY
CARTER

PREFACE

I was in college in Atlanta in the late 1950s when the civil rights movement began to unfold. I was one of a handful of whites who, together with African-American students from the Morehouse and Spelman colleges, picketed against segregated lunch counters at the downtown Rich's department store while robed Klansmen paraded menacingly across the street. The wall of resistance against integration seemed at the time impenetrable. There were occasional small victories, as when we brought the leaders of the integration movement, including Marion Wright and Julian Bond, to the all-white Emory campus and persuaded the theology school to provide a room for an unprecedented integrated meeting. What little gains were won in Atlanta, however, paled to insignificance in the face of the racist rhetoric and unyielding opposition to integration that characterized the political leadership elsewhere in the state. The racial divide, which was the defining issue in my life, seemed a yawning, unbridgeable chasm.

I followed the case of a young candidate, Jimmy Carter, who was vehemently contesting his defeat in a race for the state senate. His remarkable action suggested that he was not the usual brand of Georgia politician. I dismissed him—given his origins, he was probably a knee-jerk segregationist—despite his apparent idealism. In 1963 I left Georgia to serve in the army and to complete my medical training on the West Coast.

Military service did not suppress my activism. I served with the Special Forces on the Cambodia/Viet Nam boundary and watched B-52s carry out regular saturation bombing raids over the border while President Lyndon Johnson assured Americans that Cambodian territory was not being violated. I knew that he was either deliberately lying to the country or the Pentagon was deceiving him. In 1968 I was among the "Viet Nam Veterans for McCarthy" demonstrators who were set upon by the Chicago's billy club–swinging police during the Democratic Convention. The following year I returned to Atlanta on the faculty of Emory Medical School, but primarily motivated to get reinvolved in the civil rights struggle and politics in the state.

Jimmy Carter was gearing up to run for governor again after having lost the race in 1966. Shortly after my return, I was invited to a lunch with him.

I was told he had no chance of winning but that I would find him "truly fascinating." He was much more than that. He was the stunning antithesis of what I had expected. He condemned segregation on moral grounds and spoke movingly of the suffering of those who had no access to health care or adequate education and the hypocrisy of a judicial system that provides one law for the rich and another for the poor. Here was someone I hadn't thought could exist in Georgia politics—a man able to maintain a credible base with rural whites who shared my views on race and on a whole host of social issues affecting the poor. I did not agree with him on everything, but his sincerity and honesty shone through so that I, like many other young professionals, was deeply attracted to him. He seemed to offer a vindication for years invested in the integration struggle. Here was a goodness and decency that I had given up hope of finding.

During the gubernatorial campaign I wrote some unmemorable papers for the candidate on health policy and contributed a modest amount of money. After he was elected, Rosalynn decided to make mental health her primary focus and she sought my advice, for I had set up the first and, at the time, only federally funded mental health center in the state. Over the next several months I got to know the Carters well.

Earlier in my career I had worked with drug abusers at the Haight Ashbury free medical clinic in San Francisco and in Atlanta I ran a treatment program for heroin addicts as part of my mental health center. Drug dependence became a significant concern for Carter, and he asked me to take a leave of absence from the medical school to work in the governor's office setting up a statewide treatment program. As I did this, I became involved in Carter's broader health and human service reforms and, as this book describes, in his burgeoning political career. During the presidential race I ran the campaign's Washington office and coordinated primary races in the mid-Atlantic states. My wife, Mary King, ran the Committee of 51.3 Percent, which targeted the women's vote.

As I got to know Carter better, I realized he was unlike anyone I'd ever met. He was, in many ways, a man of extremes. He was tenacious, disciplined, physically and psychologically strong; committed to self-improvement, to living up to his religious beliefs, to not wasting a moment of his life; and more driven than anyone I had ever known to make the world a better place. As early as 1976, I decided to write a combination biography and campaign book to try to explain this unusual man and how he had made it to the White House. I had gathered a great deal of material, but couldn't begin writing because I accepted a job on Carter's staff: special assistant to the President for health issues and director of international human needs, world hunger, international health, population, and literacy programs. I helped Rosalynn Carter establish her Presidential Commission on Mental Health. My work issues, which Carter holds dear to this day, consumed all of my time and I didn't finish the book. I knew, however, that it was a project to which I would someday return. It took me sixteen years to do so.

Eventually, I left the White House in the face of a media feeding frenzy over what proved a thoroughly legal prescription I had written for one of my staff. I became an assistant secretary general at the United Nations but continued my close relationship with the Carters for the remainder of their time in the White House and after they returned to Plains.

During the early 1990s, as Carter's stock began to soar and interest in him grew, I decided to return to my deferred work. I had, I felt, gained a unique perspective over the twenty-five years of close association with my subject and a great deal of information to which others did not have access. I also believed that while Carter has been appropriately lauded for his work as a former president, his role in the White House has been unfairly denigrated. He was President during a time of remarkable change and turmoil, receiving little credit for managing those difficult times and for healing the nation after a period of profound trauma.

Through extensive interviews and reading, I sought to fill the gaps in my own knowledge. I make no apologies for the affection and admiration I have for Jimmy Carter. At the same time I have sought to exercise as much detachment and objectivity as I could muster. In so doing, I have tried to produce a sympathetic yet accurate portrait of one of the most inspiring figures of our time.

Peter G. Bourne
Washington, D.C.
December 1996

CHAPTER 1

The heritage of the past is the seed that brings forth the harvest
of the future.

—Inscription on the National Archives Building

The Carter family can be traced back to 1360 in the English town of King's
Langley. Thomas Carter, the son of a London wine merchant, emigrated to
Virginia in 1635, where three generations of Carters farmed in Isle of
Wight County. Early in the eighteenth century, as the land in Virginia
became farmed out, Thomas's grandson, Moore Carter, his wife, Jane, and
their children moved south to Bertie County, North Carolina. Moore's son
Isaac, and grandson, Kindred, farmed there until 1780, when a severe
drought prompted another move. Joining a major southward migration,
Kindred crossed the border into Georgia and settled near the town of
Augusta. There on 307 acres of land ceded from the Cherokees, he raised,
with the aid of ten slaves, cotton, wheat, and livestock.

Strongly independent, the farmers who migrated south mostly rejected the
established church to become Baptists and Quakers. Shortly after his arrival,
Kindred joined the Kiokee Creek Church, the first Baptist congregation in Georgia. He and his descendents would remain staunch Baptists.

The development of the cotton gin in nearby Savannah in 1793 made the
cultivation of short-staple cotton across the South highly profitable. Land
was suddenly at a premium and in Southwest Georgia after the Creek Indians were forcibly expelled it was allocated to eager settlers in a series of lotteries beginning in 1820. Kindred's son James and grandson Wiley became
beneficiaries, acquiring land in several locations. In the fifth land lottery, in
1827, Wiley obtained substantial acreage in newly established Sumter
County. Like most cotton farmers in Southwest Georgia, Wiley Carter had
become a wealthy man by the time he died in 1864.

The Civil War, however, destroyed the wealth of the region, returning
much of the South, including Sumter County, to a frontier existence. Once
productive farmland was neglected and overgrown. There was little civil
authority and widespread lawlessness; violence was always near the sur-

9

face. Confederate soldiers bearing the physical and mental scars of war came back to a poverty-stricken society and had difficulty earning an income or adjusting to civilian life.

Slaves, whose labors had underpinned the immense profitability of cotton cultivation, were suddenly nominally free, eliminating overnight the major capital asset of the region. Few of the newly impoverished landowners could afford to employ the former slaves and the system of sharecropping emerged in which blacks independently farmed white-owned land, sharing the profits with the landowner at harvest time. Others worked as day laborers wherever they could.

In Southwest Georgia, unlike other parts of the South, there were no great antebellum mansions or vast plantations presided over by families of wealth, education, and cultured background. Instead it was a giant patchwork of parcels of land owned in many instances by absentee landlords. The role of slaves in Southwest Georgia was as field hands. There was no separate class of slaves who served exclusively as household servants as there was elsewhere. They were almost universally illiterate, and because of the greater physical divide between white and black there compared to the great plantations elsewhere in the South, there was a much smaller infusion of white blood into the slave population. As a result, the Civil War caused much less disruption to the simple social structure in Southwest Georgia than it did elsewhere, leaving the relationship between blacks and whites little altered from the way it was under slavery. Nevertheless, economic hardship and the return of Confederate soldiers caused considerable upheaval in the white community.

It was into this cauldron of sometimes violent turmoil in Sumter County that Wiley's three sons had returned after the Civil War. One of them, Littleberry, became involved in various business enterprises. In 1874, at age 42, he was fatally stabbed in a fight. According to one version, it was the result of a conflict with a business partner over a "flying jenny" merry-go-round they owned and operated. Family sources, however, suggest that he was knifed in a drunken brawl over a gambling device at a carnival secretly operated by a foot pedal. A murder indictment was issued against D. P. McCann, who fled to South America. Littleberry's wife, Diligence, was said to have died the following day from shock and grief. Littleberry and his wife left behind four children. One was a sixteen-year-old boy, William Archibald, who was known as Billy. He became a farmer, but like many of his contemporaries, he pursued other entrepreneurial businesses off the farm.

In 1885 Billy married Nina Pratt, of Abbeville, South Carolina, who came from a somewhat genteel family, but one of modest means. Nina was very pretty with dark hair and gray eyes. She dressed neatly and it was said that anything she put on looked good on her. She was only five foot five, but "carried herself well" and asserted herself strongly by the force of her personality. Soon after their marriage they moved to Arlington, a small community established in 1873 on the border of Calhoun and Early Counties. Billy set up three sawmills, a cotton gin, and a general store. The cotton gin and one of the sawmills was in the tiny community of Rowena, 3 miles from Arlington. While Billy prospered as a businessman and farmer, Nina began to suffer repeated bouts of malaria in the low-lying swampy environment of Early County. In 1900, attempting to escape the debilitating infection, the family moved north to Cuthbert in the drier land of Randolf County. Billy would stay in Rowena during the week and commute 50 miles home by train on the weekends.

The general store that Billy ran was primarily a commissary for his employees, but after several years he decided to stop running it himself, and rented it to a man named Will Talafero. As time passed, Billy began to hear that while he was away on weekends the store was being used for gambling and drinking liquor. Billy, a strict Baptist, was furious and told Talafero to move out. He did, and built a store of his own, but took along with him a desk made out of a thread case that belonged to Billy. After considerable deliberation, on September 3, 1903, Billy sent his fifteen-year-old son, Alton, to tell Talafero that he wanted the desk back immediately because he needed to work on it in the cotton gin office. Although protesting that he had paid for it, Talafero let Alton take the desk back to the cotton gin.

Considerable tension remained in the air. In the little community Billy and Alton were living in a house between the cotton gin and Talafero's new store. About 7 P.M. on a hot sultry evening after they left the gin, the two of them were sitting on the porch talking about the desk when Billy decided to walk over to see Talafero in the hope that he could defuse the situation. They began a conversation through the window of the store, but started arguing. Billy entered the building and a violent fist and bottle fight ensued; it was later reported that a bloody handprint remained on the wall. Eventually Billy left, but Talafero pursued him out of the store with a .32-caliber Smith and Wesson in his hand. Talafero shot three times and one of the bullets hit Billy behind the ear. Billy was found to have a small, twenty-five-cent Barlow knife in his hand. Whether he had threatened Talafero with it, or even used it on him, is unclear.

Nina hired a man with a horse and buggy to drive her the 30 miles from Cuthbert, arriving in the middle of the night. Billy was then taken by the first train back to Cuthbert, but he died at home the next day. Talafero was tried three times for murder. There were two mistrials, and on the third occasion he was acquitted.

Besides fifteen-year-old Alton, Billy left Ethel, 16, Lula, 12, and James Earl, 9. In addition, Nina was pregnant, and would give birth to another daughter, Jeannette, the following year. There was a man in Cuthbert who wanted to marry Nina, but she turned him down because she did not want her children to have a stepfather. Her own mother died when she was eighteen months old, and her grandmother, in her sixties, had raised her. Her father remarried twice, and she was not close to either of her stepmothers. Nina made the decision instead to move the family to Plains, largely to be near her dead husband's brother, Calvin Jeremiah, who lived in the New Era Community in the nearby county seat of Americus. The move was accomplished with his help. He sold the farm, the gin, and the sawmills for her, raising sufficient funds for them to buy a house in the town of Plains behind the Methodist church, and 1,300 acres of farmland a few miles away in Webster County.

Calvin Jeremiah became like a second father to the family. Nina knew nothing about business and, according to Alton, had it not been for his advice and guidance, they would have "ended up on welfare." Calvin Jeremiah hired an overseer to farm the land. He insisted that the two boys go to school five days a week, and then on the weekends, first with Alton and later with James Earl, he taught them how to manage and farm the property. He had a reputation as an innovator, a risk taker, and particularly as a doer. Perhaps already shaped by the influence of his own father, Alton would grow up to be relatively conservative in business. James Earl, who had been much younger at the time of his father's death, identified closely with Calvin Jeremiah and, adopting his entrepreneurial spirit, had a broader vision, a greater eye for innovation, and a willingness to take a chance on something different.

Plains had changed dramatically since the first settlers had arrived there. In 1884, a 37-mile narrow-gauge railroad was established, connecting Americus and the tiny communities of Preston and Lumpkin. Plains was moved a mile south of its original location to take advantage of the railroad, and it became the central feature of the town with the small business district strung along a hundred yards of main street adjacent to the depot and parallel to the tracks. In the heat of summer, red dust swirled around the town, coating the buildings, and in the winter rains it turned to cloying mud along the main street. There was a general store, a drugstore, the Plains Bank, a barbershop run by the brothers Broadus and Otis Wellons, and the Timmerman and Wise Warehouse that handled seed, fertilizers, cotton, and bricks. One store that had been operated by a long-departed Jewish family was still referred to as the "Jew store." The Lebanon Baptist Church moved, becoming the all-white Plains Baptist Church; their former building became a Baptist church for the blacks living in the area. Methodists and Lutherans had also established themselves in the town. When it was formally incorporated on December 17, 1896, its bylaws contained, for the first time in Georgia, a clause to prohibit the sale of intoxicating drinks. The first well pump providing a public water supply was established on the main street in 1905.

Despite Jeremiah Calvin's admonition, Alton stayed in school for only one more year after the move to Plains, leaving at the end of the eighth grade to work as a clerk at the Oliver McDonald Company, the largest merchant in town. His starting salary was $25 a month. After four years he had sufficiently impressed the local business leaders that they were willing to finance him in setting up his own store—Plains Mercantile Company. With the guidance of his uncle, he quickly assumed the role of head of the family, and felt a serious obligation to earn money to support his mother and siblings. He would remain the patriarch of the Carter clan in Plains until his death in 1978.

Encouraged and financed by Alton, James Earl went away to attend the ninth and tenth grades at the Riverside Academy in Gainesville, north of Atlanta. When he returned to Plains he went to work for Alton at the Plains Mercantile Company, and from the start, he aspired to have a store of his own. He was reluctant to enlist in World War I because he was in love with a young woman. However, he was selected in the draft lottery and went on active duty on October 1, 1917. He completed his training, but the armistice occurred and he was discharged on November 30, 1918, as a second lieutenant in the Officer Reserve Corps. Although he had remained in the United States, he was eligible to wear the World War I Victory Medal and Victory Button, a source of pride and prestige in the military-conscious South, when he returned to Plains.

When James Earl, or Mr. Earl as he became known, returned to civilian life, he worked briefly for Alton, but was quickly able to open an icehouse as the agent of the Atlantic Ice and Coal Company, and a "pressing club," a dry-cleaning operation in which he oversaw the work of a single black employee. He opened his own grocery business, and soon was sufficiently established to raise $7,000 in credit, which he used to purchase a farm.

When Earl was twenty-five, a young woman, Lillian Gordy, came to Plains to train as a nurse at the local hospital run by the Wise brothers. The Gordys came from Richland, 18 miles away in Stewart County. The family history of the Gordys was similar to that of the Carters, and of many other settlers in Southwest Georgia, emigrating to America from England or Scotland in the seventeenth century. Around 1800, Peter Gordy moved his family from Maryland to Hancock County, Georgia. His son, Wilson, obtained land, as did the Carters, as a result of the land lotteries in the 1820s. Among their ten children was James Thomas Gordy, a farmer and Baptist like his father, but also a tax collector. During the Civil War in 1864 he enlisted as a private in Company B, 6th Georgia State Militia. He survived his brief period of service and lived to the age of 62. He and his wife, Harriet Emily, had nine children.

This new generation of Gordys, many of whom lived into the twentieth century, reflected an increasing trend in which education became the route to escape the poverty and frequent despair of the post–Civil War South. Two brothers trained as doctors, and one of them was elected a state legislator.

A third brother, James Jackson, to be known as "Jim Jack," became a life-long activist in local and state politics. At a young age he was engaged, but he stood up his fiancée at the altar and fled to Texas, where he stayed for two years. He returned more worldly and aware of the varied opportunities that existed away from the parochial life of Southwest Georgia. He married sixteen-year-old Mary Ida Nicholson, whose family would later produce a U.S. senator, Sam Nunn. He worked as a schoolteacher and part-time farmer, but eventually, through his political connections, he was appointed by Woodrow Wilson to be the postmaster in Richland, a position he held through four administrations.

Jim Jack's life centered around politics. He became known as the lead-ing political expert in Webster and Stewart Counties. While he never ran for elective office, he was a friend or acquaintance of many who did. By far his most important relationship, however, was with Tom Watson, the charismatic and controversial populist whose statue stands today in front of the Georgia State Capitol.

Thomas Edward Watson was born near Thomson, Georgia, in McDuffie County in 1856. He spent his childhood in relative comfort until the Civil War drove his family into poverty. He struggled to find the money to get an education, becoming a lawyer and establishing a successful law practice. He had a strong interest in politics and in 1882 he was elected to represent McDuffie County in the Georgia House of Representatives. He immedi-ately demonstrated a special sympathy for the state's impoverished farmers and the plight of convicts, and in 1890 the Tenth Congressional District elected him to Congress.

In Washington, Watson continued to push the Alliance agenda and his own concern for poor farmers. He introduced legislation for an income tax, free coinage of silver, and the abolition of national banks of issue, all of which he failed to get enacted. He did manage, however, to win passage of an experimental program for the rural free delivery of mail; he considered himself the father of RFD. It was, however, a concept first suggested to him by Jim Jack Gordy.

Watson attributed the defeat of most of his legislative initiatives to what he perceived to be the reactionary nature of the Democratic Party, con-trolled by the Bourbons,* standing in the way of needed reform. Toward

---

*The post-Reconstruction Democrats in the South were referred to by their detractors as Bourbons, because like the French royal family, they appeared to have learned nothing and forgotten nothing from the Revolution.

the end of 1891 he astonished Georgians by joining the newly formed Populist Party. He also founded an Atlanta weekly called the *People's Party Paper* through which he promoted his populist beliefs. His continuing sympathy was with the poor farmer, black or white, and he argued that there should be a free ballot for all citizens. Although he never advocated social integration or promised offices to black supporters, his enemies accused him of being a traitor to the white race. The Bourbon Democrats perceived the Populist movement as a profound threat to their monopoly on power across the South, and used appeals for white supremacy combined with ballot stuffing to turn back the rising Populist tide. Tom Watson was narrowly defeated for reelection in 1892 in a patently fraudulent election. Late in the campaign he had saved a black Populist from a lynch mob, and as word spread throughout the state, he became a kind of messiah for many blacks. He ran once more in 1894 and again lost a rigged election.

By now Watson was a national figure and in 1896 the Populist Party nominated him for vice president, running on a ticket with Democrat William Jennings Bryan. Watson would accept the party's presidential nomination in 1904 and 1908, but ran only token campaigns. Increasingly he withdrew into writing and publishing. He purchased Hickory Hill, a mansion near his childhood home in Thomson, leading to his sobriquet, "the Sage of Hickory Hill." He considered himself an ideological disciple of Thomas Jefferson, and like Jefferson, Watson embraced the virtues of agrarian life, the yeoman farmer, and an abiding faith in democracy. He also shared his reservations about banks, tariffs, and cities.

Around the turn of the century, Watson, who had always been the victim of depressions, morbid fears, and uncontrollable outbursts of rage, began to exhibit increasingly bigoted and paranoid behavior. It was said that he felt blacks had shown insufficient gratitude for his efforts to enfranchise them, and he turned on them. Others feel it may have been merely the reaction of a frustrated and bitter man. He campaigned venomously against both blacks and Catholics. His seeming reversal did nothing to diminish his political popularity among white Georgians, and he was increasingly seen as the political kingmaker without whose support a candidate could not be elected. Jim Jack Gordy remained loyal to Watson and in 1906 named his new son after him.

In 1913, Leo Frank, a Jewish Atlanta storekeeper, was accused of the rape and murder of a thirteen-year-old gentile girl, Mary Phagen. Frank was almost certainly innocent, but Watson's lurid denunciation of the "Jew pervert" in speeches, and in his publications *Watson's Magazine* and *Watson's Jeffersonian Weekly*, inflamed the emotions of the populace. In 1915, Frank was lynched and, in the anguished aftermath, Watson's intemperate rhetoric was used as an explanation to exonerate those who were actually involved in the horrendous act.

After the Frank episode, Jim Jack, who was already disillusioned by his friend's turn against blacks, seems to have distanced himself from Watson, although he did take young Tom Watson Gordy at age 6 to meet him at the State Capitol in Atlanta. Several years later they also made a trip to Washington, where Watson took father and son to visit the White House. In 1917, Watson, adamantly opposing U.S. involvement in World War I, ran unsuccessfully for Congress (as a Democrat). In 1920, he ran for the U.S. Senate, opposing American membership in the League of Nations and the policies of Woodrow Wilson, whom the Democratic hierarchy of the state supported. In the Senate he called for recognition of the Soviet Union, and was a staunch foe of the Red Scare, imperialism, militarism, and child labor. He was a fervent defender of freedom of speech. He died on September 26, 1922, in Chevy Chase, Maryland.

Watson reflected the complexity of political beliefs and social change at work in Georgia at the end of the nineteenth century; through his forceful personality and the vehemence of his positions, he exerted a powerful influence directly and indirectly on the thinking of subsequent generations of politicians in the state. The Bourbons, with their effort to promote economic growth and industrialization by concentrating power in the hands of the white elite, excluding the poor of both races, inevitably created a situation favoring the interests of the haves at the expense of the have-nots. The situation was ripe for a populist leader like Watson to emerge. The Bourbons were strong enough to prevent the Populists from ousting them from power, but were severely weakened in the process. The resulting vacuum was filled by the New South Progressives, who sought to blend a social concern for the rural poor with the maintenance of power in the hands of a business-oriented white elite. They would dominate southern politics for the first half of the twentieth century.

Jim Jack was a tall, dashingly handsome man with a large mustache and a penchant for bow ties. His preoccupation with politics, generally viewed in this deeply religious region as sordid, reflected a willingness to be unconventional, if not controversial. He was by all accounts a good father in a happy home presided over by Mary Ida, a small dainty woman usually clad in a "mother hubbard" with long straight hair that she wore in a bun on the top of her head. She was recalled variously by the children as sweet, warm, kind, generous, and "always pregnant." They had nine children: Susie, Annie Lee, James Albert who died as an infant, Bessie Lillian "Lilly," Walter Lemuel, James Jackson, Jr., Tom Watson, Mary Elizabeth, and Emily Frances "Sissy." Mary Ida's sister Sallie married Jim Jack's brother, David Crockett, but she died in her late twenties, leaving two young boys,

Ralph and Rex. Jim Jack and Mary Ida took them in. Mary Ida's mother also lived with them. As a result, there were frequently thirteen at the dinner table. These were hard times for everyone, and no one had extra money. However, 25 cents would buy enough steak to feed the whole family, and they never went hungry.

Jim Jack was, like his forebearers, a mainstream Baptist, while Mary Ida was a more fundamentalist "hard-shell" Baptist. They settled their differences by becoming Methodists. Mary Ida was the more devout of the two, and it was she who led the family prayers every night and taught the children about the Bible. Despite his own limited education, Jim Jack understood its importance, and placed great emphasis on learning in the family. He encouraged the children to learn one new word every day and pushed them to practice the piano regularly. It was also a family in which great value was placed on reading. Jim Jack was a voracious reader and bought as many books as he could afford.

Jim Jack was a freethinker with eclectic views. Despite his Baptist upbringing, he had an interest in the Free Religious Association set up in 1867 to propound a religion of humanity, guided by reason, aimed particularly at those who regarded themselves as too enlightened for the confines of splintered sectarian Christianity. The association fought vehemently in the 1870s for the complete separation of church and state and against an effort by Presbyterians and Episcopalians to amend the U.S. Constitution and have Christianity made the official state religion. Philosophically Jim Jack Gordy was a liberal progressive who passed on those views to his children.

Perhaps influenced by his time away from Southwest Georgia in Texas, and his willingness to accept controversy, Jim Jack's liberalism was especially expressed by an unusually progressive attitude toward blacks. He treated local sharecroppers and farm laborers, if not as equals, at least with a degree of respect that set him apart from most other whites. The children remembered an educated black man named Ben Davis, a Republican National Committee member and publisher of the black weekly *Atlanta Independent,* who would come to visit their father from Atlanta and was received in their home. Jim Jack was also friendly with a black Methodist minister, William D. Johnson, and is said to have used his influence to help him become a bishop. On occasion he and Johnson would sit on their porch having long philosophical conversations and sing hymns together. Lillian said, "That's where I got into my head that blacks were people."

Jim Jack had another characteristic that was unusual for the time. He treated the children, including the girls, with respect as individuals, and strongly encouraged them to take responsibility in making decisions about their own lives. Annie Lee died at age 25 in the Spanish flu pandemic of 1918, and as a result Lilly, who at the time was working for her father for

$66.33 per month in the post office, decided that she wanted to go into nursing.

Lilly had applied to be an army nurse, and was initially accepted on Armistice Day, 1918, but with a decline in the need for nurses, the military stopped training new women. She continued to work at the post office for another two years, still hoping to become a nurse. In 1920 she was accepted at the recently established Wise Clinic in Plains. Despite the isolation of Plains, the three Wise brothers, Burr Thadeus, Sam, and Bowman, had rapidly built an institution with a considerable reputation. Physicians came there for post-graduate training and positions in the nursing program were eagerly sought. Lilly was accepted, in part, because Jim Jack was a friend of Dr. Sam Wise. The training was very strict. There were only twelve beds when Lilly started, but by the time she graduated, a new ninety-bed hospital had been built.

With the encouragement of Dr. Sam Wise, Lilly started dating Earl. Dr. Wise said to her, "I have picked out someone for you who is going to be the most successful man here, and that's Earl Carter." Jim Jack had status in the community because he was the postmaster and his political connections, but money was always tight for him. Dr. Wise, who liked Lilly, clearly saw that Earl Carter could offer her the sort of financial security that her family and most of the other young men could not.

On their first date, they went to the Opera House in Americus to see *The Merchant of Venice*. The tickets cost $5, a stunning sum. They drove over in a Model T Ford without a top and on the way back it rained, soaking them. However, it did not dampen the relationship. Frequently he took her to see his newly acquired farmland, his second love. In 1921, during their courtship, Earl's younger sister Jeanette, then age 17, had run away and secretly married. After the death of their father, the two boys felt responsible for their mother and sisters, and Earl had particularly cared for Jeanette. That she eloped without telling him, he saw as his failure. As a result, he insisted to Lilly, "I want you to finish your training and then we'll get married."

In order to do so, she had to spend six months at Grady Hospital in Atlanta for experience she could not get in Plains. While she was in Atlanta, Earl called every Sunday and twice made the 150-mile trip to visit her. Finally he sent her an engagement ring. They could not afford an elaborate wedding and were married simply at the minister's house on September 23, 1923. It was a joint wedding with J. G. Webb, the widowed husband of Annie Lee, who was also marrying a nurse, Lillian's best friend, Gussie Abrams.

To raise money for their honeymoon, Earl had planted a crop of potatoes, but it had failed, dooming any possibility of an exotic or distant destination. So they spent their wedding night at Nina's house and the following day they moved into modest rooms Earl had rented on the second floor of a building in the center of Plains.

Lillian was eager to get pregnant, in part to avoid night duty at the hospital. She had wanted to get a college degree, but that was now out of the question. She did, however, land the prestigious job of surgical nurse, and became pregnant shortly thereafter. As the pregnancy progressed, she had increasing difficulty negotiating the steep outside stairs to their apartment, so Dr. Sam Wise insisted that they move. They rented rooms on Church Street in the home of Elmer E. Cook, who had acquired the first radio in the community.

Lilly's first child was born a year and eight days after the wedding. The day before, Earl had gone to his farm near Preston in Webster County to attend to a problem with one of the horses. When he returned he found Lilly had gone into labor at 10 P.M. He took her immediately to the Wise Clinic.

CHAPTER 2

Dear is the boyhood spot we ne'er forget.

—Lord Byron

James Earl Carter, Jr.—"Jimmy"—was born at exactly 7 A.M. on October 1, 1924, with Dr. Sam Wise in attendance.* He came home to the Cook house on Church Street, where he would spend the next two years. He was a bright, happy baby who needed no special care. His mother would breast-feed him for his first year.

The day he was born the governor of Georgia gave the keynote address at the annual convention of the Ku Klux Klan.

Plains was a bustling boomtown in the 1920s. The population had risen rapidly to 600, and businesses were thriving. In addition to the new hospital built by the Wises, a bond issue had raised $40,000 for a new school, and a two-story hotel had been opened. There were two banks, two "department stores," and a half-dozen other shops. The cotton gin operated by Luther James Cranford occupied a whole block on the west side of South Hudson Street. Wealthier citizens were building fancy wood-frame houses on Church Street. Six trains a day stopped at the depot.

Earl, stocky at five foot eight and 175 pounds, was energetic and had a constant smile on his bespectacled face. Beneath his outgoing exterior and reputation as an aggressive businessman, he was a shy, almost timid man. He was known for working harder than anyone else and he was always looking for new ways to make money. As Lilly put it, "He planned ahead every day of his life." He always reminded his children that there was a world to be conquered outside Plains, but he never saw it for himself. His own ambitions extended to being the most successful person in Plains.

His store, which sold mostly groceries, was doing well, but his real interest was in the land. A cautious and conservative risk taker, he had bought his first farm on credit, but from then on he operated entirely on a cash basis. He would buy and sell land for many years. Paying no more than $15

*He would become the first American president born in a hospital.

20

per acre for forested land, he would then cut and sell the timber to his friend Ray Sullivan. So reliable was his judgment that he developed the reputation of having everything he touched turn to gold.

Lilly, or Miss Lillian, as she increasingly became known, remained dedicated to nursing and was happy to turn much of her child-rearing responsibilities over to her black help. She also prevailed upon Earl's sister Ethel, and Ethel's son, Willard Slappey. When a second child, Gloria, arrived in 1926, just twenty months after Jimmy, Lillian's fourteen-year-old sister, Sissy, came from Richland to stay with the Carters. She attended the ninth grade at Plains High School and helped to care for the two babies.

Although he had been healthy for the first two years of his life, shortly after his second birthday Jimmy developed "bleeding colitis." He was hospitalized at the Wise sanatorium. He kept crying and saying that he wanted a baby goat. Lillian's sister-in-law, Miss Abrams, who was one of the nurses caring for him, bought a tiny kid and put it in a box at his bedside. Jimmy came home, but remained sick, and neither the local doctors nor a specialist from Macon had anything to offer. Eventually a Dr. Logan from Montezuma suggested to Lillian that she try enemas of saturated cornstarch and he was rapidly cured. It was a technique she subsequently used with great success on the many children she saw who had the same condition.

In the final analysis Earl was always the boss, but Lilly asserted a degree of independence unusual for women at that time. She was often outspoken and did not mind being thought controversial. She also raised eyebrows by showing an undue concern for the health needs of the black population in and around Plains. In small towns in the South a degree of paternalistic compassion toward black families in times of crisis was considered legitimate Christian charity. Lillian, however, took pleasure in pushing this license to its limits.

It was the clear influence of Jim Jack on his daughter that made her unafraid of controversy. "I am more like my father than any of the rest of the children. I like controversial people and my father did too," she would say. Also, it was Lillian and Sissy who most shared his interest in politics, a questionable pursuit looked upon as unsavory, if not immoral, by the more devout members of the community.

With the arrival of the new baby the Carter family needed more space and moved into a house owned by Cora Lunsford on Bond Street. Then after another year they moved to the Ballew or McGarrah house as it is now known. Finally, shortly before Jimmy's fourth birthday in 1928, they moved to Archery, a flagstop community on the Seaboard Railroad line 3 miles west of Plains and close the county line with Webster County where Earl's original farm was situated. Their house, built around 1922, was known as the Plexico Place. There was only one other white family in the community, the Watsons. Ernest Watson was the section foreman for the railroad. He and his wife had two boys and two girls, but except for one of the daughters, they were all several years older than the Carter children. From time to time other white families moved into the general area near Archery, but the Carters had little contact with them.

The simple dwelling was set back a hundred feet from a dirt road that ran from Plains to Preston, parallel to the railroad track. The low clapboard house was painted white with a shingle roof and had a front and back porch. On the front porch there was a swing and at one end a large spirea vine provided shade in the afternoon. At the side of the house was a big mulberry tree. The front and back yards were covered with white sand swept regularly to keep it neat. In the rear, also, was an aromatic "flea tree" that was supposed to keep fleas out of the house. Nearby they pumped their water from a well by hand and beyond the well was a four-holer outdoor privy. The washing was done in a big iron pot outside. An outdoor shower with rainwater trapped in a metal drum was used by Lillian and the girls to wash their hair. Later on, Earl built a makeshift tennis court next to the house, surrounding it with kumquat bushes.

Inside, the walls were painted green and the floors were covered with linoleum, except in the living room, where there was a wool rug. The ceilings were high but made of beaverboard, which sagged in places. The house was airy and cool in summer, but could be bitterly cold in the wintertime. Fireplaces within two double chimneys and a wood-burning stove in the kitchen took off only some of the chill. Jimmy slept on an iron bed in a plain room in the northeast corner of the house. In the living room Earl had a large red chair with an ottoman in which he would take a nap after lunch, and where in the evening he listened to the radio. The children were forbidden to touch the chifforobe in their parents' bedroom where Earl kept his pistol and razor blades in the top drawer. Lillian had a desk where she read and wrote.

In Archery, twenty-five to thirty impoverished black families eked out a living as farmhands or as sharecroppers. Mostly illiterate, they lived with few possessions, in primitive wood-frame shacks without running water. Hunger was a constant companion. Malnutrition and infestation with parasites, especially hookworm, were rampant. Denied access to the white-only school system, the education of black children was rudimentary at best. There was no doctor to serve them anywhere in Webster County, and high infant mortality was an accepted part of life. A few had mules and carts that served as their only means of transportation. Their survival was dependent on the largesse of the white community under circumstances that differed little from the life their ancestors had led under slavery. No black was registered to vote in Webster County (even as late as the 1950s) and they were denied any other influence over the economic and political system that defined their existence.

Intimidation of blacks was considered essential to keep the system in place, and politicians won election by preying on the irrational fears of poorly educated whites, especially exploiting the ultimate fantasy that black men were bent on obtaining sexual access to white women.

In most respects Archery did not differ from hundreds of other poor, majority-black rural communities in the Deep South, except for the presence of Jim Jack Gordy's friend Bishop William D. Johnson of the African Methodist Episcopal (AME) Church, an educated and sophisticated man who traveled regularly and who had administrative responsibility that extended as far away as Texas.

In 1921, when a new school was being built in Plains, the old wooden building was bought for $500 by Bishop Johnson and the AME Church. It was moved to Archery and reassembled adjacent to the church as the Johnson Home Industrial College. It operated over the next fifteen years as a boarding school for adolescent boys with Johnson as the principal. His reputation attracted students from several states outside Georgia.

Earl never engaged in physical labor himself except light tasks such as cutting watermelons. Gloria observed, "Daddy never worked in the fields. He said that one time he worked a half day and that was it. But he oversaw everything that was done—everything." He had a thorough understanding of farming as well as an inventive mind, developing a new design for a single-wing plow that he patented and sold, for a modest sum, to the Rone Plow Company. There were as many as 260 black workers employed on the farm at the peak of its operation. They rose at 4 A.M. to the jarring sound of the farm bell rung by the foreman, Jack Clark. The tenants, Dave Laster, Fred Howard, Johnny Will, Cooper Berry, and others, assembled with those who lived off the land. They gathered at the barn adjacent to the Carter house and by the dawn light each man assigned to a particular plow or wagon would catch his own mule and harness it. Then they took their orders for the day from Mr. Earl. The going rate for labor was a dollar a day, with women getting 75 cents and children 25 cents.

The longstanding dependence of the region on cotton was giving way in the 1920s to peanuts, which have remained the dominant crop of the area. The peanut plant was brought by slaves to the New World where, ironically, they were then forced to cultivate it so their masters could reap handsome profits. Peanuts, which grow underground, were plowed up by the mules, and the vines were shaken and hung to dry around poles set at 10-yard intervals. Sometimes the workers were paid a piece rate of 1 cent per stack for this task. A family could do as many as 300 stacks in a day.

Earl Carter operated a store, or commissary, for his workers that offered considerable convenience, but further bound them to the farm. In buying their bare essentials, almost all their meager earnings went back to their employer. As Jimmy Carter described it, "We sold overalls, work shoes, sugar, salt, flour, meal, coffee, Octagon soap, tobacco and snuff, rat traps, castor oil, lamp wicks, and kerosene. Our own farm products were kept in stock, such as syrup, side meat, lard, cured hams, loops of stuffed sausage, and wool blankets. The store was open on Saturdays during payday and otherwise was unlocked only when a customer came, almost always during mealtimes, for a nickel's worth of snuff or kerosene." (A pair of overalls cost $1 and a pair of shoes $1.50.) Jimmy would later write:

> No rent was charged for the farm houses, and garden patches and free wood to be cut in the forests helped make ends meet. In almost every family someone trapped, hunted, or fished. White corn was milled into meal and grits and wheat into flour. Soap and lard were made on the farm. Most repairs could be made with hay wire, which was everywhere.

Every July 4, Earl had a barbecue for the workers. He would roast three or four pigs and a couple of goats in an open pit, and a vat of brunswick stew would also be made. The meal was served with pickles, corn bread, and Coca-Cola. The black families who worked for him were invited to bring their relatives so there would be as many as 400 at the party. They came on foot and in their mule-drawn wagons. It was one of the few times when they could afford to amply satisfy their appetites. Gloria recalled that some would fix a plate and surreptitiously sidle over to their wagon where they would hide the food to take home, then come back for more.

At the time of the second Joe Louis–Max Schmeling heavyweight title fight, the black field hands gathered under the mulberry tree by the Carters' house. Earl put his radio in the window so that everyone could hear as Louis battered Schmeling and became the first black heavyweight world champion. After the fight the group politely thanked Earl and left. But when they reached a shack a hundred yards beyond the road, a loud jubilant celebration broke out.

In addition to cotton and peanuts they raised sugarcane, sweet potatoes, Irish potatoes, watermelons, velvet beans, and corn in substantial quantities. They had pigs, up to a dozen milking cows, a bull, a few sheep, geese, chickens, guinea fowl, and the mules that were used to plow the fields. There was a dovecote by the house with pigeons. Always looking for ways to squeeze a few extra dollars out of the property, Earl had the sugarcane stalks ground in a mule-drawn roller press to extract the juice, then cooked it in a large iron kettle heated by oak logs until the right syrupy consistency was achieved. The resulting product was bottled and sold in all the local country stores as "Plains Maid Syrup." In later years the process was mechanized with the introduction of a steam-operated mill and cooker.

The farm also produced jars of honey, goose-down pillows and comforters, tomato ketchup, and jams and jellies made from peaches, blackberries, wild cherries, and muscadines. Milk from the cow was separated into butter and cream. Mixed with chocolate powder, it was sold in 5-cent bottles at local stores and filling stations. Wool from the sheep was exchanged for finished blankets. When winter arrived, two or three dozen hogs were slaughtered and processed into cured hams, rendered lard, and pickled pigs' feet. The heads of the pigs were used for making sausages and brunswick stew.

Mr. Earl, fastidious about every dollar, had a rule that everything on the farm had to pay its way. There was, he would say, "Always a reckoning, always a reckoning." It was a lesson that young Jimmy learned well, and in later life he would attribute his fiscal conservatism to the teachings of his father during these depression years.

There was a large pecan grove near the house that Earl assigned to Lillian as her personal prerogative. Each year she would have the workers collect the nuts and sort them by size and quality. She then sold them to a man named Eli Addia and her profit was her spending money for the year.

The family ate well. There was always a good supply of meat and fresh vegetables. After dinner Earl would listen to his battery-operated radio. Glenn Miller was a favorite of the whole family, and Earl enjoyed listening to Walter Winchell, although he was invariably annoyed by him. The radio was an indispensable connection to the outside world, significantly reducing the isolation of earlier generations. Several weeks before Jimmy's twelfth birthday, he listened with his father as Alf Landon was nominated as presidential candidate by the Republican National Convention.

For young Jimmy it was a Huckleberry Finn existence. From April to October he seldom wore shoes or a shirt. He fished for eels and catfish in the Chocktawhatchee and Kinchafoonee Creeks, and, because he was an agile tree climber, he frequently went out with hunters to shake down treed possums and raccoons.

In his early years Jimmy's usual playmates were the children of the black farmhands. His closest friend was "A.D." Davis, also known as "Knock." As young children they were treated equally by the adults of both races and subjected to the same discipline. They also visited each other's homes. However, Miss Lillian differed from other white mothers in allowing A.D. and other black children to eat with Jimmy in their kitchen. As they grew older the intricate minuet of social segregation began to separate them. They continued to hunt and fish together, but when Earl built the tennis court, A.D. was not invited to play. It was school that definitively set them on separate paths.

For several years Jimmy had one close white friend, Rembert Forrest, who lived 5 miles north of Archery. They would ride by horse between their homes and stay with each other for days at a time.

On occasion Jimmy's cousins Hugh Carter and Willard Slappey came to play. They rode horses and swam in pools they created by damming the streams with sand. They regularly searched for Indian arrowheads; ghosts of the evicted Creeks were very much in Jimmy's mind as he grew up.

Jimmy twice broke his arm, and when he was six he was involved in an accident in Plains in which the school bus, driven by Sammy Faircloth, ran over both his feet, breaking several bones. For weeks he could get around only on his hands and knees.

Earl was a man of some contradictions. He was serious, driven, highly self-disciplined, and worked from sunup to sundown. At the same time he was fun loving and always looking for a good time. He enjoyed dancing and frequently took Lillian out at night to Americus or to a dancing pavilion at Magnolia Springs. He enjoyed going to the baseball games in Americus or even Atlanta and played on the local Plains team. When the Ringling, Barnum and Bailey Circus came to Americus each year, he would take the children.

At the time of their marriage Earl was a secretary-treasurer of the Plains Baptist Church and a Sunday school teacher, but he and Lillian had a drink, usually bourbon, every night before supper. Lillian drank Blue Ribbon beer with their friends, but never in front of the children.

A tough, shrewd businessman, Earl did not mind taking advantage of other people's misfortune. Yet at the same time he was remarkably generous when he knew someone was in dire financial straits. His need to feel that he had "won" in every deal tended to mask his generosity. Above all, Earl liked to feel he was in control.

Unlike Lilly, Earl was not a prodigious reader. He did, however, read the paper religiously and had a small library that included a complete set of the works of Victor Hugo, all the Tom Swift books, the *Royal Road to Romance*, all twelve Tarzan books by Edgar Rice Burroughs, and *A History of the World Series*.

Earl wanted to be liked and mostly he was. In general he was a conformist, not wanting to risk upsetting people. He shared the racist views of others in the community, but was tolerant if not supportive of Lillian's views. Ultimately, however, Earl always had the last word. On one occasion he was willing to take a stand and face potential ostracism: "They're going to open the movie on Sunday afternoon now," he told the children. "People are going to say bad things to you, and I don't want it to worry you because every Sunday afternoon we're going to go to the picture show."

From the day Jimmy was born it was clear that Earl wanted to be as successful a father as he was a businessman. He believed that involved teaching his son to be hardworking, disciplined, and respectful of authority. As

Jimmy says, "My father was a very firm but understanding director of my life and habits." From an early age Jimmy was assigned tasks such as sweeping the yard, pumping water, gathering eggs, and cutting and stacking wood in the backyard. As he grew older his father assigned him the same tasks that black children had, carrying buckets of water to the workers in the fields, turning sweet potato and watermelon vines, pruning deformed young watermelons, and carrying slop to the hogs. He spent many hours alongside his father's black field hands picking cotton. On one occasion, his aunt Sissy recalls, Earl was planning to take the family on a picnic, but he had assigned Jimmy the responsibility of pruning watermelons and the job had not been completed. Earl made him stay behind. Feeling sorry for him, Sissy stayed to help him finish.

Earl set an exacting standard for his son, although Carter has said, "One reason I never thought about complaining about the work assigned to me as a boy was that my father always worked harder than did I or anyone else on the farm." Yet similar demands were never placed on his siblings, and others noted Earl to be a harsh taskmaster compared to other fathers in the community. Carter also says of his father, "He was a stern disciplinarian and punished me severely when I misbehaved." Earl nicknamed Jimmy "Hot," short for "hotshot." Whenever his father used the name "Jimmy" it was because he was about to be reprimanded. Each of the six occasions when his father whipped him with a flexible peach tree switch are burned painfully and vividly in his memory. The transgressions included stealing a penny from the collection plate in church, spending a night in a tree house while ignoring his father's calls, arguing with his sister Gloria, even shooting her in the rear with a BB gun. Lillian said of Earl, "He hated a liar. He'd whip for lying faster than anything else."

On one of the first occasions that Jimmy hunted he shot a quail. He dropped the gun and proudly took the bird to show to his father. Earl rebuked his son for dropping the gun. Later Jimmy said, "My father loved me very much," but also acknowledged there were aspects of "my father's relationship with me that at times I resented very much."

Carter, nevertheless, says of his father, "He was always my best friend." Earl smoked three packs of cigarettes a day, but when Jimmy was twelve, he promised him a gold watch if he would not smoke before the age of twenty-one. It was a pledge Jimmy felt a moral obligation to keep. His mother continued to work as a nurse, partly to supplement the family income, but more to meet her own psychological needs. Often she would work two shifts back to back. In his mother's absence it was his father who provided much of his emotional support in his early years. It was Earl who helped the children with their homework despite Lillian's penchant for reading. On occasion when his mother was away, young Jimmy would

wake up in the night and sneak into bed with his father. The price of his
father's affection, however, was satisfying him as relentless taskmaster and
thoroughly obeying his tough disciplinary standards. Gloria fought and
argued with Earl. Jimmy did not, but as he matured he felt a growing
resentment toward his father's dictatorial ways and the high price he had
to pay for his love. As a result, he grew up both obedient to, and resentful
of, authority, happy to look for safe ways to thwart it.

When a second daughter, Ruth, was born in 1929, Jimmy was five. There
was no question that she was Earl's favorite. With curly blond hair, blue
eyes, and a captivating angelic personality, she was his little princess. He
thought she was the most beautiful child in the world and he told her so
every day. It is to Earl's credit that he managed to continue showing love to
his son, although in a different way, so that Jimmy did not grow up feeling
deep resentment toward Ruth.

Lillian's work as a nurse, either at the Wise sanatorium or doing private
duty, earned the family $4 for a twelve-hour shift, $6 for twenty hours. To
take care of the Carter children, she had hired a thirteen-year-old black
girl. Annie Mae Hollis would work for the family for twenty-one years.
Occasionally, Annie Mae, who was married four times, would get into trouble on weekends, sometimes ending up in jail in Americus. The sheriff
would notify Earl, who invariably replied, "Let her out and I'll pay the
fine." Lillian also had a series of cooks who prepared most of the meals
except Sunday dinner and, in the wintertime, the "foreman" Jack Clark
would clean out the ashes from the fireplaces and set the new fires. This
allowed her to be gone much of the time. She went to the Missionary Society, or to play bridge, or to auctions, which she particularly enjoyed.

With no doctor in Webster County, Lillian filled that role for black and white
alike. Many of the white people she nursed were able to pay her and she often
worked regular shifts at the Wise hospital. But she treated anyone who was
sick, often in collaboration with Dr. Sam Wise, who would provide his services free to people Lillian was nursing if they could not pay. If there were
any costs involved, for drugs or dressings, Earl would quietly foot the bill.

On one occasion she nursed a little black girl with diphtheria, the
daughter of a family that barely scraped a living from selling turpentine
chips. The infant eventually died. Soon after, the impoverished father came
to the Carter farm with a wagonload of turpentine chips. They had little
value but efficiently started their fires for several years.

The philosophy of volunteerism, with its roots in the ideal of Christian
service, which his mother exemplified, made a lasting impression on
Jimmy. It would be a model that he would emulate as well as a philosophy
he would expect others to pursue.

Lillian read voraciously. She instilled a reverence in her children for
reading, and felt obliged to make excuses for Earl, by saying that he had

trouble with his eyesight. Although she gave the children direction as to what they should read, there was little discussion in the family about what they learned as a result. Even at the dinner table, with the exception of saying the blessing, talking was forbidden. It was, on the other hand, acceptable to bring a book to the table and read while eating. As Gloria would later recall, "Mealtime was for eating." The experience had a lasting effect on Carter, who as an adult had a persisting tendency to eat at breakneck speed and feel discomfort with light mealtime banter.

Whenever Miss Lillian left the house she would leave notes for the children on her desk. She tried to minimize her absences, but they would tease her that they had come to believe the desk was really their mother. Sixty years later Jimmy would recall, "The strong memory in my mind is coming home and my mother not being there."

Miss Lillian was a woman of vitality and intelligence who felt thwarted and trapped by the conventions that prescribed the limited role to young white women of that era in the South. Her father had encouraged her to be independent and freethinking and in many ways had given her unrealistic expectations. Although she had sought to escape by becoming an army nurse, pressured by economic insecurity and the social demand for marriage, she had to settle for the best that was available to her. Her marriage appears to have been happy, yet it represented a trade-off in which she had accepted security for a lowering of her personal aspirations. Unlike some women who can feel fully gratified by motherhood, Lillian found it insufficient. Instead she found an outlet in nursing and in essentially being a "family doctor" to those who had no other health care. In addition, her reading was a form of escape. She was a good mother in meeting the conventional needs of her children, but she yearned for much more out of life.

In his mother's absence Jimmy was drawn to Rachel Clark, wife of Jack Clark; she was reputed to be the descendent of African royalty. "Rachel Clark was aristocratic," Gloria would later say. "Queenlike" was how Jimmy would recall her. Such was her stature, Gloria says, that her mother would never have thought of asking her to do housework. She did, however, cook for the Carters for a time and took care of the children. She was never asked, but offered when she saw a need.

Each year Earl and Lillian would go away on vacation, usually to New York or Chicago to attend major-league baseball games.* In their absence Jimmy would stay with the Clarks in their ramshackle dwelling, sharing their simple monotonous diet (the girls usually went to Earl's sister Ethel). Jimmy described Rachel as a second mother. He often went to their home before dark

---

*By chance in later years they were at the first Brooklyn Dodgers game in which Jackie Robinson played. Lillian was the only person in her section of the bleachers to stand and applaud as he came on the field.

to play cards—always Seven-Up. Rachel taught him about man's responsibility to nurture the land. She also taught him how to fish, taking him on long treks to special fishing holes. She always used seven fishing poles, but never explained why. Jack Clark taught him to hunt 'coons.

Earl and Lillian had vehemently differing views on race, although they rarely argued about it. Jimmy inclined toward his mother's perspective, but he understood she was in the minority, and that his father, whom he loved, as well as all the other white men in his life, were archsegregationists. This created an odd situation with Bishop William Johnson's son Alvan, who was in college in the North. Periodically when he returned to Plains he would visit Lillian, who received him in the front room. Earl would absent himself ahead of time as though he were unaware of what was happening.

The most important event to occur in Archery happened when Jimmy was twelve years old. It was the funeral of Bishop Johnson. An array of choirs and preachers came, some from out of state, in an armada of black Cadillacs, Packards, and Lincolns. A number of whites were in attendance. Miss Lillian took Jimmy, but Earl did not join them.

Jimmy sought to please his father by starting his own enterprises. Even before he started school he had begun selling peanuts on the streets of Plains. When he got older, Earl would give him an acre on which to cultivate his own crop. He would dig up the plants, pick off the nuts, wash away the dirt, and then after letting them soak overnight, boil them in salted water and put half a pound into each of twenty bags. He then walked barefooted along the railroad tracks to Plains where he would sell the peanuts for a nickel a bag. He quickly divided the world into two types of people: the good people who regularly bought his peanuts and the bad ones who did not. Mostly he sold them to the men sitting idly around the Timmerman service station and in front of the Swannee store.

It is a measure of the isolation of his early life in Archery that he considered little Plains a somewhat frightening metropolis. He had experiences that reinforced his distrust and sense of vulnerability:

> A wise guy at the local garage offered to buy a bag of peanuts if I could obey some hand signals that he would give me. I was only seven or eight years old. The checker players and other loafers watched while I moved back and forth and from side to side with my eyes fixed on the movement of the man's hands, until he finally guided me to step on a lighted cigarette with my bare feet. A few of the onlookers laughed while I tried not cry.

His cousins Willard and Donnell had started a weekly enterprise selling hot dogs, hamburgers, and ice cream from a little stall in a building Alton had purchased, vacated by the bankrupt Bank of Plains. Every Saturday they would make a dollar or more each, selling mostly to the black farm hands and their children who would come into town for the day. After Willard and Donnell finished high school, they turned the operation over to Hugh and Jimmy. Frequently at the end of the day they would hitchhike into Americus to see a western for a dime at the Rylander Theater.

By the time he was nine, Jimmy had accumulated enough money to buy five bales of cotton at the all-time low price of 5 cents a pound. He stored the bales in his father's barn for four years until the price rose to 18 cents per pound. He then sold them and used the proceeds to purchase, from a local undertaker, what he described as "five houses." They were, in fact, shacks housing poor black tenants. From then until he left Plains in 1943 he collected "$16.50 in rent from those five houses. Two rented for $5 each, two for $2 each, and one for $2.50."

As Jimmy spent more time in Plains he saw more of his grandmother Nina. Demanding and self-centered, she disliked being alone and the family agreed that one of the grandsons would stay with her in turn each night of the week, in Jimmy's case, Friday. As he grew older what had started as a chore became a convenient excuse to be involved in social activities in Plains and Americus. He then frequently stayed Saturday nights as well.

The family belonged to the Plains Baptist Church, by far the largest in town, with a congregation of around 300. From an early age, Earl and Lillian took Jimmy to Sunday school, but Miss Lillian frequently missed church herself. Although personally committed to her Christian beliefs, she said of church, "It wasn't too much with us. The church is the center of everything in a small town . . . it was just more of a habit to go to church." Earl, who had been the secretary-treasurer while attending the men's Bible class also taught Sunday school.

At the time Jimmy was born, the preacher was Jesse Eugene Hall, a graduate of the Louisville seminary, who, like many educated pastors of his era, read the New Testament in the original Greek. He served the Plains congregation from 1923 to 1927, preaching alternate Sundays in Richland. He would return to Plains again from 1941 to 1951. While he never used the pulpit to advocate a change in the social caste system, he exerted a moderating influence on racial attitudes.

Hall was succeeded by Jesse F. Ray who, in turn, was followed by Royall Callaway. He baptized eleven-year-old Jimmy at the end of a revival in the summer of 1935. Callaway, a member of a prominent and wealthy Georgia family, held more fundamentalist views than his predecessors. He was a pre-millennialist who preached that the Jews would soon reclaim Palestine and that Christ's return to earth was imminent. His wife, Ruby, had been the private secretary of Dr. Bob Jones, Sr., then the leading voice of southern fundamentalism and an archsegregationist.

Although Lillian asserts that Jimmy was not religious when he was young, he took his role in the church seriously like everything else in his life. With no minimum driving age in rural Georgia, he would, at the age of twelve, when he was still barely big enough to see over the dashboard, borrow his mother's large black car and round up other youngsters who did not have a ride to attend Sunday school.

Through his study of the Bible and his regular attendance at Sunday school, Jimmy acquired a broad familiarity with the Holy Land. By the time he was ten years old, he had a greater knowledge about Palestine than he did about the rest of America. It seemed a fascinating, exotic place associated with an aura of deep religious reverence. Later this childhood imagery would hold an important place in his mind and his heart.

With the start of the depression in 1929, Plains went into an economic decline from which in many respects it never recovered. The population dropped from 600 to 300. The Bank of Plains had already closed and so did the hotel. Other businesses went bankrupt. The clinic burned down and, rather than rebuild, the Wise brothers moved to Americus. Crop prices plummeted with peanuts dropping to 1 cent per pound. Respectable families were staring destitution in the face. Even Earl, despite being "land rich," was, like everyone else, unashamed to be seen around town in clothes that were frayed and repaired with "patches in his britches."

The one advantage Earl did have was that after his first farm he had bought nothing on credit and had what few others possessed—cash on hand. This enabled him to take advantage of the rock-bottom prices. By the early 1930s, he would be on the road to considerable financial success. In 1932, he closed the grocery store in Plains as it was no longer making much profit. In 1934, he purchased a farm insurance and mortgage agency that gave him significant new influence in the community. His warehousing and processing operation was expanded when he became an agent for McClouskey Mills in Americus, buying peanuts from local farmers to sell in bulk for their peanut oil business. By the time Jimmy was in sixth grade, Earl was able to build a "pond house" for Lillian, a modest building for retreat and recreation on a small fishing lake.

Although shielded from the depression's worst deprivations, Jimmy was still permanently affected by the suffering he witnessed. In later life he would cite James Agee's *Let Us Now Praise Famous Men* as his favorite book. Agee traveled through the South during those years recording the hardships of cotton tenant farmers. He wrote powerfully of the unity of suffering of both black and white, showing respect for the beauty and dignity of the poor that transcended their circumstances. Agee understood that people outside the mainstream of American prosperity could yet be richer in spiritual gratification. For Jimmy, Agee graphically summed up the lessons and values of the time that he himself would carry with him into adulthood.

CHAPTER 3

Any boy, even one of ours, might grow up to be president of the United States.

—JULIA COLEMAN

In 1930, one month before his sixth birthday, Jimmy began first grade at the Plains school. He entered an all white world. The new building, constructed in 1921 after the fire, housed the grammar school in its east wing, and the high school in the north and west wings. There were only eleven grades. As with most country schools of the period, emphasis was placed on regimentation, and obedience was taken for granted. When the school bell rang in the morning students lined up in the yard by grade and were marched into the classroom.

Eleanor Forrest was Jimmy's first-grade teacher, and she says of him, "He was a very bright boy, real easy to teach, cooperative, good. I remember him pleasantly." She was the first white woman, other than his mother, with whom he had sustained contact and he developed a strong attachment to her.

From the start he was not only an obedient and well-behaved student but also worked hard. When he was five, his godmother, Gussie Abrams, had given him the complete works of Guy de Maupassant, but it was several years before he was old enough to read them. His father constantly emphasized the importance of education to the children. From an early age Jimmy was determined to graduate from high school and go to college. "It was," he says, "the driving force in my life."

Jimmy was small for his age, sandy haired and freckle faced. Adopting the style he had seen his grandfather Jim Jack Gordy use, he would walk up to other students, stick out his hand, and say, "Hi, I'm Jimmy Carter." He was well liked, in part, because he tried hard to get along. His small stature would remain a worry to him.

At the lunch break each day Jimmy would go to the home of his aunt Ethel. Earl paid her 5 cents per day to feed the children lunch and also frequently sent meat and other supplies over from his store. Ethel's husband,

Willard, worked as a self-taught veterinarian, and in the days of the depression many farmers could only pay him in kind for his services. They gave him, among other things, possums and racoons, which he kept in cages in the back yard and fattened for the kitchen. Jimmy was often served possum for lunch at Ethel's table. On his birthday Ethel would bake him a coconut cake—his favorite.

In the third grade Jimmy won a prize for reading the most books. As part of the award the teacher, Mrs. "Tot" Hudson, invited him to her house for lunch. Sauerkraut, which Jimmy had never previously encountered, was served. He struggled to swallow it, but left most of it on his plate. His embarrassment left a lasting impression on him. He was sensitive about being raised in the country. He was in the third grade when Gloria started school and he wanted her not to tell the other children she was his sister. She "didn't talk right," as her speech reflected her almost exclusive exposure to black playmates.

Earl had a pair of 1890s vintage shoes left over in his store that were sharply pointed and buttoned up, like "witches' shoes." He made Jimmy, who was struggling for conformity and acceptance, wear them to school, where he was teased and derided. It was, he says, "one of the worst things Daddy ever did to me." By the time he was in the fifth grade, however, he was well assimilated.

The period Jimmy was in grade school was a time of considerable change for the family and for the community as a whole. With his election in 1932, Franklin Delano Roosevelt would have more impact on the rural South than any president since Lincoln. Earl was in a position to take advantage of the New Deal programs and the improving economy. He benefited in particular from a federal program that paid subsidies for enclosing open pastures. Able to buy land, when most others could not, he erected cheap barbed-wire fencing and collected $10 an acre. Much of the devalued land in that part of Georgia was bought up by outside interests, especially insurance companies.

With his growing prominence in the community, Earl was appointed to the Sumter County school board in 1936. The following year he became one of the directors of the local Rural Electrification Association (REA). The arrival of electricity in the Carter home in Archery was, according to Jimmy, "the single most important event in my life." The day no longer ended at sundown and most of the more laborious tasks on the farm, such as pumping water and building fires for cooking, were supplanted by electrical appliances. It also had a political effect. The directors of the REA wielded considerable power in determining which areas would be covered by the new electrical lines, in setting the rate structure, and in bargaining with the Georgia Power Company. It was a turning point for Earl Carter in moving from being merely a modestly successful businessman to becoming a substantial community leader.

The election of FDR did not portend well for Jim Jack Gordy. After skillfully surviving through four administrations, he finally lost his patronage job as the Richland postmaster, which posed a serious financial crisis. The family moved to a house near Archery to be close to Earl and Lillian, and for a while Lillian's brother Lem worked on the farm, although it was clear that he had no aptitude for it.

During this period, when Lem was in charge of overseeing the peanut picking, the field hands went on strike, demanding a raise from $1 to $1.25 per day. It was still the depth of the depression, with hogs selling for 1 cent per pound and cotton for $5 per bale. Despite the impoverishment of the workers, Earl's own financial survival was at stake. He felt his responsibility was to see that his employees had a roof over their heads, were clothed, and did not starve. He was little concerned for their desire for disposable income when his own was shrinking. He went around to every rent-free shack and told the workers that they had a choice: they could pay what they owed him, pack their belongings, and be gone by sundown, or be in the fields again at first light. Without exception they were back harvesting peanuts the next day.

Fortunately, within a year Jim Jack landed a job as a deputy sheriff and later as a federal district revenue officer, and they moved to Columbus. After several years, he was given a retirement job as a doorman at the State Capitol in Atlanta. Subsequently he served as a guard at the mansion of former Governor Eugene Talmadge. Lem became a traveling salesman, selling primarily long-life lightbulbs. It was a career for which his jovial personality seemed to suit him perfectly.

As the depression eased and his business again began to flourish, a philanthropic side of Earl Carter became increasingly apparent. He had always quietly helped out those he felt were in need. When Lillian's sister Sissy went away to college in 1930, he gave her $75, a substantial sum at that time. When his friend Frank Timmerman became terminally ill with tuberculosis, Earl sent him $25, and continued to send money to his widow after his death. When one of the teachers mentioned to him that she was raising money to buy a piano for the school, he asked how much she was short. "Twelve dollars," she replied. He pulled out his wallet and gave it to her. When he heard a widow was without fuel, he asked a dealer to deliver a load of coal to her anonymously and he paid the bill.

Despite his gregarious business style, Earl was reflective, somewhat introverted, and even secretive, especially about his generosity. Maintaining his anonymity in these acts was very important to him. He used Frank Timmerman's wife, Ida Mae, to keep him informed about destitute families, both black and white—a girl who could not afford a graduation dress, or a youngster who needed help with college expenses. He then had Ida Mae pay the necessary costs without divulging the source of the largesse.

Earl's motivations were clearly deeply personal. In his own mind his generosity reflected Christian charity, and his reluctance to seek recognition would have been an appropriate manifestation of humility. Such religious values were drummed into all church members, but few acted on them as Earl did. What is most significant is that in Earl's carrying out his philanthropy so discreetly, Jimmy, growing up, remained almost entirely oblivious to it.

Earl's involvement with the REA led him to have an increasingly active interest in politics generally. Like most of the white population of Southwest Georgia, he had become a supporter of Eugene Talmadge, the rising star of the 1920s in Georgia politics. "The Wild Man from Sugar Creek" was elected four times as governor of the state. Following the collapse of the populist movement of Tom Watson and the discrediting and weakening of the old Bourbon hierarchy, the so-called "New South Progressives" had seized the initiative in southern politics by stressing the need for urban industrial growth, attracting economic investment, and expanding the role of government in providing educational and other basic social services. Above all, they were seeking to create a stable social and political order in which the white elites at all levels could amass wealth and consolidate their power. They introduced the poll tax, literacy and comprehension tests, the county unit system, and most importantly the "white primary," all measures that disenfranchised not just blacks but many poor whites as well.

Talmadge embodied that new politics. He was one of the great demagogues of American politics who used blatantly racist rhetoric to appeal to small farmers and rural merchants. He appealed also to the residual populist sentiment by attacking Wall Street, bankers, monopolies, and the railroads. The votes were in the rural areas, but the control was in Atlanta, where the financial backing for Talmadge came from. The business establishment did not mind what he had to do or say to get elected because they knew they could count on him, once in office, for a stable environment fully supportive of their interests.

Talmadge espoused the Protestant ethic of hard work, piety, thrift, and individualism with which Earl and others like him strongly identified. He also advocated the preservation of a system under which blacks provided limitless cheap labor, and enterprising whites, like Earl, of only modest background and education, could prosper without ever having to engage in much physical work. Although Earl had benefitted from FDR's enclosure program, he, like many other farmers, became disillusioned when in an effort to raise commodity prices the Agricultural Adjustment Administration (AAA) called for farmers to slaughter their pigs and plow under the cotton they had planted.

Evidence that FDR, and especially Eleanor, had sympathy for the plight of blacks further alienated many southern whites. When Talmadge attacked the New Deal as "downright communism and a plain damn foolishness," it was as much a coded message about race as criticism of the merits of the economic measures. Jimmy Carter says his father did not vote for FDR after 1936. Despite his father's dominant role in all family decisions, Jimmy speculates that his mother, in the privacy of the polling booth, may have continued to vote for Roosevelt. When FDR sought in 1938 to oust longtime U.S. Senator Walter George, a native of nearby Vienna, Georgia, by backing one of his opponents, Lawrence Camp, Earl was further incensed.

As he started high school in the eighth grade, Jimmy wrote in his scrapbook six "good mental habits":

> If you think in the right way you will develop: (1) the habit of accomplishing what you attempt, (2) the habit of expecting to like other people, (3) the habit of deciding quickly what you'd like to do and doing it, (4) the habit of sticking to it, (5) the habit of welcoming cheerfully all wholesome ideas and experiences, (6) a person who wants to build good mental habits should avoid the idle daydream; should give up worry and anger; hatred and envy; should neither fear nor be ashamed of anything that is honest and purposeful.

These admonitions were very much taken to heart even at age thirteen and constitute an accurate reflection of the mental discipline he was able to impose over himself in the coming years.

At the beginning of the eighth grade he would also encounter a teacher who would profoundly shape his life. Julia Coleman had already taught a generation of children when he arrived in her class. She was probably the most admired and respected person in Plains. Born in Nacogdoches, Texas, Julia was the daughter of an academically educated man, who had been a Baptist preacher with mainly affluent congregations in Alabama, Mississippi, and Texas. Her mother was a teacher who had on occasion privately taught the children of well-to-do families. In the 1890s, her father had received a letter inviting him to come to Macon, Georgia, to become president of Mercer University, the leading Baptist educational institution in the state. They sold their possessions in Texas and moved with their two young daughters, only to find upon their arrival that the chairman of the board had convinced the other board members to give the job to his son.

Julia's father eventually became the pastor at the Friendship Baptist Church in Lumpkin. Later they moved closer to Plains, where Julia completed high school. She then went on to Bessie Tift College in Forsyth, graduating in 1908. As a little girl she had fallen from a window. The result was a broken femur that had been improperly set and that left her with one leg shorter than the other. In college she suffered from an unexplained retinal hemorrhage that made her largely blind in one eye. She graduated only because the other girls were willing to read to her.

Significantly disabled, "Miss Julia," as she became known, returned to the school in Plains to teach, first seventh-grade English, and later Latin. Subsequently, she took over the eighth grade. However, her involvement with the school and its students over the next thirty-five years was to become totally enveloping. Ultimately she would become, at different times, both principal and superintendent.

Julia Coleman had a commanding presence. She also emanated, in the limited educational environment of Plains, a touch of intellectual aristocracy. "She was nothing like any of us," says one student she taught in the early years.

She never stopped trying to broaden her own mind. Every night she would have her sister read to her on a wide variety of topics. Her family had one of the first radios in Plains and they not only read the local newspapers but had the *Atlanta Constitution* and *Atlanta Journal* delivered. They also subscribed to several national publications. She would never marry and teaching consumed her entire life. She had a special gift for challenging children to reach their maximum potential. She singled out "favorites," those she thought had particular talents, and worked with them to make the most out of their gifts. But she also had a penchant for spotting those headed for trouble and would intercede, quietly counseling them before they got into serious difficulties. Jimmy would say of her, "I have never known of a teacher who had such a profound impact on students as she did."

When Jimmy's cousin Don was in school, she noted his embryonic talents as a writer and thought it would be beneficial for him to attend a high school press meeting at the University of Georgia. This was an unusual suggestion in an era when people did not travel much, but his father, Alton, paid for him and Miss Julia to go. On their return she helped him start a school newspaper. As a result, he was inspired to pursue a career in journalism, achieving considerable distinction at the national level, and ultimately becoming vice president of the Knight-Ridder newspaper chain.

In the late 1920s, Julia Coleman went, for several successive summers, to Lake Chautauqua in upstate New York. There, started in 1874 as a vehicle for educating Methodist Sunday school teachers, the Chautauqua Institute provided university summer school courses and classes in the arts, drama, music, religion, and youth activities. Plays and operas were performed and symphony orchestras gave concerts. Associated with the summer program was a directed program of home reading and correspondence study. They also operated traveling Chautauqua programs that visited rural communities throughout the country to bring a brief taste of culture to those who otherwise would never have such exposure. Through the efforts of Miss Julia, Plains was on their itinerary for several years, until the depression made such visits impossible.

The Chautauqua program had been given new impetus and stature through the interest and involvement of Eleanor Roosevelt. One summer Julia Coleman met her there and, after Eleanor Roosevelt became first lady, Miss Julia was invited to "have tea" with her at the White House. She was accompanied on the trip to Washington by her sister's daughter Ann, then a college student. Ann recalls her trepidation, as they arrived at the portico of the White House, about her aunt Julia's ability, because of her infirmities, to handle the formalities and especially the steps she would have to climb. But when they arrived, Mrs. Roosevelt and the other women present warmly greeted her, saying, "Ah, here is the lady from Georgia," and helped her into the meeting. They spent two additional days in Washington giving her a wealth of new knowledge and experiences to share with her students upon her return to the isolation of Plains.

It was Miss Julia's ability to translate her own diligently acquired knowledge into fascinating and inspiring classroom material that made her such an exceptional teacher. Whether they were headed for higher education or not, her students had at least a rudimentary understanding of the American cultural heritage. Among her other achievements she obtained a grant one year from the Works Progress Administration (WPA) to keep the library open over the summer. She established a reading club—with the slogan "Readers Make Leaders," a message drummed into everyone who attended Plains High School—and monitored the reading level of each student, and astutely assigned books to meet their individual intellectual level. She ran the debating team and would have students come to her house in the evening to drill them on debating skills. She had a special concern about women having equal educational opportunity, leading a fight to get the conservative community to accept girls wearing basketball attire.

She saw her teaching responsibilities as including the transmission of Christian values, and she would have students memorize and recite parts of the Bible, which took on the significance of philosophical underpinnings for how to live one's life in a successful and happy way. It reflected her belief that a fulfilling existence required a strong spiritual foundation as well as the many other more concrete elements she tried to bring into the children's lives.

Perhaps her greatest attribute was her ability, when even a trip to Atlanta was a truly major event, to inspire her students to see beyond the isolation of Plains, to understand what the larger world had to offer, and to believe it was all accessible to them if they had sufficient ambition and the self-discipline necessary for hard work. Jimmy's cousin Hugh says, "I think if every schoolchild was made to memorize Rudyard Kipling's poem 'If,' as she made us memorize it, it might excite many more youngsters to fight for success and take defeat in stride until success finally comes."

In any small town, the school together with the church form the central part of the community. However, Julia Coleman accentuated that role. As the years went by she eventually had taught, except for a handful of newcomers, every man and woman in Plains, and she had shaped all of their lives to some degree. She took an interest in continuing education for the adult community, organizing round-table discussions on literature in the evenings. She took a special interest in landscaping the school grounds and under her direction the children planted flowers and shrubs to form "The Friendship Garden." A section was set aside as "Baby Row" where a tree or bush was planted for every new (white) baby born in the community.

At the end of the 1920s, Georgia schools were rated the poorest in the nation, and a state report in 1929 listed Sumter County schools as lagging behind the Georgia average in student achievement scores. The Plains school, however, produced a disproportionate number of students who went on to college and professional careers, for which Julia Coleman deserves most of the credit. Eventually the Georgia Department of Education would name Plains High School as one of the three model schools in Georgia.

It is, perhaps, a fitting reflection on just how remarkable this woman was that one of her students should become a president of the United States. In a later era with different opportunities it is unlikely that a woman of such exceptional talent would have been satisfied to remain a teacher in a small-town high school.

No relationship, other than that with his parents, was more important in shaping Jimmy Carter than that with Julia Coleman. He says of his school years, "I don't think there is any way to explain my life or to explain Rosalynn's life, or to explain our advancement after school, without understanding the Plains High School and what it meant." He was referring primarily to Miss Julia. She early spotted him as bright, self-disciplined, and an avid reader who was eager to learn. He became one of her "pets," one of those students in whom she saw her own personal investment was likely to yield a handsome reward. He, in turn, was a willing vessel into which she could pour her energies and ambitions for him.

Under the tutelage of Miss Julia, Jimmy acquired a lifelong interest in poetry, and a lasting appreciation of art and music. He became a member of the debating team that met on Friday afternoons and discussed topical social and political issues, such as whether the United States should send aid to Britain in the emerging conflict with Hitler. In this setting he overcame his natural shyness, learning to articulate forcefully his position on issues. Fifty years later, Carter still vividly recalls memorizing both the Twenty-third Psalm and, perhaps more significantly, 1 Corinthians chapter 13, which in many respects represents in its focus on selfless love, or "agape," the unique and central message of Christianity that would dictate both his personal and his political philosophy:

If I speak in the tongues of men and of Angels, but have not love, I am a noisy gong or a clanging cymbal. And if I have prophetic powers, and understand all mysteries and all knowledge, and if I have all faith, so as to remove mountains, but I have not love, I am nothing. If I give away all I have, and I deliver my body to be burned, but have not love, I gain nothing.

Love is patient and kind; love is not jealous or boastful; it is not arrogant or rude. Love does not insist on its own way; it is not irritable or resentful; it does not rejoice at wrong, but rejoices in the right. Love bears all things, believes all things, hopes all things, endures all things.

Love never ends; as for prophecy, it will pass away; as for tongues, they will cease; as for knowledge, it will pass away. For our knowledge is imperfect; but when the perfect comes the imperfect will pass away. When I was a child, I spoke as a child, I thought like a child, I reasoned like a child. When I became a man, I gave up childish ways. For now we see in a mirror dimly, but then face to face. Now I know in part; then I shall understand fully, even as I have been fully understood. So faith, hope, and love abide these three, but the greatest of these is love.

When Jimmy was thirteen, Miss Julia suggested that he read Tolstoy's *War and Peace*. Encouraged by the expectation that the book was about cowboys and Indians, he hurried to the library where he was appalled to discover that it was a 1,400-page tome about the French army under Napoléon and his catastrophic invasion of Russia. The message of the novel in Carter's words was "to show that the course of human events—even great historical events—is determined ultimately not by the leaders, but by the common ordinary people. Their hopes and dreams, their doubts and fears, their courage and tenacity, their quiet commitments to determine the destiny of the world." It was a theme that resonated strongly with the legacy of Tom Watson and the populist tradition of the region. It had a profound effect in shaping the way Jimmy Carter would see the relationship between the governors and the governed and, over the years, he would read the book three times.

In most other respects Jimmy Carter's high school years differed little from those of most students of his time. He joined the Future Farmers of America and learned the rudiments of woodworking that would later become a favorite hobby. Because the school was small, there was no foot-

ball team, and basketball was the major sport. Jimmy made the team as a
forward. His speed on the court made up for his lack of height. He was also
a reasonable pole vaulter.

When Jimmy started school he was closest to his friend Rembert Forrest, but later his closest friendships were with Richard Salter and Bobby
Logan. Occasionally he would stay overnight at their homes or they would
come out to Archery where they would hunt and fish in the woods together
or go skinny dipping in the river. As he grew older, it was the relationship
with Bobby Logan that became the most enduring and significant, even
though on one occasion they had a fistfight. He was always concerned
about getting the grades necessary to achieve his goal of going to college,
and was viewed at times by his classmates as being something of a grind,
although his mother described him as being so smart that he never needed
to study hard to succeed academically.

His first love was a classmate, Eloise (Teenie) Ratliffe, five foot three,
dark-haired, and a fellow book lover, whom he started dating when he was
thirteen. She lived near his grandmother, Nina, which made the nights
spent at her house considerably more endurable. He also would ride his
bicycle in from Archery to see her, until his father let him use their pickup.
There were only a limited number of places to go on a date. They went to
movies in Americus, or drove out to Magnolia Springs to dance or swim. Frequently they just went to Godwin's Drugstore after school. Most social
activities, if not sponsored by the school, were organized by the church.
The Baptist Young People's Union met on Sundays before the evening worship service, and was an easy environment in which teenagers could socialize. Every Friday night there was a "prom." Although for a while they were
inseparable, Teenie seems to have been the less committed to the relationship, and confided to one of her friends that she felt Jimmy was tight with
his money. Shortly afterward, a family named Taylor moved to town, and the
son, Lonnie, who was older than Jimmy, took Teenie away from him. Ultimately they were married and had children. Some years later the entire
family was killed when a plane Lonnie was piloting crashed near Plains.

Jimmy subsequently dated Ann Montgomery, who from a young age was
an accomplished pianist and went on to become a successful performer.
Then he developed a relationship with Betty Timmerman, whose parents
were close to Earl and Lillian and whose mother, Ida Lee, shared in a less
ostentatious way Lillian's concern for the black residents of Plains. On one
occasion Jimmy and Betty went together in a horse and buggy to attend
services in a black church. By then Jimmy's social life was somewhat cur-
tailed because he had a part-time job in the evenings working at the Plains
Mercantile Store. When he got off, often not until around 10 P.M., he and
Betty would go to a movie in Americus.

As graduation neared, Jimmy was one of a small group, including Teenie Ratliffe, Billy Wise, his friend Bobby Logan, and Grace Wiggins, who were academically at the top of the class. On April Fool's Day, 1941, their senior year, Teenie Ratliffe's boyfriend, Lonnie Taylor, convinced a group of boys, including Jimmy, to skip school and go for a joyride to Americus in his hot-rod. They went to a detective movie and toured the Coca-Cola plant. They made one mistake, which was to go by the office of the *Americus Times-Recorder* and tell the editor with bravado about their escapade. Needless to say, an item appeared in the next issue. Y. T. Sheffield and Julia Coleman felt some punishment was called for, although there are various versions as to what actually happened. Mr. Sheffield is said to have offered them the alternative of making up the lost time, writing a 5,000-word theme, or receiving a whipping. It is unclear what option Jimmy took.

It was widely reported in 1976 that Jimmy was to have been the valedictorian of the class, but because of the caper in Americus, Miss Julia decided the honor should be awarded instead to Teenie Ratliffe. It appears that Grace Wiggins, Teenie Ratliffe, and Jimmy all had sufficient grades to be contenders, and whether he was denied it purely as punishment is not known. The position carried with it a scholarship to Georgia Southwestern College in Americus. Jimmy, friends recall, seemed genuinely happy that his former girlfriend, who came from a family of very modest means and otherwise could not go to college, would receive the scholarship in his place.

During May 1941, the graduating class of Plains High School, accompanied by Y. T. Sheffield as chaperone, piled into the school bus and took a weekend trip to Florida, visiting the beaches in Jacksonville and St. Augustine. A few days after graduation on June 2, Earl and Lillian threw a party for the entire senior class, their friends, families, and teachers. They sat on benches at long tables in the open air eating barbecue, fried chicken, sweet potatoes, squash, collard greens, and corn bread washed down with lemonade and iced tea.

On graduation day, Miss Julia had arranged for the members of the debating team, Jimmy Carter, Doris Cosby, Billy Wise, and Richard Salter, to address the assembly. The overall theme, so reflective of her own perspective, was "Building for Today and Tomorrow." Jimmy spoke on "The Building of a Community."

CHAPTER 4

If a man advances confidently in the direction of his dreams to live the life he has imagined, he will meet with a success unexpected in common hours.

—HENRY DAVID THOREAU

Jimmy Carter has said that because of the limited financial resources of his family, he never considered anything other than a free college education when he began planning his future at the height of the depression. This was a primary reason he was attracted to a military academy. By the time he was actually ready for college his father could well have afforded to send him to the University of Georgia, where his cousin Don had gone, or even to most private colleges; but by the age of seven, Jimmy had made up his mind to go to the U.S. Naval Academy at Annapolis, and had pursued that goal with a dogged singlemindedness.

Jimmy's choice of the Naval Academy over West Point, which his father would have preferred because of his army background, was a product of his relationship with his uncle, Tom Watson Gordy. Tom had left home at seventeen to become an enlisted man in the navy. He served as a radio man on the USS *Essex* and later the USS *Boise*. Tom sent Jimmy picture postcards, letters and small gifts, a model sampan, and a box with dragons painted on it. For a little boy who lived in geographic and cultural isolation, receiving a letter—especially from a distant exotic port— was an exciting and memorable occasion stimulating fantasies about a life of adventure. A few days after Pearl Harbor, Tom was captured by the Japanese on Guam, and would not be heard from for more than four years. In the meantime, the Red Cross notified the family that he was presumed dead.

In grade school, Jimmy wrote to the Naval Academy asking about the entrance requirements without revealing his age. When he received the catalog it instantly became a treasured possession. He memorized every crucial section. The seemingly strict requirements for admission caused him to have secret and irrational fears that he would not measure up.

Some of the physical requirements listed in the catalog gave me deep concern. "Malocclusion of the teeth" was my biggest theoretical problem. When I ate fruit, the knowledge that my teeth did not perfectly meet interfered with my enjoying the flavor. There was another requirement that caused me to worry, one called "retention of urine." I was always ashamed to ask whether that last clinging drop would block my entire naval career.

Jimmy overcame his preadolescent concerns, although his small stature remained a potential problem. Throughout his school years his determination to go to the academy never wavered. "It was," he says, "the driving force in my life." He read books about the navy and sought to prepare himself for his intended lifelong career. The only concern was whether in a highly competitive arena, where political influence counted for much, he would be admitted. If not, he had decided, he would probably become a college professor, an alternative that reflects the somewhat academic self-concept he had developed.

With World War II under way in Europe and the increasing likelihood of U.S. involvement, by the time of his high school graduation in the summer of 1941, Jimmy's desire to go to the Naval Academy no longer set him apart. The possibility of military service was, by then, something that most able-bodied young men were anticipating.

The gathering clouds of war were given a sense of urgent reality when Souther Field on the outskirts of Americus was turned into a training ground for military pilots. Shortly thereafter, a contingent of Royal Air Force pilots arrived from Britain. This sudden intrusion of an incipient world war directly into their community woke the locals out of their somnolent isolationism.

To be accepted at Annapolis Jimmy needed the support of the Carters' local congressman, Stephen Pace, who in 1938 had succeeded their long-time representative Charles Crisp. Increasingly active in local politics, Earl had strongly supported Pace in his two elections, partly because the congressman was the leading advocate in Washington for the interests of the peanut farmers, but also to foster the chances of getting the needed sponsorship for his son. The appointment was not immediately forthcoming as Pace already had a candidate for that year, and Jimmy was forced to enroll at Georgia Southwestern College, a two-year school in Americus.

In the early 1940s, Georgia Southwestern College was a modest institution indeed. The campus consisted of an administrative-classroom building, two dormitories, and a gymnasium. There were only around 200 students, and after the draft was instituted, they were overwhelmingly female. The curriculum was limited: introductory chemistry and physics, math, two world literature survey courses, and English composition. In 1941, as the war gathered steam, aviation was added and, to accommodate the interests of the increasing number of girls, ballroom dancing. Journalism was initially offered during the same period. Tuition was $204 per year.

Jimmy's cousins Hugh and Don had excelled at the college before going on to the University of Georgia. Jimmy, one of his friends noted, arrived with a degree of purposefulness that was missing in other students. The day Pearl Harbor was attacked by the Japanese, a group of students stood on the steps of the dorm talking about their potential roles in the war. Jimmy astonished the others by the clarity and certainty with which he indicated his plan to become a submarine commander. He did well in school and during his second semester worked as a laboratory assistant. He continued to play basketball and, together with his friend Bobby Logan, made the "all-star" team.

Jimmy initially continued to live at home, commuting each day to Americus by car or being driven in the old Plains school bus. Lillian had had a fourth child in March 1937—another boy, William Alton, called "Billy." To escape the crowded house, Jimmy moved into the dorm for his second semester. He joined the IFT fraternity ("Ingenuity, Fidelity, and Trustworthiness") and the Investors, a group that sponsored the school dance each fall.

Jimmy became friends with Beverly Forester, a student with little money, whose parents had both died. The president of the college had arranged a job for Forester in the post office so that he could make ends meet. Forester vividly recalls Earl Carter, learning of his situation, taking a warm and paternal interest in him. Several times Earl brought him food, and on one occasion gave him $15. Jimmy's fellow students recall, by contrast, Miss Lillian asking them how their grades were and whether they were studying. One said of Jimmy, "I think he got his warmth from his father and his ambition from his mother."

Jimmy and Beverly Forester ran against each other for freshman class president. Forester won, probably because he lived on campus. Jimmy became vice president. Subsequently they competed again for the title "Mr. Southwestern" with a similar outcome. "Jimmie" (as the yearbook labeled him) directed his energies primarily toward meeting the requirements for acceptance to the Naval Academy. As he had seen his father do, he was already adopting a pattern of carefully planning all of his activities and meticulously apportioning time and energy to those that would help him achieve specific goals.

Jimmy continued to date Betty Timmerman, but then became involved with Marguerite Wise, daughter of Dr. Bowman Wise. Miss Lillian would have been particularly happy for her son to marry into the Wise medical family, but Marguerite's mother, Mozelle, was not enthusiastic about the match. "I think if Miss Mozelle had been receptive to me, I probably would have stayed with Marguerite. I really liked Marguerite," Carter says.

Jimmy also had several dates with Roxy Jo Logan, the strikingly beautiful sister of his friend Bobby Logan. The family had moved to Quitman, Georgia. On one occasion visiting at her home, and trying to impress her with his tumbling skills, he stepped in a hole and fell, breaking his wrist. Local physicians were unable to set the fracture and he was sent to Atlanta where he was hospitalized for ten days.

Jimmy was also attracted to a fellow student, Annelle Green, who was "Miss Georgia Southwestern." She was, however, going with his friend Beverly Forester. They would compete for her affections for some time.

In the summer of 1942 the appointment to Annapolis finally came through for a year hence, but it was contingent upon his completing various additional science courses in the interim that were not offered at Georgia Southwestern. The navy recommended that he attend Georgia Tech in Atlanta as a general engineering student and join the naval ROTC to take courses in navigation, seamanship, and military science that they required. His provisional acceptance at the Naval Academy came just in time to save him from the draft, which in all probability would have meant serving as an enlisted man, and rapid deployment into a combat zone.

Georgia Tech in the summer of 1942 was being swept up by war fever. Most of Jimmy's time and energy that was not taken up with physical and military training went into studying. During the three terms that Jimmy was at Georgia Tech he was in the top 10 percent of his class and made the honor roll.

"Tech was the most difficult school I ever attended," he would later write. However, he would also say, "My biggest adjustment at Tech was not so much to the school as to living in the big city of Atlanta." He did not join a fraternity, frequently went back to Plains on weekends, and did not involve himself in any social life in Atlanta away from the campus. Jimmy's roommate in 308 Knowles was Robert Ormsby, who would become the president of Lockheed Corporation. Ormsby launched him on a lasting appreciation of classical music. Jimmy also became an avid Georgia Tech football fan and remained a lifelong supporter.

At the end of the school year, Jimmy went back to Plains for two weeks. On June 26, 1943, he and Evan Mathis, a boy from Americus, boarded the Silver Meteor train for Washington, D.C. From there, filled with a mixture of trepidation and eager anticipation, they took the bus to Annapolis. Even though Jimmy had been away from home for much of the past year, his departure out of state had a wrenching emotional impact on his family. According to Rachel Clark, Earl went with his friend Raymond Sullivan to get drunk, and his mother went off by herself to go fishing and cry. Meanwhile, Jimmy and Evan Mathis took a room overnight on George Street across from the academy. The next morning, Monday, June 28, they reported for their physicals. Jimmy weighed 121 pounds, barely above the required minimum. On Wednesday, he was formally sworn in as a cadet, a member of the class of 1947. He would actually graduate in 1946 under the navy's wartime accelerated program in which the work of four years was squeezed into three. That night he wrote a long letter home to his parents describing the events of the previous seventy-two hours. He also began keeping a diary that he would maintain for most of his first year at Annapolis.

Jimmy was originally assigned to the Thirteenth Company of the Third Battalion (later he and other seniors would be reassigned to the Fifteenth Company). Each was composed of around 100 men drawn from the three classes: plebes, youngsters (second year), and seniors (third year). This was the basic organizational unit that lived together in the same section of Bancroft Hall; they ate, socialized, and played. They marched together under section leaders to their respective classes.

Life was entirely regimented. Reveille was at 6:15 A.M. Within forty seconds every individual had to be out of bed with his door open. From then until "lights out" at 10 P.M., every moment of the day was programmed in detail. There was no "free time" and even when studying they were not permitted to lie down on their beds. Because of the organizational and social structure, friendships were almost entirely restricted to classmates within the company. They could receive guests only on weekend afternoons, and only members of their immediate families.

In 1943, hazing was still a dominant aspect of life at the Naval Academy. The majority of the entries in Jimmy's diary involve his travails with the system. Real or imagined infractions were punished by beatings from upperclassmen with brooms, heavy aluminum bread pans, or long-handled serving spoons. On other occasions he was forced to do inumerable push-ups or run around the military track or obstacle course before dawn. The upperclassmen made nonsensical demands of the plebes and, if they were not performed to their satisfaction, the plebe was arbitrarily punished. As Carter has recounted it, "We never ate a peaceful meal. There were constant questions, research, songs, poems, reports on obscure athletic events, and recitations required of us." One of the most common punishments to which Jimmy was subjected was called "shoving out," which meant sitting in a normal position to eat your meal without actually touching your chair.

An upperclassman named Weidner insisted that Jimmy learn and sing "Marching Through Georgia," the battle hymn of General Sherman's army. It was an infliction not for him personally but something regularly used to humiliate every plebe from Georgia. Jimmy politely but repeatedly refused and endured "shoving out," "eating a square meal" (making a square with each forkful of food), and ultimately the inevitable flagellation. The confrontation went on for several days with Carter noting in his diary, "my rear was getting in worse shape." Eventually an upperclassman, Sammy Rorex, from Arkansas, intervened on his behalf. Much has been made of this story to suggest that Carter was a persecuted southerner in an alien Yankee environment. In fact, the majority of his classmates were southern boys, and the Naval Academy, situated in a state below the Mason-Dixon line, had a strong southern orientation like most military institutions at that time.

Discipline, physical punishment, and a sense of vulnerability to those in authority was nothing new for Jimmy. His childhood with Mr. Earl had prepared him well for the rigors of Annapolis. He dealt with both situations with quiet stoicism and a great deal of repressed anger, for what he saw as gross injustice. One of his classmates, Arthur Middleton, described how Jimmy would march to his quarters, his icy blue eyes staring ahead and his face white with fury. "But he would never let it out," says Middleton, "never kick a chair or throw a book like the rest of us." Carter has said that only his life-long commitment to a navy career allowed him to tolerate the hazing. In early August he noted in his diary, "Over 5 months to Christmas. I hope I can stand it." The disarming strategy he had learned as a child—of smiling at anyone who was bigger or more powerful than he—did not work at Annapolis. "My main trouble was that I smiled too much," he wrote. "I soon learned to concentrate on a serious subject when passing a group of the yapping 3/c [third classmen]. . . . I also learned how to 'wipe it off.' " As a way of trying to control the emotion evoked, he made himself see the hazing as a game. After two months he had settled into a strategy of anonymity, a successful survival ploy frequently used by those who see themselves as weak and impotent in the face of overwhelming domination. It also results in being widely ignored. Despite his solid record, he did not achieve prominence as a leader. "A big man on campus he was not," a classmate recalls.

Upon their arrival at Annapolis, Jimmy, Evan Mathis, and a boy named Donald Fantozzi were assigned to share 3315A Bancroft Hall, a two-room "suite." Jimmy soon had a new roommate, Don Andrews, from Iowa. In April of his freshman year he was moved again, getting a new roommate, R. L. Scott, and a new room, 2259. Scott was a concert pianist and he and Jimmy jointly purchased a record player and many classical records. They discussed the relative merits of different pianists' interpretations of a piece of music, such as a Rachmaninoff piano concerto. When they graduated, Jimmy flipped a coin and won the record collection while Scott got the player.

At the beginning of their senior year, a midshipman committed suicide by diving out of a dorm window, a deeply traumatic event for the entire community. Concerned about providing for the emotional needs of the dead man's roommate, the administration placed him with four other students who it was felt could provide this sort of support. Jimmy was one of them. His roommates that final year, in addition to Bob Scott, were Al

Rusher, Blu Middleton, and Lou Larcombe. It was a particularly compatible and happy group.

Academically he did well, finding Annapolis easier than Georgia Tech. He chose Spanish as the one elective he was allowed. He did not stand out on the parade ground, but at the end of the first quarter he had a grade average of 3.478.

He learned to handle weapons on the firing range. Physically adept from life on a farm, he rowed cutters, sailed in knockabouts and whalers. He played on the under-140-pound football team in the intercompany league. He also went out for track as a pole vaulter and high jumper, but it was in cross-country that he did best. Lean and slight of build, he was suited for the sport. It also attracts those who are introverted and loners, characteristics he possessed as well. Captain Ellery Clark, the coach, was one of the few faculty members with whom he established a close personal relationship.

The job of the academy was to turn out not just technically competent military officers but gentlemen. During his senior year, Jimmy took a course in ballroom dancing, learning from professional instructors—but without female partners—to waltz, fox trot, samba, and rhumba. He described after-dinner speaking as one of the most "fearsome requirements." A couple of times a month a group of fifteen or twenty midshipmen and officers would gather, in formal attire, for a banquet in a small dining room off the main hall. Under the tutelage of the head of the English department, and guided by a pamphlet, "Hints on After Dinner Speaking," each student came with a prepared oration. Toasts were drunk with ginger ale in the wineglasses, as one third of the sweating midshipmen would be called on arbitrarily to deliver their speech.

On weekends Jimmy went to the movies. Among the many films he saw were *The Constant Nymph* ("it stank"), *Heaven Can Wait* ("not bad"), *Holy Matrimony* ("thought it was swell"), *Stagedoor Canteen, Assignment Brittany, Mr. Lucky,* and *Slightly Dangerous.*

Jimmy stayed in close touch with his parents. His father made a welcome visit during November of his freshman year, and at regular intervals after that. Jimmy went home to Plains for Christmas. His emotional ties to Sumter County remained strong as did his continuing relationship with Annelle Green. A classmate, Dr. Francis Hertzog, said of him, "He was very well liked by his company. But he was a loner. He did not make close intimate friendships. He went out of his way to be perhaps more friendly to more people, but he didn't need other people's close bond of friendship to support his own ego and personality—he had a very strong character." In a letter home he asked Gloria not to refer to him anymore as "hot," and admonished her, "Don't write me on lined notebook paper with a pencil." His ability to feel secure in his own identity enabled him to handle the stresses of the Naval Academy, and that identity was rooted in his family and Plains. Despite the navy's efforts to remake him in the military image, they never captured his soul.

Religious belief had remained an important part of Jimmy Carter's makeup. Even though he had written in his diary that "chapel was okay," he soon elected not to attend the academy's Episcopalian services on Sunday, and went instead to a nearby Baptist church where he taught Sunday school. A fellow classmate said, "From the way he carried himself you could tell he was devout." It was also something which, in the alien environment of the Naval Academy, represented a piece of his home environment that he could rely on for emotional support.

The second and third years of Jimmy's training at the Naval Academy were devoted to actual military experience; each summer was spent on a training cruise. His first such voyage was on the USS *New York*, a decrepit old battleship driven by gigantic reciprocating engines, which produced debilitating heat and humidity in the pressurized engine and boiler rooms. In a world at war the training had a very real quality as they sought to evade German submarines. On one occasion, while violently zig-zagging to evade a sub, one of the ship's four propellers was hit by a torpedo, or struck a coral reef, shearing off a blade. Continuing the evasive zig-zag on the long journey back to port for repairs, the damage caused the ship to lurch violently on every turn.

Life aboard ship was relentlessly boring most of the time. To avoid the heat below, the midshipmen slept on deck, but seconds after reveille, saltwater hoses were turned on for the morning swabbing-down and only the nimble avoided a soaking. Jimmy and his classmates carried out their menial chores under the direction of the ship's regular crew, including learning to "holystone" the decks—rubbing a white brick back and forth on the deck to polish the wood. The midshipmen were rotated so they could have comprehensive knowledge of the ship's operation. Battle stations and cleaning stations remained the same throughout the cruise. Jimmy was assigned to man a 40-millimeter antiaircraft gun during the many alerts. He also had the regular responsibility for cleaning one of the toilets that frequently overflowed.

A necessary requirement was for the midshipmen to learn to recognize the silhouettes of enemy and allied planes, and ships as they were flashed on a screen for a fraction of a second. Carter "mastered them all." A drive for a sense of mastery in each new undertaking had emerged as a vital part of his personality that would be both an asset and a liability in the future.

For plebes dating was not allowed. After the first year, dates could come to Annapolis for academy events but midshipmen could not leave the town. Jimmy did not have any dates, maintaining only his romantic relationships back home. His freshman year, Betty Timmerman sent him her picture, even though their relationship was essentially over. He continued to harbor feelings for Marguerite Wise, despite her mother's antipathy. His most active relationship continued to be with Annelle Green. During Christmas vacation of his junior year he dated her every night. The relationship ended when she finally decided to marry Beverly Forester.

Jimmy's sister Ruth had a friend, Rosalynn Smith. Despite Ruth being two years older and her being, in many respects, Rosalynn's opposite, they were inseparable. Rosalynn was painfully shy and uncertain of herself. Ruth was extroverted and gregarious. Rosalynn, although far from plain, contrasted with Ruth's beauty and flamboyance. Ruth never had to worry about a date; Rosalynn had dates, but with no certainty. In the summer of 1945, Rosalynn was about to start her sophomore year at Georgia Southwestern College, while Ruth was still a senior at Plains High School. Ruth, however, helped to broker Rosalynn's painful access to teenage social life. Rosalynn offered her the status of association with a college student.

There were few young men around—only three in Rosalynn's class. The rest had enlisted, been drafted, or were still in high school, so Rosalynn became somewhat fixated on Ruth's picture of her handsome brother at the Naval Academy. The only real contact she had had with him was as a child when she bought ice cream from his stand in the old bank. Now during a brief leave in Plains during July of 1945, Ruth schemed with Rosalynn to get the two of them together. Panic stricken and terrified of being tongue-tied, Rosalynn was relieved that every time Ruth invited her to Archery, Jimmy had plans to be somewhere else.

Finally, shortly before the end of his vacation, Ruth called to invite Rosalynn to come to the Carter's Pond House for a picnic. Jimmy was there and Rosalynn found herself far from speechless, although he teased her all afternoon. He was twenty and she was seventeen, and she worried that he would see her as more of Ruth's age and too young. That evening Jimmy invited her to go a movie with Ruth and her boyfriend. They rode in the rumble seat of the car and on the way home he kissed her, a stunning development for Rosalynn, who had never allowed a boy to kiss her on a first date.

When Jimmy got home that night, he mentioned to his mother that he had gone to the movies with Rosalynn. When asked whether he liked her, "She's the girl I want to marry," he responded definitively. Somewhat taken aback, Miss Lillian replied, "Jimmy, she's a little girl; she's Ruth's friend."

The next night, his last before leaving, he had a date with Annelle, but Ruth convinced Rosalynn to go with the family to the train station to see him off. Jimmy walked Rosalynn down the platform away from his parents and apologized to her for having had another date that evening, adding that he would rather have been with her.

"Will you write to me?" he asked.

She promised she would. They kissed and he climbed aboard the train.

After returning to Annapolis, Jimmy immediately left on a cruise in the North Atlantic. They were at sea less than a week when all hands were summoned to hear a message "of great military importance for our nation." Hundreds of men sat on the steel decks in front of the ship's loudspeakers expecting an announcement that the long-anticipated invasion of Japan had begun. When President Truman, in his flat droning voice, said a new superbomb had just been dropped on Japan, he left his seabound audience completely perplexed. For months they had assumed that upon graduation they would be destined for the Asian theater and had speculated on how many thousands of Americans and Japanese would be killed in the final assault on the enemy. Two days later, after a second atomic bomb was dropped, it was announced that Japan had surrendered.

In Plains the news was greeted by the ringing of the church bells and people gathered to pray and give thanks to God for bringing peace. Rosalynn said a special prayer of thanksgiving knowing that Jimmy would no longer be going to war.

After Jimmy returned to port, they exchanged letters regularly, getting to know each other as well as possible through the mail. Jimmy adopted with Rosalynn a pattern of teasing which throughout his life characterized his relationship with people to whom he felt close. He would tell her at length about a beautiful woman he was going out with, only to end the letter by revealing that she was the eight-year-old daughter of the commandant. Rosalynn had dated other boys. Now she was solely committed to Jimmy, but, goaded by his teasing, she wrote him back listing the boys she was supposedly seeing, even those she only played Ping-Pong with in the afternoon. It got his attention and he angrily responded, saying he wanted her to wait for him and not go out with anyone else.

When Jimmy came home on leave at Christmas, they went to movies together, took long drives, and attended Christmas parties. Romantically they sat together in front of roaring fires and listened to "White Christmas" and "Silent Night." He joked with her about just being in love with his uniform. On Christmas morning he gave Rosalynn a silver compact in the middle of which were engraved the letters "ILYTG." It was a term of endearment, a Carter family code, that meant "I love you the goodest." It would remain a special cryptic message of love between the two of them shared only with their children and Jimmy's sisters. He had a date with one other person over Christmas, and that was Marguerite Wise. He shared with her his intention to marry Rosalynn, and she, still holding strong feelings for him, tried to talk him out of it. But his mind was made up. On one of his last nights at home he proposed.

Despite Rosalynn's love for Jimmy and her aching desire to be constantly with him, confronted with the real prospects of marriage, she hesitated. She had promised her father she would get a college degree, and hoped to graduate from Georgia State College for Women as her mother had. Jimmy's proposal seemed sudden and it aroused insecurities she had suffered since her father died when she was thirteen. She saw herself as young, naive, and unsophisticated next to his worldliness. She said no, trying to explain her fears and insecurities. Jimmy responded sympathetically and they agreed to wait and keep his proposal a secret.

After Christmas they wrote to each other almost daily. Over George Washington's Birthday weekend Rosalynn accompanied Earl and Lillian on a trip to Annapolis. There the young couple talked secretly about marriage again. Rosalynn was now more comfortable with the idea and she accepted his proposal, but they agreed not to divulge their decision to anyone. Although for Jimmy and Rosalynn it was a profoundly happy weekend spent doting on each other, Mr. Earl was distinctly annoyed that Jimmy was more interested in Rosalynn than his parents. Earl and Lillian were ambitious for Jimmy and had great expectations for his future; marrying an eighteen-year-old girl from Plains was not part of those plans. Despite her initial reservations concerning Rosalynn, Miss Lillian was more supportive once she knew Jimmy had made the decision. Rosalynn's biggest problem was with her friend Ruth. Ruth had become increasingly narcissistic and self-centered, and had difficulty facing up to the responsibilities of adulthood. Although Ruth had conspired with Rosalynn to get Jimmy's attention, when it was no longer a game and she was faced with Rosalynn becoming permanently the center of his attention, she became resentful and jealous. It would be years before they would have a normal relationship again.

Jimmy sent Rosalynn a book, *The Navy Wife*, which she carefully and enthusiastically studied. In their correspondence they began to plan their navy life together. The graduation exercises in June 1946 lasted six days, culminating in the graduation ceremony itself in Dahlgren Hall. The class of '47 received their diplomas and commissions, and then, according to tradition, threw their midshipmen's caps high into the air. A short while later they reassembled at the Japanese Bell where the closest women relatives pinned shoulder boards on for the new officers. For Jimmy, Rosalynn pinned on one side and Lillian the other.

Jimmy and Rosalynn were married on July 7, 1946, in the Methodist church in Plains. It was a private wedding to which only family and a few friends came. Jimmy always had an obsession for punctuality, which his years at the Naval Academy only served to accentuate. The wedding was scheduled for 3 P.M. Jimmy had arranged to pick Rosalynn up at her mother's house at fifteen minutes to the hour, leaving ample time for the brief ride to the church. However, as they pulled up, they heard the strains of the wedding march actually being played for the second time. Jimmy leaped from the car and literally dragged Rosalynn up the steps. At the top they had to pause to catch their breath before proceeding down the aisle. Jimmy was wearing his white navy summer uniform and Rosalynn wore a white-and-blue dress, on which was pinned a corsage of purple-throated orchids.

After the ceremony they left in a car loaned by Jimmy's father for the four-hour drive to Atlanta, where they would spend their wedding night at the Biltmore Hotel. Unfortunately, in Atlanta Jimmy ran through a red light and hit a brand-new car. He was forced to call his aunt Sissy, living in nearby Roswell, to help sort out the insurance claim. He and Rosalynn departed the next day for Chimney Rock in the mountains of North Carolina, where they had been lent a friend's summer home for a week. While there, Rosalynn saw a white woman sweeping the yard of the family next door. "It was shocking to me," she later recalled. "In Plains, Georgia, I had never seen a white woman doing yard labor or housework for a white person."

CHAPTER 5

I must go down to the sea again, to the lonely sea and the sky,
And all I ask is a tall ship and a star to steer her by.

—JOHN MASEFIELD

Eleanor Rosalynn Smith was born on August 18, 1927. Her family came from the same Anglo-Saxon pioneer stock as the Carters and the Gordys, moving, as they did, to Southwest Georgia in the mid-1800s. Her paternal grandparents, Wilburn Juristine Smith and Sally Eleanor Bell, lived in Marion County. Their son Wilburn Edgar Smith married Frances Allethea Murray, known as "Allie." Allie's father, John William Murray, known as "Captain Murray," was born in Sumter County in 1871, and married Rosa Nettie Wise, nine years his junior, of Webster County.

Allie grew up an only child on the farm her parents ran 5 miles south of Plains. She attended the school in Plains and was in one of the first classes taught by Julia Coleman. The school bus driver was Wilburn Edgar Smith, known as Edgar, a tall, good-looking young man, with dark, curly hair. In his mid-twenties, he already owned an auto repair shop in an old livery stable in Plains, and a farm on the outskirts of town, and, besides driving the school bus, he supplemented his income by working in one of the stores on weekends. He was strongly attracted to the pretty, petite, brown-eyed student that he drove to school every day, but she was determined to finish college before considering marriage. The age difference between them bothered him little as it was the same as that between his parents. For Allie it was a greater concern, although his ambition and demonstrated success counterbalanced any reservations she may have had. They married in 1926 after she had graduated from the Georgia State College for Women, in Milledgeville, with a teacher's diploma.

They moved into a simple white-frame house in the center of Plains, and a year later Rosalynn was born. They had a large backyard with a wooden barn where pigs and a milk cow were kept. Another barn housed the mules Edgar used on his farm. A small smokehouse was used to cure bacon. There was a chicken coop and a rabbit pen. Petunias, zinnias, crepe myrtle,

hollyhocks, and rosebushes abounded, as Allie loved the color and fresh-
ness they provided. In the back they grew vegetables and fruit trees—figs,
pears, pecans, wild cherries, and pomegranates.

The year Edgar and Allie married was the year the Bank of Plains failed,
wiping out his entire savings of $1,000. The growing depression hit them
the way it was hitting everyone else in the community, squeezing the profit
out of Edgar's farm operation. However, he had not only the security of his
school job but his repair business, which flourished. The family always had
a car, even if never a new one, and they grew most of their own food. It
made them feel fortunate compared with their neighbors. Rosalynn would
go to Americus, where she would sketch the dresses in the store windows
for her mother, a skilled seamstress, to copy. As a result, her clothes were
the envy of all her friends.

While Allie's mother was a Lutheran, and her father a Baptist, Rosalynn's parents were Methodists. Rosalynn ended up involved with all
three denominations. She attended Sunday school and the regular Sunday
service, prayer meetings, Methodist League, Baptist Girls Auxiliary, and
Bible school. The whole family eagerly looked forward to one of the big
events of the year, the revival meeting, organized alternately by the Baptists and the Methodists. For a whole week each summer there was preaching morning and night, and they never missed a service. In the inevitable
way that hardship drives people closer to their religion, the depression further intensified the faith of an already devout community.

Rosalynn says of this experience:

> God was a real presence in my life, especially in those revival times. We
> were taught to love Him and felt very much the necessity and desire to live
> the kind of life He would have us live, to love one another and be kind to and
> help those who needed help, and to be good. But we were also taught to fear
> God, and though I loved Him, I was afraid of displeasing Him all my young
> life. I did not think about Him as a forgiving God, but as a punishing God,
> and I was afraid even to have a bad thought. I thought that if we were good
> He would love us, but if we weren't He wouldn't.

In many respects Rosalynn's relationship with God mirrored that with
her father. Edgar was a warm, loving man who overtly demonstrated a level
of affection to his wife and children that Rosalynn never saw in the homes
of her friends, making her feel their family was special. When he came
home from work, he would rush to the kitchen, whirl Allie around, and give
her a kiss. He spent countless hours playing with and entertaining Rosalynn and her two younger brothers, Jerry and Murray. He told them stories, did tricks for them, and even on one occasion when Allie had gone to
her missionary circle baked a cake for them. He loved them and they knew

it. At the same time he was a demanding and strict disciplinarian. Each of the children had assigned chores. Rosalynn made the beds, churned the milk, swept the porch, and washed and dried the dishes, while her brothers took care of the cow and pigs and brought in the wood for the stove and fireplaces. Her father insisted that they take these responsibilities very seriously and Rosalynn constantly struggled to please him. He would spank her for misbehavior, especially for crossing a dangerous and heavily trafficked street. He would tell her not to cry, but she had difficulty keeping her feelings inside and thought he was mean and did not love her. Those thoughts caused her guilt for years. Her mother was affectionate but always supported her husband with respect to punishing the children.

When Rosalynn was eight, her father's mother, "Mama Sallie," a crotchety and difficult woman, moved in with them. Rosalynn would say of her that "she always had aches and pains, and would constantly express her displeasure, and did not particularly like the children." She had a suffocating effect on Rosalynn, who lived in fear of upsetting her by making too much noise. On one occasion Rosalynn went into one of Mama Sallie's two rooms, found a box of chocolate-covered cherries, and ate one. It was "on my conscience for years and years," Rosalynn says. "She had a real impact on my life" that contributed significantly to her timidity and the shyness she would struggle to overcome in later years.

When Rosalynn started school she set very high standards for herself and was driven by a strong desire to please her parents and her teachers. She found it very painful when she thought she had let them down. She made straight A's on her first report card and rushed home to tell her parents. She continued to shine academically and in the third grade was asked to help teach second-graders who were slow learners in arithmetic.

When Rosalynn was twelve and in the seventh grade, a businessman in Plains who ran the M and M store, and who had himself failed the seventh grade, offered a $5 prize to the student that year with the highest grades. Rosalynn was not merely determined to win but felt that her family and the teachers expected it of her. She was acutely aware of the pressure she was under, memories of which remained with her into adulthood. She won, receiving widespread adult recognition and adulation in the community. In retrospect she pinpoints this experience as teaching her, for the first time, that the satisfaction and pleasure in accomplishing lofty, seemingly unattainable goals more than compensates for the struggle and hard work involved.

Her teacher that year, Miss Thelma Macarthur, was a young, beautiful woman, who seemed to know more than anyone Rosalynn had ever met. She brought maps of the world to school and she encouraged the children to read the newspapers. The year was 1939 and she taught them about the impending war in Europe. She was Rosalynn's idol and her consuming interest in current events led Rosalynn to search for stories of interesting people and places far away from the sheltered and isolated community of Plains.

That summer Rosalynn's parents suddenly reversed an earlier decision and allowed her to go to summer camp with a group of girls from the Methodist church. On her return from Camp Dooley she discovered the reason for their change of heart. Her father was very sick and, while she was gone, had spent most of the time in the hospital undergoing a lengthy series of tests. He went to work irregularly and over the next few weeks spent increasing amounts of time in bed. He assured Rosalynn that he was doing what the doctors ordered and would get well. But she knew there was something irretrievably wrong. Toward the end of August he suffered a serious crisis, collapsing with shortness of breath. From then on he was bedridden. He delighted in having the children come to report their activities at his bedside, and he took great comfort from having the family gather around him to read the Bible together. Rosalynn worried that her negative thoughts when angry had somehow contributed to her father's illness. Unable to share her fears, she felt consumed with guilt. To assuage it, she devoted herself to him, reading to him and brushing his hair, terrified as he became progressively more frail and ashen. She prayed to God to save her father, only to question why her urgent prayers were seemingly ignored.

One evening early in October, the children were summoned to their father's bedside—Rosalynn, Jerry, Murray, and three-year-old Lillian Allethea in her mother's arms. "I want you all to listen very carefully to what I have to say and be very brave," he began. "The time has come to tell you that I can't get well and you're going to have to look after Mother for me. You are good children and I'm depending on you to be strong." Rosalynn began to sob uncontrollably as did her two brothers and their father. Telling them to dry their tears, he began talking about aspects of his life he had never shared with them before. His greatest regret was that he had never gone to college and, above all, he wanted that for his children, so they would have the opportunities in life he had been denied. He told Allie to sell the farm if necessary to see that they had the money for their education. Rosalynn left the room devastated and went outside to her frequent refuge and crying place, the privy.

In the following weeks Lillian Carter, after whom Rosalynn's sister, Lillian Allethea, had been named, became a regular presence in their house. She provided nursing care and helped Allie to look after her husband. The neighbors rallied around, and his friends took turns sitting with Edgar and reading to him. The support and warmth of the community, so typical of rural societies in a time of crisis, gave mother and children a sense of security and solace.

On the evening of her father's death, Rosalynn was sent to Archery to spend the night with Ruth Carter. In the middle of the night, Miss Lillian woke her up and took her home. Her father had died of leukemia. He was forty-four years old, Allie was thirty-four, and Rosalynn was thirteen. Forced to endure a crushing emotional loss, the family also faced an economic crisis and the challenge of assuming substantial new responsibilities. Rosalynn could not be a child anymore. In the early months her maternal grandparents shared much of the burden. Grandfather Murray rented out their farm and collected the rent. Grandmother Murray frequently stayed with them to help Allie, and on occasion the children spent time at the Murray farm. Then tragedy struck again. Within a year of Edgar's death, Grandmother Murray died of a heart attack. Seventy years old, Captain Murray could no longer run the farm by himself, so he moved in with Allie and the children. Instead of being a source of support, he increasingly became part of her burden. At the same time, however, Mama Sallie moved out into a house built for her by Edgar's brothers.

Mother Allie took charge, suddenly exuding a degree of self-reliance that significantly shaped the kind of person Rosalynn would become. They had only the income from the farm and Edgar's insurance—$18.25 a month—to live on. To make ends meet, Allie turned her hand to sewing. Later she worked in the school lunchroom and in a grocery store. Eventually she went to work for the post office, initially part-time, then full-time, remaining there until she retired in 1978.

She treated Rosalynn as an equal and a partner in the family's struggle to survive. She sought Rosalynn's advice and judgment on everything from the handling of the young children to what she should wear, even to what job she should take. Rosalynn was expected to behave as a responsible adult and not as a typical teenager. Although she frequently felt resentment, her sense of obligation to her mother and siblings dictated that she always be on her best behavior.

While growing up, Rosalynn had relatively little to do with blacks. They provided the labor on her father's farm, but Rosalynn went there only occasionally. They did use a washerwoman and took the clothes to her house, where they were washed and returned neatly ironed on Friday. Occasionally another black woman would help her mother with the housework.

When Rosalynn was in the ninth grade, a young black woman named Annie B. Floyd, who had grown up on their farm, came to the back door of their house. Knowing that Rosalynn had a typewriter, Annie came to ask if Rosalynn would type the thesis she needed to graduate from the all-black college in Forsyth. When Rosalynn looked at the paper she, as a ninth grader, was astonished by the misspelling, poor grammar, and lack of punctuation—not what one would expect from a college student. It was, for Rosalynn, a pivotal moment in which she suddenly became aware of the glaring inequity in the quality of black and white education. Ultimately, Annie B., after earning several more degrees along the way, would become the principal of the Plains all-black Rosenwald School. Yet it was hard to ignore the dramatic contrast between the backgrounds of Annie B. Floyd and Julia Coleman, and its implications for the education of the children of their respective races.

The perfection of Rosalynn's high school performance exacted a significant toll psychologically. Success in life, which previously had seemed to involve such straightforward things as making good grades and pleasing her father, had now become complex and demanding. She lost much of her earlier self-confidence, and began feeling weak and vulnerable. She became even more painfully shy and timid. Her sense of abandonment by her father was reinforced by the death of her grandmother. She questioned her relationship with God, who seemed to have abandoned her too. She felt increasingly sorry for herself and could not resolve the fundamental question of why, when she had always tried to be such a good girl, all these terrible things had happened to her. Paradoxically her father affected her behavior and thinking even more after his death than when he was alive. She found herself asking, "Would Daddy have approved of this or would he have been angry if I did that?" She vividly recalled how he, a nondrinker who only smoked a pipe, condemned those who drank and had told her how ugly he thought women looked when they smoked a cigarette. For Rosalynn, thoughts of smoking or drinking would have been a betrayal.

Rosalynn compensated by burying herself in her schoolwork. She studied relentlessly and was consistently at the head of her class. A year after her father's death, Ruth and Rosalynn were double dating at a movie in Americus when the screen went blank and an announcement was made that the Japanese had attacked Pearl Harbor. Julia Coleman, who by then had become the superintendent of the school, exhorted the students to make an even greater effort in their schoolwork as part of their patriotic commitment to the war effort. While few girls at that time dreamed of being anything other than housewives, teachers, or nurses, Julie Coleman saw the opportunities the war could offer and encouraged them to broaden their vision and prepare for life in a world that went far beyond Plains and Sumter County. Her message found its mark with Rosalynn, who began to fantasize about being an architect, a stewardess, an interior decorator, or even a famous artist. Rosalynn was particularly drawn to math and science, deriving a strong sense of gratification from her ability to understand the operation and mastery of machinery.

Rosalynn, as did most of the girls, played basketball and her self-confidence received a happy boost when she made the first team. She also worked part-time giving shampoos in the local beauty parlor, benefitting particularly from the sense of independence that earning her own pocket money gave her. But it was her academic accomplishments that did the most to rebuild her self-esteem. She ended her senior year as the class valedictorian, and she faultlessly delivered, with knees trembling, her carefully memorized speech.

She enrolled at Georgia Southwestern, riding to school each day with a neighbor and taking the Greyhound bus home. By skipping lunch she could save enough from a $4.50 per week allowance to go to the Roxy movie theater with her female classmates and swoon over Frank Sinatra.

Rosalynn had limited time to pursue a social life, but her relationship with Ruth became very close. Despite their age difference, they shared all their secrets and rarely dated except together. Ruth's self-assured bravado, especially dealing with boys, obscured Rosalynn's timidity. Rosalynn dated a classmate named Robert Mills, a platonic friend Rosalynn felt she could call on as an escort for social events. She also dated Ross Oliver, who was related to one of Plains's most prominent businessmen. He pursued her almost too aggressively and frequently. When he called on a weekend, Rosalynn would tell her mother to say she was out.

Once she met Ruth's brother, Rosalynn had no interest in other boys and dated no one else. Happy to be leaving Plains and the hardship she associated with it, Rosalynn eagerly looked forward to the challenge of married life and her husband's exciting career. Assignments for the new Annapolis graduates, to fulfill their initial requirement of two years of surface duty, were made by lottery. Jimmy drew his fourth choice, the USS *Wyoming*, an old dilapidated battleship, based in Norfolk, Virginia. It had been converted into an experimental vessel for testing prototypes of new navigation, radar, fire control, communications, and gunnery equipment.

Carter has described the assignment on the USS *Wyoming* as "wonderful training" and "interesting," but he also confesses it was "terrible duty." He was at sea from Monday to Thursday and had to stand duty every third night, which took a piece out of every weekend. As always, he was determined to make the most of every situation—to work hard and sacrifice to make a success of his navy career.

The Carters had rented an apartment at 1009 Buckingham Street in Norfolk, a pleasant middle-class area. Rosalynn, nineteen years old and living out of the rural South for the first time, felt overwhelmed and lonely. Resourceful and determined not to let her new husband down, she learned to deal with the landlord, the electrician, and the plumber. She opened a bank account and paid their bills. Jimmy's demanding schedule and salary of $300 per month, one third of which went for their rent, offered little opportunity for recreation outside their apartment. They did buy a new record player so they could listen to Jimmy's collection of classical records that he had won from Bob Scott.

In their free time, they socialized with Jimmy's fellow officers and their wives. His former roommate, Al Rusher, and his new wife, Betty, a former "Miss Arkansas," became close friends. Lou Larcombe was from Norfolk and they would visit him and his parents. They had other navy friends whose apartments they would visit for meals or parties, including Jack and Lil Weaver, Marion and Ralph Kinser, Bill and Elaine Hough, and John and Chloe Cohoon.

Jimmy expected the same self-sufficiency of others that had always been expected of him. He assumed Rosalynn would take care of her responsibilities to the best of her ability. At the same time he had difficulty discussing his own problems in the navy with her. The southern cultural style demanded that men be strong and stoic while women and mothers were to be spared involvement in the male world outside the home. It was not that he was unfeeling. He always let her know how proud he was of her and when he was home he helped with the cooking and housekeeping. Jimmy was willing to try his hand at any challenge, satisfied if he felt he had done his best. Rosalynn, by contrast, shied away from trying anything that she could not do perfectly. "Despite our love, it was not always easy for us to adjust to one another," he says.

On July 3, 1947, John William Carter (Jack) was born at the Portsmouth Navy Hospital. Jimmy took two weeks of leave to help Rosalynn with the cooking, the washing, and the care of the baby. Rosalynn adored being a mother, but once Jimmy was back on duty the responsibility of motherhood seemed at times overwhelming. They had no car and even getting groceries involved a long ride on the streetcar, taking the baby with her. She says:

> Tears, I had learned, instead of being persuasive or eliciting sympathy, had quite the opposite effect on Jimmy. He had and still has no patience with tears, thinking instead that one makes the best of whatever situation—and with a smile.

Living in the apartment beneath them was a young navy doctor and his wife, who had young children of their own. "I don't know what I would have done without them. They saved my life," she says. Betty Rusher also had a baby at about the same time and their shared experiences created a special bond between them.

The *Wyoming* had been launched in 1911 and was considered so unsafe that it was not allowed to dock at the Norfolk Navy Yard piers, but instead was anchored at the far side of the harbor. By mid-1948, the decrepit ship was decommissioned and sent to the scrap yard. It was replaced by the USS *Mississippi* on which Jimmy would serve for another year. Among other responsibilities, he was in charge of the training of enlisted men at the high school and college level, stimulating an interest in education that would be central to his future career. The captain, however, "was a martinet, who exercised his authority in an arbitrary and vindictive way." The crew resented him and morale was low.

Overall the two years on surface ships was a dreary experience. The *Wyoming* and the *Mississippi* were never allowed to leave the navy's gunnery practice ranges of Chesapeake Bay, earning them the name "Chesapeake Raiders." Jimmy says of that period:

> The postwar navy was in bad shape. It was a time of great discouragement because we were undermanned, the nation was relaxing after a long and difficult war, and funds allocated for naval operations were meager. I became most disillusioned with the navy, and the military in general, and probably would have resigned had not I, and all Annapolis graduates, been serving "at the pleasure of the president." Reenlistments in the navy were rare, and most of the ships that remained in commission were understaffed. Sea operations were curtailed, and morale was low.

Searching for other options, Jimmy applied for a Rhodes scholarship.

> I got to the final screening board [to be the selectee from Georgia] and there was another fellow in there with me. He was a tall gangly fellow, real peculiar-looking guy. We were the last two. He studied Elizabethan poetry, and the interviewing board asked something about current events, and he said he wasn't interested in anything that happened after Queen Elizabeth died. . . . They asked me every question they could think of. I answered them all—current events, philosophy, music, nuclear physics. But the other guy got the Rhodes scholarship. I didn't even feel bitter about it. But as a matter of fact, he went over there from Georgia and he had a nervous breakdown.

It was the first time in his life that Jimmy was forced to face a significant failure, and he was depressed for several weeks. His mother later recalled that the rejection was quite devastating. Jimmy, however, always has shown an unusual ability to put setbacks small or large behind him.

> That comes natural to me. . . . I don't worry about the prospects of future disappointments or embarrassments or difficulties. I take one thing at a time, do the best I can, and then if I fail, I don't dwell on it or bemoan it. I just go on.

He bounced back by quickly applying for the prestigious, and highly sought-after, submarine service. He and Rosalynn were ecstatic when he won one of the coveted positions and was assigned to a six-month submarine officer training school. They arrived in New London, Connecticut, in June 1948. All of the sixty junior officers in the class and their families were housed together in quarters on the submarine base. For the first time in their marriage, Rosalynn felt relaxed, content, and no longer lonely. Jimmy came home every evening to their apartment on base. They were within walking distance of the officers club, and there was a movie theater nearby that cost 10 cents. There were backyard parties and barbecues and the wives baby-sat for each other, giving Rosalynn a degree of freedom she had not known since Jack's birth. That Jimmy's pay was only $282 per month seemed to matter little.

Jimmy and Rosalynn were, however, remembered as "shy" and less gregarious than the other couples. They seemed content to be with each other and their young baby, without any great urge to socialize. In part it was a reflection of the values of their rural small-town upbringing, but it was also a manifestation of their individual personalities, especially Jimmy's. Pleasure was to be derived not from relaxation and well-earned lethargy but from a sense of constant accomplishment, whether it involved self-improvement or contributing to the welfare of others. It would lead people to describe him as "driven." While many of his classmates were content to spend an evening together drinking beer, Rosalynn and Jimmy preferred more meaningful activities. Their next-door neighbors were a young Peruvian couple, Manolo and Maria Piqueras. Although Maria spoke fluent English, Manolo did not. Rosalynn bought books and tapes and the four of them practiced Spanish and English together. While in Norfolk, Jimmy had ordered a commercial art course for a sailor who was studying for his high school diploma. It arrived after the man had been transferred, so Jimmy and Rosalynn took it themselves. They studied *Treasury of Art Masterpieces,* and acquired basic proficiency in the use of charcoal, watercolors, and oil paints.

The submarine course itself was very demanding and 15 percent of those who started did not complete it. Apart from classroom lectures, they went to sea every day in submarines, practicing diving and firing torpedoes in the waters of Long Island and Block Island Sounds in mock battles that the instructors compared to actual submarine actions in the Second World War. The students were an elite group and the competition was intense. Each man knew that his failure to master properly the skills or techniques being taught could ultimately put the lives of an entire crew at risk. Jimmy applied himself intensively, and graduated third among the fifty-two men who completed the course.

The Truman/Dewey presidential race occurred while Jimmy was at the submarine school and he recalls being the only one in his class to openly support Truman. Earlier, while Jimmy was still stationed in Norfolk, Henry Wallace had come to address a political rally. Jimmy casually mentioned that he would attend to his executive officer, Commander Smythe, who glared at him and demanded, "Are you prepared to give up your career in the navy?" Jimmy stammered that this was not his intention. "Then stay away from political meetings," Smythe admonished him. From then on, he generally kept his political views to himself.

Upon graduation Jimmy received his first submarine assignment, as an electronics officer on the USS *Pomfret* (SS 391), a vessel that had already earned five battle stars in the war against Japan. It would be based in Honolulu, but the assignment would begin with a three-month cruise to China. Jimmy and Rosalynn drove home to Plains for Christmas in their first car, a new gray Studebaker "Commander." Rosalynn and young Jack stayed with Miss Allie while Jimmy drove to Los Angeles and flew on to Honolulu on December 28, where he joined the *Pomfret* at Pearl Harbor. Two days later they sailed for Asia.

Almost immediately the crew ran into one of the worst recorded storms in Pacific Ocean history. Seven ships were lost. Jimmy was desperately seasick for five straight days, but as the engineering officer Warren "Red" Colegrove recalled, he would not forgo his duty. "He had a helluva time. But I will say this. He never refused to take his watch. He'd take his bucket right up on the bridge. He was a gutsy guy."

Near tragedy occurred for Jimmy during the storm. Submarines of that vintage were forced to surface each night to recharge their batteries. Jimmy was on the bridge, about 15 feet above the water, when they were hit by a giant wave rising at least 6 feet above his head. Its force tore away his grip on the handrail and he found himself swimming inside the wave, completely separated from the ship. "After I swam for a good while—it seemed forever—the wave receded and I landed on top of the 5-inch gun located about 30 feet aft of where I had been standing. I clung desperately to the gun barrel, and finally was able to lower myself to the deck and return to my watch station."

The storm also destroyed the *Pomfret*'s radio transmitting equipment so that the crew was unable to send their daily location report to Pacific Fleet Headquarters. They could, however, hear the calls from headquarters and knew that their failure to respond was causing great concern. They changed course and headed for Midway to radio their survival. The last report they heard before they arrived was: "To all ships in the Pacific. Be on the lookout for floating debris left by submarine USS *Pomfret*, believed to have been sunk approximately 700 miles south of Midway Island." The crew was desperate to assure their families of their safety. Wives in Hawaii had already been notified by the navy that the *Pomfret* might be lost. Happily, Rosalynn, far away in Plains, was unaware of the incident until it was over.

After completing repairs in Midway, they headed for the East Coast of China. There, the corrupt regime of Chiang Kai-shek was ending, and the forces of Mao Tse-tung were about to take over. The presence of U.S. and Allied navy vessels was primarily aimed at providing a symbolic gesture of support to the collapsing regime. However, for a young naval officer the geopolitics were of little concern compared to the day-to-day military responsibilities that justified their presence. Jimmy later described the experience.

We were there to operate primarily with the British and Australian navies. We provided the target for them to practice antisubmarine strategies, because the Russians' main force was submarines and they did not have any submarines of their own to practice on. So part of the cruise was to start at Hong Kong and go all the way up the coast of China visiting as many seaports as we could . . . in every one of those ports there was a small redoubt of Nationalist troops there and the city was surrounded by the communists— Mao Tse-tung's forces. We could see their campfires all around. And the Nationalists were recruiting little boys as soldiers. Several times we saw mature troops with bayonets with little boys backed up against the wall forcing them to leave home and go join the Nationalist forces who were on their last legs. This was in the spring of '49, and Chiang Kai-shek left China completely on October 1 that same year.

We spent about two weeks, if I remember correctly, in Tsingtoa, which was the furthest north port. . . . All the stores were boarded up in the front. If you wanted to buy ivory carvings, or cloisonne vases, or raw silk, or bolts of cloth, you went around to the back of the shop and you could buy them for practically nothing because there wasn't any market anymore. And every time we tied up with our ship, our captain, J. B. Williams, who was the best captain I ever had, would let the merchants come and spread their wares on the back of the submarine.

Each evening on the *Pomfret*, Commander John B. Williams and the other seven officers would linger in their tiny ward room after dinner for coffee and poker. The exception was Jimmy Carter. Says Sam Colston, who was the ward steward: "He thought four hours of poker was a waste of time. He would go back to his bunk and read a book or work on some sonar problem. He always wanted to do something constructive." Red Colegrove says, "Jimmy was not one of the guys. We didn't criticize him or anything because he was an incredibly determined and responsible officer. But he was always apart . . . he never really got close to anybody." Carter considered Williams the best captain he served under, and in later years sought to model his own leadership style after him.

At the end of the cruise, in March 1949, the *Pomfret* returned to Hawaii. Jimmy began settling into a two-bedroom apartment for married officers at 318 Sixth Street, NHA #1, Pearl Harbor. A week later Rosalynn arrived with Jack after a rough sea voyage. Jimmy met them at the pier with traditional leis in hand. He had filled the apartment with exotic blooms and had champagne chilling in the refrigerator.

Thus began a happy year and a half. When not at sea, Jimmy was usually home shortly after lunch. They had the time to travel about the islands and enjoy the beaches. The warmth of the tropical climate, the lush vegetation, the orchids that proliferated almost like dandelions, the hibiscus plant that grew its crimson blooms up to their second-floor bedroom in three months, the rainbows that appeared almost daily, were lasting memories.

Rosalynn says, "We quickly went native. I made matching shirts for Jimmy and Jack. Jimmy learned to play the ukelele, and I did the hula to songs like 'Lovely Hula Hands' and 'In a Little Grass Shack' while he strummed away."

Their social life involved almost exclusively Jimmy's shipmates and their wives. "Red" (W.R.) and Joy Colegrove were their closest friends. Their next-door neighbors in Hawaii were Paul and Mary Ellen Haines, who had two small children, and together Jimmy and Paul fenced in the backyard. Their circle of friends included other naval officers, Ed Marcus, Chick Bowling, Chuck Tisdale, and Bob Bisset, whose wife, Rosalynn recalls, was the best hula dancer among them. It was during this period that Jimmy perfected the woodworking skills he had begun to learn in high school.

> I would go to the hobby shops that the navy had at the submarine base.
> They had excellent cabinetmakers there and . . . they had . . . the right kinds
> of glue and large machines for lathe work and saws. And they would teach
> you about the different woods.

Jimmy was still studying to become qualified in submarines and this consumed much of his free time. He passed his exams and, on February 4, 1950, Rosalynn pinned his "Dolphins" on his uniform.

Rosalynn became pregnant again, and on April 12, 1950, James Earl Carter III was born. He was called "Chip" by the nurses at Tripler Army Hospital; the name stuck.

One day, toward the end of their tour in Hawaii, Rosalynn drove to the base to pick up Jimmy. She was told that there had been an emergency and no one was allowed to enter, so she went home and nervously awaited some news. When Jimmy finally came home late that night, he told her that war had started in Korea.

Jimmy and Rosalynn would have preferred to remain in Hawaii indefinitely. They had decided that it was where they would retire after Jimmy left the navy. His tour was scheduled to end in June 1950 and the *Pomfret* was to go to New London for a complete overhaul and refit. But with the sudden outbreak of the Korean War, the orders changed and the *Pomfret* and her crew were assigned instead to the shipyards in San Diego, so that the ship could remain available for immediate service in the Pacific theater. Rosalynn, with their two young sons, flew in a drafty navy transport plane with canvas bucket seats back to California. They stayed in Los Angeles with the parents of one of Jimmy's fellow officers, "Slick" Fitch, for several weeks until Jimmy arrived with the ship and found them a place to live in San Diego.

The Carters' life in San Diego was a painful contrast with the idyllic existence of Hawaii. San Diego had become the staging point for thousands of military personnel bound for Korea, who swamped the city. Housing was scarce and Jimmy and Rosalynn were forced to settle for accommodations at 18 J Street in a predominantly Mexican section of town near a row of bars. Their elderly landlady, Mrs. Johnson, lived next door and criticized Rosalynn for everything from her shopping to her housekeeping to her cooking. Jimmy was gone all week, so Rosalynn was at Mrs. Johnson's mercy. As she was reaching her wits' end, and in the midst of a visit by Jimmy's parents, orders finally arrived assigning them back to Connecticut. The most beneficial aspect of their five-month ordeal was that it gave them a chance to use their Spanish on a regular basis. It also exposed them to the urban poverty of the Hispanic and black residents among whom they lived.

As the Carters prepared to leave San Diego for the long drive across the country, they could not, because of a telephone strike, get any cash transferred from their account in Plains to a local bank. Spending their meager cash on $3- and $4-a-night motels and eating very little, they drove 700 miles in one day to reach Brinkley, Arkansas. Jimmy's old friend, Al Rusher, had left the navy to return to Brinkley, where his family owned the local bank. Not only did Jimmy and Rosalynn get a supply of cash but, as the Rusher family also owned the local hotel, the Carters enjoyed one very comfortable night on their trip.

Jimmy had consistently impressed his superiors as dedicated, hardworking, self-confident, and congenial. They routinely rated him as outstanding. For his part, he loved submarines and he enjoyed the physical and personal closeness with other members of the crew, the competitive masculine relationships, and the demand for perfection required of each man as the price of interdependence. His low-key but confident style, his retiring, sometimes introverted manner, and his sensitivity to the psychological as well as the physical needs of others made him an ideal choice for the cramped life of the submariner.

It was, however, his demonstrated talents as an engineer that led to his selection for his next assignment. In 1949 the navy had decided to build its first new ship since the end of World War II. It was to be an innovative submarine, the K-1. The navy described its mission as: "Only a little more than half as big as the navy's fleet-type sub, the K-1's job is to lie in ambush along enemy submarine lanes, spot its prey with sonar gear, then nail the enemy with homing torpedoes equipped with electronic ears." The keel had been laid at the shipyards of the Electric Boat Company in New London, Connecticut, on July 1, 1949. Jimmy arrived as the senior officer of the pre-commissioning detail on February 1, 1951, as construction was being completed. For several weeks he was the only navy person aboard. The

K-1 was launched on March 2 and commissioned on November 10 under Lt. Commander Frank A. Andrews with Lt. James E. Carter, Jr. (J.G.), as the engineering officer. He would later become the executive officer.

Once at sea, Jimmy found the new equipment that they were testing intriguing and intellectually stimulating.

> We would stay submerged for long periods of time, working in stockinged feet, with machinery in operation, controlling our depth simply by raising or lowering the periscope a few inches at a time. With a constant ship weight and a slightly varying amount of water displaced, the submarine would rise or sink very slowly as the periscope was moved. This fine balance took a lot of skill, experience, and luck, but gave us a platform of almost complete silence from which to listen to our prospective targets. We would hear all kinds of strange sea creature sounds and could detect ships at extraordinary distances.

William Lalor, a fellow crew member, recalls these periods when Jimmy, who was called Jim by his crewmates, showed both a steely nerve under pressure and a self-deprecating humor. "I can remember him being in a really precarious situation a couple of times . . . the ship would be sitting almost vertical. He'd just laugh and scratch his head and say, 'You know there's something wrong, we just shouldn't be this way.' " It was a stressful environment, and on one cruise, after they had been underwater for three weeks, an electrician's mate went mad with claustrophobia. After restraining him in his bunk for several days, they were forced to surface south of Bermuda and the man was taken off by helicopter. Carter himself has said, "I never did feel any adverse effect from claustrophobia because there was an embryonic feeling that you were protected in your isolation."

Lt. Commander Frank Andrews recalled Carter's service on the K-1 in the following way: "For Jimmy Carter I would use words like all business; no fooling around; professional; organized; smart as hell. But I sure couldn't tell you who his buddies were." He passed through the lives of his closest colleagues with utter unobtrusiveness. "Its hard to believe about anybody in the navy," says Roy Cowdrey, the executive officer, "but there are no sea stories about Jimmy Carter. The only thing I could tell you is that he really knew his manuals." Rosalynn would later describe Cowdrey as Jimmy's "special friend" on the K-1. Another officer, Charles E. Woods, however, says, "I lived in the stateroom with Jimmy, and I suppose I was as close to him as anyone on the K-1. But it was not a relationship I would call a close friendship. . . . He knew his job better, and he did it better, with less fuss and bother, than any of the rest of us. The reason was that he was always studying the ship and the power plant."

It was primarily Rosalynn who took the responsibility for maintaining the personal relationships. She recalls making several close friendships with the wives of crew members, especially with Betts Woods and Mary Callaghan, whose husband, Joe, succeeded Jimmy as the engineering officer.

It was on the K-1 that Jimmy first had the opportunity to assume a position of command. Unlike conventional military units, command in a submarine has a certain informal quality. Leadership is not exercised by autocratically handing down orders, but, in cramped quarters where a high degree of collaboration is required, has to be built on establishing mutual trust, confidence, and respect. Above all, leadership is by example and the ability to project in one's actions qualities that others can identify and emulate. The leadership style he learned in the submarine service was the leadership style he would exhibit for the rest of his career.

On one cruise K-1 docked in Nassau, Bahamas, where local British officers invited the crew ashore for a party. They made it clear, however, that a black sailor in the crew was not included. When the rest of the submariners discovered this, they unanimously decided that none of them would go. Later while on leave, during a visit home to Plains, Jimmy recounted the story to his father. Earl responded that the British had been perfectly right in their refusal to invite the black sailor. Jimmy never again discussed racial issues with his father.

Rosalynn was happy to be back in Connecticut. They had rented a comfortable house at 26 Bill Street in Groton, and on Rosalynn's birthday, August 18, 1952, their third son, Donnel Jeffrey, named after Jimmy's cousin and known as Jeff, was born. In his off-hours Jimmy pursued his woodworking skills at the base carpentry shop and made a cabinet for their record player. They bought their first television set and became avid N.Y. Yankees fans. Sometimes they went fishing for striped bass along the rocky shoreline. Much of the time Rosalynn was too busy to go and Jimmy would fish with the hospitalman's mate from the submarine.

They experienced heavy snow for the first time and enjoyed sledding with the boys. Rosalynn found the local library and made time to start reading regularly again, including, with Jimmy's enthusiastic encouragement, all 1,400 pages of *War and Peace*. In the fall of 1951 the K-1 was sent to Provincetown, Massachusetts, at the tip of Cape Cod, for the builder's sea trials. Together with Frank Andrews's wife and their three young sons, Rosalynn bundled her boys into a station wagon and drove to Nantucket Bay. "We rented an upstairs apartment in a big old house," Rosalynn says. "They had the upstairs, we had the downstairs . . . and during the day we would sit . . . upstairs and watch the K-1 diving and emerging from the sea."

While based in New London, Jimmy qualified as a submarine commander. To do this he wrote a thesis dealing with a new method of underwater range finding, using passive listening devices, which the navy later employed extensively. Years later, former navy people remarked to Rosalynn that they had to study the technique Jimmy developed.

CHAPTER 6

And you, my father, there on the sad height,
Curse, bless, me now with your fierce tears, I pray.
Do not go gentle into that good night.
Rage, rage against the dying of the light.

—DYLAN THOMAS

To Jimmy Carter life needed to be a series of challenges; he became bored once he had achieved his goal or mastered a skill. Having qualified for command, and having been promoted on June 1, 1952, to full lieutenant, he had every reason to expect that he would ultimately be given his own submarine. However, there was no predicting how many years he would have to wait. And, more importantly for him, after his previous year and a half, there was little more that he could learn. What had attracted him so much about his assignment to the K-1 was its innovative and experimental nature. It is not surprising, therefore, that when he heard the navy had created several positions for officers of his rank in its recently instituted nuclear submarine program, he applied. It was the most prestigious navy billet for anyone at his level; however, relatively few officers had the intellectual ability, technical knowledge, and engineering experience in submarines to be seriously considered.

The atomic submarine program was the brainchild of Captain Hyman Rickover, a brilliant, self-confident, effective, opinionated, pugnacious, controversial, vindictive, deeply admired, and vigorously despised individual. In 1949 he convinced the Department of the Navy to develop a nuclear propulsion plant for ships. Two prototype atomic-powered submarines were to be built, the *Nautilus* and the *Sea Wolf,* one by Westinghouse, the other by General Electric. In February of that year, Rickover had skillfully arranged to be appointed as director of the atomic submarine division of the Bureau of Ships and, at the same time, as head of the counterpart office at the civilian Atomic Energy Commission. This enabled him to send letters on behalf of the navy seeking authorizations from the AEC, then immediately dictate responses to himself providing the necessary approvals.

In keeping with the meticulous interest that he took in every aspect of the program, Rickover personally interviewed each navy applicant seeking to work under him. Jimmy went off to Washington with confidence in his qualifications and experience, but with some trepidation about facing someone with Rickover's formidable reputation. Rickover grilled him for two hours sitting at a small table in the middle of a cavernous room. He began by asking Jimmy if he had read *The Caine Mutiny*, which he had. Rickover proceeded to quiz him about the lessons that could be drawn from it about the navy and the nature of command. He then offered Jimmy the chance to choose any topics he wished to discuss. Jimmy describes what followed:

> Very carefully, I chose those about which I knew most at the time—current events, seamanship, music, literature, naval tactics, electronics, gunnery—and he began to ask me a series of questions of increasing difficulty. In each instance, he soon proved that I knew relatively little about the subject I had chosen.
>
> He always looked right into my eyes, and he never smiled. I was saturated with cold sweat.
>
> Finally, he asked me a question, and I thought I could redeem myself. He said, "How did you stand in your class at the Naval Academy?" Since I had completed my sophomore year at Georgia Tech, before entering Annapolis as a plebe, I had done very well, and I swelled my chest with pride and answered, "Sir, I stood fifty-ninth in my class of 820!" I sat back to wait for the congratulations, which never came. Instead, the question: "Did you do your best?" I started to say, "Yes sir," but I remembered who this was, and recalled several of the many times at the academy when I could have learned more about our allies, our enemies, weapons strategy, and so forth. I was just human. I finally gulped and said, "No, sir, I didn't always do my best."
>
> He looked at me for a long time, then turned his chair around to end the interview. He asked one final question, which I have never been able to forget—or to answer. He said, "Why not?" I sat there for a while, shaken, and then slowly left the room.

Jimmy returned despondent on the train to New London, where he recounted to Rosalynn how, when he had confidently told Rickover of his interest in classical music and that Wagner's *Tristan and Isolde* was his favorite opera, Rickover had bored in with questions of such detail that he could not answer. It seemed that with many of the replies he gave, which were perfectly correct, Rickover would dispute them just for the sake of argument. What he did not realize was that this was part of Rickover's technique to see how the interviewees could handle stress. Jimmy had held up well enough to impress him. In the later years Carter would himself apply the same technique on supposed experts, quizzing them to the limits of their knowledge while he watched them squirm in confused embarrassment.

In due course a letter arrived announcing his acceptance into the program, and assigning him to duty with the U.S. Atomic Energy Commission, Division of Reactor Development, Schenectady Operations Office. He was to work at the General Electric factory on the development of the USS *Sea Wolf,* the second of the prototype atomic submarines. First, however, he was sent to Washington on temporary duty with the Naval Reactors Branch of the Atomic Energy Commission from November 3, 1952, to March 1, 1953. Rosalynn, with the three boys, settled into their sixth home in six years at Mohawk Manor, Apartment 7, Duanesburg Road, Schenectady.

Carter was assigned as the senior officer of the precommissioning detail for the *Sea Wolf.* His job, and that of the other officers, involved familiarizing themselves with the nuclear technology and supervising the training of the noncommissioned officers in basic mathematics, physics, and reactor technology. He and Lieutenant Charles Carlisle took two graduate-level courses in reactor technology and nuclear physics for one semester at Union College. The noncommissioned officers came in groups of thirty or so for a twenty-week course taught by Professor Way of the physics department. Practical experience was gained at the Knolls Atomic Power Laboratory at the navy installation in nearby West Milston. There Carter and his colleagues collaborated with the General Electric employees in the construction of the prototype power plant within a huge steel sphere built for this purpose. At the General Electric factory in Schenectady, a mock-up of a nuclear submarine, complete with console, had been constructed in which the prospective crew could receive hands-on training and practice.

Early in 1952, a nuclear reactor at an experimental installation in Chalk River, Canada, suffered a meltdown and some radioactive material escaped into the atmosphere. The Canadian government made an urgent request to the Atomic Energy Commission for assistance in disassembling the damaged nuclear reactor core. Carter was a member of the team dispatched to the site. A duplicate mock-up of the reactor was constructed on a nearby tennis court, in which the men were able to practice each tedious step of the dismantling process. The intensity of the radiation at the core meant that each man could spend only ninety seconds in the reactor. In teams of three they descended far beneath the ground, where their work was monitored by closed-circuit television. Every time they removed a bolt or fitting, the equivalent piece was removed from the mock-up. Finally, Carter and his two colleagues descended into the reactor and worked furiously but methodically for their allotted time. Eventually the reactor was completely disassembled.

For months after, Carter and his colleagues had their urine and feces monitored for radiation levels. In the one minute and twenty-nine seconds that they were underground they had received the maximum annual allowable level of radiation. However, they suffered no ill effects. The experience, in many ways heroic, made a deep impression on Carter.

Jimmy's job demanded frequent travel, not only to Washington, D.C., but also to the Hanford Works in Washington State where the plutonium was produced, and to Arco, Idaho, where the reactor for the other prototype atomic submarine, the *Nautilus*, had been built. Rosalynn was kept busy caring for three children under six. Jimmy continued his interest in art and produced a painting that he sent to his mother depicting four weather-beaten trees against a bleak mountainous background with a lake and a boat. Writers would later interpret it as a reflection of his feelings in gray, industrial Schenectady.

Once again they had to start in a new location without friends or acquaintances. Chuck Carlisle, with whom Jimmy was working, had been an Annapolis classmate, but they had barely known each other. In addition, they were competitive. Jimmy had had a higher class standing at the academy, and that technically made him the superior, something Rosalynn said Carlisle seemed to have difficulty accepting.

Since their marriage, Jimmy and Rosalynn had attended church irregularly, due in part to his constant travel and the difficulty of finding babysitters. Their frequent moves also gave them little opportunity to join a congregation. In Plains, church was a central part of everyone's life. This was not true, they found, elsewhere in the country. In Hawaii, they had on several occasions attended a Methodist chapel. In Schenectady they attended an American Baptist church with some regularity, but the congregation was very different from the southern Baptists. Rosalynn was quite astonished to find one Sunday that they were selling soap and other items to raise money for the church. "In our church [in Plains] we never bought [or sold] anything on Sunday."

Carter has made much of his relationship with Admiral Rickover; his question as to why Jimmy had not done his best ultimately formed a central theme of the Carter presidential campaign. As a result, the importance of the relationship may have been overstated. Carter worked in the Rickover program for only one year and the personal contact between the two men was relatively limited. Yet there is no doubt that they shared many similar traits or that the young impressionable lieutenant modeled himself after the admiral. Carter acknowledges the significance of the relationship in his own psychological development, saying, "Admiral Rickover had a profound effect on my life, perhaps more than anyone except my own parents." The similarities between his relationship with Rickover and his father are inescapable. Jimmy says of Rickover, "He was unbelievably hardworking and competent, and demanded total dedication from his subordinates. We feared and respected him and strove to please him. I do not in that period remember his ever saying a complimentary word to me. The absence of a comment was his compliment." He would later say, "Rickover was not dissimilar from my father," adding, also referring to Rickover, "He scared me."

Carter's naval records show him to have received exemplary evaluations from all of his superior officers with the exception of Rickover. While still very positive, Rickover's sparing use of superlatives probably says more about him than Carter's performance.

Rickover was a powerful leader who led more by example than by rhetorical exhortation, a trait that would emerge as a central feature of Jimmy Carter's leadership style. Rickover worked at least as hard as his subordinates and his insistence that they know their jobs in the minutest detail was more than matched by his own obsessive grasp of every aspect of the nuclear submarine program. Carter described one occasion when, after a long day's work in Washington, he and some other junior officers boarded a plane for Seattle with Rickover.

> It was a long flight in a commercial prop-jet plane. He began to work when the plane took off, and we were determined to do the same. After a few hours the rest of us gave up and went to sleep. When we awoke, Rickover was still working.

Over the years there would be many who could describe similar experiences working for Carter.

Hyman George Rickover was an outsider. Born in 1900 in Makov, Russia, he grew up on the tough Near West Side of Chicago. He set for himself an improbable goal for the son of Jewish immigrants—winning an appointment at Annapolis. Through a combination of tenacity and intellectual brilliance he was accepted at the academy shortly after the end of World War I. After receiving a master's degree in engineering at Columbia in the 1920s and serving on several submarines, he went on to a distinguished career as perhaps the most skilled and innovative naval engineer of modern times. During World War II he was appointed as head of the electrical division of the Navy Department's Bureau of Ships. At the end of the war he did a six-month tour as assistant director of operations of the Manhattan Project in Oak Ridge, Tennessee, where the atomic bomb had been developed. He returned to the Bureau of Ships with the conviction that the navy must invest immediately in nuclear propulsion, and a singleminded determination to see that a nuclear-powered submarine was built.

Rickover inspired fanatic loyalty among those who worked for him and in return he would go to great lengths to protect his dedicated followers from the larger naval bureaucracy. Unfortunately, Rickover's arrogant self-assurance, the absolute certainty he had about his own beliefs, and his attempts to bypass anyone who thwarted him angered many people in the navy hierarchy. In the early 1950s, the Navy Selection Board twice passed over Rickover for promotion to rear admiral. How much of this was due to the enemies he had made and how much to anti-Semitism will never be known, but normally such an action made mandatory retirement inevitable. Rickover was characteristically unwilling to accept the judgment and, while Carter was working for him, mobilized a political campaign on his own behalf, resulting in the direct intervention of President Truman and senior members of Congress to assure his promotion in the middle of 1953.

At the heart of the defense establishment, yet anti-establishment, Rickover was happy to ignore, or circumvent, military procedures and chains of command when it came to dealing with those above him. Rickover's critics describe him as being a martinet with those who worked under him. He harshly punished those who disobeyed his orders and vindictively destroyed the career of at least one officer who actively opposed his plans. He tolerated fools poorly regardless of their rank or political position. With justifiable faith in his own immense intellectual capability and an insatiable appetite for hard work, he had an unswerving view that his decisions were inherently correct and in the best interests of the country. Being right was for Rickover a legitimate substitute for being political. It was a perspective on government that, to some extent, rubbed off on his subordinate Jimmy Carter.

While all who worked for him lived in awe and constant fear of his disapproval, he ran an unorthodox organization wherein rank and seniority were of little importance. The lack of formal structure was the traditional submariner's pattern with which Carter was already familiar. It was a style that made obvious practical sense in a submarine actually at sea. It made less sense as a management structure on land. Rickover, however, saw himself not so much as a manager but as a charismatic figure leading a crusade for his beliefs. He preferred the sense that he was surrounded by dedicated followers, all intensely loyal to him personally, rather than that he was building an efficient bureaucracy that could survive without him. It was a style that Carter, consciously or unconsciously, would later make his own.

Carter's modeling of himself on Rickover was clearly selective as he has never particularly manifested any of the admiral's less attractive characteristics. Rickover's example, Carter feels, made him realize what a small effort he was actually making "compared to what I could do."

Early in 1953 Jimmy received a fateful telephone call informing him that his father was unwell and losing weight. A few weeks later his mother called to say that he had been diagnosed with cancer of the pancreas and was not expected to live. Jimmy laid across his bed and cried. He immediately went to Plains.

It had been eleven years since Jimmy departed for the Naval Academy. At the time of his departure he, like many eighteen-year-olds, felt some distance from his father, whom he saw as rigidly demanding. He still felt a degree of resentment that his father's strictness had denied him some of the pleasures to which, as a teenager, he should have been entitled.* He had come home on leave and from time to time his parents had visited him at his navy postings. However, the life Jimmy and Rosalynn had been leading, the ideas they had been exposed to, the experiences they had had, only served to widen the gap with their parents. His parents' life in Plains seemed parochial, and his father's attitudes on many issues, especially race, seemed out of touch with the new post–World War II America in which he and Rosalynn had been living.

Jimmy, age 29, returned to his bedridden father and began to spend hours sitting and talking with him. He felt guilty about the chasm between them and began to become reacquainted with his father. But he discovered a different person from the father of his childhood, learning much about his life that he had never known. He saw the compassionate side of his personality and discovered for the first time how his father had quietly helped so many in the community. He was astonished at the hundreds of people, of both races, who came to express their concern with an unanticipated degree of warmth and sincerity.

Earl and Lillian Carter and sixteen-year-old Billy moved into the center of Plains, where Earl had become an increasingly substantial figure. Just before his illness, he had been elected to the state legislature. His farm holdings had grown so that he owned more than thirty parcels of land in Sumter and Webster Counties, amounting to over 5,000 acres. The seed and fertilizer warehouse was thriving, and with his willingness to extend liberal credit to farmers throughout the growing season, he served as a consequential private banker.

Miss Lillian minced no words about wanting Jimmy to come back and take over the business. She had never involved herself directly in her husband's farming and business activities, and faced with the prospect of Earl's death, she foresaw a serious crisis looming. Earl also had extended

---

*In his classic study *Young Man Luther*, psychologist Erik Erikson observed that the heavy hand of moralistic paternalism denying many of the spontaneous time-squandering diversions, daydreams, and minor delinquencies of childhood could lead, as they did in Martin Luther, to "someone with a precocious conscience, a precocious self-steering, and eventually an obsessive mixture of obedience and rebelliousness." For Carter, as with Luther, it seemed to be the formula for creating a strong moral leader later in life.

credit totaling between $50,000 and $100,000, but Jimmy saw his father tear up IOUs and forgive many of the debts before he died.

Jimmy returned to Schenectady in a state of deep anguish about his future. He spoke with several of his fellow officers, mostly those who had been on the K-1 with him. "I remember it clearly because it was just about the only time he wasn't talking about the ship or the navy," Frank Andrews recalls. The world of Southwest Georgia he described to his mostly northern urban friends sounded to them like something from another century. His friend Bill Lalor remembers:

> It was almost like a medieval idea, that one man, his father, was responsible for the souls in the town of Plains, Georgia . . . without his father those 1,500 people were not going to have any means to live. . . . He was just torn over the obligation to those people and the idea that he was picked to be the chief engineer of the *Sea Wolf.*

Jimmy's biggest problem, however, was with Rosalynn. She absolutely did not want to go back.

> I was having a great time. . . . Jimmy had good duty almost always. He was doing just what he wanted to do. . . . He was very happy and I was worried about him coming back. I was as worried about him as I was about me, because I just did not know whether he would be happy or not.

She had concerns about herself also.

> I had three little babies. And I could see . . . everyone telling me what to do. I always felt I was in the way with all the babies in my mother's house or Jimmy's mother's house and you know they are just waiting for you to leave. And I felt like it would be that way when I came home.

The navy was a meritocracy where social standing was based largely on rank and career success regardless of background. Although social position was not particularly one of Rosalynn's concerns, as the wife of one of the service's young rising stars Rosalynn was guaranteed a degree of acceptance and status, which would only increase in the future. Back in Plains, they would return to a narrow social structure where, despite Jimmy's navy career, their standing in the community was largely preordained by their family backgrounds. They would not be the most prominent couple in Plains, much less be accepted into the self-anointed upper crust of Americus. For Rosalynn their married life had helped them move beyond the petty small-town values of Southwest Georgia. To return seemed like a monumental step backward.

There were practical considerations too. Plains offered few of the amenities they had come to take for granted in the navy. It had no swimming pool, no kindergarten, no library, and it was miles from the sea. Once there, Rosalynn feared that the exciting life they had both enjoyed for the previous eight years would be over forever.

For Jimmy the situation posed a major existential crisis. The navy had served its purpose for him. It had enabled him to get out of Plains and acquire a superior education. He had earned the rewards of his hard work and was successfully climbing the navy's career ladder. The prospect for the future, however, was more years of the same relentless hard work competing with his fellow officers. Relatively soon he could expect to become commander of a nuclear submarine. The ultimate goal would be to become chief of naval operations. Also, Jimmy's success in the military won him his father's fullest approval, and it would have been very hard to consider leaving the navy during his father's lifetime.

Yet the navy had drawbacks. He saw the restrictive nature of his life when he compared it to that of his father. He had hobbies, but except for Rosalynn and the children, he had no intimate, deep, personal relationships. In Plains he had roots and lifelong friendships with which he felt much more comfortable. Military life was an existence where success was measured by relentless efficiency reports and the struggle for promotion or command, not by the degree of spiritual gratification. He felt an emptiness that another twenty years in the navy was not likely to fill.

After Earl died, Jimmy and Ruth went out to visit tenants on his land to inform them of his death. Upon Jimmy's return to Schenectady, he talked to Rosalynn about it, who says,

> That made a great impression on him . . . he did not think he could ever do anything in his life to have an impact on people's lives like his father's life had made. . . . I think he thought he could work in the navy . . . and not really make a difference to people.

There were, of course, some valid practical reasons for leaving the military. As a result of his orchestrated campaign to get his own promotion, Rickover had substantially increased the hostility toward himself. The nuclear program was under serious attack and its future proved uncertain. In addition, navy pay was low and, nearly thirty years old with three children, Jimmy was concerned about ever being able to afford the luxuries of life. Despite the Korean War, promotions were slow. The post–World War II economic boom was at its peak and, with seemingly limitless opportunities in the civilian sector, military morale was poor. Jimmy was also having some doubts about his role in the military. Within the overall philosophical reevaluation of his life, the excitement the navy seemed to offer in his youth had been replaced, as he matured, with a more sober assessment of the true military purpose. He says he came to the conclusion, "God did not intend for me to spend my life working on instruments of destruction to kill people." For Christians in the South there was always an inherent tension between the pacifist teachings of Christ and the warrior culture of the society that demanded the suppression of those inclinations. As he had become older, Jimmy was less a captive of southern culture, and was more concerned about being true to his own beliefs and values.

He had also not resolved deep-seated problems with authority, and found it difficult to work for someone else. He had done so obediently and conscientiously, but he hid the fact that he did so grudgingly. His father's death enabled him to resolve that dilemma in an honorable way.

The funeral, already emotionally traumatic for Jimmy, was further etched in his consciousness by the obvious depth of feeling that the overflowing throng of mourners had for Mr. Earl. He wondered how many people would come to his funeral and what they would say about the meaning of his life. With the continuing encouragement, if not pressure, of Miss Lillian, he made the decision to return home and pick up his father's mantle.

Jimmy and Rosalynn returned separately to Schenectady after Earl's funeral. When Jimmy got back he informed Rosalynn that he had made up his mind—he wanted to leave the navy and return to Plains. It precipitated the greatest crisis of their marriage. She vehemently opposed his decision and their heated arguments reached the point where she was screaming at him. She pleaded and cried to no avail. She knew how stubborn he was, and that once he had made up his mind, he was unlikely to change it. "She almost quit me," Carter later said of the conflict. Rosalynn could not change his mind but continued to be resentful and angry, even as she prepared for their departure from Schenectady.

Rickover was no less happy with Carter's decision. The rigors of the selection process to get into the program and the intense loyalty he engendered in his team, essentially defined resignation as a betrayal. Just to secure his release from the navy involved getting the assistance of Georgia senator Walter George.

Jimmy called his mother and said, "I have no alternative. I am coming home." She knew he would return. "He had to come back," she said. "Everything we had was on the line."

Jimmy was honorably discharged by the headquarters of the Third Naval District in New York on October 9, 1953. He had served a total of seven years, four months, and eight days. He was forced to come to New York City for his processing out, leaving Rosalynn to pack.

Jimmy went on to Washington and Rosalynn and the children followed later by car. They agreed to meet at the Washington Monument. As Jimmy appeared some distance away, baby Jeff scrambled over the luggage toward the back window so that he could wave to his father. He fell and nearly severed his tongue in two. What was to have been a happy reunion turned into a frantic search through the telephone book to find the location of Children's Hospital, where Jeff's tongue was eventually sutured together again.

The following day they stopped at the office of their congressman, "Tick" Forrester, the representative for Georgia's Third Congressional District. To their surprise, he launched into a lengthy diatribe against blacks. Then he attacked public housing projects, saying that the scum of the earth lived in them. He did not know that Jimmy and Rosalynn, with little money saved and no assured income, had arranged to move into public housing in Plains. As Rosalynn says, "He was talking about the kind of people who live in public housing and we were they!" Not only did Forrester antagonize them with his attack on public housing, but his overall bigotry and ignorance exemplified the worst in southern politicians, which did little to reassure Rosalynn about returning to Plains.

From Washington they drove South. For Rosalynn, it was not a happy journey.

> I became more and more dejected the closer we got. I didn't want to live in Plains. I had left there, moved on, and changed. But Jimmy was determined—and happy. . . . Never had we been at such cross-purposes. I thought the best part of my life had ended. But Jimmy turned to me with a smile and said cheerfully, "We're home."

The death of his father was for Jimmy a psychologically traumatizing blow compounded by his decision to break his ties with Rickover, his other father figure. He worked through his grief, preoccupied with the intense flurry of activity involved in moving the family back to Georgia. Henceforth, he would be the master of his own destiny.

It was during this period that he encountered the works of Dylan Thomas, who had also died that year. So many of Thomas's poems seemed to mirror his own thoughts as he grappled with a new sense of the evanescence of life. Reflecting on how Thomas skillfully brought to the surface the deep emotions of loss that he could not articulate for himself, he felt an affinity with the poet that would become lifelong. He was particularly drawn to Thomas's poem "A Refusal to Mourn the Death, by Fire, of a Child in London." It accentuated his appreciation of the enormity of his loss, but its perspective had a therapeutic effect in enabling him to deal with his own grief. The final line would stick indelibly in his mind—"After the first death there is no other."

CHAPTER 7

Jimmy and Rosalynn spend the first few nights back in Plains with Miss Lillian, but quickly moved into the red brick housing project a block away on Olive Street. Apartment 9A became their cramped new home. Jack was in the first grade, but Chip (age 3) and Jeff (a little over a year old) were at home with Rosalynn. The back door of their apartment opened onto a grassy yard, where the wives of the ten families in the project sat and chatted during the day, watching their children as they played. Rosalynn rarely joined them. She kept busy sewing, making slipcovers, curtains, and clothes for the children, and occasionally finding time to read. She was miserable, and her irritation at returning to Plains kept her from engaging anyone except superficially. Jimmy cajoled her, but never sympathized with her.

"It's good to be home. We will both be glad some day," he said repeatedly until she thought she couldn't stand to hear it one more time.

"I will not ever be glad! Don't say that anymore," she retorted at the top of her voice.

After several months Allie talked with Rosalynn and gently suggested to her that people felt she was aloof. Rosalynn was finding, as she knew she would, that she could not tolerate the usual small-town ways of killing time. She turned down all invitations to play bridge and had no interest in making endless small talk over coffee. She preferred doing something constructive, if only reading a book, to engaging in activities she felt were a waste of time. For men, a constant need to achieve was acceptable as a reflection of drive and ambition, but southern wives were expected to be demure yet sociable, concerned only with their husbands' interests.

Gradually Rosalynn found activities that were acceptable to the community and she made a conscious effort to heed her mother's advice. But for some people in Plains, Jimmy and Rosalynn would always be seen as a couple apart. They returned with a body of accomplishments behind them, and with different views, values, and experiences; naturally some in the community resented them.

Meanwhile, Jimmy was the executor of his father's estate. In his will, Earl had left the house in Plains and his in-town lots to Lillian. The rest of the property he wanted sold and the proceeds divided among his wife and the children. His insurance business he left to "Miss Nellie" Walters, who had faithfully run it for him through the years. Jimmy bought out Gloria and Ruth's portions of the legacy, then consolidating Lillian and Billy's share with his own, he formed a corporation with himself as the manager. He took over his father's office in the warehouse.

The problem was that they were land rich and cash poor. Jimmy and Rosalynn had arrived back at the time farmers would normally have been paying down the credit Earl extended to them at the beginning of the planting season. However, 1953 was a year of severe drought and many of the farmers did not have the money to repay their loans. Jimmy had little choice but to reextend them to the following season. The withering drought continued through 1954. The peanut, cotton, and corn crops all failed. In the navy, he and Rosalynn had been able to save $75 out of his monthly check of $300. His total profit for the first year in business was $200. This was despite the fact that he sold 2,000 tons of fertilizer in 100-pound paper bags or 200-pound burlap sacks, all of which, as the sole employee, he had bagged himself. Late in 1954, he went to Evan Mathis, father of his Annapolis classmate and president of the Citizen's Bank of Americus, to seek a $10,000 loan. He was turned down, unless he could get his mother or his uncle to cosign the note. He was angry and felt humiliated that he was not considered creditworthy in his own right. Instead, he managed to get credit from the fertilizer company, and scrimped up the remainder by delaying payment on bills and putting together every cent they had.

Money worries were a constant stress, as he recalls:

> No matter what [good] happened . . . underneath, it was gnawing away because I owed $12,000 and did not know how I was going to pay it. If I could not collect my bills that month, I could not pay for the fertilizer I had already sold. It was gnawing away at [my] guts no matter what other good things were going on.

He did, however, have one ace in the hole. Before he left the navy, senior officials at the Electric Boat Company, impressed by his work on the K-1, had guaranteed him a job if he should ever want to work for them. He knew that, if he ever really faced bankruptcy, relatively well-paid employment was assured. The real problem was the notion of failure, which was anathema to him. Worse would be to fail where his father, whom he was desperately trying to emulate, had consistently built such success.

Farming had changed a great deal since Jimmy left to go to the Naval Academy. The shift from cotton to peanuts, begun after the arrival of the boll weevil in 1926, had accelerated significantly during World War II, and there had been a dramatic increase in mechanization. The high percentage of clay in the soil demanded a skilled, more scientific approach to cultivation to achieve the crop yields necessary to be profitable. In the 1930s and 1940s, if a farmer got a ton of peanuts per acre, he could do well. By the 1950s and 1960s, he needed 2 to 3 tons per acre to survive. Jimmy found that he had to start relearning about agriculture. He enrolled in short courses at the University of Georgia's Experiment Station in Tifton and spent considerable time with the employees at the Agricultural Extension Center just outside Plains, established with the help of his father in 1952 during his brief tenure in the Georgia legislature. He also bought books on farming and spent many hours discussing the subject with his uncle Alton, the county agent, and with the men who came to buy his fertilizer. He was as determined to master the new scientific approach to farming as he had been to perfect his technical knowledge of the K-1 or the *Seawolf*.

At the beginning of 1955 the rains returned and the crops flourished. The despondency in the community was replaced by optimism. By harvest time, money was flowing again; farmers paid their bills, bought equipment, and began thinking about luxuries like family vacations. Jimmy and Rosalynn found their own circumstances transformed, as their customers made good on long overdue credit, and peanuts by the tons poured into their warehouse. However, it was backbreaking work, weighing and storing the peanuts or shipping them out to processors to be turned into peanut butter, shelled peanuts, or candy. Much of the physical labor Jimmy did himself with the aid of temporary help during the peak periods.

One day just prior to the recovery in 1955, Jimmy, without money to hire helpers, asked Rosalynn to come to the warehouse and answer the phone while he went out to visit some farmers. She had to take the children with her, but soon was doing it two or three times a week. She then began handling the billing and keeping the books, which she enjoyed and found gave meaning to her life beyond the drudgery of housework. As she gradually took over more and more responsibility, she took correspondence courses in bookkeeping and accounting. She would later tell an interviewer, "I was sure I could have passed the test for CPA . . . and I loved it. To make all those books balance? I liked it better than anything I had ever done."

Rosalynn was by no means unique in Plains or other rural communities in working in her husband's business. Several other Plains' wives helped their husbands, including Virginia Harris Williams, who owned with her spouse the peanut warehouse that was the Carters' major competition. What was significant, however, was that being forced to deal with a wide range of sometimes aggressive people in a business setting became an important aspect of Rosalynn's own maturation and development of her self-confidence. It was, too, a further palliative for the trauma of the move back to Plains.

Perhaps the major casualty of Jimmy and Rosalynn's return was Billy. He was only eight when Jimmy left for the Naval Academy and had grown up hardly knowing him. He was very close to his father, and Earl, mellowed by the years, had not demanded of him the same discipline and performance that he had of Jimmy. Billy, although very bright, had been an indifferent student in school. When Earl became sick, Billy dropped out to help take care of him, driving him around and helping out in the warehouse. Billy also went with his father to Atlanta and worked as a page for the one term Earl served in the legislature. After Earl's death, Lillian sent Billy to Gordon Military Academy for his junior year. He returned to Plains High School, but would eventually graduate near the bottom of his class.

Billy had assumed that he would ultimately take over the business, and had Earl not died when he did, that might have been the case. But he was only sixteen in 1953. Jimmy says:

> It was almost preordained that one day Daddy would turn the peanut business over to Billy. No one ever questioned that. I was very happy in the navy, and neither Mama nor my sisters had any strong interest in managing the business. . . . I feel he resented my coming back to run the business because he had thought it would be his one day. Also, he was deeply hurt that Daddy had died and left him. He ended up lashing out at the situation.

Billy was more blunt—"I was mad as hell"—but it was clear there was nothing he could do about it. "Finally, I decided to hell with it. Let Jimmy run the warehouse. He could do it without me." The day of his eighteenth birthday and two months short of his high school graduation, Billy enlisted in the marines. Jimmy and Lillian talked him into finishing school, but the morning after graduation he was on his way to Parris Island. Billy said, "I wanted to join the Marine Corps because I always heard they were bad asses, and I wanted to be a bad ass. I never did quite make it." He also wanted to marry his high school sweetheart, sixteen-year-old Sybil Squires. Again Jimmy and Lillian tried, this time unsuccessfully, to talk him out of it. Billy and Sybil were married as soon as he finished basic training.

Years before, Gloria had, like Jimmy and Rosalynn, been determined to see the world outside Plains and get away from her parents. It was an option that had not been open to her mother a generation earlier. After graduating high school in June 1945, she had gone to Georgia Southwestern College where she had studied journalism. Attractive, and perhaps the most outgoing and talented of the Carter children, she fell in love with a young air force enlisted man named Everett "Soapy" Hardy, who prior to entering the service had worked as a soda jerk in Americus. Despite strong opposition from Earl and Lillian, they ran off and married that December. After four years of moving from one air force base to another, the marriage fell apart. Gloria returned penniless to Plains with her two-year-old son, Willie, or "Toady," as he was known, in tow.

Earl expressed his strong displeasure with the mess she had made of her life, adding to her sense of guilt. Feeling considerable pressure, Gloria attended business school and acquired proficiency as a tax expert and bookkeeper. She earned a reasonable income keeping the records for a number of farms in the Plains area. However, from a young age "Toady" began to have difficulties. He was disruptive in school and would suffer outbursts of violent behavior. He was taken to several psychiatrists and, after he broke into a store and later stole a car, he had to be removed from the Plains school. He was sent to a military academy and subsequently to a school for emotionally disturbed children.

Gloria met a farmer, Walter Spann, who lived near Plains, and married him a week before her father died. She settled into the staid life of a farmer's wife. It was as though she had tried life in the larger world, been burned, and withdrew back into the security of the world of lower expectations in Plains. She also had "Toady" to remind her of the error of her ways. Yet she remained close to Jimmy, who was always willing to forgive human frailties in others more easily than in himself. Her dedication to Jimmy would be reflected in her willingness to work slavishly behind the scenes for him in his future public life.

Ruth, who had seemed as a teenager to have everything a young girl could want, had gone to Georgia State College for Women in Milledgeville. She made little effort to study; the end of her second year she met and married Robert Stapleton, a veterinarian, and moved to Fayetteville, North Carolina. Adored and overindulged by her father, Ruth had grown up expecting to be flattered and showered with success without having to lift a finger. She was completely unprepared for the responsibilities of marriage. These problems would later cause her to reexamine and profoundly change her life, but in the early 1950s she appeared to be a happily married mother of two young babies.

Jimmy regularly discussed the business with Miss Lillian and sought her advice. She, however, had no more real interest in the operation than when Earl was alive. The death of her husband of thirty years left her devastated. She was deeply depressed and her studied independence over the years had left her with few close friends of her own age who could comfort her. She felt what she later conceded was an un-Christian and unfair resentment toward Earl's brother Alton, "Uncle Buddy," and his family for failing to do more to reach out to her. "What I needed," she later recalled, "was the support of an adult, but Uncle Buddy never once asked if there was anything he could do to help." Jimmy and Rosalynn, beset with their own problems, could offer her only limited comfort. So Miss Lillian, her own emotional resources depleted, could not give Billy the support and guidance he needed. She passed her days fishing, playing bridge, baby-sitting her three grandsons, and working in her garden. But she remained bored and unhappy, with a continuing sense of emptiness in her life. Gloria convinced her to take a trip to Canada, but that provided only temporary relief.

Eventually, after two years, Lillian decided to leave Plains. Her younger sister, Sissy, was working as a housemother for a fraternity at Auburn University in Alabama, and told her a similar job was available with the Kappa Alpha fraternity. Lillian applied and was accepted. Before she departed, Jimmy bought her a new Cadillac so that no one would get the mistaken impression that she working because she had to.

In many ways it was the escape that she had sought in fantasy all her life, but had never been able to make because of her responsibilities. Now Jimmy was running the business and it was beginning to be successful. Although Lillian was Jimmy's financial partner, Rosalynn shared the work with him. Billy had left for the marines. Gloria was married again. And Ruth was a seemingly contented mother. For the first time in her life Lillian really was free to do whatever she wanted.

There was one other matter that had caused family turmoil in the years immediately following the war. Tom Gordy, Lillian's brother, who had been so instrumental in inspiring Jimmy to pursue a naval career, had not been heard from in the four years after he was captured by the Japanese in December 1941. The family had come to accept the Red Cross position that he was presumed dead. His wife Dorothy remarried. Then shortly before the Japanese surrender, the family received a letter from Tom saying that he was being held in a small POW camp at the base of Mt. Fujiyama. He had been forced to work in a Japanese mine, as the fireman on a train hauling coal. Dorothy offered to divorce her new husband and return to Tom, but most of the family condemned her for having remarried too hastily and therefore, in their eyes, having committed adultery—although Tom had been declared legally dead years before. Jimmy, characteristically, was the only one who felt Dorothy should be forgiven for an honest mistake and, if she and Tom wanted to reestablish their marriage, she should be welcomed back into the family. In the end, that did not happen; Tom eventually made another very happy marriage and moved to Florida.

From the moment Jimmy arrived back in Plains he had been active in the community's affairs. As Rosalynn overcame her initial reclusiveness, she joined him. Much of their initial motivation was to promote his business. "We wanted to have a successful business and be rich one day," he has said, summing up what was then the central goal of his life. "If any customer's daughter married, we were there; if anybody had a funeral, we were there. If anybody got sick, we sent flowers," Rosalynn says. Jimmy also encouraged customers to take the same short courses as he had at the agricultural station in Tifton, even offering to give them rides. There they could learn, as he says, "how to grow peanuts better, build fences, take care of pine trees, or have a good fish pond." At one level he understood that more sophisticated farmers would buy fertilizer and other products from him. Also, larger yields would bring more business to the warehouse. Jimmy was motivated by a sense of civic pride with a desire to emulate his father's role in the community and encourage the awareness of social responsibility.

As in every small town there were conflicts, and Jimmy and Rosalynn did not enjoy unanimous support. They competed with the Williams family who owned the other peanut warehouse. However, the rift extended beyond business, so that when there was disagreement in the community, the town divided between the Williamses' and the Carters' supporters. These divisions were minor until race began to surface as an issue.

Jimmy and Rosalynn took an interest in politics, but at a distance. In the 1954 governor's race Jimmy supported Fred Hand of Camilla because his grandfather had worked with Hand's father in the timber and turpentine business; Hand's position on the issues was not a major consideration. This represented the time-honored way political fiefdoms were built in South Georgia. However, independent and more attuned to political ideology, Rosalynn voted for a relatively liberal attorney from Brunswick, Charlie Gowan. The race was won by Marvin Griffin, a segregationist of the Talmadge mold.

In 1954, the Georgia Power Company sponsored a statewide competition, the Georgia Better Hometowns Project. Jimmy, who had joined the Lions Club, the only civic club in Plains, became project chairman and led the effort over the next year to beautify the town. A careful record had to be kept of every project that was undertaken toward this goal; Julia Coleman accepted that task. The newly elected governor, Marvin Griffin, had made the paving of rural roads the hallmark of his administration, and small grants were available to communities like Plains to pave their streets, but until Jimmy took the initiative no one had bothered to apply.

With the improvement of the local economy, Jimmy made plans to expand the warehouse and hired a local contractor, John Pope, a friend of his sister, Ruth. He also proposed to Pope that they collaborate on the building of a swimming pool for Plains. Jimmy offered to persuade the local farmers to do the excavation with their tractors if Pope would contribute his time, equipment, and expertise to supervise the project. At almost no cost they built a 35-by-75-foot swimming pool. What astonished Pope was Jimmy's ability to convince him to contribute his valuable time and at least twenty-five local men to contribute their labor. "He kind of had a way of getting you to do things," Pope says, laughing. When a similar effort was attempted sometime later in the nearby community of Ellaville, leaders there could never get more than one person to volunteer for half a day. The Plains swimming pool, of course, was open only to whites.

Inspired by their paved roads and new swimming pool, the people of Plains, in a rush of community spirit, painted their homes and cleaned up the town. Of the four categories in the Georgia Power Company competition that Plains entered, the town placed first in two and second in the others.

In addition to joining the Lions Club and heading the community development committee, Jimmy served on the Sumter County Library Board and was appointed a member of the hospital authority. A year after their return, Rosalynn's cousin, Drew Murray, a member of the county school board, accidentally killed himself with a gun he was carrying while climbing over a fence. The grand jury, which was responsible for making appointments to the school board and the hospital authority, asked Jimmy to take his place. In 1961 he was made chairman. Jimmy also acted as the scoutmaster for the Boy Scouts while Rosalynn was the den mother for the Cub Scout pack.

Working with the mayor of Plains, Jimmy also sought to find a doctor for the town, which had been without one since the demise of the Wise clinic. Jimmy convinced Dr. Carl Sills to relocate there, but had to raise enough money among his fellow businessmen to build a modest clinic. Early in 1956, Jimmy was considered for selection by the Americus Jaycees as Sumter County's "Outstanding Young Man of 1955." Although he lost, he was the only county resident living outside the tight-knit community of Americus considered for the honor and was named to the Distinguished Service Award List.

"He was always the leader of everything he got into," John Pope says of Jimmy Carter during that period, "and he would give it a lot of time that most people wouldn't." Jimmy would tell Rosalynn that you could always find time to do things you really wanted to do. In part it was his personality that drove him to fill every moment of his life with what he considered worthwhile activity. But he also wanted to show Rosalynn that despite her reticence, the return to Plains had been justified.

At an early stage Jimmy decided that instead of buying and reselling certified seed, it would be considerably more profitable if he started growing it himself. The increased income enabled him to expand the warehouse operation which, during the eight years following his return to Plains, included installing a new peanut-shelling plant, a peanut-drying system, and the purchase of three additional acres in town for peanut storage. By 1959 they were doing well enough to build a new warehouse at the corner of Main and Bond Streets, and in 1962 to install a $300,000 state-of-the-art cotton gin. Their letterhead spoke to the range of the business: "Certified seed peanuts, custom peanut shelling, peanut buying and storage, liquid nitrogen, bulk fertilizer and lime, corn buying, custom grinding and mixing, cotton ginning, fire and casualty insurance." Rosalynn acted as the financial manager, and with her aversion to being in debt, she fretted when Jimmy launched into one new project after another before the loans on previous expansions of their operations had been paid off. Meanwhile, Jimmy hired several employees— Francis Dolbeck, Clarence Welch, Frank McGarragh, Randy Coleman, and others—both black and white. He also made a point of providing jobs for several young black teenagers who came to work after school.

As soon as the finances of the business had turned around, Jimmy and Rosalynn moved out of the housing project. They briefly rented what was known as the old Montgomery house and then, in 1956, moved to the Stewart house at the edge of town on the Old Preston Road toward Archery. The large airy house standing on brick pillars with camelias in the front yard was rented from Raymond Sullivan, Earl Carter's friend and partner. It was more than a hundred years old and had once been the proud plantation home of the owner of a surrounding peach orchard. For the three Carter boys it had the added attraction of being haunted, or so legend had it. On one occasion, after removing some bricks from behind a fireplace, Jack found, to his delight, a ladder and a long-forgotten hidden room. With sheds and barns and a large open space in the backyard they had room for hunting dogs, a pony, and other pets. However, for all the pleasure the house gave in the summertime, it was cold and drafty throughout the winter. When the temperature got down to freezing and the wind whistled under the house, the pipes froze even though Jimmy had carefully lagged them with newspaper.

Although business success was Jimmy's primary goal, he, like his father, had a fun-loving tendency, and he and Rosalynn led an active social life. In Plains they were friendly with Jimmy's high school classmate B. T. Wishard and his wife, Gloria, as well as Joel Thomas and his wife, Betsy, who was Gloria's sister. They would often go fishing together or spend an evening having a cookout at Miss Lillian's Pond House. On several occasions Jimmy and Rosalynn drove with friends to Sebring, Florida, to watch the twelve-hour sports-car race.

The late 1950s was a time of somnolent self-indulgence in Southwest Georgia, as it was in much of the rest of the country. The economy was booming and successful young business and professional people had few worries. They were enjoying a steadily increasing standard of living and amount of leisure time that was quite unprecedented. They wanted to do things other than the traditional male recreations of hunting and fishing. Travel, for fun, especially to South Florida or the Caribbean, was considered exciting and adventuresome. With the influence of the church declining in people's lives, drinking, partying, and occasionally adultery became, in addition to more wholesome activities, a growing and accepted part of modern life in Americus. Heavy social drinking was a particular manifestation of the fifties and several of the Carters' close friends became alcoholics.

During the building of the swimming pool, Jimmy and John Pope ate lunch together every day for several weeks. What started as an acquaintance blossomed into a social relationship that, despite ups and downs, would prove one of the most enduring for the Carters over the years. John, his wife, Marjorie, Rosalynn and Jimmy, and a third couple from Americus, Billy and Irene Horne (whom Rosalynn had known at Georgia Southwestern), became a regular social group—three couples that Billy Horne would refer to as "the three musketeers." Both Horne, a civil engineer, and Pope were successful in their businesses. Before he and Marjorie married, John Pope had acquired a reputation as somewhat of a playboy, and the two of them loved to have a good time. The Carters, the Popes, and the Hornes would dance at the Americus Country Club, where they also took dancing lessons. John Pope says of Jimmy, "He *loved* to dance." Occasionally they went to Albany where there was a nightclub, although clubs were not Jimmy's preference. Many a Saturday afternoon John Pope would drive over to Plains and help Jimmy shovel and dry peanuts so the couples could go out that night. On one occasion they flew to Havana for two nights. They did not go to bed the second night because they had gambled away the money they intended to use for their hotel rooms. On another occasion they saved $300 and went to New Orleans. The couples agreed they would stay until the money ran out, which proved to be four days. It was four days of partying, sleeping in late, and going to jazz clubs, good restaurants, and the race track. It was, Rosalynn recalls, the first time she and Jimmy drank wine at lunch.

John's wife, Margie, was a quiet but exceptionally pretty woman who had been a "Miss Georgia Southwestern." She had the graceful ability to get the group to do whatever she wanted. According to Rosalynn, "She was just kind of vulnerable and not secure and you always wanted to do what she wanted to do and make her feel good." At the same time Rosalynn says, "She was just a neat person," adding, "Jimmy really liked her." Most who knew both couples during that period felt there was a special affection between Jimmy and Margie Pope.

Southwest Georgia remained a thoroughly segregated society in the 1950s, with blacks, most of whom lived in abject poverty, doing the bulk of the physical labor. Prior to World War II, few, black or white, had thought to question the way society operated. Awareness of the outside world began with the upheaval brought about by the war, but even then real change would be slow in coming. Military experience in a conflict that was, in part, a war against racism had exposed southerners to other values and cultures, so when they returned, many of them saw their old way of life in a new context. Frank Myers, born and raised near Plains, who would later be twice elected mayor of Americus, joked, "Growing up, I was like everyone else. I didn't believe in segregation—I believed in slavery!" When he returned after serving as a navy pilot in World War II, it was not a question for him of whether change would occur, but how.

Griffin Bell, a close friend of Frank Myers, says:

> Growing up in Americus and Sumter County before the war you never really thought anything about the race law. . . . It was just part of the way of life. . . . When I got home from the war, I for the first time . . . noticed a black school—a ramshackle building. And I had a friend in the car with me—we were law students. And I said to this other law student, "Look what we are doing to the blacks. Isn't that terrible that they would have a school like this and the whites have got these nice brick buildings." . . . And I am sure there were hundreds of other veterans . . . that started thinking that way. . . . That forecast change. You could not keep doing that.

Although recognizing the inevitable demise of the old order, this younger generation, for the most part, envisioned only modest, gradual change—white largesse that would grant a fraction of the post-war affluence to blacks by raising day wages, incrementally improving the quality of their schools, extending water and sewer lines to black houses, or paving a few roads on the other side of the railroad tracks. Yet, it was enough to deeply divide the white community largely along generational lines. As Griffin Bell described it:

> The South was divided between the people that wanted to work out of that and those that wanted to preserve the status quo. And those that wanted to work out of it I would say were the problem solvers. It was not an easy thing. . . . I never met anybody who wanted just overnight to turn the whole system upside-down. It had to be done in some orderly way.

Not all returning veterans shared the views of Griffin Bell and Frank Myers. Lawyer Warren Fortson used to frequent Georgia's Cafe, a local gathering place in Americus where people would come midmorning to drink coffee and talk:

> I remember being at a table with . . . a bunch of them in there . . . [one of the guys] had been a pilot during the war, fought in Europe . . . and somehow the subject of Jews came up . . . he thought Hitler was right in what he did. And I remember that . . . I was either going to knock the shit out of him or I was going to get up and leave. . . . And I just got up and went on. . . . Interestingly enough, in a way it was easier to argue about black folks than it was over Jews . . . because it was so rabidly extreme on Jews.

The environment occasionally bred someone at the other extreme. In 1942, the year Jimmy Carter was appointed to the Naval Academy,

Clarence Jordan, a Baptist preacher with a Ph.D. in New Testament Greek, moved to Sumter County. After finishing seminary in Louisville, Kentucky, Jordan had stayed there for a while as a missionary working with blacks who had fled the poverty of the rural South only to end up in the squalor of the city's ghettos. The experience convinced him that the ideal of Jesus he understood from his academic studies was fundamentally at odds with the social system he had grown up with in the South. Before going to the seminary he had received a degree in agriculture, so with a down payment from a friend he purchased 440 acres of land along Dawson Road, 4 miles from Plains and 8 from Americus. Jordan, his wife, Florence, and a missionary couple recently returned from Burma, moved into an old four-room house on the property, and named it Koinonia, a Greek word meaning sharing or fellowship. Jordan believed that to be judged a true Christian you must live out the teachings of the New Testament in your daily life. He credited his inspiration to Acts 2:32–37 and Acts 2:42–47. A tall, folksy man, he would say, "Religion that don't help people ain't worth a plugged nickel."

As a way of living their faith, Jordan and his companions set up a model farm where they would provide on-the-job training for any local farmer, white or black, who sought it. Florence set up sewing and cooking classes for their wives. The community gradually grew and prospered as others, mainly seminary classmates who shared Jordan's Christian views, joined them. Jordan did not initially set out to focus on blacks or to crusade against the existing social order, but having access to no other facility to upgrade their agricultural skills, it was overwhelmingly the black farmers who came to learn what he had to share. Shortly after his arrival he received a visit from two members of the Ku Klux Klan who said they had heard the couples "had been taking meals with niggers" and warned of dire consequences. However, Jordan's stature as a southern Baptist preacher, his jovial style, and his ability to relate to poor rural whites disarmed his visitors and they left without pursuing the matter further.

Over the next ten years Koinonia remained a tolerated, if not accepted, part of the community. The Jordans joined the nearby Rehoboth Baptist Church, and Clarence was invited to preach in white Baptist churches around the county. He and Florence were pleasant people who, apart from the way they treated blacks, were liked and accepted. In the pure Baptist tradition, they wanted only to live their beliefs without interference from the community. One Sunday in 1950, however, the Jordans brought with them to church an agricultural student from India who was studying at Florida State University and visiting Koinonia. Subsequently the deacons paid Jordan a visit to express their outrage for his bringing what they described as a "disguised nigger" to church. In the course of a frank and open conversation they discovered that his beliefs were far more radical than they had previously suspected. On their recommendation, the church voted that the Jordans and their friends be put out of the congregation for "disrupting the Christian spirit and unity." When Clarence and Florence continued to attend, saying, "We love you no matter what," the deacons ordered them to stay away.

On May 17, 1954, a bombshell hit the South when the U.S. Supreme Court, in *Brown v. Board of Education*, ruled that segregation in public schools was unconstitutional. With this decision the government in Washington was declaring the most radical intervention in the South since reconstruction. There were deep forebodings as howls of outrage rose from every southern state.

Jimmy was listening to the announcement on the radio in the warehouse when Rosalynn and the boys walked in. He was immediately concerned about what the reaction of their neighbors would be and Rosalynn recalls him saying with some trepidation, "I don't know what's going to happen around here." Across the entire South, groups clustered to discuss what their response to the decision should be.

Initially it was viewed by most southern blacks with no greater enthusiasm than by most whites. The case on which the Supreme Court ruled had been in the making for a long time. In the 1930s, Howard Law School dean Charles Hamilton Houston, together with his protégé, Thurgood Marshall, had conceived of the idea of a legal challenge to segregated schooling as an area of vulnerability through which the entire "separate but equal" doctrine could be overturned. But a substantial segment of black society, including many business leaders and professional people, opposed Houston and Marshall's attempt to change the system, viewing them as troublemakers. Adhering to "separate but equal," with the emphasis on "equal," they believed would do more to improve the quality of life for blacks than integration. Through years of accommodation to oppression, a black bourgeoisie had adapted itself to the system so that its members had a vested interest in the status quo and saw change as posing a threat to what little status and security they had. Black morticians who had a monopoly on black funerals, the owners of black life insurance companies, black preachers, barbers, and especially schoolteachers feared the uncertainty of change. By the 1950s the black business center on Auburn Avenue in Atlanta boasted several millionaires who were not among those pushing for school desegregation. It had taken Houston and Marshall more than twenty years to get a case to the Supreme Court, and their efforts were now about to transform the South.

In Southwest Georgia there was no visible support for school desegregation from the local black community. In part this reflected the profound nature of generations of oppression that had resulted in either an acceptance of the status quo or, for those with sufficient initiative, a determination to move elsewhere in the country. The result was that the local white community felt they could legitimately defy the Supreme Court decision as a totally unwanted intrusion in their local affairs by the federal government. Formal opposition began immediately to organize. The *Atlanta Journal,* under an Americus dateline, reported:

> Plans were outlined Wednesday at the first grassroots meeting of the States Right Council of Georgia, Inc. before a cheering overflow crowd of 600 persons jammed into the Sumter County Courthouse in this southwest Georgia city. Governor Marvin Griffin . . . said that he "did not believe in the decisions of the Supreme Court." . . . Former Governor Herman Talmadge said he felt that "regardless of what the Supreme Court says, does or thinks . . . by the grace of God, Georgia will continue running its own affairs."

The *Americus Times-Recorder* on June 10, 1954, ran a story saying that Sumter had become the seventh county in the Third Congressional District to organize a county unit of the States Right Council of Georgia. The organizing meeting was opened with a prayer by the Reverend M. F. Reeves and presided over by Herbert Moon, a former member of the state legislature. The officers of the committee were all leading citizens of the community, including Rudy Hayes, a future editor of the newspaper, and lawyer William E. (Billy) Smith.

The effect of the Supreme Court decision was to harden positions and polarize the community. Billboards calling for the impeachment of Earl Warren, the chief justice, sprouted throughout the county and across the South. Previously, whites, such as Miss Lillian, who had shown a kind and generous attitude toward blacks, were tolerated or, at worst, dismissed as eccentric. Now, those who failed to express adamant opposition to school integration were reviled and ostracized. Their businesses were boycotted and they faced the constant threat of physical attack.

After the initial furor over the Supreme Court decision died down, there were several years of relative quiescence until it became apparent that the federal government was determined to implement the decision even in the rural parts of the South. At that point a new outgrowth of the States Right Council, the White Citizens Council, emerged. Its avowed purpose was to sign up every white male to fight school integration.

In Plains, the organizers of the White Citizens Council were the police chief and the railroad depot agent, who was also a Baptist preacher. They came to the warehouse to get Jimmy to join. He declined. A few days later they returned with several of his friends and customers to inform him that he was the only white male in the community who refused to become a member. They pointed out that refusal to join could damage his business and out of concern for his welfare were even willing pay the $5 dues for him. He responded that he was not willing to join on any basis. "I would as soon flush $5 down the toilet," he told them. "I was willing to leave Plains if necessary," he would later write.

A brief boycott was organized against the Carter business, which initially was quite unnerving, especially to Rosalynn. They were just beginning to make a profit and could not afford to lose customers. In the end only two clients permanently deserted them, one a cousin of Rosalynn's. They were also subjected to other indignities; for several weeks, the filling station attendant ignored them and they had to fill their car's tank themselves.

Jimmy and Rosalynn were also expelled from the Americus Country Club, which they learned rather painfully. Rosalynn had taken Chip for a golf lesson, where, he says, "I was told we had been kicked out the night before. So for two and a half hours I sat on the curb waiting for my mother to come pick me up. It was a major moment in my life."

After years of relative tolerance, Koinonia became a convenient and accessible target for the anger and hatred of the local people who had no way of striking back at the distant Supreme Court. In September 1956 two black students had applied to the Georgia State College of Business Administration (now Georgia State University) in Atlanta. A front-page story in the *Americus Times-Recorder* announced that Clarence Jordan had signed an endorsement of their applications. In fact, he had not, because at the last minute the executive secretary of the Board of Regents had ruled he was ineligible to do so, having graduated from a different school in the university system. There followed abusive anonymous phone calls, and the Koinonia roadside welcome sign, picturing a Christian cross and a pair of clasped hands, was riddled with bullet holes and eventually torn down. Local retailers turned away Koinonia produce, and three sticks of dynamite blew up their roadside produce stand. Three hundred of their fruit trees were chopped down and there were numerous incidents in which hooded riders fired into the farm at night.

On the evening of February 24, 1957, more than a hundred members of the Ku Klux Klan drove in seventy cars and pickup trucks to Koinonia. Their spokesman told Dr. Jordan that it would be a good idea if the people of Koinonia left South Georgia. A few weeks later two young black men from Koinonia and a very light-skinned black woman strolled down the main street in Americus eating popcorn from the same bag. The citizens of Americus, assuming the woman was white, were outraged. Charles F. Crisp, the banker, declared "they deliberately tried to upset our equilibrium . . . it was a calculated affront." "The people," said Sheriff Fred Chappell, "have had it up to here."

In April 1957, a Sumter grand jury was convened to investigate charges

leveled against Koinonia, including alleged communist activities and associations, and profiting from, and even concocting, the violence against
itself. Although the grand jury failed to return an indictment, it did little to
diminish the hostility. Anyone who sought to defend Clarence Jordan's
rights, much less openly share his views, faced fearful retribution. Herbert
Birdsey, a prominent Macon businessman who owned a retail flour operation in Americus, wrote to Clarence Jordan apologizing for the boycott and
saying that his store was available to do business with Koinonia. They
bought a truckload of flour from him. A few nights later a tremendous
explosion destroyed the building at the northwest corner of Lee and
Forsyth Streets where the store was located.

Jack Singletary, an Annapolis graduate who had spent two years living at
Koinonia before buying his own farm south of Plains, was threatened, had
his produce boycotted, and was told he and his family were not welcome as
members of the Plains Baptist Church. Singletary's oldest son had leukemia
and had been sent to New York for treatment. Singletary used the phone at
a local store to call his son, but the sheriff and the Georgia Bureau of Investigation pressured the storekeeper into denying him further use of the
phone. Later, after the boy was brought back to the Americus hospital in the
terminal phase of his illness, Singletary parked his car outside to go in for a
visit. When he returned he found sugar had been poured into his gas tank.

Florence Jordan has been quoted as saying of Jimmy Carter, "He never
visited here, but his silence was no more than anyone else's." This is in fact
not true. Whether Florence Jordan was aware of it or not, beginning at the
time of his return to Plains, Carter went to Koinonia and established a relationship with Clarence Jordan. He says of their relationship:

> I went there several times . . . to try to sell him fertilizer, and seed and ani-
> mal feed, cattle and hog feed. But he was very frank with me. He said, "You
> know, Jimmy, I can buy fertilizer as cheap as you can. We buy our fertilizer
> directly from the factories in the north. Swift and Company and others will
> sell me fertilizer at the exact same price you can buy it for." But what we did
> do primarily for them was to shell seed peanuts.

The Carters were friendly with the Singletarys, primarily because of
their navy connection. When the Plains merchants imposed their boycott
on Jack Singletary, Jimmy Carter sought to get it eased and tried to convince the store owner to let him use the phone again. Rosalynn's role was
even more determined. Jack recounts:

> Our little boy finally died of leukemia. It was when the boycott was on
> and we had our friends from Koinonia come over for the funeral. Rosalynn
> came over the next morning and brought a ham. We invited her to stay and

she did: we had a very informal Quaker-type service and put the body in a little box that Koinonia had made. We took it down to a little playground there where he had played and buried him without any remarks.

Rosalynn immediately drove back to Plains and went to the home of Robert Harris, the preacher of the Plains Baptist Church, to confront him over his refusal to officiate at the burial. According to Singletary, "He said he reckoned he'd be run out of town if he did, but she made him come . . . we had a graveside service . . . that's a little insight into the kind of person she is."

There was little doubt about Rosalynn and Jimmy's position on racial matters whether they articulated it or not. Warren Fortson says:

> You just knew where Jimmy stood. You knew that Jimmy also was a person who had no truck with that kind of stuff. You knew that Jimmy was a severe critic of the way in which they treated Clarence Jordan and his folks at Koinonia. You did not have to sit down and talk about them, you just knew it. . . . Jimmy was a good, decent, fine person then. . . . He was no Jack Kennedy who once he got elected suddenly got liberal on the issue. It was that he always had strong beliefs that way.

Rosalynn has described an experience that had significant impact on Jimmy in the early years after they returned to Plains:

> One day a black farmer and customer asked Jimmy if he could borrow some money to buy shoes for his little girl, who was just starting school. He said she was going to school barefoot, but he would have to keep her out when the weather got cold. He would pay Jimmy back when he gathered his crop. A few days later, Jimmy rode down to the farmer's house. The whole family lived in a house without heat or electricity, indoor water or plumbing. There was a garden in the yard with collard greens and sweet potatoes, and Jimmy learned that that plus corn bread was the family's food. A house full of children, and none of them could remember when they had any kind of meat to eat, even chicken. This image remained in Jimmy's mind long after we bought shoes for all the children and as he worked to help our customer improve his farming operation.

How one felt and what one could do on a personal basis was very different from what one could afford to do publicly. In the 1950s, Jimmy Carter's first priority was to make his business a success. As long as he kept his views to himself, or his close friends, he could still prosper. To become a defender of the Supreme Court decision, or even to have openly supported Clarence Jordan, would have spelled financial ruin, but he walked close to the edge by continuing to do business with Clarence Jordan. He did not

seek to publicly identify himself morally with Clarence Jordan in his conflict with the community leaders. Jimmy Carter was by nature a conciliator
who avoided confrontation if it was at all possible.

What created such vitriolic feelings toward Clarence Jordan was that he
inflamed the conscience of relatively decent people as they struggled to
reconcile two incompatible but deeply held sets of beliefs—their Christian
values and their historic allegiance to the institution of segregation. His
pursuit of what many of them knew to be truly Christian ideals provoked
intolerable discomfort. On May 26, 1957, a delegation of the town's leaders
went to Koinonia. It included Chamber of Commerce President Frank
Myers, Mayor Fred Bowen, banker Charles F. Crisp, physician Dr. J. H.
Robinson, *Americus Times-Recorder* publisher James R. Blair, and County
Commission Chairman George Matthews. Crisp acted as their spokesman
in addressing Jordan:

> We came out here on the basis that you are serving what you believe to be
> Christian principles. . . . Now our philosophy is that the first duty of a Chris-
> tian would be to make brotherly love in the community. Unfortunately, your
> experiment has not done that. It has set brother against brother; it has cre-
> ated bitterness; it has created hatred; it has created every emotion that is
> contrary to my concept of Christianity.
>
> It is our belief that unless this experiment is moved to other fields that
> tempers will get to such a point that somebody is going to get hurt. . . . We
> want to appeal to your good judgment to pray over it and see if you don't
> think you'll be serving the best interests of the community, and certainly the
> best interests of the Lord, to move and leave us in peace.

Jordan was not moved and responded in a restrained manner, advising
the delegation that they would do well to remember that:

> Our forefathers were driven from Europe on these same grounds because
> . . . they wanted to be free to worship as they saw fit. . . . I think you have it in
> your power to drive us out . . . [but] to be quite frank with you, I think Sumter
> County has a great responsibility in this too.

Jordan stayed, and later when he was set upon and beaten on the streets
of Americus, it was he who was arrested and charged with disturbing the
peace. Years later, Frank Myers would say that it was one of the great
regrets of his life that he had been a part of the delegation that went to
Koinonia.

In the summer of 1954, Jimmy and Rosalynn had attended the weeklong
Baptist revival meetings. The visiting preacher was named Ben Grenade.
One night at the start of the service, he commented, "I am delighted to see
my good friend Clarence Jordan in the congregation." With that, a substan-

tial part of the congregation who had not noticed Jordan's presence got up and left. Rosalynn, however, was sufficiently impressed by Grenade's truly Christian spirit that she switched her membership from the Methodist Church to the Baptist.

The regular Baptist preacher, Tommie Jones, asked Jimmy to teach a Sunday school class of nine- to twelve-year-old boys and later to help build a youth camp for the Friendship Baptist Association. "Jimmy knew where to get the workers we needed for clearing the land," Jones says. "He was the best assistant I ever had."

When Tommie Jones left in 1955 he was replaced by Robert Harris. His wife, Ethel, was a specialist in early childhood development. Before coming to Plains, the Harrises had been in Fort Valley, Georgia. There they had arranged for a white Baptist coed to lead a vacation Bible school for the local black Baptist church. After a week, Harris received a call from the local sheriff who told him bluntly, "Get that white lady out of that nigger church or I won't be responsible for her safety." Harris, a mild-mannered man and no advocate for integration, was shaken by the experience and, because of it, left Fort Valley for Plains. It also made him very reticent to speak out on matters of race during the twelve years that he was the Carters' pastor.

On other matters Harris was outspoken. He strongly encouraged members of the church to get involved in public life. In the early sixties he was a strong proponent of the Peace Corps, an organization that many Baptist preachers opposed. His preaching inspired Miss Lillian, who later became a Peace Corps volunteer. Harris would admonish his parishioners that they must (1) place God's men in office; (2) pray God's wisdom for them; (3) help them to eradicate evils in our country; (4) reduce the crime rate and thereby reduce taxes; (5) raise the moral standard and thereby get more for each tax dollar. These were tenets that Jimmy Carter could comfortably embrace and, taken together, with some variation, would come to constitute the central values as he conceptualized public service and his political life.

Jimmy Carter and Bob Harris disagreed on one issue—alcohol. Jimmy saw nothing wrong with taking an occasional drink. Knowing full well the degree of bootlegging that went on locally, he opposed, unsuccessfully, the effort by Harris and other parishioners to keep Sumter County dry. Jimmy also believed alcoholism, an affliction from which two of his mother's brothers (Lem and James) suffered, to be a disease rather than a moral failing. Because of these views, in spite of having been previously proposed, it was not until 1962 that the congregation elected him and he was ordained a deacon of his church.

By 1961 Jimmy had achieved his business goals and made considerable money. Some of his friends thought making money was too important to him. Others felt, perhaps more accurately, that for him money symbolized success. As one friend says, "Money is what you use to keep score. But the game is success."

Jimmy and Rosalynn bought a plot of land on shaded Woodland Drive near the center of Plains and engaged an Albany architect, Hugh Gaston, who would become a close friend, to design a brick ranch-style house for them. It would become their permanent home to which they would return throughout the rest of their lives. When they moved in at the end of 1961, the modern, comfortable but unpretentious house symbolized that they had fully arrived in Plains. The years of struggle since returning from the navy were over. They were financially secure. Jimmy was a respected leader of the community and his church.

CHAPTER 8

The domination of Georgia politics by Eugene Talmadge that had begun in the 1920s when he was agriculture commissioner reached its peak in 1940 when he was elected to his third two-year term as governor. The growing U.S. involvement in the war in Europe, however, was already forcing a change in public attitudes in the state. In 1941, Talmadge made the mistake of demanding the dismissal of the dean of the College of Education at the University of Georgia for allegedly advocating the integration of the public schools. The Board of Regents refused to carry out the governor's orders. In retaliation he purged the board and fired the dean as well as several other faculty members. As a decisive statement about where he stood on the race issue, it was wildly popular with his rural constituency, but among the more educated and worldly leaders in the state, especially his financial backers in Atlanta, his dictatorial behavior did him considerable harm. The Southern Association of Colleges and Schools stripped the entire state university system of its accreditation. Thus, students faced the prospect of receiving worthless diplomas; perhaps even more telling among the alumni, the University of Georgia and Georgia Tech faced the prospect of exclusion from the football conference schedules.

Talmadge's actions generated a groundswell of support for his opponent, Ellis Arnall, a successful lawyer, in the 1942 gubernatorial campaign. Promising to insulate the university system from future political interference, Arnall won a stunning upset victory. His election was a watershed, ending the Gene Talmadge monopoly, and also suggesting a new progressive political trend around which more enlightened groups, including returning veterans, could rally. Arnall benefitted from being the first governor to serve a four-year term without the right of succession, as opposed to the earlier two-year term. He set about implementing a progressive program that included, in addition to protecting the university system, significantly aiding education without increasing taxes, establishing a new state constitution, making Georgia the first state to give eighteen-year-olds the right to vote, repealing the poll tax, abolishing chain gangs, and establishing the state merit and teacher retirement system. Of particular importance to the state's economy, he helped to break the freight rate monopoly that had for so long shackled the South. He was even briefly mentioned by those around FDR as a potential vice-presidential candidate in 1944.

Eugene Talmadge, resorting to his well-worn racist rhetoric, used his four years out of office to further strengthen his political machine in the rural counties. In the gubernatorial election of 1946, James V. Carmichael, a moderate businessman, easily won the statewide popular vote in the Democratic primary, but came in a poor second to Talmadge under the crucial county unit system that made the winning of counties, regardless of their population, the deciding factor in the election. In the general election, despite questions about his health, Talmadge won in a landslide. He died, however, before taking office.

As a precautionary measure, some of Talmadge's supporters, aware of the graveness of his illness, had organized a secret write-in campaign for his son Herman. A dispute then ensued between Herman Talmadge, James Carmichael, who had also run a write-in campaign, and the Republican candidate, D. Talmadge Bowers. To further complicate matters, M. E. Thompson, who had been elected lieutenant governor, declared that Gene Talmadge had been legitimately elected and upon his death he, Thompson, should be governor. Ellis Arnall, as the departing governor, backed Thompson, refusing to formally relinquish the office until the courts ruled on the case. In a comic opera atmosphere. Herman Talmadge seized control of the governor's office in the capitol and the mansion, changing the locks on the doors, while Thompson established his own governor's office in a downtown office building. Two months later the Georgia Supreme Court ruled in Thompson's favor but allowed him to serve only a two-year term. Herman Talmadge was then able to mobilize his father's organization to assure his election by an overwhelming margin in 1948.

Georgia's image, which had been so enhanced in the Arnall years, was reversed, and the state became an object of ridicule. Jimmy Carter recalls how it embarrassed him at the time on the USS *Wyoming*, and it was one of the reasons that he talked little about politics while in the navy. Beginning with Arnall's tenure, Georgia became polarized between the Talmadge forces and the anti-Talmadge forces. The latter were made up of the growing urban population, the more educated, liberals, the small but influential Jewish population, blacks, and younger people, especially those who had served in World War II.

After Arnall, Thompson became their standard bearer. Thompson had lived for several years in Americus and had a group of avid supporters there. One was Frank Myers, who as a veteran at the University of Georgia became student body president and a vocal and visible leader of the young anti-Talmadge, pro-Thompson forces. Returning to practice law in Americus, he ran successfully for the state legislature in 1950. As a progressive, stubborn, and often abrasive legislator, he proved a constant thorn in the side of Governor Herman Talmadge. According to Meyers, the Talmadge forces targeted him as one of their primary enemies, and in Americus they sought to destroy him politically and economically. He says that he could not get loans at banks and that they contacted his legal clients, warning them that if they gave him any further business they too would be boycotted.

They needed a candidate to run against Myers and settled on Earl Carter. With the Talmadge machine behind him and arguing that Myers was too liberal for Sumter County, Earl was elected to the legislature in 1952. Initially on election night, it seemed Myers would be reelected. The Plains district reported hours after the others and gave Earl such a large majority that he won the race overall by 2,177 to 1,936. Frank Myers believes the ballot box had been stuffed by the Talmadge people without Earl Carter's knowledge. Myers accepted his defeat resignedly, and, particularly because of a warm relationship with Lillian Carter, remained friendly with the Carters. For many years he served as the lawyer for the family business.

Earl Carter remained an unrelenting Talmadge loyalist. As a state legislator and a member of the Sumter County school board he was able to persuade Herman Talmadge, as governor, to make the graduation speech at Plains High School on June 2, 1953. On his visit the governor spent the night in the Carters' home. Upon Earl Carter's death, a delegation from the community came to Lillian to offer Earl's seat in the legislature. The offer reflected the high esteem in which Earl was held, and the assumption that, as his wife, she too would be a loyal Talmadge supporter. By ignoring her longstanding sympathy for blacks, they implied that women were accorded greater latitude in their relationships with blacks and that their views on racial matters were of no real consequence. In her grief she declined and the community rallied behind Thad Jones, a successful businessman and friend of the Carters. He completed Earl's term and was subsequently reelected several times without opposition. Jones was, however, an ardent segregationist who later organized the brief and ultimately unsuccessful boycott of the Carter business when Jimmy refused to join the White Citizens Council.

In the early fall of 1961, Warren Fortson and Charlie Smith, who ran the local radio station, drove to Plains one day to see if they could convince Jimmy to run against Congressman "Tick" Forrester. As Fortson says, "To those of us . . . a little more liberal . . . he [Forrester] was an abomination before the Lord and an embarrassment to have representing the district. . . . We wanted to see someone run against him and beat him, because . . . we thought he was vulnerable."

They found Carter in the warehouse in work clothes and a baseball cap. He was running his hands through a load of wheat contaminated with crotalaria seed, which is poisonous to cattle and other livestock. He was clearly upset and preoccupied. Nevertheless, they broached the subject they had come to discuss:

> We sat there and talked with Jimmy and he was very cool to the idea. . . . He certainly did not agree with [Forrester's] political persuasion, but said he was very very busy with his farming operation and his warehouse operation.

Carter says of the encounter more than thirty years later:

> I despised his [Forrester's] attitude and philosophy. He was as bad as Bilbo. . . . I had too much to do in Plains to consider moving to Washington . . . and probably could not have won. Warren, Charlie, and I were a small minority in a totally segregated community, and I knew this.

Jimmy, however, was to be drawn almost unwittingly into the elective process. Consolidation of the Sumter County and Americus school systems had long been under discussion. Earl Carter, when he was on the school board, had supported it as a way of giving Plains students access to a wider range of subjects and teachers. Language classes, science labs, music instruction and a school band, special education classes, as well as an expanded sports program to include a football team, were all benefits to be derived from having a single large high school. At the time Jimmy became chairman of the school board in 1961, there were three white high schools in the county with a total enrollment of 500 pupils, enough for one large school. It was opposed by the people in the small communities, for whom the local school and its basketball team was an important source of community pride, and who feared being swallowed up by a consolidated system dominated by Americus.

After the 1954 Supreme Court ruling on *Brown v. Board of Education,* consolidation took on the added implication of being, in some way, a stalking horse for future school desegregation. Jimmy, who had carefully studied the recently published reports of the commissions on American education headed by John Gardner and James Bryant Conant, had become a fervent advocate for consolidation for the same reason his father had— because he thought it would lead to better education. He and his fellow board members, together with Warren Fortson, then the county attorney and a member of the Americus school board, developed a detailed consolidation plan that needed a voter referendum to be implemented. Naively discounting the emotions involved, Jimmy believed that skeptical parents, wanting the best for their children, would inevitably accept the plan if presented with the facts. He made speeches throughout the county, while Rosalynn and other supporters made phone calls, wrote letters, and raised money for newspaper and radio ads.

His position split the Carter family in two. His conservative uncle Alton and cousin Hugh adamantly opposed the plan, and Hugh, together with the Plains High School principal, Y. T. Sheffield, became a major spokesman for the anti-consolidation forces. Fear of integration was their major weapon and Y. T. Sheffield said forthrightly that blacks would be allowed into Plains High School "over my dead body." The issue was brought to a public vote and was defeated by only 84 votes countywide, but in Plains there were a mere 33 votes in favor and 201 against.

By early 1962, two black students, Charlayne Hunter and Hamilton Holmes, had been admitted under court order, with some violent resistance, to the University of Georgia. The public schools of Atlanta were moving toward integration and the civil rights movement was gaining momentum across the South. In late 1961, the Student Non-Violent Coordinating Committee (SNCC), under the local leadership of Charles Sherrod, had moved into Albany, 40 miles from Plains. Relying on the large black student community at Albany State College, Sherrod and other black leaders under the umbrella of the "Albany Movement" began organizing a voter registration drive and repeated challenges to the continuing segregation of public facilities involved in interstate commerce—a violation of federal law.

In the first week of December, Dr. Martin Luther King, Jr., came to Albany to speak and lead a march. He and other leaders were arrested. In order to defuse the tension in Albany, King and Ralph Abernathy were moved to the Americus jail for several days awaiting their trial. Despite the actions of the Supreme Court, the southern bloc in Congress, led by Georgia senator Richard Russell, had always been able to forestall the enforcement provisions of any civil rights legislation, largely neutralizing the impact of the laws. By directly challenging the failure of the federal government to enforce its laws, a new activist breed of young blacks in the South was forcing the hands of those in Washington. The white rural population of Southwest Georgia was feeling increasingly threatened by the changes. Violence always lurked just below the surface, and during 1961 and 1962, six black churches in the area were burned to the ground in an attempt to intimidate local blacks. In the view of the young activists in SNCC, Southwest Georgia was second only to Mississippi as the most dangerous place they worked.

Rosalynn recalls that the night of the school consolidation vote she and Jimmy had gone to a high school basketball game in which their son Jack was playing. When the results of the referendum were announced in the gymnasium, the crowd broke into wild applause. As she described it:

> I sat there at the ball game with my chin up while everyone gloated over our loss, but I was crying inside. On the way home from the game, we passed

our office and noticed something on the door. It was a homemade sign: COONS AND CARTERS GO TOGETHER. I was devastated.

Jimmy had invested a great deal of himself in the consolidation issue and he took the defeat of the referendum as a personal repudiation. It was, he says, "a stinging disappointment."

Ernest Vandiver, Georgia's youngest attorney general and a progressive man by Georgia standards, had been elected governor in 1958 on the slogan, "No, not one!" meaning that he would allow not one black student in a white school. However, unlike George Wallace in Alabama and Ross Barnett in Mississippi, he did modify his stand by allowing that, however unpalatable, the courts should be obeyed. Many Georgians felt that within the law they had the option of integrating the public schools or closing them. As a result, in the early sixties all-white private "academies" sprang up throughout Georgia. Families who could afford tuition abandoned the public school systems in droves. The Carters were determined to see the public schools stay open.

Meanwhile, Jimmy was passionately committed to another education issue. Georgia Southwestern College had been crucial over the years in affording hundreds of poor students the opportunity to receive advanced education and go on to professional careers. Because the college was accredited only as a two-year school, it could not award a full degree. Community leaders in Americus had long sought to get the State Board of Regents to give the school four-year accreditation. The regional representative on the board was Bo Callaway, a West Point graduate and scion of a wealthy textile family. He was from Columbus and was eager to give the four-year accreditation instead to a relatively newly established college in that city. It was said he intended to run for Congress and Columbus had more votes than Americus. Carter was incensed that Callaway, a man of great wealth and little empathy for the poor, would allow his own personal ambitions to sway him in denying the long established and academically superior Georgia Southwestern College the four-year accreditation. Following a Board of Regents meeting before which Callaway had personally lobbied his fellow regents to vote against Georgia Southwestern's application, Carter pursued Callaway back to his family's estate and cornered him in a boathouse by a lake. A heated argument followed and Carter says that he came nearer to having a fistfight at that moment than at any other time in his adult life.

Jimmy's characteristic way of dealing with defeat was another challenge. The only way to compensate for what he felt had been a personal rejection at the polls was to look for another, larger race that he could win. Having ruled out challenging "Tick" Forrester for the Third Congressional District seat and a race against Thad Jones for the State House of Representatives, this left only the state senate. However, the position of state senator had traditionally been weak and ineffectual. The counties where Atlanta and Savannah were located each had their own senator. Throughout the rest of the state each senatorial district was made up of three counties regardless of size. Each of the three in turn elected the senator to represent the district. Senators served for only two years, so it was a body in flux with no seniority or potential to develop a long-term legislative agenda. Also, the local courthouse politicians had almost total control over who got the job when it was their county's turn. In effect, it provided an opportunity for one of their cronies, once every three years, to spend forty-five days, expenses paid, in Atlanta during the low point of the farming year. Dramatic changes were, however, about to occur in the Georgia political system, the timing of which would prove a stroke of luck for Carter.

The political system in Georgia, which had allowed demagogues like Eugene Talmadge to thrive, was the county unit system. As Carter himself has described it:

> It was this 1868 document (the new state constitution) that eliminated direct popular elections for governor and other state offices, establishing in its place the county unit system, a method of indirect election that was defended by claiming that it was somewhat akin to the electoral college in presidential elections. Except within individual counties, popular votes did not count. Instead, the constitution mandated that each of the six largest counties (changed in 1920 to eight), regardless of population, could cast six unit votes; more than a hundred of the smallest ones would have two votes apiece; and about thirty would have four. The state house of representatives was also apportioned according to this 3-2-1 ratio.

As a result, by World War I the value of a vote in Fulton County (Atlanta) had shrunk to less than a quarter than that of an average vote in Georgia as a whole. Atlanta continued to grow, and by 1960 a vote there was worth approximately a hundredth of a vote in Echols County, which had the smallest population. While there were other mechanisms for specifically disenfranchising blacks, it also meant that their votes in Atlanta were essentially canceled out by the unit votes of a county like Webster, where, despite being in the majority, not a single black citizen had been allowed to register to vote.

The county unit system had been repeatedly challenged over the years, usually under the equal protection provision of the Fourteenth Amendment. The federal courts, conservative and reluctant to interfere with the perceived sovereign right of states to run their own elections, had always ruled against the challengers. The Supreme Court had upheld their decisions. However, the increasingly apparent absurdity of the unit system, the growing political clout of major southern cities like Atlanta, and the more liberal, activist court of Earl Warren coalesced to make change inevitable. Finally, on March 26, 1962, in a Tennessee case, *Baker v. Carr,* the Supreme Court of the United States struck down the iniquitous systems that denied equal representation to individuals and communities and established what became known as the "one man, one vote" rule.

In Georgia a suit was immediately filed by Atlanta civil rights attorney Morris Abrams on behalf of James O'Hear Sanders to overthrow the county unit system. This suit, *Sanders v. Gray* (James Gray being chairman of the Democratic Party), was quickly followed by a second, *Toombs v. Fortson,* brought by a group of citizens against Secretary of State Ben Fortson (brother of Warren) seeking reapportionment of the Georgia General Assembly based on population. Because the Supreme Court had mandated judicial action in implementing their *Baker v. Carr* ruling, a three-judge panel chaired by the senior court of appeals judge, Elbert P. Tuttle, was formed on April 2, 1962, to hear *Sanders v. Gray.* Judge Tuttle appointed to the panel Judge Frank Hooper, the federal district judge in the northern district of Georgia to whom the *Sanders v. Gray* case had been submitted, and Judge Griffin Bell, an Americus native and distant relative of Rosalynn. Because the second case, *Toombs v. Fortson,* was so intimately linked to the first, Tuttle formed a second panel to hear it, substituting Judge Lewis R. Morgan for Judge Hooper.

Over the next five months these four men would completely transform the structure and nature of elective politics in Georgia, resulting in a profound shift of power from the rural to the urban areas, an indirect but dramatic enfranchisement of the black vote in the state, the destruction of a longstanding system of patronage and corruption, and an opening up of elective offices to people of backgrounds and perspectives completely different from the previous incumbents. Not surprisingly the Supreme Court decision on *Baker v. Carr* and the impending dismantling of the county unit system was roundly condemned by officeholders at every level.

The first impulse of Governor Vandiver and members of the legislature was to stall and simply do nothing. They were thwarted by the judges who intimated that if the Senate refused to come up with a reapportionment plan by April 27, the day they set for their final ruling, they would reapportion the legislature themselves. A special session was called and more than two dozen bills were introduced, most of which sought to somehow preserve the county unit system. The bickering among the legislators, who rightly saw an end coming to many of their political careers, was at times vicious, and when the House and Senate conference committee met and deadlocked, the recriminations between the two bodies were intense. Finally the House voted on its own plan and adjourned, leaving the Senate with the choice of accepting the House bill or bearing the blame for allowing the federal courts to rewrite the political map of Georgia unilaterally. They finally passed the House plan, Vandiver signed it, and it was delivered to the judges.

Judges Tuttle and Hooper were known to be progressive and their opposition to the county unit system was a foregone conclusion. What was not clear was the position Griffin Bell would take. His origins in Southwest Georgia and his intimate ties to some of the more conservative politicians in the state led to concern among opponents of the county unit system. Bell had served as Governor Vandiver's chief of staff, a largely pro forma position involving working with the legislature. During the 1960 presidential primary campaign, Georgia's top politicians—Governor Vandiver and Senators Russell and Talmadge—had fervently supported Lyndon Johnson against John Kennedy. After Kennedy won the nomination, they became seriously concerned that, should he become president, Georgia would lose all White House patronage. They realized they needed to redeem themselves by going all out for Kennedy and pledged their total loyalty to the ticket. Griffin Bell was made chairman of the Kennedy campaign in Georgia. Because of the extraordinary machine that Russell, and especially Talmadge, had throughout the state, they were able to deliver Kennedy the largest state majority in the country. As a result, Kennedy appointed Griffin Bell to the federal bench.

Despite his conservative credentials, Bell continued his evolution that had begun when he returned from World War II. Above all, he was a realist who understood that times were changing and society in the South had to adapt, especially if the region was to compete economically with the rest of the nation. It was he who, on April 28, read aloud the unanimous decision of the panel considering *Sanders v. Gray*.

Because the composition of the Senate could be changed quickly by legislation, whereas the state constitution had to be amended to alter the elective process for the House, attention focused on reforming the former body as the easiest way of complying with the court—a view encouraged by the judges in responding to queries from the plaintiffs. Because the system of rotating the Senate seat among the three counties had denied seniority based on length of tenure, opposition was limited.

The Democratic primary for governor was scheduled for September 12. In addition to conservative former governor Marvin Griffin, and progressive lawyer Carl Sanders, there had been a third candidate in the race, Lieutenant Governor Garland Byrd. Byrd had been a classmate of Jimmy Carter's at Georgia Southwestern in 1943 and was considered one of the brightest rising stars of Georgia politics—an almost certain future governor. At the height of the reapportionment dispute in May he dropped out of the gubernatorial race, citing a mild heart attack. Some saw it as a "political heart attack" brought on by the realization that under a popular vote he and Marvin Griffin would split the conservative rural vote and assure Carl Sanders's election. Byrd's doctor was Beverly Forester, who argues that the heart problem was legitimate.

Carl Sanders did win the Democratic primary. Both Rosalynn and Jimmy voted for him. Facing only token Republican opposition and clearly wanting the reapportionment issue resolved before he took office, he quickly announced that he would work collaboratively with Governor Vandiver to reconstitute the Senate. Another special session of the general assembly was called for September 27. Carter describes what happened:

> Governor-nominee Sanders, who was still serving as Senate president pro tem, was riding a crest of popularity and power, and there was little doubt that the reapportionment plan he endorsed would be passed in its general form. It called for fifty-four Senate nominees to be chosen by majority vote in a special Democratic primary October 16 and routinely confirmed by the state Democratic convention the following day. Necessary runoff elections would be held on October 23. Then these nominees would face possible Republican opponents, with the victors elected in the regularly scheduled general election on November 6. The average district would include about 70,000 citizens, but the judges permitted deviations of up to 20 percent, roughly equivalent to the disparity among the fifty states in the electoral college for choosing the president of the United States.

There remained serious discord between the two houses and individual legislators. Carl Sanders, however, was in a uniquely powerful position and forced through the plan that was signed into law by departing Governor Vandiver on October 5. Candidates were given three days, until October 8, to qualify. The election was to be held just eight days later.

Throughout the summer of 1962 the reapportionment battle was the dominant topic of conversation in the state, especially in the rural areas. Any change would have occasioned fear and anxiety, but what made matters worse was that this reform was clearly dictated by outsiders, the federal courts. Still reeling from the ramifications of the school desegregation ruling, the full impact of which had yet to reach Southwest Georgia, white people felt they were losing control of their lives and their communities. More and more it seemed that people in Atlanta and Washington, who knew nothing about life in rural Georgia, were deciding their future. Above all, they were concerned that the shift in power would mean control by blacks.

Like everyone else, Jimmy and Rosalynn had followed the reapportionment battles with keen interest. While they shared some of the fears of their neighbors, for Jimmy it also opened up a major new opportunity. Seeing, during the summer, the inevitability that some form of popular election for the state senate would be instituted, he began to contemplate actively the possibility of running.

Carter was not interested in politics for its own sake; it seemed to him a profession in which moral values were too easily compromised. In many respects it was the antithesis of the way he led his own life. If, however, it could be a vehicle for constructive change, especially with regard to education, then he could view his own potential involvement in a different light. In August 1962, Allen Comish, one of the best-known Baptist ministers in Georgia, and a close friend of Robert Harris, came to Plains as the guest preacher for the weeklong revival services. Comish came to dinner one night with Miss Lillian, Jimmy, and Rosalynn. After dinner, Jimmy and Comish discussed politics. Comish describes the rest of the conversation:

> It wasn't a structured discussion at all. He said he was thinking of running for the state Senate, but I don't remember that he asked my opinion. I certainly didn't advise him against it. I had a couple of men in my church already serving in the legislature. What I did was lay out a political life from my viewpoint as pastor and as one who had grown up in a politically active family.
>
> I must have said, "You won't find political life easy. You'll lose friends. You'll be subjected to personal attacks. You'll be pressured by special interests. You'll have to compromise a little and get a coalition to get your bills passed. Not many bills become law today on merit alone."

Carter remembers Comish as saying, "If you want to be of service to other people, why don't you go into the ministry or into some honorable social service work?" Impulsively Carter responded, "How would you like to be the pastor of a church with 80,000 members?" Comish conceded that it might be possible to stay honest and at the same time minister to the needs of the 80,000 citizens of the Fourteenth Senate District. Carter's comment reflected what would remain in his own mind a close analogy, an elected politician and his constituency and a pastor and his congregation. As a member of the Baptist faith in which preachers are not appointed by a church hierarchy, but elected by the congregation they serve, the analogy seemed to him quite apt.

September was the busiest time of the year. The peanut and the cotton harvest came in; Jimmy and Rosalynn worked with their employees for days at a time, around the clock, eating and sleeping at the warehouse and going home only to change clothes and shower. Jack, Chip, and Jeff worked in the warehouse too when they were not in school. They bought thousands of tons of peanuts from the local farmers and ginned the cotton that was brought in. Jimmy also had to carefully monitor the quality of the seed peanuts, which had become the central part of their business. With the farmers cashing in on their harvest it was also the time when Jimmy had to collect on all of the IOUs for seed, fertilizer, and pesticides for which credit had been extended earlier in the year.

The business was still the central aspect of Jimmy and Rosalynn's lives. By now Jimmy had made up his mind to run for the state senate, but still slow to share with her his innermost thoughts, did not mention his decision to Rosalynn. To have done so in the midst of the September harvest would have seemed almost dilettantish, if not selfish. It also had the potential for precipitating a major disagreement with Rosalynn, in part because it would mean Jimmy being away in Atlanta at least two months a year. He delayed saying anything as long as he could, and when he did, Rosalynn was quite unprepared.

> He got up on his birthday, October 1, put on his slacks instead of his khaki clothes to go to the warehouse. I said, "Where are you going?" He said, "I'm going to Americus to see who is running for the state senate." He came back and said nobody from our county was running . . . and we talked about it and decided he would run.

Jimmy had, in fact, while in Americus, placed a notice in the *Times-Recorder* saying that he would be a candidate. It ran in that afternoon's edition.

There were fifteen days until the election. Jimmy had never been near a political campaign. He had no staff or surrogates to campaign for him and no money except that from his own pocket. He had to work at the ware-house and had only a few hours each day to campaign. Despite her surprise at his decision, Rosalynn threw her considerable energy into the whirlwind campaign. She, more than Jimmy, had a natural aptitude for political strategy. She also brought to bear the same methodical approach that had made her such a successful manager of the business. She helped design calling cards and a campaign poster that displayed his picture and the words CARTER and SENATOR in letters large enough to be read by passing motorists. Jimmy nailed up the posters at crossroads and on the approaches to towns. There were no rallies or opportunities for set speeches. It was mostly one-on-one discussion. Never a person to waste time, he quickly learned he could easily get bogged down by people he described as "loafers" who were expert at "embroiling me in idle talk." His future campaigns would be characterized by a studied effort always to be in control of the conversations he had on the stump. Jimmy also learned that inveigling lonely disc jockeys into brief on-air conversations could be very productive. He had less success with the two newspapers in the area, especially the *Columbus Ledger,* which declined to interview him. On election eve he made a brief television announcement on the Columbus CBS station—his first experience live before the camera.

There were fifty-four Lions Clubs in southwestern Georgia, and as the district governor Jimmy was known to all of their members. He had business customers in Stewart, Terrell, Sumter, and Webster Counties. He and Rosalynn had relatives in all seven counties in the new district. He received some help from his friends, especially John Pope and Warren Fortson, but it was likely the efforts of Rosalynn and his sister Gloria were decisive in the brief campaign. Whatever Rosalynn's initial reservations, she knew how stubbornly determined Jimmy would be to win. Between her other obligations at the warehouse she called every person on the Sumter County voters list. When she found supporters, she enlisted them to call others. She and Gloria addressed thousands of letters.

Some of Carter's friends joked that he was running for the state senate to get off the Sumter County school board. With the full impact of the Supreme Court's *Brown v. Board of Education* decision about to hit Southwest Georgia, the chairman of the school board would be in the eye of a hurricane. In leading the consolidation effort, Carter had had a foretaste of the vitriolic hatreds that were likely to be unleashed against anyone seen to promote school integration, even if merely obeying the orders of the courts. Not only would he risk being widely ostracized but his livelihood could be completely destroyed. He had a family to support and, as the years had passed, his option of using his nuclear expertise to work at the Electric Boat Company had diminished. The threat of violence could not be discounted.

When he first joined the school board in 1956 Jimmy accepted the conventional wisdom that the best way to avoid court-ordered integration was to improve the black schools so that the fiction of "separate but equal" could be maintained. He did, however, show a willingness to go along with the traditional way of doing things when, for instance, he voted to buy new typewriters for the white schools while the old, used machines, like the worn-out textbooks, were passed on to the black schools. The pressure to accept blindly the inequities was considerable. "It seems hard to believe now," he would later write, "but I was actually on the school board for several months before it dawned on me that white children rode buses to their schools and black children still walked to theirs." Jimmy recalls visits that the board members made to the all-black schools and, despite the modest improvements they had authorized, how embarrassing and obviously untenable "separate but equal" was. But while he, and especially Rosalynn, could have personally accepted integrated schools, to have advocated it in any way would have been unthinkable and pointless. As Warren Fortson says, "integration back then was about like child molestation is today. If you wanted to queer something you just said it would lead to integration."

By the time Jimmy had become chairman of the board in 1961, it was increasingly clear that school integration was inevitable and that the only alternative was to close the public schools. As a result of the publicity that had surrounded the consolidation issue, he was well known throughout Sumter County. While some people despised him for those efforts and would not vote for him on any account, there were at least an equal number who were prepared to vote for him for the same reason.

Jimmy's opponent was Homer Moore from Stewart County, who was well known and widely liked in the region. He had been elected earlier in the year under the county unit system and announced that he would be a candidate under the new system. As a result, a number of prominent community leaders had publicly committed to him before Jimmy entered the race. Carter had little antipathy toward Homer Moore. In his book *Turning Point*, he says, "I was not running a personal campaign against Homer Moore, and I respected him as an honest and able opponent." He further described him as "an honest, hard-driving, ambitious, and active community leader." They were both involved in the farm supply business and had long competed for the patronage as they now competed for votes. By the time Carter recognized the extent of Moore's support, he was too deeply into the race to withdraw. Instead it just hardened his determination to win.

Homer Moore argued in his campaign literature that he had already been elected "fair and square" to the job under the old system. In so doing he symbolized the old politics and the past, an advantage throughout much of the district. By stressing his educational background, his community service, and his independence, Jimmy Carter was perceived as representing the future. In the low turnout, Jimmy's votes came heavily from relatives and people who knew him personally.

One of Jimmy's close friends and staunchest supporters was Billy Blair, whose father owned the *Americus Times-Recorder*. Billy was able to use his influence to get a particularly ringing endorsement that read in part:

> Jimmy Carter has shown his courage of conviction and stood for what he
> considered right, sometimes in the face of strong opposition among his own
> people, and still retained their respect and friendship. This is an important
> attribute for a man in public office, since win or lose, he must retain the
> respect and confidence of his colleagues and constituents.

As election day dawned, Jimmy drove to each of the seven county courthouses and key precincts, while Rosalynn continued to make calls encouraging his supporters to go to the polls. As he visited polling places, he felt he was doing well in his home county. Only in Leslie did his opponents clearly outnumber his supporters. In Webster County the situation did not look good either. Next he went to Terrell County, the site of a recent church burning and where the federal government had filed the first suit anywhere in the South against local officials under the 1957 Civil Rights Act. Jimmy had several customers and friends there. In Randolf County he knew few people except members of the Lions Club.

In late morning he checked in with Rosalynn, who told him that a cousin of hers, Ralph Balkcom, had called from Quitman County, the smallest and most distant in the district, to say that some disturbing things were going on at the county courthouse in Georgetown. Jimmy, responding to warnings that the Quitman County vote might be rigged, had asked John Pope to go there as a poll watcher. He too called in to report that gross irregularities were taking place. Jimmy asked the *Columbus Enquirer* to send a reporter to the scene, then jumped in his car and drove the 55 miles to Georgetown. He arrived at the same time as reporter Luke Teasley.

Quitman County had long been the personal fiefdom of Joe Hurst. Originally from Alabama, Hurst had moved over the state line as a young man in the 1920s. He had made a reasonable living running small establishments selling beer and under-the-counter "moonshine" whisky. Despite occasional problems with the law, he was elected in 1935 as county commissioner. Through his skill in parlaying his local political influence with politicians at the state capital in Atlanta, he received patronage jobs with the highway and revenue departments and eventually a position with the commissioner of agriculture. In 1949 he was elected to the state House of Representatives. Subsequently, when a law was passed prohibiting state employees from serving in the legislature, he used his influence to have it written in such a way that he was grandfathered in as an exception. He was a master of pork-barrel politics, bringing highways, bridges, and other benefits to the citizens of little Quitman County, where his largesse gained him near total political control.

Hurst's wife, Mary, was made the local welfare director and Joe arranged that instead of the checks going directly to the recipients, they were all sent to his wife. That way he could deliver them himself and remind the beneficiaries—more than 50 percent of the population—who controlled their livelihood, especially as an election neared. Under the county unit system, Quitman, with 2,400 residents, had political clout equal to a third of the population of Atlanta. Because Joe could deliver his county to any candidate or cause, he was one of the state's most powerful political figures. Joe paid special attention to the elections for sheriff, state superior court judge, and solicitor general (district attorney), thereby hoping to ensure a favorable outcome if his interests were ever at issue.

Many of the legislators who went to Atlanta for the legislative session from January to March each year saw it primarily as an opportunity to have a good time. The Henry Grady Hotel, owned by the state, provided free rooms to the legislators. Gambling and drinking were also big business during the session. A poker game had been run by Gene Talmadge's driver since the 1930s. When Hurst's friend Marvin Griffin became governor in 1955, Joe took over the game and its financial and political benefits. As perhaps the largest bootlegger in Southwest Georgia, Joe also managed to corner the concession on "moonshine" whisky. An official from Stewart County had the prostitution concession. Other gambling was controlled by another official from Stewart County. These three men from a tiny corner of the state brought to bear enormous pressure on the legislature.

Shortly before the election a small amount of iron ore had been found in Quitman County, and the Chattahoochee River had been dammed to create Lake Eufaula. Joe Hurst and his friend Sam Singer developed a plan to build a subdivision on the lake and a boat motel to serve both the highway and river traffic. They needed an amenable state senator to help them get the state to build free roads so they could develop their projects. They hoped that Homer Moore, Singer's former business partner and friend, would look favorably on their plans if he were elected. Regardless of whether Moore would ever have supported the development, Joe Hurst had to know that the entrance of Jimmy Carter into the race with his "clean government" approach and commitment to community service was a threat to the entire corrupt fiefdom that Hurst had taken years to build.

When John Pope entered the courthouse he ran into the county ordinary, Robert Ellis, who informed him that Joe Hurst had, the night before, indicated that he wanted the polling held in the ordinary's office instead of setting up collapsible voting booths in the main courtroom as was customary. "I know something is going on during this election, and I don't want to be any part of it," Ellis said to Pope. "I am here to vote, then I am going fishing." At the courthouse door Pope encountered Joe Hurst, overweight, wearing a white shirt open at the neck, smoking a big cigar, and sporting a gray fedora pulled low over his eyes. He greeted each voter in a cordial manner, and escorted them into the ordinary's office. There the assistant poll taker, "Doc" Hammond, would lay the ballot on the counter, saying, "Just scratch out Jimmy Carter's name. Joe wants you to vote for Homer Moore. Homer has already won this election once, and deserves to win."

A woman named Rosalynn Moore (unrelated to Homer) came in and said, "I intend to vote for Jimmy Carter!" "Doc" became very vocal about Joe wanting Homer to win. John Pope at this point said, "Let her make up her own mind and don't harass her." He added, " 'Doc' cursed me out real good and continued badgering on Mrs. Moore. She then scratched out Jimmy Carter's name."

An elderly couple named Spear took their ballots out into the hall and folded them several times after marking them. Mr. Spear reached his hand into the cardboard ballot box and attempted to hide their ballots by mixing them with those already in there. As they walked away, Joe Hurst reached into the ballot box and easily found their ballots because of the tight way they had been folded. Looking at the slips of paper he said, "You haven't learned anything about voting my way." He then tore up the two ballots and, turning to "Doc" Hammond, said, "Gimme some fresh ballots and let me teach them." "Doc" obediently tore off six ballots and handed them to him. Joe proceeded to scratch out Jimmy Carter's name on each, folded them together, and put them in the ballot box. "That's the way you're supposed to vote," he said. "If I ever catch you voting wrong again, I'm gonna burn your house down."

John Pope confronted Joe Hurst: "Don't you know I am here to try to look out for Jimmy Carter's interests?" he asked. "Don't you know that I will report all that has gone on here in Georgetown?"

"I have been running my county my way for twenty years," Joe said waving his cigar, "and no one from Sumter County, or any other county, is going to come in here and tell me how to run my county. And, Mr. Pope, I want you to know that I have put three men in that river out back for doing less than you are doing here today."

Chastened, Pope walked over to the barber shop where he talked to the barber, some customers, and the Gary brothers, known opponents of Joe Hurst, whose family had once been politically prominent in the county. There was a significant group of local citizens who strongly opposed Hurst, including Rosalynn's cousin Ralph Balkcom, who was the school superintendent and the local Baptist preacher, and Comer Williamson, who was the most vocal leader of the opposition. In later years there would be some resentment that Jimmy Carter received so much credit for overthrowing Joe Hurst. "He didn't clean up Georgetown; the local people did that," Williamson insists.

After Jimmy arrived and was briefed by John Pope and Ralph Balkcom, he walked up to Joe Hurst.

"Where are the voting booths?" he asked.

"This is such a simple election for just one office that we've decided they're not necessary today," Joe replied.

"The law requires that people vote in secret and you're watching every one," Carter persisted.

"People don't mind if we know what they do."

"You are breaking a lot of laws. Who's in charge of this election?" Carter asked.

"Well, 'Doc' here is the poll manager and I'm the chairman of the Democratic committee, so I guess you could say we're in charge," Hurst answered in a relaxed and matter-of-fact manner.

Jimmy and his friends withdrew to discuss the situation. Their one hope seemed to be the newspaper reporter, Luke Teasley, but he was sitting on the courthouse steps drinking a Coca-Cola with Joe Hurst. Obviously they were old friends. As Jimmy started detailing the irregularities, Teasley cut him off: "Mr. Carter, everybody knows it's not right, but this is the way they always run elections over here. I'm sure that the people who are for you will have their votes counted." Jimmy was fuming and demanded that he call the story in to his newspaper. Teasley insisted it was not newsworthy as he got in his car and drove away.

Jimmy briefly toured other polling places in the county and found similar irregularities occurring. Finally, in disgust, he drove back to Plains. John Pope stayed on, and toward the end of the afternoon he noted one of the poll workers busily transcribing names from the voter registration list directly onto the list of those who had voted. There were a hundred absentee ballots in the box, she explained. Pope went outside and asked Joe Hurst how many absentee ballots there were. "Not a damn one. I forgot to mail the damn things out."

Pope remained to witness the counting of the votes. It was done in a meticulous legal fashion. There was a total of 420 votes counted, while the precinct had only 410 registered voters. The ballot stubs suggested only 333 votes had been cast from the book of 500 ballots.

Warren Fortson joined Miss Lillian, Jimmy, Rosalynn, the three boys, and a few other friends at the warehouse as the vote tallies came in. Jimmy had carried Sumter County by a three-to-one margin, but only a third of the electorate had voted. He lost Webster by a substantial margin, and as the votes came in from Terrell, Randolf, Stewart, and Chattahoochee Counties, he saw his lead slowly draining away. He remained upbeat as they waited for Quitman to report. Miss Lillian, well versed over the years in the way of South Georgia politics, was not so optimistic. Sitting on the floor next to Warren Fortson, she squeezed his arm several times and said, "Warren, Jimmy is so naive, he is *so* naive." Finally, John Pope called with the news that Homer Moore had carried Quitman County by 360 votes to 136, putting him narrowly over the top in the district as a whole.

CHAPTER 9

There is no honor in politics.

—Benjamin Disraeli

Jimmy hated to lose, but even more he could not stand to be cheated. He was far from being the first to lose a rigged election in South Georgia, but while others were willing to accept their fate, he was determined to confront what, in his devout sense of right and wrong, he felt was a gross injustice. The next morning, October 17, before breakfast, he and Rosalynn discussed the cost in time and money that would be involved in challenging the election, as well as the potential perception in the community that he was just a sore loser. They decided to proceed with the challenge, more because Jimmy could not live with himself if he did not than that he believed it would overturn the results.

Reading the morning's newspapers, Jimmy realized the state Democratic Party convention was being held that day in Macon, 60 miles away. Jimmy and John Pope set off for the convention, hoping to get a hearing for their grievances. They stopped en route to talk with the editor of the *Americus Times-Recorder*, resulting in a brief story that afternoon under the headline, "Carter Considers Contesting Race." The same day a story in the *Columbus Ledger* was headed "Moore Wins."

John and Jimmy joined a milling crowd of several thousand people at the Macon Civic Center. The primary purpose of the convention was to endorse the candidates who had won the party's nomination in the primary. With only nominal Republican opposition anticipated in the general election, the event took on the character of a coronation. This was especially true for Carl Sanders, the first gubernatorial nominee to win by popular vote. Educated and polished, he symbolized the new post–county unit political era in Georgia. As the "Golden Boy" of Georgia politics, he enjoyed wide support from progressives, blacks, the business community to which he had strong ties, and, because of his many years of service in the state legislature, a surprising degree of acceptance in rural areas. To most thoughtful Georgians, Sanders seemed like the ideal person to lead the state through the dark tunnel of integration, which had become the all-consuming political issue in the state. Even many of the old politicos jumped on his bandwagon to preserve their own careers. Everyone in the convention hall seemed determined to show their unity on Sanders's behalf. No one was interested in a young defeated political outsider who, as Carter says, "was not willing to accept his own defeat with good grace."

Eventually Pope and Carter discovered the results of all the House and Senate races that had been routinely confirmed by the body that morning. As soon as it was clear they could do nothing more, they got in the car to drive back to Plains. "I don't remember any other time I have felt more out of place or when my efforts were more fruitless," Carter would later write.

That evening, Jimmy, Rosalynn, Warren Fortson, and John Pope gathered at the home of Hugh Carter to go over the situation. It was concluded that a two-part strategy was required: Every legal avenue should be pursued, and publicity needed to be generated that would put a spotlight on Joe Hurst and the institutionalized fraud in Quitman County.

In 1960, Warren Fortson, knowledgeable about Georgia election laws, had been part of the one successful election challenge in recent years. Superior Court Judge Tom Marshall, an Annapolis graduate and member of a wealthy Americus family, had been in a dead heat with his opponent, Charles Burgamy, but on the recount it emerged that six of Burgamy's votes were improperly solicited absentee ballots. Fortson had been Tom Marshall's vote counter in the successful recount. While agreeing to advise Jimmy, Fortson recommended that he also engage a more influential lawyer, in part because Fortson's increasing identification with the integration movement would only jeopardize Jimmy's chances. Hugh Carter suggested they call his brother Don, who had become managing editor of the *National Observer* in Washington. Don Carter told them about an investigative reporter named John Pennington. By coincidence, he was from Andersonville in Sumter County, and had, for a while, attended Georgia Southwestern College in Americus. Pennington, a fearless opponent of the Ku Klux Klan, had a reputation as a crusader against corruption and an advocate for social justice. John Pennington was one of a group of the brave young journalists based in Atlanta in the early sixties that included Jack Nelson, Howell Raines, Claude Sitton, and Fred Powledge. All of them were born and raised in the South. They wrote with objectivity, integrity, and deep understanding about the civil rights movement and the changing social and political situations in their native region. That night, Jimmy talked to Pennington, who agreed to come to Americus the next day.

Before Pennington arrived, Jimmy met with Wyngate Dykes, the Sumter County democratic chairman and a brother-in-law of Judge Tom Marshall. He was sympathetic with Jimmy but told him bluntly that the

Georgia law concerning the challenging of elections was very weak and allowed for little more than a recount of the votes. He pointed out two other problems: Homer Moore himself had done nothing wrong and was greatly liked throughout the district, and Joe Hurst had the power and influence to cover up his transgressions and defeat any challenge. Warren Fortson, nevertheless, urged Jimmy to go ahead on principle. They decided that they would file for a recount under Section IX, Article XII of the "Rules and Regulations of the State Democratic Executive Committee of Georgia." Ironically, under this article they would be presenting their evidence of fraud to the very people who had perpetrated it.

But time was running out. The general election was on November 6, and the challenge would have to be successfully concluded by then if Jimmy's name was to appear on the ballot. After feverishly poring over law books, with Jimmy serving as his legal assistant, by the following afternoon Fortson had prepared the requests for recounts to go to the executive committees in each of the seven counties. They put six in the mail, but delivered the one for Quitman County by hand. Over the next four days Warren and Jimmy took depositions, often from people who were reluctant to jeopardize their future relationship with Joe Hurst for what looked like a lost cause. Every time Jimmy went there, he was trailed constantly by two men. He knew that the names of everyone with whom he spoke were taken down and passed on to Joe Hurst.

At other times the process took on an almost comic character. Legal papers had to be exchanged between the two candidates, and Homer Moore was often hard to locate. On one weekend, Jimmy and Rosalynn went looking for Moore and eventually found him sitting in silk pajamas, in front of the television set with a tray of food in his lap. He did not get up but smiled and accepted the papers they had come to serve him with.

On Saturday, October 20, they submitted their petition, demanding of the Quitman County Democratic Executive Committee that the entire Georgetown ballot box be thrown out on the grounds of fraud.

John Pennington, tall, thin, and hawklike, interviewed Jimmy and Warren and went over their records. He made it clear that he wanted to conduct his own investigation to protect his journalistic independence. His reputation had been made by doing meticulous, objective research and extensively documenting his stories. Over the next five days he methodically interviewed dozens of people in Quitman County. On Monday, October 22, the *Atlanta Journal* ran a front-page story under Pennington's byline. In it he detailed how "every election law in the book" had been violated. The article brought the situation to the attention of people statewide and most especially to that of the Democratic Party leadership. It also triggered stories in other newspapers, and on radio and television.

Warren continued to advise Jimmy of the need to get a "big-gun" lawyer into the case and proposed Charles Kirbo of the prestigious Atlanta firm of King and Spalding. On Wednesday, October 24, Fortson called Kirbo, who agreed to see them, and they immediately drove to Atlanta for a meeting that afternoon. Had it not been for the publicity generated by Pennington's article two days earlier, he would probably have declined.

Kirbo, a slow and ponderous man, listened sympathetically but was noncommittal, allowing only that he was impressed by their tenacity in pursuing the case. Reflecting on that first meeting, he would later say:

> I could tell Jimmy was a well-organized fellow and he was absolutely convinced he had been cheated. . . . I was pretty well convinced that even if he had been cheated, it would be hard to prove because of the secret ballot. . . . One of the reasons I didn't want to go down there was because I did not think we could make any money out of it. It takes a lot of time and expenses and I told Jimmy that.

Nevertheless, Kirbo, who had been a classmate of Dan Carter at the University of Georgia, did agree to take the case and introduced them to David Gambrell, a junior partner in the firm, who would assist him and do the background research.

Back in Plains, Jimmy scrambled to help Rosalynn at the warehouse. The seed peanuts had to be carefully sorted according to their strain and the fields from which they had come. To preserve the lineage, careful documentation was essential. As the sole person who knew all the strains and all the fields, only he could prevent any one of a hundred trucks from unloading in the wrong place. "Nevertheless," he says, "the election challenge had become an obsession with me."

On Friday, October 26, Jimmy received a petition signed by 10 percent of the registered voters in Quitman County saying that the voting in the Senate race, as well as in past contests, had been fraudulent. They urged him to pursue his case and help clean up their county. In the afternoon, when the *Atlanta Journal* arrived, it contained an explosive article by John Pennington detailing years of abuse and voter fraud in Quitman County, setting the recent Senate race in a broad context of entrenched corruption, thereby dispelling any argument that Jimmy was merely a sore loser or that the irregularities in his race were minor, one-time errors.

Focusing particularly on the race for U.S. congressman, U.S. senator, governor, and lieutenant governor on September 12, Pennington identified the following among those who were listed as having voted: J. C. Hollingsworth, who was dead; Lloyd Hovey, who was in an Alabama prison; and Georgia Ruth Williams, who lived in California and had never cast an absentee ballot. Most interesting, Pennington pointed out, 117 people "are listed as having lined up and voted in alphabetical order, even down to the second and third letters of their name." He quoted Hurst as saying, "I don't think our poll managers would let a dead person vote. I know they wouldn't." Reflecting his journalistic astuteness by focusing on the September 12 primary, Pennington had not only demonstrated a pattern of practice but had skillfully picked an instance where the votes cast included those for federal offices, thereby demonstrating that federal crimes had been committed. Thus, his article commanded far broader attention by both state and federal law enforcement agencies than an account of Jimmy's election alone would have done.

The official hearing of the voter fraud petition under Article XII by the Quitman County Democratic Executive Committee had been scheduled by Joe Hurst for Monday, October 29. Homer Moore had now included in his legal team, in addition to his regular lawyer, Jesse Bowles, a state representative from Albany, and George Busbee, who was close to Carl Sanders, the individual who would ultimately have to rule on the final decision of the State Democratic Party. It was agreed that Charles Kirbo would remain in Atlanta to focus on the recount scheduled for November 1, and Warren and Jimmy would argue the case before the executive committee in Georgetown. They knew that with Joe Hurst presiding, the deck was hopelessly stacked against them. What they hoped to do, however, was get enough of the facts in the record so that when an adverse decision was appealed to the State Democratic Committee or the state courts, evidence of chicanery would be overwhelming.

The hearing began at 10 A.M. before about fifty local people and several reporters, including John Pennington. A number of those present were Georgetown residents, sufficiently emboldened by the newspaper coverage to testify in open hearing on Jimmy's behalf. Warren spoke first, but after a few minutes, in which he outlined the legal basis for the hearing, Joe Hurst asked Homer Moore's lawyers to respond. They naturally argued that they could see no basis for the challenge and were content to let the committee decide the matter. Hurst then called a recess with no evidence having been presented or affidavits submitted.

In less than five minutes the members of the committee were back. Joe Hurst walked over to Jesse Bowles and quietly said, "We have sustained your motion." With that they began to leave. Warren Fortson was furious, shouting and demanding that the meeting be reconvened.

"We have made a decision," said Joe Hurst. "We sustained the motion of the defendant."

"Are you refusing to hear the contest at all?" Warren replied incredulously.

"Yeah," said Hurst, and walked out of the courthouse. He had outsmarted them; with no evidence in the record, there was no basis on which they could appeal the decision. The local anti-Hurst people gathered around Jimmy, Warren, and Rosalynn to express their dismay at what had happened. Most of them cared less about the election than about the fact that Jimmy had become their champion in their long struggle to end Joe Hurst's autocratic rule. Jimmy felt obliged for their sake not to concede final defeat. Ralph Balkcom remembered his exact words: "You people have no control over things in your own county . . . but if you will help me, I'll fight this to the end. If you're not willing to get involved . . . I'll just pack up and go back to Plains."

The next day, Tuesday, October 30, with Charles Kirbo's help, they filed an appeal with the State Democratic Committee in spite of the sparse hearing record. Pennington's front-page *Atlanta Journal* piece was accompanied by a strong editorial that said in part:

> Certainly there ought to be an opportunity for airing this smelly situation. . . .
>
> It seems a shame that such conditions should leave a stain on this state at a time when it's trying to get some semblance of fairness into its system of voting and representation.

The willingness of the *Atlanta Journal* to give the story front-page placement was in part a reflection of Pennington's reporting, but also of the lingering resentment for the many years during which, under the county unit system, Atlanta had been held captive by the state's rural politicians.

On Thursday, November 1, Jimmy and Rosalynn, together with Kirbo, Fortson, and a number of other supporters, went back to the Georgetown courthouse for the recount of the election ballots. The rules called for it to be supervised by a superior court judge from an adjacent judicial district, in this case Judge Carl Crow of Camilla in Mitchell County. Jimmy's friend Billy Horne was his recount representative and Sam Singer was Homer Moore's.

To Jimmy's surprise Judge Crow wanted a complete picture of the circumstances surrounding the voting rather than merely a recount of the ballots. He allowed Kirbo to present all of the affidavits and call all of the witnesses that they had prepared for the Democratic Executive Committee. The testimony lasted four hours. Throughout this time the ballot box sat ominously on a table in front of Judge Crow and the two vote counters. Finally, he ordered the seal broken and the ballots counted. Before that happened, Billy Horne quickly interjected, "Judge, let's turn the box upside-down." When they did, it was apparent that the bottom flaps were only folded together, not sealed. The judge said nothing, but for several seconds Jimmy said, "My heart was in my throat."

When the box was opened there was nothing inside except the ballots.

The list of voters and ballot stubs that should have been there were gone. Among the loose ballots was a roll wrapped with a rubber band—a hundred votes all for Homer Moore. The recount showed 325 votes for Moore and 106 for Carter, a total of 431, although the total count on election night had been 420.

Judge Crow asked Homer Moore's lawyers if they had any comment on the count and they assured him that despite the obvious discrepancies they were quite satisfied with it. He then turned to Kirbo, who spoke softly in the slowest of southern drawls, with long pauses, catching the rapt attention of everyone in the courtroom as they leaned forward to hear. He combined a folksy rustic style with a deep knowledge of the law and a steel-trap mind. He reviewed the conflicting testimony and seeming breakdown of record keeping that had occurred on polling day. Step by step, he drew the inevitable conclusion that common sense alone demanded that the Georgetown ballot box be thrown out entirely. Then, after a long pause, he drew himself up to his full six-foot-three height, and in a louder, sterner voice began:

> Judge, I'm not talking here in Georgetown about any honest mistakes or even irregularities or illegalities. I'm talking about fraud. There is no way you can explain away the absence of all the stubs and all the voter lists.

Over the next several minutes Kirbo spelled out in detail what each person had done to fraudulently rig the vote in Homer Moore's favor. It was a masterful performance. Judge Crow called an adjournment, saying he would announce his decision the following day from his chambers at the courthouse in Albany.

When the two candidates, a few supporters, and their legal teams assembled that Friday in the courtroom, the tension was palpable. Jimmy sat squeezing Rosalynn's hand. Finally, Judge Crow, Sam Singer, and Billy Horne emerged from the jury room where they had been deliberating with somber faces. Billy, however, managed surreptitiously to give Jimmy a V for victory sign. Judge Crow read a long statement detailing the discrepancies they had found and concluded by saying, "The ballot box, showing to have been stuffed and it being impossible to separate the illegal votes from the legal votes, if any, a majority of the committee [the judge and Billy Horne] finds that the Georgetown precinct vote should not be counted."

This gave Jimmy a 2,811 to 2,746 victory districtwide. That evening there was great celebration at 1 Woodland Drive, where in honor of the judge they drank Old Crow. Jimmy and Warren swore to each other that in the future when they drank bourbon that would be the brand.

The battle, however, was not over. With the general election due in four days, on November 6, they knew Homer Moore would appeal. Kirbo met on Saturday afternoon with the new state party chairman, J. B. Fuqua.

Fuqua was convinced that the party should endorse Jimmy, but Bob Richardson, lawyer for the state party, warned him that he should do nothing without the concurrence of Carl Sanders. After finally tracking him down, Kirbo got Sanders to sign the documents declaring Jimmy Carter the party nominee for the Fourteenth Senatorial District. Within a few hours, Homer Moore's lawyers tried to get Sanders to sign similar documents for their client, only to find that they were too late.

Jimmy had received some help from his friend Brooks Pennington (no relation to John). Brooks Pennington, who lived in Madison, near Augusta, owned a seed company that would become the largest grass seed business in the United States. Jimmy had been a successful dealer for Pennington's company and, at the time he became president of the Georgia Crop Improvement Association, Pennington was elected president of the Georgia Seedmen's Association. Throughout 1962 they had worked closely together with farmers' groups all over Georgia. Pennington, too, had run for the Senate and had easily won his race. As soon as Jimmy had made the decision to challenge the vote, he called Pennington and asked him to intercede with his close friend Carl Sanders. Pennington did so and, although Sanders could not become involved until the issue reached his level, he was ready to help Jimmy when Kirbo arrived.

It was 8 P.M., but Kirbo still had one more obstacle to overcome to get Jimmy's name on the ballot. He flew to Atlanta and rushed to the home of Secretary of State Ben Fortson, who was about to go to bed. After some discussion he signed the necessary certification and sent telegrams to the ordinaries of each of the seven counties in the district to put Jimmy Carter's name on the ballot as the official nominee.

Having arrived at Carl Sanders's door too late, Homer Moore's lawyers filed an appeal of Judge Crow's ruling with the Quitman County Democratic Committee, the very body against which he had ruled. Joe Hurst issued an order that the judge's ruling be held in abeyance until a full hearing could be held on Monday. On Sunday, Kirbo and Warren Fortson filed for an injunction against the committee's decision. The superior court judge under whose jurisdiction their action fell was Tom Marshall, whose own disputed election had been won with the help of Kirbo and Fortson. Homer Moore, however, had also been instrumental in that victory, and one of his lawyers, Jesse Bowles, had been a law-school classmate and fraternity brother of the judge.

In time for the Sunday edition of the *Columbus Ledger*, Homer Moore had announced that if his name was not on the ballot he would run as a write-in candidate. Meanwhile, during the day the entire Carter family and a handful of friends went to every courthouse in the district with rubber stamps to help the ordinaries put Jimmy's name on the thousands of

ballots. As there was no Republican opposition, every stamped ballot, apart
from Moore's write-in campaign, was tantamount to a vote for Jimmy.

On Monday morning Judge Marshall held a hearing at the courthouse in
Leesburg. Jimmy and his family were still at work putting his name on the
ballots, so Kirbo went alone. The hearing went on for hours interrupted by
the judge's need to handle other cases. Finally, Judge Marshall ordered the
ordinaries of the seven counties to appear at six o'clock at the Sumter
County courthouse. With only thirteen hours to go before the polls
opened, several declined to come. Marshall ordered the sheriffs to bring
them to Americus. Increasingly convinced that Marshall intended to rule
against them, Kirbo sought to stall, in order to make it impossible to change
the ballots before the polls opened at 7 A.M. As the proceedings dragged on
toward midnight, the judge finally terminated the discussion and ruled that
both names should be removed from the ballot, creating a write-in election. All the ordinaries argued that it would be next to impossible to carry
out the judge's order. Robert Ellis, the Quitman County ordinary, was particularly forthright, saying that he was determined to right the past wrongs
in his county by seeing that the vote was fair—meaning that he thought
Jimmy's name should stay on the ballot.

Overnight both sides put together conflicting radio announcements to
run as people were going to the polls, explaining the complex turn of
events and advising them on the write-in procedure. Jimmy's name had
been struck from the ballots in all the counties except Sumter and Quitman. The votes were slow coming in that night from Sumter County, and
for a while Homer Moore was ahead. The final tally, however, gave Jimmy
a winning vote of 3,013 to 2,182. In Quitman County, where the voters
were now free from the corrupt hand of Joe Hurst and his friends, he beat
Moore by 448 to 23. In the Plains precinct Jimmy got 201 votes, but 28
people voted against him.

Physically exhausted, Jimmy spent most of the next twenty-four hours in
bed. He had lost 11 pounds in two weeks. At 9 P.M. the following evening,
he received a friendly and cordial call from Homer Moore. However, a
week after the election, on Tuesday, November 13, Moore's lawyers filed a
motion on the failure of the two ordinaries, in Sumter and Quitman Counties, to remove Jimmy's name from the ballots. A hearing on the violation of
his order was set by Judge Marshall for November 30. That morning,
Homer Moore called Warren Fortson to tell him that they had decided not
to go through with the hearing. Jimmy and Rosalynn relaxed, thinking the
ordeal was finally over. However, Homer Moore and his team had merely
decided to adopt a different strategy.

Jimmy had never met Carl Sanders or the lieutenant governor–elect,
Peter Zack Geer, who would be the presiding officer at the upcoming ses-

sion of the state senate. On the other hand, Homer Moore's lawyer, Jesse Bowles, had been a law-school classmate and fraternity brother of Carl Sanders, as he was of Judge Marshall. Bowles was a neighbor and intimate friend of Peter Zack Geer, who also owed his election in substantial part to Joe Hurst. His other lawyer, George Busbee, was a well-regarded legislator who was close to both the incoming governor and lieutenant governor. Their strategy was to convince Geer not to seat Jimmy and put the choice between him and Moore to a vote by the Senate. Jimmy knew next to no one in the Senate; Homer Moore and his lawyers knew them all.

Jimmy was proceeding on the assumption that he would be going to the Senate in January. Late in November he went to Atlanta to discuss his committee assignments with the new lieutenant governor, Peter Zack Geer, a bright young lawyer from a politically powerful family. Because of reapportionment, the Senate was made up almost entirely of new members; there was little seniority and Geer was in a position to create the Senate the way he wanted. Because of the problems with Jimmy's election, most of the other senators already had their committee appointments, including Brooks Pennington, who had been made chairman of the Agriculture Committee, and another of Jimmy's acquaintances, Ford Spinks from Tifton, who was the vice chairman. Pennington had already asked Geer to make Jimmy the secretary of the committee, which he did. In his meeting with Geer, Jimmy expressed a strong interest in the Education Committee.

Geer, slightly embarrassed by the slim pickings left on the more powerful committees, was surprised. "I haven't had many requests like this, and there's no problem putting you on the Education Committee." Jimmy asked if a subcommittee on higher education could be created, and after calling the committee chairman, Geer agreed. Before leaving, Jimmy asked him about a disputed Senate race in Savannah. Geer responded that he did not know what the outcome would be, but it would be decided by the Senate itself, not the courts. He added that it was probably not the only contested seat the Senate would have to decide. Jimmy had a sudden sinking feeling and realized his election was not as secure as he thought.

During December, Homer Moore was quoted in the *Stewart-Webster Journal* as saying that he might consider challenging the election in the Senate when it convened. Jimmy and Charles Kirbo agreed that the best strategy was to lie low and that any lobbying effort would probably backfire. Unknown to the two of them, Brooks Pennington was again talking with his friend Carl Sanders, urging him to use his influence to prevent the contest from resurfacing in the Senate. Apart from the merits of the case, the politics of Joe Hurst and Quitman County—that had been so thoroughly and embarrassingly aired in the state's media—was something they wanted to put behind them. Jimmy Carter, young successful businessman, progressive, well educated, and against corruption, had an image that was far more consistent with the "new era" in Georgia politics that Sanders wanted to symbolize.

Jimmy and Rosalynn drove to Atlanta for the opening of the 1963 General Assembly still not knowing whether he would be seated. The prospect of a protracted fight on the floor of the Senate was daunting. The night before the legislature opened, they went to the traditional barbecue party at the Henry Grady Hotel, a backslapping environment in which the whisky flowed freely—a gathering of old friends. Jimmy and Rosalynn knew few of them, and his uncertain status added to their sense of timidity. However, Jimmy strode forth with seeming self-confidence, pushing their way through the crowd toward Peter Zack Geer's suite, where he intended to introduce Rosalynn to the new lieutenant governor. As they came down the hallway, they walked into Homer Moore, Sam Singer, and Jesse Bowles coming out of Geer's suite. All three men were grinning broadly, adding to Jimmy and Rosalynn's anxiety. They soon left the party and went to bed.

The next morning, Peter Zack Geer gaveled the Senate into session and announced that he would have the members come forward ten at a time to be sworn in. He asked the senators-elect from districts one through ten to come forward, excepting the Third District (Savannah), where he said, "I have been informed that there is a contest pending." The first group stood in the well of the chamber and took the oath of office. Jimmy looked up at Rosalynn sitting on the edge of her seat in the balcony. Her eyes were closed. "Will the senators-elect from Districts Eleven through Twenty come forward." Jimmy waited for the dreaded words, "except for the Fourteenth District." They did not come and he walked forward and raised his right hand. He was finally an undisputed member of the Georgia Senate.

Jimmy Carter's victory was a tribute to his unflagging determination not to give up. He would later note: "If . . . I have one political attribute as the cause of my success, it would be tenacity. Once I get onto something I am awfully hard to change. That may also be a cause of some of my political failures."

However, it could never have happened without the federal courts and the abolition of the county unit system. Jimmy would not have entered the Senate in 1963 if those who assumed control of the state party in that year's elections, especially Carl Sanders, had not wanted him there. It almost certainly would not have happened without John Pennington's superb reportage. It would not have happened without his friends' support and the exceptional legal and political counsel he received from Warren Fortson and Charles Kirbo. His decision to enter the race in the first place reflected a certain naivete. But it was naivete born of the deeply held faith that goodwill always triumphs over evil and, as long as you keep up the fight, right will ultimately win over wrong.

Rosalynn, who also deserved enormous credit for the victory, was not merely a supportive and loyal wife; she too had a driving need to win, and had since childhood. More recently she had felt the only way she could live in Plains was if she and Jimmy were really successful, although initially she had seen this only in financial terms. She had found the racially motivated defeat of the school consolidation plan both painful and humiliating, and winning the Senate seat a way of dealing with the resentment she felt. At the same time the exposure to the seamier side of politics distressed her greatly. She would later write:

> I was totally disillusioned with the whole political process. I had been naive enough to think that politics was straight, and that sheriffs were straight, and that judges were straight, and that county officials and political figures really had the best interests of the people at heart. What I witnessed at first hand contradicted all that I believed in. Jimmy had won and I was pleased about that, and I never thought about giving up or getting out or living an easy life away from all the ugliness. But I hated the dirty politics we had been exposed to. And it was not over yet.

One day, shortly after Rosalynn returned from the opening session of the legislature, a complete stranger had come to the warehouse to sell a load of high-grade peanuts. After completing their business, he said he had a message for her. Someone, he said, wanted her to know that the last time anyone crossed Joe Hurst their stores burned down. He refused to say who sent the message and drove away. Rosalynn knew that two legal liquor stores that competed with Joe Hurst's moonshine business had both been burned down on the same night, so she knew the message was serious. Fear of the threat from Joe Hurst's people coalesced with general apprehension generated by resentment toward the family over the race issue, and she was afraid the whole time Jimmy was away. She made the boys stay with her at the warehouse after school because she did not want them in the house alone. She left lights on and barricaded doors with chairs. As Hugh Carter would later note, there had long been an unusual number of unexplained fires in Plains.

As they would ultimately discover, willingness to subvert the American democratic process was not restricted to Southwest Georgia. At a national level only the degree of sophistication of the intrigue was different.

CHAPTER 10

Every white southerner must choose between two psychic roads, the road of racism or the road of brotherhood.

—HOWELL RAINES

Relieved merely to be there, Jimmy did not make a big splash during the 1963 legislative session. He spent most of his time learning the ropes and building relationships. He worked slavishly during the forty-five-day session to learn how the state government worked and about the issues before his committees. He has observed,

> I made what later sometimes seemed an unfortunate pledge—to read every bill before I voted on it.
>
> Although the promise was made originally only to myself, I told several people about it and for four years I read them all.

He took a speed-reading course, the first of several in which he and Rosalynn would enroll over the years. It helped him plow through the 800–1,000 bills that came before the Senate during each session, and to become adroit at detecting technical errors and mistakes in the proposed legislation. He moved into the staid Piedmont Hotel, arose early for breakfast at a nearby cafe, and walked to the Capitol. To ensure that he was thoroughly familiar with the scheduled business for the day, he would arrive well before other members of the Senate.

There was a strong competitive element underlying Jimmy's diligence. He wanted to be the best member of the Senate. The quality of his fellow senators was unquestionably superior to their predecessors, yet most had business interests and other concerns that consumed much of their attention, even during the few brief weeks of the session. Rosalynn ran the warehouse with competence and pleasure as a full political partner, allowing him to devote himself entirely to state government business. The only time she called him for help was when one of their old brick warehouses collapsed, dumping several tons of peanuts into the street.

Carter's navy experience had taught him that doing his best, and being the best, was the most effective way in the long run to catch the eye of his superiors. He was uncomfortable with the backslapping of traditional insider politics and had a strong antipathy to brokering deals in the back rooms of the Capitol. However, he needed to impress Carl Sanders and other party leaders. It was they who held the power to advance his political career both in the Democratic Party and in the Senate. Carl Sanders, progressive, capable, and nationally ambitious, laid out a comprehensive program for his administration in a speech on January 16, including a revision of the state constitution, reorganization of state government, and increased funding for education, mental health, and the prisons. He also called for a bill to reform the highway department, which was notorious for its corrupt patronage. Jimmy could be counted on, along with most other members of the Senate, to vote for the governor's bills. Jimmy did cosponsor a bill with his friend Brooks Pennington to "regulate the registration, labeling, analysis and sale, and application of agricultural limestone."

Carter did differ from the majority of his colleagues in his aversion to "sweetheart" bills submitted on behalf of various special-interest groups. Private bills came up on Fridays, and Jimmy would often delay his return to Plains for the weekend so that he could oppose or modify them. To the extent that he had a political ideology, it was a perception of himself as David against Goliath. He was offended by the doctors who lobbied the Senate not to improve the health of Georgians but to protect their own financial interests, and teachers who had less concern for the standard of education than their own welfare. Unlike many of his fellow senators, and Carl Sanders, he generally had an aversion to bankers, paving contractors, insurance executives, and other wealthy businesspeople. Despite being a successful businessman himself, he felt his responsibility was to protect the interests of the rural poor, with whom he strongly identified, against the seizure or abuse of their government by these organized powerful groups. While a foe of most special-interest lobbyists, he was, in keeping with his populist bent, receptive to almost every public-interest organization.

The summer of 1963 was a time of growing racial turmoil across South Georgia. Despite the presence of the Student Non-Violent Coordinating Committee (SNCC) in Albany since December 1961, and regular demonstrations there, Americus, only 60 miles away, had remained largely untouched, even when Martin Luther King, Jr., was briefly held in the city jail. However, early in 1963, several organizers arrived in Sumter County. They were welcomed both at Koinonia by Clarence Jordan and by members of the black community, previously too intimidated to initiate any protests on their own. In April, a white student, Ralph Allen, on leave from Trinity College in Hartford, Connecticut, was beaten on the street in Americus when he accompanied a black woman to the courthouse to register to vote. Early in August, eleven young blacks tried to purchase tickets at the "white" ticket window at the Martin Theater on Forsyth Street. It was the first act of public defiance by blacks in the city's history. The police arrived and ordered the group to disperse. When they failed to do so, they were arrested and charged with blocking the sidewalk. Two days later a group of pickets marched in front of the theater while a menacing group of whites gathered across the street. On August 8, 250 blacks, organized by the SNCC workers, gathered at the black Friendship Baptist Church and marched to protest segregation in public facilities. Almost immediately the police waded into the parade, beating the marchers with billy clubs, and firing pistols into the air. They particularly targeted and repeatedly hit three SNCC workers, Ralph Allen, John Perdew, a white Harvard student, and Donald Harris, a black graduate of the Fieldston School and Rutgers University.

The next night, 175 demonstrators marched from the Allen Chapel and were again attacked by the police with guns, clubs, and electric cattle prods. Among the forty-seven blacks arrested were twenty young girls, aged nine to thirteen, who were sent to the prison at Leesburg in nearby Lee County. They were kept for a month in a cell 10 feet by 30 feet with no beds or mattresses and two broken and clogged commodes. Robertina Freeman, thirteen years old, and the daughter of an activist local minister, described the ordeal: "The guards took away our remaining beds because we were singing and praying. So then we started sleeping on the floor with no mattresses, no beds, no blankets, no sheets, no nothing. The floor was wet with waste material."

The following day, Police Chief Ross Chambliss deputized sixteen local men and armed them with night sticks. The city council, concerned with the town's image, requested all news media "not to print or broadcast news of racial disturbances without the council's prior approval." Demonstrations continued throughout August, and on the seventeenth, a white student organizer from Minnesota was arrested for encouraging blacks "to march without a permit." Subsequently, Solicitor General Stephen Pace, Jr., son of the former congressman, announced that the students and the three previously arrested SNCC workers were being charged with attempting to incite an insurrection—a capital crime in Georgia under an old law aimed at preventing slave uprisings. It was also a way to deny the defendants bond.

Suddenly Americus was the focus of nationwide attention. Two U.S. senators demanded that the Justice Department and the Senate's constitutional rights subcommittee investigate the situation in Americus. In Hartford, Connecticut, students from Trinity College marched on the state capital in support of Ralph Allen. Morris Abrams, the successful advocate

of *Sanders v. Gray,* the case that overthrew the county unit system, agreed
to represent the four defendants.

In seven weeks the situation in Americus and Sumter County had
become bitterly polarized. More than 250 blacks had been arrested. Several of the more conservative civic leaders made inflammatory statements.
"I hope they will get any outsiders for anything they can get them for until
they find out they're not wanted here," Tommy Hooks, former president of
the chamber of commerce, was quoted as saying. Banker Charles F. Crisp,
also the son of a former congressman, warned that the ultimate aim of the
black civil rights campaign was to create "an amalgamation of the people
like they have in Cuba."

In later years outsiders would question why there was no record of public comments by Jimmy Carter on these events during the summer of 1963.
In fact, feelings were so inflamed, and the pressure on all politicians to make
ill-conceived, pro-segregation comments so strong, that his very silence
was in itself a measure of courage. Not a single white minister spoke out, for
to do so, one of them said, would have made their positions "untenable." When
queried about the need to establish lines of communication between the white
and black community, one business leader responded, "If I tried to start a biracial committee here, they'd run me out of town."

The civil rights movement in its values and strategies was deeply rooted
in the Christian ethos. Many of the top positions were held by ordained
clergy. Even in SNCC, the most community-based of the civil rights organizations, the majority of the student workers, black and white, were from
deeply religious backgrounds, believing that the real test of Christianity
was in its practice.

Consistent with the historic Baptist commitment to human rights, the
Georgia Constitution had originally banned slavery in the state. However,
the immense wealth to be made from the cultivation of cotton by slaves led
to the repeal of that clause. Baptist preachers, many of them slave owners
themselves, reinterpreted the theology of the faith to legitimize slave own-
ing.* The implied message of the young civil rights workers to the white,
predominantly Baptist community, was that their racial attitudes were at
odds with true Christian values. Even well-meaning whites believed that
the docile acceptance of the local black community in the past came not
from generations of intimidation but from contentment with the status quo.
Outside agitation was perceived as the root of the problem.

---

*The Baptists lost the moral high ground and role as the primary and undisputed force
for individual and human rights in America when they abandoned their historic opposition
to slavery. Baptist leader John Leland, friend of Jefferson and Madison, said of slavery that
use should be made "of every legal measure to extirpate this horrid evil from our land."

There were a few brave individuals in Americus who were determined to find a middle ground, among them Warren Fortson, Dr. Bud Robinson, Jean Wise, B. T. Wishard, Joel Thomas, Russell and Maryanne Thomas, and Clay Mundy, the superintendent of the Americus schools. Fortson says, "Jimmy was not part of the group, but would have been had he not been sitting out there in Plains. That would have been his mentality." All felt that compliance with the law and a low-key effort to begin integrating public facilities would defuse the tension. Few shared the views of Warren Fortson, who "thought segregation was just plain wrong," but the more educated people knew further confrontation would lead nowhere.

In the eyes of most white citizens in Americus and across the South, the ultimate villain in the civil rights struggle was President John F. Kennedy. It was ironic because Kennedy initially proposed no civil rights legislation out of deference to southerners in the Congress. He even failed to make good on a campaign promise to end segregation in new federal housing, which he could have done by signing an executive order. His first judicial appointment was of William Harold Cox, a hardcore racist Mississippian, who insulted black attorneys who appeared before him. He referred to black plaintiffs in open court as "baboons" or "a bunch of niggers." Historian Harvard Sitkoff has written of President Kennedy in his book *The Struggle for Black Equality, 1954–1980:*

> Only in the battle against Communism did he think the United States should "pay any price, bear any burden, meet any hardship, support any friend, oppose any foe." Never in the struggle for black rights would he ask the American people for a commitment or a sacrifice approaching that.

Of the Kennedy administration as a whole, prior to the Freedom Rides of 1961, Sitkoff says:

> They could no longer tolerate either the deliberate failure of local authorities to preserve civil peace or the open defiance of federal law. Yet they still sought to walk a tightrope between, as the Kennedys viewed them, the unreasonable militants on both sides. . . . Racial prejudice and the inequities it fostered bothered them. They hoped to better the life of Afro-Americans— but slowly, and at the proper time. They thought demands for freedom *now* to be just as irresponsible as calls for segregation forever.

The "Freedom Rides" in May 1961, the arrival of James Meredith on the campus of the University of Mississippi in September of that year, a series of federal court rulings, and the direct action of the civil rights movement increasingly forced Kennedy, however reluctantly, to engage the full power of the federal government to ensure the federal laws he had sworn to uphold were enforced. In so doing, he became identified, in the eyes of southerners, as the instigator of the most massive intrusion by the federal government into the affairs of the South since Reconstruction. When Kennedy sent 250 U.S. marshals and subsequently 2,500 federal troops to escort Meredith onto the Old Miss campus, and to maintain order after the ensuing riots, it aroused bitter historic memories across the region.

By mid-1963, the pressures on Kennedy from both sides were intense. He desperately needed the support of the southern bloc in Congress for the passage of his legislative program as well as their backing in his delicate maneuvering with Nikita Khrushchev over disarmament, his primary concern. Also, during the first week of June, there had been 160 separate civil rights incidents. His brother Robert and Senate Majority Leader Mike Mansfield insisted that he must propose civil rights legislation or risk losing control of the situation entirely.

Matters came to a head on June 11, the day the courts had set for the admission of two black students, Vivian Malone and James Hood, to the University of Alabama. Governor George Wallace, surrounded by a hundred members of the Alabama state police, "stood in the school house door" vowing to deny the students admission. After a symbolic noon-hour confrontation between Wallace and the federal authorities, led by Deputy Attorney General Nicholas Katzenbach, the students were admitted. It had been high drama on television screens across the country, and in the aura of turmoil and uncertainty left in its wake, Kennedy overcame his earlier reluctance and accepted the advice of his aides to make a major televised address to the nation at 8 P.M. that evening.

The speech—part text, part ad-libbed—lasted only eighteen minutes, but would prove to be of profound historic significance. He began, "This afternoon, following a series of threats and defiant statements . . . two clearly qualified young Alabama residents who happened to have been born Negro . . ." He went on to describe the events of that morning, continuing, "I hope every American, regardless of where he lives, will stop and examine his conscience about this and other related incidents." Then from a memo prepared by his one black aide, Louis Martin, "The Negro baby born in America today . . . has about one half as much chance of completing high school as a white baby born in the same place on the same day, one third as much chance of completing college, one third as much chance of becoming a professional man, twice as much chance of being unemployed . . . a life expectancy which is seven years shorter, and the prospect of earning only half as much."

Coming to the crux of the matter, he said,

> This is not a sectional issue. . . . Nor is this a partisan issue. . . . We are confronted primarily with a *moral issue*. It is as old as the scriptures and is as clear as the American Constitution.

If an American, because his skin is dark, cannot eat lunch in a restaurant open to the public, if he cannot send his children to the best public schools available, if he cannot vote for the public officials who represent him . . . then who among us would be content to have the color of his skin changed? Who among us would be content with the counsels of patience and delay?

We face, therefore, a moral crisis as a country and as a people. It cannot be met with repressive police action. It cannot be left to increased demonstrations in the streets. . . . It is time to act in Congress, in your state and local legislative bodies, and above all in our daily lives. A great change is at hand, and our task, our obligation, is to make that revolution, that change, peaceful, and constructive for all.

Kennedy's speech hit the South like a bombshell. He had put aside the politics of expediency and the need to mollify the southern racist oligarchies that had so long constrained earlier presidents from speaking unequivocally on the race issue. For the first time since Abraham Lincoln, an American president had forcefully couched the issue of the racial divide in absolute moral terms. As his earlier willingness to placate the southerners in Congress suggested, he was fully aware of the price he would pay, especially in his legislative program, for rising above politics to give the nation moral leadership. His instincts had led him to one of the most consequential acts of modern American history.

For conservative white southerners the speech made Kennedy the devil incarnate. For moderates and pragmatists the speech was a clear indication that there was no going back. For the frontline activists, white and black, the speech assuaged many of the doubts they had about the sincerity of Kennedy's interest in civil rights. Kennedy reaffirmed their belief in the moral righteousness of their cause and the conviction that history was on their side. Kennedy had intended that his speech would dampen the number and intensity of their protests and demonstrations. It had the reverse effect.

The Carters were fervent Kennedy supporters, none more so than Miss Lillian. Among those who remained loyal to Kennedy in Sumter County, there were those who saw in Jimmy a local version of the president. Youth and vigor, a navy background, a charming smile, a strength of personality that drew people to him, a certain presence, even a degree of physical similarity, and a pragmatic determination to move the community forward—all were attributes they seemed to have in common. Several of Jimmy's staunchest supporters would attribute their attraction to him to his being Kennedyesque.

Shortly after 12:30 P.M. on Friday, November 22, 1963, Jimmy called Rosalynn at the Plains beauty shop to tell her there were radio reports that President Kennedy had been shot. With her hair still half up in curlers, she ran back to the office to be with him as they listened to the reports from Dallas coming in. "We felt such sorrow for the president, whom we had admired and loved, and for his family," Rosalynn recalls. Chip, who had been the Kennedy youth coordinator in Sumter County, was in class at Plains High School. When the news of Kennedy's assassination was brought to the classroom, the teacher exclaimed, "That's good!" and the students broke into applause. Chip, more volatile than the rest of the family, but reflecting the view of Kennedy he had learned at home, picked up his desk and threw it at the teacher. He was suspended for three days, but says it was the only time he got in trouble at school when his father was not upset with him. Over the next few days while the nation as a whole was in mourning, and as millions attended memorial services across the United States and around the world, not a single service or event acknowledging the president's death was held in Americus. Many southerners believed that Lyndon Johnson would surely not pursue the cause of civil rights.

In January, Jimmy returned to Atlanta for the 1964 session of the legislature. His diligence and industriousness had been noted. He was appointed by Carl Sanders as one of two legislators on a special commission to look at education in Georgia. A fellow appointee was Dr. Horace Tate, then the executive director of the black teachers' association of Georgia. Carter and Tate, who would later himself become a state senator, established a warm friendship and political alliance. Jimmy was also appointed to the State Democratic Executive Committee. Because of his willingness to take on arduous, often thankless tasks, the committee appointed him to be part of a group to rewrite the Democratic Party rules. These assignments led to his meeting two people by whom he would be significantly influenced.

The first was Marvin Shoob, a sophisticated, progressive Jewish lawyer, originally from Savannah. Shoob had been a law-school classmate of Carl Sanders and they had remained close. He had also held several of the top positions in the Fulton County (Atlanta) Democratic Party structure. He and Carter were asked to draft the document covering the new rules, a task that took nearly a year. After the legislative session finished, Jimmy would come to Atlanta to work with Shoob. Rosalynn frequently accompanied him and they would have dinner with Shoob and his wife, Janice.

For all of their travel in the military, Jimmy and Rosalynn had made no significant friendships apart from his navy colleagues. They had remained insulated and in many respects they were still thoroughly unsophisticated. Their friendship with, among others, the Shoobs started them on a road to a new worldliness. It was a process that would escalate with dizzying speed.

The second important relationship Jimmy established was with William Gunter from Gainesville, north of Atlanta. Gunter was also a lawyer, a progressive, and active in party politics, having served in the Georgia House of Representatives in the 1950s. He too was close to Carl Sanders and had been his campaign chairman in the Ninth Congressional District.

Over the next year, the Carters, the Shoobs, and Bill and Betty Gail Gunter would regularly dine together. The dinner talk was predominantly political. All three men were financially successful, but had a strong interest in public service. With a new progressive governor, the overthrow of the county unit system, and the racial turmoil, now was the time, they all believed, to radically remake the politics of the state. They were, each in his own way, idealistic populists believing that the primary responsibility of the state was to achieve social justice, with a special obligation to help the poorest residents, black and white. Yet they believed equally in the need for fiscal restraint, balanced budgets, efficiency in government, and an end to the longstanding corrupt practices and patronage system embedded in state government.

Bill Gunter, seven years older than Jimmy, had been a friend of his cousin Don at the University of Georgia. Don Carter says of him, "I recall him as being a very dedicated and caring individual. . . . I would think of him as, what I would call, a really Christian gentleman. He tried to live his religion." Gunter, a Presbyterian, was throughout his life concerned about how to translate Christian faith into political action. For Carter this was, and would remain, a recurrent agonizing quandary. In Gunter he found someone with wisdom, sophistication, and political experience who had the same concerns. Gunter became a trusted confidant and advisor. Carter, who considered Gunter "brilliant and very liberal," says, "He saw I needed some education—that I was very parochial in my attitudes."

Those who had assumed that Lyndon Johnson would abandon Kennedy's pursuit of civil rights were in for a rude awakening. A man who understood poverty and discrimination, he pressed the legislation with a fervor and sincerity that Kennedy lacked. However, when he signed the Civil Rights Act of 1964, he sadly and accurately acknowledged that he was probably spelling the end of the Democratic Party's political domination in the South. Across the region alienated white Democrats switched their support to the Republican presidential candidate, Arizona Senator Barry Goldwater. Goldwater, a vocal opponent of the civil rights legislation, knew how to use terms like "state's rights" and other code words to let disillusioned segregationists know that he was sympathetic. Overnight the Republican Party replaced the conservative wing of the Democratic Party as the new home for white racism. One of Goldwater's early supporters was Ronald Reagan. His dedicated embrace of Goldwater led ultimately to his being named cochairman of his California campaign.

In Georgia, Goldwater was endorsed by diehard segregationists from former Governor Marvin Griffin to Calvin S. Craig, grand dragon of the Georgia Ku Klux Klan. In Americus, a Sumter County for Goldwater Club was formed, headed by Charles R. Crisp, Tommy Hooks III, and other reactionaries. Among those who went, representing Sumter County to the Third District and state Republican conventions, was Jimmy's friend John Pope. Jimmy's nemesis and Pope's friend, Howard H. "Bo" Callaway, was announced as the Republican candidate for the Third Congressional District seat vacant because of the death of "Tick" Forrester. Callaway pledged "to seek immediate and complete repeal of the Civil rights Bill [sic]." According to Rosalynn, Callaway's shift to the Republicans was "sheer racism."

Even those who remained as Democrats sought to separate themselves from the national ticket. Former Lieutenant Governor Garland Byrd would ultimately get the Third District Democratic nomination for congress. It was, however, hotly contested by Ed Wohlwender, a Sumter County farmer and Columbus lawyer who warned of the "black menace, led by goatee-wearing pinkos and punks," and Stephen Pace, Jr., who announced that he might vote for Goldwater, even though he had taken an oath when qualifying for the congressional seat that he would support all the Democratic nominees.

Warren Fortson became the chairman of the Sumter County Johnson for President Campaign. They opened a small office in Americus, but could find no one willing to run it. Finally, Miss Lillian stepped in, and she and Gloria essentially became the campaign. Miss Lillian was the butt of local hostility and petty aggression. Chip bravely wore a Johnson button to school and placed an "I'm a Democrat" sticker on his notebook. He came home on more than one occasion bruised after being roughed up by his classmates. Johnson himself did not campaign in the South. He left it to his wife Lady Bird, and other surrogates.

Jimmy nominated his Georgia Southwestern classmate and Senate seatmate, Garland Byrd, at the Third District Democratic Convention, then campaigned hard for him. Byrd, however, agonized over whether to endorse Lyndon Johnson for fear that it would cost him votes. Indecisiveness hurt him even more and Callaway became the first Republican congressman from Georgia since 1874. While winning nationally in a landslide Johnson lost Georgia and the rest of Dixie to Goldwater. Unopposed for reelection to his Senate seat, Jimmy, while campaigning for Garland Byrd, attacked Callaway for using his position as a state regent to block the four-year accreditation of Georgia Southwestern. It was a way of finessing the race issue, and also of testing his own muscle against Callaway for a secretly contemplated race against him two years hence.

Jimmy's life was becoming increasingly schizophrenic. When he was in Atlanta he was involved with like-thinking people who were liberal and had a broad worldview. Their concerns were with charting a progressive course for the state. Atlanta leaders had moved aggressively to put segregation behind them. The schools were integrated, downtown restaurants were beginning to serve blacks, and the city hospital, Grady, was integrating its wards. Black or white "only" cabs were disappearing from the streets. Civic leaders were promoting Atlanta as the "City Too Busy to Hate." Even his fellow senators from the rural areas, when away from their own constituencies, were courting the friendship of their one black colleague, Leroy Johnson. As politicians, they were realistic enough to know that as blacks were increasingly enfranchised, he could be very helpful in gaining those votes for them in their districts.

Jimmy faced a different world when he was back in Sumter County. There, the local leadership, shortsighted and parochial, remained implacably opposed to integration and was far from ready to concede defeat. Since childhood, Carter had learned to accommodate psychologically opposing views on race. But never before had he been forced to face the conflict as so stark a public choice. He had no doubt about the tide of history and clearly foresaw Southwest Georgia eventually following Atlanta. However, to publicly endorse integration was political suicide. He sought, instead, a strategy that would deflect attention away from direct confrontation and buy time, in the belief that reconciling the conflict was ultimately possible. He understood well that overcoming economic backwardness was as important as federal civil rights legislation in ending the feudal system that slavery had bequeathed to Southwest Georgia. He also never allowed race to become an emotional issue or condemned those whose views differed from his own. As a result, while still inevitably despised by some, he maintained the goodwill of many segregationists who shared his views on other matters. He honed skills in conflict resolution that would stand him in good stead later in life.

Jimmy began to focus his attention on local economic development, the improvement of community institutions and public services. In January 1964, he chaired a meeting in Americus establishing the West Central Georgia Area Planning and Development Commission (WCGAPDC), and subsequently became its permanent chairman. Over the next several years the commission received grants from the state and federal government and launched the local Head Start and Neighborhood Youth Corps programs. Plans were developed to make the Andersonville prison and cemetery a tourist attraction and Lake Blackshear a recreational area. They arranged to restore an antebellum mansion and a Creek Indian village. Under the auspices of the commission, Jimmy also appointed a committee to study the development of the Flint River valley. With a group of friends, Jimmy sought, unsuccessfully, to obtain a charter for a national bank in Americus to provide banking services for the more progressive element in the county.

In the summer of 1964, the Georgia legislature was called into special session to consider the proposed Fair Elections Act and the revision of the state constitution. Jimmy used the opportunity to make what was his maiden substantive speech in the Senate. He spoke out against the notorious "thirty questions" asked only of blacks who tried to register to vote, some of which required the skill of a constitutional scholar. Some were designed merely to mock the applicant such as, "How long is a piece of string?" or "How many bubbles are in a bar of soap?" The speech was a way of venting some strongly held feelings, but reflecting the nature of the two worlds in which he lived, he says, "I spoke in that chamber, fearful of the news media reporting it back home, but overwhelmed with the commitment to the abolition of that artificial barrier to the rights of an American citizen." He hardly needed to worry. His lack of oratorical style did little to hold an audience and in Atlanta such a viewpoint was hardly news. The speech was not reported in the Atlanta newspapers or in the *Americus Times-Recorder.* It was not even recorded in the *Senate Journal,* which was done only at the speaker's request, an omission that may have been deliberate.

The House had prepared a revised version of the constitution that contained in the Bill of Rights the statement, "Every man has the natural and inalienable right to worship God according to the dictates of his own conscience." As a stickler for precision, he objected to the wording, arguing that it might be interpreted as a requirement that "God be worshipped." He suggested, as a substitution, the wording from the First Amendment to the U.S. Constitution, "No law shall be passed respecting an establishment of religion or prohibiting the free exercise thereof." His amendment was initially approved by the Senate, but twenty senators opposed it. In conference the House version prevailed. On the final vote four senators voted against the new document. Jimmy was one of them, reflecting the depth of his feeling on the issue. Years later his vote would be used against him by opponents to show that he was an atheist!

Shortly after "Bo" Callaway won the Third Congressional District seat in November 1964, Jimmy decided to run against him in 1966, a decision he shared only with Rosalynn, whom he had increasingly accepted as his political partner. Growing up in an environment where everyone had worked hard for what they had, Jimmy felt antipathy toward people of inherited wealth, especially those whom he believed used the power and influence it gave them for selfish goals. By 1964, Jimmy himself was wealthy. But the Callaways were in a different league. In addition, what seemed to be Callaway's crass opportunism in jumping on the Goldwater bandwagon to exploit the race issue was too much for Jimmy, who felt that responsible leadership in a time of turmoil demanded moderation, not demagoguery. They were also natural competitors. Callaway had gone to West Point and had been a tank commander in Europe. He had quickly emerged as the leader of the state's Young Republicans, while Jimmy was increasingly viewing himself as a rising figure among the younger Democrats.

The prospect of moving to Washington in two years was not unappealing. Jimmy and Rosalynn had established a secure financial base, and with Billy back, they had someone who could run the business for them. Jimmy and Rosalynn continued to have many friends in Plains and Americus, but except for a handful of like-minded people such as the Thomases, the race issue was always in the background. Americus remained in the stranglehold of a handful of old, established, wealthy families who were unaccepting of any change. Jimmy and Rosalynn felt they had little in common with them and the feeling was mutual.

Having made the decision to run for Congress, Jimmy launched a covert campaign over the next eighteen months. His chairmanship of the regional planning commission (WCGAPDC) provided him with an ideal cover. He spoke all over the district, promoting economic development, greater efficiency in government, and the need to balance the state budget and lessen the tax burden on rural communities. He was able to keep himself highly visible, meeting people all over the district, and identifying himself with ideas and positions with which few could disagree. His seeming openness, friendly personality, grasp of the issues, and crusading interest in the improvement of the community won him a dedicated following.

Racial incidents had continued in Americus during the summer of 1964. Mostly they involved spontaneous friction between white and black teenagers rather than organized demonstrations. A paid advertisement in the *Times-Recorder* announced that the previously public swimming pool was now private and open to members only, despite its support by taxpayers.

In May 1965, Robertina Freeman, one of those incarcerated in the Leesburg prison in 1963 and one of the token blacks admitted to the previously all-white high school, was arrested in a lovers' lane and charged with "fornication." It was just before final exams and graduation. She was kept in jail in an effort by local leaders to punish her and her clergyman father for their civil rights activities. Warren Fortson agreed to undertake her defense and that of her male companion, also a civil rights activist. He lost the case initially, but won it on appeal.

On July 20, 1965, four black women were arrested when they attempted to join a "white" voting line. In an attempt to draw media attention, the SNCC workers appealed to Dr. Martin Luther King, Jr., and the Southern Christian Leadership Conference (SCLC) for help. King dispatched his lieutenant, Hosea L. Williams, to the scene. A few days later, 300 demonstrators, protected by a cordon of police, marched to the Sumter County Courthouse to begin an all-night vigil. One of their demands was for the establishment of a biracial committee to try to resolve peaceably their differences. Focusing their attention on the more reactionary Sumter County Commission, rather than the city officials, a group of white moderates, mostly women, but led by Warren Fortson, pleaded for the creation of a biracial committee. When the request was flatly rejected, Fortson and three friends set up their own informal committee. He now became the focus of escalating hatred, a convenient scapegoat for the white leadership that felt cornered. A petition drive was started to have Fortson removed as county attorney. People ignored him in the street, some because they despised what he was doing, but most because they were afraid. Often they would call later and apologize. His private law practice dried up, and he sent his children to Atlanta for their own safety.

On August 1, a mixed group of twenty-one whites and blacks attempted to attend services at the First Baptist Church in Americus. A photographer caught the scene as the group, denied entry, kneeled, praying on the church steps, while above them pastor Hal Henderson stood with a bandolier of bullets across his chest and a riot gun in his hand. The picture was flashed around the world.

The following week they went to the First Methodist Church, where their path was blocked by a line of twelve white male elders. Warren Fortson, a member of the church, went home in disgust. The following week an emissary of the congregation visited him to ask him not to come back. They delivered the same message to Dr. Lloyd Moll, president of Georgia Southwestern College for thirteen years, who had long been the teacher of the Bible school class, but who had also criticized the refusal to admit the visitors.

On August 1, word also had reached the Baptist church in Plains that "agitators" had tried to enter a church in Americus. The deacons, fearing their church might be next, met that night and agreed that the ushers should bar outsiders. One of the twelve deacons—Jimmy Carter—was absent, having spoken that day at another church some distance from Plains. Pastor Robert Harris, in seriously declining health, was present, but the minutes do not show him to have intervened. His wife, Ethel, was later quoted as saying, "If you walked into a room and smelled gas, would you light a match?" The congregation scheduled a vote two weeks later at a time when the Harrises would be away on vacation. That weekend, the Carters had gone to Roswell near Atlanta for a family wedding. Jimmy and Rosalynn argued about whether they should go back to Plains for the vote. Rosalynn pleaded not to go, arguing that with his plans to run for Congress he did not need further controversy. "I was tired of confrontation and the threat of boycotts against our business," she later wrote. "I was not very courageous and didn't want to take the risk, but Jimmy insisted on being there."

There were more than 200 people at the church the next morning.

When the resolution was read to bar "Negroes and other agitators" from the church, Jimmy rose to urge the congregation to reject the deacons' recommendation. The vote was 54 to 6 (Jimmy, Rosalynn, and Chip, Jeff, Lillian, and Homer Harris, an old hard-of-hearing farmer who had apparently not understood the issue). Most did not vote, and later several of the younger members called Jimmy to say that they agreed with him but were too afraid to take a public position.

In mid-August the worst riots in a generation erupted in the predominantly black Los Angeles suburb of Watts. Many southerners took quiet comfort in the event as a vindication of their opposition to integration and their view of the hypocrisy of their northern critics.

Finally, on August 13, Mayor T. Griffin Walker announced that after a meeting the previous night with the city council, the Sumter County movement, a newly formed coalition of civil rights groups, had agreed to halt the demonstrations. Gradually, over the remainder of the summer, some of the black demands were met and the unrest quieted down. The week President Johnson signed the Voting Rights Act, when it appeared the federal government was about to send in examiners, the local authorities registered 1,700 blacks within a few days.

The Sumter County Commission had received a petition with nearly 2,000 signatures demanding that Warren Fortson be fired as county attorney. A petition supporting his retention contained less than 100. The commission met to discuss the issue and few were willing to defend Fortson publicly. Maryanne Thomas, "the liberal sage of Americus," was a vociferous exception, as was Jimmy Carter. Fortson says of Jimmy's appearance,

> The thing that distinguishes Jimmy from others is that there was a testing time that came. And when it did he stood up. . . . I begged Jimmy . . . "don't come down here . . . stay away." But he wouldn't do it. He came down there and, in his quiet way, he made his pitch and caught hell for it.

Early in September the county commissioners quietly transferred their business to another firm of attorneys. Fortson sent his wife, Betty, to Atlanta, and without income, he closed his office, put their elegant eighteen-room house on the market, and followed her there. Although he was hailed in the national press as a hero and as a martyr, he was vilified in Americus, despite his tireless efforts at reconciliation, for having "blackened the good name" of the city. Under similar pressure Lloyd Moll and his wife moved to Pennsylvania. Few voices were raised in their defense. One was that of the Reverend David G. Pritchard, rector of Calvary Episcopal Church, who had the advantage, unlike the Baptist clergy, of not being entirely dependent on the support of his congregation to keep his job.

At the start of 1966, Jimmy returned to Atlanta for what he knew would be his final term in the Senate. He had been voted by his fellow legislators as one of the five most effective senators, and as one of the two most promising legislators in Georgia. Reporters covering the capital had nominated him for recognition as one of the thirty-five outstanding legislators nationwide. He had advanced to a coveted seat on the Appropriations Committee, and while his relationship with Governor Carl Sanders was not as close as that of many of his colleagues, he enjoyed considerable respect.

Carter's work on the Commission to Improve Education in Georgia had culminated in legislation entitled "A Minimum Foundation Program for Education" that provided additional funding for education statewide. It also included a provision finally upgrading Georgia Southwestern to the four-year status that Jimmy had so long sought. He distinguished himself through his concern that the tax load be lightened on smaller, rural school districts; it was a position that won him strong support back home. He also advocated giving local school board members a role in selecting members of the State Board of Education.

The laborious rewriting of the Democratic Party rules that he had undertaken with Marvin Shoob was eventually completed, resulting in a document an inch and a half thick. Jimmy suggested to Shoob that they take it to Washington and have each Democratic member of the Georgia congressional delegation review it. Shoob declined the suggestion. Undeterred, Jimmy went alone, eventually seeing every member of the delegation. The trip had less to do with the Democratic Party rules than Jimmy's desire to meet all the members and to savor the expectation that he might soon be joining them.

In the 1966 session Carter also began to emerge as a fiscal conservative, reflecting more personal "penny-pinching" traits from his business background than a particular political ideology. He repeatedly asserted the need for the state to save money, balance the budget, and improve its administrative structure and management. His frame of reference in the allocation of state funds was deeply rooted in his identification with the needs of the people of Sumter County and Southwest Georgia, tending, some would argue, to obscure at times an adequate view of the needs of the state as a whole.

CHAPTER 11

On March 3, 1966, as soon as the General Assembly session was over, Jimmy announced that he was a candidate for "Bo" Callaway's congressional seat. During his time in the Senate, Jimmy became friendly with a Yale-educated reporter, originally from South Georgia, Hal Gulliver, who wrote for the *Atlanta Constitution*. Gulliver, who had left the paper in 1965, had remained Carter's friend and admirer. On the last day of the legislative session Jimmy asked for Gulliver's help in writing the press release announcing his candidacy.

Unlike the Senate race, this time it was to be a carefully planned and methodical campaign. Each day Jimmy would spend several hours meeting and talking to people. It was a systematic courthouse-to-courthouse campaign. He shook thousands of hands and whenever he could find an audience he would give an impromptu speech. He carried a small tape recorder, and as soon as he got back in the car he dictated the names, and, if possible, some personal comment about each individual he had met. Each evening, he and Rosalynn, with Gloria's help, would write a follow-up letter asking for their support. In anticipation of the campaign, Jimmy had taken a memory course and read two books on the subject to help him remember people's names. He and Rosalynn thought up different mnemonics and then would compete after an event to see how many people's names they could recall. Over the years he developed this skill to a fine art. He learned how strongly people wanted to believe he remembered their name or something about them.

With most of the wealthier and more influential former Democratic figures still committed to Callaway, an overwhelming favorite for reelection, Jimmy's campaign had to be geared to a direct popular appeal. He enjoyed meeting and talking to ordinary people far more than influential political power brokers. He had carefully researched Callaway's congressional voting record and could point out instance after instance where Callaway's votes favored vested interests rather than the ordinary citizens, especially the farmers, of the district. Race remained Callaway's strongest issue. Although the power of the federal government had prevailed in guaranteeing the rights of black citizens, the resentment of the majority of whites had diminished little. The John Birch Society flourished, in part, on the belief that integration was the result of a communist conspiracy and several chapters existed in Sumter County. The organization strongly embraced Callaway. Carter always had to reach beyond the race issue to discover the other parts of people's lives where government could make a positive difference.

On May 18, 1966, the leading candidate in the gubernatorial race, former governor Ernest Vandiver, announced that he had suffered a mild heart attack and was dropping out of the race. His major opponents were Ellis Arnall, the progressive former governor who had served from 1942 to 1946, and Lester Maddox, the ax-wielding racist restauranteur from Atlanta. Arnall, a tough, aggressive campaigner, had staked out a strong early position with support especially among increasingly active college students. With the seeming certainty that the liberal Arnall would now secure the Democratic nomination, "Bo" Callaway abandoned the congressional race and announced his intention to seek the Republican nomination for governor. The leading Georgia Democrats panicked at the prospect of having the state go Republican for the first time since 1868. They especially feared Callaway, who had strong ties to the Republican national leadership in Washington. They implored U.S. Senator Herman Talmadge to return from Washington and run. But after hearing from many of his powerful backers that they did not want him to forfeit his senatorial seniority, Talmadge announced, on May 23, that he would stay out of the race.

Two candidates immediately offered themselves as the Democratic conservative alternative to Arnall (Lester Maddox was not being taken seriously by the professional politicians in the state). They were Jimmy's friend Garland Byrd and James Gray, a conservative transplanted northerner, graduate of Amherst, who published the Albany *Herald*. A perennial fringe candidate, Hoke O'Kelley, would also join the race. Jimmy felt Gray was too conservative and that Byrd, coming off a defeat by Callaway, stood little chance. Some party leaders accepted with resignation the prospect of Callaway as governor, but not Bill Gunter. He and Jimmy had several discussions about what they saw as the desperate need to get a moderate Democrat of stature into the race. Gunter felt, after four years of progress and moderation, Callaway would set the state on a reactionary and backward course.

With Callaway out of the Third Congressional District race, Jimmy had what seemed only token opposition. Moving to Washington appeared virtually assured. A potential problem existed in that Stephen Pace, Jr., had switched parties and would be the Republican candidate against Jimmy. Beyond his racist rhetoric his appeal was limited, and he posed little threat unless a landslide gubernatorial victory for Callaway occurred and he could ride his coattails. This would be particularly true if Callaway chose to campaign for Pace to keep the district Republican. Although sharing

Gunter's concern about the future of the state, Jimmy also, therefore, had a personal interest in assuring that Callaway had serious opposition.

Jimmy took it upon himself to try to find and convince an appropriate candidate to run. He went with Hal Gulliver to talk with Gulliver's boss, state insurance commissioner Jimmy Bentley. Bentley, a protégé of Herman Talmadge, was bright, dynamic, and handsome. He was spoken of as a likely governor one day. Carter not only urged Bentley to run but promised that with his own election seemingly assured, he would spend the bulk of his time campaigning for him. Bentley, who was well along in his own reelection campaign as insurance commissioner, declined, saying that he felt it was too late and that the field was too chaotic.

Other potential heavyweights viewed the situation in a similar manner. Jimmy met unsuccessfully with the longtime influential head of the highway department, Jim Gillis, seeking to get him to run or recruit someone else.

Early one morning, he went to the governor's mansion and implored Sanders to find somebody to run; he suggested as one possibility Noah Langdale, president of Georgia State University in Atlanta. Langdale, a lawyer and man of considerable stature, came from a wealthy South Georgia family that owned thousands of acres of land. Sanders, however, had ties to Ellis Arnall and was reluctant to do anything. Some around the governor even argued that it was in his interest to let Callaway win. Sanders would then remain the preeminent figure in the Democratic Party and be ideally poised to run for the U.S. Senate, or for the governorship again at the end of Callaway's term.

Despite Jimmy's frenetic efforts, no one was interested. The recent change in the county unit system and the passage of the Voting Rights Act had changed the political landscape in drastic and unpredictable ways. Old political hands who had prided themselves on knowing instinctively how to sell themselves to the Georgia electorate, were now insecure about how to formulate the new power equation. In addition, the time before the filing deadline was running out. Perhaps most important, Callaway looked so strong that no Democrats with real aspirations to be governor wanted to throw away their chances by being a sacrificial lamb in this race.

At lunch with Gulliver, Jimmy distantly pondered, "Maybe somebody needs to get into the race who has nothing to lose." He meant himself, but Gulliver did not initially catch it. Jimmy talked with Charles Kirbo, who says, "I told him it was a big gamble, that I was afraid he didn't appreciate how much money it would take, and he said he had some money, and was willing to spend it. I think he said he had $70,000 or $80,000 to spend on it." Bill Gunter was enthusiastic, and although not wealthy himself, offered to help raise the funds. On the night of June 1, Jimmy, Bill Gunter, Hal Gulliver, and a man named Bobby Troutman met in Jimmy's room at the Riviera Motel on Peachtree Road.

Bobby Troutman was the grandson of a Methodist minister and the son of a notably liberal partner at Kirbo's law firm. Troutman, present at Gunter's invitation, had been a lawyer with King and Spalding but had subsequently gone into real estate and happened to be Joseph Kennedy, Jr.'s roommate at Harvard law school. As a result he was drawn into the Kennedy political circle and was campaign manager in Georgia for Jack Kennedy's 1960 campaign. Troutman relished being in the political arena, and what particularly attracted Troutman to Carter was that he was young and dynamic—"like Kennedy."

The four men debated the pros and cons of Jimmy entering the race for most of the night, focusing substantially on the fund-raising considerations. Finally Jimmy decided that he would run. The next day he called his friend from the Senate, Brooks Pennington, who together with Ford Spinks had been urging him during the previous week to enter the race. On June 3 the *Atlanta Constitution* under the headline "Draft Carter Movement" ran a story saying that five of his fellow senators—Brooks Pennington of Madison, Robert Smalley of Griffin, Bobby Rowan of Enigma, Ford Spinks of Tifton, and Phil Broun of Athens—had formed a committee to urge him to run. Acting as their spokesman, Broun said, "There is definitely a grassroots desire to get a middle-of-the-road candidate in this race. . . . I think Jimmy Carter is our man."

Although he was a reluctant entrant into the governor's race, Jimmy had been cultivating a statewide role for himself for some time. Trying especially to appeal to younger people, he had been speaking on college campuses, including twice at Emory, where the head of the campus young Democrats, Terry Adamson, and already the youth coordinator for the Arnall campaign, was a friend.

On June 7 the lead story in the papers nationwide was about James Meredith being shot on a civil rights march in Mississippi. In Atlanta the *Constitution* headed a story on an inside page, "Jimmy Carter Thinks He Could Be Elected Governor," which said, in part:

> Jimmy Carter is considered to be one of the most outstanding members of the Senate. He is much younger looking than his 41 years, and many think he resembles the late President John F. Kennedy. Carter has described himself as a Russell Democrat, which if taken at face value means he is fairly conservative. . . . If he does run for governor he will indeed be a long shot. . . . Carter's reported optimism may be strictly his own.

The following day the paper ran a brief story saying that the California GOP had chosen Ronald Reagan as their gubernatorial candidate to run against Governor Pat Brown.

Bill Gunter was energetically calling his friends, especially his law-school classmates, to mobilize support for Jimmy. He had first called and recruited his friend David Gambrell, whom Jimmy knew slightly from his role with Kirbo in the Quitman County case. Gunter and Gambrell, who would become the campaign finance chairmen, then went to see Philip Alston, senior partner of Alston, Miller and Gaines, an Episcopalian, and a pillar of the Atlanta establishment. Alston, busy practicing law, had not previously been active in politics, but had reached a point of success in his life where an invitation from people of the stature of Gunter and Gambrell piqued his interest. He had earlier met Jimmy and been favorably impressed. According to Alston's wife, Elkin, one of the objectives in recruiting her husband was the hope that he would, in turn, secure the support of Mills Lane, president of the Citizens' and Southern Bank, and one of the most wealthy and powerful people in the state. This, however, did not happen.

On the morning of June 12, Jimmy went to a committee room in the southeast corner of the gold-domed Capitol, and there, before about 100 cheering supporters, announced his intention to run for governor. In his prepared statement he pledged to work for improvement in public education, mental health services, highways, and the state tax structure. It was hardly an original platform but did not need to be. Everyone knew that the only real agenda was that he was the moderate who could beat Callaway and the questions from the press reflected this. Did he think he was the only one who could beat Callaway? "I think I can beat him worse than anyone else." Did he think he was a conservative or a liberal? "Conservative, moderate, liberal, and middle-of-the-road. . . . I believe I am a more complicated person than that."

Apart from his fellow senators, Kirbo, Alston, Gunter, Gulliver, and members of the press, most of those present were young idealistic professionals attracted by his charm, energy, and image as a symbol of the new politics. One such individual was John Girardeau, an Emory University law student, who knew of Carter's reputation, but had never met him. He hoped to get a job in the campaign for the summer. On his way to the event he stopped to see a lawyer at a downtown law firm. It happened to be Gambrell's law firm, and when he heard of Girardeau's interest, he wrote a note, handed it to him, and said, "Find a man called Kirbo at the announcement and give this to him." By the next morning, Girardeau was starting his new job as the candidate's driver, confidant, and the campaign's first paid staff member.

Jimmy's decision created several problems for him. Rosalynn, who had her heart set on moving to Washington, was not happy. It also meant committing a substantial portion of their savings to something that was a staggering long shot. John Pope, who despite his switch to the Republican Party had agreed out of personal loyalty to help Jimmy in the congressional race, had also accepted the position as Sumter County chairman of the

"Callaway for Governor" campaign. Now they were directly against each other. Jimmy also had several friends who had helped him put together his campaign and had looked forward not only to getting rid of Callaway but to replacing him with a progressive of whom they could be proud. By abandoning the race when it was all but won, they felt he had betrayed them. It seemed he had ignored their concerns about the district to pursue his own quixotic ambitions. "They were *very* angry with me," he says.

Jimmy called Marvin Shoob to ask for his help in Atlanta, but Shoob had already committed to Ellis Arnall and saw breaking the commitment as too great a breach of integrity. Janice Shoob, however, felt she was not bound by the same commitment and pledged her support and assistance to Jimmy.

With exactly three months to go before the primary, Jimmy convinced Brooks Pennington to be his campaign manager. They set up the headquarters in Suite 562 of the aging but once elegant Dinkler Motor Hotel, where coincidentally James Gray also had his headquarters. Pennington was a tough, successful businessman, well versed in the ways of Georgia politics. He and Jimmy put together a volunteer committee in each of Georgia's 159 counties, and every Sunday they met with the volunteer coordinators from around the state. Initially only a handful of them would make the effort to come. But over several weeks the meetings grew in size and soon the committees in the different counties were competing in fund-raising and volunteer recruitment.

After a good deal of fence mending back in the Third Congressional District, Jimmy was able to turn most of his congressional campaign organization into a strong regional base for his gubernatorial effort. Even many previous enemies were taken with the idea of a local candidate running for governor and, putting aside past animosities, jumped on his bandwagon. Most striking was his ability as a conciliator in getting people of opposite extremes to unite behind him. He convinced William E. (Billy) Smith, the archconservative who had resigned from the Americus school board when an integration plan was presented, to be one of the cochairs of his campaign in Sumter County. The other equally conservative cochair was Frank Chappell, Jr., from Plains. At the same time, Russell Thomas, Jr., who, with his wife Maryanne, had only a year earlier been vilified as an integrationist, served as the campaign treasurer and provided office space. Frank Myers, whom Mr. Earl had defeated in 1952, and who had been a Johnson delegate in 1964, was a major financial backer and an active volunteer.

In late June, Philip and Elkin Alston hosted a dinner at the elite, and still segregated, Piedmont Driving Club to introduce Jimmy and Rosalynn to the leaders of the Atlanta establishment. The club was a living vestige of antebellum plantation life at which old, moneyed Atlanta families were dutifully waited on by a legion of meticulously trained and immaculately dressed white-gloved black waiters, waitresses, and assorted doormen and footmen. By all accounts the evening was a disaster. The assembled guests represented the very wealthy, powerful interests that Jimmy in his populist rhetoric railed against. He was, at the same time, overawed and uncomfortable in the setting. As one guest said, "He kept thanking us over and over again for having him there." As one longtime observer of the Atlanta power structure has noted, "They do not want petty favors or corrupt government. They want a prosperous, stable environment, in which business can prosper and grow . . . support is a blend of personal preference and realism." In Jimmy they did not see the kind of stability they sought or, more important, they did not see someone who looked like he could win.

Shortly after the campaign began, Bill Gunter, walking on Peachtree Street, encountered an old law-school classmate, Bob Lipshutz, an influential figure in the Atlanta Jewish community. "Come with me. There's someone I want you to meet," Gunter said. He took Lipshutz to the Dinkler to meet Jimmy Carter; he agreed not only to support him but to help raise money for the campaign. Pennington's ties to the Sanders and Vandiver people enabled him to recruit former Sanders speechwriter Bob Short as the headquarters coordinator, handling mainly the press and public relations, and also Mrs. Merle Meacham to head the women's division of the campaign, a function she had previously had with the Vandiver campaign before it folded. Jimmy's Aunt Sissy helped to coordinate the volunteers.

One night at the end of June, Jimmy Carter gave a speech at the Elks Club in Albany. In the audience was a young student attending the University of Georgia, where he was active in campus politics. Hamilton Jordan, a resident of Albany and a nephew of Clarence Jordan, had a summer job spraying mosquito breeding sites. With the help of Hugh Gaston, Carter's friend who had designed his house, Clarence Jordan arranged for Jordan to become the youth coordinator for the Carter campaign.

A campaign trip to the mountains of North Georgia was scheduled to coincide with a meeting of the regional planning and development commission (the local equivalent of the WCGAPDC in Americus) at Berry College in Rome. One attendee was Bert Lance, president of the First National Bank of Calhoun. Lance, the grandson of a Methodist circuit rider in the Blue Ridge Mountains and the son of a small, North Georgia college president, walked over to introduce himself to Jimmy, who was standing under the shade of a large oak tree. Lance liked what he had read about Carter and told him so. As they talked they had much in common—deep religious faith, high energy, ambitions much larger than the communities into which they had been born, and a strong desire to stamp their own imprint on the future of the state. Lance pledged his support.

Girardeau, Jordan, Lance, and many others who were attracted to

Jimmy Carter in 1966 represented a new generation of young Georgians from rural or small-town backgrounds who had acquired good educations and who identified with what he was and what he symbolized more than with what he said. They knew social change was inevitable and needed. For Girardeau, who came from Claxton in Southeast Georgia, a town not much bigger than Plains, Jimmy was a powerful role model.

> There was a lot I admired—single-minded, unbelievable discipline. I heard what he said privately; I heard what he said publicly. The private person and the public person was one. I liked what he said. It was idealistic, but there was enough practical in it to improve the lives of Georgians.

Since it was the summer, and Billy and Sybil were running the warehouse business, Rosalynn and the three boys were able to come to Atlanta and work full-time on the campaign. The office ran with great informality as Rosalynn would sit with her stocking feet tucked under her, making phone calls around the state, then dashing up and down the back stairs of the hotel because the elevators were too slow. Kirbo was a regular presence, and others, like the Gunters and the Langfords, also made it a family commitment with wives and children as much a part of the action as their husbands. It was small-town style to involve whole families in any endeavor, but it was also characteristically the Carter style. With little money, and relying almost exclusively on volunteers with whom enthusiasm substituted for political sophistication or experience, the personal dedication to Jimmy Carter, rather than belief in an ideology or position on issues, became the glue that held the campaign together. An almost cultlike fervor engulfed the loyalists, so that the venture took on more the quality of a crusade than that of a political campaign. Jimmy understood the strength of this attribute and knew that his most powerful weapon was the impact he had on people in a one-to-one exchange.

In an article that has remained one of the most enduringly insightful about Carter's approach to politics, *Atlanta Constitution* columnist Bruce Galphin wrote, in part, on July 2:

> It is hard to meet Senator Jimmy Carter and hear him talk about state government without liking him and admiring his integrity. . . . For those who hadn't known Senator Carter before, his appearance at the Atlanta Press Club Thursday was a startling experience. Here was a breed of politician new to Georgia's big contest: subdued, frank even about his deficiencies, refusing to torture the traditional whipping boys.
>
> When he got to talking about Milledgeville State Hospital, he said the plight of patients there made him choke up, and indeed his voice faltered and his face reddened a shade.

. . . But many of the assets of Jimmy Carter the man may be deficits for Jimmy Carter the political candidate.

His honesty is almost painful. He admitted the unique problems of big cities were new to him. He said he had been boning up on them in the last few weeks, and you could believe he can learn fast. But it was a deficiency, politically speaking, he shouldn't have admitted.

He said Viet Nam wasn't an issue in the Georgia governor's race—an honest position—but then went on to talk about it, to admit it was complex and finally to confess, "I don't have any solutions." He would have done better to stop after saying it wasn't an issue.

It apparently didn't occur to Senator Carter—as it had to Lester Maddox, Bo Callaway and Ellis Arnall before him—to pack the Press Club luncheon with friends. So the room was embarrassingly bare before TV camera eyes.

Jimmy had set a frenetic pace for himself racing from one end of the state to another. He would later say that he and Rosalynn had shaken the hands of 250,000 people—"to let people know I am interested in them and their problems."

Jimmy Carter's campaign theme was simple: "We need in the state a competent, compassionate, caring government that is as good as its people." He then presented himself and his background as evidence that he was the person who could bring that about. His campaign literature itemized his qualifications under five headings: Jimmy Carter as Outstanding Georgian; Success in Business; Leading State Legislator; Lifelong Churchman; Devoted Family Man. A special box emphasized his religious background, ending by saying, "He deeply believes that a man's faith, whatever his creed, is his greatest strength"—a view that would become increasingly true throughout his life and would play an important part in his political decision making.

In a speech on July 14 to fifteen teenage campaign workers in Hall County, he said, "If I ever let you down in my actions, I want you to let me know about it and I'll correct it. I promise never to betray your trust in me." They were lines that he would use with slight variations throughout his political career. Interestingly the campaign material was entirely devoid of any discussion of issues, as were, for the most part, his speeches early in the campaign. Rather than stake out a specific position on crime, he talked movingly about the tragic toll it took in the state and assured his audience that he had confidence in state and local officials to control lawlessness. He always sought to emphasize the spiritually uplifting over the adversarial. The bottom line for Jimmy Carter was a conviction that if people knew him they would vote for him.

A Quayle poll done at the end of July showed that despite his vigorous efforts to sell himself to the electorate, Jimmy was still trailing badly (Arnall 32%, Maddox 15%, Gray 12%, Byrd 8%, Carter 5%, O'Kelley 3%, and undecided 25%). More disturbing, the argument that Jimmy was the candidate who could most easily beat Callaway was severely undermined by polls continuing to show Arnall well ahead of Callaway. It was clear that a more aggressive assault on Arnall was needed, particularly to lure away some of his supporters by painting him as too liberal. He castigated Arnall for saying those who attack the federal government or disagree with him can go to Russia. He described Arnall, age 59, as "bald, squat, and old," saying he had little support in South Georgia, a veiled way of saying he was too liberal. When he accused Arnall of spending state highway funds politically when governor, it backfired because he had difficulty proving it when challenged. He called Arnall "wild with promises and money," and claimed the state constitution written when he was governor had to be amended 250 times.

Garland Byrd, who had learned the price of sitting on the fence in his 1964 race with Callaway, was fighting with Gray and Maddox for the most conservative segment of the electorate. He announced that he would work against the reelection of Lyndon Johnson, and on August 6, he predicted riots if the federal school integration guidelines were enforced in the fall. On August 12, all members of the Georgia congressional delegation, with the exception of Atlanta congressman Charles Weltner, voted against a new civil rights bill. On August 16, Byrd announced that Lyndon Johnson was supporting Arnall, and Bobby Kennedy was behind his longtime friend and erstwhile supporter Jimmy Carter. His only evidence for the latter was the involvement of Bobby Troutman in the Carter campaign. "Any man who would accept support from either Johnson or Kennedy is not worthy of serving in public office in this state," Byrd said. Jimmy dismissed the assertion of Kennedy involvement through Troutman as "ridiculous." Maddox joined the effort of the conservatives to label Arnall and Carter as too liberal by saying, "There's no difference between Mr. Carter and Mr. Arnall except in years." At the same time, Maddox was negotiating with Gray to try to get him to drop out.

On August 24, as the race heated up, Jimmy showed that he was not above using some of the same tactics to brand Arnall as too liberal: "Ellis Arnall's image represents everything Georgia voters dislike about President Johnson, the National Democratic Party, and the Georgia Democratic Party." However, he added: "The Democratic Party must have a candidate who has the respect of a majority of the responsible Negro and white voters."

Apart from Ellis Arnall, Jimmy was the only candidate who actively sought the black vote, but he did so more aggressively than Arnall. A report from the Voter Education Project of the Southern Regional Council indicated that in 1966 there were 275,000 black voters in Georgia, 34,000 of whom had registered in the previous year. John Girardeau described Jimmy's deliberate effort to appeal to that constituency.

> He would seek people out. . . .When he went into a restaurant, for example, he would shake hands with folks in the restaurant, with the owner of the restaurant, then work his way back into the kitchen. . . . There were times when he would almost go out of his way to recognize a black person in face of what might have been circumstances that politically would have been better left alone.

On the afternoon of August 16, Jimmy had a long meeting with a group of black Baptist ministers at Atlanta's Wheat Street Baptist Church. Although most of them had already committed to Ellis Arnall, the religious background he shared with them enabled him to establish a strong rapport and create a positive impression. In the evening he went to the all-black Morris Brown College for the celebration of the first Episcopal service in the Joe Louis Gymnasium by Bishop Ernest Lawrence Hickman. Later this same year William Winter, a progressive candidate in Mississippi, would lose his race for governor, in significant part because he was willing to publicly shake hands with blacks.

The campaign received a major boost early in August. Jimmy Bentley had hired a bright young advertising man named Gerald Rafshoon to handle his reelection effort. Rafshoon, who had never previously done the publicity for a political race, designed a sophisticated statewide campaign geared in part to the contingency of Bentley entering the governor's race. Bentley, with only token opposition in his race for insurance commissioner, did not want to use it. Gulliver suggested to Rafshoon that he contact the Carter campaign, but Carter already had an agency and Rafshoon was hesitant to do so. Then, as he describes it:

> I was riding along in the car . . . on a Saturday and I heard a jingle come on the radio. It was country and western singers, "Jimmy Carter is his name, Jimmy Carter is his name" (to the tune of "Davey Crockett"). I thought this is really a lot of horse shit . . . you don't just repeat the guy's name over and over like that. I got so upset that I pulled over to a service station and I called Hal Gulliver . . . and I said, "Boy your friend Jimmy Carter needs help." And he said, "He sure does."

A couple of days later Rafshoon received a call from the Carter campaign asking if he could come the following morning with a proposal. They had $70,000 to spend. Taking the plan developed for Bentley, Rafshoon and his creative director, Jack Kaplan, worked all night to convert it into a 120-page proposal to sell Jimmy Carter using modern, innovative advertising concepts and techniques that were completely new to the Georgia political scene. Essentially, Rafshoon proposed putting all the money into an intensive television campaign over a three-week period portraying Jimmy as attractive and dynamic in a variety of action sequences around the state. A voiceover would say that the experts thought he could not win, but the voters needed to learn about him, and if they liked what they saw, they should prove the experts wrong.

When Rafshoon made his presentation, Jimmy asked questions that Rafshoon found perceptive and impressive. Bobby Troutman, the largest contributor to the campaign, was more critical, saying that he preferred the traditional approach. In the ensuing heated discussion Rafshoon became exasperated and was about to tell Troutman he was out of date and that if he didn't appreciate the creativity they had to offer he did not need the business. "I felt someone kick me under the table," he said. "I looked over and there was Jimmy just smiling." Rafshoon then tried to draw some analogy with the 1960 Kennedy campaign and Troutman, rising imperiously, said, "Don't you tell me about Kennedy. I knew John Kennedy." He then left the room. Immediately Jimmy said to him, "There's only one person you have to satisfy and that's me. I like it. Go ahead and do it." For Rafshoon it was a major breakthrough.

> Here I was a struggling advertising man always having to compromise with clients . . . and here was a guy who respected my professional judgment enough to put it in my hands. That was one of the things that really attracted me to him. We went to Plains and Columbus and we put together a campaign in about three or four days. During that weekend Jack Kaplan and I stayed over at Miss Lillian's and talked to Jimmy a lot. He really charmed us.

Rafshoon's television spots coincided with and contributed to a marked surge for Jimmy. The effort by all of the other Democratic candidates to paint Arnall as too old and too liberal had clearly had an impact. Jimmy's appeal was particularly to young people who were ready for change, and to women. On August 28, the *Atlanta Constitution* described "girls too young to vote leaving the headquarters in a swooning condition."

Progress in the polls spurred Jimmy on to more intense campaigning even though he was becoming physically depleted. Rosalynn, still timid and shy, had forced herself to speak before small groups and was maintaining her own campaigning schedule. Of the many forums offered the candidates, Jimmy accepted almost all, Arnall very few.

One night Girardeau was driving Jimmy, exhausted, back to the headquarters after a heavy rainstorm. As they approached the front of the hotel in the car with a large "Vote for Jimmy Carter" sign on the roof, they went through a large puddle completely drenching one of two pedestrians who had just emerged from the building. Jimmy turned ashen and Girardeau could see the artery pulsating in his temple, which his friends had all learned indicated a state of severe emotional agitation. "Stop, stop, stop!" he demanded, jumping out of the car. Girardeau watched in the rearview mirror as Jimmy pursued the two men on the street. Suddenly when he was halfway there he stopped, turned around, and came back to the car with a broad smile on his face. "It was James Gray," he said.

For the three months of the campaign the relationship between Jimmy and Girardeau was intense. Often spending twenty-four hours together in a car or plane during the day and sharing a room at night, there was the kind of intimacy that Jimmy had not experienced since he was in the submarines. Despite the rigors of the campaign, he was lonely away from Rosalynn, and he and Girardeau talked about their families, their childhoods, their fears and their aspirations, in addition to the politics. To save money they often stayed in the homes of supporters, or shared a room in a motel. Jimmy, who slept in his underwear, would kneel by the side of his bed to pray. He would be asleep in a matter of minutes, no matter how stressful the day or pressing his worries.

For Girardeau the three months were "a life-changing experience for me . . . even though it was a short period of time I felt a strong connection, affiliation, support, like he was an older brother or perhaps father—but more like a brother. I felt very close to him." Even though they would see each other infrequently in later years, Girardeau continued to feel the same way. "It was something that he burned into me. That's remained and always will."

Money was a significant problem. Without additional funds it was clear they could not mount the kind of media blitz Rafshoon was recommending and without it the chances of success were slim. Finally, David Gambrell, Brooks Pennington, Philip Alston, and Bill Gunter cosigned a note for $50,000 to keep the campaign afloat.

Brooks Pennington had managed an effective campaign, primarily from his business office in Madison with the help of his secretary Joan Hunicutt. Less of a populist than Jimmy, he and Ford Spinks focused their efforts heavily on getting members of the state House and Senate to support Jimmy and to use their influence on Jimmy's behalf in their own districts. He also contacted all of his friends and clients in the seed business not only asking for their vote but getting them to contribute financially. Some of the contributions he obtained were from outside Georgia. Pennington was shrewd, skillful, and willing to engage in some of the traditional Georgia campaign practices that were out of keeping with the high moral ground the candidate was staking out. As an associate says, "He was a conniver." Pennington understood that for a candidate who started almost unknown it was essential to be perceived as having a chance, and to be making steady progress against the opposition. He devised a strategy in which he would have weekly polls from the "Voter Research Institute" available for the press that invariably showed Jimmy gaining momentum. But nobody ever asked what the Voter Research Institute was.

As one of his fellow campaigners says, "It was completely fictional . . . it was totally a creation of his office." Toward the end of the campaign he was able to draw on legitimate, if unrepresentative, polls such as one conducted with 900 employees at the Atlantic Coal Company.

Georgia's two U.S. senators had stayed out of the race except to express their desire to see Callaway defeated. Pennington prepared a message without consulting them:

> We are very concerned that Ellis Arnall will, if elected, take control of our Georgia Democratic Party and mold it into the image of the National Democratic Party. We cannot afford to have this happen.
>
> We have carefully analyzed the governor's race. We are now of the opinion that our only hope to block Arnall in his drive for power is to support the one candidate who can defeat him—State Senator Jimmy Carter. There are other acceptable candidates, but we are convinced that Senator Jimmy Carter is the only man certain to defeat Ellis Arnall. We have waited until the last moment for the clearest picture possible of this race—therefore as our friend you must act quickly— today call at least ten of your friends, have them call and spread the word. Defeat Arnall with Carter.
>
> —Concerned friends of Dick Russell and Herman Talmadge

The message was printed on thousands of postcards that Pennington arranged to have mailed from Washington, D.C., and Lovejoy, Georgia, Talmadge's hometown, as well as Atlanta, to maximize the impression that this was, indeed, an endorsement by the two senators. In Atlanta, Pennington was thwarted when Arnall supporters working for the post office put the cards aside until the day after the election. When asked about the postcards, Carter told the press, correctly, that he had no knowledge of them.

Under the state Democratic Party rules candidates had to get a clear majority of the votes to secure the nomination, or there was a runoff between the two highest vote getters. By the end of August it was looking increasingly as though Arnall could be held well below 50 percent, and that Jimmy might eke out second place. The campaign did its best to foster this impression, as the *Atlanta Constitution* gullibly reported on August 30:

> Carter's state headquarters in Atlanta released the result of a poll taken by the Voters Research Institute which showed him in second place. . . .
>
> The poll showed Arnall with 17%, Carter 15%, Lester Maddox 11%,

James Gray 9%, Garland Byrd 8%, Hoke O'Kelley 1% and undecided 39%. The Carter headquarters statement also said the results showed Carter out-polling Callaway 43% to 39% with 20% undecided.

Bobby Troutman prepared a two-page analysis of the black vote. In the August 25 document, he argued that blacks would be wasting their vote by giving it to Arnall, because he ultimately could not beat Callaway. The other Democrats were racist, therefore, voting for Jimmy, who was both sympathetic to their cause and could beat Callaway—this was the only thing that made sense. Jimmy spoke to a group of black leaders in Dalton. Speaking without a text, as he always did, he said:

> I think responsible Georgians believe in treating everyone fairly .... The State Merit System should not be rigged for anyone. When I am governor, people will be hired and appointed to state positions on the basis of qualifications rather than their race.

Six days later he was the only candidate to attend a rally at the Wheat Street Baptist Church. Throughout that week the campaign was crowded off the front pages of the Atlanta newspapers by the activities of SNCC in Atlanta. Increasingly militant, having expelled whites from its leadership, the organization was now headed by Trinidad-born Stokely Carmichael. He championed the term "black power," which to southern whites was thoroughly incendiary. Carmichael's confrontational style led to a riot on September 6 in the Vine City section of Atlanta and Carmichael was arrested on September 7. While the other candidates rushed to exploit the situation, Jimmy remained quiet, except when pressed for a comment, he said, "I think he should have been arrested. Anyone who incites a riot should be." He did use the opportunity to attack James Gray as a "rabble-rouser," accusing him of trying to stir up "racial unrest."

On September 7, the *Atlanta Constitution*, citing his exceptional, progressive record as governor during his previous term, endorsed Ellis Arnall. Coming from men of his own generation, who called him "a source of pride for Georgians in World War II," it was not an unexpected setback. On September 12, Jimmy did receive a long-sought-after public endorsement from William Bowdoin, a pillar of the Atlanta establishment—too late to make any real difference.

Jimmy spent a good part of the following day, the last of the campaign, greeting workers in the rain outside the Scripto plant in Atlanta. That evening in a talk with campaign workers he told publicly, for the first time, the story of his interview with Hyman Rickover. He related it to their efforts, in saying that the only thing that mattered was whether or not you had done your best, but it was as much a statement about himself. Win or lose, he had really done his best. He was utterly exhausted and had lost 22 pounds. On election day he and Rosalynn voted in Plains, then returned to the headquarters in Atlanta. That evening after dinner they returned in an optimistic mood to the Dinkler to await the returns. Arnall was predictably in the lead, but Carter was running second, making a runoff look assured. But as the night wore on, and the rural vote came in, Maddox crept up on and overtook Carter. A quiet fell over the assembled families. By the early hours of the morning it became clear he had lost. The dedication of the true believers turned to devastating disappointment. John Girardeau found Jimmy in the hallway and both, in tears, hugged each other. Officially the vote was too close to call and Jimmy did not concede.

Edna Langford described the feeling the next morning: "A funeral-like pall hung over us . . . with still lingering disbelief." Jack, incredulous, said, "How could they choose Lester Maddox, who is less qualified in every way than my dad." Part of the explanation was that with no Republican primary (Callaway was nominated at a state party convention) Republican voters had crossed over and supported the candidate considered easiest for their man to beat. Maddox, who had first come to national attention using pick-ax handles to drive away blacks who sought to integrate his restaurant, and had previously lost races for lieutenant governor and mayor of Atlanta, was perceived as a far weaker candidate than Jimmy Carter.

Despite the loss, the media were duly impressed: "Carter was the big surprise of the night"; "the moderate candidate [Carter] who undoubtedly ran one of the most surprising races in Georgia in decades"; "Regardless of Carter's loss, his showing means a new Democratic star is born"; "He has joined the heavyweights."

At 2:45 P.M. on Thursday, September 17, two days after the election, Jimmy called a news conference at the headquarters. Sitting on a folding steel chair with Rosalynn next to him firmly gripping his arm, he formally conceded and answered a barrage of questions.

The following Sunday, Jimmy and Rosalynn met with over a hundred of his supporters from around the state. After the meeting he announced that he would not endorse anyone. Some had urged him to seek the chairmanship of the Democratic Party to keep his name before the public. "I only want to go back to Plains," he said. He added, however, "I cannot rest, because I have to pay off the campaign debt."

The official vote tally was:

Arnall	231,480	(29.4%)
Maddox	185,672	(23.5%)
Carter	164,562	(20.9%)
Gray	152,973	(19.4%)
Byrd	39,994	(5.1%)
O'Kelley	13,271	(1.7%)

In the runoff scheduled for September 28, Maddox made a public statement implying that Jimmy had endorsed him. Jimmy denied it. Passions were powerfully stirred by Maddox. Congressman Charles Weltner of Atlanta resigned from the Democratic ticket because he felt he could not honor, as a matter of conscience, the Democratic Party's pledge to support *all* of the ticket. A story in the *Atlanta Constitution* on September 27 said that Maddox was campaigning around the state in a plane provided by segregationist supporters in Americus. The same week a Baptist pastor in Macon was voted out by his congregation for allowing a black student to attend services.

Maddox did defeat Arnall for the Democratic nomination, but in the general election in November diehard Arnall supporters launched a write-in campaign. Callaway narrowly defeated Maddox in the popular vote by 49 percent to 48 percent, with Arnall holding the 3 percent balance. Under the Georgia Constitution, if a candidate did not get 50 percent, the election was thrown into the State House of Representatives. The overwhelmingly Democratic House declared Lester Maddox the new governor.

Jimmy and Rosalynn returned to Plains profoundly depressed. Not only had he lost the governor's race, he had abandoned the almost certain congressional seat, expended most of his and Rosalynn's savings, and four of his friends were still personally carrying a substantial bank loan for him. In addition, if he had not been in the race, Arnall would have won the nomination without a runoff and quite possibly the general election. Having Maddox as governor was the worst of all possible outcomes, and he was responsible for it.

Reflecting both his gratitude and his depression he wrote to John Girardeau:

> John, there is no need for me to tell you that you occupy a special place in my heart, second only to my own family. Someday, whether I ever amount to much or not I hope to be able to repay you for all that you have done for me. I am always here and available if you need me.
> —Jimmy

CHAPTER 12

He that is humble ever shall
Have God to be his guide.

—JOHN BUNYAN

Jimmy returned to the bosom of Plains as a place of retreat, renewal, and replenishment, drawing strength from the rural environment of his childhood. Despite the local conflicts of the recent years, he felt more compatible with the residents of Sumter County than with people anywhere else. In victory or defeat it was where he came to lick his wounds or share his glory.

As before, he sought to deal with failure by immediately embracing a new challenge. As he has written, "I remembered the admonition, 'Show me a good loser, and I will show you a loser.'" Despite his despondency, within a month he began to plan for the 1970 governor's race. In one respect he had little choice. If he was to raise funds to pay off his and his friends' debts, there should be some expectation that he had a political future. Brooks Pennington and Bill Gunter, still burdened by the note they had cosigned, organized an "Appreciation Dinner in Honor of Jimmy Carter." Such an event, to pay off a campaign debt, was unprecedented in Georgia politics. It was held at the Dinkler Motor Hotel on November 4, 1966, and at $50 per head, to everyone's surprise, there was a sellout crowd of 500. For the printed program Bill Gunter chose a verse by Robert Browning:

One who never turned his back but marched breast forward,
   Never doubted clouds would break,
Never dreamed, though right were worsted, wrong would triumph,
Held we fall to rise, are baffled to fight better,
   Sleep to wake.

One of the featured speakers at the dinner was Dr. Horace Tate, Jimmy's black colleague on the education commission. His presence and that of a

166

handful of other black supporters made it among the first integrated dinners for a white statewide candidate.

For Jimmy it was a time of serious psychological introspection.

> The prospects of my winning in '70 were dismal. I was determined to run, but thought most likely I was facing another defeat. . . . I had arrived at a point in my life when I did not get much pleasure out of success or victories, and I felt personally responsible for all the small failures and defeats. I had very little genuine interest in other people and I was quite disconsolate and dissatisfied with myself.

To deal with these feelings he turned increasingly for solace to his faith. At a crossroads, he was struggling to find meaning and purpose. Psychological and spiritual gratification seemed to offer a more secure sense of fulfillment than the traumatic vagaries of public life.

There followed a series of events that would reshape both his relationship with his faith and the central guiding motivation in his life. The first of these occurred when his sister, Ruth, came to visit six weeks after the election loss. As he describes it:

> Ruth suggested that I could change my whole attitude, that I was not taking advantage of my deep religious conviction that would alleviate my problems if I were sincere and could accept it. As a result of the meeting which was not tearful or emotional or anything, I decided, along with Ruth, that I would try to reassess my relationship with God, and did. I began to try much more than I had ever tried before.

Ruth would later embroider the story, describing it as a much more pivotal and emotional event than Jimmy recalls.

Ruth herself had recently relied on religion in overcoming serious personal problems. She later wrote, "I had been raised to believe that I was God's gift to the world, the most beautiful child ever born . . . the queen of the universe." This reflected the tradition of the southern belle, a relic from a bygone era when women were waited on by servants and adored by male admirers, but lacked any preparation for the responsibilities of modern womanhood.

After she married and moved to Fayetteville, her life seemed outwardly happy enough. She and her husband had a modern house, a cabin retreat in the woods, and eventually a vacation home in Portugal. Ruth, however, could find no internal peace. Her first pregnancy filled her with anxiety and fear of responsibility. With each successive child she suffered severe postpartum depression, and her marriage became increasingly rocky.

Since her adolescent years she had been obsessed with Henry David

Thoreau, carrying a copy of *Walden* with her much of the time, and spending increasingly long periods alone at their lakeside cabin. Depressed and anxious, she felt overwhelmed by the demands put on her as a mother and a wife, and thoroughly unfulfilled as a person.

Ruth decided to go back to college, majoring in English and religion; eventually she received a master's degree and taught high school English. On her lunch hours she took a Bible class at the Fort Bragg Army Base and became, over time, fixated on religion. Ultimately she was fired from her teaching job, because she spent more time talking about God than about English. When the teacher of the Bible class left for Vietnam, Ruth took it over and for the next seven years she taught Bible classes throughout the Fayetteville area, attracting a substantial following. "I was very religious," she says. "All I did was pray, read the Bible, and speak." But she remained depressed and empty. She saw a psychiatrist, but achieved little relief.

Early in 1966, she was driving to the Fayetteville airport to pick up a psychologist and spiritual leader whom she had invited to speak to her Bible class. In what she suggests may have been a suicide attempt, she jumped from the car because "the brakes failed." As she described later, in her book *The Gift of Inner Healing,* she sat through the class with her bandaged leg propped up on a chair. The speaker later came back to her house to talk and over several hours she was finally able to unburden herself about her relationship with her parents and the stultifying effects of Earl's overindulgent love. From that moment on, Ruth no longer felt "crippled" and her symptoms of depression began to lift. She believed it was Jesus who healed her and her faith in him that had made the difference.

Ruth had a powerful attractiveness, a gentle warmth, and a high level of charismatic energy with a strong sexual component to it. Blond haired and well dressed, she drew people to her. Capitalizing on these characteristics she was able to create a unique role for herself as a psychological counselor, preacher, faith healer, and inspirational orator, although she disavowed any of these labels. Over the next fifteen years she would travel widely throughout the world developing a devoted following and becoming relatively wealthy.

In her conversation with Jimmy after his election defeat, she empathized and offered solace based on the experiences of their shared childhood and her own struggle. She stressed that achieving a deepened religious faith was central to achieving inner peace and regaining a sense of pleasure out of life. She urged him to strive for a "fresh, intimate, personal, loving, caring relationship with Jesus Christ." She said, she later recalled, "You've got to be willing to accept God's will, Jimmy, no matter what He should want you to do."

After this discussion, Jimmy, already a diligent reader of the Bible, began to spend more time seriously studying it and thinking about the meaning of its teachings. Soon after, Pastor Robert Harris preached a sermon on the apostle Peter's imprisonment by King Herod. He reminded the congregation that Christians were still being imprisoned for their beliefs, and cited as an example two southern Baptist missionaries, Herbert Caudill and his son-in-law David Fite, who had been imprisoned in Cuba. Then looking at the congregation, Harris asked, "If you were arrested for being a Christian, as Peter, Herbert Caudill, and David Fite were, would there be enough evidence to convict you?" The question stuck with Jimmy, who mulled it over for several weeks. "I finally decided," he later wrote in his book *Why Not the Best?* "that if arrested and charged with being a committed follower of God, I could probably talk my way out of it! It was a sobering thought."

A few weeks later he was asked to address a group of Baptists in Preston about "Christian Witnessing." Every year before the weeklong summer revival, he and his fellow deacons would visit their neighbors in Plains, read the Bible, talk about their beliefs, promote the revival, pray, and try generally to get their hosts to recommit themselves to their religion. As he prepared his speech, Jimmy added up the number of families with whom he had "witnessed" during the fourteen years since he returned from the navy, and it amounted to a total of 140 people. It seemed like a commendable number until he compared it to the 250,000 with whom he and Rosalynn had had personal contact during the gubernatorial campaign. He felt ashamed that he had reached out to so many in pursuit of his own political interests, while he had contacted so few for Christ. The self-aggrandizing element in politics was a difficult burden to bear for someone whose religion demanded humility. How do you reconcile a lifelong belief that deep humility is an essential part of achieving God's kingdom on earth with the egotistical self-promotion of politics, he regularly asked himself. It was a dilemma that had festered in his psyche since prior to the Senate race.

Slowly he began to deal with this painful paradox. He was recommitting himself to Christ, through deep ongoing study and meditation about Christ's life, out of which he sought to gain the fullest possible understanding of what the Christian message meant in modern life. He also committed himself to living a life emulating that of Christ and the values for which he stood. By his own example and leadership he hoped to bring those values to others. In this way he believed he could use his role in politics to spread his Christian values, in which case the seemingly self-serving nature of politics would be obviated. Central to the Christian message that he sought to embrace was the concept of agape, or Christian love toward one's fellow human beings. It is a concept of disinterested love in which the individual seeks not his own good but the good of his neighbor.

These developments, which changed the quality and degree of his faith, constituted being "born again" in his mind and that of his fellow Baptists. As Jimmy himself has said, Baptists "believe that the first time we're born as children, it's human life given to us, and when we accept Jesus as our savior, it's new life. That's what 'born again' means." Baptists reject infant baptism on the grounds that a child should be old enough to understand the significance of being baptized and able to make a conscious decision about accepting Christ. Having come into the world in a state of original sin and lived in sin, as defined by Baptist leaders, ordinary believers could only achieve salvation by accepting Jesus, who died for all their sins, as their personal savior. Then they could enter the kingdom of heaven and avoid a future of eternal damnation. The biblical underpinning lay in the story of Nicodemus, a wealthy and profligate man who came to Jesus to ask how he could be saved. Jesus answered that he must be "born again," essentially starting his religious life over in a state of enlightenment.

There were other important aspects of the Baptist faith, its history, organizational structure, and theology, that shaped Jimmy's perspective. Roger Williams, who can be considered not only the father of the Baptist denomination but also the father of human rights in America, felt there must be no constraints placed on the individual conscience and that the separation of church and state should be total and absolute. Central to Baptist belief is the notion of soul liberty or soul competency, which holds that individuals have the ability, based on their reading of the scriptures, to directly search out their own relationship with God, unimpeded by the role of a priest or the hierarchies of church or state.

Jimmy believed, like other Baptists, that Jesus wanted people to experience God directly. He once told a Sunday school class, "The teachings of God are simple and personal. They apply to us. You don't have to have a preacher. You don't have to have a Sunday school teacher. You have to have simple faith." Griffin Bell, whose father and grandfather were Baptist ministers, says that the publication of the King James version of the Bible in English "did more to democratize the world than anything that ever happened—letting the people have the Bible." Baptist leaders like Virginia preacher John Leland fully supported the efforts of Thomas Jefferson and James Madison to incorporate the Bill of Rights, guaranteeing separation of church and state, into the Virginia and federal constitutions. The "American Creed" characterized by liberty, egalitarianism, individualism, populism, and laissez-faire owes much to the forceful influence of the Baptists.

Unlike the established faiths, the Baptist church has no hierarchy, with each congregation being an independent entity. Historically there was no central doctrinal or management control. There are no Baptist bishops and each congregation is free to elect its own pastor. Missionary work and evangelism are a central concern.

Jimmy continued his dialogue with Bill Gunter about how to achieve a psychological reconciliation between his religious faith and life in politics. Early in 1965, Gunter had lent him a copy of *Reinhold Niebuhr on Politics,* a 1960 collection of excerpts from theologian Niebuhr's political writings. The book offered some specific answers to the questions with which Jimmy had long struggled. This first contact with Niebuhr had had such an impact that he told Gunter it was "the most amazing thing" he had ever read, later describing the book as his "political Bible." He would go on to read *Justice and Mercy,* a selection of Niebuhr's later sermons and prayers edited by his wife, Ursula, and June Bingham's 1972 study of Niebuhr's life and thought, *Courage to Change.* All three books he heavily underlined. Later, in August 1976, Jimmy would write to the then-widowed Ursula, saying of her husband, "He contributed to my private education more than you could know."

Niebuhr had served as pastor of the Bethel Evangelical Church in Detroit in the early twenties, and became radicalized by seeing the suffering and exploitation of workers in the automobile industry, prior to unionization, and unprotected by social legislation. He became a socialist, forming the Fellowship of Socialist Christians and running for elective office several times on the socialist ticket. In 1928 he joined the faculty of Union Theological Seminary, where he remained for the rest of his life. A fervent opponent of Nazism, he split with the socialists at the start of World War II over their pacifist and noninterventionist foreign policy. By the 1940s he had become a left-wing anticommunist Democrat. He was a founder of Americans for Democratic Action and served for a time as the vice chairman of the New York State Liberal Party.

It was, however, Niebuhr's writings and teachings on the relationship between moral values, Christianity, and politics that established him as what political scientist Hans J. Morgenthau described as "the greatest living political philosopher of America." For Jimmy, who sought precision and clarity in everything he did, Niebuhr seemed to answer the perplexing question of how a deeply committed Christian could conduct himself in politics without compromising his religious values. Most Georgia politicians Jimmy had encountered seemed to have abandoned the Christian faith in pursuit of their political goals. Love, or agape, was unattainable, Niebuhr contended, in the political sphere. Justice, he argued, was the nearest equivalent, and was therefore the way to apply love to politics and should become its highest value. In Jimmy's copy of *Courage to Change* he heavily underlined, "Justice must be the instrument of love."

Niebuhr also emphasized the need for Christian political involvement as exemplified by his own life. "Theology and politics are not really separate fields," he wrote, "but two perspectives on a single reality, each helping to illumine the data of the other." It reinforced the message Jimmy had heard several years earlier from his own pastor, Bob Harris. Niebuhr also undersocred the tendency for sin, in the form of destructive pride, to appear on every level of human achievement. He accentuated the good that could be achieved through collective humility and the overcoming of pretensions. People sin and ought to be humble, he said, reaffirming the Baptist teachings with which Jimmy was so familiar. Perhaps more important, Niebuhr said, was the inherent danger in the pride of nations, and he warned against American arrogance, calling for "a contrite recognition of our own sins." Collective humility would become an increasingly central theme of Jimmy's later political beliefs, especially in the international arena.

Niebuhr understood the complexities of political life, and emphasized the inevitable tension between idealism and realism. He criticized Woodrow Wilson, whom he admired, for stubbornly adhering to principle in the face of political reality. It was a crucial consideration for Jimmy. As he said on one occasion and alluded to frequently, "We must always combine realism with principle." Critics would accuse him at times of seemingly abandoning his stated moral values in an overeager pursuit of practical political goals. Jimmy saw no contradiction. As Burns Stanfield has written, Jimmy appreciated Niebuhr's remark that "Man is the kind of lion who both kills the lamb and dreams of when the lion and the lamb shall lie down together." Determining the point at which principle must yield to political reality is left to the individual. Detractors argue that this too easily enables one to claim that one is acting out of the highest principle while engaging in politics as usual.

Historian Arthur Schlesinger, himself a friend of Niebuhr's, would later dismiss Carter's interpretation as superficial, saying that Niebuhr would have labeled Jimmy's campaign rhetoric as "the most errant sentimentalism." But this was beside the point. Jimmy did not pretend to be either a theologian or an intellectual. He was not looking to replicate the views of Niebuhr, but rather to take from them whatever would help him to achieve his own perfectability as a Christian. He was seeking the self-knowledge and understanding that would give him inner security and make him a better, more comfortable Christian in the political arena. Among Carter's political predecessors, an ardent Niebuhr adherent was Adlai Stevenson.

Although their impact did not compare with that of Niebuhr, Jimmy, over the years, also read Dietrich Bonhoeffer, Martin Buber, Karl Barth, Hans Küng, Søren Kierkegaard, and Paul Tillich. He has particularly cited his appreciation of Tillich's observation that religion is a permanent search for an ever closer relationship with God and our fellow human beings. Despite Ruth's fascination with Thoreau, Jimmy rejects the notion that he consciously adopted any of his philosophy, although he did read *Walden*. The notion of taking a principled stand regardless of what others may think and paying the consequences, a characteristic he later exhibited, he attributed more to his Baptist heritage than Thoreau. He was, however, very aware of the aggregation of Christian beliefs, Gandhian nonviolence, and Thoreau's call to civil disobedience that underpinned the philosophy of the civil rights movement sweeping the South at the time.

One day in the spring of 1966, Miss Lillian came to the warehouse and announced to Billy, Jimmy, and Rosalynn that she planned to join the Peace Corps. Impressed by the television ads, she was determined to go somewhere where "the people were black." Since returning to Plains from Auburn University, she had managed a successful small nursing home in Blakely, Georgia, but she was bored and found the local community narrow and stultifying. In November, she went to the University of Chicago, where she was trained in Hindi to teach nutrition in a program in India. Then, because Indian prime minister Indira Gandhi wanted some volunteers assigned to a family planning program in Maharashtra, she was switched, requiring that she also learn the Marathi language.

Miss Lillian was sent to the small town of Vikhroli outside of Bombay. She was unprepared for the depth of the poverty, ill health, and malnutrition that confronted her, and her early letters conveyed a sense of her difficulty adjusting. By the end of her tour, however, she had become thoroughly assimilated. Writing to the family on August 15, 1968, shortly before her return, she said:

> I didn't dream that in this remote corner of the world, so far away from the people and the material things that I had always considered so necessary, I would discover what Life is really all about. Sharing yourself with others, and accepting their love for you as the most precious gift of all.
>
> If I had one wish for my children, it would be that each of you would dare do the things and reach for goals in your own lives that have meaning for you as individuals, doing as much as you can for everybody, but not worrying if you don't please everyone.

On her return Miss Lillian was treated as a celebrity by the news media. She was profoundly affected by her tour and would tell Gloria, "If it weren't for leaving home again, I'd spend the rest of my life in India—I'm still torn between this life and my life there."

Early in 1967, Rosalynn found she was pregnant. She had had surgery for a benign uterine tumor, and this enabled her to have the baby for which she and Jimmy had been hoping. Amy Lynn was born on October 19, 1967. Jack, age 20, Chip, age 17, and Jeff, age 15, were waiting with Jimmy as Rosalynn was wheeled out of the delivery room with Amy in her arms. There were tears of joy, especially over the fact that the baby was a girl. The following six months were among the happiest of Rosalynn's life. She worked at home on the warehouse books so that she could devote herself fully to Amy. She also began what would become a lifelong interest in birdwatching.

Jimmy, like his own father, had high expectations of his children. While he did not interfere in their decisions, he found it hard to show sympathy for their difficulties and provide them with psychological support. Rosalynn, who provided much of the emotional nurturing to the boys, described Jimmy's typical attitude, "If he told one of the boys to go to Mr. Tanner's farm and pull in two trailerloads of peanuts, even if the tires blew out and the tractor broke down, that boy wouldn't come back without the peanuts. . . . He was kind and patient, but he let us know that if he had to explain all the details of the job to us, he might just as well do it himself."

When Chip was in the eighth grade he failed his midterm Latin test. According to Chip, "When I got home Dad became very incensed. . . . He spent a week learning it and then tutored me every night and I ended up making a 'B' in the course." However, as Jimmy became increasingly busy with politics, he had less time to focus on his sons' problems.

Jack had, at his father's urging, enrolled as an undergraduate at Georgia Tech, but switched to Emory University, hoping the courses would be less technical. Yet he was still dissatisfied and had considerable difficulty studying. He was disillusioned with politics after his father's defeat and shared many concerns of those opposing the Vietnam war, especially that it was being fought by the poor and minorities while wealthier white boys got student deferments. To his parents' shock he called one morning and announced he was joining the navy. He ended up on a buoy tender off Vietnam.

While bitter resentment still smoldered, integration under federal mandate was slowly proceeding in rural Georgia. The Plains school was integrated in the fall of 1966, when two black children were admitted amid the menacing presence of the state patrol and the local police. However, when Dr. Martin Luther King, Jr., was assassinated in April 1968, a local watering hole gave away free beer. And, in the presidential election that fall, Georgians voted for the independent candidacy of segregationist George Wallace over Democrat Hubert Humphrey and Republican Richard Nixon.

Jimmy's life was now increasingly oriented around the 1970 governor's race. This effort was planned and calculated as a meticulous four-year venture. Planning became the central theme in his life, and later when people would ask him about his profession, he would identify himself as "basically a planner." He intensified his work with the WCGAPDC, in part because it provided a convenient cover for campaigning and building networks throughout the region. During the 1966 campaign, one of his supporters,

Senator Phil Broun, introduced him to Frank Moore, who was running a similar commission covering several counties in northwest Georgia. After the election Jimmy convinced him to move to Americus and become the director of the WCGAPDC. Frank became a loyal friend and participant in Jimmy's campaign planning, even though his primary obligation was to the nonpartisan planning commission.

Jimmy helped to organize a statewide planning society and was elected its first president. He visited communities around the state to help them develop public/private collaboration, improve social services, better exploit natural resources, and increase economic development and social justice. He also became the state chairman for the March of Dimes, giving him further visibility. He had been a member of the Plains Lions Club since the week he returned from the navy. He was elected chairman of the six regional governors for the state. With 180 chapters, most in small communities, Lions now offered him ready-made audiences statewide.

The careful building of his base for the gubernatorial race paralleled the growth in his evangelical activities. His faith offered, in part, an emotional safety net if he should lose the governor's race.

During October 1967, Jimmy and a hundred other laypersons attended a three-day retreat at the Toccoa Baptist Camp in the North Georgia mountains focusing on evangelical missionary work. Six months later he returned for a second retreat sponsored by the Southern Baptist Home Mission Board to discuss Project 500, an outreach program designed to establish 500 new churches and missions. He agreed to join a lay team for ten days and was assigned to a three-man group that would go to Lock Haven, Pennsylvania, a town of 37,000 in the mountainous coal-mining area.

Jimmy arrived at the Marriott Hotel in Atlanta to meet Hoyt Robinson, a dairy farmer from Dahlonega, the only other Georgian on the project. The timing was bad for both of them—Jimmy was committed to giving three speeches that day, and Robinson had just qualified for the state senate. In the end, Robinson drove alone to the orientation meeting in Williamsburg and Jimmy later flew there to join him. Jimmy suggested that he and Robinson be paired with more experienced partners, so Milo Pennington, a peanut farmer and cattle rancher from Elkhart, Texas, and Claude Perry of Plainview, Texas, were assigned by the project director.

On May 27, 1968, the four of them drove to Lock Haven. Each morning they divided up the 100 cards listing prospective members. Then they went out two by two, as Jesus had sent out his disciples, to present the Gospel and discuss the plans for a new Southern Baptist Church. Those who responded positively were invited to come to the YMCA for services at night.

Jimmy's partner was Milo Pennington, who described the experience several years later to W. A. Reed, religious editor of the *Nashville Ten-nesseean,* for a series of articles:

> Jimmy and I would pray as we sat in the automobile before we went into a home. Sometimes he led the prayer and sometimes I did. . . . Jimmy . . . acted all the time like he was on the mountaintop for the Lord. He was never one to talk politics. We were just witnessing for the Lord. We went into ten or fifteen homes each day and we were there ten days and Jimmy and I heard fourteen persons make professions of faith and accept the Lord.

When Jimmy knocked on a door, he said, "I'm a peanut farmer from Georgia." He did not mention his political life. However, Robert and Thelma Farwell observed that his clothes, his manner, and the way he carried himself suggested he was not the average South Georgia farmer. The Farwells invited Jimmy to dinner and Thelma recalled that "He was just like one of the family," and noted his love of Christ "shone on his countenance."

The whole experience had an uplifting effect on Jimmy. He told Hoyt Robinson that the first day had been the greatest of his life. He would later write to the Farwells that their town would always have a "special place" in his life, because it was "where I first experienced in a personal and intense way the presence of the Holy Spirit in my life." In a later interview he would say:

> The whole week was almost a miracle to me. I felt the sense of the presence of God's influence in my life. . . . It was a new sense of release and assurance and peace with myself and a genuine interest in other people that I hadn't experienced before. I felt then and ever since that when I meet each individual person, they are important to me. I found myself able to say, "What can I do to make this person's life even more enjoyable?"—even people I met on an elevator or in a chance encounter in the street. In the past I had a natural inclination to say, "What can I get from them?" Or to wipe them out of my mind. Now it's just a different feeling altogether. It's hard for me to express it.

On the drive back to Atlanta with Hoyt Robinson, Jimmy told him that he now grasped, in a practical way, how his role in politics meshed with the implementation of his religious beliefs—doing what he believed was right to fulfill human needs. The distinction between witnessing for Christ and political campaigning became increasingly narrowed.

Shortly before Thanksgiving 1968, Jimmy received a call from Elias Golonka, an immigrant preacher of Polish origin. Would Jimmy be willing to go for a week's mission to Springfield, Massachusetts? About two dozen men had been chosen for a campaign among Spanish and other foreign-language-speaking minorities. Jimmy had used every opportunity to maintain a degree of fluency in Spanish over the years. Although engaged with his gubernatorial campaign, Jimmy said yes. The ailing Robert Harris had resigned as the pastor of the Plains Baptist Church in June 1977, a resignation hastened, some said, by his proclamation on February 12 of "Race Relations Sunday" when he preached on "The Kingdom Without Clan." His replacement was John Simmons, a stocky, dark-haired navy veteran who differed from Harris in talking much more about soul-saving evangelism. Simmons eagerly volunteered to go to Springfield, as did two other members of the congregation, Jerome Ethridge, an agriculturist at the Georgia Agricultural Experiment Station, and Edwin Timmerman, a minister of music. Hoyt Robinson also agreed to participate.

The project in Springfield represented a new strategy. The Baptist Home Mission had found that seeking to establish large multilingual, multiethnic congregations in the North was not particularly successful. Instead they had decided to try to start a new church for each of the major ethnic groups in a city, holding services and Sunday school classes in the people's own language. This approach, which respected people's sense of ethnic identification as they struggled to assimilate into American culture, impressed Jimmy and would influence his later political thinking.

Jimmy was assigned initially to work with Jose Reyes, a Puerto Rican. Together they had considerable success with the Spanish-speaking community. Later in the week he worked with Eloy Cruz, a tough, muscular, macho-seeming Cuban refugee preacher who planned to move from Brooklyn to start a church in Springfield.

The week started inauspiciously with the community preoccupied by an approaching northwester that brought in cold rainy weather. The reception from the English-speaking community was equally cold with several groups getting doors slammed in their faces. On Thanksgiving morning the four men from Plains decided that they would go door to door in a more affluent Anglo suburb of Springfield. One homeowner called the police, who accused them of soliciting without a license. They were taken to the station house where there was some embarrassment when their legitimacy as Baptist missionaries was revealed. For good measure they left behind copies of the New Testament.

For Jimmy the most important aspect of the week was meeting Eloy Cruz, who impressed Jimmy with his gentle nature and caring for people. Later in his autobiography, Jimmy would recount how he asked Cruz, "How can a man as tough and rugged as you be so sensitive and filled with love?" Embarrassed, Cruz answered, "Our savior had hands that are very gentle, but he cannot do much with a man who is hard." Jimmy went on to say, "Sr. Cruz was one of the best men I have ever known. He had a remarkable ability to reach the hearts of people in a very natural and unassuming way, and quickly convinced them that he loved them and that God loved them. I observed him closely as we spent that inspiring week together." Later, frequently reflecting on the nature of this man, Jimmy would see him as a metaphor for the way he felt government should be: efficiently managed with tough financial discipline and control, but at the same time "with the sensitive and effective service needed to alleviate affliction and to enhance the development and use of capabilities of our most needy citizens."

Others who participated in the mission that week in Springfield were impressed by the depth of Jimmy's sincerity and the impact that the experience obviously had on him. Reverend Peter Miccoli recalled how intensely Jimmy felt the needs of the people they encountered and how tears were in his eyes as he prayed for the Spanish-speaking people. Jimmy recalls frankly, "I was . . . overwhelmed . . . and several times had tears running down my cheeks."

Jimmy's deepening involvement with his faith, intellectually, emotionally, and practically, gave him back a sense of meaning in his life. Increasingly he conceptualized politics as a vehicle for advancing God's kingdom on earth by alleviating human suffering and despair on a scale that infinitely magnified what one individual could do alone. His most frequent prayer was that his life be meaningful in the enhancement of God's will and in the lives of fellow human beings.

If he was to use the governor's office to advance God's work, he had to be elected first. His absolute determination to win became less a troubling matter of egotistical ambition and more a prerequisite for fulfilling the commitment he had made to carry out God's work. Although he would disavow such an interpretation, he would, in practice, tolerate far greater latitude for political expediency in campaigning than in governing.

Jimmy consciously sought to maintain a separation between his evangelical activity and his political campaigning, observers noted that one of his greatest political attributes was an ability to give each individual his undivided attention, looking intensely into their eyes as he shook hands and spoke to them. He never looked around to see who else, particularly those of importance, might be there. It was a powerfully endearing quality, dismissed by cynics as merely the acquired attribute of many a skilled campaigner. But as Jimmy described it, he tried to "truly love" that person for the brief period of their interaction, a direct outgrowth of his evangelical experience.

By the time the gubernatorial race was moving into high gear in 1970, any ambivalence Jimmy may have had about a career in politics had been replaced by a steely determination to succeed. It increasingly manifested itself in an unshakable self-confidence that some criticized as smugness.

Jimmy had evolved for himself a very personal set of religious beliefs.

He had devoted far less time to formulating a coherent political philosophy. To a large degree his religion was his politics. He was not, as one friend noted, a person who particularly understood or identified with "the great social or political movements of the time." His politics were personal and his values and beliefs were enduring, unrelated to changing political circumstances. He would pose a perplexing enigma for analysts and reporters who sought to pigeonhole him according to the traditional categories of liberal, moderate, or conservative. "I try to utilize my own religious beliefs as a constant guide in making decisions as a private or public citizen," he said.

He believed that government should aspire to the noblest ideals, and for Jimmy, that meant those taught by Jesus. As he readily admitted, many decisions in politics and government do not lend themselves to biblical dictates. However, in the often complex and rapidly changing circumstances of public life, he would note, "My faith does not change. It is a stabilizing factor in my life." In the context of the political and social turmoil of the late 1960s in the South this was of particular relevance. As a practical matter, staking out hard political positions, or embracing any particular political ideology under such fluid circumstances, was highly risky and cost many a promising political career in Georgia during that period. Embracing more enduring and unassailable values such as those embodied in Christian teaching was not only safer but also provided a philosophical underpinning from which most political decisions could be derived without the uncertainty of trying to guess the sentiments of the electorate at any given moment. That Jesus was a social revolutionary and a populist who presented a peaceful but brazen challenge to both the Roman rulers and the Jewish elite was something that Jimmy understood and appreciated.

CHAPTER 13

The day after Carter lost the 1966 governor's race he received a call from a man named David Rabhan. Rabhan had provided his private plane to Ellis Arnall during the campaign and had heard Jimmy's stump speech many times. He was so impressed he would have switched allegiances had it not been for his sense of personal loyalty to Arnall. Now he offered his support, his financial backing, and his services as a pilot should Jimmy decide to run again.

By any standard David Rabhan was an unusual man. The same age as Jimmy, he had a shaven head and habitually wore a blue jumpsuit. Born in Savannah to a well-established Jewish family, he was distantly related to Marvin Shoob. Shoob describes the Rabhans as not merely orthodox but the most devout family in Savannah. David went to the University of Georgia where he majored in agriculture and art. He was a gifted artist and a successful farmer of land in Swainsboro, near Savannah, that had been in his family since the 1800s. His real skills, however, lay in business. In his late twenties he started a discount operation. One of his partners, who also owned a nursing home, kept giving him bad checks, so he took part ownership in the nursing home. He soon had several nursing facilities, in addition to his discount venture, a substantial income, and a second home in the Bahamas. Concerned about the elderly people in his care, he went back to the University of Georgia for a master's degree in nutrition. Rabhan took an interest in politics, selectively supporting more liberal candidates. He backed Arnall partly out of personal friendship, but more because of Arnall's progressive record as governor during World War II.

In 1967, David Rabhan was building a nursing home in Cairo about 65 miles south of Plains. After that initial phone call to Carter, he would stop en route to visit with Jimmy and Rosalynn, usually staying with Miss Lillian after her return from India. Gradually he got to know all of the Carters and developed a special relationship with Ruth, visiting her several times in North Carolina. Eventually he put a secretary on the Cairo nursing home payroll whose sole job was to work on the embryonic campaign. Long before Jimmy was a formally announced candidate, Rabhan was flying him around the state to speaking events in his new Cessna 310. Jimmy frequently took the controls and invariably served as the navigator. Rabhan was an intrepid pilot and on several occasions they flew to scheduled events when the weather conditions were below the required standards. It was often a memorably alarming experience for accompanying staff, but Jimmy treated it with equanimity, having the greatest faith in Rabhan's skills and a certain tendency to believe in his own invulnerability.*

By most estimates Rabhan's combined direct and indirect contributions, including the loan of a luxury apartment in the Landmark Tower in Atlanta, would make him by far the largest financial backer of the campaign. Although such largesse was entirely within the law at the time, worried about Rabhan's eccentric image, Kirbo expressed concern to him about how the scale of his support might be perceived. Rabhan was unmoved and kept no account of what he gave.

During the long hours of flying together, Jimmy and David Rabhan developed a strong personal bond. Rabhan was one of the few people in the campaign who felt free to address him as an equal, and he had a frank irreverence in saying bluntly whatever was on his mind. They shared many characteristics. Both men were soft-spoken and unassuming on the surface, but were tough as nails at their core. Both had a populist, anti-establishment view of politics and a belief that achieving social justice was the primary rationale for political involvement. Although his deepest values had been profoundly shaped by his orthodox background, as he became more sophisticated Rabhan had, unlike Jimmy, rejected the more simplistic and hypocritical aspects of organized religion. He was one of the few people who ever said to Jimmy, "I do not know how an educated person like you can believe all that stuff."

In particular, Rabhan questioned the seeming hypocrisy of Jimmy's loyalty to the Southern Baptist faith, which he saw as a bulwark of segregation. They rarely argued. Jimmy, when he disagreed, just sat listening to Rabhan's comments without responding. Chip says that Rabhan "packed his [father's] head with liberal ideas." Actually their beliefs were similar, but they differed in their approach; Jimmy believed in evolutionary change and remaining close enough to the mainstream to build bridges. Rabhan was a gadfly and was less concerned with what others believed. Nevertheless, the two men had a strong rapport. What to others were Rabhan's strange eccentricities, Jimmy found endearing and stimulating qualities.

On one occasion at age 11, Rabhan and his father passed the body of a black man draped over a barbed-wire fence. Later he heard the man had

---

*The elements never deterred Rabhan. During the 1966 campaign he flew at night through a thunderstorm to drop off Ellis Arnall near his home in Newnan. The experience so unnerved Arnall that he refused ever to fly with Rabhan again and the plane was used subsequently only to fly campaign workers.

been "lynched." Whether actually lynched, or just killed by whites, the experience had a searing emotional impact on David Rabhan. As he reached maturity he not only made a point of treating blacks as equals, he went out of his way to work with black leaders around the state. He was never publicly outspoken on the issue, but pursued his beliefs in his own somewhat unorthodox style.

At the time he began flying Carter around the state, Rabhan had an office in the complex next to the Ebenezer Baptist Church on Auburn Avenue in Atlanta. The pastor was Martin Luther King, Sr. ("Daddy" King). Like many established leaders of Atlanta's black community, he was a Republican, as their families had been since emancipation. Their endorsement had given them standing with Republicans nationally, but with the Goldwater revolution they were in an anomalous position, as the attraction to the party of Lincoln began to turn sour.

Younger black leaders were lining up behind Carl Sanders, already the runaway leader for the 1970 gubernatorial race, who had been relatively progressive on racial issues during his earlier term. However, his main attraction was that he looked like a sure winner and they believed their best interests would be served by an early commitment. Rabhan urged them to consider Jimmy Carter instead.

Rabhan pressed "Daddy" King to meet with Jimmy. "I'm not going to him. He has to come to me," King responded. Carter quickly accepted, becoming the first white candidate running statewide to visit the Ebenezer Baptist Church. It was a risky move in 1969 with little short-term political advantage. Martin Luther King, Jr., assassinated only a year earlier, was still reviled by the majority of white voters in the state. "Daddy" King gave his support, although he remained skeptical about Carter's chances.

Not since Tom Watson, had a white Georgia politician so actively sought black support. As Jimmy says, "David Rabhan knew every influential black preacher in Atlanta and a lot of other places in the state. . . . Cameron Alexander, for instance, said if you want my people to vote for you, come to church. I went to his church and I would give a Baptist sermon." In addition to Cameron Alexander, one of his most active supporters in the black community was the Reverend Fred Bennett, who worked long and hard to secure the black electorate for Carter.

Some observers would consider Carter's decision a shrewd calculation—that the number of whites offended would be smaller than the number of black votes he would attract. Also to beat Sanders, he had to win a significant segment of the black vote. However, Carter was driven far more by a sense of moral imperative than by political expediency. In 1966, during a period of greater racial tension, Carter had openly sought out black voters with even less regard for his overall political welfare.

It was part of the paradox of the time that Carl Sanders was viewed as the more liberal candidate. As governor, he had avoided racist rhetoric, and unlike several other southern governors of the early sixties, he was committed to keeping the public schools open. He kept a tight rein on the legislature to prevent the passage of inflammatory anti-integration laws. When they voted to invite George Wallace to address the body, Sanders vetoed the invitation and prevented Wallace from coming to Atlanta. On the other hand, he convinced President Kennedy to cancel a speech at Georgia Tech because he thought the association with Kennedy might hurt him politically. Yet at the Southern Governors Conference in August 1963, he led the efforts to block a resolution sponsored by George Wallace censuring Kennedy for his integrationist policies.

But his positions were politically determined and he had little empathy for the plight of the black population. His affluent lifestyle afforded infrequent contact with blacks who were not servants or other menial workers. As governor, he showed scant interest in advancing blacks in state government and he seemed uncomfortable campaigning in black communities. Sanders testified before the Senate Commerce Committee against the "public accommodations" section of the 1964 Civil Rights Act. When Charlayne Hunter (later Charlayne Hunter Gault) went to Cleveland shortly after graduation from the University of Georgia to marry Walter Stovall, a white college classmate, Sanders called the marriage a "disgrace" and a "shame." His attorney general threatened to prosecute her under Georgia's anti-miscegenation law if she ever returned to the state, and there was discussion of revoking her diploma.

The period between the start of 1966 and the end of 1970 was one of racially contradictory signals in the South. Despite his relatively progressive public positions, Carl Sanders ended his term at the start of 1967 as a very popular figure. Many people interpreted this to mean that the integration issue was behind them and that the people of Georgia were prepared to move forward, especially economically. The election of Lester Maddox refuted this notion. He sustained his own substantial popularity by rekindling racist sentiment and support for resistance to federal integration laws. In a throwback to the Talmadge rhetoric of the 1930s, he labeled integration as "un-American, un-Godly, and even criminal," a view that made him immensely popular with much of the rural white population. In the 1968 presidential race, George Wallace, backed by Maddox, handily won Georgia with his diehard segregationist message, although nationwide Wallace received only 13.5 percent of the vote.

Unable by law to succeed himself as governor in 1966, Wallace had orchestrated the election of his wife Lurleen, but she died of cancer in office and was succeeded by Lt. Governor Albert Brewer. Although hand-picked by Wallace, Brewer proved to be considerably more progressive than his mentor, and yet was popular with most Alabamans. When he announced that he would run for a full term in his own right, most people thought he would win reelection handily. The conventional wisdom held that Wallace would not run against his protégé and that, in any case, his racist message was passé and he would be defeated. But on June 3, 1970, George Wallace scored a stunning upset against Governor Brewer in the Democratic primary. Shaken, Brewer, whose popularity had been based on his ability to lead the state beyond segregation, said, "It was nigger, nigger, nigger all over again."

The Wallace victory cast a long dark shadow over the Georgia governor's race. Overnight Sanders's progressive credentials began to look like a liability. One prominent Georgia politician said in the *Atlanta Constitution,* the day after Wallace won, "There is only one issue and you spell it NIGGER."

Although Sanders was more conservative than his public image suggested, it was hard to remake people's perceptions. Carter was considerably more liberal on race, yet it was clear that only a more conservative candidate could defeat Sanders. The big advantage Carter enjoyed was that, while Carl Sanders's record on the issues was well known, Carter's positions were not. He had come out of the 1966 race having taken very few hard positions. Apart from Sumter County, he had a clean canvas on which to paint for the Georgia electorate whatever picture of himself he wished. This was true in spite of having traveled around the state since 1966 talking to groups and building a base of support.

In 1968 he had scribbled down his thoughts about Sanders's perceived liberal bent on a yellow legal pad, ending with, "Some of these are conflicting, but right now we just need to collect all the rough ideas we can. Later we can start driving a wedge between me and him." Driving the wedge would be the core of the campaign.

At Kirbo's suggestion, Jimmy hired Washington pollster William Hamilton, who between September 1969 and October 1970 would conduct five statewide surveys. The first of these revealed that 84 percent of voters had a favorable view of Sanders, and 20 percent rated his performance "excellent" during his first term as governor. It was, Hamilton noted, "one of the best job ratings I have ever seen given a former governor after three years out of office." If the election were held at that point, Sanders would have gotten 53 percent, Carter just 21 percent.

There were other candidates in the race: Dr. McKee Hargrett, a conservative osteopathic physician; Linda Jenness, a Socialist Workers Party candidate; Jan Cox, an attractive bearded young man without name recognition; J. B. Stoner, an attorney and avowed racist from Savannah; and most importantly black attorney C. B. King from Albany. King, one of only three black attorneys in the state outside Atlanta, had played a prominent role in the Albany Movement in 1962 (a coalition of the NAACP Youth Council, SNCC, and the Southern Christian Leadership Conference). Although highly respected, blacks were divided over whether to support him. Recognizing that he could not win, most of the more conservative black leaders felt a pragmatic need to support Sanders.

Jimmy chose as his campaign chairman his cousin Hugh, who had succeeded him as the state senator from the Fourteenth District and was not known for having liberal sympathies. Hugh had also established important friendships at the statehouse with some of his more conservative fellow senators, although most established Democrats in the state had close ties to Sanders dating from his first term as governor, or before. Brooks Pennington supported Sanders out of loyalty and pragmatism. He also felt that Jimmy, by running, was showing a considerable degree of ingratitude for Sanders's help during the disputed Senate race. Neither could Marvin Shoob betray his lengthy friendship with Sanders, although Janice was again an ardent Carter campaign worker.

Hamilton Jordan had left after the 1966 defeat to join the International Voluntary Service and was sent as a civilian community worker to Vietnam. While there he exchanged occasional letters with Carter. After a few months he was evacuated because of a medical condition involving severe enlargement of lymph nodes in his neck. After several months back in Albany he recovered and in mid-1968 he started going to Plains to help with the rapidly growing volume of campaign mail. He and a secretary, Sara Lee, were the campaign staff. During that period he talked with Carter about the futility of running for governor and suggested that he think about lieutenant governor or agriculture commissioner, but Carter was adamant.

However, over the months Jordan demonstrated a growing political astuteness and eventually would be named campaign manager. With Hugh Carter he put together a grassroots organization in every county in the state. Hugh had a successful business raising and selling worms to fishermen all over the Southeast, and the campaign shared the office of the worm business. Twenty-five years old, affable, rotund, and self-deprecating, Jordan was well liked. He not only lacked the polish that Carter had acquired but pointedly eschewed any inclinations in that direction. Also, he was a self-described "late bloomer" on the race issue after having actively opposed the integrationist efforts of the Albany Movement in his hometown. Both Jordan and Hugh Carter were assets in gaining the confidence of the rural white vote upon which the success of the campaign depended.

Carter, who wanted to be simultaneously above and a part of politics, saw it only as a means to an end. Jordan offered a perfect match. He enjoyed politics and had little compunction about doing what was necessary to win—those things that Carter found so antithetical to his self-concept.

Jody Powell was born in Vienna, 25 miles northeast of Plains, and the home of the state's longtime U.S. Senator Walter George. Jody's father, Joe Powell, farmed 500 acres of peanuts and cotton. His mother, June, was a high school civics teacher. Bright and ambitious, but with limited family resources, Jody had successfully sought admission to the Air Force Academy. However, one semester from graduation, he was expelled over a minor honor code infraction. It was difficult and humiliating to return at Christmastime 1964 to a region where honorable military service was highly revered. He finished his undergraduate degree at Georgia State University in Atlanta and soon started a graduate course in political science at Emory. Writing a paper on George Wallace and southern populism, Jody talked to Senator Hugh Carter, who convinced him that Jimmy embodied many of the characteristics he admired in Wallace and could win the governor's race. He drove to Plains and offered his services.

Jody was hired to serve as driver and personal assistant to the candidate, performing essentially the role that John Girardeau had in 1966. He had only his thesis to complete to get his Ph.D., but decided to wait. Jody, twenty-six, blond, good-looking, and more urbane than Hamilton Jordan, would increasingly become Jimmy's alter ego. The similarity of their backgrounds made them naturally compatible, and their analysis of politics was remarkably similar. However, while they were both churchgoing Baptists, Jody's faith was less a factor in the way he viewed the world. The Civil War was the defining factor in his view of southern politics while Carter almost never mentioned it. Carter was charming and fundamentally shy; Jody was pugnacious often to the point of offense.

Over the years many who met Carter thought his smiling, open, warm approach to them invited a closer relationship. Mistaking friendliness for friendship, they were stunned, and often hurt, when they encountered an iron barrier as they tried to cross some unseen and unspoken threshold. Despite an ever-growing army of devoted followers, he would hold them all emotionally at arm's length. Jody crossed that barrier with greater success than anyone else in Jimmy's inner political circle. It resulted in fanatic loyalty and ferocious attacks on those, especially in the press, who he felt had unfairly criticized Carter. He would also come to guard jealously and ruthlessly the relationship against anyone he felt might be encroaching on his territory.

Charles Kirbo, David Gambrell, Philip Alston, Bob Lipshutz, and Bill Gunter continued to raise money and serve as senior advisors. State Senator Ford Spinks, who had encouraged him to run in 1966, Senator Lamar Plunkett, and 1966 veterans Beverly Langford, now himself a senator, and his wife, Edna, out of personal devotion nurtured the vital statewide network. Lamar Plunkett's daughter-in-law, Connie, an attractive strong-willed woman, would coordinate the western part of the state. Cecil McCall from Americus, became the campaign treasurer.

Carter was finally able to get the meeting that had eluded him in 1966 with Mills Lane, the wealthy president of the Citizens' and Southern Bank. Carter made his pitch for support, following which Lane rose and said, "Mr. Carter, it's an interesting world." He then left the room. It was only when he did not return that Jimmy uncomfortably realized the meeting was over. The experience only served to deepen the dubious view Carter already had of bankers and the corporate world.

In Atlanta, a young lawyer, Stuart Eizenstat, volunteered his part-time services, writing issues papers. Son of an Atlanta shoe wholesaler, a graduate of Grady High School and Harvard law school, Eizenstat had worked briefly as a researcher on the staff of President Lyndon Johnson. Subsequently he coordinated candidate research in Hubert Humphrey's 1968 presidential campaign. Early in 1970, at age 27, he sought out candidate Carter and after a lengthy discussion Jimmy asked for his help. Introverted, almost monkish, Eizenstat was in nearly every respect the antithesis of the South Georgians around Carter. Well connected in the Jewish community and with a political perspective that went beyond Georgia, he was the first person to begin inserting serious analysis of issues into the campaign. James Clotfelter, a political scientist on the Emory faculty, who would later write with considerable insight about this period in Georgia politics, also helped to shape the issues for the campaign.

Another Harvard-trained lawyer involved with the campaign was Jack Watson. Born in Arkansas, he had come to Georgia in 1966 to join King and Spalding, Kirbo's law firm. A Kirbo protégé, Watson had gone to Plains late that summer and spent a Saturday walking and talking with Jimmy, in the fields around Plains, in the warehouse, and at his home. Over the next three years when Carter was passing through Atlanta on his way to a speaking engagement he would often call Jack. Jack's reaction to Carter was similar to that of many: "I was fascinated with him, with his intellect, with his voracious appetite for reading and learning . . . by his singleness of purpose. There were many things about him that utterly intrigued me."

Jack Watson also knew Carl Sanders, with whom he frequently played handball at the YMCA in Atlanta. In early 1970 Sanders asked Jack if he would be willing to be filmed with him for a campaign commercial. Flattered, but embarrassed, Jack was forced to tell Sanders that he was supporting Jimmy Carter.

Like Watson and Eizenstat, Paul and Carol Muldawer were part of the growing group of young moderate Atlanta professionals attracted to Carter. The Muldawers held a biracial fund-raiser at their house in November

1969—an event that would have been almost inconceivable anywhere outside Atlanta. That evening Carter met for the first time the Reverend Andrew Young and Vernon Jordan, an Atlanta native, who was expected to announce his candidacy for the Fifth Congressional District seat. Jordan did not announce, and ultimately Young entered the race. Carter campaigned with him, and although Young lost, he would win the seat in 1972, becoming the first black congressman from the South since Reconstruction.

Speeches Carter made to rural audiences, reported in the newspapers, periodically caused serious misgivings among his liberal Atlanta backers. He needed frequently to attend events in Atlanta where he was able to shore up that support by his persuasive one-to-one contact. As then senator Max Cleland remembered, "He could charm the scales off a snake." It required considerable skill to hold together, by sheer force of personality, a constituency that extended from liberals to segregationists.

Charles Hamilton's polling had shown that despite his massive lead, between 20 and 25 percent of Carl Sanders's support was "soft." He had weaknesses. He was arrogant and aloof, an image that was compounded by his campaign slogan, "Carl Sanders ought to be governor again." One of the former governor's closest supporters says of him, "Sanders was a cold person . . . as he became governor he became even more distant and impersonal in his relationships. Carter was just the opposite, a very warm and caring person. . . . Sanders antagonized an awful lot of people with his attitude." His regal air angered even the establishment of the Georgia Democratic Party, the bedrock of his support. According to Carter,

> Sanders had alienated . . . particularly the supporters of Dick Russell. Russell was a patriarch, almost worshipped in the state political system, removed from Georgia because he had become a national figure. When Russell had made his previous reelection announcement, Sanders made it very clear that he was going to run against Russell. And it really hurt Senator Russell and it made his fervent supporters furious. . . . A lot of them came to me and said, "We will give you help." So I capitalized on that.

The Russell supporters were mostly older Talmadge-era veterans. Supplanted and antagonized by the younger reformist progressives associated with Carl Sanders, they naturally gravitated to Carter, giving the Carter campaign a more conservative cast.

One of Charles Hamilton's early polls showed that 81 percent of the Georgia electorate felt alienated from government. They were also concerned about high taxes and welfare. In April 1970, 54 percent felt integration was moving too fast. As Clotfelter and Hamilton would later write, describing the "new populism" of that era, "More important . . . than specific issues was the selling of populist symbols. The common ingredient was voters believing the candidate cared about what they cared about, that he was one of their own and would not forget them." The fine line that Carter sought to walk was to use those symbols to make ordinary rural and urban-blue-collar-worker voters believe he shared their views and values by mentioning the race issue. "These are my folks. . . . I convinced the average working man and woman that I was their friend, that if I was elected, I would understand their problems." Carter said this convincingly because it was exactly how he felt. In a later interview he would say, "One of the standard speeches I made . . . that Georgia people are conservative, but their conservatism does not mean racism . . . that we hide our heads in the sand and refuse to recognize that changes are inevitable in a fast and technological society . . . that we are callous or unconcerned about our fellow man . . . Georgians are conservative. So am I." To the contention of some, including close supporters, that he ran a campaign covertly appealing to racists, he would state vehemently, "No one ever heard me say any word that could be interpreted as racist."

Rafshoon, who had transformed political advertising in Georgia, continued to excel over his competition. Early in the campaign the peanut emerged as Carter's symbol. Supporters wore gold peanuts in their lapels and women had peanut necklaces. It was a way to affiliate himself with the rural electorate. Rafshoon set out to "drive the wedge" between the candidates that Carter had referred to in his 1968 notes. He designed a media campaign that reflected a deft understanding both of Jimmy Carter and the political mood in the state. It was aimed at drawing the starkest counterpoint between the two candidates, relying almost entirely on image and symbolism, while ignoring any differences on issues. One commercial showed Jimmy harvesting peanuts on his farm, while the voiceover said,

> Jimmy Carter knows what it's like to work for a living. He still puts in twelve hours a day in his shirt sleeves on the farm at Plains during the peanut harvest. . . . Can you imagine any of the other candidates for governor working in the hot August sun? No wonder Jimmy Carter has a special understanding of the problems facing everyone who works for a living. . . . Isn't it time someone spoke up for you.

A parallel commercial opened showing an elegant but tightly closed door while a voice said, "This is the door to an exclusive country club, where big-money boys play cards, drink cocktails, and raise money for their candidate, Carl Sanders." The doors swing open and the camera zooms in on a well-manicured hand, French cuffs and elegant cufflinks, writing a check while the voice says, "People like us aren't invited. We're too busy working for a living." The scene changes to show Jimmy Carter talking to an "ordinary working person" while the voiceover says, "That's why our votes are going for Jimmy Carter. Vote for Jimmy Carter, our kind of man, our kind of governor." Use of the phrase "our kind of man" was not by chance; it was the slogan that had described George Wallace in his gubernatorial campaign. It instantaneously linked Carter to Wallace.

"Cufflinks Carl" became the label the Carter campaign tried to hang around Sanders's neck. It had been first applied to him by a Republican, and in a speech on June 8, 1970, Sanders had used it in referring to himself. Twenty years later Sanders would concede the success of Jimmy's strategy.

> He pictured me as a corporate lawyer in Atlanta who had capitalized on being governor and who was now representing the fat cats and he was out there representing the average citizen. That's a pretty hard thing to overcome.

The whole strategy had a visceral appeal to Carter—the outsider battling the establishment and especially the rich. In a way it was a comfortable recapitulation of the way he had felt about running against Bo Callaway.

Carter formally announced his entry into the 1970 race on Friday, April 3. Carrying two-year-old Amy in his arms and followed by Rosalynn, he strode into the Supreme Court room in the State Capitol packed to overflowing with his supporters. In his statement he called for building a better school system and for obeying school desegregation laws. He spoke against inequities in the tax system and said he would veto any increase in the sales tax as regressive.

He also fired the opening salvo in what would be the pivotal battle of the campaign—the effort to undermine the credibility of Carl Sanders. "Georgians never again want a governor who will use the tremendous power and prestige of the office for his own personal wealth." He repeatedly returned to the theme that Carl Sanders had "used secret information to get rich." Campaigning at a bank, Jimmy peered into the vault and quipped in the presence of reporters, "Looks like Carl Sanders's basement." In a television program on May 8 he charged that Sanders had used his connections with the Johnson administration to influence the granting of TV licenses, that since his term as governor he had been receiving large retainers from major businesses, and that he had bought property knowing in advance that highway construction would appreciate its value. He announced that he would release a complete financial statement within a few days; Sanders could only complain that his finances were not a part of the campaign. On June 18 at the Atlanta Press Club, Carter released his records showing assets of $455,000.

The attacks on Sanders continued almost daily. On June 28, at a meeting of the Georgia Press Association, Carter asserted that Sanders was more interested in Richard Russell's Senate seat than a second term as governor.

Using information developed by press secretary Bill Pope, he also claimed that the registration number of Sanders's private plane was out of the usual registration sequence, and applied somewhat tortuous reasoning to suggest that it represented a veiled message of Sanders's ambition. The story received wide coverage, reinforcing the image of Sanders as a wealthy man and reminding Russell loyalists that he clearly coveted their man's Senate seat. Perhaps most out of character was Carter's statement explaining the bitterness of his attacks. He blamed Sanders and the then Democratic Party chairman, J. B. Fuqua, for his loss in 1966, saying that they had not only failed to support him but even urged him not to get into the race. "If they had supported me . . . I would have been elected," he insisted. Personalizing the issue did not show good judgment by Carter.

Carter also criticized Sanders for having been too close to the national Democrats in Washington. With an eye to a possible presidential appointment, Sanders had sought to foster a close relationship with the Johnson administration. Even though he himself had voted for Humphrey, Carter criticized Sanders for his support of the national Democratic ticket in the 1968 presidential race, implying that he should have supported Wallace. The explicit message to the electorate was that Sanders had been more interested in promoting his national ambitions than in the people of Georgia; implicitly it linked him to the integrationist policies of the national Democrats.

During the last few weeks of the campaign Carter promised "proof" of his accusations that Sanders had used the governor's office to enrich himself and his friends. On August 26, Carter presented to the press his "proof package." It included minutes of a board of directors meeting of the Willingham Finance Company held on June 15, 1964, attended by then-Governor Sanders, at which the president of the company, J. B. Fuqua, had been authorized to buy the assets and the license of WROZ Radio Station in Evansville, Indiana. Copies of documents filed with the FCC were provided that supposedly showed Sanders had used his influence to get approval. Other material indicated that Jones and Fellers, architects identified as Sanders's "political cronies," had received $1,282,853 in fees from the state in 1966—"a major percentage of all fees by the state to architects." Further documents showed that at the beginning of the Sanders administration, the state had shifted deposits to the Georgia Railroad Bank—which Carter claimed was because it made loans to Sanders's friend, J. B. Fuqua.

The heavily hyped "proof" proved a major letdown. There was no evidence that Sanders either owned stock in or benefitted financially from the success of the Willingham Finance Company. Carter was forced to admit that he had no evidence of illegality, but insisted that the package showed a "consistent pattern of combining political and business interests on behalf of Mr. Sanders."

The *Macon Telegraph* accused Carter of having "overpromised and underdelivered." The *Macon News* described Carter as "a classic example of a good man whose high standards have been undermined by political ambition."

Carter's critics have accused him of being disingenuous and of running a campaign against Sanders that was essentially groundless and vicious, even by southern political standards. Nearly twenty-five years later Carter would say that he had no regrets about the way he conducted the 1970 campaign. "I never criticized the job Sanders did as governor; in fact, I felt he was a very good governor." Technically that was true. Sanders remains bitter and resentful about Carter's tactics.

Of more enduring controversy was the manner in which the campaign sought to attract the Wallace/Maddox voters. Early in the campaign Carter criticized Sanders for refusing to allow George Wallace to address the state legislature, and even for seeking to prevent him from addressing private groups. Carter had complained,

> I was a member of the Georgia Seedmen's Association. We rented a National Guard Armory and asked Governor Wallace to address us. At the last minute, Governor Sanders sent us word that he would not allow Governor Wallace to speak on Georgia state property. I don't think it is right for Governor Sanders to try to please a group of ultra-liberals, particularly those in Washington, when it means stifling communications with another state.

Carter pledged repeatedly during the campaign that as governor he would invite Wallace to Georgia to redress the slight that had been done.

Following a press conference on June 10, Bill Shipp would write the next day in the *Atlanta Constitution*.

> And another sheet of paper was being quietly and anonymously passed around. It was a copy of a newspaper photo showing a Negro basketball player pouring champagne over Carl Sanders's head.
>
> In the context of the sports pages, it was a routine shot. One of the team's owners [Sanders] was being given a traditional champagne dunking by a victorious player. But in the context of this political campaign it was a dangerous smear that injected both race, alcohol, and high living into the campaign . . . this smear was being mailed to every preacher, police chief, sheriff and [white] barbershop in the state.

Several sources indicate that Bill Pope was responsible for preparing the leaflets and Hamilton Jordan directed their mailing. Dorothy Wood, a former vice president of Rafshoon's advertising firm, recalled seeing the pamphlets stacked in boxes of several hundred in the office. Jordan and Pope deny any involvement, as does Rafshoon, stating that because his company's offices were adjacent to part of the campaign operation, material was stacked everywhere regardless of its origin. Bill Abernathy, another vice president at the time, later suggested the agency did play a role in what Carter campaign workers would come to refer to as the "stink tank" operation. Bill Shipp described riding in a rural part of the state with Bill Pope, who Shiff says insisted on stopping at a Ku Klux Klan rally so that he could distribute the leaflets.

The Carter campaign also created the "Black Concern Committee" that prepared pamphlets mailed statewide to black barbershops, pool halls, churches, and funeral homes accusing Sanders of having not kept promises made to black voters in his 1962 campaign. It included cartoons linking Sanders to the death of a black prison inmate in Putnam County in 1966, which Carl Pederson, an artist with the Rafshoon Agency, said he drew. At the same time, to pry black votes away from Sanders, Abernathy claimed that under Rafshoon's direction he prepared and paid for radio spots for C. B. King.

On June 14, the *Atlanta Constitution* reported that Carter denied any knowledge either of the leaflet picturing Carl Sanders or the mailing from the fictitious "Black Concern Committee," saying that what was important was to adhere to the issues in the campaign. There is nothing in the record to suggest that Carter was aware of what Bill Pope, Hamilton Jordan, and others were doing. Indeed, during this period he was engaged in frenetic campaigning that left him little or no time to be concerned with what was happening at the campaign headquarters in Atlanta. Bill Pope would later tell the *Washington Post* that he had run a "nigger campaign" for Carter and Rafshoon. Conley Ingram, a Carter friend, who ran the campaign in Cobb County and subsequently became a Georgia Supreme Court judge, would say twenty years later that he still associated Bill Pope's name with "suspicion, mistrust, and fear." Effecting a South Georgia accent and humorously mimicking his campaign colleagues, Rafshoon would say, "We coulda won by a lot more if we'd bin able to stop Jimmah saying so many nahs things abaht nigguhs."

While public attention was focused primarily on the battle with Sanders, the methodical organizing of the state was the real key to victory. It had been a four-year campaign in which Jimmy and increasingly self-confident Rosalynn had used every opportunity to travel the state, meeting, talking to, and recruiting support from a broad range of voters, especially those in the middle- and low-income brackets. He says of the campaign,

> I think Sanders was caught by surprise, because I had a meticulously developed campaign organization—all 159 counties—no one had ever done

this before. And Rosalynn and I figured conservatively that we shook hands with 600,000 people . . . and we visited 600 cities and towns in Georgia. So that was the basis on which I predicated my success.

His greatest assets were his charm and his willingness to listen. He won over many with differing views, because they assumed his ability to listen meant he agreed with their position. He hated to lose anyone's support, so often he would add qualifiers to his positions to assuage any doubts they might have. This enabled supporters to take what he had said and interpret it to fit whatever they believed. It also reflected his urge for conciliation even with people with whom he fundamentally disagreed.

Critics would later accuse Carter of tailoring his positions to fit his audiences in various parts of the state. Usually the story was more complex. White-only private academies were springing up all over the state in response to the integration of public schools. Early in the campaign Jimmy said that he was "opposed to putting a single dime of taxpayers' money in private schools." Through Charles Kirbo, a group of people came to him who represented private schools that had been started for nonracial reasons. After visiting one such school, he told a rally late in the campaign, in Fittin, Georgia, "Don't let anybody, including the Atlanta newspapers, mislead you into criticizing private education." In his own mind he was stating two not incompatible positions. To his critics it was a craven attempt to have it both ways.

Carter understood that good people could be prisoners of their history, culture, and background, causing them to do bad things that did not reflect their entire character. His religion taught him also that opposition to evil acts must be separated from feelings against the people who happen to be doing the evil. He believed that poor whites were as much the victims of segregation as poor blacks, that forgiveness and reconciliation was the only way forward. He would later say that if he had attacked white southerners for the sins of racism he would not have received 10 percent of the vote. "The point I am making," he said, "is that the South, including Georgia, has moved forward primarily because it hasn't been put in the position of having to renounce itself. You've got to give people credit for the progress they make and the change in their attitudes." In his future career dealing with parties in conflict he always carried this lesson with him. Trust could only be built if you did not ask people to repudiate themselves, but once you had their trust you could often lead even the most recalcitrant to accommodation.

He did not win everyone's support. On one occasion while campaigning at a shopping center in an Atlanta suburb he was hit by a full right hook to the jaw that sent him reeling to the ground. His assailant was a former marine with a history of psychiatric problems. Later Carter went unannounced to the state mental hospital in Milledgeville to visit the man and offer his forgiveness.

Carter also failed to win the support of the Atlanta newspapers. Reg Murphy, editor of the *Atlanta Constitution,* had harbored an antipathy toward Carter since they first met during the 1963 legislative session. "I used to dread to see Jimmy Carter coming down the hall," Murphy says, "because he was going to tell me about some comma or fault in the newspaper—some little nitpicking thing, instead of dealing with what I considered to be the important thing, whether we were getting mainly the tempo of issues right. We just never got along." Murphy saw Carter as self-righteous, ambitious, and ruthless. He was, however, a close friend of Carl Sanders. Carter says,

> Reg Murphy was fanatic in support of Carl Sanders. And he abandoned, in my opinion, all rationality. And as I became stronger and stronger . . . Murphy assumed that I was a peanut farmer from Americus, Georgia, which was a hotbed of John Birchers, and that I was a racist. So his theme in the *Atlanta Constitution* was you've got this nice clean, enlightened, successful, experienced former governor who's willing to serve our state again and you've got this red-neck, racist, ignorant bumpkin who's unsuccessful and all he does is grow peanuts, running against him.

Carter repeatedly attacked the Atlanta newspapers and on June 27 wrote a letter to the editors of the *Constitution* accusing them of pro-Sanders bias, implying it was because the son of the president of the Atlanta Newspapers Inc., Jack Tarver, Jr., was Sanders's law partner. They did not publish it. Carter then used the annual convention of the Georgia Press Association, at which all the candidates were invited to speak, to read the letter. "It was my worst mistake . . . and counterproductive," he admits. However, he adds that outside Atlanta, "It was not totally a negative because a lot of people saw the *Atlanta Constitution*'s endorsement as a negative factor."

Already by June 16, Bill Shipp reported that Carter's attacks on Sanders were paying off. More than 50 percent of people now believed Sanders had personally benefitted from his term as governor. Now money began to flow more freely. J. Paul Austin, chairman of the Coca-Cola company, contributed $4,000 and other senior executives in the corporation gave lesser amounts. The president of Delta Airlines gave $4,995. During the general election Ann Cox Chambers, chairman of the board of the Cox Broadcasting Company, and her husband, Robert, made the largest contribution of $26,500 even though the Cox newspapers owned the *Atlanta Constitution* and *Atlanta Journal.*

On election night, September 9, Carter supporters gathered at the Quality Inn on Tenth Street in Atlanta. At 11:15 P.M. Carter appeared raising his hand in a V for victory sign. The final tally showed Carter with

388,280 votes, or 48.6 percent, and Sanders with 301,179, or 37.7 percent. The *Atlanta Journal* described it as the most stunning upset in years. Carter missed avoiding a runoff by less than 10,000 votes. He carried 135 counties to Sanders's 23. He won significantly with all segments of the white vote, but received only 5 percent of the black vote. C. B. King came in third with 70,424 votes.

Suddenly Carter found himself the favored candidate. Sanders, betrayed by his overconfidence, became the candidate on the attack. He referred to Carter as a "slaver" (referring to his slave-owning ancestors), a slum landlord (the shacks he had owned and rented in his youth), and, most curiously, as an atheist because of his insistence on the adoption of the First Amendment's wording regarding separation of church and state in the new Georgia constitution. He accused Carter of being a liar and a hypocrite. "The last time Carter worked in the fields in the hot August sun was when his slick advertising agency took the pictures you see on television every day," he sneered.

Sanders eagerly sought a televised debate with Carter, who deftly side-stepped the issue, first saying he did not have the time available, and later, "I don't think in his present frame of mind it would be right to engage in a personal name-calling exercise on television." Sanders appeared anyway with an empty chair for Carter. The absent Carter came out the victor when he was quoted as saying, "Some folks say the chair was ahead."

The race issue remained persistently present. Sanders labeled Carter an ultraliberal, trying to pass himself off as a hardworking farmer yet at the same time exploiting blacks who worked for him. Carter responded by inviting the press to Plains. The *Atlanta Journal* sent a team of reporters, as did the Sanders campaign, although they did not help their candidate's cause when they arrived in a limousine. The newspapers' judgment was that the Carters were fair landlords and bosses, certainly no worse than other rural businesses.

Sanders again raised the issue of the Carter campaign having paid for radio spots for C. B. King to siphon off black votes and accused him of getting high-profile black activist Hosea Williams, of the Southern Christian Leadership Conference (SCLC) to attend a fund-raiser for Sanders in order to create a backlash. Sanders's workers distributed leaflets showing Carter with Hosea Williams. Carter campaigners printed leaflets reproducing an article in which Sanders had paid tribute to Martin Luther King, Jr. (a seemingly hypocritical act given Carter's relationship with King's father, but of which they were unaware). C. B. King, who had accused both Sanders and Carter of running racist campaigns, declined to endorse either one. However, on the last weekend of the campaign, Carter encountered him at the Daugherty County Fair in Albany and they had a warm exchange. When asked for his comments, Carter replied that while he would appreciate them, "I can win this election without a single black vote."

The following day, a week before the runoff, he met with Roy Harris, the former chairman of Georgia's White Citizens Council, the Georgia director of Wallace's 1968 presidential campaign, and editor of the racist *Augusta Courier*. Harris was, however, a very bright and capable man widely respected as a savvy politician. After the meeting he announced that he had voted for Carter in the primary and would do so in the runoff and the general election. The Sanders campaign had a field day, distributing a cartoon showing Carter getting into bed with Harris over whose head was a sign "White Citizens Council." Carter did little at the time to dispell the impression the meeting left, as with most voters it was an asset. Years later he denied that race was discussed in the meeting or that there was any discussion of a quid pro quo concerning Harris's role as a member of the state University Board of Regents, a position that he cherished. It appears in retrospect, that Harris, perceiving Carter as the next governor, merely saw an opportunity to solidify his chances for reappointment. Also given a choice between Carter and Sanders, whom he had known for years in Augusta, Carter seemed the more conservative.

Subsequently, speaking before a largely hostile audience of students at the University of Georgia, Carter won their applause by announcing that he did not intend to reappoint Harris to the Board of Regents. According to Harris, Carter called him the following day to apologize and assure him that he had made no decisions about the Board of Regents. A week later, speaking before an overwhelmingly black audience at the Atlanta Hungry Club, where heavy press coverage was guaranteed, Carter defended Roy Harris as having had a long interest in education, and as having initiated the first statewide minimum foundation programs.

As with other issues, Carter again appeared to want to have it both ways, winning the substantial constituency of pro-Harris voters and those who opposed him as well. He made a similar gambit with regard to the powerful and controversial state highway commissioner, Jim Gillis, citing him as an example of the kind of entrenched state employee he would replace as governor. Later when Gillis endorsed him, he retracted the commitment.

On election day, September 23, Carter again triumphed over Sanders, winning 60 percent of the vote. However, despite the efforts of Dr. Horace Tate, Fred Bennett, and other black supporters, Carter still garnered only 7 percent of the black vote to Sanders's 93 percent. Lester Maddox, unable to succeed himself as governor, emerged as the Democratic nominee for lieutenant governor. Sanders remained permanently bitter over his defeat. However, Sanders's friend, former party chairman J. B. Fuqua, later a strong Carter supporter, would say, "Jimmy beat him fair and square."

On the Republican side the winner was a political novice, Atlanta television newsman Hal Suit. He stunningly upset Jimmy Bentley. The increasingly conservative Bentley had opportunistically switched parties, but Georgia Republicans opted for the more moderate, longtime party loyalist Suit.

Fate was very much on Carter's side. While Bentley would have been a tough opponent, Suit, pleasant, moderate, and little known outside Atlanta, posed little threat. Surprised by his success in the primary, Suit was underfinanced and lacked the burning desire to win. He conducted a gentlemanly but low-intensity and ineffectual campaign. He did seek support from President Nixon, but the Republican leadership had already written off the Georgia race.

On October 1, Carter's forty-sixth birthday, he received a call from Robert Woodruff, octogenarian chairman of the board of the Coca-Cola Company, who said he was sending his Rolls-Royce to bring Carter to meet him. Woodruff, who had been instrumental in getting Eisenhower to run for president and in persuading him to make regular use of the Augusta National Golf Course, represented the pinnacle of corporate power in the state. He wanted nothing, he said, but with Carter clearly bound for the governorship, he just "thought it was time we got acquainted." Carter was euphoric with the vote of confidence from the corporate power structure this meeting symbolized.

Confident of an easy victory, Carter nevertheless spent the final weekend campaigning with great intensity. Driven by Jody Powell and accompanied by Terry Adamson, now a reporter with the *Atlanta Constitution,* he went to five Friday-night football games in Southwest Georgia and a county fair. At 5:30 A.M. on Saturday, they attended a dawn rally in the Americus town square where several hundred Sumter County supporters were about to travel around the state extolling Carter's virtues in what was called the "Hi Neighbor Program." At a massive rally on the Baldwin County Courthouse square in Milledgeville, featuring the venerated congressman Carl Vinson, Carter talked of the three great heroes in his life: Vinson, Rickover, and Russell.* On to Augusta where he shook hundreds of hands at the Richmond County Fair and did several television interviews. Finally to Atlanta where he appeared in a business suit at the Georgia Press Association's "Cracker Crumble," a show of political parody and skits. He

---

*Carter had frequently referred to himself as a "Dick Russell Democrat." Russell was a die-hard segregationist, but his many years in Washington, his courtly style, and his avoidance of inflammatory rhetoric had enabled him to sidestep either the label or image of a racist. Carter could safely link himself to Russell in a way he could not with Wallace, although their views on race differed little.

worked the crowd of journalists, businesspeople, and lobbyists with the same fervor he had the football games and county fairs in the previous twenty-four hours.

On voting day, November 3, Carter received 60 percent of the vote. Lester Maddox, however, received 73.5 percent of the vote for lieutenant governor.

Black state Senator Leroy Johnson, who had supported Sanders in the primary, said in an interview with the *Atlanta Constitution:*

> He [Carter] is going to be one of the greatest governors this state has ever had. I served with him in the Senate . . . he wasn't a racist then. And I know now that he is going to do more for blacks than any governor has ever done. . . . I understand why he ran that kind of ultra-conservative campaign . . . you have to do that to win. And that's the main thing. I don't believe you can win this state without being a racist. Five years from now, perhaps—but not now.

On a day late in the campaign, David Rabhan was flying Carter across the state. During the flight Carter turned to Rabhan and said, "What could I do for you as governor to thank you for everything you have done for me in this campaign?" "I don't want anything," Rabhan replied. "Well, there must be something," Carter persisted. After a moment's reflection, Rabhan said that he wanted Carter to say something in his inaugural address about removing the millstone of racism from around the necks of the Georgia people. Carter took a flight map and, after a few moments' thought, wrote in the margin,

> At the end of a long campaign, I believe I know our people as well as anyone. Based on the knowledge of Georgians north and south, rural and urban, liberal and conservative, I say to you quite frankly the time for racial discrimination is over.

"How would this be?" he asked, handing it to Rabhan. "Sign it," Rabhan replied. Carter did so.

CHAPTER 14

January 12, 1971, was a cold and windy day with rain threatening. Jimmy Carter stood on the raised platform appropriately adjacent to the statue of Thomas Watson in front of the gold-domed Georgia capitol. At his side was Rosalynn, holding three-year-old Amy's hand. Next to them was the departing governor and incoming lieutenant governor, Lester Maddox. Behind them were arrayed Miss Lillian, Jack, Chip, Jeff, and other members of the Carter family. John Simmons, the pastor of the Plains Baptist Church, and Nelson Price, a Baptist preacher and Carter friend from Marietta, offered prayers. The Naval Academy choir from Annapolis sang. On the dot of noon Jimmy Carter was sworn in as Georgia's seventy-sixth governor. To administer the oath of office he had chosen Robert Jordan, a judge of the court of appeals and the brother of Koinonia founder Clarence Jordan. Like a mythological omen, as Carter rose to give his inaugural address the clouds parted and the sun shone down. Only eight minutes in length, it was one of the most important speeches of his life. He began:

> It is a long way from Plains to Atlanta. I started the trip four and a half years ago, and, with a four-year detour I finally made it.

He focused primarily on the human needs of the people of the state:

> Every adult illiterate, every school dropout, every untrained retarded child is an indictment of us all. Our state pays a terrible price for these failures. It is time to end this waste. If Switzerland and Israel and other people can eliminate illiteracy, then so can we.

Then to stunned gasps from his audience, Governor Carter went on to repeat the words he had pledged to Rabhan that he would include, adding:

> No poor, rural, weak, or black person should ever have to bear the additional burden of being deprived of the opportunity of an education, a job, or simply justice.

The speech, which he had written himself, was a lucid statement of his philosophy and concerns: protection of the environment; the need to apply "business principles" to government: "the function of government should

200

be administered so as to justify confidence and pride," "taxes should be minimal and fair"; and, reflecting his concern for conciliation, "rural and urban people should easily discern the mutuality of their goals and opportunities"; his self-concept as a planner: "we should take future actions according to carefully considered long-range plans and priorities."

> Government is a contrivance of human wisdom to provide for human wants. Men had a right to expect these wants will be provided by this wisdom.
>
> The test of government is not how popular it is with the privileged few, but how honestly and fairly it deals with the many who must depend on it.

Carter's emphatic statement that the era of racism was at an end drew nationwide attention, but it also angered a significant segment of the electorate that had voted for him believing he shared their views on race and now felt betrayed. But for the Atlanta business establishment and the black leadership, it was an unexpected, if welcome, break with the past.

Carter was only one of the progressive southern governors elected that year, including Reuben Askew in Florida, John West in South Carolina, Dale Bumpers in Arkansas, and Lynwood Holton, a Republican in Virginia. Referred to collectively as the leaders of the "New South," their elections had not been as dramatic as Carter's, but they all shared similar views on the race issue. *Time* magazine decided to do a cover story on the "New South Governors," using either a picture of Reuben Askew or small portraits of each. J. Paul Austin, president of Coca-Cola and an increasing admirer of Carter, who was all too aware of the benefits to his corporation of emphasizing the new enlightenment in Georgia, called Andrew Heiskell, editor of *Time,* and convinced him to put Carter alone on the cover. As a result, on May 31, 1971, he had the rare distinction for a southern governor of being featured in a glowingly positive light before a national audience.

Nine days after his inauguration, Carter faced his first political crisis, when Senator Richard Russell died in office after a long illness. Former Governor Vandiver, who was married to Russell's niece, understood that Carter would appoint him ostensibly in return for his endorsement in the gubernatorial race. Carter denies there was any such agreement. Carter's friend, State Senator Lamar Plunkett, a wealthy patrician who liked to see himself as above the fray of politics, considered himself the natural choice. Charles Kirbo declined the seat but suggested his former law firm associate and chairman of the Georgia Democratic Party, David Gambrell. Although a lengthy list was prepared of potential candidates, the choice came down to Gambrell and Carter's cousin Hugh. However, Carter was counting on Hugh to be one of his legislative leaders in the state senate.

When Carter finally settled on Gambrell, Hugh was deeply disappointed, although his appointment would have done little in Washington to enhance Carter's image.

Under the eccentric and neglectful Maddox, much of the governor's power had gravitated to the legislative branch. Carter was determined to restore power to the governorship and set about the mundane task of launching a much-needed reorganization of state government. This had not been undertaken since 1929, when Governor Lamartine G. Hardman's extensive reorganization plan had been blocked by the legislature. His successor, Richard Russell, got it passed and parlayed the credit he received into a U.S. Senate seat. For Carter, who styled himself as a "Richard Russell Democrat," historical precedent held considerable allure.

During the campaign, Republican Hal Suit had made reorganization his issue. Carter had mentioned it in his 1966 campaign, but in 1970 had no desire to promote his opponent's platform. Immediately after winning the election, however, he announced a long list of reforms he planned to carry out in office. He studied Hardman's reorganization plan methodically and announced modernizing the state government would be the centerpiece of his program. He proposed to reduce the number of state agencies from 300 to 22, saving an estimated $50 million per year. "Reorganization," he said, reflecting a growing tendency to hyperbole, "is as important to the future of Georgia's state government as education is to the future of our young people." Previous governors had given lip service to reorganization because the political capital required was substantial, and, mindful of their future ambitions, they had been unwilling to assume the risk. Self-confident and seemingly unconcerned about the political hazards, Carter undertook the challenge because it was "the right thing to do."

Carter knew that to put his own stamp on the state government and to honor a campaign pledge he had to fire those most visibly associated with the old patronage system, including longtime highway commissioner Jim Gillis. He was nervous as he walked to Gillis's office, but aware of the inevitable, Gillis, a savvy politician who understood that the era he symbolized in state government was over, proved gracious in acceding to Carter's wishes. What Carter needed was someone both loyal to him and capable of running a modern and increasingly technically complicated department. He appointed the ebullient and energetic Bert Lance, whose effective role as a campaign fund-raiser had tightened the growing bond between them.

Carter also sought to staff his administration with recognized and qualified experts from around the country. He wanted to transform the state's deservedly maligned penal system and recruited as commissioner of corrections Ellis MacDougall, a well-regarded professional who had held a similar post in Connecticut. When the legislature initially resisted Mac-Dougall's salary demands, Carter paid the difference from his own pocket.

Toward the end of the gubernatorial campaign, Hamilton Jordan asked Rabhan to raise with Carter his wish to be his executive assistant in the governor's office, to which Carter readily agreed. Jody Powell became his press secretary. After the inauguration, Lansing Lee gave up his scheduling role to become an administrative assistant. Landon Butler would later join his staff to handle special projects. Carter asked Charles Kirbo to be his "chief of staff," a traditional, prestigous, but honorary position without line authority, involving mainly advising the governor and working with the legislature. In appointing Lansing Lee, a young campaign aide, as his scheduler during the transition, Carter warned him, "I'm going to make you the horse's ass. I'm going to tell everyone I'd like to meet with them and then you're the one who's going to have to tell them 'no.' "

A particularly consequential appointee to his personal staff was Cloyd Hall, hired initially to handle relations with the city of Atlanta, but who later took over responsibility for "community relations," natural disasters, civil disorders, and a variety of other functions. "I was," Hall says, "a vacuum filler."

Hall, previously an employee of the county government of Bibb County (Macon), was a short, slight man with thinning gray hair and a withered right arm. A person of sensitivity with a deep empathy for human suffering, he had natural skills as a negotiator and little interest in self-promotion. With ties both to black leaders and to conservative rural elements, he mirrored more the private than the public face of Jimmy Carter as he quietly and relentlessly worked on closing the racial divide in the state. Hall's success in helping to maintain racial tranquillity would later enable him to play an instrumental role in convincing foreign corporations, especially Japanese, to invest billions of dollars in Georgia for which Carter would get the credit.

Sanders still had many friends in the Georgia House and Senate, who had little love for Carter after the bitter primary fight. Eugene Holley, state senator from Sanders's hometown of Augusta, was chairman of the powerful Banking and Finance Committee, and the leader of the Sanders loyalists. In addition, there were many in the legislature and the state government who were Talmadge supporters. They feared that the natural next step for this ambitious, popular, young governor (allowed by law at the time to serve only one term) would be to go after their man's U.S. Senate seat, and they had little interest in allowing a successful governorship to become a launching pad for such a campaign. A further problem for Carter was that the president pro tem of the Senate was Hugh Gillis. A few days after the general election, the Senate Democratic Caucus met to select its leaders for the 1971 legislative session. Eager to displace Hugh Gillis prior to firing Gillis's father, Carter endorsed a longtime friend and supporter,

Senator Robert Smalley, for the job of president pro tem. Smalley was defeated, 27 to 17, and Gillis retained the position. Through poor judgment and political naivete, the prestige of the governor-elect had suffered a serious self-inflicted blow.

Carter's biggest headache throughout his tenure would be his lieutenant governor, Lester Maddox. During his campaign, Carter went out of his way to avoid conflict. At a state Democratic meeting toward the end of the campaign, on October 29, Carter praised Maddox: "He has brought a standard of forthright expression and personal honesty to the governor's office and I hope to measure up to this standard." On election eve, Carter announced he was going to vote for Maddox, and there were areas of genuine agreement. Carter shared Maddox's opposition to pari-mutuel betting and also affirmed that he would, if elected, continue "Little People's Day," a populist gesture by Maddox that set aside one afternoon a week when any citizen could come, without appointment, for a couple of minutes of the governor's time. They also agreed on the need for electoral reform of the Democratic Party.

Even before the general election, however, Maddox was sniping at Carter. As lieutenant governor, Maddox would not only preside over the Senate but would also refer bills to committees of his choosing and appoint the members of standing and ad hoc committees. When Carter stated that he was going to want some say in naming committee members, Maddox warned that he would not accept "encroachment of the executive branch of state government over the legislative branch." When Carter endorsed Smalley, it was exactly the sort of interference Maddox had warned Carter against. The two had several meetings before and just after the inauguration in an effort to resolve their differences and to convey an impression of cordiality. However, after one meeting Carter told his staff and some of his Senate supporters, "He's *really* mad." For all practical purposes they engaged in open warfare throughout Carter's term.

Carter adroitly announced that rather than appoint his own floor leaders, as governors had traditionally done, he would instead use the present Democratic leadership in both houses. It brought Senate majority leader, Al Holloway, and Speaker of the House, George L. Smith, into the Carter camp, enhanced their power and stature, and completely disarmed the diehard Carter opponents. Both Holloway, elected in 1962 in the same freshman class as Carter, and Smith, an accomplished lawyer, were thoughtful individuals who understood that the reform of state government was long overdue. Carter liked both men, especially Smith.

Because most state agencies existed by statute, any reorganization plan required authorization from the General Assembly. After considerable negotiation between Carter and the House Policy Committee, an authorizing bill, House Bill No. 1 (HB 1), was submitted, giving the governor authority to propose extensive reorganization. His reorganization plan was to be submitted to the General Assembly at the beginning of the regular session in January 1972. Legislators would have ten days to veto any provisions they found unacceptable. Crucially, those provisions of the plan not vetoed during this time would automatically become law.

Throughout the legislative session Carter met each morning at 8 A.M. with his cousin Hugh and other floor leaders to plan strategy. With the help of Holloway, Smith, and Senate majority leader, George Busbee, the bill eventually became law, but not without several seriously weakening amendments. Constitutional officers (including the commissioners of Labor and Agriculture, elected rather than appointed to their positions) were given the right to veto any proposed statutory changes in their own departments, and the veto period for the legislature was increased from ten to fifteen days. Smith was able to deliver the bill from the House of Representatives with only minor changes. However, in the Senate, Maddox marshaled the anti-Carter forces in an attempt to kill the bill. At an unprecedented Sunday evening news conference, Maddox claimed a conspiracy between Carter and key legislators:

> Persons who engender fear and cowardice and lust for power, who conceived the plot in defeat and nurtured it in iniquity, in raw and rotten collusion . . . they would set up a dictatorship, a monarchy . . . they would sell their souls for a mess of porridge [sic].

The *Atlanta Constitution* ran a headline: "Carter and Maddox put the political heavyweight championship of Georgia on the line." Maddox's antics only enhanced Carter's contrasting image as thoughtful and seriously concerned about responsible government. Three previously uncommitted senators immediately joined the Carter forces.

By mobilizing his grassroots network of supporters and the business community, Carter was able to get the bill passed, signing it into law on February 15, 1971. His victory was widely interpreted as a major defeat for Maddox. On his voting tally sheet Carter underlined the names of four senators who he felt had lied to him about how they would vote. Maddox banished all 23 senators who voted with Carter to desks in the capitol basement with a single secretary among them.

Carter had made the right decision in forcing an early showdown with Maddox, who would never again pose the same threat. However, what struck observers was Carter's unflinching audaciousness in pursuit of such a high-risk course of action. Winning vindicated him, but few others would have dared to try it, a reflection of his enormous self-confidence and his tenacity. Wanting always to see the good in people, he tended to believe that even his most ardent opponents were as committed to the common good as he, but were either under pressure from special interests or simply lacked adequate understanding of the issues.

Carter's job might have been a good deal easier if he had been willing to engage in traditional backslapping, trading favors, and massaging egos. As Hamilton Jordan said of him, "He doesn't understand the personal element in politics." Bert Lance observed, "His personal curiosity was about process, not about people." "He wasn't big on small talk. It was total, total business," says Cloyd Hall. Ironically his election campaigns were rooted in personal politics and loyalty, but with those who opposed him, he responded with frustrated annoyance. As one friend said of his attitude toward the legislature, "He didn't like to fool with them. . . . He didn't like it, didn't enjoy it, didn't respect them."

Carter supporters in the legislature became increasingly frustrated at his reluctance to woo the opposition. Finally, his friend Senator Ford Spinks, who had remained deeply loyal, arranged with Bert Lance for the three men to have lunch together. Carter invited them to his office, a room with a deep-piled carpet in vivid blue, an overstuffed black leather couch, and chrome and leather chairs. On the wall were four pen and ink drawings of simple shacks lived in by rural blacks across the South. The drawings were by David Rabhan. Reflecting Carter's frugal nature, after bringing in ham and cheese sandwiches and a Coke for each of them, secretary Mary Beazley said, "That will be $2.78." Although forewarned by Lance, Spinks jumped right in: "Governor, . . . I've been observing you lately in the way you've been dealing with the senators and the members of the House. Governor, you aren't paying enough attention to them. You aren't stroking them enough. You aren't inviting them down to your office to chat and pass the time of day. Governor, you've got to love these folks more."

Carter became flushed and the artery on his forehead throbbed visibly, indicating his anger. "Ford," he said deliberately, "I want to tell you that as long as I'm governor of this state, don't ever tell me again what I ought to do and what I ought not to do with the legislature."

Early in the session Carter had invited all the members of the legislature to a dinner at the mansion. The meal was served on paper plates with Cokes out of a "wash tub." They were disappointed and many were affronted that he had treated the event like a "South Georgia barbecue." It was not so much that Carter did not know better, but that he was, because of his own priorities, curiously insensitive to how important the trappings of power were to the legislators. After the faux pas was pointed out to him, he and Rosalynn invited them back in small groups and used the china and crystal.

To direct the development of the reorganization plan, Carter appointed

Tom Linder, whom he had recently made the director of the Bureau of State Planning and Community Affairs. Linder had previously served as executive director of the Middle Georgia Area Planning Commission, a counterpart to the authority Carter had helped to set up and chair. It was through these planning organizations that the two men knew each other.

Consulting with other states that had carried out reorganizations, Linder found three different groups had been used, separately or in combination—professional management consultants, state employees, and business executives. Carter instructed him to involve them all. Arthur Anderson and Company was picked as the management consultant firm. Linder then wrote to all the major businesses in the Atlanta area asking them to contribute personnel for periods of two to six months. Despite the fact that Carter had often run against the business community, forty-eight organizations contributed a total of sixty-five people. There was little concern about conflict of interest even though several of these firms were doing business with the state. The only objection was from organized labor, but Carter was meeting regularly with campaign supporter Herb Mabry of the Georgia AFL-CIO and they arranged for labor representatives to be involved. Carter viewed the effort as a crusade, and he expected everyone to share his enthusiasm and vision, volunteering their efforts in a selfless way. It would never have occurred to him to try to profit from the reorganization, and he assumed the same was true of others. By and large it was.

Jimmy Carter loved being governor. Having campaigned so hard and so long, talking and listening, he felt utterly confident that he knew the people of the state better than anyone else. During his two terms in the Senate he had acquired a sense of mastery over the bureaucratic process, and enjoyed working directly with people at all levels in his administration. As one aide observed, Carter was quite willing to accept "the bureaucratic establishment, but not the legislative establishment." Those who worked with him on the reorganization initiative were astonished with his grasp of even the tiniest details. At press conferences he was rarely asked a question on any topic where he was not more conversant and substantially better informed on the issue than the questioner. He radiated the sort of self-confidence that came from feeling fully in command of the job.

Carter read an article about "zero-based budgeting" being used by the Texas Instruments Corporation. Implementing it as part of the state budgeting process, he required department heads, for the first time, to justify their budgets from scratch each year.

Carter had Cloyd Hall go immediately whenever a disaster struck in the state—an explosion at a Thiokol plant that killed 26 black women, a ship severely damaging a road bridge near Brunswick, a lethal explosion at a chicken processing plant near Claxton. Carter usually quickly followed.

Evidence of Carter's immediate concern, according to Hall, meant that "with the people, *the people,* it created a great reservoir of love and respect for the man."

After their modest home in Plains, the Carter family quickly adjusted to the comforts of the $2 million three-year-old governor's mansion. It was staffed by black servants who were serving time in the Georgia prison system. Amy was the adored center of family attention, especially for Jimmy, who frequently referred to her, some felt inappropriately, when speaking in public. It reflected, however, the depth of his pride and affection for her. Both Jack, back from the navy and at Georgia Tech, and Chip, a student at Georgia State University, married while they were living in the mansion. Jack's wife, Judy, was the daughter of Beverly and Edna Langford, who had been central to the Carter gubernatorial effort since 1966. Miss Lillian regularly came to stay and surprised the Atlanta elite by attending professional wrestling events.

Rosalynn's shyness, although diminishing, belied a drive and political sophistication that were inapparent to most outside the family. Few were aware of what a significant role she played in their political symbiosis. Rosalynn chose to make mental illness her primary issue. Reflecting a long-standing interest derived, in part, from having a relative in the notorious state mental hospital at Milledgeville, Jimmy early appointed a Governor's Commission to Improve Services to the Mentally and Emotionally Handicapped. Rosalynn hired an assistant, Madeline MacBean, and began working closely with the commission using her position to draw public attention to the problem. She also worked as a volunteer one day a week at the Georgia Regional Mental Hospital near Atlanta.

Rosalynn did, however, find the early months in the governorship a serious strain. Her self-imposed demand for perfection, public scrutiny, enduring security that prevented anonymity, missing her previous relaxed relationships with friends, and dealing with incessant official entertaining, became too much for her. After a year she was seriously depressed. She reorganized her life and relinquished the more unrealistic demands she was placing on herself. She achieved this primarily through her religious faith, turning to friends in a Bible class she was attending and to writings from Jimmy's sister, Ruth. Rosalynn would later write of this period,

> . . . that experience and that lesson saved my life. I have been in many situations since that were very difficult, that could have been very lonely and defeating, but I am constantly aware that God is with me to help me through the difficult times.

Whisked from one part of Georgia to another by the state patrol or by the planes at his disposal, accompanied by his personal bodyguard, Stock

Coleman, Carter maintained a frenetic pace, ready day or night to rush to the site of a disaster or to address meetings of county commissioners, sheriffs' associations, or health workers. He was energized, as he had been campaigning, by constant contact with ordinary people. He began his day at the Capitol no later than 7:15 A.M., without eating breakfast, and was obsessed with both punctuality and not wasting time. His day was minutely planned, even having precisely thirty minutes set aside on his schedule on Tuesdays when he read *Time* and *Newsweek*. Wasting time meant not doing his best, a betrayal not just of the standards he had set for himself but of the obligations he had set for himself with God.

The governorship attracted diverse and fascinating people to the mansion. Jimmy and Rosalynn, always eager to broaden their horizons, were willing hosts to the famous, the not-so-famous, and even the controversial, if they were sufficiently interesting. Jimmy was like a sponge, absorbing whatever he might from anyone who crossed his path. Their first distinguished guest was Van Cliburn, who became a loyal friend and subsequently sent flowers on the anniversaries of his visit. Although Carter's favorite piece of music at the time was the classical *Recuerdos de la Alhambra* by Francisco Tarrega, he enjoyed the company and music of the Allman Brothers, Paul Simon, the Marshall Tucker band, and several country and western artists. Social critic Bob Dylan's poetic lyrics intrigued Carter. His songs "Bound for Glory" and "Ode to Woody Guthrie" struck in him the same chord as Agee's *Let Us Now Praise Famous Men.* Other guests ranged from Margaret Mead to Henry Kissinger, and from artist Peter Max (beginning a longstanding relationship) to Eunice Shriver.

The Carters joined the Northside Baptist Church in Atlanta. The pastor, Forrest Lanier, was a well-educated and worldly individual who, although from South Georgia, had established himself as a progressive on the race issue. Carter disagreed with him, however, over the church's proposed multimillion-dollar building program; he was inherently cost conscious, especially when it came to putting money into buildings. The majority, however, supported the construction project, and at the groundbreaking four-year-old Amy turned the first shovel of dirt. Carter's greatest interest was in seeing the affluent congregation expand its missionary work significantly. A friend from Plains, Dr. George Mims, had recently made a missionary trip to Honduras. At Carter's invitation he came to Northside to talk about the trip. Inspired, Forrest Lanier led a group of twenty-five young people, including Chip and half a dozen doctors and dentists, to Honduras for three weeks in June 1971.

In 1968, Carter had attended a Jaycees award banquet in Marietta, and shared the program with a young dynamic preacher, Nelson Price, pastor of the Roswell Street Baptist Church. They sensed a strong mutual compatibility and had agreed to keep each other in their prayers. As governor, Carter would appear from time to time unannounced at Price's church. On one occasion, Carter, a stock car racing enthusiast, invited Price to the Atlanta Raceway, where he gave a brief sermon to more than 100,000 race fans before riding with Carter in the lead car at 160 miles per hour.

For Carter there was no doubt about the natural blending of his religious faith and improving the quality of life for the people of Georgia. The new social programs he implemented he saw as "an extension of the gospel, problem solving combined with Christian charity." Prayer was an important part of his personal struggle to achieve his goals. There was a little private office behind the large ceremonial office of the governor where he would later tell people he spent more time on his knees than he had during the rest of his life added together.

Bert Lance rapidly slipped into the pattern of coming to Carter's office at the start of each working day. They talked about the day's news in general, the doings in the legislature, or the reorganization initiative. At the end of the day, Bert would also frequently go to the governor's mansion, where they would play tennis, usually with Hamilton Jordan and Lansing Lee or other members of Carter's staff. As one of them said, "Carter played to kill as he did in the campaign and as governor." Bert became one of the few Carter confidants, but he, like the others, was kept in many ways at arm's length. Apart from Rosalynn, Carter chose to operate in isolation.

He did not like meetings. His preferred style was to work individually with staff members. There were no regular staff meetings to plot political or administrative strategy. Bert Lance says, "I finally got him to have lunch once a month with all the department heads and constitutional officers not because he could exercise any control over them but because there just ought to be some communication."

Carter wanted the most experienced and competent appointees to fill visible positions in his administration, yet on his personal staff he went to the other extreme, placing a premium on youth, energy, and loyalty. Powell, Jordan, and Lee were all under thirty and had little employment experience apart from the campaign. Jordan, while widely liked, was quickly overwhelmed by the demands placed on him. Friends described him as a "thinker, not a manager." Dozens of unreturned phone calls piled up and on occasion he would slip out of the back door of his office to avoid meeting with people. Fortunately, Lansing Lee, who was organized, would call people back on his behalf.

Carter was remarkably tolerant, rarely castigating his young staff for their sometimes publicly embarrassing errors. On one occasion the older Cloyd Hall went to the mansion to brief Carter on a current emergency. The governor was in the shower and his tuxedo was laid out on the bed.

Carter made a couple of minor criticisms of the way Hall had handled the matter. "Governor," Hall asked, "how come you're always criticizing me, but you let Hamilton and Jody get away with murder?"

"It's just that I expect a lot more from you Cloyd," came the terse reply from the shower stall.

In September 1971, a nasty racial conflict developed in Hancock County, southeast of Atlanta. The population of the county was two-thirds black, while Sparta, the county seat, had a white majority. John McGown, the black Hancock County administrator, who was also the head of the Georgia Council on Human Relations, was an energetic, charismatic organizer. He had taken full advantage of the range of "anti-poverty" programs being funded out of Washington, and with substantial additional moneys from the Ford Foundation, launched an impressive array of small businesses, job creation projects, and other economic development initiatives, mainly for blacks across the county. Feeling suddenly threatened, a group of the white citizens in Sparta led by Mayor Buck Patterson, a funeral home director, purchased ten submachine guns with privately raised money for the city's reluctant six white police officers. McGown's response was to place an order for thirty submachine guns ostensibly for the use of the newly formed "Hancock County Sporting Rangers." Fearing a pointless bloodbath, where he would be caught in the middle, the Sparta police chief took a thirty-day leave of absence.

Nevertheless, hardliners were edging toward violent confrontation, creating a potentially explosive situation that could have had devastatingly negative consequences for Carter not just in Georgia but to his national "New South" image. The traditional approach would have been to send in hundreds of state troopers and even the National Guard. That, Carter believed, had the potential to trigger the very conflagration he wanted to avoid.

Instead he dispatched a three-man civil disorder unit, led by Cloyd Hall with Robert Insley, a black Justice Department agent who was a specialist in civil disturbances, and Ray Stevens of the Georgia State Patrol. The unit had already had considerable success around the state defusing tense racial situations. Over the next three weeks, facing suspicion and hostility on both sides, the three negotiators identified the people of goodwill and the bridge builders in the community as a slow process of "conflict resolution" was started. Each night, and often several times a day, Cloyd Hall was on the phone to Carter reporting on their progress and planning the next steps. Eventually, Buck Patterson, who had the weapons stored at his funeral home, agreed to surrender them, asking only that Hall not publicly embarrass him for seeming to have backed down. McGown immediately agreed to cancel their order for guns.

For Carter, already deeply committed to Christian reconciliation, it was a pivotal experience in convincing him that, with tenacity and sufficiently skilled negotiators, confrontation between even the most intransigent opponents could be resolved without violence, whether in Hancock County, Georgia, or anywhere in the world.

Supreme Court justices in Georgia are elected, although the governor has the authority to make appointments to fill unexpired terms. Carter's first appointment was Robert Jordan, who had administered to him the oath of office. He filled the next vacancy with his friend Bill Gunter, who had also been his campaign chairman in Hall County. In August 1973, he would appoint another friend, Conley Ingram, who described Gunter's influence on Carter as "substantial." Gunter and Carter saw eye to eye on most things. They differed, however, over the death penalty. During the campaign Carter had said, "I favor retention of capital punishment," the only realistic political position he could have taken given the public's attitude. Rosalynn, however, remained personally opposed. Gunter, after long reflection, had concluded that his religious beliefs forced him to oppose it. He would persist in trying to change Carter's view, and he sent him a lengthy letter laying out the moral and legal issues as he saw them. Gunter found himself in a minority of one on the court and ultimately would resign in frustration over the issue. Ironically, during his four years in office Carter was never faced with having to impose the penalty. Twenty years later, he says, "I do not know what I would have done."

Carter took a special interest in reforming the judicial system, which had been attempted in Georgia since the turn of the century without success. He scrapped the old system by which governors could appoint judges regardless of their qualifications. He established instead a Judicial Selection Commission chaired by one of the most highly respected lawyers in the state, Henry Bowden, who had endorsed him at the last minute in the 1966 gubernatorial race. Anyone could nominate candidates for a judicial appointment by submitting their names to the commission, which in turn submitted a list of the five most qualified to the governor.

Receiving less than 10 percent of their vote against Sanders, Carter owed little politically to the black community. Yet as his inaugural speech had indicated, he saw race as the great unhealed scar of American society, and saw one of his primary objectives as governor to transform the role of African Americans in the state. He hired a young black woman, Rita Samuels, to help identify potential appointees. At the start of his administration there were only three blacks serving on major state boards and commissions. When he left there were fifty-three. At his instigation the number of black state employees increased from 4,850 to 6,684. He particularly appointed blacks to bodies that affected the lives of black citizens: the Board of Pardons and Paroles, the State Welfare Department, and the

State Board of Regents (from which he also dropped Roy Harris). State Senator Horace Ward, who had been denied admission to the University of Georgia Law School because he was black, was appointed to a judgeship. Carter opened up the state patrol to blacks and made a black state trooper part of his security detail. When he received a call from the Macon Country Club where he was scheduled to give a speech, asking him not to bring that trooper, he deliberately did so and then proceeded to lecture his audience on the evils of racism.

However, during his first two years in office, while the reorganization plan hung in the balance, Carter held back on more controversial measures lest he antagonize conservative legislators whose votes he desperately needed. Where he could make points with conservatives without compromising his principles, he did so. He opposed forced busing, calling it "the most serious threat to education I can remember." He did, however, support the voluntary busing program in Atlanta that enjoyed the support of most black leaders. At the National Governors Conference in Puerto Rico on September 15, 1971, Carter, George Wallace, and Republican Winfield Dunn of Tennessee cosponsored an anti-busing amendment, consideration of which was refused. On November 10, at the Southern Governors Conference, Carter supported a resolution praising the U.S. House of Representatives for passing a bill denying funds for school busing. He also called for an anti-busing plank in the 1972 Democratic Party platform, saying, "It would be difficult for me to ask the people of Georgia to support the ticket without a guarantee that the South would receive the same treatment as the rest of the country."

During his first two years in office Carter's future was uncertain, and running against Herman Talmadge for his U.S. Senate seat was a likely option. In that light, Carter was reluctant to burn his bridges to conservatives.

It was still a time of bitter racial hatred, and many Georgians resented that Carter reached out to blacks. It was Jordan's job to notify legislators when Carter appointed a person from their district to a state board or commission, a particularly delicate problem when black appointees came from the districts of racist representatives whose votes Carter still desperately needed. On one occasion Jordan was overheard telling a North Georgia legislator over the phone, "I wanted to let you know we're going to do something real nice for one of your niggers up there." It was a clever and effective way of deflecting the anticipated explosion of wrath, yet it would have seriously disturbed Carter had he heard it. However, his ignorance enabled him consistently to take the high road, while Jordan held together the conservative support he needed.

Another difficult dilemma was posed in early 1971, when Lt. William Calley was court-martialed in Atlanta for his role in the My Lai massacre.

There was widespread public support for Calley in Georgia. The state commander of the Veterans of Foreign Wars called on Carter to declare a day of public support for Calley, and Maddox appealed to President Nixon to free him. Carter would later say, "I never thought Calley was anything but guilty. I never felt any attitude toward Calley except abhorrence. And I thought he should be punished and still do." Yet the situation put Carter in a tight spot. He called a press conference on April 2, 1971, at which he expressed concern that there were those, by implication in the anti-war movement, who sought to exploit the Calley situation "to cheapen and shame the reputation of American servicemen." He said Calley was being made a scapegoat and that his superiors should be held equally accountable. Instead of calling for a "William Calley Day" he proclaimed an "American Fighting Men's Day," asking Georgians to demonstrate their support by driving with their car headlights on. It was a skillfull and successful ploy that defused the situation.

Tom Linder and his corporate team had put together a 2,500-page comprehensive reorganization package containing 300 proposals for governmental reform. Carter had devoted more than 200 hours to sifting through and discussing with team members every recommendation. From the beginning he had stressed that priority should be given to structural reform, reducing the total number of government agencies. He also repeatedly urged the team members to make their recommendations purely on the basis of merit without regard to cost-saving or political considerations. "I have no intention of making a recommendation simply for political expediency, nor to avoid confrontation," he told a reporter. Carter did not necessarily believe in smaller government, but he did believe it could be made infinitely more efficient and responsive to people's needs.

The plan called for the existing sixty-five budgeted agencies to be consolidated into twenty agencies, and the functions of more than 200 unbudgeted agencies were to be transferred to one or more of the twenty line departments. By far the most controversial, and perhaps sensible, recommendation was for a Department of Human Resources that would consolidate into a single delivery system physical and mental health, welfare, probation and parole, drug treatment, and housing. It meant abolishing the State Board of Health, whose members were nominated by the Georgia Medical Association, and replacing it with a Board of Human Resources made up of other health professionals and consumer representatives, on which private physicians would be a minority. The chairman of the Board of Health was Dr. Beverly Forester, Carter's friend and classmate from Georgia Southwestern. A loyal supporter, he was willing to step down, but the Georgia Medical Association, heavily Republican, mounted a vicious campaign in an attempt to preserve their control of the Health Department.

George Kaiser of Arthur Anderson, who had participated in numerous such studies in other states, told Tom Linder that it was one of the most well conceived and comprehensive plans he had seen. However, no matter how good or needed, reorganization had no natural constituency. To get it past the legislature, and Lester Maddox, Carter would have to create active support. Cloyd Hall, as Carter's man for all seasons, took responsibility for coordinating a statewide Public Awareness Program. In some ways the effort paralleled Carter's race for governor. It sought to bring together a broad populist coalition behind the notion that reorganization was a laudatory step forward in the interests of a broad cross section of ordinary Georgians.

Much of the success of this effort was again attributable to Gerald Rafshoon, who masterminded the public relations campaign. By mid-August he produced an eleven-minute film which, drawing on a poll that showed 85 percent of Georgians felt government generally neglected the average citizen, emphasized "responsiveness of government" as one of the primary benefits of reorganization. His agency also produced 145,000 brochures emblazoned with the slogan "Economize, Revitalize, Reorganize State Government." Later 200,000 copies of a twenty-page brochure detailing the plan and accompanying its release were sent out. Originally Rafshoon had reserved the central role in the awareness campaign for Carter, but the governor wanted the focus instead on the legislature, to imply unity of purpose and to dramatize their crucial role.

As much as Carter differed from conventional politicians in his willingness to gamble his political career on reorganization, he was equally determined to leave no stone unturned to assure he did not fail. With an intensity that was unprecedented in the state for any previous initiative, he hosted hundreds of groups at the capitol and at the mansion explaining the details of reorganization. He taped a fifteen-minute radio interview that was run by virtually every radio station in the state. Tom Linder was talking everywhere to any group in the state that would listen. A Citizens' Committee for Reorganization (actually a reactivation of the 1970 Citizens' Committee for Jimmy Carter) was chaired by Robert Lipshutz, Carter's friend and fund-raiser. They put out a newspaper with a cartoon showing Carter as St. George slaying a multiheaded dragon, labeled "Waste, Inefficiency, Special Interests, and Petty Politics." The headline said, "Jimmy Carter Needs Your Help." Perhaps the most important organizational endorsement came from the Georgia Jaycees. Through their publications and statewide network they mounted a letter-writing and media campaign directed at the legislature, producing a swelling momentum in the weeks before the legislature convened. They also organized pro-reorganization exhibits at fifty-nine county fairs.

Carter solicited and won the support of all of the predictably pro-good-government organizations such as the National Council of Jewish Women of Georgia and the American Association of University Women, but he considered particularly important the backing of the League of Women Voters and Common Cause. Their backing, especially that of the league, would carry considerable weight with some legislators, and being national organizations they offered the potential for gaining national recognition. The two organizations were run by a husband and wife, Sidney and Leah Janus. Carter won their early support and that of both organizations, but not until after Leah Janus had expressed serious concern about the lack of women at any senior level in the reorganization planning. Jordan acknowledged the failing and promised to remedy it, although little was done.

The governor's staff prepared articles and editorials to run in publications all over the state, including a piece for the *Christian Index,* the publication of the Georgia Baptist Convention, with a circulation of more than 130,000. On July 8, 1971, the Carters entertained 200 Georgia broadcasters and their wives at the mansion, and a week later they held a similar event for 170 members of the print media.

Carter still had to obtain the support of the popularly elected heads of the constitutionally established departments, who had been granted veto rights under HB 1. The strongest opposition came from Jack Nix, state school superintendent, and Ben Fortson, both of whom publicly denounced the plan several months before its final release.

Ben Fortson, white haired and in a wheelchair since an automobile accident in 1929, had been a widely liked fixture in the capital for twenty-five years. He was the older brother of Carter's friend and lawyer Warren Fortson. His opposition boiled down to his feeling that he had been stripped, in a publicly humiliating way, of the responsibility for the flower gardens around the capital in which he had taken great personal pride over the years. After Warren Fortson complained to Carter about the insensitive treatment of his brother, Richard Harden, Carter's talented strategist and troubleshooter for reorganization negotiated a face-saving compromise.

An additional problem was posed by Sam Caldwell, the labor commissioner, with close ties to Herman Talmadge. He was one who had hoped that Carter might appoint him to Richard Russell's Senate seat, and was determined to block the reorganization any way he could. Calling it a "power grab" by the governor, he exercised twenty-nine vetoes out of the forty-five cast by all department heads.

Despite the overall success of the Public Awareness Program, Carter's aversion to one-on-one politicking left him without the support of several powerful House and Senate figures. Carter's unwillingness to wheel and deal was a source of great frustration to both his friends and his enemies. As one Carter friend said, "The Speaker is a horse trader. He wants to do something for you, if you want to do something for him. Jimmy is not like that. He doesn't like to trade. He's stubborn."

Carter's unwillingness to deal is exemplified by one situation involving Senator Culver Kidd, one of Carter's most implacable foes, who suddenly announced that he might be willing to sponsor an amendment assuring passage of the Human Resources part of the plan in return, he told the press, for some new staff allocations at the Milledgeville State Hospital in his district. The offer disappeared as rapidly as it had surfaced, only to reemerge seven years later when Carter gave videotaped testimony against Kidd when he was under federal indictment for conspiring to obstruct state gambling laws. In his testimony Carter said that during the debate he was approached by Senator Holley, who conveyed the message that Kidd was willing to support the proposal in return for advance notice of gambling raids by state agents in his district. Ray Pope (brother of John), then Georgia public safety commissioner, supported Carter's account. Holley's and Kidd's stories differed significantly, and Kidd was ultimately acquitted. He was, however, the only senator to end up voting against the administration on every single roll-call vote. Carter could have gone public with his charges against Kidd at the time, but did not.

With increasing pressure from his supporters, especially his cousin Hugh, Carter admitted he had a problem. He told newsmen that he had been concentrating on the reorganization study and the state's revenue crisis, and as a result had not had "enough time to work adequately with the legislature. But this is a deficiency I am trying to correct." He held a series of conciliatory meetings with legislators, even inviting Senator Gene Holley to stay overnight at the mansion. Carter, who could perform superbly as a mediator in resolving other people's conflicts, found it very difficult to compromise when he was one of the protagonists. Bert Lance, more outgoing and gregarious, together with Kirbo, took on the heavy lobbying for him. As state highway director, Lance had control of highway construction projects as well as considerable influence in banking and business circles, and was effective because he did not hesitate to use whatever sticks and carrots were at his disposal to pressure uncommitted legislators. By contrast, Carter sought to stop the Highway Department from paving the main street in Plains for fear that it would look like favoritism. He did not stop Lance from this activity, but he did not want to be a party to it.

By the end of 1971, the prospects for reorganization looked bleak to most observers both in the legislature and the media. Bill Shipp reflected the general sentiment when he wrote in the *Atlanta Constitution* on September 23, "Unless he [Carter] pulls off a political miracle by January, his government reorganization will be doomed in the regular session of the General Assembly."

In the face of such pessimism, Carter's persistent optimism seemed curiously out of place. "I'm going to get it because it is right," he said. His charm offensive had worked relatively well in the House where conciliation had always been possible; but in the Senate the confrontation had gone too far, while Maddox continued to use every procedural trick he could.

At noon on January 11, Carter walked quickly and purposefully into the House chamber to deliver his "State of the State" address to a joint session of the legislature that had convened the day before for its 1972 regular session. The atmosphere was tense and Carter received only perfunctory applause. He reviewed the accomplishments of his administration during the previous year, leaving any mention of reorganization to the end. He then launched into an aggressive, harsh defense of the plan. The blood vessel on his forehead throbbed as he denounced those who opposed the plan with flashes of anger. Reverting to his deep-felt populist beliefs, he said, "The choice we have is to yield to the pressures of . . . special groups of interest and tell the people their rights are denied, or we can summon our courage and act for the people."

Testfying before the Senate Economy, Reorganization, and Efficiency in Government Committee, Ben Fortson made a statement about Carter that would become the most widely quoted concerning his term as governor. He said:

> Don't pay any attention to that smile. That don't mean a thing. That man is made of steel, determination, and stubbornness. Carter reminds me of a South Georgia turtle. He doesn't go around a log. He just sticks his head in the middle and pushes and pushes until the log gives way.

Fortson had colorfully and aptly predicted Carter's tenacious grind over the next two months. Inch by inch he would drive the reorganization plan through the legislature on its merits, seeking primarily to shame legislators into supporting it. Carter created a dilemma for many by including in his 1973 budget proposal the $55 million in savings that he claimed the reorganization proposals would achieve. By opposing reorganization they would seem to be opposing the savings. Former Governor Marvin Griffin helpfully commented favorably on this strategy in a newspaper column.

At the start of the session Carter removed Hamilton Jordan from the traditional legislative liaison role of the executive secretary. Legislators were complaining about Jordan's failure to return phone calls; they thought that he was over his head, and his age was a drawback in dealing with veteran politicians old enough to be his father. He was also caught in a very difficult position trying to represent Carter's new style of politics when his natural inclinations were closer to the style of the legislators. Thus, in the effort to line up votes, he often seemed to better represent the interests of the legislators to Carter than vice versa. Early in the administration, Carter had established the policy that the state would no longer pay for cost overruns on state-financed local projects. When a cost overrun occurred on a project of the West Georgia Airport Authority in Carrollton, on behalf of the local legislators, Jordan urged Carter to waive the policy as a way of garnering votes in the upcoming General Assembly. Carter refused on the grounds that the integrity of the policy was more important. Similarly when Jordan wanted to oppose an appropriation sought by the Central Savannah River Area Planning and Development Commission to punish legislators who had voted against the administration's programs, Carter rejected the notion on the grounds that ultimately it would only hurt ordinary citizens. As Carter had shown in his meeting with Spinks, although willing to listen to anyone's views, he resented being told what to do.

As he came down to the wire, Carter was willing to make some substantive compromises in the details of the plan to gain the support of wavering legislators, provided he felt it was not doing violence to the real meat of each reorganization measure. He had his own standards for determining what was acceptable in arm-twisting legislators, mainly based on whether he thought he was supporting or opposing the public good. He was willing to use his $2 million contingency fund to pay for items which, although relatively cheap, were of enormous importance to the image of legislators in their own districts. These included such things as funding a high school band to go to the Rose Bowl parade, repairing and expanding athletic facilities, and improving water and sewage systems. He was equally willing to block the pet projects of those who opposed him.

By January 26, the end of the fifteen-day period specified in the "reverse veto" provision of HB 1, the whole reorganization package remained relatively intact. Carter had sustained thirty-four vetoes in the House and eleven in the Senate. Most of those in the House were the result of negotiated agreements that had Carter's support, involving relatively minor elements in the plan conceded in order to preserve the overall structure. It was the vetoed portions in the Senate that posed a greater problem because they tended to be more substantial and were intended by his enemies to strike at the heart of the whole initiative. Overall, however, 198 of the 243 provisions in the bill remained intact, an accomplishment that astonished many observers. The General Assembly then recessed, planning to reconvene on February 21 to complete the constitutionally mandated forty days of its regular session.

Carter's opponents sought to obstruct the passage of this new legislation by bottling it up in a Senate committee. Eventually Carter supporters, by threatening a legislative maneuver to bring it directly to the floor of the Senate, were able to get committee chairman Stanley Smith to report a version of the bill. But it contained a substitute provision relating to the Department of Human Resources that was totally unacceptable to Carter. As Carter and his staff listened tensely in his office, the substitute went down by a vote of 28 to 27 on the Senate floor. The Carter version then passed 29 to 26 when two of the usual Carter opponents decided to put themselves on the winning side.

The mandatory ending of the session was drawing near and Lester Maddox and the other Carter opponents thought that by stalling they could deny a Carter victory. On the last day of the session, a Senate/House conference committee was still required to reconcile the relatively minor remaining differences between the bills passed in each house. Maddox delayed all day in appointing the Senate representatives on the committee. At 9:05 P.M., with less than three hours to go, Senator Holloway took the floor to introduce a motion instructing the "yet to be named" Senate members of the conference committee. Maddox still stalled. In an atmosphere of escalating drama, a Carter loyalist, Senator Julian Webb, rose to move that the Senate instruct the "conference committee to be named" to report to the Senate in one hour. At 10:31 P.M. he informed Maddox for good measure. To expedite matters, Carter reluctantly agreed to one last compromise—exempting the computer system of the labor department from a plan to consolidate all the state's computer and printing systems.

At 11:50 P.M., ten minutes before mandatory adjournment, the committee reported back to the Senate. However, the fight was still not over. Senator Stanley Smith, a diehard Carter foe and one of the Senate conferees, had suspiciously disappeared. The head of the House delegation, Majority Leader George Busbee, threatened to stand in the well of the Senate, preventing adjournment until the sergeant-at-arms found the errant senator. Cloyd Hall rushed frantically through the capitol and eventually produced Smith, who then signed the conference report. The omnibus reorganization package was passed literally on the stroke of midnight.

CHAPTER 15

Destiny is not a matter of chance, it is a matter of choice. Destiny is not a thing to be waited for, it is a thing to be achieved.

—WILLIAM JENNINGS BRYAN

In the spring of 1972, Sam Nunn came to see Carter. He intended to run in the Democratic primary against Carter's appointee, U.S. Senator David Gambrell. Nunn was uncertain about his chances, but told Carter he wanted to at least lay the groundwork for a future statewide race. Carter was ambivalent. Nunn had been a loyal supporter in both of his gubernatorial races, and had been his Houston County chairman in 1970, delivering a substantial majority. Nunn had succeeded him as the second president of the Georgia Planning Association and Carter had also appointed him to head his "Goals for Georgia" program. He was in many respects an ideal successor for Carter in the governor's office, which would clearly be Nunn's next objective if, as was likely, he lost the Senate race.

Carter was also mildly miffed with Gambrell for taking positions critical of him, although philosophical about the need for Gambrell to establish an independent political identity. He was less sympathetic about Gambrell's opposition to the proposed supersonic transport plane that would have been built, in large part, at Lockheed's Marietta plant near Atlanta. While Carter agreed that the plane was probably not needed, he felt it was politically inept of Gambrell, while running for reelection, to vote against a project that involved so many Georgia jobs. The thirteen-man field also included former governor Ernest Vandiver, who consistently argued that the seat was rightfully his. Although a Gambrell defeat would be mildly embarrassing, Carter gave Sam Nunn his blessing.

With the reorganization plan successfully achieved, Carter could afford to focus on broader political vistas. He successfully hosted the Southern Governors Conference in Atlanta. His fellow governors elected him to serve on key regional boards including the Southern Regional Education Board, the Appalachian Regional Commission, the Coastal Plains Regional Action Planning Commission, and the Southern Growth Policies Board. In the summer of 1972, when Governor John West hosted the Southern Governors Conference at Hilton Head, South Carolina, a resort for the wealthy, Jimmy and Rosalynn left the group for an afternoon to visit the nearby impoverished counties of Beaufort and Jasper. These two overwhelmingly black counties had become the focus of a federal anti-poverty project after they had been identified as among the poorest in the nation, with severe malnutrition, parasite infestations, and an absence of running water and health care. Media coverage of Carter visiting destitute blacks only minutes away from where his golfing fellow governors were residing in the lap of luxury made him the focus of an otherwise unremarkable event. To him it was a legitimate interest; to several of his colleagues it was grandstanding.

Following the uproar at the 1968 Democratic National Convention in Chicago there was strong pressure within the party to open up the delegate selection process, enabling ordinary citizens to play a greater role in party affairs. The changes were particularly directed at blacks, women, the young, and other groups traditionally excluded by party regulars. Within guidelines, each state was permitted to establish its own process. During the campaign, Carter had enthusiastically embraced the move, promising to "return the Democratic Party to the people." Traditionally in Georgia, as in many states, the governor and the party chairman appointed their cronies to be delegates. The reforms for 1972, instituted by Georgia Democratic Party executive director Zell Miller, under Kirbo's chairmanship and with Carter's backing, called for delegates to be picked simultaneously at "caucus" sites in the state's congressional districts. Registered Democrats could announce their candidacies for specific delegate slots, identifying themselves as pledged to specific presidential candidates or as uncommitted. On March 11, voters could go to the designated location in their congressional district and vote for the delegates of their choice.

Under the plan the governor and the state party chairman were automatically to be a part of the delegation. However, because of Carter's highly touted commitment to this new democratic selection process, he announced that he and Kirbo should run for election in their districts like everyone else. Two of the leading presidential candidates, Senator Edmund Muskie and Senator George McGovern, had for several weeks been organizing delegates to run. Carter put together a slate of "uncommitted" (but loyal to him) delegates from among his supporters, the votes of whom he intended to use for bargaining purposes at the convention in Miami. He had let most of them know he was leaning toward Senator Henry ("Scoop") Jackson, whom Kirbo favored. The majority of Georgians preferred George Wallace, but he made little or no effort to organize delegates in the state. Wallace says this was because he had a deal with Carter that in return for staying out of the state Carter would nominate him at the convention, and then presumably would get the votes of the Carter-loyal delegates. Carter will neither confirm nor deny that such a deal was discussed.

On Saturday, March 11, a sunny but cold day, only a minuscule percentage of the Georgia electorate turned out to vote in the district caucuses. Those who did were overwhelmingly the more liberal party activists, particularly the young and blacks. Black students across the state had organized behind the candidacy of New York congresswoman Shirley Chisholm with devastating effect. In the Fifth Congressional District, encompassing most of Atlanta, with the exception of the nationally known black legislator Julian Bond, running officially uncommitted but leaning toward McGovern, they took every other position. All the Carter-loyal candidates, including Kirbo, the primary architect of the new system, were defeated. The Fourth Congressional District, covering mostly white suburbs of Atlanta, was swept by McGovern-pledged delegates.

At the Americus High School gymnasium, where the Third District meeting was being held, Carter arrived to find a similar situation. The problem had been compounded by the fact that local insurance executive John Amos, angry with Carter for not appointing him to the state party executive committee, had hired buses to help bring in black college students. It suddenly looked as though the governor might go down to embarrassing defeat by one of two college students—Mike Blackwell or Thomas Dortch. The voting was a slow and tedious process that allowed Carter supporters to put out an urgent distress call. Miss Lillian and Gloria played a crucial role in rallying people to vote. Carter won a majority with 653 votes, avoiding a potentially disastrous runoff by only 15 votes. Later some tardy students would correctly argue that there had been a deliberate effort by the local party officials, mostly Carter's friends, to close the first round of voting before they arrived. Not a single Wallace- or Muskie-pledged delegate was elected in Georgia, although some of those elected as "uncommitted" were Wallace supporters.

In the next two months, McGovern, an architect of the new rules, emerged as the likely nominee. Carter was in a period of surging ambition. Highly competitive, he felt the declared presidential candidates and other national political figures were a surprisingly unimpressive group. They were certainly not Jeffersons or Madisons. He intended to use the presidential campaign to generate national visibility for himself. He even fantasized that with a liberal like McGovern heading the ticket, the choice of a progressive southerner to provide ideological and geographic balance seemed a natural conclusion. As Kirbo recalls, they discussed Carter's prospects:

> At the time Jimmy and I discussed it, we were trying to get "Scoop" Jackson nominated, which did not look very likely. I recall telling Jimmy that I

thought we needed to continue to try to do a good job in electing "Scoop." I did not think that would hurt him, that it wouldn't influence or prohibit him from being selected as the vice-presidential candidate.

Carter pursued a two-track strategy. He needed to maintain communications with the McGovern supporters on the Georgia delegation while promoting himself in the national media as leading the "stop McGovern" movement. Running the McGovern campaign in Georgia and across most of the South was thirty-two-year-old Bebe Bahnson Smith. The Bahnsons were a prominent and politically active Americus family. Bebe had become a social activist as a teenager when her Episcopal congregation sought to fire their priest, Reverend Paul Ritch, for his defense of Clarence Jordan; she and a handful of others avidly defended Ritch. Although Bebe's unorthodox and outspoken mother often played poker with Miss Lillian and Gloria, Bebe had never met Carter and he did not know her by her married name.

A few weeks after the caucus meetings, Carter invited the successful McGovern delegates to the mansion. While Carter, Kirbo, and Jordan had had their differences with Lester Maddox and other members of the Georgia legislature, they at least spoke the same political language. The McGovern delegates might just as well have been from another planet. Having worked in the Arnall campaign, Bebe was the only one with any background in traditional Democratic politics. Most of the others were involved only because of their strong anti-war sentiment, or to challenge the white, male political establishment. The atmosphere was one of instant mutual hostility.

Kirbo addressed them in a condescending manner, saying that while what they had done in taking advantage of the new rules was enterprising, it was time now to join the party leaders in getting behind "Scoop" Jackson. That Kirbo could be so oblivious to their idealism and that he could suggest supporting Jackson, who symbolized everything they were against, left them dumbstruck. As Bebe Smith says, "They went into orbit. It was a *very* tense little evening after that."

As they were preparing to leave, Bebe approached Carter, who had said little and barely smiled all evening. "You know I'm from Americus. I lived there all my life."

"No?" he responded with surprise, then asked in southern colloquial style, "Who's your mama?"

When she told him, he rolled back his head laughing and said, "Well that explains it all." He hugged her and then started reintroducing her around to everyone, saying he knew her mother and Bebe was just like her. She says, "From that moment on, he was wonderful to me. . . . He hated George McGovern. He did everything he could to derail George McGovern, but treated me with warmth, kindness, and humor."

In June, Carter generated considerable publicity at the National Governors Conference trying to gain opposition to McGovern, who he argued
could not be elected in the South. With encouragement from some organized labor groups, Carter became identified as the leader of the "ABM"
(Anyone But McGovern) movement.

In early July, en route to the Democratic convention in Miami, McGovern campaigned through the South and stopped in Atlanta to address a
rally. Carter did not attend. However, he did invite McGovern, accompanied by his key fund-raiser, Morris Dees, to spend the night at the mansion,
a necessary act of hospitality that southerners would not perceive as any
form of endorsement. Carter found himself much more compatible with
George McGovern than he had expected. McGovern, whose father had
been a minister in the Wesley Methodist Church, an evangelical, fundamentalist faith, had himself spent some time in a seminary. Both men saw
the melding of their Christian beliefs and politics in a similar way. Carter
subsequently told reporters that he felt McGovern might carry Georgia,
adding that McGovern had made an important concession, namely that as
president he would see that civil rights laws were enforced throughout the
country and not just in the South. While remaining coy about his aspirations, Carter did nothing to discourage his staff from pursuing the possibility of his being on the ticket with McGovern.

On May 15, George Wallace had been shot while campaigning at a shopping center in a Maryland suburb of Washington. For a while it was uncertain whether he would continue as a presidential candidate. When he did,
it was no longer as a potent player galvanizing conservative southern sentiment against the liberal takeover of the party, but rather as a figure invoking compassion and sympathy. Whatever assumptions Wallace may have
had about an agreement on Carter's part to nominate him, it now made little sense from Carter's perspective to do so. However, shortly before he
left Atlanta, Carter received a telegram from Wallace asking him again to
put his name in nomination, or at least make a seconding speech. Carter
sent him back a handwritten note saying he planned to remain uncommitted. Wallace claimed in 1976 that the telegram was sent not by him but by
some of his aides without his knowledge. Several newspaper editorials in
Georgia urged Carter, in view of the heavy vote for Wallace in the state in
1968, to be his nominator. Flying on a state plane to Miami, Jody Powell
asked Carter to nominate Wallace, to which Carter responded, "If you
think George Wallace is fit to lead the American people, you tell them. Not
me." Carter recalls that Hamilton Jordan also supported the idea, but Jordan later said he saw it more as a last resort in order to get Carter national
visibility on the podium, if no other opportunity developed.

With the exception of Wallace, "Scoop" Jackson was the only candidate

Carter had previously known, and that was only a brief encounter when Carter was working for Rickover and Jackson was a young senator. Richard Russell saw Jackson as somewhat of a protégé and had told Carter that Jackson was someone to watch. The family of Jackson's wife were also from Georgia. The Russell imprimatur, Jackson's pro-military stance, and his wife's kinship made him look like a potentially attractive candidate in the South to Carter. In February 1972, long before McGovern was seen as a credible candidate, and with pressure from Kirbo, Carter had come close to publicly endorsing Jackson as a way of preempting efforts to force him into the Wallace camp. When Jackson had come to Atlanta in the spring of 1972 and stayed at the mansion, the notion of Carter nominating him was raised. As Carter recalled, "I encouraged it, but I don't think I committed myself to do it."

As a faculty member at Emory Medical School, I had met Carter and contributed issue papers to the gubernatorial campaign. After his election, I had worked with Rosalynn as she launched her mental health initiative. Subsequently, Carter asked me to take a leave of absence from my academic position and join his staff in setting up a statewide program for treating drug addicts and handling other health matters. Over time my friendship with the Carters grew, as well as the scope of my involvement with his political career. I never returned full-time to academia.

In the days before leaving for Miami, Hamilton Jordan, Gerry Rafshoon, Landon Butler, and I discussed how we could further the effort to get the McGovern staff to consider Carter as his running mate; it would have been out of character for Carter to have indulged in such scheming. More important, it was completely improbable. Jordan, who read Carter's intentions with precision, knew very well that his failure to discourage us was a green light to go ahead.

Regardless of the vice-presidential possibility, having Carter make a prime-time nominating speech was important for his political future. We also needed to make a pitch to the senior McGovern campaign staff, and none of us had an entree to his inner circle. The best we could do was for Landon Butler to obtain a letter from a former aide to Robert Kennedy, extolling Carter's attributes, for me to give to Gary Hart, McGovern's campaign manager. I never did see Hart personally and ended up giving the letter to a young campaign aide.

Carter arrived in Miami at 1 P.M. on Saturday, July 8. He went almost immediately to a meeting of Democratic governors where, eager to carve out a visible role for himself, he pushed through a resolution calling for the appointment of a committee of six governors to help resolve credential fights. Carter was himself embroiled in a challenge to the composition of the Georgia delegation, implying racial discrimination, brought by Julian

Bond and Bebe Smith, which had the backing of the McGovern campaign. Carter needed visibility, but not in a major floor fight with Julian Bond, which would have been reminiscent of a similar fight between Bond and Lester Maddox in 1968. Carter negotiated a formula that allowed a number of people, black and white, myself included, to be placed on the delegation even though we had not been elected. It meant the Georgia delegation would be seated and able to vote on a much more consequential challenge, that to the composition of the California delegation.

After attending church on Sunday, Carter received a call from "Scoop" Jackson asking him to make his nominating speech. Carter promised to give him a definite answer by the end of the day, following which he and Rosalynn left for a lunch aboard a yacht belonging to the Coca-Cola Company. That evening, Hamilton Jordan and I were driving to a restaurant when he received a message from Carter on a two-way radio asking him to call Jackson's staff and accept the invitation to nominate him. We stopped at a pay phone, but neither of us had a dime. We pleaded with a passerby to give us change so the call could be made.

Neither Carter, Kirbo, nor any of the rest of his immediate staff had ever been to a national party convention. When this one opened on Monday evening, we walked out under the glaring lights onto the convention floor flushed with excitement. Amid the red, white, and blue balloons, brightly colored signs, loud festive music, and mingling celebrities of politics and media, it was seemingly a moment to savor for a lifetime. It was, however, instantly apparent that the convention was dominated by delegates more akin to Bebe Smith and her group than to Carter, Kirbo, and the other more conservative members of the Georgia delegation: Of the 3,194 delegates, 39.7 percent were women, 21.4 percent were thirty years old or younger, and 15.2 percent were black. It was the ultimate moment of triumph for the anti-war movement and they wanted to make the most of it. It was obvious to Carter and to the rest of us that these young pro-McGovern delegates reviled "Scoop" Jackson and were likely to feel the same way about anyone identified with him.

The following morning we gathered in the Carters' suite with serious ambivalence about the decision to nominate Jackson. However, there was little alternative but to make the most out of the situation. As the person closest to McGovern ideologically, and therefore considered to have the greatest affinity with the McGovern delegates, I drafted the nominating speech. I decided to make scant mention of Jackson until the last sentence, when Carter would have to say he was nominating him. Instead I focused heavily on Carter's own attributes, beliefs, and accomplishments, linking them and him to the Kennedy ethos and memory—a theme I felt would be acceptable to virtually all of the delegates. Many delegates wished Ted Kennedy were the nominee, and I tried to show Carter was acknowledging that. Rafshoon and Carter made some minor additions, but when the speech was sent to Jackson for his review, he understandably insisted on giving his name and his own accomplishments greater mention. Nevertheless, as Leslie Wheeler suggests in her book *Jimmy Who?*, the basic objective was still achieved:

> Carter's speech is interesting in terms of what it reveals about his thinking at the time. . . . [It] shows that Carter had Kennedy very much on his mind, a man who could bring the diverse elements of the party back together again. McGovern was not the man to do this, and neither—Carter must have realized even as he gave the speech—was Jackson. It was the right speech, but for the wrong man at the wrong time.

Our efforts to promote Carter as the vice-presidential candidate continued. Carter had told the *New York Times* the previous day that Wallace had assured him he would not make a third-party effort. Carter also said that he now believed if McGovern campaigned in the South, and did not antagonize Wallace voters, he could win. The implication was that if he was on the ticket it would make McGovern acceptable to the Wallace supporters. On Wednesday morning, July 12, Jordan and I arranged to have breakfast with Bill Dougherty, the lieutenant governor of South Dakota and a McGovern intimate. He was encouraging, telling us that Carter's name was certainly on the list. More than a year later we learned that Dougherty had been a staunch supporter of Wisconsin Governor Patrick Lucy and adamantly opposed consideration of any southerner.

Andrew Young, running for the Fifth Congressional District seat in Atlanta, arrived that afternoon. As Carter later recalled,

> I . . . asked Andy Young to help me put my name forward as a possible vice-president. When my name was presented to McGovern there was some vile language used and my name was immediately rejected, which was reported to me. I never tried anymore to have my name put forward.

Rafshoon and Jordan showed Pat Caddell, McGovern's twenty-one-year-old pollster, some rather dubious poll data purporting to indicate that Carter would be McGovern's strongest running mate. Caddell responded with what he later conceded was feigned enthusiasm. Black Atlanta vice-mayor Maynard Jackson told the *Atlanta Journal*, "It ought to be Jimmy Carter. And I'm working hard on it." Morris Dees, an Alabaman whose revolutionary fundraising techniques had contributed greatly to McGovern's success, genuinely believed that Carter would be a good choice and actually pressed his cause in the McGovern circle, but his enthusiasm was not shared by others.

Ted Kennedy, so as not to steal the limelight from McGovern, had announced that he would not come to the convention until the last night, but even in his absence he overshadowed the proceedings as the dominant figure of the Democratic Party. That same morning five southern governors, including Carter, had breakfast with McGovern and urged him again to pick Kennedy as the only person who could help the party ticket carry their states. Knowing that Kennedy had adamantly on several occasions refused, Carter could easily go along with his fellow governors without compromising his own chances.

On the opening night of the convention, Governor Reuben Askew, already under discussion as a vice-presidential possibility, gave an inspiring keynote address, immediately boosting speculation that if McGovern did decide on a southerner, Askew would be his choice. To our surprise and pleasure that morning, Askew withdrew his name from consideration. At midmorning, Carter and Jackson appeared at a press conference to announce that Carter would make the nominating speech, which we awaited with eager anticipation.

Each night the convention had been running further and further behind schedule, continuing into the small hours of the morning. By the time Carter went nervously to the podium to give his speech, most of the television audience had gone to bed. The McGovern delegates, smelling their final victory, were impatient and milled about on the convention floor, largely drowning out the speakers. The headline the next day in the *Atlanta Journal* read "Carter's Speech Goes Unnoticed."

McGovern's victory was formally ratified in the early hours of Thursday morning. The final vote of the Georgia delegation was 14½ votes for McGovern, 14½ for Jackson, 12 for Chisholm, and 11 for Wallace. Despite political differences, the general level of compatibility on the delegation had been remarkably high. Black radicals, anti-war activists, and conservative Wallaceites found that when forced to talk together they had much more in common than any of them anticipated. Most would become loyal Carter supporters.

During the day on Thursday, July 13, Jimmy and Rosalynn remained in their suite waiting with lingering optimism for the elusive phone call. We heard rumors that McGovern had selected Congressman Wilbur Mills of Arkansas, then Leonard Woodcock, head of the United Auto Workers, and then Senator Fritz Mondale. Carter stayed busy with state business, never acknowledging what we were all hopefully waiting for. Finally, we heard McGovern had definitely picked Senator Thomas Eagleton of Missouri. Hamilton Jordan and I walked over to the formal announcement, feeling only mild disappointment that our infinitely long-shot candidate had not made it onto the ticket. Asked for his reaction, Carter declined to discuss the choice, "until I can find out his record and his stand on the issues."

On the final night, McGovern's acceptance speech, with the refrain

"Come home America," provided a fitting climax to the week, but it would prove the high point of his campaign. Ted Kennedy, whose absence throughout the week reflected the distance he wanted to maintain from McGovern, arrived to deliver a similarly rousing speech. His unequivocal message to traditionalists, however, was that he, not McGovern, was the true leader of the party. Few doubted he would be the nominee in 1976.

My personal loyalty and affection was with Carter, but my ideological sympathies were closer to McGovern and his followers, although it was clear that the enthusiasm of the McGovern loyalists at the convention was not shared by the rest of the country. The McGovern campaign was a necessary vehicle to exorcise the anger of a war-weary generation of young people, but Carter was a conciliator committed to healing old animosities rather than aggravating them. In his approach to politics, which relied on bringing adversaries together to solve problems, emotions got in the way. When I looked at those of us around Carter, there was Kirbo, deeply committed to "Scoop" Jackson; Jody Powell, who had wanted Carter to nominate George Wallace; Landon Butler, who early on had been the Georgia coordinator for Edmund Muskie; and myself, a McGovern sympathizer. Yet all of us saw qualities in Carter that were compatible with our own views. It again reflected Carter's enjoyment of being surrounded by people of disparate, if not utterly opposing, views. He did not particularly care if they were compatible with each other. He was the unifying force.

Over the next two weeks I would think increasingly about the fundamental changes that were happening in the country as a whole and in the political process in particular, precipitated by the war in Vietnam, the civil rights movement, and the youth-oriented revolution of the previous ten years. I also thought specifically about the unprecedented new rules, still undergoing revision, that were transforming the presidential nominating process in the Democratic Party and the as yet unexplored new possibilities that this created. The McGovern people had put together a unique campaign and had used it to seize power from the party establishment in a revolutionary way. What they had done was impressive, but they had only begun to exploit the full potential of what the rules now made possible, especially for a dedicated populist.

Another event with ongoing implications had occurred a month before, on June 18, 1972, when a group of wiretappers had broken into the Democratic National Headquarters in the Watergate complex in Washington. To that point, what President Nixon's staff dismissed as a "second-rate burglary" had received relatively little press attention, but over time it would cause an explosion of skepticism toward traditional politicians and result in changes in the campaign finance laws that would open the door for a complete outsider to be elected president for the first time.

Within ten days of the convention it emerged that Senator Tom Eagleton had a history of psychiatric hospitalization on three separate occasions for depression and had received electroshock therapy. Under increasing pressure, McGovern removed him from the ticket. On a Sunday afternoon at the height of the crisis, I received a phone call from Rosalynn Carter asking if she could come to see me at my house. I offered to go to the mansion, as I had always done in the past, but she insisted on coming to me. She arrived alone except for her driver/security guard. She came quickly to the point, telling me she was convinced Eagleton's departure from the ticket was inevitable and imminent. She wanted to know if I would be willing to pursue with my contacts in the McGovern camp the possibility of their considering Jimmy as Eagleton's replacement. I was not encouraging and after a couple of calls was convinced this was out of the question. The same day, Carter invited State Representative Julian Bond to come to the mansion and he asked Bond also to intercede with McGovern on his behalf. Bond tried, but had no greater success than I. McGovern soon selected Sargent Shriver.

Relieved of any doubts I might have had about the Carters' ambition, I prepared a ten-page memo for Governor Carter, noting what seemed a unique, open opportunity for an outsider to run for the presidency and urging him to begin planning immediately for the 1976 race. The majority of people drawn into politics by McGovern were there to stay; it would not be politics as usual after McGovern's anticipated defeat in November. Favored by the rule changes, grassroots activism was likely to be more important than traditional coalition building. The opportunity would be there to build a new constituency based on a populist appeal, but it would require a real risk taker. The time also seemed right for a southerner who, unlike Wallace, could hold a biracial southern base but still appeal to the rest of the country. While the conventional wisdom assumed Kennedy would be the nominee, there were many reasons to think this unlikely.

I then made a series of recommendations, by far the most important being that a decision to run needed to be made as soon as possible to allow the time to build the base for a successful campaign. I also urged Carter to write an autobiographical book that could help people get to know him and to develop expertise in a couple of areas such as health care or the environment in order to become a national spokesperson on those topics. He needed to travel the country, accepting as many speaking engagements as he could, campaigning for Democratic candidates and especially helping to raise money, building relationships by capitalizing on his greatest asset—his personal charm. I concluded:

> No southerner has captured the presidency because he has not been will-
> ing to take the drastic step away from traditional southern politics that is
> necessary. What is critical is the psychological and emotional decision to

take the risk and run for the presidency to win, whatever the eventual outcome might be. I hope you will consider it and I think you can win.

With the democratizing changes that have occurred in American presidential politics over the last twenty years, it is now difficult to recapture a
sense of the lofty isolation with which the presidency and the pursuit of it
were still viewed in 1972. While there were titanic struggles over who
would assume the office, it was seemingly always between men of great
stature and of longstanding national prominence. The idea of someone virtually unknown outside his own state, out of office and having little or no
ideological base, running successfully for president seemed, in the old context, so absurd as to not even warrant discussion. How poorly known
Carter remained outside of Georgia was reflected by the fact that when, in
early 1973, he appeared on *What's My Line?*, the panel could not guess his
job. The prospect of a southerner winning the presidency for the first time
in more than a hundred years seemed highly improbable. Carter, while
someone of confidence and ambition, remained genuinely committed to
humility as a cardinal virtue. Without some independent validation of the
idea from anyone around him, other than Rosalynn, to pronounce suddenly
his intention to run for president would have seemed almost an act of irrational egotism. Even to begin discussions he needed to feel he had the
license, afforded by the faith of others.

Those who might have suggested to Carter that he run could not bring
themselves to raise the issue directly with him. Charles Kirbo understood
Carter's remarkable talents as well as anyone. What he did not fully appreciate was the revolution occurring in the country and in presidential politics, something Carter himself grasped much better.

Prior to becoming governor, Carter had never met a president. During
1971 he had two brief ceremonial meetings with Richard Nixon. He still
held the presidency and its occupants in considerable awe. He wrote in
Why Not the Best?, "Great presidents like Washington, Jefferson, Lincoln,
and Roosevelt have always been historical figures to me, and even the intimate biographical information published about them has never made them
seem quite human." He noted that in early 1972, "I began comparing my
own experience and knowledge of government with the candidates, not
against 'the presidency' and not against Thomas Jefferson and George
Washington." Rosalynn was more emphatic: "Jimmy knew a lot more about
a lot of things than did these men who were running for president."

After a meeting with Carter on other business, I handed him my memo.
I heard nothing for ten days. Then Hamilton Jordan said to me, "Jimmy
showed me your memo." He had also already discussed it with Rosalynn.
Once the proposition was in writing and Carter had not dismissed it out of

hand, Jordan eagerly embraced it. We began to discuss what would be involved and how to get Carter to make the necessary early decision. In addition to the two of us, Landon Butler and Gerry Rafshoon attended our early meetings, held at our homes and not at the office. Jody Powell was invited, but did not come. He not only had reservations but he also had practical concerns as to what the reaction of the press, the legislature, and other groups would be if word of such a scheme leaked out. With two years left on the gubernatorial term, he was primarily concerned about protecting Carter from what would likely be wild derision from Lieutenant Governor Lester Maddox and others if they found out Carter was so presumptuous as to think he should be president.

On October 17, Carter invited Jordan, Butler, Rafshoon, and myself to the mansion. We arrived around seven in the evening. We settled into the overstuffed chairs, Jordan and Butler sitting opposite Carter, Rafshoon and me on either side. The conversation began awkwardly. Hamilton Jordan took the lead: "Governor, we have come to talk to you about your future," he said with a touch of humor. "I don't know any other way to say this, and it's hard to bring myself to say the words, but I guess I will just have to say it." He paused, his hesitancy reflecting the enormity and audacity of what he was saying. "We think you should run for president." Carter nodded.

Jordan then proceeded to review Carter's options. The Georgia constitution prohibited him from seeking a second term, so he would be out of office in January 1975. He could, as most people in Georgia anticipated, run against Herman Talmadge for his Senate seat. However, his chances against such an entrenched icon would not be good. Besides, even if he were to win, being back in a legislative body as a junior senator would not be satisfying. It was almost unprecedented for someone out of office, much less out of a job, to run for president, and we talked about the possibility of Carter trying to secure a university presidency for a while as Eisenhower had done. On the other hand, without other responsibilities he could campaign full-time, something other candidates would not be able to do.

We all agreed that McGovern and Shriver, facing an overwhelming defeat, would have little residual strength after November. Wallace and Kennedy loomed as the most imposing figures for 1976, although both had striking vulnerabilities that made their prospective roles uncertain. If Wallace ran and remained healthy, he would pose a special problem, because he would have to be beaten in the South if Carter was to achieve credibility as an acceptable southern alternative. Kennedy remained an enigma. He was the overwhelming favorite for the nomination, yet rumors persisted that fear of assassination, the impact of Chappaquiddick, and other personal problems would discourage him from running.

Others who seemed decided long shots were Senator Walter Mondale (too liberal), "Scoop" Jackson (too old), and Hubert Humphrey, who had lost in 1968. Of the other "New South" governors, only Dale Bumpers of Arkansas, whom we knew to be ambitious, and Reuben Askew, whose intentions seemed obscure, offered any concern. Two political newcomers, Jay Rockefeller, running for governor of West Virginia, and John Glenn, the astronaut seeking a Senate seat in Ohio, were long shots we felt bore watching. We concluded that whatever hurdles Carter had to overcome, no one was necessarily in any better position for a primary race that was still more than three years away.

Perhaps Carter's biggest potential liability would be if Lester Maddox were to again be elected governor. Being constantly undercut by the governor of his own state would make it almost impossible to maintain credibility in a presidential race. Bert Lance had expressed interest in running for governor and Carter told us that he felt helping Lance to succeed him had to be a top priority. We also discussed the problem of fund-raising. With his characteristically frugal mentality, Carter talked about operating on a shoestring and relying heavily on volunteers. He felt that he could raise enough money from a handful of his wealthy and most loyal supporters because they liked him and they really believed he could be elected president.

We also talked quite frankly about Carter's shortcomings, which he openly admitted. While he was superb talking one on one or to small groups, he lacked forcefulness and dynamism when he addressed large audiences, especially when he spoke from a prepared text. He also generally did poorly on television and agreed he needed help. Although he had considerable interest in foreign affairs and was in the process of starting trade missions for Georgia in several foreign countries, his knowledge was hardly sufficient to stand up to the tough scrutiny of a presidential campaign. He would also have to give special attention to the field of economics, where he was hardly in a presidential league.

Although the general election of 1972 was still more than two weeks away, with so much to accomplish time was crucial and Carter could not afford to squander it. At several points in the meeting I pushed to get a definitive commitment from him that he would run. But as was his style, he held back, absorbing everything we discussed but keeping control in a tantalizing way. The meeting broke up around midnight. The four of us talked in the dark parking area for several minutes. We all knew the decision had been made even though he would not say it. Later he would describe the decision: "It was kind of an evolutionary thing."

On election night, November 5, I had dinner with Jimmy and Rosalynn and we watched the returns on television. McGovern and Shriver went down to their predictable defeat. Although he had taken the unpopular position in Georgia of supporting the ticket, it helped Carter significantly with the Democratic Party nationally. Andrew Young won and so did Sam Nunn, who had pulled an upset victory over Gambrell in the Democratic primary. Elsewhere, Jay Rockefeller failed in his bid to become governor of West Virginia, causing Carter to comment with a wry smile, "That's too bad." In discussing McGovern's defeat, on network television Senator Hubert Humphrey extolled the virtues of Fritz Mondale, saying that the junior senator from Minnesota was his personal choice for president in 1976. It boosted Mondale to an early, but highly tenuous, front-runner position.

The day after the election, with Carter's decision to run now taken for granted, he called a meeting at the mansion to discuss where he stood in light of the results. This time we were joined by Charles Kirbo, Philip Alston, and Bert Lance. Much of the meeting centered on Bert Lance's intention to run for governor. Preventing a Maddox comeback remained a preoccupying precondition of the presidential strategy. We did agree that Herman Talmadge should be told immediately about Carter's plans so that he would not, in the mistaken belief that Carter wanted his Senate seat, do anything to undermine Carter or Lance in the state. Toward the end of the meeting there was an open discussion in which everyone was throwing out ideas, some thoughtful, some spontaneous, about the presidential campaign. We all remained so overawed by the revolution we were contemplating that we persisted, as we would for months, in using the euphemisms "our national effort," and "seeking higher office." Don Carter, Jimmy's cousin, then the editor of the *Lexington* (Kentucky) *Herald,* was mentioned as someone who should be talked to about strategy with the national news media. Finally Carter asked Hamilton Jordan to put together all of our thoughts and suggestions for him in a coherent way.

Kirbo contacted Herman Talmadge and arranged for Carter to meet him. Flying back from a ceremonial event in Tifton, Georgia, the state plane landed at a little airstrip near the senator's hometown of Lovejoy. As Carter recalled it:

> Senator Talmadge met me there, and we sat in the front seat of his automobile for about an hour. I described to him what my plans were, that I was not going to run for the U.S. Senate, that I was going to run for president. He and I both agreed that it was a long-shot prospect and I told him that I was quite determined to pursue it. At that time we thought that Kennedy and Wallace would be the logical opponents. . . . Herman expressed his appreciation that I was not going to run against him. We both agreed that he would probably win in Georgia for the U.S. Senate and he said that when I needed him to help in the presidential election he would be there to help me.

Hamilton Jordan spent the Thanksgiving holiday completing a seventy-page summary memo as Carter had suggested. He combined my original memo to Carter, one from Rafshoon dealing with his perception and image, plus additional material that the two of us gave him. He also talked to Kirbo at considerable length as well as to Don Carter. The result was a blueprint for securing the Democratic nomination over the next four years.

The memo began by reviewing our earlier discussions deriving from the conventional wisdom that Wallace and Kennedy would be the front-runners in 1976. Jordan was convinced, correctly, that if Wallace could overcome his medical problems he would run again. He added, "It is my guess that George Wallace resents you a little, as we used him effectively in our campaign, but refused to nominate him at the Democratic convention. We should make every effort to court Wallace and gain his friendship and trust. . . . I would hope you might gain his support if he saw in your candidacy an extension and continuation of his earlier efforts."

Kennedy, he said, had many problems, the most significant of which was that he would have great difficulty in winning the general election, although he could probably get the nomination. As I had earlier suggested to Carter, establishing an early relationship with Kennedy, nevertheless, had potential pluses. Jordan wrote,

> I'm of the opinion that Kennedy probably would like to see someone from the South other than Wallace make a national effort. He knows that he cannot depend on the southern states for any initial support for the nomination and would rather have someone like yourself to deal with than with George Wallace. . . . I would place a high priority on an early meeting with Kennedy and a discussion on the future of the party and your intentions to play an active role in the 1976 elections.

Jordan continued with a review of the role of the Democratic Party predicated on the assumption that McGovern's choice as cochairs, Jean Westwood and Pierre Salinger, would be replaced by the recently ousted party treasurer Robert Strauss, a Texan with a receptive attitude to fellow southerners. What was essential, Jordan astutely stressed, was to see that the party remained open to all factions, thereby preventing the leadership from prematurely consolidating around the interests of a single strong leader and potential candidate, such as Teddy Kennedy.

By Christmas 1972, the decision had been made, Jimmy and Rosalynn had informed the members of their family, and the plan was in place.

CHAPTER 16

Justice is the bond of men in states, for the administration of justice, which is the determination of what is just, is the principle of order in political society.

—ARISTOTLE

Point 9 of things to do in Hamilton Jordan's memo was "Meet with Dean Rusk." By coincidence Rusk, who had been John F. Kennedy's secretary of state and was now a distinguished professor at the University of Georgia, called Carter early in 1973 and said he needed to see him; they met that evening at the mansion.

Distinguished, mannerly, and thoughtful, Rusk said, "I've been thinking about this a great deal. I have been talking to my friends around the country, and I think it's time for you to consider running for national office."

"There is only one national office you can run for," Carter replied.

"That's right," said Rusk.

"Well, I must admit I have been thinking about it," Carter allowed.

Rusk then outlined his own thoughts as to why he thought Carter would be successful. Carter, considerably reassured, would later say of the meeting:

> It greatly strengthened my belief that I could have a good chance, because Dean Rusk knew the Kennedy group, and the Washington scene, and the people I would need for financing. It was encouraging for me to know, independently of the input from our side, that Rusk had come and suggested it.

Carter had begun to work on his autobiography, which he was writing entirely himself. At the same time he received an invitation to speak at the National Press Club in Washington. He used the opportunity to lay out for his lunchtime audience on February 9, 1973, his vision for America, testing some of the themes that he was putting in the book. It was his first opportunity to address a Washington audience on national issues, and, although not more than five people in the room knew it, it also amounted to the clandestine kickoff of the Jimmy Carter presidential campaign.

Carter reviewed his accomplishments as governor at roughly the midpoint of his term. He talked about the failures of Richard Nixon, and of revenue sharing, and the lack of understanding in Washington for the real needs of people in the country. He implied that if our national leaders had done the kinds of things he had done in Georgia, the country would be in a much happier condition. He stressed the value of his particular fascination, zero-base budgeting as a management tool: "A zero-base budgeting system should be implemented by the executive branch of government, and a maximum spending limit adopted by both houses of Congress could provide clear and firm restraints on total congressional appropriations."

It was a compassionate speech tinged with populism in which his concern for frugality with the tax dollar was balanced by his sensitivity to the suffering of poorer Americans. He talked of the mentally afflicted child deprived of treatment, the mothers of dependent children forced back on welfare by federal cuts in emergency employment programs, the dairy farmer and the construction worker whose livelihood had been severely compromised by insensitive decisions in Washington. He talked about "benevolent conservatism," which never caught on as a label, but was an apt description of his own philosophy.

In the middle of the speech, Congressman Andrew Young wrote on his place card, "I'll be damned if he's not running for president." In contrast to most of the audience made up of Washington insiders, Young understood the potential that the times offered Carter. To end his speech Carter quoted Niebuhr's statement that the sad duty of politics was to establish justice in a sinful world, and that of Chinese philosopher Kuan Tzu, who said, "You give a man a fish, he has one meal; if you teach him how to fish, he can feed himself for life." Afterward Carter worried that these two quotes might seem a little pretentious coming from a Georgia governor, and that somehow the press would guess that he was running for president and write something ridiculing him, causing embarrassment. A few days later I spoke to my friend Jack Nelson, Washington bureau chief of the *Los Angeles Times,* who had introduced Carter at the luncheon. He understood our desire to keep our plans confidential, but observed frankly and accurately, "Your biggest problem is not going to be whether anyone knows Jimmy Carter is running for president; it's whether anyone gives a damn."

On April 3, 1973, the core members of the planning group met again with Carter. This time it was expanded to include several new members including Robert Lipshutz, Jody Powell, Jimmy's cousin Don Carter, Bill Schwartz, a successful Atlanta realtor and Carter contributor, Frank Moore, Steve Chandler, an administrative assistant in the governor's office, and Rosalynn. We were very aware of Jesse Unruh's observation that "Money is the mother's milk of politics." Lipshutz suggested we create a committee to "Keep Jimmy Carter in Politics" that could be used as a fund-raising vehicle without having to divulge our plans to Carter's friends who would be approached for contributions. Notwithstanding the claims that Gambrell's father had paid it off, there was also still a debt from the 1970 campaign to be taken care of.

In March 1973, Carter had invited Stuart Eizenstat to join the group. He had handled "issues" for Andrew Young's successful congressional race, and spent many hours with Carter interrogating him about his views. He taped the replies, which were then transcribed. Together they reviewed the roughed-out positions and, where they seemed weak, Carter would read more or discuss the topic further with experts.

An area of obvious weakness that was discussed at the April 3 meeting was foreign policy. In April 1972, Carter led a delegation with Georgia's trade commissioner, Lewis Truman, to Mexico, Costa Rica, Colombia, Brazil, and Argentina. Jimmy and Rosalynn diligently brushed up on their Spanish before leaving on the trip. In Brazil, where Georgia had a sister-state relationship with the state of Senora, the Carters were particularly well received.

The success of this trip suggested that further overseas visits were essential to prevent criticism that he lacked knowledge in foreign affairs. A trip was planned for May 1973 to London, Brussels, West Germany, and Israel, billed as another trade mission. The Carters stopped first in London, where they visited the House of Commons, toured the underground (subway), and had lunch with the directors of Lloyds. "They explained to me," he said on his return, "how, although Great Britain is no longer a great military or political power, economically their ties went throughout the world."

In Bonn, Carter met with Chancellor Helmut Schmidt. Carter was interested in the possibility of getting Volkswagen to build a plant in Georgia. According to Carter, "he said 'why don't we talk half the time about Watergate . . . and we'll talk half the time about German investment in Georgia.'" Schmidt offered to arrange for Carter to go to Wolfsberg to meet the directors of the Volkswagen company. To do this, however, Carter had to cancel one of his two days scheduled in Heidelberg. It was agreed that Rosalynn would carry out that part of the schedule alone, and Carter would take their luggage with him. He got up early, dressing and packing in the dark, and left. When Rosalynn awoke, she found he had inadvertently taken all her skirts and slacks, leaving her with only one pair of his trousers. She had a blouse and a short topcoat, which she wore all day, nervously declining to remove it, so as not to reveal that she had on only the blouse underneath. "When we met that night in Berlin," he recalls, "she was hysterical with laughter, and had had narrow escapes all day, sure that someone would find out she didn't have on a skirt or slacks."

Their stop in Israel, the highpoint of their trip for both political and religious reasons, was a profoundly moving experience for both of them. As Carter would later describe, "We had a remarkable visit there with Mrs. Meir, and Mr. Rabin, who came back from South Africa a day early to meet with me. . . . We spent five or six days traveling in Israel." Visiting the Golan Heights, the strategic importance of the site made a significant impression on him.

A fortuitous event at this time immeasurably enhanced Carter's credibility on foreign policy and dramatically bolstered his knowledge in the field. David Rockefeller had established the Trilateral Commission to bring together business, political, and academic leaders from the three developed areas of the world—Western Europe, Japan, and North America—to foster dialogue and cooperation on common problems. The commission members met twice a year to discuss topical world issues such as North–South relations, the law of the seas, the Middle East, world population problems, and the world monetary system. According to Zbigniew Brzezinski, the director of the commission, they wanted to have two governors as members. They had already chosen a Republican, Daniel Evans of Washington State, who had a special interest in Japan, and were anxious not only to have a Democrat but particularly a governor of the "New South." The choice was between Carter and Reuben Askew.

On April 13, 1973, Commission Secretary George Franklin flew to Atlanta to talk to leaders of the business community and Peter White, head of the city's World Affairs Council, about Carter. Shortly thereafter, during the trip to London, Carter met Rockefeller at dinner. Rockefeller, impressed by Carter's aggressive effort to open trade offices, recommended Carter be chosen.

Carter's involvement with the Trilateral Commission affected his prospects for the presidency in several ways. He approached his participation with characteristic intensity. He studied the reading material meticulously, in part because he felt inadequate dealing with a group of people who had primarily devoted their careers to foreign policy. The result was that he achieved a competitive facility with the issues that the commission addressed. While some commissioners admitted he made little or no impression on them, others were surprised by how conversant Carter, as an obscure governor, was with the details of some of the complex international problems before them. These powerful people became important advocates for Carter in their own spheres of influence once he officially announced his candidacy, effectively neutralizing the charge that he knew nothing about foreign policy. This would prove particularly valuable when his conservative detractors tried to argue that a one-term southern governor could not possibly know enough to be entrusted with the security of the nation.

Among the members of the commission from the academic community, Carter made important friends who were willing to educate him, and later draft speeches and serve as advisors in the campaign. They proved to be a crucial asset in being able to identify, in addition to Brzezinski, Professor Richard Gardner of Columbia, and international economist Richard Cooper from Yale, as being among those he consulted on foreign policy.

Carter has often been accused of lacking a sense of humor. Many members, however, remembered him best from a commission meeting in Washington in December 1974, when Secretary of State Kissinger met with the group. During a question and answer period, Patrick Gordon Walker, a distinguished but elderly former British foreign secretary, began a long discourse, which was not so much a question but a rambling, tortuous statement. He went on talking for more than five minutes as people moved uncomfortably in their seats amid mounting embarrassment and tension. As Kissinger finally rose to respond, the clear voice of Jimmy Carter was heard from the back of the room: "Mr. Secretary, would you mind repeating the question?" The room broke up in laughter.

Throughout 1973, the small group around Carter continued to meet every month or so. Andrew Young came on several occasions. Apart from Rosalynn, who attended every meeting and exerted considerable influence, no other woman was involved. Indeed there were no women at a significant level on Carter's staff or in the state government. Concerned about the impression this might later create, Jean Cahill, whom Carter had appointed to head the Georgia Commission on the Status of Women, was briefly invited to attend. While Carter himself was relatively comfortable with women in authority, most of the men around him found it impossible to break with their traditional southern views of the role of women. Unless they were the wives of powerful men, women were treated condescendingly, made the butt of crude jokes, or simply cut out of any decision making. Blacks would prove easier to accept in prominent roles than women.

In May 1974, Teddy Kennedy came to Georgia as the featured speaker at the unveiling of a portrait of Dean Rusk, a part of the Law Day celebrations at the University of Georgia. Carter was asked to be in a lesser role as the lunch speaker. He reluctantly accepted, and only because his son Jack would be in the audience as a member of that year's graduating class.

Kennedy and his large entourage stayed the night before at the mansion and met Carter for the first time. Carter remembers, "Everyone thought he was going to be the next president." Yet, in fact, Kennedy had already made the decision not to run. Ironically, it was Carter, treated politely but with mild disdain as an inconsequential southern governor by Kennedy's staff, who had already made the decision to enter the race.

The next day Carter discovered that Kennedy's carefully prepared talk "was basically the same speech I was going to make." Carter withdrew to a small office and jotted some new thoughts on the back of an envelope. Whether moved by competitiveness with Kennedy, or his anger at being preempted, a surge of emotion surfaced in a powerful speech in which he hit: "Things that really concerned me about the judicial system. I thought it was grossly inequitable and unfair. And I went in and just let my hair down to that crowd in a totally extemporaneous way. . . . I think it is probably the best speech I ever made."

One of those in Kennedy's entourage who shared that perception was the usually cynical journalist Hunter Thompson, who later wrote, "I have never heard a sustained piece of political oratory that impressed me any more." Before 200 stunned alumni, who comprised some of the most distinguished and conservative lawyers and jurists in the state, Thompson said, "[Carter] railed and bitched about the system of criminal justice that allows the rich and privileged to escape punishment for their crimes, and sends poor people to prison because they can't afford to bribe the judge."

Carter bored in on the issue of what really constituted right and wrong in the world. He cited instance after instance where he had found the judicial system failed in its responsibility to protect the ordinary citizen. In a seeming effort to deliberately provoke his staid audience, he said that from listening to records by "a friend of mine," Bob Dylan, including, "The Lonesome Death of Hattie Carroll," "Like a Rolling Stone," and "The Times They Are A-Changin'," he learned to appreciate the dynamism of change in a modern society. He again quoted Niebuhr that the sad duty of politics was to bring justice to a sinful world.

It was a defining speech in Carter's career embodying his deepest beliefs and values, and his rationale for being involved with politics. "It shook up that audience," Carter would later say, smiling. It was, as Hunter Thompson summed it up, "a king hell bastard of a speech."

For Carter to launch his presidential campaign it was increasingly necessary to find some activity that would allow him to travel the country, build contacts, and achieve some visibility. Jordan had suggested the possibility that Carter try to become chairman of the National Governors Conference, but it did not work out. Governor Terry Sanford had been appointed chairman of the newly created Charter Commission, and Barbara Mikulski was made the chair of the Rules Commission of the Democratic Party, closing those two options.

Following McGovern's defeat, Carter had lent his support to Bob Strauss to become the new Democratic Party chairman and invited him to Atlanta as the Jefferson-Jackson Day banquet speaker on March 5, 1973. Carter describes what happened early that evening:

He [Strauss] and I were sitting on the back porch at the mansion, just talking about the Democratic Party. We talked about the need for the DNC to actually give candidates for the first time tangible help. I told him about how completely ignorant I was when I first went into politics running for governor. I did not know how to run, did not know how to raise money, did not know how to make speeches, did not know how to organize or advertise, or use country radio stations. . . . Most people when they get into politics are like myself. . . . We both decided it would be good to set up a committee and he said he would set up the committee if I would agree to be the chairman of it.

A few weeks later Strauss called Carter and said that he wanted to announce his appointment as the national campaign chairman for the 1974 midterm elections at the upcoming Democratic Governors Conference. Carter worried that if it was merely Strauss's decision the position would carry little weight, so he said he would do it if the Democratic National Committee would pass a resolution making it an official appointment. Such appointments had traditionally been merely figurehead positions, so Strauss did not think he was giving much away. To Carter it was just the opening he needed and he intended to make the most of it.

I did not intend for it to be an honorary thing, so Hamilton and I and Jody and Kirbo . . . put together a list of about seventy-five things that the candidates really needed to run a successful campaign. And I remember Strauss made the comment that if you can do 10 percent of this it will be the best effort ever made, and I said I intended to do it all.

Hamilton Jordan resigned his job as the governor's executive secretary and went to Washington to join the Democratic National Committee as the staff director for the National Campaign Committee. Lansing Lee, who had so efficiently backstopped Jordan, had gone back to law school, creating a major vacuum. Without Lee, exhausted from eighteen-hour days, under increasing criticism, concerned about his own career identity, and with his marriage in difficulty, Jordan told friends he was thinking about leaving Carter's staff completely. The opportunity to go to Washington provided a timely solution. Frank Moore, to whom Carter felt deep loyalty, aggressively sought Lee's job, and when Jordan left, Moore succeeded him as Carter's executive secretary.

Under difficult circumstances, Jordan skillfully blended together an impressive program to fulfill the commitment to help Democratic candidates and to advance Carter's interests. Strapped for money, he nevertheless hired two associate directors, Bob Russell and Knox Pitts, and recruited a group of interns, including Joel Solomon, Ken Hays, Marc Cutright, Ellen Metsky, and Jim Gammill, all of whom, except Bob Russell, would play important roles in Carter's presidential race. He also worked with a bright, unassuming young Ph.D. candidate, Rick Hutcheson, deputy director of the research division. Hutcheson would later turn out to have an encyclopedic knowledge and understanding of the ramifications of the new complex delegate selection rules.

With the Watergate scandal over, 1974 was shaping up as a banner year for the Democrats, with a new crop of attractive candidates seeking House, Senate, and gubernatorial seats. The Rules Commission under Barbara Mikulski was holding hearings around the country. Carter and Jordan decided they would hold regional training sessions for candidates in conjunction with those meetings. They brought in experts on polling, the media, fund-raising, and other topics crucial to the candidates and their staff. As Carter further describes it:

> We asked every group of Democrats, "What can we do to help your state win the election in November of '74?" We accumulated a list of things that needed to be done . . . "we don't know how to deal with the abortion issue," "we don't know how to deal with gun control," "we don't know how to deal with the Middle East conflagration." So I decided then on my own initiative that I would start working on issue papers . . . thirty-four of them on different questions: agriculture, education, elderly, and so forth. And I put together a group of advisors—about a hundred people.

It meshed nicely with what he was doing with Eizenstat to prepare himself on the issues for the presidential campaign.

> Later we had a series of meetings in Washington . . . to go down . . . 503 elections. . . . We brought together . . . all the labor leaders . . . the environmental groups, education groups. . . . It was tedious business from eight o'clock in the morning until six o'clock at night. No break for lunch.

Carter himself campaigned for the Democratic candidate in sixty-two congressional races. The prodigious expenditure of time and effort over and above his continuing responsibilities as governor, and completely on his own time, was remarkable. Carter, who never held a press conference, understood well that the relationships he was building were more important than immediate publicity.

He liked to see harmony when often it was only skin deep. His issue papers were good, but drew criticism from the "Democratic Policy Committee," which in theory should have been producing something similar. Carter and Jordan were doing a very commendable and needed job, but their very success pointed out what the DNC had not been doing. Although Carter was probably unaware of it, there was a deliberate effort to marginalize Jordan and his coterie of interns at the DNC. Strauss, expecting Carter to treat the job as largely symbolic, was quite surprised by his creation of a mini-empire, and ultimately by the recognition that Carter was using the position to lay the groundwork for a presidential bid. Strauss was already committed to fellow Texan Lloyd Bentsen, and executive director Bob Keefe was planning to be the campaign manager for another run by "Scoop" Jackson. While neither took the Carter prospects seriously, they also had no reason to help him. Carter and Jordan did, however, find a friend in Marc Siegel, Keefe's deputy.

No longer needing the support of the few Republicans in the Georgia legislature, Carter was now willing to begin taking more partisan positions, becoming the first governor to call for Nixon's impeachment and referring to him as "the worst president in my lifetime."

On Friday, March 15, 1974, using Carter's role with the DNC as a cover, Hamilton Jordan and I, together with his wife, Nancy, and Mary King, whom I would later marry, went to New Hampshire. It was our first trip and the ostensible purpose of it was to establish contacts for a subsequent visit by Jimmy and Rosalynn Carter, who also had not been there previously. Our broader purpose was to obtain a feel for the state, assessing Carter's prospects two years hence, and looking at how we might put together an organization in the state.

We had the names of only three people in all of New Hampshire: David LaRoche, the young Democratic state party director; Richard Winter, a political science professor at Dartmouth; and Lucille Kelly, the co-owner of the public relations firm of Kelly and Cohen in Manchester. Mary King had obtained an introduction to Lucille from her friend Ann Lewis,* an aide to Mayor Kevin White of Boston. We invited Lucille to have dinner with us in Manchester. She had never heard of Jimmy Carter, and was clearly dubious about the prospects for any southerner in New Hampshire. A fascinating woman, she had been a key figure in Jack Kennedy's 1960 New Hampshire primary victory and subsequently had been a speechwriter for Rose Kennedy. Earlier she had worked for William Loeb, the controversial conservative publisher of the *Manchester Union Leader,* who torpedoed Edmund Muskie's 1972 campaign. Despite Lucille's Democratic associations, she remained friendly with Loeb.

With continuing misgivings, Lucille reluctantly agreed to meet with the Carters when they arrived. However, when they met a month later, they had instant rapport and the Carters invited her to visit them in Atlanta. She did and remained at the mansion for ten days, which happened to be when the Carters were hosting a meeting of the Organization of American States. Before she left she wrote to friends in New Hampshire, saying, "I have met the next president of the United States."

---

*Ann Lewis, whose brother, Barney Frank, would later become a prominent member of Congress, would herself emerge as a national figure in the Democratic Party.

In the next two days we talked to several dozen New Hampshire residents—waiters, hotel staff, store owners, anyone who would take a few minutes to talk about politics. We visited shoe factories in Manchester. We drove to the coast and talked to people at the site of a projected oil refinery, opposed by the local community and environmentalists. We drove through snow to Hanover to meet with Richard Winter, an energetic, young political scientist who offered us a more liberal view on the state's politics and agreed to arrange for Carter to speak at Dartmouth.

By Sunday evening we were ecstatic. New Hampshire was a small state ideally suited to the intensive personal style of campaigning that Jimmy and Rosalynn had perfected in Georgia. The state was a good deal more conservative than the past successes of McCarthy and McGovern had led us to expect. When we asked people why McGovern had done so well in 1972, they said that when he shook a person's hand he looked them straight in the eye and they could tell he was an honest, sincere individual. This had been much more important to most of them than his position on the issues. For Carter, New Hampshire seemed tailor-made.

On election night, November 5, 1974, the Democratic victory, fueled substantially by Watergate, was overwhelming. The Democrats had gained 4 seats in the Senate, increased the majority in the House from 248 to 291, and taken the number of statehouses from 32 to 36. That night at the DNC headquarters, Strauss gave interviews to the media while Carter remained in a back room calling candidates for whom he had campaigned, congratulating them and solidifying his relationship with them for the future.

Campaigning in thirty-two states, Carter had met, in addition to the candidates, the young party activists who were working for them. His obvious sincerity and his often staggering ability to remember people's names after a single meeting had a powerful and flattering effect on them. He spent relatively little time with party power brokers because he knew that they would stick with the more obvious front-runners and not support his insurgent campaign. Through 1973 and most of 1974, Ted Kennedy remained the overwhelming favorite of the serious politicians for the nomination. Based purely on personal persuasion, Carter did obtain the support of some important figures, including that of Bill Dodds, the respected political action director of the United Auto Workers. He also built sound relationships with major figures such as Mayor Richard Daley of Chicago.

In Georgia, Carter's appointment by Strauss provided a convenient excuse for opening what amounted to the first Carter presidential campaign office in a back room of Robert Lipshutz's law firm at 64 North Pryor Street. So small it could hardly accommodate two desks, it was staffed by Steve Chandler and Suzanne Grasty. In taking the job with the Democratic National Committee, Carter had stressed in Georgia that he would keep his national role completely separate from his responsibilities as governor. The office, used as a base by Hamilton Jordan when he was in Atlanta, was displayed as evidence that he was doing that, and no other questions were raised about its function. Steve Chandler ran Carter's out-of-state schedule to campaign for candidates and usually accompanied him on those trips.

National organizations regularly held their conventions in Atlanta, and as Carter's intentions became increasingly public, he used them as opportunities to reach thousands of people, demonstrating expertise or concern in their areas of interest. He would invariably send a personal note afterward to the officers of the different organizations and associations he addressed. These contacts frequently had significant payoffs. Maryland State Senator James Clark, for instance, at odds with his own governor, Marvin Mandell, made a commitment to Carter after he heard him address the National Convention of State Legislators, returned to Maryland to begin recruiting support among his fellow assembly members, and would later become the state campaign chairman.

As the monthly meetings at the mansion continued into 1974, Carter assigned responsibility for different areas to individuals in the group. A list was prepared of all national associations and organizations with memberships over 10,000. A letter went out with Carter's signature to the executive directors of each group soliciting information about the concerns of the membership. With those who responded particularly positively, Carter would follow up with a personal note or phone call.

During the summer of 1973, Lansing Lee, on vacation from law school, categorized every piece of out-of-state correspondence Carter had received while in office. The names, addresses, and phone numbers of all friendly contacts were entered in a "Black Book" organized state by state. To this he added lists of Democratic Party officials in every state, and the names of Georgians with national standing who had their own network of contacts elsewhere in the country. The "Black Book" became a fundamental campaign document containing every potentially useful political relationship in the country, and formed the primary source for those Carter would contact when he went into another state. By the end of 1973, there were nearly 17,000 names; Madeline MacBean, Rosalynn's assistant, and Chip's wife, Caron, sent holiday greeting cards to everyone on the list.

Landon Butler researched the primary and caucus states. National party rules as well as state laws were undergoing change as was the relationship in several states between the popular vote and the allocation of convention delegates. A thorough understanding of the new procedures and their ramifications for the Carter campaign was essential. Determined to prevent a repeat of 1972, party regulars were endeavoring to reassert their control over the process, including in Georgia. Alarmed by the manner in which the Chisholm and McGovern candidates had outmaneuvered the system, they scrapped the congressional district caucuses and proposed a conventional primary instead. However, an early primary in Carter's own state where he might be embarrassingly defeated by Wallace was out of the question. In the legislative session of 1974, Carter convinced the legislature to let him appoint a committee to set the date, which they did for May 4. By then Carter would either be doing so well that he would easily carry Georgia, or the nomination would already be lost.

Throughout 1973 and 1974 the ever-present prospect that Maddox might again become governor dogged the presidential plans. Bert Lance, Carter's chosen successor, was not doing well in the race. Both Jordan and Lance believed Carter could not have been reelected even had the constitution allowed him to run again—a view not shared by Carter himself. His transparent liberalism on the race issue had lost him considerable public support, and for Lance to be seen as his protégé was a mixed blessing.

On election day, August 13, 1974, Lance came in a close third behind Maddox and State Representative George Busbee. It was depressing that night at Lance headquarters not just because of our close emotional involvement with his campaign but because it potentially put the presidential plan in serious jeopardy. Neither Maddox nor Busbee had received a majority, so they faced a runoff. Now the priority for the presidential effort was to assure Busbee's defeat of Maddox, which happily occurred.

The Maddox loss turned out to be much more than just a tactical victory for Carter. Because of Maddox's close association with George Wallace and the "Old South," the election was interpreted as having strong symbolic significance, a theme that was picked up by writers across the country. It was seen as evidence that the South was finally moving into the mainstream and out of its preoccupation with the race issue. The election of the "New South" governors in 1970, and of Andrew Young in 1972, was now seen as part of a trend, and not a series of flukes. Maddox was seen as a stand-in for Wallace and the race as a referendum on the "old" versus the "new" South. The Maddox defeat was widely perceived as a serious setback for Wallace.

An editorial in the *Washington Star* on September 19 effectively captured the feeling:

> Lester Maddox . . . as the last notable champion of cornpone racism, was known to be fighting an uphill battle for the governorship. But few observers foresaw the sweeping dimensions of his defeat. . . . Its disposition of Maddox is but the latest in a series of political episodes that have elevated bright progressive men to governorships all across the South. But Lester, nonetheless, was symbolic. His overwhelming defeat may have been the clincher—the ultimate proof of transformation. Already there is talk that it may embolden

the "New South" governors to challenge any 1976 presidential maneuvering in that region by Governor Wallace, who is trying to modify his own gravelly image.

More importantly the South—the fastest-growing part of the country—may well be headed for new stature in national politics, especially in the affairs of the Democratic Party. Its ambitious new figures, who undoubtedly hope to vie for the 1976 ticket, no longer will be hampered by the old crippling mark of regionalism (which essentially was racism), and some of them may be very hard to stop.

Although unsigned, the editorial bore the clear mark of Jack Germond, one of America's most insightful political journalists, who was almost alone at that point in looking seriously at Carter as a presidential prospect. On June 2, 1974, Carter had appeared on *Meet the Press*. He did not particularly impress the audience, but he had a significant impact on the host, Lawrence Spivak. They established a friendship through which Spivak gave Carter considerable advice about handling the media, and he warned his own circle of distinguished senior journalists in Washington to ignore Carter at their peril. Journalists with a southern background caught the potential earlier than most. Charles Houston wrote in the *Richmond News Leader* on November 2, 1973:

> Governor Carter is something new to me in southern politics. Some call him a populist and he calls his philosophy "enlightened conservatism." He's a working Baptist in person and on paper, he appears to be the kind of innovative politician who bears watching.

A poll of Democratic Party leaders in November 1973 had shown that Senators Jackson and Humphrey were making some inroads on Kennedy's lead, but as pollster Martin Hanan said, noting that none got more than a quarter of the vote, "the situation is ripe for a dark horse." As late as November 1974, less than a month before Carter would formally announce his candidacy, a Harris poll listed thirty-five potential candidates. Carter was not among them.

Most journalists seemed not to grasp the profound social and political currents affecting the country. The impact of Vietnam, Watergate, the change in race relations in the South, and especially the profound opening up of the political process seemed largely ignored, and candidates were examined only within the context of the old political paradigm. Speculation was ill-informed and almost universally inaccurate, including among several nationally respected columnists, to whom the notion that anyone not already in Washington and not personally known to them could be elected president seemed inconceivable.

Watergate had played no role in Carter's decision to run for president, but as the scandal unfolded in 1973 and 1974, it proved to be extremely fortuitous. Public resentment blossomed not just toward Nixon but more broadly toward Washington and career politicians. Also, because so many of those associated with Watergate were lawyers, they as a class were impugned. Soon one of Carter's most popular lines was: "I am not from Washington, I do not hold public office, and I am not a lawyer."

In the closing weeks of the 1974 election campaign, Carter met with the editorial board of the *New York Times*. For an hour and a half they discussed his role as campaign chairman, getting his projections for the outcomes of various races, and the impact of Watergate on voting attitudes in the country. As the meeting was breaking up, James "Scotty" Reston in an offhand way, asked, "Governor, what do you plan to do when these elections are over?"

"I plan to run for president," Carter replied, stunning the room into a state of suspended animation. People's jackets were quickly removed and, resuming their seats, they invited Carter to stay and talk about it. He did so for another hour, impressing them with the logic of why he believed he would win, but leaving them, for the most part, incredulous.

From the moment the decision was made in late 1972 to run for president, Carter's perspective and posture as governor changed. He no longer had to pander to a highly conservative audience to get his reorganization bill through the legislature. He was running on his record as having been a good and competent governor of the state, so he could not neglect state affairs. However, his actions were now aimed at a national rather than a Georgia audience. He was freed to do those things in which he had natural interest rather than those that might win him votes in the legislature. There would be no more sponsorship of anti-busing amendments at governors' conferences.

Carter had a longstanding interest in conservation and the outdoors. Overall, during his term as governor, Carter felt he spent more time on conserving natural resources than on any other issue. He worked hard to preserve the Georgia coastline, and helped to arrange for Cumberland Island, his and Rosalynn's favorite vacation spot, to be given to the state. With the help of Landon Butler, he presided over the acquisition of several key sites on the Chattahoochee River that runs near Atlanta, turning them into state parks for the benefit of canoeists, rafters, muskrats and wood ducks, rainbow trout and fishermen. Before his intervention this entire historic river area was threatened by uncontrolled land development. He also established the Georgia Heritage Trust to assess and preserve more than 2,000 historic sites in the state.

Carter's most important act, however, which brought him to the attention of environmentalists all over the country, was his decision to veto plans by the U.S. Army Corps of Engineers to build a large dam on the Flint River. Plans had been under way for years to build the Spruell Bluff dam. The Corps of Engineers argued that it was a way to open up the economy of the area and create a large recreational lake. Carter appointed a commission to study the issue and, based on their report, and after making two canoe trips himself down the river, he decided that the arguments in favor of the dam were largely spurious, and that preserving the last free-flowing stream in that area of Georgia was of far greater importance. The veto was a stunning surprise to the corps of engineers—no governor had ever before vetoed such a project. It also gave him instant name recognition with environmental activists as far away as California.

In late 1973, Carter recruited to the presidential effort Jane Yarn, the Georgia director of SAVE (Save America's Vital Environment), who would later head "Environmentalists for Carter," and Barbara Blum, already a contributor and supporter who had led the fight to preserve the Chattahoochee River. Together with Landon Butler they arranged for Carter to meet a group of environmentalists from around the country in Washington, D.C. Carter revealed to them that he was planning to run for president and asked for their help. It was the first group outside Georgia to whom he had made an open statement of his intentions.

On Sunday afternoon, February 17, 1974, the portraits of Dr. Martin Luther King, Jr., and two other distinguished black Georgians, educator Lucy Craft Laney and Bishop McNeal Turner, were unveiled by Carter in the state capitol as a small group of robed Ku Klux Klansmen paraded outside. It was a moving ceremony in which Secretary of State Ben Fortson, an old-style southern politician, spoke eloquently about the accomplishments of Dr. King, and the meaning of his life, especially for African Americans. Then he and Carter joined the racially mixed audience in singing "We Shall Overcome."

In the final months of 1974, Carter began meeting in Georgia with groups of friends and supporters from his gubernatorial campaigns to share his plans to run for president. Many reacted like his mother, who asked, "President of what?" When invited to a small luncheon of key professional and business leaders put together by Philip Alston and Bob Lipshutz at the Commerce Club, and when told that Carter planned to discuss his intention to run for president, Marvin Shoob initially assumed it was for president of the chamber of commerce.

In another meeting at the mansion, Carter was asked whether a lack of knowledge of economics could be a liability in his campaign. He responded that he had obtained a textbook used at the University of Georgia in an introductory course on economics and was determined to master the subject. There were those in the audience who marveled at his belief that this could be sufficient preparation to manage the world's largest and most complex economy, but also at his serene conviction that he could overcome any shortcoming by sufficient study, discipline, and exposure to the best experts. By nature Carter saw no challenge as too great. He approached everything with brimming self-confidence, gave his best effort, and moved on. Sometimes he fell short in the performance, but he shied away from nothing.

On Saturday, November 17, 1974, Carter went to Washington to hold a press conference at which he intended to issue a major statement on energy policy. It was the hot topic of the moment and President Ford was also known to be preparing to address the subject. In part the intention was to use the event as a dry run for the formal announcement of his candidacy a month later. Jody Powell was particularly interested in assessing the degree of press attention that Carter could generate. The assumption was that with the president about to make a major speech on energy, and with a high degree of public interest, Carter's thoughtful statement would be widely picked up as an important alternative Democratic position on a vital national issue. Anticipating that his position, which was quite critical of Ford policy, might get major media coverage, Carter called Ford as a courtesy. He told the president that he planned to call for a cutback in U.S. oil consumption of 2 million barrels a day.

"How did you come up with a figure like that?" asked Ford. Carter explained that he had arrived at it after careful deliberation with advisors at the Brookings Institution.

The news conference was sparsely attended. Robert Kuttner, a young economics reporter from the *Washington Post,* filed a lengthy story, but it ran in only one edition of the paper the following day, in the "B" section. The statement received no other national coverage. Carter was disappointed. The following Tuesday, President Ford released his own energy statement to nationwide media headlines. Among other things, he called for a 2-million-barrel-a-day cutback in oil consumption. When pressed by reporters, Ford's advisors said they were surprised by the figure and did not know where the president had obtained it.

In the early meetings at the mansion, Kirbo had repeatedly stressed that Carter should not predicate his campaign on what other candidates might or might not do. Everyone around Carter assumed Kennedy would be his main competition for the nomination, but agreed that he had to pursue his own strategy regardless. On July 4, Kennedy had gone to Dothan, Alabama, for a joint appearance with George Wallace. The meeting produced a deluge of critical mail from the liberal wing of the party, but also, more to his surprise, widespread reference to the Chappaquiddick affair.

While he remained the favorite for the Democratic nomination, there were serious new doubts about whether he could win the general election. Other factors began to weigh on him. His son Teddy, Jr., had developed cancer in 1973, requiring the amputation of his right leg, and was still undergoing therapy. He was also endeavoring to play the father role for the thirteen children of his two slain brothers. In addition, his wife, Joan, had a serious drinking problem, for which several efforts at treatment had proven ineffectual. Death threats were frequent and a presidential campaign might prove too great an invitation to a potential assassin.

Matters came to a head in mid-September when Kennedy went to California to campaign for Democratic candidates. The press covered his trip almost exclusively in terms of his anticipated presidential bid. Having long since made up his mind against running, he was increasingly uncomfortable with the charade. On September 23, at the Parker House in Boston with Joan at his side, he announced that he would not be a candidate, saying, "My primary responsibilities are at home."

Kennedy's departure was a stunning, if welcome, surprise to the Carter camp. Two weeks after the November elections the campaign received another boost when Senator Fritz Mondale also withdrew from the race. Mondale had anticipated that with Kennedy's withdrawal he would pick up much of his liberal support, but this did not happen. In addition, he was having difficulty raising money. Offering the widely quoted explanation that he could not take another year "sleeping in Holiday Inns," Mondale faced the inevitable and ended his campaign before it really began.

Two years after the original decision was made that he would run for president, and before he had even officially announced his intentions, Carter's prospects looked increasingly rosy. With Kennedy and Mondale out of the race, and serious questions about whether Wallace's health would allow him to run a full-scale campaign, the field seemed wide open. As much as there was one, "Scoop" Jackson now seemed the front-runner, but there remained deep antipathy toward him among liberals. Carter might still be a dark horse, but his chances now looked as good as anyone's.

CHAPTER 17

The 1974 Conference on Democratic Party Organization and Policy, or "mini-convention," was held over the weekend of December 6–8, 1974, in Kansas City, Missouri. The primary purpose of the meeting was to approve a new party charter and delegate selection rules based on recommendations of commissions cochaired by Governor Terry Sanford (North Carolina) and Congresswoman Yvonne Braithewaite Burke (California) and by City Councilwoman Barbara Mikulski (Baltimore), respectively. It was also an opportunity for Bob Strauss to demonstrate that he had, if ever so tenuously, achieved party unity.

Carter and Jordan considered the mini-convention an important opportunity to market the Carter candidacy to party regulars. Preparations had been under way for four months. In a memo to the staff Jordan noted, "The goal of our program will be to make contact with targeted delegations, discuss and hopefully recruit people to the Carter effort."

Gerry Rafshoon had prepared a glossy eight-page color brochure depicting Carter in Kennedyesque poses with a description of his accomplishments in Georgia. With a cover letter from Carlton Hicks and Connie Plunkett, the Georgia Democratic committeeman and committeewoman, it was mailed a week ahead of time to every delegate.

Nearly 2,000 people stopped by a hospitality suite on the twenty-third floor of the Holiday Inn. A story in the *Kansas City Star* erroneously accused the Carter contingent of plying delegates with "alcohol and pretty girls," mistaking national committeewoman Connie Plunkett, hardworking and professional but also a strikingly attractive blond, with being a specially imported lure for the delegates. Rosalynn was also concerned with the impression that the campaign was providing free-flowing alcohol and decreed that hard liquor should not be offered at future events. Finally, journalists, too, in significant numbers, wanted to talk with Carter.

Carter made the maximum use of his time. In two and a half days, in addition to his role in the formal business of the convention, he addressed seventeen delegations and gave more than a dozen interviews.

The creation of the Charter and Delegate Selection Commissions had grown out of the dissatisfaction among party regulars with the way delegates to the Miami convention had been picked. Abandoning most of the earlier ambitious reforms, the Charter Commission agreed that state parties would be allowed to pick a quarter of the delegates to the 1976 convention. Still in contention was how to ensure in the charter the representation of minorities, women, and youth. The AFL-CIO leadership argued that "quotas" had produced chaos in Miami and wanted to return control to the traditional party power brokers, a move they knew would aid their candidate "Scoop" Jackson. Unresolved, the issue resulted in a walkout of blacks and their allies, led by California Assemblyman Willie Brown, at the final meeting of the commission in August.

In an attempt to avert further conflict, Carter had pushed a resolution through a November meeting of the Democratic governors urging the Charter Commission to adopt the wording of the report of the Mikulski Commission, already a compromise, and that those rules be made applicable through the 1980 convention. It put Carter in a central role at the mini-convention even though his compromise was opposed by Strauss and by the AFL-CIO. After considerable behind-the-scenes negotiating, he won broad approval from the delegates. Strauss, ultimately more concerned with preserving the image of unity than his obligations to labor and Jackson, accepted Carter's settlement. Carter's success dealt a camouflaged but significant blow to Jackson's presidential prospects. In so doing, he made a lasting enemy of AFL-CIO political director Al Barkan, and its president, George Meany, a problem that would dog him for the next five years.

Carter left Kansas City having recruited supporters in virtually every state. Some were people of considerable consequence in the liberal wing of the party, including Patt Derian of Mississippi, a longtime activist and party reformer, Anne Wexler, a McGovern operative who had recently been referred to in the media as "the most influential woman in American politics," and Marjorie Craig Benton, a wealthy contributor and McGovern supporter from Chicago.

Four days after the mini-convention, December 12, Carter formally declared his candidacy for the presidency. A great deal of thought had gone into the timing of the announcement, so it would occur before he ended his term as governor on January 13, 1975, but prior to the midterm elections in November. It could not be right before the mini-convention, which would look as though he sought to usurp attention at a party event, and he wanted to avoid the distraction of the holidays. The Carter camp had assumed his announcement would be the first—and the earliest—in history, but had not considered Congressman Morris Udall, who preempted him by a week.

The announcement location was also a topic of lengthy deliberation. To maximize coverage and minimize Carter's regional image, Washington was the first choice, but there was no way to produce a large partisan crowd in the capital. Plains was considered: "It would convey the image of the non-politician from rural America contrasting sharply with the Washington crowd whom the country sees as jaded and tarnished," said one document, which reflected the campaign's central Jeffersonian theme but ignored the need for national media coverage.

Carter talked to Lawrence Spivak, who accurately advised that Georgians would resent their governor making his announcement in Washington. Carter compromised by making a major noontime speech at Washington's National Press Club, and that evening formally declaring his candidacy before a large partisan audience at Atlanta's new Civic Center.

On December 11, Carter had breakfast in Washington with Bardyl Tirana, a lawyer and former member of the District of Columbia school board. The meeting was typical of the self-confident way Carter was now recruiting expertise and personal support. Tirana, a part owner of the Executive Jet Corporation, had worked in Bobby Kennedy's 1968 campaign, and had organized McGovern's campaign transportation. He and Carter talked about leasing Lear jets and Boeing 727s, and when such equipment would be needed. Tirana was taken aback that Carter talked with such certainty that he would still be in the race at that stage. "I don't intend to lose," Carter said emphatically. Then, he pinned Tirana with his strong blue eyes and said forcefully, "I need your help." Tirana, who had agreed to the meeting "just to take a look," made an unconditional commitment on the spot.

Later that morning, Carter had a meeting with Senator Edward Kennedy, who reaffirmed that he had no intention of running in the 1976 campaign. Carter, perhaps remembering the Law Day events, or because he had long anticipated Kennedy would be his main competition for the nomination, had a degree of antipathy toward him. At the mini-convention when Kennedy addressed the delegates, Carter was overheard to comment to one of the Georgia delegation, "I'm glad I don't have to kiss his ass to be president." The following morning, December 12, Carter was the guest at the "Sperling breakfast," a weekly Washington institution organized by Godfrey Sperling of the *Christian Science Monitor* at which the city's leading political journalists grilled political newsmakers. He made an impressive showing, but the journalistic gurus were universally skeptical of his chances.

In his speech at the National Press Club, he set a lofty tone asserting his belief in the "greatness of our country" and Americans as a "great and diverse people." But, he said, we had lost our way and deviated from the path that made us great: "We have dared to dream great dreams for our nation. We have taken quite literally the promises of decency, equality, and freedom of an honest and responsible government." But, he added, "Our commitments to these dreams have been sapped by debilitating compromise, acceptance of mediocrity, subservience to special interests, and an absence of executive vision and direction."

The great dreams still lived in the hearts of the American people, he said, but the leadership was not up to those dreams. By implication he was offering himself as the leader who embodied those dreams and values. After Watergate and with America's 200th birthday just ahead, it was time, he asserted, "to reaffirm and to strengthen our ethical and spiritual and political beliefs." Quoting from the Bible, he said, "If the trumpet give an uncertain sound, who shall prepare himself to the battle."

He then checked off a series of specific proposals, some traditional Democratic offerings, others reflecting his own populist ideas. In the context of the mid-1970s politics, several sounded anti-establishment, but they were notions he perceived as representing a pure thematic trail from the thinking of the drafters of the constitution down through the southern blend of populism and Protestant individualism:

> We need an all-inclusive sunshine law in Washington so that special interests will not retain their exclusive access behind closed doors.
>
> Absolutely no gifts of value should ever again be permitted to a public official.
>
> Complete revelation of all business and financial involvements of major officials should be required. . . .
>
> Regulatory agencies must not be managed by representatives of the industry being regulated. . . .
>
> Public financing should be extended to members of Congress.
>
> The activities of lobbyists must be thoroughly revealed and controlled.
>
> Minimum secrecy in government must be matched with maximum personal privacy for private citizens.
>
> All federal judges, diplomats, and other officials should be selected on a strict basis of merit.

(In a speech on November 12 to the Commission on Foreign Relations, Carter had said in connection with U.S. ambassadors he had personally observed, "It is a disgrace to our country to have had in some of those cities people representing our own nation who obviously knew very little about the people, their attitudes, their hopes, their aspirations, and their customs.")

He talked of the need for efficient management of the federal government and cited his accomplishments as governor. He called for a comprehensive national energy policy and reform of the welfare system. "The word *welfare* no longer signifies how much we care, but often arouses feelings of contempt and even hatred. Is a simplified, fair, and compassionate welfare system beyond the capacity of our American government? I think not." Saying "I expect the next Congress to pass a national health insurance law," he asked, "Is a practical and comprehensive national health program beyond the capacity of our American government? I think not."

Concerned at being perceived as a regional candidate, or worse, that he showed the racist views of other southerners who had sought the national limelight merely to "send a message," he quoted from his inaugural speech as governor, beginning, "The time for racial discrimination is over." Then he added, "We must meet this firm national commitment without equivocation or timidity in every aspect of private and public life."

Lest anyone had missed that Carter was drawing a direct philosophical line between himself and the founding fathers, basing his candidacy on a reaffirmation of the fundamental values in which they believed, he told the story of a recent trip he had made to Philadelphia.

About three months ago I met with the governors of the other twelve original states in Philadelphia. Exactly 200 years after the convening of the First Continental Congress we walked down the same streets, then turned left and entered a small building named Carpenter's Hall. There we heard exactly the same prayer and sat in the same chairs occupied in September 1774 by Samuel Adams, John Jay, John Adams, Patrick Henry, George Washington, and about forty-five other strong and opinionated leaders.

Carter concluded by retelling the story of his initial interview with Admiral Rickover, ending with the question Rickover had asked, which he in turn posed to the audience: "Why not the best?" The speech was politely but unenthusiastically received, getting token coverage in the national media.

That evening in Atlanta it was a different story. An integrated crowd of 3,000 cheering supporters drowned him out as he announced, "I am planning to run for president." Most were Georgians, but there were supporters from around the country, including Lucille Kelly from New Hampshire; Margaret Hobelman, Harriet Terry, and Marie Vickers from Kansas, who in September had driven all the way to Atlanta to urge him to run; Cecil Partee, the black president of the Illinois State Senate; and astronaut "Buzz" Aldrin (an Annapolis classmate), prompting Carter to comment, "I even have someone here from the moon for my announcement."

Carter's first trip as an announced candidate came a week later when he went to San Francisco to address a conference on alcoholism and drug abuse. He stayed at the Hilton and walked to a breakfast meeting three blocks away; he was not recognized by a single person en route. At a press conference he was questioned relentlessly about what was to become a recurring topic: George Wallace. How was he going to beat George Wallace? How did they differ on the issues? Was Wallace's paralysis an issue? In a lunch meeting with the stuffy editorial board of the *San Fran-*

cisco Examiner, after a few perfunctory questions about the economy and defense, the discussion reverted to Wallace for the rest of the meeting.

The entire family gathered in Plains over Christmas to plan each of their roles in the coming campaign. Rosalynn would, of course, be an equal partner, and unlike the wives of previous presidential candidates she would set a precedent by maintaining a completely separate campaign schedule. Still somewhat reserved, she saw every challenge as surmountable if you applied an iron will. Jack and Chip, with their wives, Judy and Caron, would campaign especially in the southern states. Jeff, who worked in Seattle for a time, had returned home, married Annette Davis from Arlington, Georgia, and was enrolled at Georgia State University. He would work at the Atlanta headquarters between classes. Miss Lillian once again would campaign as hard as her health would allow. Jimmy's aunt Sissy and his sisters Ruth and Gloria would also help. Billy's primary responsibility would be to keep the family business operating to enable the rest of the family to be gone.

On January 13, 1975, George Busbee was formally inaugurated as governor. In addition to reorganization, the centerpiece of the Carter administration, Jimmy had compiled a considerable array of accomplishments. Despite deeply entrenched opposition in the legislature and among several state officials, 85 percent of all administration bills had passed. The resulting legislation included:

> A complete overhaul of the ad valorem tax system to equalize tax assessments and open appeals procedures to the poor as well as the rich
>
> Environmental protection laws, generally conceded to be among the toughest in the nation at the time
>
> Removal of tax advantages for large corporations that immediately increased state tax revenues by $28 million per annum
>
> Age of majority legislation to provide full citizenship for eighteen-year-olds in Georgia
>
> Full funding for a testing and research program to eradicate sickle-cell disease
>
> A comprehensive package of prison reform legislation
>
> A coordinated statewide network of drug abuse treatment centers, and a comprehensive law giving greater flexibility in dealing with first offenders, with stricter penalties for drug pushers.

Carter had established international trade offices in Germany, Belgium, Brazil, Canada, and two in Japan. He had actively sought foreign investment, especially from the Japanese, who in 1973 invested $125 million in manufacturing enterprises in the state. Together with Rosalynn he had

actively sought federal support to establish community mental health centers around the state and to expand the regionalization program for state
mental hospitals. He had launched the so-called "Cripplers and Killers
Program" to identify and reduce the major causes of death and disability.
He sponsored legislation to equalize education funds between richer and
poorer counties, to raise the salaries of schoolteachers, increase the number of special education teachers, and provide more financial aid to higher
education. He also launched an early childhood development program to
provide better teaching and medical care for preschool children, which he
considered one of the most important accomplishments of his administration. He initiated the writing of a new history of Georgia for the U.S. bicentennial under the direction of Kenneth Coleman and a group of historians
at the University of Georgia.

Carter himself had few regrets about his term. He was disappointed that
he failed to get the Forestry Department incorporated into the new
Department of Natural Resources—his only significant reorganization failure. He cites "lack of success in improving the school system" as the one
area in which he would have liked to do more. He wanted to establish
mandatory testing at the fourth grade and implement multicounty school
consolidation, which he had fought for in Sumter County, but he says, "it
was politically impossible." However, despite Carter's success, Bert Lance
would comment that he was "more of an outsider when he left the governor's office than when he came in."

On January 15, Carter and Jody Powell left on what would be close to
two years of almost continuous frenetic and often lonely travel. They
returned to Washington for a dinner at the home of Bardyl Tirana with a
group of the city's political leaders including Lillian Huff, Julius and Tina
Hobson, John Hechinger, and Marion Barry. With the improbable
prospect of a southern governor trying to prove himself to a group of veteran civil rights activists, the evening started somewhat tensely. By the
time he departed, he left a group of astonished, if tentative, supporters.
The next morning Carter appeared on the *Today* show, evoking little interest, and met with the editorial board of the *Washington Post*. After explaining his strategy for winning the nomination, he then piqued their interest
by suggesting that, after the experiences of Watergate, the attorney general
should be made completely independent, perhaps serving for just one year.
Bob Maynard, a black member of the board, would comment afterward, "I
was not expecting much, but was enormously impressed."

Before Carter left Washington at the end of the day, he had also met with
Jack Conway, the executive director of Common Cause, Reuben Johnson
of the National Farmers Union, and Glenn Watts, president of the Communications Workers of America. Both Conway and Watts were part of the

liberal establishment that Carter needed to convince he was not another southern racist and was their best hope for blocking Wallace, since he alone had the potential to defeat the Alabama governor in the South. Carter returned to Plains for the weekend and on Monday left for the West Coast, giving speeches in New Orleans, Baton Rouge, and Houston along the way, and adding an important side trip to Albuquerque.

Landon Butler had for some time been urging Carter to hire and put in place a field staff, a view shared by both Jordan and Powell. Carter strongly resisted, saying, "I can do this with volunteers." Money was a consideration, but it also reflected a curious naivete about what was involved in mounting a nationwide presidential campaign. It also showed a side of Carter's character in which he believed that he could attract an almost evangelical following of people who would be willing to contribute their savings, give up their jobs, or devote all of their spare time to making him president—and many did. He thought of "field staff" as people who made their living from politics and were not personally devoted to a specific candidate. Professionals represented the aspect of politics that he had always found most distasteful. As in the governor's race, he wanted a campaign of devoted disciples no matter how inexperienced, not experts selling their talents. On a trip returning from a South Carolina fund-raiser, Butler said, "Governor, I want to talk to you again about putting a field staff in place." Carter responded testily, "I don't want to talk about it. I told Hamilton I was through with that subject. Why does it keep coming up?"

Butler persisted, pointing how crucial such an organization had been to the McGovern campaign, how hard they worked, how relatively low the cost was, and that the right paid staff could be as loyal as volunteers. Finally, at the end of the evening, Carter looked at him and said, "All right, damn it, but you've got to find them."

That night Butler called his sister-in-law in New Mexico, Rhetta Richards, who had worked for Robert Kennedy and McGovern, and she recommended two young field workers there. So en route to the West Coast, Carter traveled from Houston to Albuquerque. Rhetta and her husband, Ken, had organized a reception at which Carter was introduced to Tim Kraft and Chris Brown, the two proposed "field staff." Both would prove crucial to Carter's ultimate victory.

At a San Francisco news conference on January 25, Carter's comments reflected his continuing concern about prejudice against the South and being written off as a regional candidate. The fact that he was a southerner should not detract from his candidacy, he said, continuing:

> Again and again the experts have underestimated the people. Those who
> say Americans will refuse to give a fair hearing to a candidate from the South

are making the same mistake again. Place of birth in this country should not, and, I believe, will not be a qualification for the presidency in 1976.

Carter drove from San Francisco to Sacramento to attend the Democratic state convention accompanied by Jack Germond of the *Washington Star* and Tom Ottenard of the *St. Louis Post Dispatch*. Both saw a potential in Carter that other political reporters did not. At the convention Carter walked up and down the lines of delegates waiting to register, introducing himself, "My name is Jimmy Carter, and I'm running for president." It was a reasonable approach since most of them had not the least idea who he was.

Carter's formal speech made little impact on the mostly liberal delegates. Of the announced or prospective candidates present, former Oklahoma senator Fred Harris was the only one to stir the audience. However, as the *San Francisco Chronicle* headlined the next day, "Democratic hopefuls gather, but it's Governor Brown's show." Enigmatic Edmund G. "Jerry" Brown, Jr., had not attended either the mini-convention or the Democratic governors' conference. Making an asset of being outside the traditional political structure, he largely ignored the presidential candidates, but he knew this was his crowd and in a rousing speech he made the most of it. "Scoop" Jackson did not attend, but when asked about his absence, an aide, to Jackson's considerable detriment, was quoted in the *San Francisco Chronicle* as saying, "He doesn't need California; California needs him."

Carter made some progress. He resonated well with the farm-oriented members of the rural caucus that he addressed. Hispanics appreciated his modest abilities in Spanish, and he attracted some interest from black delegates, most of whom still had close family ties in the South. Carter, unlike many liberals who were strong advocates of civil rights but dealt with few blacks individually, was thoroughly at ease. Paul Wieke, a writer for the then-liberal *New Republic*, was persuaded to come to Plains to do a story on Carter. His subsequent piece proved an important milestone in establishing Carter's credibility among liberal intellectuals.

On April 14, Rosalynn and Edna Langford, Jack's mother-in-law, set out for Florida in Rosalynn's green Chevrolet, having decided Edna's more comfortable Cadillac would create the wrong impression. As Rosalynn describes it:

> Edna and I just drove from one town to the next. We had a few receptions
> ... lined up, but very few.... The first ... was in Tallahassee. I had a friend
> who lived down there ... [Eleanor Ketchum, who had taught both Jimmy
> and Rosalynn at the Plains school. She sent out 400 invitations, hoping 50
> would attend. On the day, 308 showed up.] and Edna had some friends
> [Doug and Judy Henderson] and they had a reception.

Armed with a copy of the 1974 Florida Almanac of Democratic Party officials and a slowly expanding list of contacts, they went from town to town introducing themselves to Democratic Party officials, passing out brochures, and giving interviews to the media.

As Rosalynn descended, sometimes without warning, on disc jockeys and reporters, announcing, "I'm Mrs. Jimmy Carter and I thought you might want to interview me," she found they were often at a loss as to what to ask her. She solved the problem by preparing a list of a half-dozen questions that allowed her to focus on the points she wanted to make. Nine times out of ten the interviewers used them verbatim.

Rosalynn and Edna had set themselves a relentless schedule, and often drove much of the night to make the next morning's commitments. Exhausted and anxious, Rosalynn sometimes woke up nauseated. Occasionally she was so tired she could not remember where she was. Eventually she learned to write down the day's entire itinerary so she could answer such questions as, "Mrs. Carter, where have you been today?" or "Where do you go from here?" She won the hearts and support of many people, especially other women who empathized with her tackling an obviously frightening task with courage. That she had a sincere interest in people, was by nature friendly, and was attractive helped her also.

At the end of two weeks, Rosalynn and Edna returned to Plains with hundreds of new names on the blue three-by-five cards. For Rosalynn it was a revelation to discover that people were similar everywhere and that campaigning in Florida was not very different from the gubernatorial campaigns in Georgia. She brimmed with a new self-confidence, telling Jimmy, "I know we can do it." She also noted some campaigning lessons:

> Stop at courthouses. In small towns they tend to be the center of political activity and gossip.
>
> Insist on the front page of the newspaper. Don't let them fob you off to the society editor or the women's page.
>
> Head for the large radio and television antennas, usually the most visible landmark in town.
>
> Stay in people's homes. You saved money, learned about people's real concerns, established close ties and loyalty, and ended up with access to a network of their friends and relatives. [Al and Shirley Seckinger of Tampa, whom she had known in Plains, were the first of hundreds of "Carter Innkeepers" across America who hosted Jimmy, Rosalynn, and other members of the Carter family.]
>
> Be intrusive—on meetings, events, carnivals, any place people gather. Rosalynn and Edna had invited themselves into an all-male Rotary Club weekly meeting. They found the group delighted to have Rosalynn address

them. On another occasion Rosalynn introduced herself at a cattle sale and persuaded the auctioneer to stop long enough for her to address the crowd.

After a week at home with Amy, Rosalynn left for Iowa. From Iowa she went back to Florida. By the time of the primary, she had spent 75 days in Florida and visited 105 communities in Iowa. She spent weeks on end in New Hampshire, Maine, Vermont, Massachusetts, Mississippi, Pennsylvania, Ohio, Illinois, and Wisconsin. By the end of the campaign she had been in forty-two states.

The odyssey of Jimmy Carter and Jody Powell was similar, flying tourist class, staying in private homes, and often speaking to very small audiences. During 1975, Carter stayed with fifty-one families, some of them very poor. "I was embarrassed," he said, "when some people were so poor, to impose on them." For most, however, the honor of having even a long-shot presidential candidate stay in their home outweighed the inconvenience. On one such visit, Carter got a phone call after everyone had gone to bed. Jack's wife, Judy, had just had a baby boy, Jason, and Jimmy and Rosalynn were grandparents for the first time.

Carter remained supremely self-confident even in the face of daunting setbacks: "I remember the first reception we had in Des Moines. We rented a very large hotel ballroom and we had enough food for several hundred people. And four people came. So I stood around embarrassed."

Jimmy and Jody spent countless hours in shopping centers and at factory gates often in the bitter cold. Carter would hold out his hand, "Hello, my name is Jimmy Carter. I'm running for president." Jody would hand them a brochure, and if they expressed interest, he would add them to the file of blue index cards. He spoke to small groups in people's homes or addressed civic groups or other organizations. His schedule kept him permanently on the verge of exhaustion.

Carter campaigned more on his personality and his character than on the issues, relying on his warm smile, his charm and, as he had done in his two gubernatorial races, on the sense of sincerity and integrity that he emanated. He frequently deflected detailed substantive questions by saying the real issues were competency and trust. Watergate and the conduct of the Vietnam War had produced a dramatic increase in the skepticism Americans felt for their government. They had been lied to and deceived. Carter offered to restore honesty to the presidency.

Carter's short discussions with individuals, or small groups, informed him as well. As the year wore on, and he had interacted with thousands of individuals, there was an increasing precision to his understanding of what was on the minds of the American people.

George McGovern's pollster, the now aging child prodigy Pat Caddell, met with Carter and agreed to join the campaign. "The [two] thing[s] that really attracted me to him personally," Caddell said, "were . . . one, was that he had the best understanding instinctively—viscerally—of the country of any politician I had ever met. . . . The other was Jimmy's tremendous grasp of . . . secondary and tertiary impacts in certain sectors." During 1974, Caddell's Cambridge Research Group had conducted in-depth surveys around the country, interviewing 2,000 people for two and a half hours every ninety days. It was aimed at uncovering deep "pattern" movements in economic and political attitudes. Caddell was considerably frustrated trying to interest members of Congress running for reelection in the results of his studies. With Carter it was the reverse. Caddell says:

> Jimmy is . . . asking, and he's learning, and he's absorbing and he picks it up . . . he'll pick up odds and ends of things that I never expect anyone to pick up and question me about . . . they are so insignificant.

Caddell's studies had identified the emergence of two fundamental themes that concerned the American people: a desire for nonideological change and the restoration of values. (They would persist as concerns ebbing and flowing for the next twenty years as politicians grappled, largely unsuccessfully, to respond to them.) Carter had instinctively sensed these trends and had already woven them into his basic stump speeches. Caddell's data served primarily to reaffirm Carter's self-confidence that he was on the right track. His instincts also told him things Caddell had not seen. He asked Caddell to survey for the public's concern about reorganization and mismanagement of the federal government. Caddell was dubious:

> I tested only because Jimmy insisted that we look at it. I thought it was a stupid issue. I didn't think anyone cared. . . . And then it scored just tremendously high. It ranked like second on the intensity scales. . . . It was a major reason people thought the economy was in trouble. . . . It was really an eye-opener. It was clear Jimmy had instincts and defined an issue that . . . was carrying all kinds of other connotations to it.

During the early seventies, *The Waltons*, the story of an Appalachian family in the depression, was a widely popular television series. They exemplified the values of honesty, decency, concern for each other's welfare, and commitment to the Protestant work ethic, enabling them to overcome or endure hardships, deprivations, and repeated setbacks. They embodied values that many viewers saw as quintessentially American, but that were increasingly absent in society. Many felt the Carters, coming from a rural southern background and espousing many of the same values, touched a similar chord.

Carter's naturally frugal nature meshed well with the strict, post-

Watergate campaign financing laws, under which all expenditures had to come under the allowable maximums and be documented. Meticulous budgeting and tight centralized control were required. Fund-raising was very difficult through much of 1975. As late as March of that year, an event in Washington, D.C., attended by 300 people at only $10 a head, nevertheless raised more money ($3,000) than any previous event outside Georgia. Bob Lipshutz, the campaign treasurer, managed the limited resources with such skill that Kirbo described him as "the only person indispensable to the campaign." Richard Harden, who had distinguished himself in implementing the reorganization plan, had a background with Arthur Anderson and Company and brought tight management to the day-to-day campaign expenditures.

In May 1975, Carter was scheduled to attend a meeting of the Trilateral Commission in Japan. It was to be the only overseas trip of the campaign. Jody Powell's father had tragically died a few days earlier, so I was to accompany Carter because I had made previous visits to Japan; I also was one of the few insiders who had a passport and therefore could leave at short notice. We stopped en route in California for a series of campaign events. One afternoon was spent in the Imperial Valley as a guest of Bob Myers, a wealthy farmer and early supporter.

That night Carter spoke at a dinner organized by Myers at the country club in El Centro. Bobby Kennedy was the only other presidential candidate to have visited the town, a fact not lost on the 250 people, many of them Republicans, who attended the event, or on the editorial board of the local paper with whom Carter had a brief meeting. It underscored the advantage of holding no official office and being able to campaign full-time, a completely radical notion in the eyes of conventional politicians at the time. Carter gained loyal supporters of diverse political backgrounds merely because they had the chance to shake his hand and were flattered by his attention to their community.

The following day, spent in the Los Angeles area, included a small reception at the Beverly Wilshire Hotel hosted by Harold Willens, Max Pavlevsky, and other members of the so-called Malibu Mafia, a group of wealthy liberal businessmen who had backed George McGovern. The group was less interested in Carter than in their preoccupying fear, following the departure of Ted Kennedy, that George Wallace might end up as the Democratic nominee. Although they discounted his prospects and were uncomfortable with his southernness, they found Carter the single best hope for blocking Wallace, enabling a "true" liberal ultimately to get the nomination. After Carter spoke, there was considerable surprise that he shared their own liberal social views and could also relate to them as businessmen. He won over several key members of the group who would later provide an invaluable fund-raising nucleus in southern California and also provide an important entree to the Hollywood community.

The next morning there appeared a front-page story in the *Los Angeles Times* by Robert Shogan headlined, "Carter: The Religious Moralist Candidate for President." The story detailed Carter's religious background and his sister Ruth's evangelical work, making the point that his faith and his morality set him apart from the other candidates. Mindful of the sophisticated liberals we had met with the day before, I expressed my deep concern about the damage the article could do to his efforts in California. "You're wrong," he said with assurance. "It will help me—even in California."

That night we flew to Hawaii, where once again Carter was the only candidate to have visited the state. Though the stop was short, the symbolism of his presence and the brief flurry of local publicity it generated was enough to launch a substantial following in the state.

The Trilateral Commission was to hold two days of meetings in Tokyo and then move on for two days in Kyoto. At the airport we were met by the representatives of the YKK zipper company, which had opened a large plant near Macon, Georgia, when Carter was governor. Carter had developed a personal friendship with Tadeo Yoshida, the president of the company, who had converted to Christianity and devoted much of his profits to philanthropy. On the way in from the airport one of the Japanese asked Carter if there was anything he wanted particularly to see or to buy while he was in Japan. Merely by way of conversation Carter mentioned that he did hope to buy a small color television set for Amy while he was there. We had hardly checked into our hotel room when a brand-new portable television set was delivered, a gift from Mr. Yoshida. Although its value was modest, I expressed concern to Carter that as a presidential candidate he could not afford to have it written that he was accepting gifts from Japanese businessmen. He fully agreed and told me to arrange to have it returned. However, the Japanese staff members of the Trilateral Commission told me it would cause great offense to return the gift. In the end we agreed that Carter would keep it, but that when he returned to Georgia he would send Mr. Yoshida a gift of comparable value, which he did.

In the lobby of the hotel I encountered Eugene Patterson, formerly publisher of the *Atlanta Journal* and then with the *St. Petersburg Times*. He was a member of a delegation of senior newspaper and magazine editors and publishers on their way to China, who by sheer coincidence were stopping over for two days at the same hotel. He agreed to convene the group that evening for a meeting with Carter to discuss his campaign. Carter made a strikingly positive impression. Ironically, it would have been impossible to convene such a prestigious and influential group of media moguls for that purpose in the States.

The trip to Japan had been looked upon as an opportunity for Carter to make a major foreign policy speech that would hopefully be covered by the several distinguished journalists in Tokyo for the Trilateral Commission meetings. Originally the planned audience was the Overseas Correspondents Association, but we arrived in Tokyo to find they had chosen another speaker. I frantically sought a substitute venue, finally convincing the American Chamber of Commerce to hold a special lunch for the purpose. It was not well attended. The speech was a solid and substantive statement carefully prepared with significant help from Zbigniew Brzezinski and Richard Gardner. Although several journalists attended the luncheon, and Tom Oberdorfer of the *Washington Post* filed a long story, it resulted in only a picture of Carter and a single-sentence caption that he had made the speech. It received no other coverage in the United States.

Carter visited the Diet and was eager to meet with government leaders, but they were not convinced it was worth their time to meet with him. Eventually he was received by Foreign Minister Masayoshi Ohira, Vice Premier Takeo Fukuda, and Prime Minister Takeo Miki. We also met with former Prime Minister Kakuei Tanaka, who would later be indicted for his role in a bribery scandal involving the Lockheed Corporation, but who took more seriously than the others Carter's prospects as a presidential candidate. He inscribed for us copies of his autobiography, but we later laughed as we realized, not reading Japanese, that we did not know which book was intended for which of us.

Ultimately the most important aspect of the trip would be the opportunity it provided for Carter to enhance his relationship with his fellow commission members. Although he had met most of them at previous meetings, in spending four days together he got to know them in greater depth. We discussed the potential that several obviously had for appointment to a Carter administration, among them Cyrus Vance, Warren Christopher, Harold Brown, Michael Blumenthal, Richard Cooper, Leonard Woodcock, Lloyd Cutler, Anthony Solomon, Paul Warnke, Lucy Wilson Benson, and Henry Owen of the Brookings Institution. Later in the summer Owen would arrange for two several-hour briefings for Carter by his fellow scholars at the Brookings Institution, one on foreign policy, the other on domestic issues.

Richard Holbrooke, managing editor of *Foreign Policy* magazine, made a point of talking at length to Carter. He volunteered his efforts and support and would subsequently play a prominent role in the campaign. Carter's attention was naturally focused primarily on the American members of the commission. He enjoyed the Japanese, but he was least drawn to the Europeans, who in turn were relatively aloof and uninterested in him. One exception was Mary Robinson, a young member of the Irish Senate, who would later become her country's president and who shared Carter's concern for the Third World.

Leaving Japan, a two-hour wildcat strike by TWA employees forced Carter, who was always irritated by any delay in his schedule, to cool his heels in the airport VIP lounge. There, an American traveler, after staring at Carter for a long time, walked over to introduce himself, and said, "I know you are somebody, but I just can't figure out who." We considered it progress.

Flying overnight from Tokyo to Anchorage, Carter attended a birthday party for U.S. Senator Mike Gravel. Democratic activists at this fortuitous event had come in from all over the state, allowing him to meet them in a way that would have been impossible short of traveling all over Alaska. Many of them were schoolteachers, who in small isolated towns and villages were often the most educated and influential people in the community. As in Hawaii, he was the only Democratic hopeful to visit and he tailored his remarks to reflect his own longstanding interest in education. It helped him in Alaska and, as word filtered back, it also helped him with the growing support he was receiving from the National Education Association in Washington.

We arrived in Seattle at 5 A.M. and had a several-hour layover there. The VIP room was closed, so we went to the airport chapel, stretched out on the floor, and slept for two hours. Late that afternoon we arrived at the airport in Albany, Georgia, exhausted. Carter would take one day off before leaving on another intensive campaign swing around the country.

CHAPTER 18

The winds are always on the side of the ablest navigator.

—EDWARD GIBBON

Carter benefitted immeasurably from the unique circumstances in the elections of 1976. It is unlikely that he could have succeeded in any other year.

Under the new rules, delegates in primary states were chosen by congressional district, with candidates receiving 15 percent or more of the popular vote being eligible for delegates in proportion to the percentage of the vote they received. In contrast to earlier years, there were no "winner take all" primaries. The implication was that it was crucial to enter every primary and to file a slate of Carter delegates in every congressional district. Even a relatively poor showing in the popular vote could now yield delegates as long as the 15 percent threshold was achieved. Several candidates who would beat Carter in the popular vote would come away with fewer delegates from a state because they had not grasped the full significance of the new "democratized" rules or had failed to meet the early deadlines for filing slates of delegates. Of the 3,071 delegates to the 1976 Democratic convention, 75 percent were to be picked in primaries and the remainder in twenty-three states that planned to hold caucuses.

Even more important was the legislation spawned by Watergate that established public financing for presidential elections. To be eligible, primary candidates were required to raise a minimum of $5,000, in amounts of $250 or less, in at least twenty states. Most importantly, individual contributions were limited to $1,000, except for the candidates themselves, who could contribute up to $50,000. The federal government matched funds raised by eligible candidates. Then the campaigns had an expenditure ceiling of $10 million. For the first time, dark horse candidates were competing on an equal footing with national figures. Even the wealthiest contributors could give only the $1,000 limit. New fund-raising techniques were required that targeted the largest number of people who could give at the $1,000 level. Unlike most of the candidates, Carter had no very wealthy backers, so the new rules favored his grassroots campaign, enabling it to raise small amounts of money from ordinary people.

Carter and Jordan, thanks to the Mikulski Commission and the "mini-convention," were thoroughly familiar with the subtler ramifications of the new delegate selection process. With the $10 million limit on expenditures, the careful budgeting of time and resources was vital. Jordan, in a lengthy and sophisticated memo, produced a complex weighting for states:

> In a campaign to win the Democratic nomination for president, there are three major factors to be considered: the relative size of the states and their delegations to the Democratic National Convention; the sequence of the primaries and the sequence of the delegate selection process in nonprimary states; and our own campaign strategy. . . . This memorandum is an attempt to account for these factors and reconcile them through development of a formula that will guide us in the allocation of the major resources of the campaign.

The plan referred to as "percentage of effort targeting" became central to the campaign strategy in apportioning money, staff, media buys, and the candidate's time. During that period, representatives of the other candidates and I attended briefings held by the Democratic National Committee. The others seemed wedded to the rules of the past and had little grasp of the more complex implications of both the new delegate selection and campaign financing rules. The ability to master detail was, however, also inherent in Carter's nature in a way that it was not for the other candidates. It proved an enormous asset.

More broadly the Carter strategy involved the following elements: Having consolidated his southern base and built contacts and name recognition nationwide during 1974 and 1975, he would win the Iowa caucuses on January 19, 1976; maintaining that early momentum by coming in first or second in the remaining early caucus states, Mississippi, Oklahoma, Maine, Alaska, and South Carolina; winning the New Hampshire primary, boosting him to front-runner status and showing he was not just a regional candidate; beating George Wallace in Florida, wresting from him leadership of the region. The expectation was if this could be accomplished, then the field would be so narrowed and the momentum so irresistible that Carter would be unstoppable in the industrial states. He had repeatedly said early in the campaign that he was confident there would be no more than two viable candidates besides himself after the Florida primary.

Carter had made the decision to keep the campaign headquarters in Atlanta rather than move to Washington; with a growing paid staff they took over offices on Peachtree Street. Having limited contacts around the country, Carter relied heavily throughout 1975 on the network effect of having his Georgia friends contact their personal and business acquaintances to promote him as a serious candidate. Carter even asked every supporter to contact the people on their holiday card lists.

Particularly in states where he was barely known, there was a separate need to recruit enough people to run as his pledged delegates by the filing deadlines. With little money for travel, the campaign relied significantly on those traveling for other business to line up support. In May 1975, I spent a day sitting in a Wyoming motel room calling Democratic activists around the state, following up with either a meeting or a brief note about Carter. The Wyoming Democratic Party was small, and no other candidate had yet bothered to solicit their support. That the Carter campaign with its distant southern base did so, helped him in the same way it did in Hawaii and Alaska. Sometimes such contacts paid off handsomely. I met Ted Sorensen as a coparticipant in a seminar at the Aspen Institute in Colorado. After hearing my passionate advocacy of Carter's candidacy, he agreed to meet with him a week later. Sorensen, impressed, then agreed to be the New York campaign chairman, greatly enhancing Carter's standing with liberals and Kennedy supporters. Similar personal contacts by others in the year before the first primaries paid off handsomely by the time the voting actually began.

The inability to sustain a steady flow of cash is what ultimately breaks most presidential campaigns. In an effort to beat the January 1, 1975, deadline, Bentsen and Jackson had furiously raised money from wealthy contributors during 1974. Although Jackson "limited" himself to accepting donations of $3,000 per person, or $6,000 per married couple, he had put together the bulk of his $6 million primary campaign war chest before the new law went into effect. By contrast, Carter announced that he would abide by its provisions immediately. It was, in fact, not much of a concession as he had virtually no wealthy backers who could finance him at the level Bentsen and Jackson were achieving. In 1974, Carter pledged his own allowable limit of $50,000. Philip Alston, Bill Schwartz, and a few other relatively wealthy Carter friends in Georgia made contributions up to the $1,000 level. However, apart from Carter's contribution, the campaign collected only $47,000 in all of 1974. When Frank Moore left the governor's office in late 1974 and asked to join the campaign, he was told there was no money to employ him. He joined anyway, in charge of fund-raising. Getting a paycheck for himself was a powerful motivator.

Because he was given so little chance of success, according to Moore, Carter had to "grub for every penny." Chip Carter, the most effective family fund-raiser, says he would literally stop people on the street and say, "My daddy is running for president, and would you give him $10?" Every member of the campaign staff was working at a considerable financial sacrifice out of the loyalty that Carter inspired in them.

A $100-a-couple dinner held in Atlanta in March 1975 boosted income for the first three months of the year to $180,989.72, but collections for the next three months fell to $150,615.75. As Carter had no financial base outside Georgia, he was forced to return repeatedly to those who had backed him for governor, yet during the last five months of 1975 the donations averaged only $75,000 per month. Gradually, however, the $5,000 level was achieved in twenty states. Finally, on August 18, Rosalynn's birthday, Carter was able to call a press conference in Washington to announce that he had qualified for federal matching funds.

Unfortunately, although he was now entitled to receive $500,000 from the Treasury, the money would not become available until January 1, 1976. The financial situation was desperate. Jordan and other top campaign staff went without paychecks for September, October, and November. Telephone, rent, and the salaries of junior campaign staff had to be paid to keep up appearances, so reporters wouldn't write the campaign obituary before the first primary. To compound the problem, a huge effort was needed in Iowa and New Hampshire if Carter was to pull off his planned upset victories.

Two developments saved the day. Phil Walden, president of Capricorn Records based in Macon, Georgia, offered to hold a series of rock concerts to raise money. The arrangement was worked out by Cloyd Hall, who at the end of Carter's term had taken an executive position with the astoundingly successful record company in his hometown. Under the new law the cost of each ticket counted as an individual contribution to the campaign and therefore could be federally matched. The first event was held at the Fox Theater in Atlanta on October 31. It began at midnight with the Amazing Rhythm Aces. Then Carter came on stage.

> Tonight is the night for music, not politics. I just want to say four things: (1) I'm running for president. (2) I don't intend to lose. (3) I need your support. (4) I'd like to introduce my friends, the Marshall Tucker band.

The event was a sellout, with 4,000 people at $6.50 for advance tickets, $7.50 on the performance night.

There were subsequent concerts on November 23 in Providence, Rhode Island, with Grinderswitch and the Allman Brothers (10,000 tickets, $8 each), and January 14, 1976, in Atlanta with Charlie Daniels and the Outlaws. At the event in Providence, Carter was introduced by Geraldo Rivera. Because of his relationship with ABC, Rivera was supposed to be neutral. However, once on stage he got carried away by the enthusiasm of the crowd and gave Carter his backing, making him the first nonsouthern celebrity to do so. Apart from the much-needed funds that were raised, the campaign recruited more than 200 volunteers, achieved for Carter the endorsement of most college newspapers in New England, and generated invaluable free publicity. Not to be outdone by the rock stars, Robert Shaw, conductor and director of the Atlanta Symphony, gave $1,000.

Jack Watson organized a statewide fund-raising telethon for February 14, 1975, with the slogan "Georgia Loves Jimmy Carter." Ten-dollar tickets were sold to more than 100 parties in people's homes around the state, at which the guests watched the telethon combining Carter and the stable of entertainers from Capricorn Records, including Greg Allman, Peggy Cass, and James Brown.

The other significant development was the recruitment of Morris Dees. Dees, who had revolutionized direct-mail political fund-raising when he worked for the McGovern campaign, was described by Gary Hart as "one of the few bona fide geniuses" he had ever known. In November he received a call from Charlie Kirbo asking for his help and agreed to become the national finance chairman for a campaign that was, for all practical purposes, broke.

In both December and January, $100,000 was needed if the campaign was to survive, and it was the worst time of year to be soliciting contributions. Dees found that 1,900 people had contributed $100 or more and that 1,450 of them lived in Georgia. With no exciting news to attract new donors, he knew that he would have to go back to those people. He decided to ask every past contributor to give the same amount again. "Double-up-for-Jimmy" became the battle cry as bleary-eyed clerks under the direction of a dynamic young black woman, Eddie Poe, prepared file cards on each of the greater-than-$100 givers. Dees prepared a draft two-page letter from Carter mailed on December 12 to each contributor. A mixture of hokum and hard sales pitch, it said in part:

> A bumper crop of peanuts, I learned years ago, is not made at harvest time, but in the early spring when you prepare a good seed bed. . . .
>
> I believe so strongly that our government can be decent, truthful, fair, compassionate, and efficient and I need your help so urgently that I am going to ask you and each donor to make a personal sacrifice.

It ended:

> Will you reach out your hand to me, once again? Rosalynn and I will do our best to never disappoint you.

On December 15 a group of volunteer Carter loyalists—lawyers, physicians, business professionals—began making follow-up calls to every recipient of the letter. Despite early skepticism of Dees's effort, checks poured in. During December, $176,000 was raised, and in January, $125,000, averting the crisis that would have doomed the campaign.

Dees then started to build a long-range fund-raising structure, beginning by setting up finance committees in each major city. Then dividing the country into eight regions, he appointed a team of national finance directors to supervise them: Bill Albers, Roger Altman, David Dunn, Joel McCleary, Paul Porter, Steve Selig, Mort Zuckerman, Jack Watson (Georgia finance chairman), and Doug Huron, who was responsible for working with political action committees. Under the direction of these people, more than 100 finance committees were set up in major cities and states. By the end of the primary season, this had mushroomed to over 600.

Dees was able to quickly enlist several of his old wealthy liberal friends from the McGovern campaign. He argued that it was not so much a contribution to Carter but an investment in someone who could defeat Wallace in Florida. In a matter of a few months, more than a million dollars was raised. One New York woman, Alice Mason, a committee member with no political fund-raising background, personally raised over $75,000 for the campaign.

Georgia, however, was to remain the key to Carter fund-raising until after the Pennsylvania primary in April. Jack Watson was central to that effort. Dees says of him:

> Watson is absolutely the best organizer I have ever worked with. He organized Georgia in a three-week period and, directly from his efforts, over one million dollars poured into the campaign.

Despite Dees's indispensable contribution, his very success began to expose serious rifts in the campaign. For the first time in three years the Carter inner circle was in serious debt to someone not from Georgia and not part of the original group. Dees was very committed to seeing Carter become president, but he was not an original diehard loyalist. To Hamilton Jordan, Frank Moore, and those around them, Dees was seen as an ultraliberal with influential friends around the country whose talents they desperately needed, but with whom they did not want to share any power. Partly it was ideological, partly it was the inherent battle of egos that grips every presidential campaign, but it signaled the start of a series of serious rifts among the staff. Despite being the savior of the campaign, Dees's role was both praised and subtly denigrated with reporters. On one occasion, when asked if Dees would be attending an important strategy meeting, Frank Moore responded, "Dees is not part of the campaign. He just raises money."

Carter had done very well as a thematic, as opposed to an issues, candidate. However, as he appeared increasingly consequential, reporters pressed him to clarify the specifics of his positions and identify who his advisors were on substantive matters. Steve Stark, a former reporter, had been the full-time "issues coordinator" since late 1974. Stu Eizenstat, while still practicing law, continued to help Carter refine and articulate his positions on a range of topics. He and Stark, with the help of "issues committees" of volunteer experts set up by the small staff in the campaign's Washington office, prepared position papers and identified experts with whom Carter could talk and obtain advice. These included Philip Handler, president of the National Academy of Sciences; economists Charles Schultze and Lawrence Klein, of the University of Pennsylvania; Leon Keyserling, a Truman advisor; and Mary Dublin Keyserling, who would draft key campaign speeches for Carter on health care and welfare reform. Carter also consulted with foreign policy expert Milton Katz at Harvard.

Preoccupied with political organizing and fund-raising, "issues" received scant attention from the staff at the Peachtree headquarters. In June 1975, Hamilton Jordan visited Washington. One of his meetings was with a group of student leaders at American University, who peppered him with questions relating to Carter's position on a range of topics. Jordan, who rarely accompanied Carter on a campaign trip, was hard-pressed to respond to a single query and was painfully unfamiliar with Carter's positions. Finally he volunteered that he was "not an issues person," saying that he could only comfortably discuss political strategy (at which he excelled), but would send issue papers to anyone who wanted them after he returned to Atlanta. Jordan was not unique. It reflected how little the deep loyalty among those closest to Carter had to do with ideology and how compartmentalized the campaign had already become. One journalist wrote, referring to the Atlanta staff, "Very few of them seem to have much interest in why Jimmy wants to be president, or even in what he might do after he wins."

Earlier Eizenstat had asked me to intercede with Jordan. I wrote:

> Stuart Eizenstat is upset about the way the development of the policy operation is going. He feels that his group has operated in a vacuum, and that they are extremely handicapped by not having enough interaction and feedback with the governor either to adequately brief him or to allow him to refine his positions that would be consistent with his own beliefs. He also feels that there is too much gap between operations and policy, so that there is not only not enough thought given to the situations where the governor could really get the greatest mileage by saying the right things to the right people, but that he could get badly burned by being caught ignorant and without a fully defined position on some crucial issue.

My entreaties were largely ignored, and it was not until Eizenstat joined the campaign full-time in April 1976 that he began to assert his role more forcefully. Even then, he and his staff were used primarily when a major speech was required. Carter floated above the conflicts in the campaign, narrowly and intensively focused on his own role. He addressed these organizational problems only rarely and reluctantly. Bert Lance would observe, "He could have cared less about what was going on with the staff."

The Iowa caucuses had been established in 1972 as a part of the democratizing process. That year, Edmund Muskie was the clear Democratic front-runner and his anticipated victory caused little stir and minimal media coverage. In 1976, with a crowded field and no obvious front-runner, it became a crucial test of who would first emerge from the pack.* From the moment Tim Kraft moved to Iowa in August, his role as a full-time professional organizer proved pivotal. Following the strategy outlined in the comprehensive operational manual that Hamilton Jordan had prepared, he began by organizing a nucleus of committed volunteers in each congressional district, then establishing a statewide steering committee, then similar committees in each congressional district, and, as time permitted, developing smaller committees at the county or community level. In many instances they never met as a group, partly because they could not get along among themselves.

In Iowa, Kraft put together a statewide committee that included Charles Hammer, a physicist who had been a McGovern organizer and anti-war activist, Soapy Owens, the retired chief of the Iowa United Auto Workers, Jim Schaben, a conservative who had been the 1974 Democratic nominee for governor for whom Carter had campaigned, and James Maloney, auditor for Polk County, a member of the old-line "courthouse crowd" in Des Moines. Getting commitments was not always easy, as Rosalynn describes:

> On my first trip . . . Tim was putting together the [state] steering committee and he had some people he wanted me to see. We talked to Charles Hammer, who was very liberal. . . . I went out to dinner with Charles and his wife, Hazel [who at that point was actively identified with the Harris campaign]. . . . I really liked her and I think she liked me. . . . When I got home I told Jimmy to call Charlie Hammer and see if he would be on the steering committee. He said it wasn't any use to call him because he was so liberal. And I said, well we can call him. It won't hurt. Jimmy talked to him, and he said . . . that he was undecided, but that he would think about it and call back on Sunday. . . . He called back on Sunday and said he would do it.

Another committee member was Fred McLain, a farmer who lived near Ames. He came home one day to find that Carter had left a handwritten note pinned to the front door. They'd met only once before, but the gesture was enough to get him to agree to be on the committee. However, as Rosalynn recalls, "[He] had always been a Humphrey man. But by then we had his name on the letterhead."

*The other announced candidates at this point were Senator Birch Bayh, Senator Lloyd Bentsen, former Senator Fred Harris, Governor Milton Shapp, Sargent Shriver, Senator Henry "Scoop" Jackson, Congressman Morris Udall, and Governor George Wallace. An additional candidate, Terry Sanford, had already dropped out at this point.

That Carter could not be easily pigeonholed ideologically made it possible for him to appeal to people across a wide political spectrum. In this agricultural state, corn and hog farmers identified with Carter because of his background. For fiscal conservatives his talk of waste and inefficiency in the nation's capital was appealing. When he spoke of the need for integrity and honesty in government, and for new ideas and faces, it appealed both to conservatives and to liberals. McGovern supporters liked his call for a reduction in defense spending and his criticism of the Central Intelligence Agency, especially its connections to the Watergate scandal. In Iowa, a state with a high percentage of deeply religious people, Carter's devout beliefs had wide appeal even though Southern Baptists were a rarity in the state. Others, like Hammer, were attracted by a man running for president who shared with them a scientific background. And to intellectuals Carter's manifest brainpower was an attraction. As he had done throughout his political career, Carter presented himself to the electorate, as frankly as he could, to show what he was as much as to say in what he believed.

By presenting himself as an "ordinary citizen" rather than as a career politician, people identified with him, and he attracted those who had never before been involved in politics. Floyd Gilotti, a longtime political activist in Des Moines, told of attending a Carter meeting at which he knew only 4 of 160 people present. Carter believed that the absolute dedication and loyalty of a person who had no power base or political experience was at least as important as the lukewarm support of a small-time political boss looking to advance his own position.

The only significant institutional support Carter had in Iowa was from the United Auto Workers. On an early visit, Carter had stayed with Soapy Owens, who although retired from the union subsequently mobilized the state leadership. The UAW membership would vote 99 percent in favor of Carter, but perhaps more important, they had the organizational structure for the crucial task of getting Carter supporters in sufficient numbers out to the caucuses. The national UAW leadership would later get behind Carter, in part because he promised that as president he would back comprehensive national health insurance.

The turning point of the entire campaign probably occurred on October 27, 1975. That morning the *New York Times* ran a front-page story by the highly respected political reporter, R. W. (Johnny) Apple: "Carter Holds Strong Lead Going into Iowa Caucuses." It was an object lesson in the power wielded by the press in the presidential selection process. Because of who the writer was and his forum, as much as the piece's coverage of the campaign's success in building grassroots support, Carter was boosted immediately into an undisputed front-runner position. Apple later readily admitted that he was aware of the impact the story would have and thought long and hard about writing it. He felt, however, that the facts were inescapable.

Reporters of more modest stature writing for lesser publications had written similarly about Carter's emergence from the pack, but they had been largely ignored. Now, suddenly, the television networks assigned camera crews to follow Carter everywhere he went and he was inundated by requests for interviews. The lonely duo of Carter and Powell had become a full campaign entourage. One of the brightest and most energetic volunteers who had appeared in the Washington office was Greg Schneiders, the former owner of a Capitol Hill bar. So that he could now focus full-time on the press, Jody Powell hired Schneiders as Carter's traveling personal assistant. Although lacking previous campaign experience, he was not only efficient but proved a source of valued mature political judgment for the candidate.

A straw ballot at a preliminary caucus meeting early in the summer had been won by Carter. At a Jefferson–Jackson Day dinner in Ames in October, where seven of the nine candidates spoke, a poll by the *Des Moines Register* among 1,094 attendees showed Carter the choice of 23 percent. His closest rivals were write-in candidate Hubert Humphrey with 12 percent followed by Birch Bayh with 10 percent.

With few topics having aroused much passion in the campaign, the two weeks before the January 19 caucuses were suddenly dominated by the contentious abortion issue. Early in his term as governor, Carter had strongly supported family planning programs including abortion. He had written the foreword to a book, *Women in Need,* that favored a woman's right to abortion. He had given private encouragement to the plaintiffs in a lawsuit, *Doe v. Bolton,* filed against the state of Georgia to overturn its archaic abortion laws. Together with the more famous *Roe v. Wade* case from Texas, it had gone to the U.S. Supreme Court and formed the basis for the 1973 landmark decision on the issue. Subsequently, after being viciously attacked in a public meeting and repeatedly exposed to anti-abortion literature showing the humanoid features of early fetuses, Carter began to reassess his personal feelings on the subject. During 1975, however, he had generally supported the Supreme Court decision and opposed a constitutional amendment to reverse it. In Iowa, a state with 528,000 Roman Catholics, he came under criticism for his position. In the final days before the caucus, the situation seemed to favor a late surge by Sargent Shriver, the only Catholic in the race, at Carter's expense.

The week prior to the caucuses, Carter was quoted in the *Catholic Mirror,* the Des Moines diocesan newspaper, saying that he would support a "national statute" to prevent abortion—a somewhat ambiguous statement, seemingly in conflict with his earlier comments. It clearly worked to Carter's advantage. The word was passed from Catholic pulpits throughout the state, the Sunday morning before the caucuses, that Carter was the one to back. In addition, his statement was distributed after mass, stapled to parish bulletins. Columnists Evans and Novak would later say, "The anti-abortion movement made the difference between first and second place for Carter in Iowa." Carter staff, however, disputed this conclusion.

Elsewhere in the country, Carter's statement created an uproar. The women's movement was already skittish about Carter, but had kept an open mind in view of the strong support that he and Rosalynn had expressed for the Equal Rights Amendment. The movement leadership was indignant about his apparent reversal on the issue that was the sine qua non to many for their support. After he had safely won the caucuses, Carter explained that the story in the *Catholic Mirror* was the result of a discussion with a group of priests in the basement of the Holy Spirit Church in Des Moines. They asked a whole series of improbable hypothetical questions ending up with: "Are there any circumstances under which you might support a national statue against abortion?" to which he said he replied, "Yes. I suppose it is possible, although I cannot think of any."

Critics saw in the way he handled the abortion issue a replay of his attempt in the 1970 gubernatorial race to obfuscate where he stood on race in order to keep the support of liberals while appealing to the Wallace vote. However, it was probably less a calculated political ploy than an inherent psychological need to resolve conflict by accommodating opposing views in his own mind.

An urgent need now existed to mend fences with his supporters, especially women, in the more liberal states, such as New York and California. After considerable deliberation, he worked out with Mary King, his advisor on health and women's issues, a statement he used for the rest of the campaign.

> I have consistently stated that I oppose constitutional amendments to overturn the Supreme Court's decision on abortion. However, I personally disapprove of abortions and do not think government should do anything to encourage abortions.
>
> The Supreme Court left many questions unresolved. As president, I would be guided and bound by the courts' decisions on these and other questions pertaining to abortion services.

As a result, women's groups dropped their overt opposition to Carter. In the end, however, the biggest problem he faced over abortion was not his standing with women but the eroding effect it had on his greatest asset—his integrity. The man who had inspired the support of so many by saying, "I will never tell a lie," had, in the eyes of many, come dangerously close to shading the truth. Jack Germond wrote in the *Washington Star,*

He [Carter] is, as those who have known him longest have been saying all along, an icy-hard politician with a knack for recognizing and exploiting political targets of opportunity. . . . Somehow he picked just that time to suggest that, although he opposed a constitutional amendment restricting the right to abortion, he might not be opposed to a "national statute" on the same subject.

Sargent Shriver was said to feel he had been robbed by Carter, and one Catholic priest was quoted the morning after the caucuses as saying, "I think I've been sandbagged."

On the evening of January 19, 1976, as Iowans gathered in 2,530 locations—meeting halls, schools, and even the front rooms of people's homes—to vote, Carter was in New York City. He attended a fund-raiser and after a brief meeting with his top New York supporters he went to bed. At 2 A.M. Jody Powell called to say the first results clearly showed Carter the winner. Greg Schneiders, who woke Carter to give him the news, says, "He was very happy, but not jumping up and down." Powell called again at 4 A.M. with further results, but they let Carter sleep. He was up at six and went to claim his victory on the breakfast television shows.

The final results gave Carter 29.1 percent, Bayh 11.4 percent, Harris 9.0 percent, Udall 5.8 percent, Shriver 3.1 percent, and uncommitted 38.5 percent (mostly Hubert Humphrey loyalists who hoped he might eventually enter the race). Carter's unprecedented victory gave him instantaneous national recognition and celebrity status as his picture appeared on the covers of both *Time* and *Newsweek*.

The Iowa caucus had grabbed the public attention, but between that evening and the New Hampshire primary on February 24, there were less heralded caucuses scheduled in Mississippi, Oklahoma, Maine, Alaska, and South Carolina. The first, in Mississippi, was scheduled for Saturday, January 24, just five days after Iowa. It had particular significance for Carter because, after winning in Iowa, he needed to demonstrate in his own region that he had the strength to take on George Wallace.

Carter had made his first campaign visit to Mississippi early in 1975, where despite being the recent governor of a nearby state, he remained virtually unknown. His leading, and almost only, supporter in the state was Patt Derian, a progressive advocate of integration whom he had met at the "mini-convention." Ken Dean, president of WLBT-TV in Jackson, arranged for him to be interviewed on his station. Dean, originally recruited by Chip Carter, was a Baptist preacher, and a courageous figure who believed his faith demanded that he work for integration, yet he maintained a conciliatory stance toward the segregationist forces and enjoyed cordial relations with the leaders of the Ku Klux Klan in the state. He and Carter had a natural affinity. Hodding Carter III (no relation), another progressive, whose family owned the *Delta-Democrat Times* in Greenville, also became an early supporter. None of these could particularly help him with the Wallace vote. (Wallace had won 63 percent of the vote in Mississippi as a third-party candidate in 1968.)

A complex situation existed in Mississippi. There were now essentially two Democratic Parties: the Loyalists, who had been established as a predominately black group known as the Mississippi Freedom Democratic Party and loyal to the national party just prior to the 1964 convention; and the Regulars, who had maintained an independent white party. The caucuses in 1976 were aimed at reuniting the two factions with the strong support of moderate Governor Cliff Finch. Since the Goldwater victory in 1964, the Republicans were increasingly seen as the party of segregation, and many white Mississippians were switching their allegiance. The terms *caucus* and *mass meeting* and the expectation of heavy black participation seemed initially to be discouraging much white involvement. In addition, the rules for participating were too complex for many people to understand.

For interesting historical reasons, Sargent Shriver appeared to have the early lead. As director of the Johnson administration's war on poverty, he had been responsible for the development of several federal programs primarily to benefit blacks in the state. His relationship with the Kennedys further strengthened his appeal with the Loyalists. Longstanding friendships with Aaron Henry and other black leaders helped him in putting together his campaign.

Lloyd Bentsen, who had the endorsement of his two fellow senators from Mississippi, Stennis and Eastland, hoped to make an impressive showing to salvage his dying campaign. Fred Harris believed his low-budget, populist campaign would spark some biracial interest. George Wallace, however, remained the big imponderable. Widely popular among whites, his past success had been largely due to his demagoguery, and grassroots organizing was not thought to be his strong point. It was thought he might ignore the caucuses altogether, but instead he sent in a highly competent young organizer, Steve St. Amand, who had previously worked for Edmund Muskie.

While Carter's campaigning in Mississippi was important, it was Rosalynn who proved the more important asset, although she visited only twice. Southern chivalry led white political leaders to accord her, as a woman and wife of a former governor, a level of hospitality they would not give to Carter. It was much easier for her to meet with garden clubs, religious groups, and small business owners—those most likely to turn out for the caucuses. She also demonstrated her political acumen on her second visit when, noting that the lack of black organizers was jeopardizing their effort, she called state Senator Ben Brown, the senior African American in

Jimmy Carter's maternal grandfather, Jim Jack Gordy. (Jimmy Carter Library)

Earl Carter with Jimmy, Gloria, and Ruth. (Jimmy Carter Library)

Lillian Carter holding the infant Jimmy. (Jimmy Carter Library)

Rachel Clark surrounded by Jimmy (*upper left*), his sisters Ruth and Gloria, cousins Hugh Carter and Willard Slappey. (Special Collections, Robert W. Woodruff Library, Emory University)

Jimmy at age thirteen.
(Special Collections, Robert W.
Woodruff Library, Emory University)

The Plexico house
where Jimmy spent
his childhood.
(Special Collections,
Robert W. Woodruff
Library, Emory University)

The Carter family
store on Main Street
in Plains, 1925.
(Jimmy Carter Library)

Carter as a midshipman,
with an inscription to Rosalynn.
(Jimmy Carter Library)

Miss Julia Coleman and Y. T. Sheffield.
(Jimmy Carter Library)

Jimmy and Rosalynn
on their wedding day, 1946.
(Jimmy Carter Library)

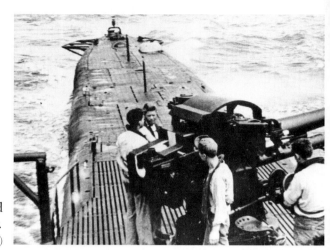

Carter aboard
the USS *Pomphret*.
(Jimmy Carter Library)

Carter at the Plains cemetery.
(Special Collections, Robert W.
Woodruff Library, Emory
University/Charles Rafshoon)

Shoveling peanuts
in the Carter warehouse.
(Special Collections, Robert W.
Woodruff Library, Emory
University/Charles Rafshoon)

VOTE FOR

JIMMY CARTER

CANDIDATE FOR

State Senator

PRIMARY OCTOBER 16th, 1962

Your Vote and Support Will Be Appreciated

Carter's first
campaign poster.
(Jimmy Carter Library)

Jimmy Carter
finally sworn in after
his contested race
for the Georgia senate.
(Jimmy Carter Library)

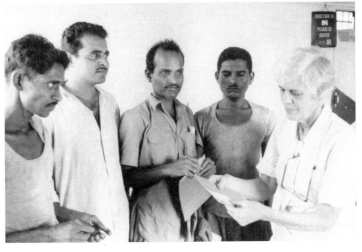

Miss Lillian in India,
working as a Peace
Corps volunteer.
(Courtesy of the Peace Corps)

Carter is inaugurated as Georgia's
seventy-sixth governor, January 1971.
(Jimmy Carter Library)

"Jimmy Carter is the most effective
one-on-one campaigner I have
ever known": Andrew Young.
(Special Collections, Robert W. Woodruff Library,
Emory University/Charles Rafshoon)

A rare moment of cordiality with Lt. Governor Lester Maddox.
(Special Collections, Robert W. Woodruff Library, Emory University/Charles
Rafshoon)

Governor Carter with key aide, Cloyd Hall.
(Courtesy of Cloyd Hall)

The picture of Carter, with his trademark smile, that would be used to launch his presidential bid.
(Special Collections, Robert W. Woodruff Library, Emory University/Charles Rafshoon)

Nicoletta Hansbury holds Carter's hand as he campaigns in the Baltimore Old Town Mall, 1976.
(Courtesy of the *Washington Post*/Ken Feil)

President Carter helps
Amy with her homework
in the Cabinet Room.
(Jimmy Carter Library)

Carter with Gloria Steinem
and deputy campaign
director Barbara Blum
at the Carter campaign
headquarters in July 1976.
(Special Collections, Robert W.
Woodruff Library, Emory
University/Charles Rafshoon)

The Carters set a precedent
by walking from the inauguration
on Capitol Hill to the White
House. (Jimmy Carter Library)

Presidential aides *(left to right)*
Gerald Rafshoon, Stuart Eizenstat,
Jack Watson, and Jody Powell.
(Jimmy Carter Library)

The Carters welcome
Admiral Hyman Rickover
and his wife to
the White House.
(Jimmy Carter Library)

Secretary of State Vance
and National Security
Advisor Brzezinski
discussing the SALT II
negotiations with Carter.
(Jimmy Carter Library)

Carter felt a special personal bond with President Anwar Sadat of Egypt.
(Jimmy Carter Library)

As the Camp David negotiations falter, Carter pleads with Begin and Sadat to continue their efforts.
(Jimmy Carter Library)

The Carters visit the Panama Canal— June 17, 1978; behind them is treaty negotiator Sol Linowitz.
(Jimmy Carter Library)

Carter, Begin, and Sadat
celebrate the signing
of the Middle East
peace treaties.
(Jimmy Carter Library)

In his relationship
with Walter Mondale,
Carter transformed
the role of the vice
presidency.
(Jimmy Carter Library)

Bert Lance was Carter's
right-hand man
as governor and during
his first year in the
White House.
(Jimmy Carter Library)

Ambassador Andrew
Young discussing
the independence
of Zimbabwe
with the president.
(Jimmy Carter Library)

The Carters tried
to make life for Amy
as normal as possible
in the White House.
(Jimmy Carter Library)

Hamilton Jordan
and Carter working
to recruit support
for energy legislation.
(Jimmy Carter Library)

The leaders of the
industrialized world at
their summit in London
in May 1977 (*left to right*):
Chancellor Helmut
Schmidt, Prime Minister
Pierre Trudeau, President
Valéry Giscard d'Estaing,
Prime Minister James
Callaghan, Carter, Prime
Minister Giulio Andreotti,
and Prime Minister
Masayoshi Ohira.
(Jimmy Carter Library)

Carter with
Leonid Brezhnev
at the signing
of the SALT II Treaty
in Vienna 1979.
(Jimmy Carter Library)

Tension in the Oval Office
during the final hours
of the hostage crisis.
(Jimmy Carter Library)

With minutes left in his presidency, Carter celebrates the news with Rosalynn that the hostages will be released. (Jimmy Carter Library)

Carter leads an immunization drive for The Atlanta Project. (1993 Michael A. Schwarz)

Jimmy and Rosalynn during a fishing trip in Tregaron, Wales, 1986. (Peter G. Bourne)

Carter meets West African
villagers in his campaign
to end river blindness.
(Bill Van der Decker)

Building houses
for Habitat for Humanity.
(Photo by Ray Scioscia)

With Senator Sam Nunn
and General Colin Powell
in Haiti.
(The Carter Center)

Carter meeting
with North Korean
President Kim Il Sung.
(The Carter Center)

Carter, with Chairman
Yasir Arafat, as leader
of the international
monitors during the
Palestinian elections
in January 1996.
(Billy Howard, 1996)

Carter celebrates his
seventieth birthday
on October 1, 1994.
(Peter G. Bourne)

the campaign. At her instigation he put together a team of black campaign workers, including other elected officials, who descended on the state in the final days, and were probably responsible for drawing away enough black support from Shriver to allow Carter to beat him.

With the Iowa victory, money was flowing in. This enabled Carter to feel more comfortable about the need for paid "field staff" and in the final week he had thirty salaried workers in Mississippi. Among them was a small cadre of young skilled organizers who would spend the early months of 1976 moving from one caucus state to another. Ken Hays, Joel Solomon, Lisa Bordeaux, and Maggie Cadoux made up the core team of "caucus-state experts" with a rapidly learned but sophisticated knowledge of how to organize and manage a caucus-state campaign. In Mississippi, however, they faced a two-step problem. They had to first convince people to support Carter and then get them to attend the caucuses. The Wallace staff only had to get their people to the meetings. His advertising simply said, "You know George Wallace. If you want to help him, come to the caucuses." A particularly frustrating problem, as Ken Hays pointed out in retrospect, was that the vigorous and visible organizing on Carter's behalf did much to inadvertently awaken Wallace's large latent support. The Carter campaign efforts to educate people about the importance of participating in the caucuses paid off, but the people they convinced to attend the meetings did not necessarily support Carter.

Throughout the Saturday of the caucuses, Carter expressed confidence about the outcome while campaigning in Vermont. As the early results were phoned to him, however, it became evident that his optimism was misplaced. The final results were: Wallace 44 percent, Carter 14 percent, Shriver 12 percent, Bentsen 1.6 percent, Harris 1.1 percent, and uncommitted 27 percent. Seeking to console Carter, who was downcast over the unexpected Wallace success, Schneiders told him he thought this result did not matter much, to which Carter replied, "I know, but I hate to lose anything." For Bentsen, who had spent considerable money and had the backing of the white Democratic power structure, it was a humiliation.

The Oklahoma caucuses on February 7 would have drawn little attention had it not been for the fact that this was Fred Harris's home state and he needed to win there. David Hales, the local Carter campaign organizer, had conducted careful research and realized it made no sense to allocate resources in congressional districts where a candidate stood no chance of reaching the 15 percent threshold. Correcting an error the Carter campaign had made in Iowa and Mississippi, Hales had identified and intensively organized the precincts where Carter was strong and ignored others, especially those around the University of Oklahoma in Norman and Oklahoma State University in Stillwater, two Harris strongholds.

Carter was better known in Oklahoma than Mississippi. Governor David Boren disliked Fred Harris and leaned toward Carter with whom he had worked as a gubernatorial colleague. He appeared on the verge of an endorsement, but then backed off, it was said, because Carter would not support deregulation of natural gas. More likely it was because he was still unconvinced Carter was ultimately going anywhere.

This was Bentsen's last gasp. Wallace had significantly less support in Oklahoma than in Mississippi and no organization. The other candidates, assuming Harris would win, had ignored the state. Harris, who had drifted to the left since Oklahomans had elected him to the U.S. Senate in 1968, was running an unorthodox and colorful campaign that appealed mostly to young college students. The result was that he had lost much of the middle-class support he once enjoyed. The more moderate Carter became a natural beneficiary of their disillusionment.

Oklahoma has a large Baptist and evangelical population with whom Carter had a natural affinity. In addition, widely known in the state because of her own evangelical teaching and the recent publication of her book *The Gift of Inner Healing,* Ruth had a lengthy mailing list. She spent days writing and calling people with whom it was more of an asset to be Ruth Carter Stapleton's brother than the former governor of Georgia. Carter spoke as a guest of evangelist Oral Roberts at Oral Roberts University, a plus in the eyes of many Oklahomans.

Carter enjoyed strong support in Oklahoma's small black community. A particularly poignant moment occurred at a rally in Tulsa when Carter was introduced by a local resident named Fannie Hill, who had been born in Plains. In a moving statement she told how, when she was growing up, Miss Lillian had been the only white person who would go into black homes to help people when they were sick. With tears in her eyes, she told what it meant to her to see that woman's son running for president.

In Elk City, Oklahoma, virtually the entire community turned out for a Carter rally. Carter was so moved that he promised the people that as president he would return to see them. He did.

Sensing the potential for an outright victory and thereby dealing Fred Harris a knockout blow, Carter mounted an all-out effort in the final week. Both Jimmy and Rosalynn spent hours every day on the phone, calling potential backers. On the morning of the caucuses, Rosalynn called twenty people in Tulsa, creating a significant ripple effect, as those to whom she spoke could not refrain from bragging to their friends that they had received a personal call from her.

The final result was Carter 18.5 percent, Harris 17 percent, Bentsen 12.8 percent, and Wallace 10.4 percent. Forty percent were uncommitted, mostly backers of David Boren, who would ultimately deliver them to

Carter. Because of erratic and slow reporting, the Harris staff were able for two days to convince the media that the contest was still a toss-up. The *Washington Post* ran a headline: "Carter, Harris Lead in Oklahoma." However, Carter had, for all practical purposes, put an end to both the Harris and Bentsen candidacies.

Three days later, on February 10, Alaska held its caucuses. Carter's twelve-hour visit there, on his way back from Japan in May 1975, bore significant fruit. Diane Anderson, an energetic schoolteacher, had organized a strong constituency for Carter, made up mostly of fellow teachers and those who had met him at the birthday party for Senator Mike Gravel. At the time of the caucuses, however, there was considerable unwillingness to elect someone committed to a specific candidate. Most of the Carter supporters, including Diane Anderson, were elected as uncommitted delegates. The final result—Jackson 6 percent, Carter 4 percent, uncommitted 90 percent—concealed the fact that Carter had actually won overwhelmingly, although he got little credit in the media.

The caucuses in Maine differed from those elsewhere in that they took place in different communities throughout the month of February, early meetings being held in Portland and those in more rural areas occurring later in the month. Carter had made several trips to Maine over the preceding two years, including as the keynote speaker at the state party convention in 1974. As an outdoorsman who enjoyed hunting and fishing, he particularly liked the state. Carter's aunt Sissy (Mrs. Emily Dolvin) had remained there for three weeks until the caucuses were over. She became a familiar figure, speaking in her warm grandmotherly style. Frequently she appeared on the same podium with Edmund Muskie, who was running for reelection to the U.S. Senate. A few weeks later, when Muskie encountered Carter in Washington, he commented, "I wish you would lend me your aunt. She's been more places in Maine than I have."

Carter also had the support of Kenneth Curtis, the governor of Maine who, like Boren, was a friend from the National Governors Conference. With intermittent help from the staff working in New Hampshire, Aunt Sissy and Curtis managed to engineer an overwhelming victory for Carter at the first round of caucuses in Portland on February 1. The media reported it as another outright caucus victory for Carter. In subsequent meetings outside Portland, Carter's percentage dropped statewide as more delegates ran uncommitted, but the press was on to other events.

In some respects Maine just fell into Carter's lap. With other candidates picking and choosing which races to enter, Carter won almost by default. He and Jordan had been amply vindicated in their early decision to contest every primary and caucus. With the new financial restrictions, other candidates had opted to save their money and spend it only in selected states where they had a chance to win. But by the time the caucus and primary schedule reached those states, the Carter momentum was irresistible. Also, as an unknown and discounted candidate, he had to establish his credibility by a series of early victories. He understood that once he had established himself as a front-runner, the intense national publicity, together with the bandwagon effect, would virtually guarantee breaking the 15 percent threshold in the later states in every congressional district. Delegates would then multiply, creating an arithmetical inevitability that those who had chosen to enter only some primaries or caucuses could not possibly overcome, no matter how great their individual victories.

The impression created in the media was that every week after mid-January Carter was coming in first or second in a caucus somewhere and in all regions of the country. Under the old rules it would have been impossible for someone essentially unknown to become the leading contender in a matter of weeks for the presidential nomination of either party. Carter would receive more coverage in the next three months than any other candidate in history. At the same time, many politicians, still steeped in the past, could not reconcile that someone who had not been a long-established figure in the national party could conceivably win the presidency. As one congressional leader said at the time, "I don't see how he could possibly become president. I've never even met him."

Politicians and journalists continued to point to the high uncommitted vote in several states as evidence of Carter's weakness. Carter himself had little concern, believing correctly that the majority of these delegates were people who just wanted to be with a winner and would automatically support him once they saw his nomination as inevitable. Some delegates, however, were a matter of concern. They were people who were loyal to Hubert Humphrey. The possibility that Humphrey might make one final run for the presidency was to loom in the background throughout the primary season. He desperately wanted to do so, but unknown to the public, he was terminally ill.

CHAPTER 19

In New Hampshire, in May 1974, Lucille Kelly had begun the improbable task of recruiting support among her friends for an as-yet-unannounced Carter presidential bid. Carter made his first trip there as a formal candidate on February 11 and 12, 1975. He stayed at Lucille's house in Manchester as he would seven more times over the next year. At different times she was also host to Rosalynn, Chip and his wife Caron, Aunt Sissy, and Edna Langford. After a day of campaigning, Carter would return to her home, kick of his shoes, put his feet on a hassock, and have milk and cookies. They would then discuss the next day's strategy.

In March 1975, when Chris Brown arrived in New Hampshire, Lucille took him on a state tour and successfully urged him to establish the headquarters in Concord rather than Manchester where campaigns were traditionally centered. The Carter campaign was different from others, and this was a way of further setting it apart.

Brown, a slight twenty-eight-year-old perfectionist, was ideally suited for the careful methodical planning that was necessary to build, community by community, a grassroots state organization. Most campaign workers relish the opportunity to share the limelight with their candidate, but Brown had little interest in being around Carter. When he was, unlike the voluble Tim Kraft, he rarely opened his mouth. Even Carter, who eschewed frivolous discussion, complained after spending a day with Brown that he had nothing to say. However, Carter and Jordan held his organizational skills in high regard.

At the end of the school year in May 1975, Chip and Caron, a teacher, moved to New Hampshire where they would remain for eight months. Their arrival gave the organization a surge of momentum at a critical time. Chip was also able to serve as a surrogate for his father as he had done in forays across the South. Volunteers trickled in, and a group of "interns" arrived headed by Scott Douglas and Gary Avery. Each received $125 per month. They lived together in a large dilapidated house in Concord that became known as "Camp Carter."

During the 1970 Georgia governor's race a group of Carter's Sumter County friends traveled around the state on weekends and provided personal testimony as to his character, talents, and their belief that he would make an outstanding governor. These weekend sallies were known as the "Hi Neighbor Days." In late 1975, Landon Butler suggested that a similar initiative might be launched in New Hampshire. Carter was initially cautious, concerned that the cultural chasm might be too great to overcome and fearing that the lack of polish of some of his South Georgia friends might serve to reinforce his image as a country redneck, or worse, a racist. Jordan and Butler, however, convinced him of the plan's merits.

Thus, the "Peanut Brigade" was born, a first in American politics. The lowly peanut had already given Carter a unique identity in the presidential race. The call went out in the late fall for volunteers to pay their own way to spend a week in the winter cold of New Hampshire. By the end of the year, ninety-eight Georgians had responded. Most came from the same relatively affluent background as the Carters—business and professional people in their middle years. The group was put together by Landon Butler and Connie Plunkett. Among them were John Pope and his new wife, Betty; Sam Singer, veteran of the disputed state senate race, and his mother, Ann; Richard Denny, a lawyer and longtime Carter organizer; Margaret Broun, wife of State Senator Paul Broun, who had been among Carter's first gubernatorial supporters; Hoyt Robinson, Carter's fellow missionary on their evangelical trip to Lock Haven, Pennsylvania; Shirley Miller, whose husband, Zell, was the lieutenant governor; Maxine Reese of Plains, who had known Jimmy all of his life; plus Hamilton and Nancy Jordan, Aunt Sissy, Hugh Carter's son Hugh Jr., and Jimmy's sister Ruth.

The "Peanut Brigaders" were greeted in Manchester by a barrage of television cameras and a covey of curious print reporters who had run out of other stories. In spite of three feet of snow on the ground and temperatures as low as nineteen below zero, the campaigners preached the Carter gospel. For most the message they delivered was simple and straightforward: I know Jimmy Carter, he is a good man, he is a good Christian, he was a good governor, please vote for him. When people were not at home they left personal notes.

On Tuesday night, January 6, Carter arrived in Manchester and joined the group at a rally in the convention center. John Pope spoke to Carter and told him that the only problem they had was responding to questions about the candidate's position on the issues. On most subjects they did not know where he stood. "Just wing it," Carter advised.

By the end of the week, they had contacted more than 18,000 Democratic households, and between them they would write 6,000 follow-up letters after they returned to Georgia. There were countless stories of unlikely successful conversions. When silver-haired, seventy-year-old Mrs. Cile Crouch, from Albany, Georgia, knocked on the door of Judge Henry Sullivan, he was so taken with her that he invited her to a restaurant for lunch. "If you're for him, honey," he said, "then I'm for him and I'm going to work for Jimmy Carter."

Starlett Mackendree found that when people saw her on their doorstep shivering in the bitter cold, they would invariably invite her in for tea or coffee. One sympathizer told her, "Bless your heart, *we* don't even go out in this weather."

While others in the race had small armies of eager young volunteers, few had the kind of personal relationship with their candidate that the Peanut Brigaders had with Carter. Generally more mature, they spoke from personal knowledge and conviction. The February 2 issue of *Newsweek* summed up the Peanut Brigaders' visit by saying that Carter might have made "the most dramatic impression in the campaign so far by fielding a force of 98 Georgians to sing his praises door-to-door all over snow-blanketed New Hampshire," going on to quote an Exeter Democrat, Robert Curran, as saying, "If that many people thought that much about him [Carter] to come all the way up here . . . then he must be a good man." Jordan considered the Peanut Brigade the single most important factor in Carter's victory. Landon Butler says, "We were never behind after that week." A second contingent was organized to return to New Hampshire for the week immediately preceding the primary.

Among Carter's opponents in New Hampshire, Congressman Morris "Mo" Udall was considered the biggest threat. His strategy was modeled on that of two previous liberal Democrats, Gene McCarthy and George McGovern, both of whom had used a strong early showing in New Hampshire as a launching pad for the remainder of their campaigns. Like Carter, he had started to organize in the state early, and had spent even more time there. Having allocated a significantly higher portion of his budget to the contest, he had a larger paid staff, and his son, Brad, had moved there full-time to campaign on his behalf. However, in 1976 the race did not start in New Hampshire, and despite a furious last-minute effort, Udall had come in a disappointing fourth in Iowa. He had not contested any of the other caucus states, fearing negative results, but this meant he had almost no media coverage in the month prior to New Hampshire. In addition, it was a crucial fund-raising period and Carter's string of successes helped him as much as it hurt Udall. He was further handicapped by the fact that New Hampshire is not a liberal state. The relative success of McGovern and McCarthy had been largely an aberration produced by their opposition to the Vietnam War, and neither of them had actually won the primary.

Birch Bayh benefitted from being better known than the rest of the field. But he started late and failed to build an adequate campaign organization, and because of the demands on him in the Senate, he could not devote

much personal time to the effort. Harris had some support around Dartmouth College and the University of New Hampshire in Keene. Shriver
had even less support in the state.

As Jordan and I had noted on our initial visit, with only 130,000 registered Democrats, New Hampshire was perfect for Carter's style of "retail"
politics. On the ideological spectrum he would seem nearer to the majority
of the population than the four more liberal candidates. As Jordan pointed
out, "The heart of the Democratic Party here is over in the factories in
Manchester. . . . If you took a profile of the Democratic voters in New
Hampshire you would find a working person, probably thirty-five to forty,
white, who would have an easier time identifying with Jimmy Carter than
with the other candidates."

With every voter expecting to meet each candidate at least once, Carter
could maximize his greatest attribute: his personal impact on people. "I
just like him," said a woman near Concord. "He seems nice and somehow
is reassuring to me. . . . But I remember how I voted for Lyndon Johnson
when I didn't like him, and then how I voted for Richard Nixon, although I
didn't like him at all. I did it because everybody said it was the sensible
thing to do. Well it didn't turn out that way after all." She could have been
speaking for thousands of Carter voters not just in New Hampshire but
nationwide.

A curious twist occurred on the Wednesday before the vote. Lester
Maddox arrived in Manchester on a one-man stop-Carter mission. Maddox
called a news conference at the Carpenter Hotel to note that he too was
thinking of running for president. He blasted what he described as Carter's
failures as governor and, zeroing in on Carter's pledge to never tell a lie, he
said Carter was one of the most dishonest people he had ever met. Rumors
circulated that Maddox, who declined to say who funded his trip, had
either been sent by Wallace supporters to sabotage the Carter effort, or
more cynically, that Carter backers had paid his way to help Carter with
the liberal vote by emphasizing his striking contrast with the likes of Maddox and Wallace. Both theories were far-fetched and seriously underestimated the true Maddox eccentricity. Jody Powell, standing in the back of
the room with a group of reporters, said almost under his breath, "Being
called a liar by Lester Maddox is like being called ugly by a frog." On the
CBS evening news that night it was Powell's riposte, not Maddox's statement, that received the coverage.

When Carter returned to the state for a final four days of campaigning,
he skillfully portrayed himself as still behind Udall. He urged his supporters to make that extra effort so that he could catch up. Until the results
were announced, Carter and Powell were able to adeptly manipulate the
press into believing what they knew to be certain victory into a seeming

upset. Close observation of a driven Carter during those final days showed that, although physically exhausted, he was emanating a particularly infectious psychological euphoria. On the eve of the election, as he spoke to high school students in Manchester, and worked his way handshaking through a shoe factory, then swept through the offices of an insurance company in Keene and on to an auditorium of college students, he was gliding on a surge of energy and excitement that would be there, with rare exceptions, for the next nine months.

The vote statewide that day was relatively heavy. Chris Brown climaxed his year in the state with an effective get-out-the-vote effort. Around 8 P.M. a crowd began to gather in the ballroom of the Carpenter Hotel in Manchester. As the votes were reported a Carter victory became an increasing certainty. Jimmy and Rosalynn had dinner that night at the home of Clifford and Joan Ross, his Manchester coordinator. They arrived at the Carpenter Hotel at 11:40 P.M. As Carter stepped to the podium, he had his left index finger held high: "We're number one, we're number one," he said, starting a chant among the cheering supporters. He thanked them for their help, and then with his family pressing around him, he added, "You're all just like part of my family yourselves." That indeed is how it was. The majority of those in the room that night were not New Hampshire voters but Georgians, most of whom had worked for Carter since he ran for governor and were there because of their deep personal loyalty to him.

The final vote gave Carter 29.4 percent, Udall 23.9 percent, Bayh 16.2 percent, Harris 11.4 percent, and Shriver 8.7 percent. Detractors argued that Carter's victory was made relatively easy by the fact that he had a monopoly on the conservative and moderate vote, while his four opponents were dividing up the more liberal voters in the state. It was argued that Carter would not have won had Jackson and Wallace been in New Hampshire. However, we had been confident for two years that Carter would win in New Hampshire no matter who the opposition was. That Udall did so well was a tribute mainly to his ability as a tough campaigner. This first primary ended the presidential quest of Birch Bayh.

Four days later, on Saturday, February 28, South Carolina held its caucuses. Carter had enthusiastic support from his friend former governor John West, and party chairman Don Fowler, and he expected to do well. With resources stretched thin and believing no other candidate would make a serious challenge there, Jordan had made the decision to de-emphasize South Carolina. Sensing an opening, George Wallace launched an intensive last-minute campaign designed to embarrass Carter, taking the shine off his New Hampshire victory, and creating for himself momentum in the South going into the crucial Florida primary. A counterblitz late in the week, including heavy advertising on black radio stations, enabled

Carter to avoid a significant defeat. The result was Wallace 27.6 percent, Carter 22.9 percent, and uncommitted 48 percent.

The date of the Massachusetts primary had been in doubt for much of the previous year. Initially there had been discussion of a New England primary, with all states in the region voting on the same day. When this was rejected, it was assumed the primary would be left until late in the season as in 1972. When several state legislators wanted to make the Massachusetts primary the first in the nation, the New Hampshire legislature responded by passing a bill that made their primary a week earlier than that of any other state. Massachusetts settled for March 31.

Because of the uncertainty about the date, Massachusetts never received the attention and analysis it probably deserved. Chris Brown had been designated the New England coordinator and had spent a day a week in Massachusetts. Some ardent supporters were recruited, including the Republican mayor of Pittsfield, Evan Dobbell, and his wife, Kit, who changed parties to work for Carter, but the feeling in the Atlanta headquarters was "we will get by somehow" in Massachusetts. New Hampshire had no television stations, so viewers relied on Boston stations; it was there that Carter's $130,000 worth of campaign ads had run. Because they were also seen statewide by residents of Massachusetts, the campaign media felt that additional expenditures in that market were probably unnecessary. Some early polling by Caddell also suggested that, while his support was soft, Carter could do well in the state.

In Massachusetts there was no shortage of Democratic political operatives and power brokers. Few were naturally inclined toward Carter, and the feeling was generally reciprocated. At the same time, the state was so large that his inherent style of trying to reach every voter in some personal way could not succeed. Carter received some support from Governor Michael Dukakis, who he had found shared his own views at the National Governors Conferences about efficiency in government. Fran Meany, a key Dukakis backer, chaired the Carter effort. But Dukakis had many detractors and even among those loyal to him there was a propensity to use the Carter campaign primarily for their own political ends. They sought to run a largely autonomous campaign that put them in direct conflict with the headquarters staff in Atlanta.

It was the fear of creating and funding just such self-serving independent entities that had been one of Carter's concerns when he expressed his early reservations about the need for setting up local campaign structures. Veterans of earlier presidential campaigns, where the free flow of campaign money was used for a variety of questionable purposes, deeply resented the strictures that the new finance law required Atlanta to impose on them. However, while Jimmy and Rosalynn seemed to accommodate themselves comfortably to people of any background anywhere in the country, Jordan and some others in the Atlanta headquarters had difficulty bridging the cultural gap between themselves and Carter's liberal supporters in the North. While Carter desperately sought to paint over differences and sell himself to liberals, his staff tended to react to the cultural and ideological dissonance with barely disguised contempt and ridicule. By the same token, it was in those same heavily liberal parts of the country, mainly New York, Massachusetts, and California, where Caddell's polls showed the greatest anti-southern sentiment and cynicism about Carter's campaign.

Carter support, as Caddell's polls suggested and knowledgeable writers had been saying for some time, was broad but "soft." The campaign staff prayed for good weather on primary day. Not only were the prayers unanswered but there was a blizzard. Without an effective grassroots organization to get out the vote, identified Carter supporters stayed away from the polls in droves. For the first time, Carter was faced with the fact that people who had been attracted to him as a fresh new face were also the first to desert him when the going got tough. He came in a disappointing fourth with just 14.2 percent of the vote, well behind Jackson with 22.7 percent, Udall with 18 percent, and Wallace with 17.1 percent.

While Carter was busy in New Hampshire, Jackson had chosen to reserve his time and money to make a stand in Massachusetts, and had put together an effective campaign structure. In addition to Jewish and union support, he had Daniel Patrick Moynihan, fresh from a highly visible stint as the U.S. ambassador to the United Nations, campaigning for him and attracting Irish voters. Jackson successfully drew some support away from Wallace by taking a hard line against busing. It was something Carter could not afford to do, and it would hurt Jackson later.

As Jackson had Moynihan, Udall had Archibald Cox, Boston Brahmin and pillar of the academic liberal establishment. Cox had received considerable recent national attention as the Watergate special prosecutor fired by Nixon in the "Saturday night massacre." He was persuaded to campaign for Udall, endorsing him as the candidate of integrity, thereby countering Carter on the characteristics with which he was primarily identified in people's minds, namely truthfulness, honesty, and decency. The press ignored the fact that Carter had called for Nixon's impeachment the day after Cox was fired, while Udall had waited nearly nine months and spoke out for impeachment only three days before Nixon resigned.

Carter's loss was in some ways made worse by the sense of confidence he had conveyed in the euphoric moments after the New Hampshire victory. That evening, before his victory announcement, Powell and Kraft had warned him that Massachusetts was not looking good and it might be better not to mention it. Carter responded, "I cannot let the people of Massachusetts think I do not care about them when I've promised to run in every primary." He then implied in his victory speech, breaking one of the cardinal rules of elective politics, that he expected to do well in Massachusetts the following week. It was a pattern that would trip him up throughout his career. Whenever he was coming off a success, he would lose his usual self-discipline and frequently make extravagant and ultimately self-destructive statements.

Carter *had* expected to do well in Massachusetts. And when he received the bad news at a special CBS election center on the fifteenth floor of a new bank building in Orlando, Florida, he was clearly shaken. "That's too bad, that's too bad," he repeated several times to reporters. "He was really off-balance and upset," Caddell said later. "He wasn't angry. He was stunned and disappointed, because he thought things were going so well." Schneiders recalled that "I think he was unhappier that night than any in the campaign." The one silver lining of the day was that he did win the largely uncontested primary in Vermont over Sargent Shriver. Carter as usual was able to put the loss immediately behind him, in part because, "We were so obsessed with Florida."

Florida was the linchpin of the Carter strategy. Defeating Wallace there was not just a tactical necessity for Carter. He wanted to make it a referendum on the "New South" versus the "Old South." It was the struggle with which his whole political self-concept was entwined. He wanted to use Florida to show the country that the South had really changed and that he was the region's new and legitimate representative.

Rosalynn's early trips to Florida had been followed up by Connie Plunkett, who was able to use relationships she had made as a Democratic national committeewoman to raise money and generate a nucleus of support for Carter, especially in the Miami area. Long before the "Peanut Brigade" was formally established, Carter friends from Georgia would make weekend trips, mostly to northern Florida and the panhandle, to campaign for him at their own expense. In Miami, Carter had early recruited Roger Volker, a Lutheran minister, and two young energetic organizers, Mike Abrams and Sergio Bendixen, who particularly targeted the Jewish and Cuban populations. His most consequential Cuban-American supporter was Bay of Pigs veteran Alfredo Duran, although perhaps his most ardent was a red-headed Jewish Cuban-American, Bernardo Benes.

Because name recognition was still a problem in the early part of the campaign, Rafshoon had developed unprecedented five-minute spots to introduce the candidate. They had proven highly effective in Iowa and New Hampshire, where many viewers thought they were watching documentaries. Florida was now deluged with them.

In June 1975, Phil Wise, a twenty-six-year-old engineering student whose family owned a farm next to the Carters, was sent to Florida to open a headquarters in Orlando. Although he had worked for Carter as governor, he had done only a brief stint in the Atlanta headquarters, where he helped develop a computerized system for listing supporters. Several people questioned the wisdom of entrusting such a crucial responsibility to someone who had so little political experience. The choice reflected Carter's perspective. He had known Phil all his life and saw in him cultural compatibility, loyalty, intelligence, and commitment—attributes that far outweighed lack of political organizing techniques. Carter knew someone as bright as Wise would quickly pick them up, and Wise more than justified the faith placed in him.

Wallace had easily won the 1972 Florida primary over Hubert Humphrey, but he had done so with little on-the-ground organization. While he still had a solid core of support, especially in the panhandle, his inability to maintain the frenetic pace that Carter had set and the sight of him being carried on and off his campaign plane were constant reminders to people of his infirmity. Although Carter assiduously avoided mentioning Wallace's paralysis, even when others urged him to do so, there was widespread concern about his ability to campaign much less serve as president. On one occasion in Pensacola he was dropped by his state-trooper handlers, a humiliating experience, which undercut any attempt to project a presidential image. Seduced by the lure of an early upset, Wallace, who had expended a substantial sum on a third-place finish in Massachusetts, now lacked the resources that might have saved him in Florida.

Wallace seemed slow to comprehend that he could no longer do in Florida in 1976 what he had done in 1972. At the State Democratic Party convention in November 1975, the delegates were to hold a presidential straw ballot. Carter supporters seized the opportunity to organize backing for him among the delegates while the Wallace people did nothing. The result was a 67 percent to 6 percent victory for Carter. The vote got national press attention and should have been a warning for Wallace, but it did not seem to concern him. At his first campaign rally in Florida in January 1976, he could fill only half of a 3,000-seat auditorium, whereas four years before he had spoken to an overflow audience.

Although Caddell's polls were showing Carter in the lead, fear that Wallace might actually end up as the nominee of the party, or at least play a kingmaker role, caused consternation, if not outright panic, among party liberals. Many Democratic leaders still thought it inconceivable that Carter would be nominated. They found it expedient, however, to help Carter block Wallace, assuming Carter could be stopped later and someone else—an established national figure more to their liking—would ultimately claim the nomination. "Back Jimmy Carter through Florida" was a plea the campaign effectively made to liberal and moderates around the country. Carter urged the other candidates to stay out of Florida and let him take on Wallace head-to-head, although by now Udall and Jackson were the only other viable contenders. Udall stayed out completely and Jackson had largely restricted his efforts to the two counties around Miami where he was competing for the Jewish vote against Pennsylvania's Governor Milton Shapp, whose modest campaign never got off the ground.

Carter faced a paradox in seeking liberal support. Most white southerners found themselves culturally comfortable with him, but they disagreed with his views on race. Liberals were attracted to him on the issues, but found it difficult to disassociate Carter from the stereotypical views they held of southerners, especially Southern Baptists. L. C. Hobgood, a supporter in Plains, told reporters, referring to the way Carter was viewed locally, "I think most of 'em think he's a little on the liberal side, and it just don't sit too well." At the same time, an ardent supporter in New York said, "I think he's just great, except that all that religious crap gets in the way." The one group that fully shared Carter's liberal views and had a familiarity with southern culture, especially the religious aspects, was blacks. In Florida, as long as Wallace was the only real competition, Carter was the automatic black choice. All he had to do was convince them he truly was different from Wallace and get them to care enough to go to the polls.

In the fall of 1975, Carter had, at the invitation of Congressman Andrew Young, met with the Congressional Black Caucus and attended the group's annual dinner at the Washington Hilton. Carter was the only candidate to go to the dinner, and it won him warm support from most who met him that night. Leading black politicians, including D.C. delegate Walter Fauntroy and New York Congressman Charles Rangel, went to Florida to campaign for him. Carter had the early endorsement of Martin Luther King, Sr. (although he privately added the proviso that if Nelson Rockefeller entered the race he would be obliged to switch his allegiance). Georgia State Representative Ben Brown, and Ernest Withers, an early supporter from Washington, D.C., put together an effective organization in the black community. Carter campaigned hard on black college campuses and had several dozen black students working for him.

The crucial player, however, was Andrew Young. Young and Carter had had a personal, political, and religious affinity since their first meeting in 1969. Young was the only member of the Georgia congressional delegation (apart from Talmadge) who was informed of Carter's presidential intentions at an early stage and the only one invited to the early planning meetings.

An ordained minister who had achieved national prominence as an aide to Dr. Martin Luther King, Jr., at the Southern Christian Leadership Conference (SCLC), Young came from a very different background than the parochial black leaders who had previously supported Carter. Young had grown up in a mixed neighborhood in New Orleans, where his father was a successful dentist, serving both black and white patients. He had both Native American and Jewish blood in his background. Whereas most of Jimmy Carter's early childhood friends were black, most of Young's were white. "My parents wanted to escape black culture," he recalls. Young went to Howard University in Washington, D.C., a bastion of the upwardly mobile black bourgeoisie, where he found that despite his refined middle-class background, he was looked down upon because he was from the South. Subsequently, in 1951, he graduated from the Hartford (Connecticut) Seminary Foundation as a Congregationalist minister. The prim northern Congregationalist style of theology was, on one level, a far cry from that of Jimmy Carter as well as most black Baptist congregations in the South. However, the presence of Congregationalist missions across the South had been the result of zealous New Englanders eager to assist the plight of freed slaves during Reconstruction. In that missionary tradition Young had returned briefly to the South as the pastor of a church in Thomasville, Georgia, before joining Dr. King.

Despite their disparate backgrounds, Young and Carter had remarkably similar political philosophies and visions for America. They shared a deep regional pride and knew that the South could not achieve acceptance on a par with other regions of the country until segregation was thoroughly laid to rest. Young believed that this goal could be immeasurably advanced if a progressive southerner was elected as president. For both, their beliefs were deeply rooted in their Christian faith, feeling that most conflicts can and should be healed through reconciliation. Young was quoted as saying:

> Religion is about life. When you pray the Lord's prayer, you say, "Thy kingdom come on earth." And in a democratic society, if the kingdom is going to come on earth, it's going to come by voting and by legislative action that appropriates taxes humanely and spends money on life and development rather than on death and destruction.

Carter had come to his belief through Niebuhr. Young had found his own way there.

Young and other national black leaders had one serious problem. Of all the announced or potential candidates, the one to whom they had the greatest historical obligation and loyalty was Hubert Humphrey, whose intentions remained uncertain. Young was still a more widely recognized national figure than Carter, and for him to endorse unequivocally this one-term governor, who might still be going nowhere, could look politically naive, diminish his stature among his peers, and seem a betrayal of Hubert

Humphrey. The notion, however, of supporting Carter just through Florida, with the objective of defeating Wallace, gave Young and other national black leaders splendid cover.

Young's vigorous and visible campaigning was not only crucial in mobilizing the black vote in Florida but sent a powerful symbolic message about Carter to doubting blacks and liberals around the country. With Young, Rangel, and others campaigning for Carter, the labor unions felt safer supporting him. After carefully negotiating an agreement as to what Carter's position on national health insurance would be, UAW president Leonard Woodcock went to Florida to campaign with him. After spending a day together, Woodcock's support became as much personal as organizational.

After Carter won in Iowa and New Hampshire, what had been shaping up as a relatively easy victory over Wallace was suddenly turned on its head when Jackson decided to expand from the Miami area and make an all-out statewide effort. He committed most of his remaining funds to a massive media blitz. It appeared, however, to be a spoiling tactic. He must have known he could not win in Florida, but he could try to prevent Carter from beating Wallace. Jackson surely realized a Carter victory over Wallace would make him almost unstoppable. Publicly, Jackson argued that he entered the race merely to sustain his momentum after Massachusetts.

Carter was angry that Jackson, who he felt had little chance of getting the nomination, should prevent him from having his long anticipated and decisive showdown with Wallace. Wallace's vote was relatively solid and Jackson was only going to eat into Carter's support. That meant Carter would now be forced to fight on two fronts, as Jackson's attacks on him picked up.

At a press conference in Washington on August 18, 1975, Carter had mentioned in the context of a flat-tax proposition the possibility of eliminating the deductions for home mortgages. This was not reported because Carter was not being taken seriously by the press at that point. It was not until he mentioned the flat tax again at a debate sponsored by the League of Women Voters in Boston on the eve of the Massachusetts primary that it became a major issue. Jackson seized upon Carter's comment and, removing it from the broader context of overall tax reform, used it as a way of successfully scaring middle-class homeowners.

Carter felt Jackson had been less than honest, which considerably angered him. Rafshoon rushed to Florida and found a small private studio where he and Carter spent the evening taping TV spots refuting Jackson's charges and outlining Carter's broader tax plan. The spots started running the next day and ultimately would help to blunt the Jackson barrage. Carter, however, remained angry as the attacks continued. Greg Schneiders recalled the week prior to the primary:

I remember we were in Tallahassee and Jackson had really been hitting hard on the mortgage deduction. The telephone canvassing was showing "favorable" down slightly, and "unfavorable" going up. . . . So it did not look as though we were going to be able to reverse what seemed to be the tide. . . . The whole argument that Carter was the only one who could stop Wallace was diminished and people began looking at Jackson as an alternative.

Jimmy was tired and getting kind of strident. He was really lashing out at Jackson a lot. . . . I think that that Friday was probably the most discouraged anybody was throughout the entire primaries. The feeling was that if we did not win Florida the thing was going to unravel. And it looked very likely that we would not.

Carter accused Jackson of having won in Massachusetts by focusing on the volatile and divisive busing issue. "Senator Jackson ran a campaign around the busing issue, one that has racial or racist connotations. . . . I don't think he is a racist. I think he recognized an emotional issue and capitalized on it." Carter's comments sought to paint Jackson as having the same views as Wallace in the hope that it would draw some Wallace support over to Jackson, and at the same time reiterate in the minds of the increasingly crucial black electorate, as well as the estimated 10 percent liberal white vote, that he, Jimmy Carter, was the only one they could reasonably vote for.

With the specter of more than two years of work going down the drain and his presidential ambitions in ruin, Carter girded himself for a final superhuman effort. In the last week he visited thirty-eight cities across the state, putting in a minimum of sixteen hours a day. But by Friday night, March 5, he was suffering from a severe cold and a kidney infection. He went to Plains to rest for twenty-four hours and to attend church and Sunday school. He came back to Florida on Sunday afternoon. The staff noted that he was more relaxed and made only mild jabs at Jackson in his speeches.

After its success in New Hampshire, the "Peanut Brigade," under the leadership of Dot Padgett and Jordan's wife, Nancy, had made several trips to Florida. Except for a skeleton staff, the Atlanta headquarters was emptied as carloads of additional workers flooded into the state. No one underestimated the importance of the vote on Tuesday, March 9. It would either be the beginning of the end or the end of the beginning.

Carter spent election day in North Carolina laying the groundwork for that state's primary two weeks hence. Shortly after noon, the *New York Times*/CBS exit poll reported Carter with a 10-point lead. The relief was staggering. At 8 P.M., still suffering from his cold, Carter, who had flown back to Florida, joined the rest of the family at the Carlton House in Orlando as CBS was about to project him the winner.

"It's hard to believe," Carter said with obvious relief, and then as he pored over the detailed results from the Tallahassee area, in an uncharacteristic display of excitement he yelled out to Rosalynn, "Hey, Rosie, it's 53 percent in Bear County!"

The family stayed glued to the television for the next two hours, breaking only when Aunt Sissy and campaign worker Ellen Metsky arrived with Amy. As Metsky described:

> As I opened the door to bring Amy in, Jimmy looked happier than I have ever seen him and he shouted, "Look who's here. It's Amy baby!" He hugged and kissed her and talked about how happy he was to see her.

When he finally went to the ballroom to make a victory announcement, he said, "It's not only a sign of a new South, it's a sign of a new America," which was very much the way he saw the importance of his win. Despite the lesson of overconfidence after his incautious statement on primary night in New Hampshire, he predicted, "I'll be number one on the first ballot in New York." When asked if he now considered himself the front-runner, he said, "I don't see anyone ahead of me," then added, "but we still have a long way to go. We found out following Massachusetts that a success in one state does not necessarily carry over to another one." Carter was also careful not to crow over Wallace and was gracious in his comments about him.

The final tally showed Carter 35 percent, Wallace 31 percent, Jackson 23 percent, Shapp 2 percent, and Udall 2 percent. A *Washington Post* survey of 487 Democratic voters showed Carter had appealed to an exceptionally broad-based constituency that represented virtually every social class, age group, and political ideology. Among voters at every economic level, Carter led the other candidates. He received close to 75 percent of the black vote.

Two elements seemed paramount in Carter's victory, apart from hard work and the superb organization that Phil Wise had put together. They were a perception in the minds of six out of ten who voted for Carter that Wallace was not physically capable of being president, and that economic issues, particularly unemployment, were not that important to Florida voters. Overwhelmingly, the survey showed Floridians listed honesty in government as their top concern. While Jackson was talking about jobs, Carter had focused consistently on the integrity issue.

Caddell also cited as significant his polls that showed Bayh, Shriver, and Udall, though not campaigning in Florida, still drew in 8–9 percent of the vote because their names were still on the ballot. Carter desperately needed those "wasted" liberal votes. Caddell believed that Carter either consciously or unconsciously then took the risk of attacking Jackson, implying he was a racist, primarily as a way of trying to change his image in the eyes of these vital liberal voters. As Caddell saw it, "It is exactly what paid off. Just his brilliance as a politician is there more in that single example, both in his understanding of the survey data and his ability to absorb it and his understanding of his own instincts politically."

The other winner in Florida was the man who was not there, Hubert Humphrey. As the sentimental favorite of party regulars and Washington journalists, there was an inclination to create scenarios through which he could still become the nominee. There was increasing talk of the illogical likelihood of a brokered convention. *Time* commented, "James Earl Carter, Jr., one of the most phenomenal politicians to rise on the American political scene this century," but went on to express doubts about whether he would be "granted the nomination," as though the votes of the people were ultimately irrelevant in the process. What Carter was really after, they rationalized, must be the vice-presidential nomination, a more seemly aspiration for an upstart southern governor. Columnist Joseph Kraft flatly predicted a Carter vice-presidential nomination. This was despite Carter's repeated emphatic assertions that he had no interest in the vice presidency. The favored scenario had it that familiar Hubert Humphrey, who was continuing to send mixed messages to his supporters, would ultimately enter the race, winning the later primaries, and gather up all the uncommitted delegates. At that point the bosses of the party, especially the experienced and Washington-wise Bob Strauss, would surely see he got the nomination. The democratization of the process had done away with that type of king-making forever, but they seemed unable to comprehend.

However, to an increasing number of more politically savvy converts, Carter was now reckoned as the horse to bet on. As it had after Iowa and New Hampshire, the crucial flow of money to sustain the momentum picked up dramatically. In contrast to the meager amounts raised at events six months earlier, people would now contribute handsomely merely to shake hands with Carter: March 31, Milwaukee, cocktails, $10,000; April 9, Cleveland, breakfast, $15,000, and Columbus (Ohio), cocktails, $20,000; April 16, Louisville, dinner, $50,000; April 19, Atlanta, National Finance Committee meeting, $100,000; April 19, New Orleans, cocktails, $10,000; April 20, Houston, breakfast, $20,000, and Pittsburg, dinner, $20,000; April 23, Memphis, dinner, $20,000. "The mother's milk of politics" was simultaneously drying up for the other candidates and flowing in an increasing stream for Carter.

Although exhilarated by the Florida victory and the sense that only some unforeseen catastrophe could now deny him the nomination, Carter was exhausted, still recovering from the kidney infection, and rapidly losing control over the moment-to-moment decisions in his life, all of which made him increasingly irritable. As the magnitude of the campaign had grown, the scheduling staff and media advisor were making decisions about how to use his time, frequently without consulting him. So many more consequential decisions had to be made and so many influential people wanted meetings. He was getting less and less sleep. There was relentless pressure for press interviews. His every move was increasingly having to be choreographed with the Secret Service. For someone who found it important to always be in control, it was a difficult adjustment. Plains remained his refuge, but instead of a rest day and his cherished attendance at church, he had been scheduled to fly to New York on Saturday evening, March 13, to be on the CBS news show *Face the Nation.* The next morning he excoriated the staff member responsible. It was a rare outburst, but it reflected both the growing pressure he was under and the importance he attached to spending his Sundays at home.

In Washington, an entrenched elite who had been at, or close to, the center of power since the days of Franklin Delano Roosevelt began to realize that in January 1977 there could be a new president who was a complete stranger to them. Their own political power, social standing, and often their income had always derived from having a longstanding acquaintance and/or friendship with the man in the White House, Democrat or Republican. Carter's primary victories were hardly good news to them. Tremors of apprehension rattled through Georgetown.

Richard Holbrooke, Carter's acquaintance from the Trilateral Commission, had become a valued advocate for Carter among the rich and powerful in Washington. He suggested that Clayton Fritchey, a distinguished and influential columnist with the *Washington Post,* and his wife, Polly, the widow of Frank Wisner, one of the founders of the CIA, would be willing to host a dinner at their Georgetown home for a group of about twenty of Washington's most powerful unelected figures. In Atlanta, Hamilton Jordan asked contemptuously, "How many primaries can they help us win?" Carter appreciated that winning the presidency would also require governing the country and agreed to attend.

It was an illustrious gathering, on March 28, which included Clark Clifford, Katherine Graham, Joseph Alsop, Eric Sevareid, Sol Linowitz, Averell Harriman, Benjamin Bradlee, Barry Bingham, and Bishop John T. Walker of the Washington Cathedral, the only African American invited. Spouses were not included. Oysters, pink lamb, and vanilla soufflé were served to the guests seated at three circular tables. Carter moved from one table to another between courses so that all of the guests had a chance to hear him patiently reassure them about his views on the economy, regulation of corporations, the Middle East, and the threat of communism. He was a stunning success. The evening had an equal impact on him and, he later commented with a degree of awe, "Almost everyone there was someone whose name has been familiar to me most of my life, but whom I never thought I would meet."

CHAPTER 20

James Wall, Methodist minister and editor of the *Christian Century,* was born in Monroe, Georgia. In 1972, as an anti-war activist, he had chaired the Illinois McGovern delegates. In May 1975, he met Carter and felt a powerful empathy with his fellow Georgian. In October, Carter asked Wall to become his state chairman, and together with wealthy McGovern contributor Marge Benton, he began to organize the state for Carter.

Wall warned Carter that, having suffered serious embarrassment at the 1968 Chicago convention and exclusion from the state's delegation in 1972, Mayor Richard J. Daley was determined to stay in control in 1976. Illinois was an anomaly in the already unconventional and confusing delegate selection process of 1976. There was to be a nonbinding popular vote, referred to as "the beauty contest," among the presidential contenders, about which Daley cared little. Delegates, on the other hand, were to be elected in unrelated races in the congressional districts. To achieve a delegation over which he and Daley would have full control, U.S. Senator Adlai Stevenson was running slates of delegates pledged to him as a favorite son. Especially in the Chicago area, those delegates would be Daley-picked. Wall advised Carter to run in every congressional district except in the Chicago area. Carter assured him, "I'll take care of that. The mayor and I have a good relationship."

Carter had first met Daley five years earlier and was curiously comfortable with this archetypical big-city boss, an exception to his general disdain for political power brokers. When Daley suffered a stroke in 1974, Carter offered him the use of a friend's house in Sea Island, Georgia, to recuperate. When Carter addressed the Illinois delegation at the mini-convention in Kansas City, Daley had introduced him with a surprisingly warm and generous statement. Carter met with Daley in October 1975 and told him that while he was going to run slates statewide, he would not compete directly with the Daley machine in Chicago, and that his delegates would subsequently support the election of Daley as head of the Illinois delegation. This satisfied both the mayor and Wall. However, at the time Daley probably thought that the Carter candidacy would be long gone when the Illinois primary came around on March 16, 1976.

Instead Carter scored a victory that stunned even him, winning fifty-five delegates. The campaign had spent only $130,000. Carter had devoted little personal time to the state, but that most intangible and invaluable of political assets, momentum, had come surreptitiously into play. The real importance of Illinois was that it was the first victory for Carter in a northern industrial state. At the same time, the inexorable logic of the delegate arithmetic, the ultimate arbiter of victory or defeat, was steadily marching on, still largely ignored by press and public alike.

Two who misread that arithmetic were California Governor Jerry Brown and Idaho Senator Frank Church. Brown had been publicly toying with the idea of getting into the race for several weeks. After Florida, Carter called Brown to urge him to stay out. Instead, having said that he would run in California as a favorite son, Brown now announced he would be running a national campaign. Church, whom Carter liked, especially for taking on the CIA in a series of recently concluded hearings, announced two days after the Illinois vote that he too was entering the race. Both Brown and Church knew they could not win the nomination outright starting at this late date, but they believed the continuing misconception that there would be a brokered convention.

The primary marathon moved on to North Carolina, Ruth's home state, for its vote on March 21. Throughout the campaign she had been writing letters to her extensive network of religious friends and contacts around the country. She wrote in part:

Dear Friends,

You may already know that my brother, Jimmy Carter, is running for the position of President of the United States.

My reason for writing you is to acquaint you with an important facet of Jimmy, one that couldn't possibly be pursued with any depth by the press and television, and that is his quality of deep personal commitment to Jesus Christ and his will to serve Him in whatever capacity he finds himself.

. . . our nation's greatest need is for a President who will provide spiritual leadership. This, in my opinion, is one of Jimmy's greatest qualifications.

As one who knows the importance of Christ in your personal life and who I'm sure wants our nation to be under His blessings and guidance—please pray for Jimmy. And if you share my feeling that he is the best candidate, I urge you to actively support him.

Sincerely in Christ,
Ruth Carter Stapleton

Ruth's efforts had gone largely unnoticed despite their effectiveness, especially in Oklahoma. Now as the national press corps descended on North Carolina, Ruth was suddenly thrust into the limelight. Myra MacPherson, after an extensive interview, prepared a long piece for the *Washington Post* in which she described Ruth's evangelical work and her "inner healing" ministry, her lengthy talk with Jimmy after he lost the 1966 governor's race, and his missionary forays in the North. Because of the potentially explosive and inevitably controversial nature of the piece, the *Washington Post*'s editors asked Jules Witcover, their lead political reporter covering the presidential race, to confirm the more dramatic aspects of the story with the candidate. Carter supported its basic accuracy, but suggested Ruth might have exaggerated certain aspects for effect. However, alerted that the story was to run, when asked that night at a fund-raiser about his religious beliefs, he talked at length about the same issues he knew Ruth had discussed, putting his own perspective on them. His version then became the lead news story while Myra MacPherson's piece, which would have grabbed the headlines with all of Ruth's unvarnished comments, became more of a colorful sidebar. What some would see as an adroit tactical move, Carter would acknowledge only as a spontaneous response to a question, apparently unwilling to admit to himself or others that there was any element of calculation. He says disarmingly of that evening:

> I was out on a back terrace . . . and some Yankee reporter asked me if I was "born again." And I said, yes, and it was headlines all over the nation. And I began to be concerned about it. I did not want to mix in religion and my duties as a president.

Although the story did not differ greatly from the one Robert Shogan had written in the *Los Angeles Times* in May 1975, people were not paying attention then. Now Carter was at center stage, the public was intensely interested in knowing more about him, and for many it crystallized a lurking dissonance they had felt with him since he first emerged as a serious candidate. The response to the story portrayed dramatically how partitioned the country was in terms of differing historic religious and political traditions. Separating themselves from control by the established church, Baptists, Quakers, and later the Methodists, with their emphasis on the primacy of the individual and the separation of church and state, had migrated south, spawning from their religion a populist political philosophy. There, for more than 200 years, that historic component of early America had remained, despite the Civil War, in isolation and largely unchanged. In the meantime, the North and West had been infused with new waves of immigrants who came from sharply different cultural and religious heritages that made them more concerned with group, rather than individual, identity. In general, they had little knowledge or understanding of the beliefs of the earlier arrivals.

On the rare occasions when southern evangelical and fundamentalist Christians were examined under the national spotlight, as they were during the Scopes "monkey" trial in the 1920s, their beliefs were held up for ridicule, causing them to draw back over the next fifty years from the secular world outside the South. Many of them eschewed politics, believing it was a corrupt pursuit incompatible with their deep Christian values. In 1840, de Tocqueville observed that Christianity exerted a greater "power over men's souls" in America than anywhere else and he believed that for Americans their deep religious beliefs were indispensable, both for the preservation of liberty and for democracy to function. In the backwater of Southwest Georgia, the life, religion, and values that de Tocqueville had described had probably been preserved more intact in the intervening 130 years than anywhere else in the country. The low-key missionary work of the type that Carter had been involved in reflected an incipient change in that attitude. In Jimmy Carter that time warp was coming face-to-face with a larger America that had moved on in many different directions.

In modern American politics, this had created a problem that law professor Stephen Carter has succinctly described: "Our politicians are expected to repeat largely meaningless religious incantations," but, he says, there is simultaneously in modern society a prevailing rhetoric "that refuses to accept the notion that rational, public-spirited people can take religion seriously." He adds, "The message is that people who take their religion seriously, who rely on their understanding of God for motive force in their public and political personalities—well they're scary people."

Carter was aware of this minefield he was getting into when he moved outside the South, but says:

> When I . . . got into politics . . . in Georgia, and obviously in the Fourteenth Senatorial District, nobody even asked if you were Christian or if you were Baptist, or if you were born again. That was a ridiculous question to ask. It was assumed that you were.

Sally Quinn, who spent much of her own childhood in Savannah, Georgia, began a follow-up article in the *Washington Post*: "Relax, Eastern Establishment. Jimmy Carter's OK. He's not crazy. He's just Southern." Especially for Jews, the evangelical tradition of Baptists, as well as the history of deep-seated anti-Semitism in the region, made them highly suspicious of Carter, despite the involvement of Jews in key positions in his campaign.

Fear of being misunderstood outside the South had made Carter reluctant to address his religious beliefs in any depth earlier in the campaign. When asked questions about his Baptist convictions, he gave short, simple

replies about keeping his religious beliefs separate from politics. He and Rosalynn knew that sooner or later he would have to face the matter head-on
and in depth. His hand was now forced, but North Carolina was an ideal
environment in which to deal with the issue. He would later tell a reporter:

> The people in North Carolina knew what I was talking about and I didn't
> have to define terms or explain to them the basic tenets of a Southern Baptist
> or of the Methodist faith. . . . I didn't have to tell them that the Baptists
> believe in separation of church and state and we have no hierarchical
> arrangement that might tend to dominate me from the church structure.

For Carter, who believed one's faith was a personal matter, public discussion of his religion was difficult. One journalist said, "He is uncomfortable talking about religion to reporters, lapsing into embarrassed smiles,
blushing, even looking away to avoid a cynical gaze." Yet he had no illu-
sions about the need to get the issue out in the open. "The people have a
right to know about the religious beliefs of their future president," he told
Martin Schram of *Newsday*. "And this was a legitimate inquiry when Al
Smith ran and when John Kennedy ran, and when we have our first Jewish
nominee that's going to become an issue, and I think that it is expectable
and certainly proper."

The North Carolina primary was Wallace's last chance to keep his campaign alive. In the previous week he had received phone calls from several
national figures, each with his own motivation, urging him to stay in the
race. Humphrey wanted Wallace to keep the Carter delegate total held
down, so as to maintain his own option for a late entry. Jackson wanted Wallace to slow the Carter momentum until the New York and Pennsylvania
primaries, where he anticipated inflicting devastating defeats on Carter.
Bob Strauss, who had no love for Carter and who must have been embarrassed by what the new rules allowed, promulgated under Strauss's leadership, seemed to be desperately maneuvering for a brokered convention at
which he could play the kingmaker role. Apart from their personal ambitions, Humphrey, Jackson, and Strauss, pillars of the Democratic establishment, were galled that Carter, a relative newcomer to the national party,
was on the verge of capturing its most valued prize. Carter's repeated
assertion that he had a special relationship with the people, and it was they
who would give him the nomination, was an implicit repudiation of party
leaders who previously had determined the nominee. In a March 24
memo, Caddell stressed what he saw as the vital importance of winning a
first-ballot victory; otherwise, he warned, "This party will deny us the
nomination. Popular with the elites we are not."

Still angry at Carter's "betrayal" in not nominating him at the 1972
Democratic convention, Wallace mimicked him on the stump, saying in a

voice dripping with sarcasm, "I will never lie to you; I will never mislead you." Wallace also attempted to resurrect accusations that six years earlier in the Georgia governor's race Carter had portrayed himself as a conservative to attract Wallace voters. "He was my friend when I was popular," Wallace complained. He savaged Carter for hanging the portrait of Dr. Martin Luther King, Jr., in the state capitol, which helped to solidify Carter's hold on the black vote.

However, if there had not been a George Wallace "sending a message" from the South in 1964, 1968, and 1972, there probably would not have been a Jimmy Carter in 1976. Carter understood this and was always restrained in his criticism of Wallace. But his era was over and North Carolina was his last hurrah. Carter won 53.6 percent of the vote, the first time he achieved a clear majority, to Wallace's 34.7 percent. At a press conference the next day, a broadly smiling Carter confidently predicted that he expected to have "maybe a thousand" of the required 1,505 delegates needed for nomination by the time of the New York convention in July.

The day after the North Carolina primary, March 22, the Court suspended the distribution of federal matching funds to candidates. Earlier the Supreme Court had declared unconstitutional the method for choosing the members of the Federal Election Commission, but on February 27 it had given Congress three more weeks to come up with new legislation allowing continued disbursement of the matching funds during that time. Congress had failed to do so. The decision worked very much in Carter's favor. All his funds to that point had been matched and, with the momentum he now had, money was no longer a serious problem. Brown and Church had come in too late to get any matching funds, and continuing uncertainty about the ability of Congress to act in a timely manner had a chilling effect on their fund-raising.

On April 6, Carter faced an assault on two fronts. In Wisconsin a showdown battle loomed with the liberal Mo Udall, and in New York he was up against Jackson, who could count on Jewish and labor support as well as that of most of the Democratic machine politicians. Udall had skipped Florida, Illinois, and North Carolina, concentrating on Wisconsin in the hope of making it his first primary victory, and it appeared he was making a late surge. Concern about Carter's religious beliefs, growing criticism of his lack of specificity on the issues, ambivalence about southerners, and continuing hope that Humphrey might still be a factor, all contributed to the electorate taking a second look at Carter and having some reservations about him.

Following the victory in Florida, Phil Wise and several of his staff had moved to Wisconsin. Wise stopped en route in Washington to seek advice from Gene Pokorny, now a partner of Caddell's who had run McGovern's successful Wisconsin campaign in 1972. The "Peanut Brigade" was again mobilized. Billy Carter, irreverent and hard drinking, went with them and found natural affinity with blue-collar workers in Green Bay, many of whom had voted for George Wallace in the past.

By election day the race seemed like a toss-up. As the results came in, a celebration began at Udall headquarters at the Marc Plaza Hotel in Milwaukee. He was beating Carter 2 to 1 in the Second Congressional District around the University of Wisconsin in Madison, was slightly ahead in Racine and Kenosha, and was running even with Carter in Milwaukee. ABC and NBC were projecting Udall the winner. Late in the evening, Carter went to the local NBC affiliate to tape a statement for the morning news shows. He wanted to tape two—one to be used if he won, the other if he lost—but the station refused. The Carter campaign had not set up its own reporting system, so they did not know which parts of the state still had returns outstanding. At the Pfister Hotel headquarters, Caddell was poring over what records they had and his own polls. Suddenly he grabbed the phone and called the television station to tell Carter not to concede. Carter instead taped an ambiguous statement.

The returns not yet counted were those from the rural western part of the state, and as they trickled in during the night, the Carter total slowly crept up and eventually passed Udall. Knowing that the *Milwaukee Sentinel* would have had to go to press before the outcome was clear, Carter had Jody Powell call the paper to check the early morning edition headline. It was: "Carter Upset by Udall." Powell rushed out to obtain copies. At 2 A.M., Carter appeared in the ballroom where his supporters waited, including the Peanut Brigaders. Holding the newspaper high above his head, Carter claimed victory. The resulting picture evoking the memory of Harry Truman holding the *Chicago Tribune* with the premature headline, "Dewey Beats Truman," grabbed the front page of newspapers across America. Carter not only won the vote, he also scored a decisive public relations victory.

The final vote was: Carter 37 percent and Udall 36 percent. However, Carter won by a margin of only 7,449 votes out of a total of 740,528 cast. Under Wisconsin law, besides the names of Udall and Carter, the ballot was required to show the names of all of the original candidates—Wallace, Jackson, Shapp, Bayh, Harris, McCormack (an anti-abortion candidate), and even Bentsen. Harris's vestigial campaign did make an effort to rally some support, netting him 8,185 votes. Two days later he would formally withdraw from the contest. Had Udall persuaded Harris to pull out and pledge him his support a week earlier, and had he received the few thousand votes scattered among the other liberal candidates, he would have defeated Carter.

Carter's success in Wisconsin was important in counterbalancing the day's other developments in New York. New York had been, from the start, the most difficult and alien battleground for Carter. It was a state of political machines and big- and small-time bosses who were concerned about patronage and payoffs, not spiritual renewal or "making the government in Washington as good, honest, decent, capable, and filled with love as the American people." The Democratic machine had arranged to have the delegate candidates listed on the ballot in each of the thirty-nine congressional districts without any indication as to which presidential candidate they were pledged to, thus favoring delegate slates of party regulars with name recognition—few, if any, of whom were for Carter. The campaign challenged this blatant effort early to rig the election against outsider candidates like Carter, and he milked it in the media for all it was worth. Finally, on March 11, Governor Hugh Carey, under pressure, signed into law a bill revising the primary rules to allow identification of a delegate's preference.

The size of the state did not lend itself to Carter's one-to-one campaigning, and he remained dependent on a skeptical media to reach the electorate. He was particularly ill at ease in New York City, where his core support was made up of liberals who either had no history of political involvement or, like Ted Sorensen, were identified in the public mind with the Kennedys. Jordan and Powell, more than Carter, were distrustful of these people, who were urbane, sophisticated, and politically powerful in their own right. Sorensen urged Carter to appoint lawyer and earlier supporter William vanden Heuvel to run the campaign in New York. Jordan, however, was committed to Midge Costanza, a feisty deputy mayor of Rochester whom he and Carter had met in 1974 when she ran a quixotic campaign against the long-entrenched Republican congressman Barber Conable. It was decided that the state would be divided, with the prestigious liberal, vanden Heuvel, handling the downstate area, and the maverick but less threatening Costanza handling the rest.

Knowing he could not win the primary, Carter wanted only a share of the state's enormous delegate pool of 206. Jackson desperately needed a big win to keep his moribund campaign alive. Exuding little charisma or excitement, he made boring copy and seemed to embody the politics of the past. Angry and frustrated by Carter's success, he repeatedly lashed out at him.

More consequential for Carter was the shadow of noncandidate Hubert Humphrey, who continued to hold a place in the hearts of a generation of loyal Democrats. Torn by a desire for one last shot at the presidency, encouraged by supporters and friends, privately battling a malignancy, and appreciating Carter's increasing stranglehold on the nomination, he still continued to anguish over what to do. Meeting with reporters in Washington two weeks before the New York and Wisconsin primaries, Humphrey said, "Candidates who make an attack on Washington are making an attack on government programs, on the poor, on blacks, on minorities, on the cities. It's a disguised new form of racism." Although he later said, "I was primarily talking about Reagan and Ford," it was a thinly veiled attempt to stir doubts about Carter. Carter shot back, claiming that Humphrey was encouraging support for Udall in Wisconsin to keep an opening for himself. He reiterated his earlier statement that Humphrey still carried the image of a loser (from the 1968 presidential race) and that he would be a weak candidate if he did not enter the primaries.

In the end, Humphrey's efforts hurt Jackson more than Carter. When the New York results were counted, Jackson had only 38 percent of the vote, winning 104 delegates; after a desperate last-minute scramble, Udall had 25.5 percent and 70 delegates; and Carter had 12.8 percent and 35 delegates. Twenty-three percent of the votes went to 65 uncommitted delegates, at least 16 of whom were Humphrey loyalists. To add to Jackson's disappointment, Carter's narrow win in Wisconsin became the day's big political story.

Four days before these two primaries, on April 2, as the Carters' campaign plane was approaching Schenectady, Sam Roberts, chief political writer for the New York *Daily News*, had asked Carter his opinion of building low-income, scatter-site housing in the suburbs. Carter said he preferred a program "oriented primarily where the housing is needed most—downtown areas of deteriorating cities. There's a need to protect the family entity, the neighborhood."

"Can a black central city survive surrounded by all white neighborhoods?" Roberts asked.

"Yes. My neighbor is black," Carter responded. "It hasn't hurt us—provided you give people the freedom to decide for themselves where to live. But to artificially inject another racial group in a community? I see nothing wrong with ethnic purity being maintained. I would not force racial integration of a neighborhood by government action. But I would not permit discrimination against a family moving into the neighborhood."

The quote ran toward the end of the story on page 134 of the Sunday edition. It would probably have remained unnoticed if Marty Plissner, the political editor of CBS news, had not read it and suggested to their correspondent on the campaign plane, Ed Rabel, that he ask Carter to clarify his use of the phrase "ethnic purity." On election day in Wisconsin and New York, after being up at 4:45 A.M. to catch a shift change at an auto body plant in Milwaukee, Carter had gone to campaign in Indiana. At the first stop, a press conference at the Indianapolis Hilton, Rabel asked his question. Oblivious to the implications, Carter used the same words again, saying, "I have nothing against a community that's made up of people who are Polish,

Czechoslovakians, French Canadians, or blacks who are trying to maintain the ethnic purity of their neighborhoods. This is a natural inclination on the part of people."

The context of Carter's thinking about urban ethnic groups in the North had clearly been shaped by his experience with the Southern Baptist Home Mission Board in Pennsylvania and Massachusetts. He had learned that attempts to establish large multilingual, multiethnic congregations were unsuccessful. When they started churches for a specific ethnic group in a city, holding services in the people's own language, and understanding the importance of a group's sense of ethnic identity and cohesiveness, the churches succeeded. Feeling generally insecure about his knowledge of urban problems, Carter had fallen back on the one piece of solid experience he had had. Either he was not consciously aware of the thought process behind his comment, or he felt to divulge it would only create further problems.

The media continued to press Carter on the issue all day and he became increasingly testy. Exhausted and worried about the outcome of the day's vote in Wisconsin and New York, he became more and more exasperated with the reporters in his entourage who, smelling blood, were spurred on to even more persistent interrogation. Carter had still not answered the question of what he meant by "ethnic purity," and did not seem to understand it was that phrase rather than his position on the housing issue in general that was the problem. Greg Schneiders and Powell's assistant Betty Rainwater were traveling with him. At a stop in South Bend, Schneiders handed Carter a note pointing out the inflammatory connotations of the phrase. Carter's characteristic stubbornness came to the fore and he huffily told both Schneiders and Rainwater that he did not think the words were offensive and certainly did not intend them in that way.

Both of the aides separately got on the phone to Powell in Milwaukee and Jordan in Atlanta. Powell, who had finely tuned antennae for signs of trouble with the press, immediately saw the problem, but being unable to talk to Carter directly, there was not much he could do. When Rainwater spoke to Jordan, he responded, "So what?" Later he observed, "I suppose it showed maybe we were provincial or that we had a little bit of a cultural problem in not understanding the politics of big cities. It was just an unfortunate remark, but it took me several days to realize how serious a problem it was."

That night's election results temporarily eclipsed "ethnic purity," giving the campaign a day's breathing space and the delusion that if Carter and the staff kept quiet it would go away. The following day, however, when Carter arrived in Pittsburgh to campaign for the Pennsylvania primary, he was immediately confronted by ABC news correspondent Sam Donaldson, who asked, "Are such phrases as 'ethnic purity' and 'alien group' almost

Hitlerian?" Carter tensed up, and holding back obvious anger, he repeated his previous answers and concluded by saying without his usual smile and with his cold blue eyes flashing, "If anyone derived from my statement the connotation that I have an inclination to racism, then I would resent that because it's certainly not true."

It was now a crisis that would not go away. Andrew Young, who had been warned by other black politicians not to go out on a limb for Carter, found himself in an embarrassing position. Characterizing the remarks as a disaster, he said, "Either he'll be repentant of it or it will cost him the nomination. . . . I don't think he understood the loaded connotation of his word. They summoned up memories of Hitler and Nazi Germany. I can't defend him on this." In a move to salvage his own credibility, Young joined sixteen other members of the Congressional Black Caucus in sending Carter a telegram condemning his statement.

Charles Kirbo arrived at the Atlanta headquarters to consult with Hamilton Jordan. In his interminably slow drawl, he expressed the view that issuing further clarifications would only fan the flames and keep the issue alive. Later that evening, April 7, in the Bond Court Hotel in Cleveland, Carter had just washed out his socks and underwear when he received a phone call from Rosalynn. She was clear and emphatic that he needed to apologize. It was the same advice he had received from Andrew Young and Vernon Jordan earlier in the day.

The following morning as he arrived in Philadelphia he issued a statement:

> I think most of the problem has been caused by my ill-chosen agreement to use the words *ethnic purity*. I think that was a very serious mistake on my part. I think it should have been the words *ethnic character* or *ethnic heritage*, and I think that unanimously my black supporters with whom I discussed this question agree that my position is correct. . . . I do want to apologize to all those who have been concerned about the unfortunate use of the term *ethnic purity*.

Returning to Plains for the weekend, Carter and the staff, with the help of black businessman Jesse Hill, organized a major rally to be held at noon the following Tuesday, April 13, in Hurt Park in the center of Atlanta. Carter addressed the largely black crowd, preaching about a land that grew up in slavery and had struggled to overcome that burden and create one nation. Then Martin Luther "Daddy" King, Sr., rose, and to cries of "Amen," "Tell it like it is," and "That's right," he talked of repentance and forgiveness: "I refuse to have any envy or strife in my heart against anybody. I have a forgiving heart. So Governor, I'm with you all the way." There was a sense of true communion between the two men and the shots of them together on the nightly news went a long way to lay the issue to rest.

Some people argued later, including Julian Bond, that Carter had used his comments as a calculated signal to attract conservative voters. Carter vehemently denied it at the time and several years later Andrew Young said the suggestion had no credibility in his mind. It was an honest mistake born of Carter's parochial background. He had successfully neutralized the issue for the moment, satisfactorily mending fences with the black community. A longer-lasting problem was the doubt it sowed in the minds of liberals and moderates who were beginning to be converted into Carter supporters, but who now backed off and believed their earlier wariness was justified.

Especially for Jews, who continued to have a vague unease about Carter, but up to then had been unable to point to anything concrete to justify their distrust, the "ethnic purity" issue suddenly gave them something tangible to which they could attach their anxieties. For liberals generally, the seeds of doubt had already been sown by an article in the March issue of *Harpers* magazine. Author Steve Brill had reviewed Carter's record in Georgia and particularly his efforts to attract the Wallace vote during the 1970 gubernatorial race. Although it contained little new factual information, it was cast in a way that implied Carter was at best duplicitous and possibly consciously willing to play the race card.

A lengthy rebuttal prepared prior to publication by Jody Powell, whose profound loyalty tended to make him overreact, proved a double-edged sword. It corrected the record and refuted several of the charges, but also drew far greater attention to the Brill piece than it might otherwise have received. Because Carter had been in the public awareness so briefly, people had not had time to feel they knew him or fully shape their feelings about the kind of person he was. Similar comments by other candidates thoroughly familiar to the public would probably have been quickly dismissed as inconsistent with what the public had come to know about their character over the years. Indeed, when Jackson claimed to have been "shocked" and "appalled" by Carter's statements, the *Washington Post* pointed out he, himself, had said in December 1975:

> If we destroy the various ethnic neighborhoods in our cities, including black neighborhoods, we destroy not only a rich tradition in American life but an anchor for stability in an increasingly unstable society.

The comments had not even caused a ripple.

A further confusion, especially for the press, was created by the seeming inconsistency between Carter's views and values and those of the so-called "good-old boys" on his staff, especially Jordan and Powell. In most campaigns the staff are there because they share the beliefs and ideology of the candidate. In this instance, they were there, first and foremost, out of history, shared cultural background, and deep personal loyalty, despite often differing sharply with Carter in their personal values and beliefs.

Powell did little to hide his sympathies for George Wallace. Jordan, who fully understood the political importance of the black vote and was generally liked by blacks in the campaign, could not resist telling racist jokes. Even during the week of the "ethnic purity" flap, he thought it hilarious when he wisecracked to fellow staffers that the reason blacks voted for Carter was because they thought he had a big warehouse full of watermelons in Plains. After the press began writing about Carter's profound religious beliefs, Jordan referred to this with reporters as the "weirdo factor," fueling the very suspicions and incredulity Carter was trying to allay. One staffer told a reporter, "Jimmy won't lie to you, but I will."

While Carter openly showed his deep affection for Rosalynn and talked frequently about the sanctity of marriage, members of the staff clearly had different values. Attractive young women with few relevant skills would arrive at the campaign headquarters in Atlanta and were promised jobs by male staff members. One young female volunteer received a plane ticket from Hamilton Jordan to attend a key meeting he would be at, to the utter astonishment of her state coordinator, whom Jordan had explicitly told he could not attend because no funds were available.

Since his days as governor, Jimmy and Rosalynn had actively supported the Equal Rights Amendment, and during the presidential campaign they had sought the backing of members of the women's movement. Next to Jimmy, Rosalynn was the key strategist and decision maker. Yet, at the same time, a deeply embedded southern attitude, manifested by serious discomfort with strong women in positions of authority, pervaded the campaign. The handful of older competent women, including Barbara Blum and Connie Plunkett, were demeaned and regularly excluded from meetings where substantive campaign decisions were to be made. It was an attitude that carried over adversely to dealings with the press corps. The most highly competent women members of the media were given short shrift. Even the venerated White House correspondent, Helen Thomas, complained that most Carter aides would not give her the time of day. Twenty years later, a senior reporter with a national newsmagazine recalled, "The Carter campaign was where I really learned what male chauvinism was all about." When one female reporter complained that another woman had been given a long interview with Carter in her place, she was told by a member of the inner sanctum, "The trouble with you is you don't sleep with the right people like she did."

The irreverence, the lusting, the drinking, the profanities, the disdain for the intellectual, the disorganization, often facilitated the rapport between the staff and much of the traveling press corps who were not always averse to many of those vices themselves. What it did not engender was respect. Except as a matter of degree, the Carter campaign was probably not that different from those of other presidential candidates over the years. What was different was that it was so much at odds with the image Jimmy and Rosalynn were seeking to convey. Especially for those reporters who had joined the campaign after Carter became the front-runner and had little direct interaction with the candidate, what they saw in dealing with the staff cast serious doubts upon the sincerity of the lofty public statements Carter was making on race, religion, the role of women, honesty, and other moral issues. This skepticism was inevitably conveyed, often subtly, to the reading and viewing public. The suspicion of hypocricy would continue to weaken Carter's credibility and moral authority for the rest of the campaign.

Thirty-five-year-old Tim Kraft, the architect of Carter's Iowa victory, had been a gypsy on the campaign trail for more than a year. He arrived in Philadelphia a month before the primary. During 1975, Jack Sullivan, an Annapolis classmate of Carter's, had put together a skeleton organization, with just one storefront Carter office in Philadelphia, on Twenty-second Street, and one in Pittsburgh where the mayor, Pete Flaherty, had early endorsed Carter. Now Sullivan and Kraft blitzed the state, opening twenty-two new offices and bringing in dozens of campaign workers from the sites of earlier Carter victories. They rang doorbells, distributed literature, and made over 300,000 phone calls. Jordan argued in a strategy memo that this was the state in which Carter would eliminate his only remaining significant opposition.

The once affluent Jackson campaign was now down to its last $100,000. Jack Watson and Connie Plunkett mobilized an all-out push to raise funds for the final showdown, especially in Georgia. Bob Lipshutz also arranged to borrow heavily: $100,000 as a personal loan to Carter, $175,000 to the campaign, and another $500,000 in federal matching funds, which it was assumed would start to flow again at some point. Although they would be the source of some later controversy, the Supreme Court then permitted such loans. It would result in Jackson being outspent more than 3 to 1.

Pennsylvania Governor Milton Shapp had hoped to survive long enough to secure his home state's 171 delegates, but he had been forced out. He gave lukewarm support to Jackson, then left on a trade mission to Germany. Pennsylvania, however, was really Humphrey territory. In a state with a huge ethnic, blue-collar population of orthodox Democrats, the labor unions and especially the AFL-CIO dominated politics. They were overwhelmingly loyal to Hubert Humphrey. Ed Toohey, head of Philadelphia's AFL-CIO Council, even had the initials HHH tattooed on his chest. On April 8, Humphrey had addressed the state AFL-CIO convention in Pittsburgh, where 2,000 delegates gave him a standing ovation and chanted, "We want Hubert, We want Hubert." A Gallup poll the following week showed Carter leading Humphrey by just one percentage point, 32 to 31. Two congressmen, Paul Simon of Illinois and Bob Bergland of Minnesota, announced that they intended to open a draft-Humphrey headquarters in Philadelphia only to find the Federal Election Commission required that they have the candidate's approval, and he remained reticent.

Since Humphrey was not on the ballot, Jackson seemed like the natural beneficiary of the Humphrey groundswell. Labor made a halfhearted attempt to mobilize backing for Jackson as part of a stop-Carter movement, but Jackson chafed at being sold as a stalking horse for Humphrey. Carter rubbed salt in the wound and greatly irritated Jackson by repeatedly deriding him as merely a stand-in. In an interview with a reporter from the Philadelphia *Bulletin*, after saying that Humphrey had overwhelming support with labor rank and file, Toohey went on with faint praise to add, "That does not detract from Senator Jackson. You can't find a nicer guy than Jackson." Frustrated that Humphrey was not on the ballot, labor could never engender the level of enthusiasm that the Carter campaign had achieved around the state. The final count gave Carter 37 percent of the vote to Jackson's 25 percent, Udall's 19 percent, and Wallace's 11 percent.

The Carter family gathered to watch the returns in rooms 2154, 2156, and 2158 of the Sheraton Hotel in Philadelphia. A majestic winding staircase led down to the ballroom where Carter supporters from all over the country had gathered. Shortly after 8 P.M., with NBC having projected Carter the winner, Jimmy and Rosalynn appeared at the top of the stairs and walked slowly down the wide staircase, holding hands, to the cheering throng. It added theatrical drama to what was one of the emotional high points of the campaign. People were shedding tears of joy knowing that this victory, for all practical purposes, gave Carter the nomination.

The following Thursday, at 8:10 A.M., Bob Keefe, Jackson's campaign manager, called Hubert Humphrey to say that Jackson had decided to call it quits. The same day, an editorial in the *Washington Post* ended by saying that Humphrey could only bring discredit on his distinguished career by entering the race now. The day before, Humphrey had convened a group of nine of his closest friends and advisors in his Senate office. Most wanted him to get in the race, entering the New Jersey primary, which had a filing deadline of 4 P.M. the next day. But the more they talked, the more they split. The following afternoon, accompanied by Walter Mondale, his fellow senator from Minnesota, Humphrey went to the Senate caucus room and read a statement saying that he would not enter the primaries. He reiterated, however, his availability. "If my party should need me, or should nominate me, I am prepared to serve."

Carter was triumphant but not without problems. He was coming under increasing attack for lacking specificity on the issues. He knew very well where he stood on most issues. But the pressure was coming largely from liberals, and his positions, especially on economic matters and the role of government, were not their positions. In addition, his natural inclination as a conciliator, as in Georgia, led him to articulate his views in a way calculated to offend the smallest number of people. To liberal ideologues this made him sound fuzzy. He had successfully routed the field by running on his character and personality, and his tendency was to attack his opponents not on the basis of their ideology but by impugning their motives and accusing them of being subservient to this or that powerful interest group. Nevertheless, he now faced a problem.

Caddell had repeatedly warned of the need to change gears as the campaign evolved. On March 24, he had written Carter, under a heading "Speech, Issue Themes": "This area of the campaign is the one in need of the most attention. We have passed the point when we can simply avoid at least the semblance of substance." He followed up on April 8, referring to his latest surveys:

> We noted only two disturbing notes. First, the leading Carter negative on open-ended responses was the category "not specific, wishy-washy, changes stands," which went from 3% in our first poll to 11% in our last survey. Also, the agreement to the projective statement, "Jimmy Carter always seems to be changing his position on the issues," rose from 23% in survey 1 to 33% in survey 2. . . . This pattern must be overcome. We must defuse the "no specifics and changes positions" arguments. They seem to be rising. And inevitably unchecked lead to perceptions of Carter as "untrustworthy" and "dishonest."

To remedy the situation, Stuart Eizenstat was brought into the campaign full-time to beef up the issues operation.

Caddell had also advised, "This campaign needs now at least one excellent, brilliant writer, who can pull together ideas and statements and who has good political sense." He volunteered his twenty-nine-year-old friend, Bob Shrum, from the McGovern campaign. Shrum had also been a speechwriter for Edmund Muskie and New York mayor John Lindsay. What Caddell failed to consider was that Shrum, a diehard liberal, was not particularly attracted to Carter, and epitomized the kind of professional political worker with whom Carter always felt ill at ease. Shrum stayed with the campaign for just nine days.

Shrum's involvement would have passed unnoticed had he not chosen to send Carter a letter explaining the reasons for his departure. He shared a copy with the press, together with a ten-page critique of his experience, which he later expanded into an article for *New Times* magazine. Shrum's problem was in part purely ideological. He could not accept Carter's private beliefs that the defense budget might have to be raised after publicly stating that he would reduce it, or his comment that as president he would have vetoed the child-care bill as Ford had done. Perhaps worst in Shrum's eyes was Carter's rejection of a statement Shrum prepared advocating automatic black lung benefits to all miners with thirty years of service.

There was also a problem of style. Shrum was used to preparing set speeches for his previous ideologically compatible bosses that were read verbatim. Carter did not work that way. He was his own speechwriter and would rework anything submitted to him to be sure it reflected his own style and went no further than he wanted to go. Carter wanted to unify the party by bringing the liberal backers of Humphrey and Udall behind him, but he did not want to go further than necessary for fear it would hurt him in the general election.

Shrum took a number of cheap shots accusing Carter of acting in a Machiavellian way, shading his position on issues in return for political endorsements and support, something that should hardly have surprised a person with Shrum's experience in politics. He related a conversation in which Carter was bemoaning the fact that despite his efforts to solicit the Jewish vote and to stress his support for Israel, he had not been able to wean that constituency away from Jackson. Shrum quoted Carter as saying, "I don't want any more statements on the Middle East or Lebanon. Jackson has all the Jews anyway. It doesn't matter how far I go. I don't get over 4 percent of the Jewish vote anyway, so forget it. We get the Christians." Coming in the aftermath of "ethnic purity," Shrum, himself Jewish, clearly intended to foster the image of Carter as anti-Semitic. The night Shrum left, he did so only after drafting a stirring speech for the Pennsylvania victory.

In the afterglow of the Pennsylvania victory and the withdrawal of Jackson and Humphrey, the Shrum fiasco did little lasting damage to Carter. Shrum's most significant impact was on the campaign itself, which became even more closed and inward looking, distrustful of outsiders, especially "liberals," and preoccupied with maintaining absolute control in the hands of three or four people around Carter.

The Carter juggernaut was now rolling with ever-increasing momentum. On May 1, he won the Texas primary, picking up 122 delegates to 8 for Lloyd Bentsen, who had remained on the ballot as a favorite son. It was a campaign that had begun two years earlier when Chip Carter had met with a Baptist preacher, Dr. James Dunn, to ask if there might be other preachers in the state who would be interested in helping his little-known father. Now Carter's Texas coordinator, Bob Armstrong, was quoted as saying, "We're riding a fast horse. All we have to do is hold on and wave our hats."

At a Dallas rally sponsored by Southern Methodist University Law

School, someone got up with the obvious intention of embarrassing Carter and, pointing out that Texas had a large Spanish-speaking population, asked condescendingly if he had anyone on his staff who spoke Spanish. With hardly a pause, Carter responded, "Yo si hablo español, y con todo gusto, los oficiales de mi oficina le enviaran ponencias sobre cualquier tema que usted solicite." (Yes, I speak Spanish myself. And my staff will be happy to send you position papers on any issue you wish.)

Three days later, Carter swept the conveniently delayed Georgia primary with 83.9 percent of the vote. With an election-eve endorsement from Birch Bayh, he won Indiana with 68 percent to 15 percent for Wallace. In the District of Columbia he achieved an unexpectedly large victory over Udall with 39.7 percent of the vote to Udall's 26.1 percent. Even in Alabama, he pulled 27.4 percent against Wallace's 50.8 percent. In one week Carter had picked up another 258 delegates.

Senator Frank Church, who had made his decision to enter the race predicated on the expectation of a brokered convention, or perhaps to highlight himself as a vice-presidential possibility, had elected to make his initial stand in Nebraska on May 11. With Caddell's polls showing him well ahead, Carter had made only one visit. Church, however, convinced Nebraskans in the final week that, unlike him, Carter was ignoring them. Carter was attending a Democratic congressional fund-raising dinner in Washington when the results came in. Powell called him off the podium into a little side room where he and other staff members broke the news that Church was the surprise winner with 38.8 percent of the vote to Carter's 37.8 percent. It was not a consequential setback, but Carter still hated to lose. He sat for some time leaning against the wall, reflecting both dejection and anger that the staff, misreading the situation, had failed to reschedule him in Nebraska and prevent a 2,000-vote loss. "Well let's get it over with," he finally said, getting up and going out to the waiting press corps, where he told them, "I can't win them all." He did keep alive his record of never having a completely losing primary night by taking the race in Connecticut over Udall.

The one primary he did not contest was also decided on May 11—West Virginia. Senator Robert Byrd, who had at one point briefly suggested he was running as a national candidate, had withdrawn into the role of favorite son. Knowing he would ultimately get Byrd's delegates, and not wanting to antagonize the prideful Byrd, Carter did not campaign in West Virginia.

The other late entry, Jerry Brown, posed a perplexing problem for Carter. He was singing the same tune as Carter, but in a different key. He was simultaneously able to attract many of those who liked Carter and those who had become identified as part of the "ABC" (Anybody But Carter) movement. Both Carter and Brown presented themselves as anti-politician politicians. They both eschewed the trappings of power, presenting themselves as men of the people. Brown declined to live in the California governor's mansion, staying instead in a small apartment, and he drove a 1974 Plymouth from the state motor pool instead of a chauffeured limousine. Carter carried his own suit bag and stayed in people's homes instead of expensive hotels. Both emphasized that they were not from Washington and both believed in smaller, more efficient government. Carter, the Southern Baptist modulated by Reinhold Niebuhr, and Brown, a Jesuit-trained Catholic who dabbled in Zen Buddhism, seemed to offer a spiritual message that appealed to elements of the electorate. Both were populists benefitting from the rule changes. Both were elusive when it came to pigeonholing themselves on the ideological spectrum, and both seemed equally able to attract liberals, moderates, and conservatives.

Jerry Brown had remained astonishingly popular as governor of California, maintaining an extraordinary negative rating of only 7 percent. However, his campaign manager, Mickey Kantor, an experienced political operative, felt he needed to establish himself in a nonwestern state before the California primary. They chose Maryland.

On a minuscule budget, the Carter campaign had been organizing there for over a year, and Carter himself had made several visits. He had the active backing and organizational skills of state senators Jim Clark and Rosalie Abrams, and Joy and Red Colegrove, Carter friends from their navy days in Hawaii, who lived in the Third Congressional District near Annapolis. A *Baltimore Sun* poll as late as the first week in April showed Carter leading with 24 percent and Brown fifth behind Wallace, Jackson, and Udall. The only cloud on the horizon was Governor Marvin Mandel, who although under indictment on charges of mail fraud, bribery, falsifying federal income tax returns, and a "pattern of racketeering activity," remained in control of a powerful statewide political machine. Mandel was the only one of his fellow governors Carter really disliked, and the feeling was mutual. Mandel was happy to help anyone who could derail Carter.

Brown had sought advice about entering the race from Humphrey, who told him, "They [the public] want something new, Jerry. And you come into this ball game and you'll get the attention like nobody ever had it."

Humphrey was absolutely on target. Brown, who did not even go to Maryland until April 29, was greeted by Governor Mandel, Ted Venatoulis, the Baltimore county executive, other top Democratic officials, labor leaders, and a huge press entourage at the Baltimore International Airport. Brown offered an exciting alternative for all those who were opposed to, or bored with, Carter—liberals and government employees in the Washington suburbs, Jews in the Pikesville area of Baltimore, Polish and other Catholic ethnic groups in the city, even many blacks.

Meanwhile, the Carter campaign was in disarray. Jordan and his staff had not returned even the most pleading calls from the Maryland staff in more than three weeks. Overwhelmed by the avalanche of demands on him, Jordan was vanishing for longer and longer periods of time. A fellow staffer recalls seeing him return from a trip to find more than a foot of mail on his desk, all of which he shoveled unopened into the trash. He did not want to answer phone calls or meet with anyone. His assistant, Caroline Wellons, who found him kind and considerate, also considered him "vulnerable and insecure." He preferred to be on his own, drafting long thoughtful strategy memos, and told her, "Your job is to protect me from all these people [the campaign staff across the country]." Finally, as it became clear what inroads Brown was making, Phil Wise arrived in Maryland with a detachment of the "Peanut Brigade." The last-minute scramble, including media buys, occurred devoid of consultation with the existing campaign operating in the state. This resulted in essentially two Carter campaigns in Maryland working at cross-purposes. Those who came from outside, especially the "Peanut Brigade," were best equipped to win the support of Wallace supporters and other conservative elements who had already switched to Carter. They knew little about the local politics and were not attuned to dealing with urban ethnics, Jews, and liberals—the volatile element that had swung to Brown. A visit by Eizenstat to address Jewish groups proved the only constructive contribution from Atlanta.

Oblivious to the staff problems, Carter saw it in purely personal terms:

> I made . . . a serious tactical mistake in Maryland. Going in and running against Brown and running against the establishment. . . . If ever there was a state in the nation that the political establishment's still dominant, it's Maryland.

Brown won the popular vote by 48.3 percent to Carter's 36.9 percent. More serious was the meltdown in the campaign organization.

In Michigan that same night, with the support of Detroit mayor Coleman Young, Carter had every reason to anticipate a sizable victory. However, Michigan was a state that allowed "crossover voting," permitting the electorate to vote in either the Democratic or Republican primary regardless of party registration. With a tight race developing for the Republican nomination between Gerald Ford and Ronald Reagan, many Democrats crossed over to vote for Ford. They were overwhelmingly Carter supporters. On election night, Carter squeaked by yet again with 43.5 percent to Udall's 43.2 percent. The race was most notable for a hard-hitting Udall commercial that showed different pictures of Carter while a narrator enumerated his switching positions on various issues. It had a long-lasting effect on people's perception of Carter that would adhere to him far beyond the Michigan primary.

On May 25, Brown took Nevada, Church had Idaho, and Carter won Tennessee, Kentucky, and Arkansas, where his organizers included his Annapolis roommate, Al Rusher; Jackson Stephens, another Annapolis graduate; and Bill Clinton, then running for attorney general. The real contest was in Oregon, where Brown had mounted an unprecedented and complicated write-in campaign. Udall pulled out, hoping that Church and Brown would stop Carter. Before the success of Brown in Maryland, and Church in Nebraska, Carter was comfortably ahead in the polls. However, his lead was mostly by default. Carter was unable to generate much intrinsic appeal among voters anywhere in the West except on the environmental issue. As a result of the disarray in Atlanta, there had been no support for a statewide organizing effort. As the vote in Oregon approached, Caddell's polls indicated Carter had slipped to within 2 points of Church. He had planned to spend the final weekend back in Plains, but he remained and campaigned to avoid the possibility that he might even come in an embarrassing third.

Church, from next-door Idaho, won with 34.6 percent of the vote. Happily for Carter, he managed to hold off the Brown write-in by 27.4 percent to 23.3 percent.

In the final stretch, with just ten more days left in the primary season, Jimmy's stamina seemed superhuman, although he was becoming increasingly exhausted. Rosalynn was determined to fight for every last delegate. She called Jimmy, resting in Plains, to tell him that she was convinced South Dakota could be won against Udall if he would make just a brief stop there, and that while people in Democratic Rhode Island told her they would vote for Jimmy in the fall, a small turnout now threatened him in the primary. On Memorial Day he flew to Providence and then on to Sioux Falls and Rapid City before ending the day in Sacramento. On June 1, Carter won South Dakota (41.1 percent to Udall's 33.5 percent), he lost Montana to Church (59.9 percent to 24.8 percent) and, as Rosalynn predicted, in Rhode Island a low turnout enabled an "uncommitted" slate of delegates but favoring Jerry Brown, who had entered too late to be formally on the ballot, to win 31.4 percent to Carter's 29.9 percent.

June 8 was the climax of the primary season. Races in Ohio, New Jersey, and California would yield 540 delegates, the largest tally for any single day. With its 152 delegates, Ohio had always looked good for Carter, who had the enthusiastic support of the state's dynamic, young lieutenant governor, Dick Celeste. As the presumptive nominee, Carter also attracted many politicians wanting to get on the bandwagon. He swept the state with 52.2 percent of the vote (and 119 delegates), to Udall's 21 percent and Church's 13.9 percent.

In New Jersey, another state dominated by a Democratic Party

machine, state party chairman James P. Dugan, a diehard Humphrey loyalist, had put together an "uncommitted" slate of delegates with the wist-
ful hope that lightning might still strike for his man. Humphrey himself just
could not let go, telling R. W. Apple of the *New York Times*, "If Carter does
well Tuesday, fine, that's it. . . . But, if not, I'll try to get the answer to some
questions: What is the true state of the uncommitted? Are they really
open or have they made promises? How solid is Carter's support?" Dugan
desperately needed a candidate to campaign in the state for his slate and
convinced Jerry Brown to do so. The "uncommitted" slate then was, in
effect, a Humphrey and/or Brown slate. Capitalizing on the ballot confusion, Dugan and his lieutenants were able to get enough people out to win
by 48 percent (83 delegates) to 28 percent for Carter (25 delegates).

Whatever hopes Carter might have had in California had been dashed
when Brown entered the race. The situation was made worse by the organizational breakdown in Atlanta. In 1974, while still chairman of the DNC
Campaign Committee, Carter had met college professor Rodney Kennedy-
Minot from Hayward near San Francisco. As one of Carter's earliest and
most loyal supporters, in 1975 he was made the California campaign chairman. However, Terry Utterbach, a political consultant with less of a personal commitment to Carter, was given responsibility for the southern part
of the state. Subsequently, in an attempt to build bridges with the party
regulars, Jordan appointed state Senator Omer Rains as western states
cochairperson and Los Angeles county supervisor Ed Edelman as cochairperson of the California campaign. Then in order to try to keep personal
control he brought in Ben Goddard from Colorado with the titles of western states regional coordinator and California state coordinator. He was, in
theory, to be Kennedy-Minot's number two but was also to handle the day-
to-day operation. One of Jordan's colleagues in Atlanta was quoted as saying, "California was one state Ham was intimidated by. Hamilton kept
letting these people join and he kept giving them titles and each thought he
was running things. They all fought most of the time and little grassroots
organization developed." With no chain of command and Jordan largely
incommunicado, anarchy reigned.

Little, however, would have changed the outcome. Brown won 59
percent of the vote (204 delegates) while Carter received 20.5 percent
(67 delegates).

Carter gave his best speech of the campaign on June 1 before a mostly
black audience at the Martin Luther King, Jr., Hospital in Los Angeles. It
was prepared with the help of Patrick Anderson, a writer and novelist who
understood Carter would not deliver anything that did not have his personal stamp on it. My wife and I had generated Anderson's interest in
Carter a year earlier, and he had written a very well-received profile of

Carter in the *New York Times Magazine*. Then, having sold the paperback rights to his latest novel for a substantial sum, he offered his services, gratis, to the campaign as a speechwriter. There was still some trepidation after the experience with Shrum, but Jody Powell, more comfortable with Anderson, who was a Texan, was willing to give him a chance. The speech, vintage Carter, couched in the mellifluous phrases of a skilled wordsmith said in part:

> We are here today to honor a man with a dream.
>
> We are here to honor a man who lived and died for the cause of human brotherhood.
>
> Martin Luther King, Jr., was the conscience of his generation.
>
> He was a doctor to a sick society.
>
> He was a prophet to a new and better America.
>
> He was a southerner, a black man, who in his too-short life stood with presidents and kings, and was honored around the world, but who never forgot the poor people, the oppressed people, who were his brothers and sisters and from whom he drew his strength.
>
> He was the man, more than any other of his generation, who gazed upon the great wall of segregation and saw that it could be destroyed by the power of love.
>
> I sometimes think that a southerner of my generation can most fully understand the meaning and the impact of Martin Luther King's life.

Carter continued with an account of his own life and the impact that segregation had had on it, his mother's role as a nurse, and the changes that began to occur when he returned from the navy. He talked of the role of John F. Kennedy in enforcing the court orders, of Martin Luther King's March on Washington and his "I Have a Dream" speech, and of Lyndon Johnson's support for the Voting Rights Act, adding:

> It made it possible for a southerner to stand before you this evening as a serious candidate for president of the United States.

He went on to talk about King's opposition to the war in Vietnam, and his continuing struggle for the economic rights of the poor, King's assassination, and that of Robert Kennedy, but he said,

> The dream lived on.
>
> It could be slowed, but never stopped.

He talked of what he had done as governor to appoint blacks to high positions including judgeships and his hanging of the portrait of Martin Luther King, Jr., in the state capitol. But, in a reiteration of his Law Day speech in May 1974, he warned:

For all our progress we still live in a land held back by oppression and injustice.

The few who are rich and powerful still make the decisions, and the many who are poor and weak must suffer the consequences. If those in power make mistakes, it is not they or their families who lose their jobs or go on welfare or lack medical care or go to jail.

We still have poverty in the midst of plenty.

We still have far to go. We must give our government back to the people. The road will not be easy.

But we still have the dream, Martin Luther King's dream and your dream and my dream. The America we long for is still out there, waiting for us to find her.

I see an America not only poised at the brink of a new century, but at the dawn of a new era of honest, compassionate, responsive government.

I see an American government that has turned away from scandals and cynicism and finally become as decent as our people.

I see an America with a tax system that does not steal from the poor and give to the rich.

I seen an America with a job for every man and woman who can work, and a decent standard of living for those who cannot.

I can see an America in which my child and your child and every child receives an education second to none in the world.

I see an American government that does not spy on its citizens or harass its citizens, but respects your dignity and your privacy and right to be left alone.

I see an American foreign policy that is firm and consistent and generous, and that once again is a beacon for the hopes of the world.

I see an American president who does not govern by vetoes and nega- tivism, but with vigor and vision and affirmative leadership, a president who is not isolated from our people, but feels their pain and shares their dreams and takes his strength from them.

I see an America in which Martin Luther King's dream is our national dream.

Carter's overwhelming support among blacks as a champion of social jus- tice stood in sharp contrast to the continuing suspicion with which he was viewed by Jews. No matter what he did or said, there remained a hurdle he seemed unable to overcome. On May 28, the day after the Oregon primary, Carter met at the Waldorf Astoria Hotel in Manhattan with Israeli prime min- ister Golda Meir. Mrs. Meir, wishing to avoid being used in domestic Amer- ican politics, made it clear the meeting was "purely private." Powell, however, made sure the papers carried a picture the next day of Carter leav- ing the hotel, quoting Carter as saying that the prime minister was an "old friend" (based on his meeting with her in Israel as governor). With the help of William vanden Heuvel, Carter had also secured the endorsement of New York mayor Abraham Beame. He had met with countless small groups of Jewish leaders in several states to provide reassurance, especially with regard to Israel, reminding them that Harry Truman was a Baptist. As early as November 7, 1975, he had sent a handwritten note from Plains on his personal stationery to potential supporter Jerry Hornblass that read:

> Our total commitment to Israel must be maintained as a cornerstone of our nation's policy and the world should be kept aware of this commitment. . . . The major leaders of Israel [Meir, Allon, Rabin, and others] can vouch for my longstanding and continuing commitment of interest and friendship.

He had not deviated from this position throughout the campaign. An article by Richard Reeves in the May 24 issue of *New York* entitled "Is Jimmy Carter Good for Jews?" brought the topic into national focus. Reeves quoted Carter's New York finance chairman, Howard Samuels, who described how he had invited 150 northeastern Jewish leaders to a meeting with Carter to have, much to his embarrassment, only forty show up. "They don't want to listen. They totally misunderstand the man and they're scared to death of him." Reeves also noted that in the Jewish community there was the same regional prejudice against the South that there was in the country at large. When he pointed out to national Jewish leaders that three of Carter's top lieutenants were Jewish (Rafshoon, Lipshutz, and Eizenstat), the response was that he had no northern Jews around him. With growing frustration, on May 30 Carter met with yet another Jewish group prior to a fund-raiser at the Beverly Wilshire Hotel:

> I'm going to tell you something you don't like. I'm a devoted Southern Baptist. There has been a great deal of concern expressed to me by Jewish leaders about my beliefs. . . . I'm a devoted Baptist. . . . I ask you to learn about my faith before you permit it to cause you any concern. . . . There is no conflict between us [concerning] the separation of church and state. . . . I worship the same God you worship.

On election day Carter called Richard Daley. He told the mayor that he expected to lose California and New Jersey, but win big in Ohio. He asked Daley for his public support to put the events of the day in the best light. When he hung up, Daley immediately called a news conference at which he suggested the race in Ohio was the only one that really mattered and went on to say:

> This man Carter has fought in every primary, and if he wins in Ohio he'll walk in under his own power. . . . I've known him for years. He's got courage.

I admire a man who's got courage. . . . He's got a religious tone in what he says and maybe we should have a little more religion in our community. . . . The man talks about true values.

Carter arrived back in Plains after midnight to a tumultuous reception and street party. Miss Lillian handed him a message that said George Wallace wanted him to call, no matter how late, and had left his bedside number. Carter called from the old train depot that had served as the Plains campaign head-quarters. Wallace congratulated him and said that he would be announcing his endorsement in the morning. Carter felt no animosity toward Wallace and, apart from the issue of race, he felt closer to him than any other candidate.

Udall and Church congratulated Carter and acknowledged the race was over. Jackson promised his support and the release of his delegates. Hubert Humphrey announced, "The primaries now are over and Governor Carter has a commanding lead. He is virtually certain to be our party's nominee." He then unequivocally withdrew himself from contention. Only Jerry Brown continued to campaign as though nothing had transpired.

Carter's successful route to the nomination differed in only minor details from the plan worked out at the Georgia governor's mansion in the last months of 1972 and early 1973. The victory also owed a great deal to a com-bination of luck and the bad judgment of the other candidates. Some observers attributed the appeal of the Carter message to the post-Watergate atmosphere in the country. Whatever the plans, the expectation of victory was there long before Watergate became an issue.

Newsweek magazine quoted George Reedy, the former press secretary to Lyndon Johnson, as saying, "The real issues in the campaign are spiri-tual rather than economic and social. The average American today is lost. He doesn't know what to believe, where to go, what to do." The same arti-cle quoted Marquette University sociologist Wayne Youngquist as calling these spiritual concerns collectively a "meta-issue—an issue above issues. It involves tone, honesty, decency, truthfulness, morality, religion." In times of turmoil and change, people turn for a sense of security to a reaffir-mation of their fundamental values. The Vietnam War, desegregation, empowerment of the underprivileged, democratization of long privileged institutions, including the elective process, revelations about the deceit of the CIA, and Watergate had all contributed to a state of confusion for the American people. Power was shifting in unpredictable and frightening ways. Right and wrong were no longer clear. Institutions, once reliable sources of truth and trust, were now fonts of lies. From his own cultural heritage and beliefs, Jimmy Carter offered a reaffirmation of the secure fundamental values that people craved, values that had shaped the think-ing of the Founding Fathers and upon which the nation had been built.

CHAPTER 21

When you belong somewhere, there is no need to pretend who you are. It gives you a base from which to tackle any future storm.

—LUCILLA LADY NOBLE

Carter had a month before the July 12 convention in New York City. He used the time to attend relaxed fund-raising events to liquidate his debt, negotiate an uncontroversial platform for the convention, and carry out the most careful and methodical process in history for choosing a vice-presidential running mate.

A man of few pretensions, Carter returned happily to Plains. Chip notes, "Plains is like a big family for him." Carter told me at the time:

> There is no way I could abandon my roots, as a Georgian, as a farmer, or as a resident of Plains. I found when I was governor . . . that my ties back home were a stabilizing force. We tend to lose perspective when we are transferred into the center of a political position with constant deference and constant respect, constant attention given to your needs, and constant honor because you are the governor of the state. To go back home and to walk the streets of Plains where nobody defers to me and to go to the same Sunday school class, and eat barbecue chicken, and come to Billy's filling station, and talk to farmers about their crops is a kind of reaffirmation of my own status as a private citizen who's no better than anyone else. And I always try to do some manual labor when I go home, with an axe, or a shovel, or walk in the woods, or walking in the fields. In a nice way it's a humbling experience.

To savor glory was to commit the sin of pride for which the only antidote, in his mind, was to commit himself to a sense of his own humility.

Carter also wanted the reporters and the American voters to see him exactly the way he was and judge him accordingly. Having the nation's media installed in Plains for the better part of three months had the potential to reinforce many of the stereotypes about Carter. Beer-drinking Billy at his Amoco station, always ready with an irreverent quote, was lionized by the reporters, but his deliberate efforts to play the rural bumpkin renewed questions about what Jimmy was really like. Gloria, who rode a Harley-Davidson, was widely liked, but hardly fit the conventional image for a sister of the president of the United States. At the same time, the warmth and hospitality of the community, the close-knit nature of the Carter family, and particularly the charm of Miss Lillian gave Carter a human context to which reporters had often been oblivious. The intimacy of small-town living convinced most of them that there was nothing hidden about Jimmy Carter. He was what he seemed.

A sign had been erected above the stores of the town's one commercial street: "Plains, Georgia. Home of Jimmy Carter, Our Next President." The residents of Plains were taking full advantage of the economic bonanza that had befallen them. There were paid tours of the points of interest, and plenty of people willing to assist well-known TV network figures and journalists with large expense accounts.

Stuart Eizenstat had been Carter's representative at the meetings of the Platform Committee. Unlike 1972, there had been few disputes over platform content, in part because Carter delegates were in a heavy majority. The one area of contention was over the handling of those who had opposed the Vietnam War. Sam Brown, state treasurer in Colorado and a former leader of the anti-war movement, wanted to approve a "full and complete pardon" for all those in "legal and financial jeopardy." This was further than the cautious Carter wanted to go. Brown and Eizenstat worked out an amendment allowing the president to consider pardons for deserters on a case-by-case basis, which Brown acknowledged would allow "a much broader number of people to support the platform."

The country was concerned in 1976 about the manner in which vice presidents were picked. Kennedy chose Lyndon Johnson quickly, and with more thought to how he could help the ticket than what sort of president he would make. Yet he became president. Richard Nixon had picked Spiro Agnew, who was poorly qualified, and was forced to resign in disgrace. McGovern's haphazard choice of Eagleton destroyed his campaign before it even got started. Ford had been chosen by Nixon and confirmed by the Senate, yet, unelected, had become president. Rockefeller, also unelected, was now the vice president.

In many respects, Carter saw the choice of his running mate as being the first act of his presidency. He was also determined to use it to demonstrate to the country the methodical, careful manner he would use to handle matters of great import in the White House. At a strategy meeting of the senior campaign staff and advisors held at Sea Island, Georgia, on June 17, he asked members of the staff to submit recommendations as to who he should choose. A comprehensive list of 300–400 prominent Democratic mayors, governors, members of the House and Senate, as well as other party notables, was also compiled. Carter called many of these people, partly with an eye to flattery, but also with a legitimate desire to hear their views. A list of two dozen prospects was ultimately prepared.

During the primaries, Carter had said that he would pick a vice-presidential running mate who was, in order of priority, someone qualified to become president, someone with whom he felt politically and personally compatible, and, least important, someone from outside the South who would give the traditional balance to the ticket. In a memo to Carter in early June, Jordan added that he thought it crucial that Carter have clearly in mind exactly how he would use his vice president and what kind of role he would have him play. Carter had concluded that he should choose a senator who brought the Washington expertise he lacked. Those on his list were Glenn, Church, Jackson, Ribicoff, Stevenson, and Walter "Fritz" Mondale. One long shot was Congressman Peter Rodino, chairman of the House Judiciary Committee. Congressman Brock Adams of Washington, whom many respected people had recommended to Carter, was considered but was not well enough known.

Carter was inclined toward Frank Church, who he felt was well qualified, had a strong political base in the West where Carter was weak, and was seen as a liberal. Prior to Church's entry into the primaries, Carter had made a point of meeting alone with him in his Senate office, to get a feel for the man, whom he had never met. The issue of the vice presidency was not raised. Carter left the meeting with positive feelings about Church. The Carter family held a straw ballot while playing Scrabble during their vacation weekend at Sea Island. Church was the unanimous winner, except for eight-year-old Amy, who favored Glenn.

On June 22, Charles Kirbo went to Washington where he met with James Rowe, Jr., advisor to several Democratic presidents, who had assisted Johnson in choosing Humphrey. Together they compiled a questionnaire of financial, medical, and other matters aimed at avoiding the difficulties of other presidential nominees. On June 28, after refining the questionnaire with his law partner, Griffin Bell, Kirbo personally interviewed the senators on the list, leaving them with the questionnaire. Ribicoff politely declined any interest. Kirbo also went to see Muskie to get his views on the candidates. To his surprise, Muskie was upset that he was not on the list. Kirbo added him and arranged for him to receive the questionnaire.

By way of making up for this slight, Carter decided to invite Muskie to come to Plains first, for an interview. He and his wife, Jane, arrived on July 4. They talked for several hours and walked with Carter around Plains. The Muskies were pleasant enough, but he was not particularly prepared and lacked the energy level that Carter instinctively sought.

My own choice was Mondale, who I knew was also favored by Hamilton Jordan. I was convinced he was the one person who could reunite the party, especially bringing the Humphrey supporters back into the fold. Following the Sea Island meeting, I had made a strong pitch for him to Carter. I was worried, however, that others would convince him Mondale was too "liberal." Yet, without enthusiastic support for the ticket from the liberal wing of the party, I was sure Carter would lose.

Sol Linowitz, whom I had come to know and respect, was close to Mondale. He arranged for the two of us to have lunch with Mondale and his chief of staff, Dick Moe, in the senator's office. For three hours I prepared Mondale for his meeting with Carter. I went over the members of Carter's family, his personal and political history in Georgia, and many of his personal idiosyncrasies. I told Mondale that he should be thoroughly familiar with *Why Not the Best?*—Carter's autobiography published in early 1975. We discussed Carter's views on busing and various other specific issues. I warned him to have a good explanation for Carter, who valued tenacity above most other virtues, of why he had dropped out of the 1976 race at such an early stage. I was able to reassure him about concerns he had that Carter might be upset about the aggressively critical role he had played toward the FBI and the CIA, concerning their illegal activities during the recently ended Senate investigation. Carter, I told him, at least in private, would thoroughly agree with him and urged him to discuss openly with Carter his role on the Oversight Committee. I also encouraged him to be ready with a clear statement as to the role he would expect to play as vice president. I warned him that Carter would press him on any topic they discussed and that he should be thoroughly prepared with the answers he would give.

Most important by far, I told him, was for him and his wife, Joan, to establish a compatible personal relationship with Jimmy and Rosalynn. He needed to emphasize their shared rural, small-town background and, as the son of a Methodist minister, to discuss his own sincere faith as the source of his political values. I reminded him that Rosalynn was a Methodist. Joan was also the daughter of a minister. I knew that Carter would like the fact that Mondale was one of the poorest members of the Senate, having done absolutely nothing to enrich himself during his many years in politics. Mondale's conventional "straight-arrow" lifestyle would also appeal to Jimmy and Rosalynn.

Mondale went to Plains on the morning of July 8. It was oppressively hot, and the ubiquitous gnats were out in force. The meeting went well for Mondale. Carter would later write:

> I thought he was better prepared to answer questions than any other person. He had obviously very carefully considered the proper role of the vice

president. I thought he was completely frank about assessing his own strengths and weaknesses, and was also remarkably forthright in assessing the qualities of the other persons that I was considering. I asked each person that I considered what they thought about the other five. Some of them were excessively complimentary, some of them were very reluctant about saying anything good or bad, but Mondale had no constraint about it at all. . . . I think that showed a degree of maturity that was refreshing. He and I got along well together. . . . I read his book about government and found some of his ideas to be both interesting and compatible with mine. But I just felt if I was president then he was the one I wanted to work with me. I felt he would be adequately independent and also adequately loyal.

As he emerged from 1 Woodland Drive with Carter next to him, reporters asked Mondale how things had gone. "We were about to get to the question of who he wanted as vice president," Mondale quipped. "Just as he was about to tell me, time ran out."

As he had done with the Muskies, Carter walked, handshaking with the Mondales, through the center of Plains. Standing in the shade of a loading dock next to the campaign headquarters, Mondale heard Carter tell reporters, "I don't think there would be any philosophical incompatibilities that would prevent us running as a harmonious ticket."

Mondale's position was significantly enhanced when John Glenn came to Plains later the same day. Glenn was generally well prepared, but had not bothered to learn the names of the Carter children and there was little chemistry between the two men. Carter would interview the other candidates when he went to New York. Rodino would tell him that because of his wife's illness he was not interested, and by this point the meetings with Jackson, Stevenson, and Church were largely formalities.

The Carter family arrived in New York on Saturday, July 10, and were ensconced on the twenty-first floor of the Americana Hotel. The convention coincided with the nation's bicentennial celebration, which had been highlighted the previous week in New York by the stunning visit of the "Tall Ships." It left a residue of euphoria and party spirit on which the Democrats and Carter capitalized. Convening without serious conflict for the first time in twelve years, they were determined to make the meeting a love-fest.

The following morning, Jimmy and Rosalynn attended services at the Fifth Avenue Presbyterian Church. The preachers were two black Baptist ministers. One of them, Dr. Kenneth L. Folkes, would admonish in his sermon, "The day of prosperity for the privileged few must end."

As well as continuing his vice-presidential interviews, Carter met delegations of different constituent groups, including Hispanics, blacks, and women. He talked to Chicanos and Latinos in Spanish. He promised blacks that he would keep Basil Patterson as vice chairman of the Democratic National Committee. When Jesse Jackson expressed his feelings that it would have been nice, if only symbolically, to have had a black among the finalists coming to Plains to be considered as the vice-presidential nominee, Carter, somewhat taken aback, was able to say that while Mayors Thomas Bradley and Coleman Young were on his original list, he had decided early on that it had to be someone from Washington.

After he met with the National Women's Political Caucus, New York activist Bella Abzug said:

> I consider this a very important first of a series of meetings he will hold with us. I think women can expect a real commitment from this nominee. . . . He will involve women in his campaign and he strongly believes in an active involvement of women in his administration. . . . He said LBJ eliminated many of the legal barriers against blacks, and as president he would want to eliminate legal barriers against women.

Betty Friedan would later tell writer Kandy Stroud, "This is so different than it was eight years ago. I was moved to tears by Carter. He made a commitment to us in such a substantive way that unless he's an absolute liar, he'll do something for women."

Ted Kennedy, attending the first Democratic convention in twenty years where a member of his family was not a major factor, left after his offer to nominate Carter was summarily declined. Instead Carter was nominated by Peter Rodino, whose House Judiciary Committee experience during the Nixon impeachment hearings made him an ideal symbol of honesty and integrity in government. Seconding speeches were given by Andy Young and Midge Costanza.

As Ohio put Carter over the magic number of 1,505 votes, wild cheers went up from the staff trailer where Jordan and others were coordinating their troops on the convention floor. Carter was watching on television at the hotel with Amy and grandson Jason on his lap. He jumped up and hugged his mother and said, "It's been a long time. I'm glad it's Ohio." Rosalynn and the rest of the Carter family were sitting in Madison Square Garden. Rosalynn, who had worked as hard as anyone for that night, later wrote, "I couldn't wait to get back to the hotel. I wanted to be with Jimmy."

At 8:26 A.M. the following day, he called Mondale in his suite at the Carlyle on a direct line that Mondale had had specially installed in order not to miss the call. He picked it up after one ring to hear Carter say, "Did I wake you up?"—a phrase he characteristically used when calling people early in the morning to gently remind them that whatever they were doing he was already up and working. "Would you like to run with me?" he continued. Mondale turned and gave a thumbs-up sign to Joan and Dick Moe.

Shortly before announcing his selection in the press room at the Americana, Carter walked across the street to the City Squire Hotel. There he met with more than 200 Georgia supporters and delegates. With his eyes welling with tears and a crack in his voice, he thanked them for making his success possible. "When no one felt I had a chance, you were the people who believed," he told them.

Carter wanted to write his own acceptance speech, but told speechwriter Patrick Anderson before leaving Plains to solicit ideas from people around the country. "Call bright young people you know," he said. "Read my old speeches, too, the ones from the governorship. . . . I want to say my campaign started with nothing, and formed an alliance with the people, and I don't fear being president as long as I can keep my alliance with the people." He also criticized Anderson for using "they," as other presidents and nominees had done, instead of "we," when referring to the American people. "I am one of the American people," he reminded him.

Carter had written a twenty-five-page draft on yellow legal paper that had been photocopied for the staff. While he used some of the thoughts from those Anderson had culled, he rejected as inauthentic the rousing, elegant prose some were urging. He needed to reach out to every segment of the Democratic Party, but he was unwilling to be presented as something he was not. At 5 P.M. on Tuesday, July 13, Carter, Anderson, Rafshoon, Caddell, Powell, and Chip gathered around a coffee table in Carter's suite. Carter read the most recent draft of the speech aloud, asking the others to interrupt him with suggestions as he went along. When he read, "I have spoken many times about love, but love must be aggressively translated into justice," Anderson commented that he thought the line was "wonderful."

"It ought to be," Carter responded, without looking up. "It's Niebuhr."

Anderson had inserted into Carter's original draft, "Our people have suffered too much and too long at the hands of the political and economic elite that has made decisions without being accountable for its mistakes." In a redraft he had softened the wording, only to have Carter reinsert the original. "I have a strong visceral feeling about that section," he said. Rafshoon, observing that Carter, himself relatively well-off, always identified with the poor and oppressed, recalled the discussion with amusement:

> I got hot at him. We were working . . . "powerful political elites." I was for keeping it in, but someone said to him if you put that in you're going to have to say who they are. And he said, "Well, I can say who they are." So I said, "Well, tell me who they are." And he said [to chide Rafshoon], "Rich advertising executives." I said, "I'm not a rich advertising executive." He said, "You send your kids to private schools." And I said, "Jimmy, you don't have a corner on poverty. I paid for my own education. I didn't get a free education from the government."

As they proceeded, Carter said he wanted the word *explicitly* removed. " 'Explicitly' is too fancy," he said. "I want to use words that people down in Plains can understand."

On Thursday evening when Carter stepped up to the microphone it would be his opening line, suggested by Rafshoon's friend Jack Kaplan and his partner John Barrett, that would become the most vivid and lasting memory of the speech. "My name is Jimmy Carter and I'm running for president." They were the words with which his lonely odyssey had begun. Initially addressed to one or two individuals, now to the entire nation. Summing up so succinctly the struggle of the previous sixteen, if not forty-eight, months, they drove the Carter delegates wild and brought many to tears.

He talked about injustice and obliquely referred to Watergate. In the early drafting of that section, he had told Anderson, "Make it mean." What he told the delegates harked back again to his Law Day speech in 1974. "I see no reason why big-shot crooks should go free while the poor ones go to jail."

The one moment of soaring oratory came when he said:

> It is time for America to move and to speak, not with boasting and belligerence, but with a quiet strength—to depend in world affairs not merely on the size of an arsenal but on the nobility of ideas—and to govern at home not by confusion and crisis but with grace and imagination and common sense.

It was a piece of pure Ted Sorensen, solicited from him by Anderson, that had survived the many rewrites, but this was Jimmy Carter, not JFK, and it seemed almost out of place.

Carter talked of immigrants and mentioned Italians, which he pronounced "eye-talians," prompting some gasps and a few jeers. Was it just a slip or a way of assuring his South Georgia friends that he had not forgotten his roots?

The speech was a smashing success. Caddell's polls showed it was given a positive rating by 78 percent of Americans. The evening ended in an orgy of unity and euphoria with leaders of all factions of the party crowding the podium. "Daddy" King, invited to give the benediction, provided a stem-winding oration in the best Baptist tradition. "Surely the Lord sent Jimmy Carter to come on out and bring America back where she belongs." Together with Coretta Scott King, "Daddy" King then led the delegates, holding hands, in singing "We Shall Overcome." The absence of Ted Kennedy was the only blemish on the face of perfect unity the Democratic Party was presenting to America.

Mondale had made the decision that he would integrate his staff into Carter's for the fall campaign instead of setting up a separate operation. On July 23, the Carter and Mondale staffs began a two-day retreat to plan and get acquainted at the Sea Pines Plantation on Hilton Head, South Carolina. Carter and Mondale played tennis each day and the two men and their wives spent most of the time getting to know each other.

Carter had made it clear that Jordan would have overall responsibility for the campaign. Mondale set the tone for his own people by showing him considerable deference. With the candidates initially absent, Jordan convened a meeting of the staffs of both men. The Mondale group was led by Dick Moe and Jim Johnson, mature, refined, professional men, tall, well dressed in business suits, and ten years or more older than most of the Carter staff, including Jordan. Patrick Anderson would write of the same meeting, "And then there were Jody and Ham, looking like a couple of raw-boned narrow-eyed South Georgia thugs. There was always a hint of violence in them." There could hardly have been a greater contrast.

Jordan, who had not bothered to change from his shorts and tennis shoes, opened the meeting by introducing members of the Carter staff, beginning with Tim Kraft, who he announced would take on the highly responsible position of field director for the fall campaign.

Then he added, "In the Carter campaign we encouraged our staff to save money on hotel bills by sleeping with our supporters. And this fellow slept in a different bed every night of the campaign." Then, lest anyone missed the double entendre, he added, "It got so bad that in the end we stopped paying him and just sent him bottles of penicillin." There was a ripple of ingratiating laughter from Hamilton's immediate staff. On the Mondale side there was stunned and embarrassed silence. Tim Kraft rose and uncomfortably responded, with Jordan's wife, Nancy, sitting in the front row, "Thanks a lot Ham. You're the one who inspired us all," which was followed by further laughter.

Jordan then introduced Patrick Anderson, who merely raised an acknowledging hand. "Stand up, Pat," Jordan instructed. Anderson rose, whereupon Jordan, in a thinly veiled message to the Mondale staff, added, "Notice how well he obeys orders—that's why he's Jimmy's speechwriter." Anderson would later write of this humiliation:

> Why did this smart, powerful young man behave like such an ass? Because he was insecure and/or a natural-born boor? Because after the success of the acceptance speech he thought I needed humbling? Because he was trying to impress a sweet young thing we'd all spotted on the Mondale staff? All of the above?

Moe and Johnson symbolized "the political and economic elites" Carter had attacked in his speech. With all of their pluses, Jordan and others also brought into the campaign the dark side of the South, a regional inferiority complex reflected as resentment and paranoia. Moe, Johnson, and the rest of their staff were the cultural enemy, who nevertheless had to be accommodated. Holding in his hands the political future of these ambitious, liberal northerners, Hamilton Jordan appeared determined to show them that it was his culture, not theirs, that was going to dominate in the campaign. His treatment of Kraft and Anderson was a way of showing it, seemingly calculated deliberately to make the Mondale staff squirm. Moe would later say:

> It was a clash of cultures. . . . There always was. We were northern, inclined to be liberal, Ivy league educated, and we reflected Mondale. . . . On the other hand, we had been around politics for a long time and we knew this was a big diverse country. . . . It was an interesting weekend.

Subsequently, Moe and Jordan worked well together and came to respect each other's talents.

The following Monday, July 22, Carter began a series of three day-long meetings with national experts in the areas of defense and national security, economics, and foreign policy/international economics. For each meeting Carter had invited a dozen or so individuals who paid their own airfare to the Atlanta airport where they were met by a chartered bus that drove them the three hours to Plains and then along the dusty red dirt road to Miss Lillian's "Pond House." For most of these members of the Democratic policy establishment, it was the first time they had been to Southwest Georgia, and a long time since they had ridden a bus to go anywhere. But such was the allure of meeting with the nominee to parade themselves as potential appointees that they were willing to subject themselves to the indignities involved.

The first group included Paul Warnke, former assistant secretary of defense; Paul Nitze and Cyrus Vance, who had both held high positions in the Defense Department; Harold Brown, a former secretary of the air force; two highly regarded young Washington lawyers, James Woolsey and Walter Slocombe; Barry Blechman from the Brookings Institution; and Lynn Davis from Columbia University. While the ever-growing press corps waited patiently outside, they presented to Carter (and Mondale, who told his staff how much he hated making the arduous trips to Plains) their views on security matters and especially U.S./Soviet treaty commitments. Carter took notes as he peppered them with questions. At the conclusion of the meeting, beginning, "Here's what I learned today," he gave the media a fifteen-minute detailed summary of exactly what had been said in the six-hour session. His ability to absorb, assimilate, organize, and concisely regurgitate their complex material stunned most of his distinguished guests.

A day later he did the same thing with a group of economists that included Laurence Klein from the University of Pennsylvania; Arthur

Okun, former chairman of the President's Council of Economic Advisors; Charles Schultze, a former budget director; Richard Cooper of Yale; Lester Thurow of MIT; and Albert Sommers of the Conference Board. Carolyn Shaw Bell of Wellesley College was not able to attend, but had provided him with a study showing that unemployment could be reduced a full percentage point without increasing inflation. He was particularly intrigued by it and sought the reaction of his guests. With a one-day interval, he had a third meeting, on foreign policy and international economics, where the attendees included Zbigniew Brzezinski; Richard Gardner of Columbia; Tony Lake with International Voluntary Service; Michael Blumenthal; Milton Katz; Robert Pastor; and again Richard Cooper and Cyrus Vance. One of the more impressive participants was Richard Holbrooke, who was in the process of joining Stu Eizenstat's "Issues Staff" in charge of foreign policy, and had been largely responsible for putting together the list of invitees for these meetings.

During the intervening day, George Bush, the director of the CIA, had come to Plains to give Carter the standard briefing accorded presidential nominees. A few days earlier, Carter had made an attack on the Republican administration for the dubious (but common) practice of appointing candidates repudiated at the polls to high political office, citing George Bush as a prime example. Carter felt obliged to begin the meeting by apologizing.

A four-day trip to the West Coast was scheduled. At the planning meeting it was mentioned that Carter had accepted an invitation to stop en route to the Atlanta airport at Lake Sinclair, near Macon, for the annual picnic organized by Phil Walden, president of Capricorn Records, sponsor of several key fund-raising concerts during the primaries. Jody Powell expressed concern that with a raft of rock stars and entertainment people attending, there might be some drug use. With the large national media entourage now following the candidate, Powell worried about the potential for a damaging story. Carter's response was succinct and to the point: "Phil is my friend and some things are more important than politics. I'm going."

The West Coast trip began on August 22 in Los Angeles. He first went to a dinner organized by Bob Strauss and hosted by Lew Wasserman, which was attended by a group of movie industry executives eager to talk to Carter about tax shelters. He was then whisked by limousine to a late-night reception at Warren Beatty's apartment in the Beverly Wilshire Hotel. Among the fifty guests were Faye Dunaway, Robert Altman, Diana Ross, Sidney Poitier, Hugh Hefner, Norman Lear, Neil Simon, Tony Randall, Peter Falk, and Dennis Weaver. In his introduction Beatty made clear that his friends were the liberal element of the Hollywood elite, referring to them jokingly as "being pinkos, leftists, commies," but as having a "rising enthusiasm" for his guest. Carter made some preliminary comments and answered questions, many of them thoroughly fatuous, with lighthearted banter. Then Jerry Brown arrived. As if provoked by Brown's presence, Carter then concluded with a serious and passionate statement:

> If we make a mistake, the chances are we won't actually go to prison, and if we don't like the public school system, we put our kids in private schools. But the overwhelming majority of the American people are touched directly and personally when government is ill-managed or insensitive or callous or unconcerned about those kinds of problems.
>
> When the tax structure is modified, which Congress does almost every year, you can rest assured that powerful people who are well organized, who have good lawyers, who have lobbyists in Washington, don't get cheated. But there are millions in this country who do get cheated, and they are the very ones who can't afford it.
>
> We take our transportation for granted. We can go out and get into our Chevrolet or our Buick or our Cadillac or our Rolls-Royce and go anywhere we want to. A lot of people don't have automobiles. I can go a mile from my house, I can go 200 yards from my house, and people are there who are very poor, and when they get sick it is almost impossible for them to get a doctor.
>
> There's a need for public officials—presidents, governors, congressmen, and others—to bypass the lobbyists and the special-interest groups and our own circle of friends who are very fortunate, and try to understand those who are dependent on government to give them a decent life.
>
> When people organize, there's an almost built-in separation from the kind of people I've just been describing. Doctors really care about their patients, but when doctors organize and hire a lobbyist, the lobbyist doesn't give a damn about the patients.
>
> The same thing with lawyers. They really take care of their clients. But when those lawyers organize, get a lobbyist, those lobbyists don't care anything about clients. The same thing with farmers and people in business.
>
> So, I say, public servants like me, and Jerry Brown, and others have a responsibility to bypass the big shots, including you and people like you and like I was, and make a concerted effort to understand the people who are poor, black, speak a foreign language, who are not well educated, who are inarticulate, who have some monumental problem, and at the same time run the government in a competent way, well organized, and efficient, manageable, so that those services which are so badly needed can be delivered.

Carter did not need to make such a passionate outburst, but he felt provoked. Although he was barely the nominee, Strauss and Wasserman were already subjecting Carter to wealthy businessmen pushing for self-serving tax breaks. The movie stars might consider themselves liberals, but in Carter's perception they lived in a gilded cage that shielded them from really understanding the hardships and deprivations of ordinary Americans. At another level he felt their liberalism lacked either considered thought or the Christian underpinnings that had shaped his own beliefs. His reference to "the big shots, including you and people like you and like I was" suggested he had undergone a change they had not, which allowed him to lecture them. Before he left Los Angeles, Carter told the Secret Service that he no longer wanted to be driven around in a limousine and that a standard sedan would suffice.

Carter went on to Seattle to address the annual convention of the American Legion. He was accompanied by triple-amputee Vietnam veteran and former Georgia state senator, Max Cleland. At that time a staff member of the Senate Veterans Committee, Cleland describes how Carter, wearing an American Legion hat, surprised the audience by saying that he was proud to address them as a fully paid-up member of his American Legion Post in Americus. As Cleland recalls:

> He went through about twenty or twenty-one points in which he called for improving the VA, hospital care, sensitivity to Vietnam veterans, and the like. Twenty-one points that they applauded. But . . . when he got to that one line, "and I plan to pardon draft evaders to heal the nation's wounds," the entire American Legion audience got up and booed as a massive chorus.

The vehemence of the reaction stunned and frightened Cleland. The open venting of such raw anger against a presidential nominee seemed not only unprecedented and inappropriate but alarming. Carter merely stood at the podium with a wry smile on his face until, after three long minutes, the boos eventually subsided. In contrast he was followed to the podium by Ford's running mate, Senator Robert Dole, a wounded World War II veteran. "The president's position is unequivocal," Dole said. "No blanket pardon, no blanket amnesty, no blanket clemency." The legionnaires cheered wildly. But it was Carter's statement that got the coverage on the nightly news, and what he lost in the hall he gained with an electorate who shared his desire to start healing the nation.

Democratic standard bearers traditionally opened their campaigns with a Labor Day speech in Detroit's Cadillac Square. Carter decided that he did not want to launch his effort in Gerald Ford's backyard. Patrick Anderson had suggested as an alternative Franklin Roosevelt's "Little White House" at Warm Springs, Georgia, about 60 miles from Plains, and Carter liked the idea. At a superficial level it would send a symbolic message to that element of the party still rooted in the New Deal. Unremarked by the press, there was a deeper link. It was while driving around Southwest Georgia during the incipient years of the depression, when he was living at Warm Springs, that FDR was first awakened to the poverty and suffering that gripped much of rural America. It transformed his thinking and played a significant part in the genesis of the New Deal, among other things, leading to the rural electrification program that so changed the region and the early life of Jimmy Carter.

For an event at which a local son was launching a presidential campaign, the crowd was modest, mostly local friends and longtime supporters. Carter gave a conventional speech paying tribute to Roosevelt and Truman, attacking Ford for being like Herbert Hoover and failing to provide leadership for the country. He cited the Truman statement, "The buck stops here," as symbolizing his own leadership, and he would carry the phrase with him to the White House. His biggest applause came when he said, "When there's a choice between welfare and work, let's go to work." He repeated, as he had done throughout the campaign, "I owe the special interests nothing. I owe the people everything."

In Atlanta, the campaign had moved into the luxurious combined office building and hotel Colony Square, at the corner of 14th Street and Peachtree. As he did for the primaries, Jordan had developed a detailed formula for allocating the time of the two nominees, money for the field operation, and media buys based on the electoral college votes of each state and its traditional Democratic potential. Under the new campaign finance law, each campaign received 21.8 million federal dollars and was not allowed to conduct other fund-raising activities. This was a distinct advantage to Carter, who could never have competed with the Republican fund-raising potential. At the same time, $21.8 million was not much to gain the attention of the American public against an incumbent who could command media coverage at will.

Tim Kraft began hiring experienced Democratic operatives to run the field operations in the states. Among those he met with were Bill Clinton, who had just won the Democratic nomination for attorney general in Arkansas, and his wife, Hillary Rodham. Clinton was offered the chance to run Texas for Carter as he had done for McGovern in 1972, but decided instead to stay in Arkansas to work with Carter's Annapolis classmates Jackson Stephens and Al Rusher. Hillary Rodham, however, joined the campaign as a deputy field director.

Most of those whom Kraft hired had worked for Carter's opponents in the primaries. It was one way of bringing the party together, and these people had relationships with the party regulars, labor, and other key constituencies necessary to win a general election. The downside was that they were often ambivalent about Carter himself, while wanting only to be allied with a winner. Few were ever trusted by the Georgians. Many early Carter loyalists found themselves shunted aside in favor of the newcomers. A sense of angry betrayal gripped grassroots Carter workers, many of whom had worked hard for two years to help him secure the nomination, but now found the campaign in their states taken over by those who had worked for the opposition.

The problem was caused by Carter's perception that his success was primarily due to his own efforts and those of people immediately around him. This view was reflected in the limited use the campaign was to make of the most popular party figures, including Carter's primary opponents, purportedly because there wasn't enough money to pay their campaigning expenses. Many Democratic stars received a perfunctory call from Carter and then were left to sit out the campaign.

Bob Strauss was no fan of Carter and had been willing to support anyone who might deny him the nomination. He had also treated Jordan contemptuously during the 1974 congressional campaign. Therefore, it was anticipated that Carter would replace him with someone more compatible. However, right after the convention, Carter asked Strauss to remain on the job, calling him "the greatest party chairman I have ever known" (actually the only party chairman he had ever really known). There were practical considerations for this. Strauss was good at the job, he had the trust of most party leaders, and continuity going into the general election was important. Anne Wexler, deeply indebted to Strauss for past favors and a rising force in the Carter campaign, actively lobbied for his retention. However, more significant, Carter and Jordan saw Strauss as the quintessential opportunist whose loyalty would be absolutely predictable as long as they had the power. Although Jewish, Strauss was also very much a Texan, and the Georgians found him more on their cultural wavelength than most of the northern liberals.

Stu Eizenstat had continued the process begun during the primaries of gathering around him an impressive array of substantive experts. They churned out impressive position papers, but they had considerable difficulty in getting Carter to utilize any of their material in his campaign speeches. Carter needed strong support from the liberal wing of the party. He tried to hold them with the rhetoric of social, and particularly racial, justice without spelling out specific programs. He was equally cognizant of the need to appeal to moderates and conservatives. More than anything, however, he was most comfortable with what had consistently worked for him in the past. Jody Powell said, "There'll be no surprises. He just told people what he believed and what he meant to do, and he isn't going to fool around with any other approach." Similarly Hamilton Jordan said to Patrick Anderson after Carter had given a very well-received substantive speech on human rights, "I wouldn't care if Jimmy never made another speech like that. I just want to hit our basic themes over and over." It was a view echoed by Rafshoon, who believed that if Carter avoided making substantive speeches the press would be forced to write only about "the basic themes." In fact, without substance the press tended to search relentlessly for negative stories as it was the only way of making news.

On the Thursday before Labor Day, there was a strategy meeting at Carter's house where Kirbo, in particular, expressed concern that the public was seeing him as too liberal. Carter described it as "an assessment of the obvious attempt by the Republicans . . . to picture me as a spendthrift, ultraliberal candidate and the agreement among us was just to return to the basic themes I had pursued throughout the primary months." Perhaps not surprisingly, Mondale, who was used to concrete programs and proposals, would say that while his own campaigning was going well, he just did not understand what those basic themes were that he was now supposed to be articulating. Although Carter asked Anderson to write up for Mondale an outline of the key issues they were running on, it was an impossible task, because there was really only one theme—faith in Jimmy Carter and the sense of hope he sought to inspire in the American people. In the following days, however, adhering to Kirbo's advice and at the risk of alienating the liberal support he had carefully cultivated, Carter did talk more about the need for a balanced budget and other traditional Republican concerns.

There was a certain irony in the fact that Carter, who had a consuming interest in the issues and prided himself on being thoroughly knowledgeable on every subject, did not like to make set speeches detailing his positions. "Just get me back to the shopping centers and the factory shifts," he said to Jordan repeatedly. He was thoroughly energized by the one-to-one contact, while a major speech was just something to get through. Unfortunately, this approach that worked so well in the primaries was not appropriate to the general election where people expected speeches that laid out a candidate's intentions. The general election also differed in that network television relied on set-piece speeches to provide the single sound bite for the evening news. One-to-one campaigning provided almost nothing.

As the campaign began in earnest, the members of the Carter family again spread out across the country. It was very difficult for Jimmy and Rosalynn, who counted so much on each other's emotional support, to be apart for another eight weeks. Rosalynn, however, had continued to mature as a seasoned political campaigner. In March, she had turned down an invitation to address the Women's National Democratic Club, saying, "I don't think I am ready for an audience like that." By September, she comfortably appeared on *Meet the Press*. While there was always some trepidation among the staff when Jimmy was to appear on a network program, there was never any such apprehension about Rosalynn, because she always seemed the more surefooted. Jimmy was the first to acknowledge her skills:

She has always had the same qualities and confidence that she has become recognized [for] by the public. I have never seen a political performance as good as hers on *Meet the Press* in my life. . . . She even has a better awareness of people and issues than I do. I'm too encapsulated by staff and the Secret Service, local officials, and so forth. She's there, is more intimate with the average voting citizen than am I during this part of the campaign. Her advice on debate points and techniques and emphasis is almost infallible.

Carter's rhetorical commitment to women was unassailable as evidenced by the accolades he received from feminists at the convention. His attention had been drawn to a study by Edith van Horne of the UAW, which showed that since the Vietnam War, wives, daughters, and mothers were no longer necessarily voting the same way as the male union members. Later this would be labeled the "gender gap." Prompted by this evidence, Carter established the Committee of 51.3 Percent (the percentage of women in the population) to woo women as a separate constituency for the first time.

However, for all the abstract commitment to women, they were marginalized in the national campaign and excluded from any major decision-making role. Thoroughly fed up, one of them from Georgia eventually leaked a story on this hypocrisy to Al Hunt of the *Wall Street Journal*. Hamilton Jordan convened a meeting to deal with the ensuing uproar. According to Connie Plunkett, he opened it by making an intendedly humorous but derogatory statement about the role of women, leading to a heated confrontation with her. He spent the remainder of the session focusing not on how to improve the role of women in the campaign but on who might have leaked the story. Despite their anger at the repeated humiliations, the women sought to put the best public face on the situation, because they believed that Carter, as he showed in his partnership with Rosalynn, did not share Jordan's attitude.

Part of the problem was that as long as his own needs on the campaign trail were met, Carter was happy to leave the organization to Jordan. Carter was fortunate to have recruited Jim King as chief of scheduling and advance, an experienced professional who had previously worked for Teddy Kennedy. King kept the plane on schedule and Carter happy. Patrick Anderson would later write of the operation as a whole, "I've been in Mexican whorehouses that were better organized than the Carter campaign." He was close to the mark.

On July 21, Robert Scheer, a free-lance journalist doing a piece on Carter for *Playboy* magazine, conducted the first of a total of five hours of interviews with Carter. When Scheer's interview request was granted, it was felt that every effort should be made to reach as broad a constituency as possible. Carter was also concerned that the reporting on his religious beliefs made him seem moralistic, prudish, and judgmental, which he was not. Doing a series of relaxed interviews for *Playboy* during the lazy days of summer was seen by Carter and Powell as a way to explain his religious views, while showing that he was a "regular guy." A recent similar interview with Jerry Brown in *Playboy* had been very favorably received. Powell also says he understood that he would be allowed time to review and comment on the finished article before it went to press. However, the next time he heard about it was on September 10 when *Playboy* editor Barry Golson, called to say he and Scheer would be talking about it the following morning on the *Today* show. Scheer, an aggressive, incisive journalist, claimed he had agreed only to provide Powell with a copy of the article before the magazine hit the newsstands, and therefore had honored his commitment by arranging to have a copy, as it was appearing in the magazine, delivered to Powell's hotel room at New York's Statler-Hilton.

The following morning, Carter and his entourage were departing from Penn Station on a whistle-stop trip through New Jersey and Pennsylvania intended to invoke memories of Truman's 1948 campaign. Jody passed out copies of the *Playboy* interview to journalists, seeking to minimize its significance. The more savvy reporters, especially Charles Mohr of the *New York Times*, realized that they were sitting on a keg of gunpowder.

Scheer had skillfully engaged Carter in several long intellectual discussions concerning his religious faith and its potential impact on his role as the nation's top public official. The two men were like people from different planets and each regarded the other as quite strange. Struggling to have Scheer and, through him, his readers understand his religious beliefs, Carter not only made personally revealing statements but resorted to a vernacular that was quite outside his normal usage, in an attempt to reach people on their terms. On the surface the interview seemed a straightforward recitation of Carter's Christian beliefs and values. However, Scheer had pressed Carter on how his religious views concerning adultery, homosexuality, and "victimless crimes" might influence his decisions as president in such matters as appointing judges or the enforcement of federal laws, to which Carter responded:

> Committing adultery, according to the Bible, which I believe in, is a sin. For us to hate one another, for us to have sexual intercourse outside marriage, for us to engage in homosexual activities, for us to steal, for us to lie, all these are sins. But Jesus teaches us not to judge other people. We don't assume the role of judge and say to another human being, "You're condemned because you commit sins." All Christians, all of us acknowledge that we are sinful, and the judgment comes from God not from another human being.

As the interviews wore on, Carter became increasingly frustrated with Scheer's apparent inability to grasp that he could separate his personal religious views from decisions he would make as president, and even more important, that he did not judge or feel superior to those, who by his Christian standards, sinned. Perhaps because of Scheer's own different background, he seemed unable to understand how important the sin of pride was to a Christian like Carter, and how critical the issue of humility was as an antidote. Scheer was apparently unknowingly touching a raw nerve with Carter, who was struggling to come to grips with the transformation in his self-image from former governor to presidential nominee to potential president.

As the final interview was ending, and Scheer and Golson were walking to the door, Carter, unaware Scheer had turned his tape recorder back on, made one last effort to get through to them by showing that he considered himself as much a sinner by Christ's standards as anyone else and by using language that he thought might reinforce that view. Part of what he said was:

> The thing that is drummed into us all the time is not to be proud, not to be better than anyone else, not to look down on people, but to make ourselves acceptable in God's eyes through our own actions and recognize the simple truth that we are saved by grace.
>
> . . . And Christ set some impossible standards for us. Christ said, "I tell you that anyone who looks on a woman with lust has already committed adultery." I have looked on a lot of women with lust; I've committed adultery in my heart many times. This is something God recognizes I will do—and I have done it—and God forgives me for it. But that does not mean I condemn someone who not only looks on a woman with lust but leaves his wife and shacks up with somebody out of wedlock.
>
> Christ says don't consider yourself better than someone else because one guy screws a whole bunch of women while the other guy is loyal to his wife. The guy who is loyal to his wife ought not to be condescending or proud because of a relative degree of sinfulness.

At an earlier time in the campaign the article might have caused little stir, but in the white heat of the general election what should have been a sincere and frank explanation of his beliefs became a sensation. First, it enraged many in Carter's most bedrock constituency, southern evangelical Christians. That he would do an interview for *Playboy* at all upset them. Mixing up religious values with talk about love in a magazine dedicated to the commercialization of lust and using such terms as "screw" and "shack up" made many conservatives question his real sincerity as a Christian.

The Reverend W. A. Criswell, the hardline fundamentalist pastor of the nation's largest Baptist congregation, the First Baptist Church of Dallas, said, "I am highly offended by this. I think he's mixed up in his moral values, and I think the entire church membership will feel the same way. The whole thing is highly distasteful." Few Baptists wanted to defend him. Even Nelson Price, Carter's close friend and pastor of the Roswell Street Baptist Church in Marietta, Georgia, would not speak up. "I had a million-and-a-half-dollar building campaign going," he said. "I guess I just got cold feet."

Among others who had accepted Carter's devout religious views, but were not Southern Baptists, his use of the terms "screw" and "shack up" seemed to undermine his image of moral purity. For cynical sophisticates his talk about lusting in his heart and equating it with actual infidelity seemed not only patently absurd but added to what Jordan had earlier labeled the "weirdo factor." For Jews fearfully sensitive to proselytizing by evangelical Christians, there was something slightly unnerving about the unquestioning sincerity and vehemence with which Carter had sought to sell two Jewish reporters on his Christian beliefs. The cynics in Carter's media entourage questioned how he was going to provide moral leadership for the country when he could not even convince his senior staff about the sins of adultery and fornication. What should have been an article that enabled the country to have a better in-depth understanding of the real Jimmy Carter ended up hurting him with almost every group.

Carter left the campaign train in Pittsburgh and returned to Plains to prepare for the first debate with Gerald Ford. He tried to ignore the *Playboy* story to focus on his review books, but it would not go away and his refusal to talk with other reporters was criticized as stonewalling. Between the boost that the Republicans received coming out of their convention, the *Playboy* interview, the disarray of the Carter campaign, and various other missteps Carter had made, the hefty lead Carter had once enjoyed— the largest ever recorded in a presidential race—was completely evaporated by September 21, the Tuesday before the Thursday debate. By Wednesday night, Caddell's surveys showed Carter behind. Carter himself summarized his perceptions of reasons for his crash in the polls:

> The Republican Party was divided . . . about 30–35 percent said they were not going to vote for Ford, and vote for me. But after the Republican convention they were united and the Reagan voters naturally went back to Ford. . . . We have been hurt by apparent confusion in our campaign, a lot of publicity about our intrastate coordinators not doing a good job, characterization of the campaign as being confused, accusations made against me by the Republican convention that I had shifted from a moderate conservative candidate to an ultraliberal . . . some reporter said they mentioned my name 113 times at that convention. It made an impression on the American people. They said to

themselves, I presume, that maybe the Jimmy Carter we knew in the primaries is not the real candidate; maybe he is really like the press says. Also, the assumption by me of the role as titular head of the Democratic Party has obvious advantages, but also has disadvantages in that where I was an unestablishment person by myself, I became blessed or saddled with support of all Democratic members of Congress and U.S. senators, the Democratic Party apparatus, a vice-presidential candidate who is running with me, the labor unions, and so forth [which] went against the Washington-outsider-going-against-the-establishment-candidate advantage.

And then there was a time when nobody realized Ford was not campaigning; he seemed to be conducting a very calm, well-managed, organized, unshakable campaign. I always seemed to be fluctuating and uncertain. There is a growing realization that the reason Ford seems to be calm and unshakable is that he is not doing anything except hiding in the White House, while we have been out in every corner of the United States.

Carter was confident that if he could break the "rose garden" strategy and contest Ford man-to-man without the aura of the White House, he could prove smarter, better informed, more decisive, and generally more qualified to be president. The debates, three between the presidential and one between the vice-presidential aspirants, seemed to offer that opportunity. There had been no presidential debate since the legendary contests between Nixon and Kennedy in 1960, so the public interest and media hype were intense, with an anticipated television audience of 100 million. Ford had prepared by having mock debates using stand-ins for Carter. Carter, on the other hand, with a certain serenity, had limited himself almost exclusively to studying briefing books on the issues, characteristically believing that being more knowledgeable was more important than his style or presentation.

Lengthy negotiations over the specifics of the debates had taken place between the two camps under the auspices of the League of Women Voters. They covered such minutiae as an agreement that there be an especially deep well for the water glass on Ford's podium to guard against the chance that he might knock it over, reinforcing his image of an ill-coordinated "klutz." The first debate took place at the old Walnut Street Theater in Philadelphia on September 23 before an invited audience of 450 people. The candidates were to be questioned by Elizabeth Drew of the *New Yorker,* Frank Reynolds of ABC News, and James Gannon of the *Wall Street Journal.* Perhaps because of the legendary Nixon/Kennedy debates, everyone present was gripped by the sense that they were witnessing a moment of history. There was an electric tension in the theater as the two candidates came onto the stage.

As the questioning began, Carter seemed exceedingly tense, answering a question about unemployment with a deluge of statistics, but in a stilted and rote manner. He was clearly uncertain of himself and unduly deferential to Ford. He would later say:

> The only thing that ever concerned me about the first debate was an overwhelming respect for the presidency and an inability in the first fourth or third of the debate to treat Mr. Ford as an equal. There was a surprising deference that only became apparent when the debate started. I think my having been in the navy so long, and my having been from the South, probably accentuated a natural inclination to respect the office of the president and the one who is in the office. It was only after Mr. Ford made a couple of answers that were personally critical of me that I relaxed and enjoyed the rest of the debate, and realized that he was running for president the first time, like I was, and that he was the nominee of his party, as I was, and although he was the incumbent, that, as far as the debate went, we were equals, and once I removed that reticence and treated it as a contest, I didn't feel ill-at-ease or nervous anymore.

Just as Carter was hitting his stride, the sound system went inexplicably dead. For an astonishing twenty-seven minutes, while 100 million viewers waited and television technicians fumbled, the two candidates remained on stage silent and without talking to each other. When the debate finally resumed, Ford still had the edge, but the debate ended in what for all practical purposes was a draw.

The next morning Carter flew to Texas where he had to deal with another aspect of the *Playboy* interview, in which he had said, "But I don't think I would ever take on the same frame of mind that Nixon or Johnson did, lying, cheating, and distorting the truth." He had already called Lady Bird Johnson to apologize, but equating Nixon and Johnson was hardly a prudent move for a Democratic nominee, especially in the eyes of Texas Democrats for whom Johnson was still a towering party icon. In Houston he sought to convince a group of local reporters that *Playboy* had condensed his comments about Johnson and Nixon, implying that "lying, cheating, and distorting the truth" referred to both men when he had meant it to apply only to Nixon. According to Carter "It completely distorts my feelings about him [Johnson]." The national press corps, now out for blood, knew the record did not support his statements and interpreted his efforts to salvage the situation as damaging for the man who promised, "I will never tell a lie."

Carter's comments about Johnson reflected a longstanding tendency on his part to make, often gratuitously, extravagantly negative comments about people in major positions of power and authority, especially if he did not know them or saw them as representing some repugnant special interest. As governor and as an unknown presidential candidate, it rarely mattered when he made comments such as calling Richard Nixon "the worst president in my lifetime." Now such jibes came back to haunt him as with George Bush and Lyndon Johnson, causing both embarrassment and political damage. Early in the general election campaign he had lambasted Ford, linking him to Nixon by referring regularly to the "Nixon–Ford administration." After the Republican convention he accused Ford and his staff of making "an almost unprecedented personal attack on me." Hamilton Jordan convinced Carter to tone down his language, arguing that the American people saw Ford as an honorable, decent man struggling to do what was right in a job he had not sought. Attacking him personally was only likely to make Carter seem mean-spirited and hardly the candidate of conciliation and love.

That Carter would feel overawed when confronted with Ford in person, or as he had when meeting the Washington power structure at the Fritcheys' house, suggested that Carter still had difficulties modulating defiance versus respect in dealing with authority. Part of it related to his meteoric political ascent, leaving him little time to learn when to be strident and when to be deferential in order to advance his own political interests. But even as he moved toward the ultimate position of authority in the country, he still had an ingrained anti-establishment anti-authority bent.

The *Playboy* problems were suddenly alleviated for Carter on September 30. John Dean, the former White House counsel, had written an article on the Republican convention for *Rolling Stone* magazine in which he described a conversation between himself, singer Pat Boone, Sonny Bono (later a Republican congressman), and a Ford cabinet member. Pat Boone had asked the cabinet member why it was not possible for the party of Lincoln to attract more black supporters. "I'll tell you why you can't attract coloreds," the cabinet member replied, "because coloreds only want three things: first, a tight pussy; second, loose shoes; and third, a warm place to shit." The story went largely unnoticed for a month until a reporter for *New Times* identified the cabinet member as Agriculture Secretary Earl Butz. A TV network reporter then called the only black member of the U.S. Senate, Republican Edward Brooke of Massachusetts, and asked for a comment. Within a week, on October 4, Butz would resign. Carter attacked Ford for his delay in firing him, implying Ford had some sympathy for what he had said, which the president resented and said was unfair.

Ford was personally very distressed by Butz's comment as it was quite antithetical to his own views and cast him and his administration in an embarrassing light. In addition, it lost him the votes among the few blacks who might have voted Republican and those of an indeterminate number of independents. The Butz affair had the effect of precluding the possibility of the Republicans playing the race card to appeal in the South and elsewhere. While Ford, a decent man, might not have done so in any case, he would be the only Republican presidential candidate during a thirty-year period not to make that appeal; if he had, he might have beaten Carter.

The second debate took place on October 6 in the San Francisco Palace of Fine Arts. Ford was distracted by the Butz matter, and by attacks on him for his financial dealings as a congressman. The subject of the debate was foreign policy and his advisors encouraged him to make an issue of Carter's lack of experience and the risk the American people would be taking in turning over the nation's security to him.

Pumped up by his staff, as the debate started Carter was immediately on the attack. Both men fielded the questions without significant advantage until Max Frankel of the *New York Times* asked Ford about the Helsinki Agreement. After a fairly routine statement concerning the limitation of nuclear weapons and grain sales to the Soviet Union, he added:

> And what has been accomplished by the Helsinki Agreement? Number one, we have an agreement where they notify us and we notify them of any military maneuvers that are to be undertaken. They have done it. And in both cases where they've done so, there is no Soviet domination of Eastern Europe and there never will be under a Ford administration.

Incredulous, but assuming Ford had merely misspoken, Frankel gave him an opportunity to correct himself and clarify his position. Ford merely dug himself into a deeper hole.

> I don't believe, Mr. Frankel, that the Yugoslavians consider themselves dominated by the Soviet Union. I don't believe the Romanians consider themselves dominated by the Soviet Union. I don't believe the Poles consider themselves dominated by the Soviet Union. As a matter of fact, I visited Poland, Yugoslavia, and Romania to make certain that the people of the United States are dedicated to their independence.

There were audible gasps in the theater. Carter, suppressing his glee, took full advantage of the situation, coolly taking Ford's statement apart step by step. When the debate concluded, Ford seemed still oblivious to his error as were most of the viewers. An early poll suggested they thought Ford had won by 11 percent. However, as soon as the media analysts started pointing out the faux pas, and Polish-American and other ethnic groups began expressing outrage, public opinion turned heavily against the president. The following morning in Albuquerque, New Mexico, Carter launched into a sustained attack on Ford.

During our recent debate . . . Mr. Ford said, and I quote, "There is no Soviet domination of Eastern Europe." He referred to Yugoslavia, to Czechoslovakia, and to follow he said, "Each of these countries is independent, autonomous." Well, the Berlin wall is still there. There are twenty divisions and 300,000 Soviet troops in Eastern European countries.

It was a turning point for Carter. Polls showed the public, by a massive margin of 45 percent, now believed he had won the debate. While Ford struggled to mend fences with different ethnic groups, inviting angry delegations to see him at the White House, Carter hammered away to the point of overkill. "Apparently when Mr. Ford went to Poland, as happened to Mr. Romney last time, he was brainwashed," Carter crowed, using what had in political lore become shorthand for gullibility and incompetence. A Gallup poll on October 15 showed Carter had regained the lead 48 percent to 42 percent.

The same day an unprecedented debate was held between the vice-presidential candidates in Houston. It was a highly partisan affair, with Dole going a long way to establish a reputation for meanness that would cling to him for years to come. Having attributed all America's twentieth-century wars to Democrats, he said, "I figured out the other day if we added up the killed and wounded in Democrat wars in this century, it would be about 1.6 million Americans, enough to fill the city of Detroit." With reporters after the debate, Mondale remarked, "I think that Senator Dole has richly earned his reputation as a hatchet man tonight. Does he really mean there was a partisan difference over our involvement in the fight against Nazi Germany?" Pollsters estimated Mondale's performance had added a 3-percentage-point advantage for the ticket.

Ford launched an upbeat campaign aimed at making people feel positive about the country and implying that it was in good hands without need for change. His most effective TV ad showed a marching band playing on a warm sunny day while voices sang "I'm feeling good about America." For those nervous about change and particularly about Carter it had a powerful appeal, and its patriotic theme tended to offset concerns generated by his misstatements in the second debate.

The Carter camp was increasingly concerned about their candidate's problems with the women's vote. Despite Carter's strong support for ERA, his position on abortion, and the activist role that Rosalynn had played in the campaign, he had been hurt by the *Playboy* interview, and word of the marginalization of women on his campaign staff had leaked out to the feminists who had been so taken with him at the convention. The Ford people sought to exploit the situation. Columnist Jack Anderson said on ABC on October 11, "President Ford's campaign aides have been researching Jimmy Carter's past for a sex scandal. They have also used me in a scheme to get the story published." Anderson went on to describe how the Ford staff had provided him with the name of a woman with whom Carter "had had an affair." Later they gave him four other names. He had mentioned the tip to no one, but suddenly found reporters from all the major publications calling him to say Republican sources had told them he was about to break a major sex scandal on Jimmy Carter. A feeding frenzy had been created with every reporter terrified of missing out. Anderson then said he was prompted to carry out his own thorough investigation and had concluded, "I have found no truth to the sex charges against Carter."

Carter was furious about the rumors, which took on a brief life of their own. The anger he felt was substantially directed at Gerald Ford, and it helped overcome any reticence he had about being aggressive toward him in person, which was reflected in the second debate.

Ford was hurt again by a member of his own administration, chairman of the Joint Chiefs of Staff, General George Brown. Two years earlier, Brown had told an audience that Jews had too much influence in the Congress and that they owned "the banks in this country, the newspapers." He now told an interviewer that Israel and its armed forces had "got to be considered a burden" to the United States. Both candidates dismissed it as an inconsequential comment, but it played to Carter's advantage with a segment of the electorate that still had serious doubts about him.

Despite his brief surge, Caddell's polls were again showing Carter sliding in the big states by the last ten days of October. The final debate was scheduled for October 22 at the College of William and Mary in Williamsburg, Virginia. Barbara Walters was the moderator and, to Carter's pleasure, one of the panel of three questioners was Jack Nelson, Washington Bureau chief of the *Los Angeles Times*. Carter took the opportunity to confront the *Playboy* issue head-on, describing it as a mistake and saying, "If I should ever decide in the future to discuss my deep Christian beliefs and condemnation and sinfulness, I'll use another forum than *Playboy*." Neither candidate landed any telling blows.

In the remaining days of the campaign, Carter sought to shore up his support in the South, where he was counting on regional pride to give him the solid electoral college bloc he needed. Ford had tried to make inroads, especially in Virginia and Mississippi, where Wallace supporters, still bitter over Carter's usurpation of their hero, were likely to vote for Ford, or stay home. Jim Free, one of Carter's southern coordinators, had tried to get Wallace to campaign for Carter, but he had responded, "Well, you know my friends just aren't excited about the Carter presidency." Finally Carter called George Wallace and persuaded him to go the panhandle of Florida and to Mississippi. In a speech in Jackson, Wallace said, "It's all right to be a conservative Democrat and vote for Jimmy Carter."

Election day, November 2, dawned bright and sunny. After voting in Plains, Jimmy and Rosalynn arrived at Atlanta's Omni International Hotel around 5 P.M. and, with the rest of the family, settled into the Capitol Suite on the fifteenth floor. There was nothing left to do but wait. It had been an extraordinary odyssey since the five of us had met four years and a matter of days earlier at the Georgia governor's mansion, when, so overawed by the audacity of our own vision, we could not even bring ourselves to utter the word *president*. Now, while standing on the threshold of victory, despite all the work and sacrifice, we knew it could prove to have been an illusion and a mirage.

As expected, Carter established an early lead in southern and eastern states, then Ford began a comeback, winning the prairie states and the traditional Republican strongholds of New Hampshire and Vermont. By midnight things had stalled with a number of key states in the balance. Carter was calling mayors Daley and Beame to get their reading of their states; he would lose Illinois and win New York. By 2 A.M., Carter was still a few electoral votes away from victory. The two key outstanding states were the traditionally Democratic Hawaii and Mississippi. Carter sat holding Rosalynn's hand in front of the television. Downstairs in the World Congress Center more than 3,000 restive campaign workers and supporters had gathered. Finally, in an attempt to slow their impatience, Jody Powell mounted the podium and said, "We have waited more than a hundred years for this moment. We can wait a few minutes more." The largely southern audience roared its approval. Powell understood better than anyone that this was not just the victory of one man, but the final chapter in an entire region's return to the Union.

Finally, at 3:30 A.M., Cliff Finch, the governor of Mississippi, called to tell Carter that he had won Mississippi. Simultaneously Carter watched John Chancellor of NBC announce, "And nine and one half hours after the polls began to close today, we now have a projected winner in the presidential race. NBC news projects James Earl Carter of the state of Georgia, elected president of the United States." Jim Free noted, "I think we won Mississippi by less than 12,000 votes." He attributed that margin to George Wallace. "We owe him a lot," he added. The man whom Carter had worked so hard to replace as the leader of the South had almost certainly played the crucial role in enabling him to ascend to the presidency.

After addressing his exhausted but still exuberant supporters in the World Congress Center, Jimmy and Rosalynn had one more stop to make. Just as dawn was breaking at 5:30, they arrived in Plains. Hundreds of people had waited all night on the main street in front of the old railroad terminal that served as the campaign headquarters. Many had to be at work in a couple of hours. Political campaigns are always emotional experiences for the people closest to them, yet the triumphant homecoming of Jimmy and Rosalynn that morning had an epic impact on everyone present. As dawn was breaking and the Americus high school band played "When the Saints Go Marching In," Jimmy, Rosalynn, and the rest of the Carter family arrived, to be greeted by John Pope and Maxine Reese, who ran the campaign headquarters. What made it so moving and poignant was its symbolism. Here was the American dream come true—the small-town boy who through hard work and tenacity had made it to the presidency, and who moreover had returned to share his triumph with those among whom he had grown up.

Rejecting special-interest support, he had revalidated the nation's faith in populist democracy. For veterans of the civil rights struggle here was a white southerner, whose father was an avowed racist, who had been able to unite blacks and whites and was explicitly committed to ending the racial divide. It was a sight that would have been inconceivable less than ten years before, bringing with it the end of the hundred years of regional isolation inflicted on the South since the Civil War. Jimmy Carter had made America whole again.

CHAPTER 22

For every appointment I get one ingrate and make a hundred
enemies.

—THOMAS JEFFERSON

On May 11, 1976, almost a month before the last primary, Jack Watson had
sent a memo to his law partner, Charles Kirbo, headed, "Preparing for the
Presidency: Some Thoughts on Organizational and Action Requirements,
June 1, 1976, to January 20, 1977." Its genesis, Watson later said, lay in a
thought he had after Carter's Pennsylvania victory. "I said to myself," he
recalls, "good glory. . . . He is going to become president with no networks,
with no government experience beyond the governorship, no *federal* government experience, never been a cabinet officer, never been a congressman, never been a senator. . . . What can we do to alleviate that problem,
that set of problems."

Watson worked on the memo for hours with Jule Sugarman, the administrator for the city of Atlanta, who earlier had had years of federal experience.
The memo meticulously reviewed the relevant legislation and detailed the
steps necessary for a smooth transition of power. He suggested individuals
whose talents could be utilized such as John Macy, former director of the U.S.
Civil Service Commission and personnel director in the Johnson White
House; Dr. Walter Held of the Brookings Institute; and Vernon Jordan,
executive director of the Urban League. Watson concluded by stressing:
*"By all odds the most important recommendation in this document is that Jimmy
Carter immediately designate a Transition Planning Group composed of a coor-
dinator and six (6) lead persons each responsible for a functional area."*

Kirbo passed the memo on to Carter. On June 10, Carter asked Watson
to fly with him from Atlanta to Plains to discuss his proposal.

"I very much like what you proposed. I think it makes sense, and I want
to do it," Carter said, adding, "I want *you* to do it." Watson was taken aback.
His presumption had been that the person Carter should ask to lead such
an effort would be "a thoughtful, respected Washington insider—like John
Gardner [former president of the Carnegie Corporation and former secre-

tary of HEW]. He was the pluperfect example of whom I had in mind, and was specifically whom I had in mind." Watson had envisioned himself continuing to practice law and serving as executive assistant to a figure like Gardner. "All the subjects that needed to be learned and put together, all the networks that needed to be created, all the information that needed to be put together and summarized, needed someone far more knowledgeable than I. I was more of an outsider than Jimmy Carter and fourteen years younger. I was utterly not the right person to do it—in my concept."

"Jimmy, that misses the point," Watson responded. "I'm not the right person to do this. I'll help the person, but the right person is some important, knowledgeable insider." Carter replied:

> No. Wrong. I want you to do it. You have something unique that John Gardner does not have. You know me. And I know you. You know how I want it done. You know my mind. You know my approach. That's why I want you to do it. . . . You need not worry about getting all the help you need. All you have to do is ask and all the John Gardners of the world, the McGeorge Bundys, the Clark Cliffords, and anybody you call will help.

Throughout the summer and fall, Watson quietly assembled a team of young accomplished experts from around the country, including Bowman Cutter, Anthony Lake, Bruce Kirschenbaum, Harrison Welford, and Kurt Hessler, who compiled sets of briefing books and policy analyses relating to each of the major government departments and functions. In a follow-up memo to Carter concerning personnel recruitment, Watson wrote, "This is *the* most important aspect of our entire preparation for your presidency." To address this need he set up the Talent Inventory Program (TIP), a computerized system for handling the names of the most talented potential presidential appointees and those who submitted their own resumes for consideration. The day after the election, November 3, he provided to Carter a series of documents, "Some Thoughts on Selecting Your Cabinet," "Some Thoughts on Organizing the Executive Office of the President," and "Transition Overview," a detailed work program and schedule for the ten weeks prior to the inauguration. These documents were the result of countless hours of discussion Watson and his team had had with former cabinet officers and White House staff, members of Congress, and academics, including Richard Neustadt, Ted Sorensen, Steven Hess, and Joe Califano. No president-elect before or since had ever been so comprehensively staffed in preparation for taking over the office.

The very quality of Watson's work generated profound problems for him. Hamilton Jordan saw Watson creating the government-in-waiting with a degree of management skill, sophisticated knowledge of governance, and acquaintance with the best and the brightest that he could not hope to match. Preoccupied with winning the election, Jordan had volunteered little advice to Watson's operation nor had Watson sought it. An equal, if not greater, problem existed with Stuart Eizenstat, whose issues staff of talented experts paralleled Watson's operation in their abilities and ambitions. Several meetings were held between Watson and Eizenstat and their staffs to try to mute the obvious competition that was developing, but to little avail. Both Jordan and Eizenstat saw Watson as a serious threat to their own roles in a Carter White House. Although Watson denies it, by all appearances, he had launched a masterful power play to become the central figure of the new administration.

Although deeply loyal to Carter, Watson's primary relationship was with Charles Kirbo, on whom he relied to clinch his role with the new president. Bubbling over with talent and ambition, Watson had never been able to assuage Carter's perception of him as opportunistic. On election night in the Carters' suite, Kirbo sought to press Watson's cause, arguing that Watson should be the White House chief of staff. Carter brushed him aside and refused to be pinned down, finally saying sharply, "I can guarantee, Charlie, there will be a role for Jack in the White House, but I don't want to talk about it anymore."

Jimmy and Rosalynn departed immediately after the election for a ten-day vacation on Cumberland Island. Before leaving, Carter dispatched Watson to Washington to oversee the actual transition of power. Watson in turn asked Barbara Blum from Jordan's campaign staff to be his deputy. They tried to call Jordan, but could not reach him on his post-election vacation. Already creating a favorable impression for Carter with the political establishment in Washington, Watson moved into two floors of the HEW building on Constitution Avenue and began to assemble the team to take over the government. The transition, an emotionally traumatic maelstrom of ambition and envy for every incoming administration, would prove particularly so for those who had aligned themselves with Watson.

Watson prided himself on having marshaled the best objective advice he could in preparing the material he had submitted to Carter. However, when it came to the question of the White House staff, he was in a quandary. Carter's preference was to have no chief of staff. It was the one instance in which Watson, concerned about overplaying his hand, compromised his objectivity.

> I went along with what I knew Carter was going to do anyway. . . . I said, "You don't want to have a chief of staff. You don't want to impede access by your other senior staff members to you." But I knew it to be wrong. Why did I know it to be wrong? Not because I'm a genius, but because everybody I had ever talked to said, "It won't work."

Watson felt he could not talk bluntly to Carter the way Kirbo, eighteen years his senior, could. He had also never been a paid staff member like Jordan, Powell, Eizenstat, and Moore, yet he felt they were enough his peers that it would seem inappropriate for him to be criticizing their qualifications for specific White House jobs, especially that of chief of staff. For Watson to suggest, contrary to Carter's inclinations, that there be a chief of staff inevitably begged the question as to whether Watson himself was not the obvious choice. He had assumed, correctly, that Kirbo would act as his advocate.

Carter, however, had a precise vision of what he wanted and stuck to it, saying later:

> I never have wanted to have a major chief of staff between me and the people who worked for me. I have always wanted to have a multiple like seven or eight, or maybe as many as ten people who had direct access to me all of the time without having to go through an interim boss. And I appreciate working that way. I don't even mind if those ten or twelve people are incompatible with each other.

Carter's decision would have profound implications for his presidency, but it was an organizational format that had many roots. President Kennedy had preferred a similar structure, seeing presidential power as being like "the spokes of a wheel," a phrase Carter would regularly use. In contrast to the traditional perception of the military as inherently hierarchical, Carter's most positive naval experiences had been in the submarine service with bright young officers operating as a team around the captain, or around Rickover in the case of the nuclear program. The Baptist church had no hierarchy, with each congregation being autonomous and the preacher being supported by a group of deacons. There was, of course, the obvious parallel of Christ and his disciples. For both Carter and Kennedy, however, it was more a manifestation of their personalities. Neither man was by nature an autocrat. Both relied on their seductive charm that, one on one, they could invariably use to get their way. Both thrived on a certain amount of chaos and both had a distrust of formal structure. At the center of the wheel rather than the top of the pyramid they felt they could exert maximum control while deliberately leaving people in ignorance of exactly where they stood in the overall scheme.

Carter wanted everyone working for him in a functionally limited pigeonhole. Policy, politics, and strategy was to come together only in the Oval Office. He did not want someone, like Watson, with a broad range of talents, integrating and synthesizing under him. Much less did he want an old Washington hand, with political standing in his own right, in that role. A former member of the Georgia congressional delegation observed, "Carter did not like to have people around him whom he felt intimidated by, who he felt were smarter than he." It was more a reflection of his lone-wolf nature and his need always to feel completely in control. His thinking was more like that of a spiritual than a political leader or a manager.

What Carter did not appreciate was the vital role played by the White House chief of staff in organizing the president's time, helping him set priorities, managing the paper flow, and limiting access to those officials who needed decisions only the president could make. Carter did not want a repetition of the excesses of Erlichman and Haldeman that occurred under Richard Nixon. He went, however, to the other extreme. Griffin Bell says, "You would have had absolute chaos if he had not been so intelligent and had he not worked twelve hours a day. . . . He made everything come through him . . . but he was very proud of his system." Carter's intelligence and insatiable capacity for hard work notwithstanding, many argued that chaos was the result.

From the moment Watson arrived in Washington, he was under intense pressure from members of a still distrustful Congress who wanted to open lines of communication with the president-elect. During the general election campaign, affable Frank Moore had served as the liaison with Congress. The day after the election, the *Washington Post* ran a story highlighting Carter's failure to mobilize congressional Democrats behind his campaign as the reason he dropped 20 points in the polls and barely won. Moore would later recall, "They went on to cite how I had done such a poor job, hadn't returned phone calls . . . it's true. . . . I was worrying about getting elected. I wasn't worrying about kissing some freshman congressman's ass." Rightly or wrongly, members of Congress expected to be coddled. Failure to do so meant Carter was coming to Washington as alienated from many members of his own party as from the opposition.

Watson knew that to accomplish his legislative program Carter needed to turn things around and generate a spirit of goodwill on the Hill. Watson was unanimously advised that to reassure the members, someone of stature and prominence, well known to and trusted by Congress, should be appointed as rapidly as possible to be in charge of congressional relations. He called Carter in Plains, and as forcefully as he could he conveyed the message. Carter turned aside Watson's advice and responded sharply, "Frank Moore is my man. He will be there Monday morning and I want you to have an office ready for him." He hung up. Watson was shaken. He liked Moore, but says, "I don't think he should have been head of congressional liaison. I think it was a terrible mistake." One Carter intimate said, "I knew the Carter administration was finished the day I heard Moore was to be in charge of congressional relations."* As one Georgia congressman says, "It immediately signaled the Congress that this was a bunch of ama-

---

* Despite his problems heading Carter's congressional relations, in later years Moore would go on to become a respected and powerful lobbyist for private industry.

teurs coming to town." Asked why Carter did not pick someone like Robert Strauss, an old friend said, "He did not want to put up with Strauss telling him to do this or do that."

When Jordan returned to Atlanta after his vacation, he told Carter of his concern about Watson's role. He was furious that Watson had submitted a budget for the transition allocating him only one staff slot. While Watson did a highly effective job preparing briefing books on the issues and identifying the top talent, Jordan argued, he had failed to address sufficiently the political considerations involved, and especially the need to reward the campaign staff and other supporters who had made the victory possible. Watson, he claimed, was willing to give away that victory to the "liberal establishment," rather than keep control in the hands of their own troops.

With Eizenstat's crucial support, Jordan was able to convince Carter, on November 15, to strip Watson of authority for the top appointments including the White House staff, and assign it to him instead. Stories began to appear in the press portraying Watson as a "walking dead man" who, while still nominally the head of the transition, had lost his power and was no longer the person to see. Behind Watson's back, Jordan began lining up his own appointees for the administration with the aid of his friend Marc Siegel and others. Nevertheless, presidential scholar Steve Hess would later describe Watson's efforts for the Carter transition as "the best in history," and his work would become a model for future administrations.

Jordan also was out in a difficult position. He wanted the power, but had neither the background, knowledge, nor interest in being chief of staff. He equally did not want anyone else in that role. He was happy with Carter's "spokes-of-the-wheel" approach. He envisioned himself in an advisory role, writing thoughtful memos and developing narrow political strategy for Carter as he had done during the campaign, but not having to assume any managerial responsibility. He would later say, "Here I was from South Georgia and was being exposed to all these problems at the very highest level without having any background for understanding a lot of these things." Jordan and Carter, however, understood each other well and Jordan's considerable abilities as a tactician were crucial to Carter, whose desire to do what was right, often lost sight of the political realities necessary to get the job done. With Jordan, many years his junior, he could take or reject his suggestions in a way that he could not so easily have done with a peer. "One of my strengths is my ability to conceptualize, to see an objective and plan how to get there," Jordan says, noting at the same time his lack of management skills. Of their relationship Jordan says:

> I felt completely free to argue with him and differ with him on anything. . . . He pushed people and expected a lot from them. The best thing

about working for him was that you always knew where you stood. He was very direct and straightforward. If you did something he did not like, he would tell you.

During the transition, Dick Cheney, the departing chief of staff, assuming Jordan would be filling that seat, told him, "You've got to get other people to write for you. You don't have time to sit down all day and compose and write yourself." But that was what Jordan planned to do, that was what he was good at, and that was one of the things Carter needed. Recalling his days in the governor's office, Jordan said:

> If I went into the governor's office and had five arguments against something, I wouldn't get beyond point one before he'd be arguing back with me. I'd never get to points two, three, four, and five. When I had a subtle point to make, or a complicated thing to try to influence him on, I'd usually resort to writing it. I knew he couldn't argue with a piece of paper. He'd have to sit down and read it all.

As when he sent the untried Phil Wise to run the primary campaign in Florida, Carter firmly believed that cultural affinity, deep loyalty to him, and reasonable intelligence could transcend lack of knowledge or experience. Carter relied heavily on Jordan in deciding who the other senior White House staff members would be, even for such posts as the president's science advisor. Watson was relegated to a secondary role as the cabinet secretary and assistant for intergovernmental relations. Jody Powell was the unquestioned choice to be press secretary. He had six years of experience handling the press for Carter and had demonstrated his competence throughout the campaign. When he dealt with the media, there was no question that he would be speaking for the president. Stu Eizenstat was rewarded for his loyalty to Jordan by being named the president's assistant for domestic affairs, but fortunately his qualifications and talents were beyond question. Bob Lipshutz became White House counsel; Hugh Carter, Jr., was put in charge of administration. Jordan, to his credit, was willing to make competent Landon Butler his primary deputy.

Jordan filled most of the remaining top White House positions with token appointees to please different interest groups. Midge Costanza was named the constituency liaison, fulfilling Carter's pledge to put a woman in a high-profile White House position for the first time. To demonstrate commitment to minorities, Jordan sought a Hispanic and a black. Joe Aragon, a mild-mannered individual who had worked in the campaign, was picked as a special assistant to the president with unspecified responsibilities, but primarily to serve as a liaison with the Hispanic community.

Jordan and Carter wanted a black woman for the staff and were considering Eleanor Holmes Norton, a highly regarded lawyer, or Martha "Bunny" Mitchell, a campaign worker from the District of Columbia who had been a Udall supporter in the primaries and was a friend of Jordan's. Carter would have won acclaim for appointing Norton, who was widely recognized as both professional and competent and commanded considerable influence with both blacks and women. She was, however, someone of strong views who would not hesitate to express her opinion. "Bunny," on the other hand, while lacking the professional stature or experience of Norton, was expected to be more compliant. Later, when Jordan indicated to me that the job had gone to Mitchell, he added, "I guess we wanted someone we could control."

By filling jobs with people who had no federal government experience, or who were weak, ineffectual, or there solely through loyalty to Jordan, Carter was denied the range of talent and expertise he desperately needed in dealing with Washington. Such appointments occur in every White House, but are less consequential to a president who is already a Washington insider.

One appointment Carter made personally was Esther Peterson as special assistant for consumer affairs. Already in her seventies and with experience in both the Kennedy and Johnson administrations, her name had become synonymous with consumer activism. Carter wanted to establish a Consumer Protection Agency, telling her, "I want the federal government to think like the consumer would think." Carter would form a closer attachment to this warm, decisive woman than he would with any of his non-Georgian appointees. She would reminisce of their relationship: "I can't underline strongly enough my belief in this man." At the 1988 Democratic convention he would ask her to speak as the representative of his administration, saying that she embodied the very best of what it stood for.

In the months since the primaries Carter had read several books on the presidency. Truman, who like himself had entered the presidency with very little preparation, was his favorite and the man with whom he most strongly identified. He admired Woodrow Wilson, who had also assumed office in troubled times, calling for a return to principles and whose presidency was strongly shaped, as Carter's would be, by his own spiritual values.

At the post-convention retreat in Hilton Head, Mondale had spelled out for Carter the activist role he wanted to play as vice president, yet warned by Hubert Humphrey, he feared he might be sidelined as were his predecessors. Now, when he and Dick Moe saw the president-elect in late November, Mondale brought with him, as Carter had suggested, a detailed description of the power-sharing role he wanted to play. In an unprecedented move that would permanently transform the nature of the vice presidency, Carter accepted all of Mondale's suggestions. He assigned him an office in the West Wing, and agreed that Moe would be not only Mondale's chief of staff but also a member of his own senior staff. As vice president, Mondale would be a confidante and participant in all major meetings and policymaking. Carter also told his own staff that an order from Mondale should be treated the same way as an order from the president. Carter also agreed to appoint two Mondale friends to his cabinet, Bob Bergland as secretary of agriculture and Joe Califano as secretary of health, education, and welfare.

Reviewing past inaugural addresses, Carter was impressed that President Wilson had called for national repentance, and decided to use a biblical quote in his own speech. He initially chose II Chronicles 7:14: "If my people, which are called by my name, shall humble themselves, and pray, and seek my face, and turn from their wicked ways; then I will hear from heaven, and will forgive their sin, and will heal their land." It would have pleased Reinhold Niebuhr, but speechwriter Anderson and others thought it overly pious and Carter reluctantly dropped it. On a bitterly cold January 20, in his brief, eight-minute address, largely reiterating the themes of his announcement speech two years earlier, Carter quoted instead from the Old Testament prophet Micah: "He hath showed thee, O man, what is good; and what doth the Lord require of thee, but to do justly and to love mercy, and to walk humbly with thy God."

Senator William Proxmire, a physical fitness advocate, had written to Carter that it would set a good example for the nation if he and Rosalynn were to walk the 1.2 miles from the Capitol to the White House following the inauguration. The symbolism of the act appealed to Carter. Leaving the armored presidential limousine at the edge of the Capitol grounds, Jimmy and Rosalynn walked hand in hand down Pennsylvania Avenue accompanied by their children. It proved a profoundly popular act, creating a sense of trust and proximity between the president and the people that had long been absent.

A new administration takes over the White House at the moment of the swearing in of the president. Before the inaugural parade ended, the Carter family had arrived in the residential quarters. Impatient to go to the Oval Office, Carter did not know how to get there. He solved the problem by announcing to the Secret Service that that was where he was going and then following as the agents led the way.

This first act was symbolic. During Carter's early months as president, studied self-confidence and his skill at picking up information wherever he could concealed a significant lack of familiarity with the way the federal government operated, particularly the larger Washington political arena. He was far more knowledgeable about the issues than the process, and this, together with his abilities as a fast learner and a willingness to work back-breaking hours, enabled him to hide his insecurities and project an image of self-assurance.

When Carter arrived in the Oval Office, he stood silently looking around for a couple of minutes with a combination of wonderment and awe. The equally overwhelmed staff members quietly withdrew, leaving him in soli-tude to contemplate the enormity of the responsibility now on his shoulders.

Carter's first scheduled meeting at four that afternoon was with Max Cleland to whom he planned to offer the job of administrator of the Veter-ans Administration. After happily accepting the position, Cleland then said to the president, "Senator Cranston asked me to warn you that there is growing opposition among members of the Senate to your plan to grant amnesty to draft dodgers and draft evaders."

Carter leaned down to Cleland in his wheelchair and said, "I don't care if all 100 of them are against me. It's the right thing to do." The following morning Carter signed the executive order granting the amnesty. A firestorm of protest descended on the White House, with Senator Barry Goldwater calling it "the most disgraceful thing a president has ever done." Janet Pleasant in the correspondence section was handling five telephone lines that day and recalls that "90 percent of the calls were very negative, and there was much emotion, anger, and frustration involved." But the furor quickly dissipated. Carter was seen, even by opponents, as strong and decisive, both honoring a campaign pledge and standing on a matter of principle. As an act of forgiveness and reconciliation to heal the nation, it came from the core of Jimmy Carter's personality.

The antipathy among Carter loyalists to sharing power with outsiders persisted, especially the "political establishment" that had been at the heart of the battle between Jordan and the more pragmatic, governance-oriented Watson. Griffin Bell would later say, only half-facetiously, "I think he [Carter] would have been better off if he had only appointed people from Georgia. But there just wasn't enough of them." Jordan had told Robert Scheer of *Playboy,* "If Cyrus Vance were named Secretary of State and Zbigniew Brzezinski head of National Security in the Carter adminis-tration, then I would say we failed, and I would quit. But that's not going to happen."

Jordan was wrong. While Carter gave him free rein in the White House to place loyalty and submissiveness above competence, Carter was com-mitted to finding, for his cabinet, both the most competent people and those who would bring luster and credibility to his administration. In this respect, he structured his administration in Washington exactly as he had in Georgia. Carter cast as wide a net in seeking suggestions for those appointments as he had when choosing Mondale as his vice president. He also established a "Personnel Advisory Group" that included Atlanta friend Vernon Jordan and Marion Wright Edelman, to review his short lists. Including blacks in such an influential role was an unprecedented step for any president up to that time.

Their appointment reflected one of the unequivocal objectives Carter brought with him to the White House—to increase dramatically the percentage of senior positions in the federal government filled by minorities and women. This particularly included federal judgeships. It would be one of his lasting legacies. He began by appointing Juanita Kreps as secretary of commerce, Patricia Roberts Harris as secretary of HUD, and Andrew Young as ambassador to the United Nations.

In seeking excellence, Carter had no choice but to pick some cabinet officers whom he barely knew. Except for his insistence on the high ratio of blacks and women, he compounded the problem by giving them considerable freedom in naming the senior political appointees in their departments, often people loyal to them but not to Carter. One observer noted, "In his goodness he would ask someone to be in his cabinet, then give away the candy store." As Jordan ruefully reflected, "We almost tried to duplicate in the administration the chaos and the fragmentation that existed in the party."

The two cabinet positions where loyalty counts most to a president, attorney general and director of the Office of Management and Budget, Carter filled with Georgians, Griffin Bell and Bert Lance. Kirbo, who declined any formal role for himself, wanted his law partner, Griffin Bell, to be the attorney general. Even though his relatively conservative record as a federal judge and his membership in a whites-only country club initially caused considerable consternation among liberals, including Mondale, the nature of Carter's relationship with Kirbo made any other choice difficult.

On December 28, Carter had invited the cabinet nominees and their wives to join him at Musgrove Plantation at Sea Island, Georgia, owned by Carter supporter Smith Bagley. It was primarily a get-acquainted session, but Carter took the opportunity to talk about his plans for economy in government, including a 30 percent cutback in the White House staff. For a president determined to bring efficiency to government it was an important symbolic gesture, but the reduction in staff would similarly reduce the capacity of the Carter White House to govern.

Despite Carter's intentions, the failure to appoint a chief of staff quickly created a power vacuum that inevitably filled itself. Jordan was unquestionably the dominant force in the White House with the greatest influence on the president. The nebulous nature of his role, combined with his penchant for infighting to assure his primary position, undercut the effectiveness of the new administration.

When Carter came to Washington in January 1977, there were several elder statesmen in the city who volunteered not only their services but also the benefit of their many years of experience there. For the most part, they wanted nothing in return. Yet their offers were largely shunned because it was felt that if the White House appeared to rely on those veterans of former administrations, it would seem that Carter was not capable of handling the job himself.

Following the success of his inauguration day walk, Carter continued to portray himself as a president close to the people. He carried his own suit bag when he traveled. He and Rosalynn placed Amy in the D.C. public school system. He ended the practice of having "Hail to the Chief" played whenever he made a public appearance. He sold the presidential yacht *Sequoia*. He publicly ordered wide-ranging economies in the White House, reducing the number of assigned limousines and television sets in staff offices. When the press criticized the high salaries paid to young former campaign workers with minimal qualifications, he ordered all White House staff to take a 10 percent pay cut. It created some ill-feeling among the older professionally qualified members of the staff who were already making a considerable financial sacrifice by being there. Carter himself did not volunteer to take a 10 percent reduction in salary.

Carter's attempts to democratize the presidency met with mixed reviews. After the imperial presidency of Richard Nixon, a significant segment of the population liked Carter's gestures of humility (a significant motivating factor) and his efforts to diminish the distance between the president and the ordinary citizen. Others, like the White House press corps, whose own perceived importance derived from the president's, were angered and claimed he was diminishing the stature of the office. Some said the moves reflected Carter's subconscious reservations about his fitness for the job, and that he was lowering the presidency to a mundane level rather than raising himself to the level of the office. There was no doubt that by eliminating some of the symbols of his office he reduced his own real power, especially in Washington.

From the start, Carter felt isolated from the ordinary citizen. His advisors, including Vice President Mondale, encouraged him to pursue his image as the "people's president." However, for him it was much more than a public relations strategy. Throughout his political career he had required constant contact because it provided him with needed feedback about what was on the average citizen's mind, giving him a sense of confidence about his own positions. Later in his presidency, as such contact declined, he often seemed adrift. He had wanted to institute something akin to the "Little People's Day" in Georgia where he could meet regularly with ordinary citizens, but the Secret Service flatly vetoed the idea.

Carter's victory coincided with a decade-long trend in which party structures had weakened and more and more Americans viewed themselves as independents. While nominally a Democrat, in many respects Carter had run and won as an independent. As Jordan noted, "Carter was not the first choice of any Democratic constituency." He had no natural body of support in Washington. He was forced to turn to the very elite against whom he had campaigned in order to run the country.

From the start, strains appeared in Carter's relationship with Congress. For head of the CIA, he proposed Ted Sorensen, a link to the Kennedys and whose early support had been vital with liberals, especially in New York. A sterling reputation and a brilliant mind made Sorensen a likely star of the new administration. However, his confirmation was jeopardized when it became known that when he had registered for the draft he did so only for a noncombatant role and that he had removed classified documents at the end of his service in the Kennedy White House. What he did was legal at the time, but subsequent laws made such actions illegal. Eager to embarrass Carter before he took office, Republicans and several hostile Democrats declared their opposition to the nominee. Frank Moore and his fledgling staff had neither the respect nor the experience to mobilize support for Sorensen. In addition, the Georgians around Carter were ambivalent about how hard to fight for this "New York liberal." Sorensen felt that Carter himself also did nothing to defend his nominee. When Carter withdrew the nomination on January 17, perhaps prematurely, it was perceived as an act of weakness in his first confrontation with Congress. Committee chairman Senator Robert Byrd "just wanted to teach Carter a lesson," a junior Democratic senator explained to *Time* magazine.

Lacking an overriding ideology other than his own personal moral philosophy, Carter saw improving the efficiency and responsiveness of the government as his primary objective. During his presidency, the aspects of his personality acquired from his mother—his general commitment to the interests of blacks, women, and the poor—were eclipsed by the cost-conscious business orientation that was his legacy from Mr Earl. Contrary to most Democrats, he believed that while there was a vital role government could play in alleviating human suffering, there was a real limit to what it could do for people without going bankrupt, and he was preoccupied with cost efficiency and improved management.

In an interview, Stu Eizenstat grouped Carter's concerns into three areas: lack of long-range federal planning, openness in government, and governmental reorganization. Simplification and predictability were key objectives Carter had regularly talked about in connection with government reorganization, citing the need for "drastic simplification of the tax structure," "simple, workable housing policies," "simplification of the laws and regulations to substitute education for paper-shuffling grantsman-ship," a "simplified system of welfare," and a "simplification of the pur-poses of the military." He praised state and local governments for having achieved "simple organizational structures." He said he believed in "long-range planning so that government, business, labor, and other entities in our society can work together if they agree with the goals established. But at least it would be predictable."

Carter was, with other Democrats, committed to reducing unemploy-ment, but even more to controlling inflation. He believed deeply in balanc-ing the budget and reducing the deficit. At the same time, he had a sophisticated understanding of the transcendent impact of the vagaries of the international oil market on the American economy. Establishing a long-range energy policy for the nation was one of his first priorities.

In addition to lacking a natural constituency among Democrats in Con-gress, Carter's view of legislative bodies was indelibly shaped by his expe-rience with the Georgia legislature. As Bert Lance has observed, "His dealings with the legislature in Georgia then were mirrored by his rela-tionship with the House and Senate in Washington. He didn't like to fool with them. . . . Didn't like it, didn't enjoy it, didn't respect them."

In theory, with a Democratic majority in both houses of Congress, he should have been able to mobilize solid backing for his legislative program. He complained later that he held dozens of meetings in the first few months with members of Congress, perhaps more than any other incoming president. What he did not appreciate was that these often fleeting meet-ings, where he succinctly argued the merits of his proposals, did not sub-stitute for the day-to-day servicing of congressional concerns by the White House. He did not appreciate that a photo in the Oval Office, a seat in the presidential box at the Kennedy Center, a ride in Air Force One, a set of presidential cufflinks, or a pen used in a signing ceremony were often as likely to sway a congressman's vote as his painstaking elaboration of the merits of a piece of legislation. He was about more lofty matters than dealing with someone's petty ego and he expected them to rise above their own self-interest to embrace the high-minded goals he espoused. But they did not.

During December, Carter had paid a courtesy call on House Speaker "Tip" O'Neill, who explained to him that he needed to put aside the anti-Washington rhetoric of the campaign and start to work closely with the Congress. Carter responded that when he had difficulty with the Georgia legislature, he had gone over their heads directly to the people. He would not hesitate, he said, to follow the same course with the Congress. Tip O'Neill was taken aback: "You don't mean to tell me you're comparing the House and the Senate with the Georgia legislature?" He later wrote, "I tried to explain how important it was for the president to work closely with the Congress; he didn't seem to understand."

Relations were further soured early when O'Neill asked Hamilton Jordan for tickets for a pre-inaugural gala at the Kennedy Center and was sent some in the last row of the second balcony. The Speaker was outraged. Jordan swore it was an error, but O'Neill was never convinced. To Jordan, O'Neill symbolized the old politics that Carter had run against. He was a liberal, and he was from Massachusetts, where Carter had received his most crushing defeat in the primaries, something Jordan could not easily forget.

There was a certain irony that while Carter touted coordination and managerial efficiency as the ingredients he was bringing to the federal government, it was the absence of these elements in the White House that was doing most to compromise his relations with Congress. Under most administrations a close working relationship between the president's top aide and the Speaker, especially when they are of the same party, would be considered mandatory. O'Neill later wrote that he saw Jordan, whom he had taken to referring to as "Hannibal Jerken," only three times during the four years Carter was in office. Despite the notion of the "spokes of the wheel," Frank Moore was perceived as being "Jordan's man," as he always had been. Members of Congress initially saw Jordan, not Moore, as the person to contact. Repeating his pattern in Georgia, Jordan rarely returned their phone calls, arguing that it would undercut Frank Moore if people thought they could bypass him. A nominee to a federal judgeship, invited to lunch at the White House, was astonished when Jordan related with amusement that a senior Democratic senator had been calling him for days and he was ignoring his calls merely to show "who had the power."

The confusion was compounded by Carter's relationship with Bert Lance, who was the only person in the administration considered a friend and peer by Carter. As he had when Carter was governor, Lance would frequently stop by at the end of the day to talk informally with the president about a range of issues not necessarily related to his formal responsibilities. Lance, extrovert, gregarious, and a born deal-maker, was comfortable on Capitol Hill, where he was widely liked. Carter used Lance to help formulate political strategy, to represent him with groups such as businesspeople, to garner congressional votes, and to head up his plans for reorganizing the White House—all functions more normally associated with a chief of staff. He would direct members of Congress and other powerful people to "talk to Bert about that." Yet Carter kept Lance at arm's length in OMB rather than having him formally on his immediate staff.

Lance, whose supportive friendship was extremely important to Carter in the early months of the administration, says, "As a matter of preference in that complex makeup, he operates on the basis that those close to him will have partial knowledge—but only partial—of his plans and objectives. Only he and Rosalynn will know the whole picture in any particular situation." Carter individually met on a regular basis with the spokes of the wheel, but during the first two years in the White House they never met as a group with or without him. As a result, there was never a cohesive plan involving all the top staff to achieve any political or legislative goal. During that same period of time, there was only a single occasion when Watson and Jordan met together with Carter, and that was for a largely ceremonial event.

The White House became increasingly compartmentalized with little or no lateral communication. Phone calls from one "spoke" to another were often deliberately never returned. Except through Carter, coordination was minimal. This led to destructive competition and undercutting through leaks to the press that served Carter poorly. Jordan, Powell, and Moore considered themselves the "political people" as opposed to the "policy people" that included Eizenstat, Watson, Brzezinski, and others. Policy recommendations were forwarded independently to Carter without assessment of their political implications, and political advice was given by people who often had little grasp of the issues involved.

Carter did not like group meetings and especially rejected them as a vehicle for decision making. The cabinet convened once a week, but involved primarily cabinet members giving a brief report of the recent activities of their departments. Brzezinski described them as a complete waste of time, a view that was widely shared even by Hamilton Jordan, who told Carter in a note that they were wasteful, duplicative, and covered only what was already in their weekly written reports. At the same time, Carter's style inspired extraordinary loyalty and dedication. He never told people to work hard; he just made sure that everyone on the staff knew he was working harder than they were.

Carter's problems with Congress were far from one-sided. The abandonment of the old seniority system meant there was no longer a handful of powerful patriarchs, whose delivery of winning votes could be guaranteed by courting them. Members of both parties were now less disciplined and often inclined to vote independently. The majority of Democrats had been elected since Lyndon Johnson's term and, having dealt only with Nixon and Ford, had acquired a reflex adversarial attitude toward the presidency no matter who held the office. Some senators still found it difficult to accept Carter as president, particularly the majority leader Robert Byrd, who himself had briefly entered the presidential race. Similarly, "Scoop" Jackson regularly sought to oppose and undermine Carter's legislative program. According to Charles Kirbo, the reason was "jealousy, sheer jealousy."

With a precise perception of the priority needs for the country, Carter was determined to hit the ground running. However, he wrote in his diary a week after taking office, "Everybody has warned me not to take on too many projects so early in the administration, but it's almost impossible for me to delay something that I see needs to be done." During the campaign Carter had made what he considered "promises" to the American people; he had Stu Eizenstat prepare a "promises book" of those he felt he had a moral obligation to keep. During his first six months in office he would present the Ninety-fifth Congress with a lengthy legislative agenda, including proposals to create an agency for consumer affairs, executive reorganization authority, hospital cost-containment legislation, programs of urban and welfare reform, an ethics in government bill, changes in social security, a comprehensive energy program including the creation of a cabinet-level Department of Energy, and plans for cuts in federal water projects.

Carter's first major conflict with Congress was not long in coming. The Ford budget had proposed the construction of 320 dams and other water improvement projects around the country. The transition team had identified sixty as candidates for elimination, and from his experience in Georgia with the Corps of Engineers, Carter felt many were unnecessary. After he took office, all but nineteen were axed at a savings of $5.1 billion to the taxpayers. To Carter, those pork-barrel projects seemed to epitomize the waste and inefficiency he had promised to end.

His inexperienced congressional staff failed to warn him of the vehement reaction his proposed cuts would generate when they were revealed in Congress at the end of February. In his diary on March 10, Carter would note, "Had a rough meeting with thirty-five members of the Congress on water projects." It was an understatement. What to Carter was a classic example of waste was Congress's time-honored way of doing business. The harshest criticism came from fellow Democrats, including Senators Russell Long and Edmund Muskie. Majority leader Robert Byrd, the master of pork-barrel politics, warned Carter, "The road can be smooth or the road can be rough." Carter conceded that he should have consulted more with the congressional leaders ahead of time. To accommodate Speaker Tip O'Neill, he impulsively accepted a compromise plan. Later in assessing his mistakes with Congress he would write, "One that I still regret is weakening and compromising that first year on some of those worthless dam projects." The compromise, he says, "was accurately interpreted as a sign of weakness on my part, and I regretted it as much as any budget decision I made as president."

For Carter it was a clear matter of principle. For the Congress his refusal to play by the rules was further evidence of his insensitivity to their needs. For the media, accustomed to the regular compromise of principle in Washington, that he canceled any of the projects suggested naivete.

The inflation rate had dropped from 12 percent in 1974 to 6 percent by the time Carter took office. However, the economy remained sluggish and unemployment was at 7.8 percent. The number of people living below the poverty line had climbed in the previous two years from 11.2 percent to 12.5 percent. These were the Americans whom Carter felt he was primarily in the presidency to help.

In order to spur the economy and reduce unemployment, Carter and congressional leaders agreed early on to a quick tax rebate of $50 per person. The measure rapidly passed in the House, but was delayed in the Senate. In the meantime, the economy improved and inflation became a far greater concern. In April, getting conflicting economic and political advice, Carter decided to withdraw the proposal. Battling inflation for the remainder of his term, Carter never regretted it as the right economic decision. It reflected Carter's willingness to modify his position when circumstances changed. However, it cost him politically as his flexibility was labeled as inconsistency. His decision also angered many in Congress who felt they had gone out on a limb to support him only to have him saw it off. As his personal secretary, Susan Clough, would accurately observe, "In the presidency every error counts."

Carter's fiscal conservatism came as a surprise to those, including Mondale, who assumed that because of his fervent advocacy of civil rights and social justice, he would favor increased expenditures on government social programs even if it meant deficit spending. They had conveniently ignored his campaign statement:

> There will be no new programs implemented under my administration unless we can be sure that the cost of those programs is compatible with my goal of having a balanced budget by the end of my first term.

Liberal Democrats had seen the Nixon/Ford years as an interruption in the normal way of doing business. With a Democrat back in the White House, they expected spending patterns to return to those of the Johnson years. Carter believed that was a prescription for economic disaster from which everyone, especially the poor, would ultimately suffer. Liberal groups felt betrayed; union leaders, in particular, who had backed Carter in part because of his commitment to implement comprehensive national health insurance, found he was proposing a considerably more modest plan to be introduced much more slowly than they had been led to believe. He cut back on aid to the cities and public works programs, angering the U.S. Conference of Mayors and the AFL-CIO, which described his plan as "a retreat from the goals we understand President-elect Carter to have set during last year's election campaign."

Carter inherited from Gerald Ford a budget deficit of more than $66 billion, the largest in history. The transition team had predicted that by holding government spending down Carter would not only be able to balance the budget by 1981, he would actually have a surplus of $52 billion. It was, however, predicated on an annual growth in the gross national product of between 5.5 and 6 percent, which would prove overly optimistic. Carter saw balancing the budget as vital to the country's interests, and if this meant angering liberals in the Congress by limiting spending on social programs, so be it.

Carter wanted also to move rapidly on his proposed plan to reorganize the federal government. Based on his accomplishment in Georgia, this was an area to which he brought considerable knowledge and experience. He again sought "reverse legislation," enabling him to submit reorganization plans to Congress that would automatically become law unless the House or Senate specifically rejected them. Despite strong opposition from Congressman Jack Brooks, chairman of the House Government Operations Committee, he had enough Republican support that the legislation passed and was signed into law on March 31, 1977. Brooks subsequently worked closely with the administration, helping to ensure that of the eleven reorganization plans submitted, ten were accepted.

The assertion of power by the oil-exporting nations and the resulting "oil shocks" of 1973 and 1975 had shaken America's self-confident view that it was invulnerable to global interdependence. For several years the nation's energy policy had been one of Carter's leading concerns. Now, as president, he would later reflect, "There was never a moment when I did not consider the creation of a national energy policy equal in importance to any other goal we had." Deeply concerned that during the four years prior to his assuming office, U.S. dependence on imported oil had risen from 35 to 50 percent, and that the U.S. economy was becoming increasingly captive to decisions made outside its borders, Carter accurately perceived a profound threat to the nation's security.

His efforts to create a national energy program over the next four years saw him at his best and exposed some of his greatest weaknesses. He offered decisive leadership in his understanding of the urgency with which the nation needed a comprehensive energy policy that would cut energy consumption, develop new domestic energy sources, and reduce the nation's dependence on foreign oil. His instincts as a long-range planner and his wide-ranging intellectual knowledge about the subject served him well in working with his energy advisor, James Schlesinger.

He was helped initially by the severe winter weather of 1976–77. At the end of January, he sought emergency authority to deregulate the price of gas piped across state lines. Six days later, on February 1, Congress passed the Emergency Natural Gas Act. The following day, Carter used the occasion of the signing of the legislation to have a "fireside chat" with the American people. Wearing a cardigan sweater and sitting by an open fire in the White House library, he explained the nature of the energy crisis that the nation faced. He announced that within ninety days he would send a comprehensive energy program to Congress, including the creation of a cabinet-level Department of Energy.

The Roosevelt style was warmly received by the public, and he was applauded for providing strong, clear leadership in an area that his predecessors had largely avoided. He had, however, set an almost impossible timetable. To meet his self-imposed deadline he worked relentlessly and punishingly with Schlesinger, Eizenstat, and his staff. The resulting plan was too complex and had several flaws. It was produced largely in isolation, with little time allowed for coordination with cabinet members whose departments it would impact. Even less attention was paid to involving members of Congress. Carter took for granted that others would see that the interests of the nation would be immeasurably served by a comprehensive energy program. The plan, he believed, should sell itself on its merits.

On March 16, Carter held a "town meeting" in Clinton, Massachusetts, and spent the night with a local family. The following day, he met with a community group in Charleston, West Virginia. During the height of the winter cold he visited the places hardest hit, and derived renewed inspiration for his energy proposals after hearing firsthand about people's suffering.

In an address to the nation on April 18, he said:

> Our decision about energy will test the character of the American people and the ability of the president and the Congress to govern this nation. This difficult effort will be the "moral equivalent of war," except that we will be uniting our efforts to build and not destroy.

Two days later, on April 20, Carter presented his comprehensive energy package to a joint session of Congress. He followed it with a series of public forums within the White House and around the country. But by his own admission, "It was like pulling teeth to convince the American people we had a serious problem." By wearing a sweater for his fireside chat and ordering the thermostats turned down in the White House and all federal buildings, he sought to convey a sense of shared sacrifice.

The plan faced fearsome opposition in Congress. Carter was astonished to find that in the House it potentially faced review by as many as seventeen committees and subcommittees. Speaker O'Neill cooperated by creating a special ad hoc committee to review the total package that would then be referred to just five major committees, before going to the floor of the House. In the Senate the two key players were "Scoop" Jackson, chairman of the Senate Energy and Natural Resources Committee, and Senator Russell Long, chairman of the Finance Committee. Neither man had much interest in helping Carter achieve public acclaim for averting a major energy crisis. Jackson's opposition was in part due to his continuing personal grudge against Carter; his own extensive knowledge enabled him to get political mileage out of the many technical shortcomings in the hastily prepared plan.

Russell Long was primarily concerned about protecting the interests of the oil and gas industries. Carter would note in his diary on June 9, "The influence of the special-interest lobbies is almost unbelievable, particularly from the automobile and oil industries." As Carter sought to make compromises that might satisfy Long and the energy companies, liberals were squeezing him from the other side. They accused him of selling out to industry, and demanded tighter restrictions on gas-guzzling automobiles and a pledge that revenues resulting from deregulation go into social programs.

In the House, through the efforts of Tip O'Neill and Congressman Lud Ashley, chairman of the special ad hoc committee, the omnibus energy bill was passed on August 5. Both houses also approved Carter's plan for a Department of Energy and his nomination of Schlesinger as the first secretary was approved. However, in the Senate, where industry lobbyists had focused most of their attention, the comprehensive plan would remain stalled for the rest of the year.

The Carter family settled comfortably into the White House. Amy, the first child to live there since the Kennedy children, received constant attention from the media. The Carters joined the First Baptist Church of Washington, D.C., near Scott Circle. Organized in 1802, it was the "Baptist church of presidents" attended by Martin van Buren, Franklin Pierce, Lyndon Johnson, and Harry Truman on a regular basis. Carter would attend services there seventy-three times while president and on fourteen occasions would teach the Sunday school class.

The Carters, however, still had church problems back in Plains. The pastor of the Plains Baptist Church, Bruce Edwards, was in trouble. He had spoken out in support of Carter's candidacy, offering a prayer at a campaign rally and saying he had to "speak up for his Christian commitment"; he had also defended Carter over the *Playboy* interview. Carter opponents in the congregation argued that Edwards should stay completely out of politics.

A week before the election, a black pastor from Albany, Clennon King, had sent a letter to the parsonage saying that he was planning to apply for membership in the still all-white Plains Baptist Church. Clennon, the brother of Carter's former gubernatorial opponent C. B. King, was a self-identified Republican, with a history of eccentric behavior and a prison record for nonsupport of his children. Edwards had recommended to the deacons that they rescind the 1965 ban on admitting blacks and accept King for membership to avoid embarrassing Carter. Edwards and his wife had adopted a half-Hawaiian baby and, just the Sunday before, he had preached that there should be no "color line drawn in worship." With several deacons resenting both his support for Carter and his liberal views on race, they voted instead to cancel the worship service for the following Sunday, two days before the election. The pressure was growing to fire Edwards.

In the hectic final moments of the campaign, Carter kept the issue at arm's length. A story in the *New York Times* quoted Billy Carter as saying, "90 percent of the preacher's trouble" was the mixed-race baby, although he later denied making the comment. On November 18, with the national press gathered outside, the congregation voted down a motion to fire Edwards by 100–96. At the same time, they voted to open the church to people regardless of race, but establish a committee to screen people for their "suitability" for membership. Carter, who had argued that not opening the church would result in massive demonstrations, declared after the vote, "I'm completely satisfied with the votes. I'm proud of my church, God's church. We voted to keep our pastor, and more important to open the doors of our church to any person to worship. I think now our church will be unified."

Carter's optimism was misplaced. Edwards received national acclaim for his stand and was seen as a martyr by millions. On inauguration day he presided over a nationally televised "People's Prayer Service" that featured a sermon by Martin Luther King, Sr. His celebrity status, however, only further inflamed the conservative members of the church who continued to push for his ouster. On February 13, the president returned to Plains to support Edwards in a new vote. Edwards opponents managed to get it delayed a week when Carter would be back in Washington. By then, seeing his situation was hopeless, Edwards resigned. Subsequently the Carters and others in the congregation would leave to form the separate Maranatha Baptist Church.

Rosalynn had decided that she would continue her concern for the mentally ill as her primary focus in the White House. It was agreed the president would create a presidential commission that she would chair. An extensive analysis of all past presidential commissions, their legislative history, their budgets, and their staffing patterns were prepared for her. A budget of $1 million was proposed, below the previous average. In the first week in the White House, eager to begin work right away, Rosalynn wanted the president to sign an executive order creating the commission. There were, however, no available funds without waiting for a specific appropriation. An interim solution was for the president to provide $100,000 from his emergency fund.

"I can't come into office and give my wife $100,000 for her pet project," responded Carter, whose frugality bordered on the unrealistic. "I thought we were going to use volunteers for this." Eventually, Rosalynn prevailed, the $100,000 was provided, and the Presidential Commission on Mental Health and Mental Retardation was established.

Not since Eleanor Roosevelt had a first lady played such an activist role. She set a precedent with the commission, which held hearings around the country, and by testifying before the Congress in support of the resulting legislation. There was considerable criticism from traditionalists when it became known that she was sitting in on cabinet meetings, although she took notes with the staff and never spoke. As she had in the campaign, she was carving out a new role as an activist partner with her husband, paving the way for future first ladies, notably Hillary Rodham Clinton.

During his first three months in office, despite all of the internal problems in the administration, Carter had restored the faith in the presidency. He had brought integrity, honesty, and respect back to the office. He had demonstrated strong leadership in laying out a full legislative agenda that addressed some of the nation's most pressing problems, especially the energy issue. He faced an array of powerful enemies in the Congress, the media, the business community, the unions, and from many liberals. But the American people liked what they saw. By the end of April, a Harris poll showed Carter with a 75 percent approval rating.

CHAPTER 23

As a one-term southern governor with no national experience, it was presumed Carter came to office with little knowledge or interest in foreign policy. In fact, Carter saw foreign affairs as the most exciting and intellectually stimulating challenge of his presidency. He benefitted from having no one in his Georgia inner circle with a foreign policy background, forcing him instead to pick advisors purely on the basis of their proven ability and expertise. As a result, his capacity to function effectively and decisively in the realm of foreign affairs was substantially enhanced.

Carter, however, did draw heavily on the friendships and acquaintances he had made through the Trilateral Commission in choosing his appointees. No potential cabinet appointee enjoyed such near unanimous support among those he consulted as Cyrus Vance, his secretary of state. As his assistant for National Security Affairs he named Zbigniev Brzezinski, the executive director of the Trilateral Commission. Early in the presidential campaign, Brzezinski had let several of the Democratic candidates know that he was available as a foreign policy advisor. At the May 1975 meetings in Japan, Carter invited Brzezinski to review the speech he was to give to the American Chamber of Commerce. Brzezinski was impressed with it, and by the insightful interventions that Carter made during the formal sessions of the commission, especially on the Middle East. Carter stressed the need for "fairness" in achieving a settlement between Israel and her neighbors, a nuance unnoticed by others, but not by Brzezinski.

Brzezinski, in many respects the most talented and original foreign-policy thinker of his generation, had a crisp, incisive way of looking at problems that strongly appealed to Carter. Lacking the ponderous caution of most diplomats, Brzezinski had the ability, through his articulation of creative and often provocative ideas, to stimulate intellectually those to whom he spoke. Carter was determined to run his own foreign policy, but in the mercurial Brzezinski he saw someone who could both educate him and also provide a constant source of cerebral enlivenment. Carter envisioned that he would select from the menu of options that flowed from Brzezinski's fertile mind to formulate his foreign policy decisions, then use the stolid, lawyerly Vance and the State Department to carry them out.

Unlike his most famous predecessor, Henry Kissinger, Brzezinski had an attractive self-deprecating sense of humor that also appealed to Carter. However, like Kissinger, he would turn out to be a person of considerable ego and a tenacious political infighter for which Carter was not fully prepared. One colleague says, "Brzezinski was a very disconcerting presence in the White House," adding, "You could not have a meeting with the president of the United States without [Brzezinski] barging in to whisper in the president's ear just to show that he could." Susan Clough was driven to distraction by his efforts to ferret out of her the president's tennis-playing schedule or any contacts on foreign policy matters he might have had that did not come through Brzezinski's office. Over time he would systematically capture primary control of the foreign policymaking apparatus, marginalizing Vance's role and subverting Carter's original operating plan.

Brzezinski's own intellectual rigor led him to choose an impressively qualified team of experts to support him. He also had his own press and congressional relations staff; he was largely compartmentalized from the rest of the White House, needing to relate only to Carter and to a lesser extent Mondale. It was, on the surface, an example of the "spokes-of-the-wheel" concept working.

Immediately after the election, Henry Owen, Richard Gardner, and Brzezinski prepared a memo for Carter outlining what goals they thought the Carter administration should pursue in foreign policy. The document became the basis for the first informal meeting of the incoming National Security Council on January 5, 1977. It was chaired by Mondale. The meeting concluded that Panama and the Middle East should be the top priorities. Both were highly compatible with Carter's personal inclinations.

In 1903, Washington had imposed on Panama a treaty that had, in effect, given the United States control in perpetuity over the Panama Canal and the surrounding zone. Over the years Panamanians had grown increasingly resentful, and in 1964 there had been large-scale anti-American riots. Negotiations for a new treaty were begun shortly afterward. They progressed slowly, but by 1974 a set of principles had been agreed to. The process had then been stalled by domestic considerations on both sides with Panamanian nationalists demanding immediate transfer of control from the United States, while conservatives in the United States opposed any concessions to Panama. That opposition had crystallized around Ronald Reagan during his unsuccessful bid for the Republican nomination in which he blended an appeal to a sense of inherent national superiority over the Panamanians with a concern that they were inherently leftist.

The Panama Canal issue had taken on a symbolic significance throughout Latin America in which it was seen as the test of the willingness of the

United States to move beyond the legacy of gunboat diplomacy to an acceptance of a new era of partnership with its neighbors in the hemisphere. Critics would later argue that Carter paid too high a price politically to get the new treaties ratified, and that he should have deferred action until a second term. However, intelligence reports at the time suggested that a breakdown of the talks would lead to riots in Panama, possible attacks on the canal, and a furious surge of anti-Americanism throughout the region. Urgent action to complete the treaty negotiations was unavoidable.

For Carter it was a prime opportunity to apply moral values to foreign policy. He saw the existing treaty arrangement as profoundly unfair and unjust. Applying Reinhold Niebuhr, he felt the Panama Canal Treaty "exemplified those morally questionable aspects of past American foreign policy which the United States as a nation should humbly acknowledge in its striving for higher moral ground." In his book *Morality, Reason and Power,* Gaddis Smith noted that Carter believed a settlement of the canal dispute would be in effect "a gracious apology" for "past wrongdoing." Carter himself, speaking to a class of theology students at Emory University, would later illustrate Niebuhr's point that a society's highest norm must be justice, using the Panama Canal issue as a specific example. Brzezinski would say that the signing of the new treaties "represented the ideal fusion of morality and politics."

The foreign policy team's second priority had equal appeal to the president. Carter's religious beliefs and especially his deep knowledge of the Bible made the Middle East a region of unique consequence and interest to him. Carter would later write, "Rosalynn and I had long been interested in the area through our weekly Bible study." This was very much an understatement as he had not just an interest but a passionate affinity for the region. He would also write, "For me there is no way to approach or enter Israel without thinking first about the Bible and the history of the land and its people." His sense of special relationship with the Holy Land had intensified following his 1973 visit to Israel at the invitation of Yitzhak Rabin.

Through his involvement with the Trilateral Commission and other sources, he was conversant with the various peace options under discussion in academic circles. Vance and Brzezinski had drawn on a range of experts, including leaders of the American Jewish community such as Phil Klutznick and Rita Hauser, to develop a framework for a comprehensive settlement plan. Previous administrations had pushed the process as far as they could, but it had become seriously stalled. Carter believed that despite the numerous complex problems and competing interests in the Middle East, the time was ripe for reconciliation between Israelis and Arabs. So strong was his commitment that on several occasions he said he would be willing to lose the presidency for the sake of genuine peace in the

Middle East. To establish working relationships and to pick up the threads from the previous administration, Vance was dispatched to the region in mid-February.

Carter had criticized the Nixon and Ford administrations for making foreign policy in secret and had specifically labeled Henry Kissinger a "cowboy." He would later write, "I was deeply troubled by the lies our people had been told; our exclusion from the shaping of American political and military policy in Vietnam, Cambodia, Chile, and other countries; and other embarrassing activities of our government, such as the CIA's role in plotting murder and other crimes."

As part of his commitment to openness in foreign policy, on January 12 at the Smithsonian Institution, Carter had convened a meeting with the congressional leadership. Drawing on those discussions, the earlier memo, and lengthy discussions with the president, Brzezinski eventually developed a forty-three-page document outlining the administration's full range of priorities and goals. The list included achieving a settlement of the Cyprus conflict with the reintegration of Greece into the NATO command structure by the end of 1978; ratifying a new SALT treaty by early 1978; normalizing U.S.–Chinese relations; moving South Africa toward a multiracial democracy and helping to achieve majority rule in Zimbabwe, reflecting the Trilateral influence; engaging Western Europe, Japan, and the other advanced democracies in closer political cooperation; achieving a more accommodating and equitable relationship between the wealthy nations of the North and the developing nations of the South; and making human rights a major focus of U.S. foreign policy. The size of the list stunned the career diplomats in the State Department.

The incorporation of human rights into a central role in American foreign policy would become the most widely acknowledged and enduring legacy of the Carter presidency. With his Baptist background emphasizing individuality and his years of involvement with the civil rights struggle in Georgia, a globalization of his personal concern was natural. For Carter, being a devout Christian, a Baptist, and an American was inseparable from being committed to human rights.

In a speech at Notre Dame in May 1976, Carter had said, "We cannot look away when a government tortures its own people, or jails them for their beliefs, or denies minorities fair treatment or the right to emigrate or the right to worship." During the general election campaign, he made a speech to a B'nai B'rith convention in Washington. Stu Eizenstat, who was primarily concerned about the plight of Russian Jews, had strongly urged him to give the speech, which was drafted by Dick Holbrooke; Holbrooke significantly broadened the focus, which Carter liked. Holbrooke did, however, tone down the harsher rhetoric, specifically cutting a reference to human rights abuses in Iran, expressing concern lest "it tie my hands" in dealing with the Shah. In his inaugural address, however, Carter said, "Our commitment to human rights must be absolute."

In the early weeks of the administration the issue increasingly crystallized as a central feature of Carter's thinking in foreign policy, leading him to say at the town meeting in Clinton, Massachusetts, in March 1977:

> I want to see our country set a standard of morality. I feel very deeply that when people are put in prison without trial and tortured and deprived of basic human rights that the president of the United States ought to have a right to express displeasure and do something about it. . . . I want our country to be the focal point for deep concern about human beings all over the world.

Carter's position represented a profound shift in U.S. policy. Throughout the cold war, ideological loyalty in the global struggle against communism had become the preeminent criterion by which Washington judged any regime. That many of the most fervently anti-communist governments were also among the most egregious violators of their people's human rights was of little concern. Indeed those who raised this issue as a moral concern were for many years considered subversive by America's leading foreign policymakers. The matter was compounded by the continuing violation of a significant number of Americans' rights. As the nation began to resolve this in the sixties and early seventies, there was greater willingness to address human rights overseas, but largely in an effort to embarrass the Soviet Union. The Jackson–Vanik and Stevenson Amendments to the Trade Act of 1974 were intended to do just that. There was, however, growing dissatisfaction in the country, reflected among younger more liberal members of Congress, with a foreign policy predicated on might to the exclusion of morality. The Harkin Amendment to the Arms Control Export Act of 1976 specifically restricted military and economic aid to any nation that showed a "consistent pattern of gross violations of internationally recognized human rights."

Carter's view that "Our country has been strongest and most effective when morality and a commitment to freedom and democracy have been most clearly emphasized in our foreign policy," touched a powerful chord with the American people. The day after the inauguration, Vance would send Carter a message saying he was "struck by the degree of interest, even sharpness, on human rights issues. Since we have announced that we will speak out on selected human rights issues, we will of course be asked continually why we are commenting on some and not on others." Carter would be criticized on the one hand as naive for his commitment to human rights, and on the other for being inconsistent, criticizing harshly some regimes while tempering his comments toward others where the United States had overriding security or economic issues at stake. Carter would say, paralleling his belief in the imperfectability of man, "We live in a world that is imperfect and which will always be imperfect—a world that is complex and confused and will always be complex and confused. I understand fully the limits of moral suasion." What he did not say was that acceptance of such necessary compromise of ideals was an inherent part of his Niebuhrian theology.

On May 22, 1977, Carter made the major foreign policy speech of his presidency at Notre Dame. The core elements of Carter's foreign policy were a commitment to control and reduce armaments, especially nuclear weapons, close and enhanced relations with traditional allies, human rights, and an equitable incorporation of the Third World into America's international dealings. Of the five specific priorities, he listed "America's commitment to human rights as a fundamental tenet of our foreign policy" as number one. In the same speech, Carter emphasized that America could no longer accept a system where the industrialized nations shaped global policy in their own interests while ignoring the majority of the world's population living in the developing nations.

In a sharp departure from the Kissinger-dominated policies of the previous decade in which Third World nations were seen as puppets to be manipulated in our interest, irrespective of the populations involved, Carter talked of an unprecedented working partnership with the "newly influential countries in Latin America, Africa, and Asia." It was time, Carter argued, to recognize the new sense of national identity existing "in almost 100 new countries formed in the last generation."

Carter sought to awaken Americans to the new reality of the world, before most of them were ready to hear it. He said, "Abraham Lincoln said that our nation could not exist half slave, half free. We know a peaceful world cannot long exist one-third rich and two-thirds hungry." As Carter was transforming the U.S. government by appointing blacks, Hispanics, and women in unprecedented numbers to top positions, he was now reaching out to invite the leaders of the poorer and largely dark-skinned nations to share in global governance. His appointment of Andrew Young as his ambassador to the United Nations not only symbolized that commitment but reflected the connection between the social transformation in the United States and what he sought to achieve globally. As assistant secretary of state for human rights he appointed Patt Derian, an early supporter and longtime civil rights activist from Mississippi.

In the same speech, Carter also said, "We are now free of that inordinate fear of communism which once led us to embrace any dictator who joined us in that fear." He was, in effect, renouncing the fundamental pillar on which U.S. foreign policy had been based since World War II. He sought to define a new more constructive role for America. Historically it was a watershed, but it was a role that the American public would only reluctantly begin to accept over the next twenty years.

The Soviet leadership found Carter's commitment to human rights perplexing and suspicious. It was incomprehensible to those brought up in the rigid, disciplined communist system that any world leader would be able to impose his personal moral values, especially those that were religiously derived, on a nation's formal foreign policy. After years of dealing with Kissinger, whose approach was as geared to realpolitik and as devoid of sentiment as their own, the politburo could conceive of only two explanations for the behavior of the new president. Either Carter was hopelessly naive and incompetent with no comprehension about the rules of international diplomacy, or, more probably, his constant reiteration of the human rights issue was a tactical ploy reflecting the influence of "Scoop" Jackson and other hardliners who had consistently used human rights and Jewish immigration as a way to embarrass and goad the Soviet Union.

The Soviets also were deeply suspicious of Brzezinski. They knew him to be a first-rate thinker and strategist, but presumed he had an inherent bias against them. Quite apart from the U.S.–Soviet context, they were convinced that having witnessed as an eleven-year-old boy their invasion of his homeland, like many Poles, he would view Russia as an implacable enemy. Whatever Carter did, they suspected the presence of Brzezinski's Machiavellian hand in the background.

On January 18, two days before Carter's inauguration, Brezhnev had given a conciliatory speech at Tula, stressing the Soviet desire to continue detente. He also expressed his hope for a rapid negotiated reduction of the outstanding issues that remained following the signing of the earlier Vladivostok treaty that would lead to a SALT II agreement. Brezhnev's worldview had been indelibly shaped by the excruciating suffering he had seen in World War II, and he felt he bore a personal responsibility to prevent a recurrence of such human tragedy. The only time he had revealed the depths of his feelings with a Westerner was in a unique one-on-one meeting with Richard Nixon in 1974. He had had to fight a titanic struggle with Marshall Grechko and the other military leaders to wring the necessary concessions from them to achieve the Vladivostok agreement. Returning to Moscow after the signing, he suffered a mild stroke, reinforcing not only the belief that he had given his all but making him more emotionally committed than ever to SALT II as his legacy to humankind.

In an exchange of letters six days after the inauguration, Carter told Brezhnev that he intended to continue the policy of detente (although in the United States a rising tide of conservatism had led to an abandonment of the term). Almost immediately afterward, the State Department accused Czechoslovakia of violating the 1975 Helsinki accords on human rights by harassing a group of intellectual dissidents. Two days later, after Carter received a letter from Soviet dissident Andrei Sakharov, he responded with a personal note stressing his support for human rights worldwide. Although urging that his language be toned down, the State Department issued its own statement warning the Soviets that any effort to intimidate Sakharov would "conflict with accepted international standards of human rights."

The Soviet leadership was furious. In their view, Carter had broken a longstanding informal agreement between the superpowers not to criticize each other's internal affairs in public. Carter argued that by signing the Helsinki Agreement, the Soviets had accepted human rights as a legitimate subject for public discussion. The Soviet ambassador in Washington, Anatoly Dobrynin, would later say, "President Carter continued to attack us in public, in public, in public, always in public." Dobrynin met with Vance to complain. From Carter's standpoint he was articulating a universal human value; the Soviets saw it as a weapon to derail detente. Robert Pastor, director of Latin American and Caribbean Affairs on the National Security Council, points out,

> One interesting element of the human rights policy was that almost every government in the world felt that it was applied selectively to itself. I heard it from many governments in Latin America, "Why are you doing it only to us? If you were really serious about human rights," the Argentine generals would say, "Why aren't you applying it to the Soviet Union? You're not saying anything about the Soviet Union."

The Soviets saw human rights as an unnecessary and disruptive obstacle thrown in the way of the serious business of arms control. According to Dobrynin, "The most important issue for us was continuity of the detente process." He added that he believed (incorrectly), "President Carter was so sure of our devotion to detente that he had convinced himself that we would swallow anything for the sake of detente." Referring to the Soviet leadership, including Brezhnev, he says, "This constant repetition of human rights slogans got to them."

The major players came to the disarmament issue with differing perspectives. Carter saw the number of nuclear weapons in the world as an unnecessary and fundamental evil. In his inaugural address he had pledged, "And we will move this year a step towards our ultimate goal—the elimination of all nuclear weapons from this earth." In his diary he noted, "I went over the complete inventory of the U.S. nuclear warheads, which is really a sobering experience." He later wrote,

It was always obvious that both nations had far more weapons than would ever be needed to destroy every significant military installation and civilian population center in the lands of its potential enemies, and in the process kill tens of millions—perhaps a hundred million—people on each side. . . . That horror was constantly on my mind.

Achieving a profound reduction in the absolute number of nuclear weapons was Carter's primary concern. Brzezinski was relatively unconcerned about nuclear weapons per se, but saw SALT as the principal test of Soviet intentions and possibly a way to halt what he viewed as their continuing military buildup. For him it was a way of forcing the Soviets to make a choice: "cooperation or confrontation." Vance was more concerned with the broader issue of containing Soviet expansionism and moderating U.S.–Soviet tension.

By contrast, the Soviet leadership was not only unconcerned about the mere level of nuclear weaponry as a threat to humankind, they saw the size of their own stockpile as an important element of Soviet status in the world. "SS-18s were very close to Brezhnev's heart," one Soviet leader has since said. Plagued by their historic sense of inferiority with regard to the United States, they felt they now had rough military parity for the first time. The Vladivostok agreement provided ceilings of 2,400 missile launchers on either side above which they agreed not to build. For the Soviets this agreement built in the parity they had so long aspired to and assured that the United States would not move ahead of them again.

Carter's convictions made him want dramatic cuts in weapons on both sides. There was also an element of competition on his part, and especially on that of Brzezinski. After fiercely criticizing Ford for failing to drive a hard enough bargain with Moscow, they wanted to show they could negotiate a better deal than Kissinger. Carter's view was reinforced by a twenty-three-page memo sent to him by "Scoop" Jackson on February 15 and a follow-up meeting on the subject. Jackson said he favored pressing for dramatic weapons cuts and a continuing stress on human rights. In retrospect, however, it appears he was largely driven by his longstanding antipathy toward the Soviet Union and wanted to use Carter to push for reductions he knew they could not possibly accept. He was also the Senate's leading advocate for the defense industry, whose leaders had no interest in reducing arms production.

On February 15, Carter had sent Brezhnev a letter talking about substantial weapons reductions and attempting to explain his commitment to human rights. On March 15, in a speech to the United Nations, while reiterating his commitment to the existing arms control process, he said, "My preference would be for strict controls or even a freeze on new types and new generations of weaponry and with deep reduction in the strategic arms of both sides." Brezhnev had endured what seemed like a relentless battering over the human rights issue, and the suggestion that Carter now wanted to move away from the carefully negotiated Vladivostok agreement devastated him, since he had spent so much of his internal political capital to achieve it, and had such a vested personal interest in it. Carter's comments left members of the politburo dumbfounded and angry. In a letter back to Carter, Brezhnev said, in effect, "Deep reductions? We're not going to make any deep reductions." "Brezhnev thought it was outrageous," says Dobrynin. They were convinced Carter had caved in to right-wing pressure from Jackson and others whose interest was only in worsening U.S.–Soviet relations. As one official complained, "There was no continuity with the previous administration"—something unthinkable in the Soviet context.

When Vance arrived in Moscow a few days later with a new comprehensive plan involving deep bilateral weapons cuts, including a 50 percent cut in the cherished multiple-warheaded SS-18s, the Soviet leadership had already decided that they had no choice but to reject the proposal out of hand. Dobrynin says,

> The new proposal was unbearable to Russia. . . . Our leadership was offended. They felt they weren't being taken seriously. . . . The members of the politburo were outraged . . . they simply didn't want to discuss it. Brezhnev in particular did not want to discuss it. . . . I want to stress that there was no deliberation of the precise merits of the U.S. proposal. It was venting of emotions at the outrageous proposal and manner of the Americans.

Vance had brought with him a fallback plan based on the Vladivostok agreement, but he never got to present it. The Soviets felt Carter, with his annoying preoccupation with human rights and his apparent repudiation of the Vladivostok agreement, had set out to embarrass them publicly. The Soviets were accustomed to tough bargaining and criticism in private, but in public it was completely unacceptable. The politburo wanted to similarly embarrass Vance, and through him, Carter. Vance was extended the briefest and most superficial of courtesies. Then Brezhnev canceled all of the scheduled negotiating sessions, forcing Vance to cut short his stay in Moscow. Carter's critics in the United States immediately pounced on the situation as evidence of his ineptitude in foreign policy.

It was a serious public relations setback in the short run, but in retrospect a vital and inevitable turning point in U.S.–Soviet relations. According to Viktor Komplektov, head of the U.S. Department of the Soviet Foreign Ministry at the time, "Because of the initiative that began in March 1977, the entire sphere of arms control and disarmament negotiation was enlarged through the establishment of several working groups, dealing with chemical warfare, conventional arms, and so on." Ultimately SALT II would be signed, and over the next ten years agreement dramatically reducing nuclear weapons became possible. "The foundations for these discussions were laid during that period, in the Carter era generally and at the March meeting in particular." The Vance visit was, in retrospect, the point of transition between the artificial state of euphoria in the 1970s and a more realistic and clear-cut relationship between the two countries. From that moment on, substantial bilateral arms reduction became the central feature of U.S.–Soviet negotiations. For all of the discomfort and protests of the Soviet leadership, Vance also made it clear that Carter did not intend to back down on his public commitment to human rights.

Carter's uncompromising stand inspired dissidents and human rights activists in the Soviet Union and Eastern Europe. It allowed for the creation of the Charter 77 group in Prague, Solidarity in Poland, and the Helsinki Watch in East Germany and the Soviet Union. Pressure by Carter allowed 118,591 Soviet Jews to emigrate during his presidency. Secretly Carter ordered the CIA to expand its support of dissident groups and to flood the Soviet bloc with books and periodicals by and about human rights activists. He met considerable resistance from both the State Department and the CIA, who found his emphasis on human rights as unconventional in the traditional diplomatic context as the Soviets. Vaclav Havel credits Carter's actions with initiating the breakup of the Soviet empire. In his book *The Cold War: A History,* Martin Walker would say:

> Americans should recall . . . the real historical legacy of Jimmy Carter as one of the men who won the cold war. He was the president who really set in train the mixture of policies which the Reagan administration then pursued in the 1980s.

It was not just Carter's unyielding commitment to human rights that dramatically hastened the ultimate demise of communism. In April 1977, he pressured the NATO allies to rearm, demanding a solid commitment of a 3 percent annual increase in their defense budgets, which he would later match in the United States. He also boosted U.S. forces in Europe, sending an additional 35,000 troops to raise the American NATO contingent above 300,000, more than reversing cuts made by Nixon and Ford. Long after "Star Wars" became a household term, Carter's demand that the Pentagon leap a generation in weaponry—stymieing the Soviet lead in quantity with a U.S. breakthrough in quality—shook Moscow's military planners, convincing them they could not sustain the arms race. What stunned the Soviet military experts more than any other event was the awesome display of U.S. technological superiority over the Bekaa Valley when the Western-armed Israeli air force, suppressing Soviet-built radar and missile sights, shot 70 Syrian MIGs and Sukhois out of the sky without losing a single plane.

Carter matched the military buildup with a systematic escalation of diplomatic pressure on the Soviets. Formal diplomatic recognition of China, support for China's attack on Soviet ally Vietnam, covert support of the Afghan resistance to the Soviet invasion, cancellation of the U.S. presence at the Moscow Olympics, imposition of the grain embargo, Carter's hotline warning against Soviet intervention in Poland, and skillful diplomatic maneuvering to break Romania away from the Warsaw Pact all rocked the Soviet leadership into a stunned defensiveness for the first time since before the Vietnam War.

Carter operated on the cusp between idealism and realism. He was willing to give the Soviets every chance to make peaceful coexistence work, provided they acceded to his demands on human rights. Only when his most reasonable efforts failed did he move toward the tools of coercion.

With the Panama Canal, Carter's idealism would triumph. Negotiations on the canal treaty were started but moved slowly. Reluctant to oust the aging but revered Ellsworth Bunker, who had been involved with the negotiations for fourteen years and had been Ford's negotiator, Carter asked Sol Linowitz, chairman of the Commission on U.S.–Latin American Relations, to become co-negotiator. One of the most respected figures in Washington, Linowitz brought energy, a sharp legal mind, imagination, and considerable trust and respect throughout Latin America to the negotiations.

On April 14, Pan-American Day, Carter spoke before the permanent council of the Organization of American States. To the significant appreciation of his audience, he opened his speech in Spanish, and reminded them of the call for cooperation and consultation he had made when he had addressed the same group in Atlanta three years earlier. In a dramatic departure from the traditional rhetoric of previous presidents, which had invariably implied a right of U.S. hegemony throughout the hemisphere, Carter spoke of the first element in his administration's policy toward Latin America being "high regard for the individuality and the sovereignty of each Latin American and Caribbean nation." He assured them, "We will not act abroad in ways that we would not tolerate at home in our country." He went on to say, "One of the most significant political trends of our time is the relationship between the developing nations of the world and the industrialized countries. We benefit from your advice and counsel, and we count on you to contribute your constructive leadership to help guide us in the North–South dialogue." He stressed again his commitment to human rights in the region and announced that the United States would sign the

American Convention on Human Rights and Protocol I of the Treaty of Tlatelolco (prohibiting the placement of nuclear weapons in Latin America).

Carter's speech not only generated considerable goodwill but bought some maneuvering room to pursue the Panama Canal issue. As the negotiators explored the Panamanian position and began to formulate the U.S. response, it became evident that the security significance of the canal had declined while its symbolism as a source of heated emotion with Latin Americans had increased. If a new treaty was delayed too long, Panamanian passions could threaten the canal making it even more difficult for the United States to negotiate without looking as if it were giving in to a small nation. Exchanging respect for Panamanian sovereignty for the right to intervene militarily to keep the canal open, two treaties were agreed to. The first transferred control of the canal to Panama after 1999. The second gave the United States rights to defend the canal militarily. The final sticking point was over a financial settlement. As the talks dragged on, Carter sent a letter to Torrijos warning him not to push any harder. It was intended both to send Torrijos a message and to show Americans that Carter was achieving the best possible deal for the United States. The treaties were signed in September 1977.

As a way of building public support for the treaties, Carter invited Omar Torrijos and the leaders of all the hemispheric nations to come to Washington during the first week in September for the formal signing of the treaties. Underlining his differences with those still committed to gunboat diplomacy, at the ceremony Carter said that the treaties marked the commitment of the United States "to the belief that fairness, and not force, should be at the heart of our dealings with the nations of the world."

Of the eighteen heads of state who attended, close to half were dictators and several had a sordid background of human rights abuses, including General Pinochet of Chile. Carter's fervent advocacy of democracy and human rights, while aimed at the people of Latin America, made several of his guests uneasy. Torrijos himself had come to power in a military coup. Yet he and Carter had an instant rapport and Carter would later describe the general as one of the three heads of state he met as president to whom he felt personally closest. (The other two were Egyptian President Anwar Sadat and Japanese Prime Minister Masayoshi Ohira.)

In an anteroom before the signing ceremony, an emotional Torrijos had tried to thank Carter for ending generations of frustration and humiliation among the Panamanian people. Before he could finish, he broke down in tears and sobbed as his wife held him. The ceremony was covered in its entirety by Panamanian television and later, as he arrived for the state dinner, Torrijos turned to Carter and said, "Mr. President, I can tell you without fear of being wrong that more than a million Panamanians wept this evening during the ceremonies." The experience thoroughly convinced Carter that he was doing the right thing despite the domestic political cost.

Substantial opposition to the treaty had been generated by Ronald Reagan in his attacks on President Ford during the Republican primaries. "When it comes to the canal, we built it, we paid for it, it's ours, and we should tell Torrijos and company that we are going to keep it," he said repeatedly to cheering Republican audiences. The canal had become a deity in the conservative pantheon. Carter "giving away the canal" was lumped with his support for the Equal Rights Amendment and his perceived softness on abortion as wedge issues in undermining his support with Christian fundamentalists. More thoughtful conservative spokesmen, like William F. Buckley, Jr., supported the canal treaties, and John Wayne wrote to his friend Ronald Reagan, "I'll show point by G.d. point on the Treaty where you are misinforming people." Reagan, however, sent radio and television tapes to hundreds of stations and traveled the country exploiting the emotional volatility of the issue. He helped to mobilize members of the John Birch Society, the Liberty Lobby, the National States Rights Party, and other extremist organizations. These were many of the same groups that Carter had struggled against over the integration issue since the start of his political career, and the jingoistic appeal they now mounted in opposition to the treaties had a strong subtext of racism.

The effect of this orchestrated campaign was that 78 percent of the people opposed "giving up" the canal, and only 8 percent favored relinquishing it according to a Gallup poll of the American people. As a result, many Senate members were already on record against ratification. Because the treaty negotiations had spanned several administrations, there was some bipartisan support. Leaders of the moderate wing of the Republican Party backed Carter, including Gerald Ford and Senate minority leader Howard Baker, as did Henry Kissinger and most of the foreign policy establishment. Carter noted in his diary on August 9 that he had sent a telegram to all members of the Senate urging them not to speak out against the treaty until they knew the details of the agreement, adding, "Apparently it worked with most of them except a few nuts like Strom Thurmond and Jesse Helms."

Facing what seemed like insurmountable odds in getting the two-thirds majority in the Senate for ratification, Carter approached the problem with a two-pronged strategy focusing on the legislators and going directly to the people. With several months before the votes would come up, he instructed Landon Butler to begin organizing a massive nationwide campaign to mobilize public support for the treaties. Hundreds of groups, including union leaders, college presidents, editors, state and local political leaders, and religious organizations, were brought to the White House. Carter specifically asked senators which groups to invite in order to make it easier for them to vote positively. Central to the effort were Carter contributors and campaign workers, who were again asked to do battle for their hero, as though it were another election campaign.

Meanwhile, other foreign policy matters pressed on Carter. During the campaign, he had promised to reduce the number of U.S. troops in the Korean peninsula. His position had been based on estimates provided to him by several sources, including George Bush, director of the CIA, which showed South Korean defense capability was more than adequate to defend against any potential attack from North Korea. As Carter related it,

> So, very shortly after I became president . . . I expressed . . . my ambition to reduce the level of armaments in South Korea, and let that wealthy country, comparatively speaking, with its technology, defend itself and slowly withdraw the American troops. I wanted to get nuclear weapons out of South Korea as well. Another ambition I had, that is still not realized, was that that might be a step toward reconciliation between North and South and the unification of Korea.

Carter's proposed troop reductions caused a firestorm of protest from hawkish anti-communists. Their conservative allies in the administration began suddenly to produce new enhanced estimates of North Korean military capabilities. Carter recalls, "Within a few months the North Korean armed forces had more than doubled in size and far transcended the capability of South Korea. It was quite a reversal of . . . the intelligence estimations I had when first inaugurated." Carter did not believe the accuracy of the reports, but as he says, "They were from my own security apparatus." To make matters worse, the inflated estimates were leaked to the *Washington Post* and *New York Times*, making Carter's call for troop cuts seem indefensible and creating the impression that he had either flip-flopped on the issue or had not properly thought through the security implications. The Japanese also expressed displeasure that Carter should have talked publicly about troop cuts without prior consultation with them.

In May, General John Singlaub, the third-ranking army officer in Korea, told the *Washington Post* in an interview that he believed removing 32,000 ground troops would lead to war. Carter immediately relieved him of his command and ordered him back to the United States. Despite his high rank in the U.S. military, Singlaub was an eccentric figure who, it would later emerge, had strong ties to a network of neofascist groups around the world. His comments legitimized the opposition to troop withdrawal expressed in Congress, including that of Democratic Senators Gary Hart, John Glenn, and Sam Nunn. Knowing that his original decision was correct, and stubborn by nature, Carter refused formally to reverse himself, but with growing opposition on the Hill during the summer, he quietly deferred implementation of his decision.

For more than a decade there had been an argument raging in Washington about whether to build the B-1 bomber. In 1976, Congress had finally left the incoming president to decide by June 1, 1977, whether or not to proceed with the project. Carter spent countless hours listening to the pro and con arguments, sharing his own views with no one. As the deadline approached and his enigmatic silence became the talk of Washington, he played tennis late one afternoon with Hamilton Jordan. As they left the court the suspense was ended when he matter-of-factly revealed that he had decided to cancel the project.

He had made the decision entirely on the basis of a careful assessment of the technical aspects of the system and its cost effectiveness. "I was convinced that the B-1 bomber was a waste of money. . . . We did not need it strategically, and I thought the technology was too expensive for what we got." It was a view strongly shared by Defense Secretary Harold Brown. Carter paid almost no attention to the adverse domestic political consequences resulting from his decision. He is, however, happy to point out, "Later, of course, when President Reagan came in office, he resurrected the B-1 and wasted probably $40 billion of U.S. taxpayers money."

Carter faced a similar difficult decision with regard to the neutron bomb. However, he paid a price for his less-than-deft handling of the issue. On July 17, 1977, he sent a letter to Senator John Stennis, chairman of the Senate Armed Services Committee, in which he described the neutron bomb as "in this nation's security interests." Brzezinski and Brown took the letter, in the absence of any contrary statements by Carter, to mean that he was committed to deployment of the bomb, and they began discussing it with the NATO allies. As Carter says, "I felt I was confronted with a decision that had gone far beyond what I personally had decided." With regard to the Stennis letter, he later said, "I was constantly signing letters to members of Congress, maybe ten or fifteen a day to key members . . . and I have to say that sometimes I didn't meticulously study every letter."

Carter was concerned about the "anti-human aspects of the neutron weapon." He was also very much aware that, "Although it was not nearly so dramatic a technological change as going to multiple warheads, it was symbolically much more important in the public mind because the average American, even peanut farmers, can understand the difference between a weapon that destroys property and one whose penetrating radiation is basically designed to kill human beings." NATO leaders, especially Chancellor Helmut Schmidt, had encouraged U.S. development of the bomb, but when it came time for actual deployment, for domestic political reasons they did not want such an emotionally symbolic weapon on their own soil. "We did not have anywhere to put them," Carter recalls. Ultimately this was the primary determining factor in Carter's decision to cease further production.

Carter's decisions to "give away" the Panama Canal, reduce defense spending, lower troop levels in Korea, cancel the B-1, and not deploy the neutron bomb were immediately seized upon by his critics, especially conservative Republicans, as evidence that he was weak on defense and putting the nation's security in jeopardy. When he held a news conference at the end of June to announce his decision to discontinue the development of the B-1 bomber, it had a stunning effect on the reporters present and on members of Congress. Never before had a president killed so large a weapons program so near to production.

Tip O'Neill warmly congratulated Carter as "the only president who doesn't have to rely on the Pentagon to make his military decisions." What astonished most observers was Carter's willingness to buck the hugely powerful economic interests with a stake in the immense project, potentially alienating them permanently from his presidency. Washington had long become inured to the view that it was better to spend money on such projects regardless of their merits, or cost, than risk alienating the influential defense establishment. Opponents of the B-1 hailed his decision as courageous. Hard-bitten cynics called it naive. Carter was not unaware of the political price he might pay, but he had been elected to make such decisions on their merits. To him it fell into the same category as when he told Hamilton Jordan back in Georgia, "I was not elected governor to give a job to some guy's brother-in-law."

Shortly after the inauguration, Carter had dispatched Mondale on a trip to Japan and Europe. It was an unprecedented symbolic endorsement of the new role Carter had created for the vice presidency. At the departure ceremony Carter stressed that he wanted the leaders of other nations to understand that "Fritz indeed speaks for me." Although it was, as Mondale described it, "the first big foreign policy assignment I ever had," he carried it off with considerable skill and aplomb. He reassured America's traditional allies, understandably nervous of a president about whom they knew so little, and who had often been portrayed in the European press as an uncultured hayseed. Mondale stressed Carter's desire to pursue an activist foreign policy, but emphasized his commitment to consultation and collaboration. He reaffirmed the new administration's continuing commitment to the Atlantic alliance, and promised that the days of Kissinger's secret and private diplomacy were over. He also sought to reassure the Japanese that, despite the furor over the proposed troop cuts in Korea and the continuing scars of Vietnam, Washington would not turn its back on Asia.

Early in May, Carter went to London for what would become the annual economic summit of the seven industrialized nations—the G-7. Perhaps aided by low expectations, he proved a stunning success. In his typical style he had prepared meticulously, and he immediately impressed the other leaders with his knowledge of the issues and especially his grasp of economic problems. His willingness to listen and his natural charm enabled him to establish warm rapport with most of his peers.

His most significant preexisting relationship was with Chancellor Helmut Schmidt, who in the long run would also prove to be the European leader with whom he had the most difficulty. Schmidt, a cantankerous man with an outsized ego, saw himself as the senior member of the group and as the leader of an increasingly resurgent West Germany entitled to a degree of deference even from the president of the United States. Although they got along well when Carter had visited him as governor of Georgia, Schmidt had made no secret of his support for Ford in the election. On his earlier trip, Mondale had put pressure on Schmidt to stimulate the German economy as part of a global effort with the United States and Japan to prevent a global recession. Carter now increased that pressure, and as part of his nuclear nonproliferation strategy, he also sought to block the sale by West Germany of a $4.7 billion nuclear fuel facility to Brazil.

Schmidt took the lead in expressing the concern of the European leadership about Carter's emphasis on human rights, saying that it had unnecessarily upset the Soviets and jeopardized detente. Later, on July 13, he would bring to Washington a message from the leaders of all the Common Market countries urging Carter to moderate his human rights campaign. It was a message partly stimulated by the Soviet leadership, but orchestrated by Schmidt.

Among the European leaders, it was James Callaghan, the British prime minister, with whom Carter got along best. Part of it may have been the absence of a significant language barrier, but they were both populist politicians who shared similar Protestant sectarian roots. Another British prime minister, Harold Wilson, had once said that British socialism owed more to Methodism than to Marx, and this was strongly reflected in Callaghan.

Carter had planned to spend two extra days in Britain following the summit. Callaghan had asked ahead of time if there was any place Carter would particularly like to visit, and Carter responded that he would like to see Laugharn, the small Welsh village where Dylan Thomas wrote much of his poetry and where he is buried. When Carter arrived in England, Callaghan asked if he would instead accompany him to Newcastle-upon-Tyne, where a tight by-election was under way, as he believed a visit by an American president could swing the election for the Labour Party. Carter did, however, go to the poet's corner at Westminster Abbey, where he assumed there would at least be a memorial to Dylan Thomas. He was astonished when the dean said they would not consider honoring someone with such a sordid personal life as Thomas's. Carter brusquely responded that he noted this had not stopped them from honoring Lord Byron. As a result, a plaque was later installed and Carter made the pilgrimage to Thomas's grave after he left the presidency.

Callaghan wore pinstripe suits in which the stripes were made up of minute J.C.s, his monogram. Sharing the same initials with Carter, he gave him a bolt of the cloth that was made into a suit, which became a treasured Carter possession.

Apart from his relationship with Callaghan, and, to some extent with Valery Giscard d'Estaing, Carter never really warmed to the European leadership. He had little in common with their urbane cultural style, their general desire to maintain the interests of their own elites, and their skepticism about his religious beliefs and desire to introduce morality into foreign policy. In contrast to the intensive study he devoted to understanding the politics of other regions of the world, especially the Middle East, he would later say, "I never was an expert on internal European political affairs." In March 1977, Brzezinski had sent Carter a memo concerning the rising power of the Communist Party in Italy and their effort to push their dream of a "compromiso historico" with the Christian Democrats, describing it as "potentially the gravest political problem facing the United States in Europe." It stirred little reaction from Carter, partly reflecting his discounting of Brzezinski's obsession with communism, but more because he felt no passion for the region.

When Margaret Thatcher became the leader of the Conservative Party in Britain, Carter had a disastrous meeting with her during which she sought to lecture him on foreign policy. He subsequently ordered his staff never to schedule another meeting with a foreign opposition leader. Later when Callaghan was defeated and she became prime minister, he felt even further distanced from European affairs, which he increasingly left in the hands of Brzezinski and Vance's successor Edmund Muskie.

As he sought to demonstrate his creation of the new vice-presidential role, Carter also underscored a new, unprecedented role for a first lady by sending Rosalynn on a substantive policymaking trip to Latin America at the end of May 1977. Prepared by hours of briefings and accompanied by Robert Pastor and Terence Todman, assistant secretary of state for Latin American affairs, Rosalynn visited Jamaica, Costa Rica, Ecuador, Peru, Brazil, Colombia, and Venezuela—countries either with democratic governments or moving toward democracy. She spent seven hours in substantive talks with Michael Manley, the Jamaican prime minister, on topics ranging from Cuban involvement in Africa to the economic impact of fluctuating international oil prices. Word quickly spread to the leaders of the other countries on her itinerary that this indeed was not a traditional goodwill social trip as they believed. Despite considerable discomfort and with some trepidation, the male Latin American leaders on the rest of the tour prepared themselves for serious discussions rather than ribbon cuttings and visits to children's hospitals. In Colombia, Rosalynn confronted President Lopez-Michelson with CIA evidence of drug-related corruption at the highest levels of his administration and in the judiciary. She negotiated a follow-up action plan.

The trip was a startling success, dumbfounding many of its critics in the State Department and in Congress. While there were strong complaints from traditionalists who felt she should not be playing any formal role in affairs of state, consistent with the changing times, Rosalynn had set a precedent and opened the door for a completely new role for first ladies.

CHAPTER 24

If the Lord didn't have him in his hands, he wouldn't be where he is.

—Rachel Clark

Despite the plethora of issues Carter had undertaken in the early months of his presidency, none would consume him as did his desire to achieve peace in the Middle East. The initial objective that he and Brzezinski sought was to reconvene the Geneva conference co-chaired by the United States and the Soviet Union. Following Vance's early fact-finding trip to the region, aimed at laying the groundwork for a Geneva meeting, Carter invited the key players to visit him in Washington. Israeli prime minister Yitzhak Rabin was the first to come on March 7–8. Although he had warmly greeted Carter during his trip to Israel in 1973, and had seemed flexible when he met Vance, he now proved cold and stiff. Carter used every ounce of charm he could muster in an effort to warm up his guest. Although part of the problem was Rabin's personality, it would later emerge that he was deliberately stonewalling to test Carter's resolve. Rabin had been encouraged to believe, by elements in the American Jewish community, that because of Carter's inexperience and his rocky relationship with the Jewish electorate, he could be made to bend to Israel's wishes.

It was a misjudgment. Carter felt his commitment to Israel's security was absolute. Over several years he had expended more time than any of his predecessors studying the issues involved and had looked forward to having an informative, in-depth discussion with Rabin. The rebuff of his sincere efforts to reactivate the peace process only angered him and was one of the factors that led him to say a few days later at a town hall meeting in Clinton, Massachusetts, "There has to be a homeland for the Palestinian refugees who have suffered for many, many years." It was something Carter sincerely believed must be part of any settlement, but it was a provocative statement to make publicly.

Between April 4 and May 24, Carter met with President Anwar Sadat of Egypt, King Hussein of Jordan, Crown Prince Fahd of Saudi Arabia, and, at the Intercontinental Hotel in Geneva following the May London economic summit, with Syria's President Hafez al-Assad. In seeking merely an exchange of views, Carter found the Arab leaders considerably more forthcoming than Rabin. With Sadat, the meeting began a friendship of deep mutual respect and affection. Part of the affinity between the two men, one a Christian, one a Moslem, was due to their shared devoutness in their respective religions. Even with Assad, shrewd, wily, infinitely cautious, and grudging in his concessions, Carter felt he was able to have an open and frank discussion.

Carter believed that any lasting peace in the Middle East must be based on clear principles of justice and fairness. He felt that because, unlike Israel, Arab leaders had little or no organized constituency in the United States to lobby their cause, it was incumbent on him to expose himself thoroughly to their point of view. However, Carter's statement about a Palestinian homeland, his refusal to sell anti-personnel cluster bombs to Israel, the restrictions he placed on the sale of a new fighter plane with U.S. components, and his rapid scheduling of more than token meetings with Arab leaders caused considerable disquiet among a segment of the American Jewish community. Jordan asked Mark Siegel, already working as one of his deputies on political appointments, to become the White House liaison to that constituency. With Siegel's help, Jordan prepared a forty-one-page memo submitted to Carter in June 1977, addressing the impact of Middle East policy on the Jewish vote. In it he noted,

> I would compare our present understanding of the American Jewish lobby (vis-à-vis Israel) to our understanding of the American labor movement four years ago. We are aware of its strength and influence, but don't understand the basis for that strength nor the way it is used politically. It is something that was not a part of our Georgia and southern political experience and consequently not well understood.

Carter tended to view the pro-Israeli lobby as he did all other self-serving constituency groups, as threatening to distract him from what he believed was the right thing for the country as a whole. At Jordan's urging he met with Jewish leaders to explain what he was doing. As in his dealings with Congress, he assumed that as reasonable people, if they understood his approach, he would earn their support. What he was not willing to do was let them deter him from the course of action he sincerely believed was right in the long run for all the players, including Israel—even if it meant confrontation. Taking advantage of this, on October 1, 1977, Brzezinski convinced Carter, as part of the strategy, to reconvene the Geneva talks and, as a way to improve U.S.–Soviet relations, to release a joint U.S.–Soviet statement on the Middle East. Quietly negotiated by the State Department and Brzezinski, without any other White House involvement, it proved a domestic political bombshell and an object lesson in the limitations of the spokes-of-the-wheel approach to managing the White House. The first Mark Siegel knew about it was when he heard the news on the radio driving into Washington from National Airport. He pulled over to an emergency phone and had the White House switchboard connect him with Jordan at a speaking engagement in Florida. Siegel accurately warned that publicly embracing the reentry of the Soviet Union into the peace process would enrage the Jewish community. "If I could have had twenty-four hours, if I could have gotten the leadership on the phone, I could have tried to explain it . . . but they heard it on the radio like I did." Jordan was initially incredulous that it could have been done without his knowledge. Siegel's credibility with the American Jewish community had been irreparably damaged.

In the face of a firestorm of criticism, the next day Jordan convened a meeting in the Roosevelt room that included Eizenstat, Lipshutz, Siegel, Mondale, and, astonishingly, the Israeli ambassador, Simcha Dinitz. Brzezinski was invited, but as one participant noted, "He was set up." It was, he added, "a total humiliation of Brzezinski . . . a deliberate attempt to humiliate him in front of a foreign ambassador." Brzezinski's defense was that the president did not want domestic politics to interfere with foreign policy.

Jordan then insisted to Carter that he be included in the weekly foreign policy breakfast he held with Vance, Brzezinski, and Mondale. As one colleague recalled, "From that point on, Hamilton used that incident, exploited it, manipulated it to insert himself into the foreign policy decision-making process. Very skillfully." Mondale, himself a fervent advocate for Israel who was deeply dismayed by Carter's failure to use foreign policy to curry favor with domestic constituency groups, backed the involvement of Jordan. "In general, Carter rarely, if ever, thought of foreign policy in terms of domestic politics, while Mondale rarely, if ever, thought of it otherwise," one observer noted.

In the Middle East, Menachem Begin had succeeded Rabin as prime minister of Israel and proved even more unyielding than Rabin. Arab nations saw White House backpedaling after the joint U.S.–Soviet statement as evidence of a lack of sincere commitment to the peace process. At the end of October, when the United Nations was considering a resolution criticizing Israeli construction of settlements in the occupied territories, Carter, encouraged by Vance and Brzezinski, ordered Andrew Young to vote for the resolution, despite opposition from Eizenstat, Lipshutz, Mondale, Siegel, and Jordan. Carter believed the settlements were illegal and added further unnecessary obstacles to the peace process, and said so. He was also frustrated and angry at Begin's intransigence. At the same time, he wanted to regain the trust of the Arabs and prove that he was capable of brokering a just peace.

During the same week he sent a handwritten note to Sadat appealing to him to make a bold statesmanlike move to help break the logjam. Sadat attached considerable significance to the communication, considering the request a test of their personal friendship. On November 3, Sadat proposed a world summit in East Jerusalem to include the major powers, the moderate Arab states, and the PLO. Carter and his advisors saw it as a disappointing and unrealistic proposal.

After a two-week hiatus, searching for other options and under continuing pressure from Carter, Sadat announced to the Egyptian parliament that he was ready to go himself to Jerusalem. Begin responded through Carter with an invitation for Sadat to address the Knesset. Publicly Sadat credited Carter's personal note for inspiring his initiative. Later, however, he would confide to one acquaintance that it was the joint U.S.–Soviet communique that had convinced him that he had to take some dramatic action to steer the peace process away from Geneva. "I'd just spent two years throwing the Soviets out of the Middle East and now the United States is inviting them back in. I'm taking this back into my own hands," he reportedly said. At the same time, he understood the domestic political jeopardy Carter was in, and his strong sense of friendship impelled him to try to respond helpfully.

On the morning of Sadat's historic speech, November 20, Carter made a point of going to the early morning service at the First Baptist Church and publicly praying for peace. It was the breakthrough Carter had desperately sought, but he was disappointed in Begin's tepid response, offering Sadat little or nothing for the enormous courage of his gesture. Over the next several months, follow-up discussions failed to capitalize on Sadat's high-risk gambit, which had left him thoroughly ostracized in the Arab world.

Carter was devoting increasing amounts of time to the Middle East peace process to the detriment of other priorities, especially the energy package. By late 1977, he was paying the price for having put so many balls in the air in the first three months of his presidency, yet the pursuit of the peace process held an irresistible attraction. During a trip to the region at the start of 1978, both he and Sadat made upbeat statements with carefully crafted phrasing that they thought Begin might accept. After having shown some earlier flexibility on the issue of settlements in the Sinai, Begin retreated from his position in December, claiming pressure of internal Israeli politics when he met with Sadat in Ismailia on December 27. By the end of January, Sadat was feeling discouraged, and only the most urgent entreaties from Carter kept him from pulling out of the whole peace process.

Carter was not willing to accept failure. Meeting with Jordan, Mondale, Vance, and Brzezinski on February 3, Carter stood alone in his desire to move more aggressively on the Middle East. He believed that the best prospect was to develop an "American plan" and then convince Begin and Sadat to adopt it as their own. That weekend, when Sadat came with his wife, Jihan, the Carters took them to Camp David. In that relaxed atmosphere Carter used the strength of his personal relationship with the frustrated Egyptian, whom he increasingly regarded as a personal friend, to persuade him to accept his new strategy.

With Begin the situation remained difficult. Both Foreign Minister Moshe Dayan and Defense Minister Ezer Weizman were far more moderate and practical. In their discussions with Vance, Brzezinski, and Carter, they would offer positive and constructive suggestions only to be reversed by Begin. Carter told an aide, "If I only had to deal with Weizman, I would have a comprehensive peace settlement in a week." When Begin and his wife, Aliza, came to Washington in late March, the Carters devoted most of the time trying to build a personal relationship with them. Carter learned about Begin's life, the loss of his family members in the Holocaust, the time he had spent in prison, and the depth of his religious convictions. As with Sadat, Carter found it was the latter aspect of Begin's character that he could most easily relate to. Begin returned at the beginning of May for the celebration in the United States of the thirtieth anniversary of the founding of the state of Israel. They each shook hands with 1,200 guests on the south lawn of the White House. In an emotional speech, Carter reaffirmed permanent U.S. support for Israel and promised to establish an American memorial to the Holocaust.

None of this advanced the peace process in the short term. Carter continued to expend a significant portion of his time on the issue, receiving little thanks and paying an increasing domestic political price. In early June, Carter met with a group of Democratic elder statesmen who told him, "Stay as aloof as possible from direct involvement in the Middle East negotiations; this is a losing proposition." Democratic congressional leaders urged Carter to abandon his efforts to seek peace and instead repair the damage he had done to the party and to U.S.–Israeli relations. In June, Carter had to cancel Democratic fund-raisers in Los Angeles and New York because so many of the mostly Jewish party members had canceled their reservations.

Despite the political damage, Carter continued to be irresistibly drawn back to the issue. He saw the historic opportunity and felt an obligation to seize it. On May 1, he wrote in his diary concerning his discussions with Begin:

> I told him that peace in the Middle East was in his hands, that he had a
> unique opportunity to either bring it into being or kill it. . . . My guess is that

he will not take the necessary steps to bring peace to Israel—an opportunity that may never come again.

Mondale returned from a trip to the Middle East in which he worked hard to give Begin a better understanding of Carter, but returned empty-handed. Vance held a meeting of the foreign ministers of Israel and Egypt on neutral territory at Leeds Castle in England. He found the positions of both sides had become too frozen for useful negotiations. He advised Carter that he now accepted Carter's earlier premise that the United States must be more than a mediator and should develop its own peace plan. Carter talked the situation over with Rosalynn, who knew and understood the issues and the players as well as he did. They agreed together that he should make one more all-out effort even though the inherent risks were enormous.

At a meeting with Brzezinski on January 23, Carter had raised the possibility of inviting Sadat and Begin to a long session at Camp David, but both agreed the other demands on Carter's time made such a meeting impossible in the short term. Now he decided to gamble on such a meeting. The stakes were enormous and the prospects of success were slim. Failure would compound the perception of Carter as inept. Traditionally heads of state or government attended summits only after underlings had worked out agreements. It was unprecedented to bring them together to do the negotiating themselves. In addition, Begin and Sadat were so personally incompatible that their meetings had become fruitless. Carter was counting on his personal rapport with each man to bridge that gap. He dispatched Vance with handwritten invitations to Begin and Sadat, both of whom quickly accepted. He also asked them to restrain their hostile rhetoric against each other.

The thirteen days of the Camp David summit and the resulting accords would be hailed as the single greatest accomplishment of the Carter presidency. Success was achieved, in large part, because of specific personal traits that Carter brought to the negotiations: unrelenting tenacity, a fierce aversion to failure, a capacity to invoke trust as an honest broker, a deep belief in the power of reconciliation, and a capacity to school himself in the minute details of the proposed agreements to a degree that exceeded even that of the other two principals.

Sadat arrived at Camp David first, his credibility in the Arab world dependent on achieving a peace settlement, even if not a perfect agreement. He viewed himself as a man of destiny and was scornful of the petty indecisiveness of other Arab leaders. He was also angry and embittered over Begin's apparent failure to understand the enormous risks he had already taken and his frustrating reluctance to make concessions on the remaining obstacles that stood in the way of an agreement that could win them both the accolades of history. As an autocratic ruler he did not fully appreciate the varied domestic political pressures Begin was under.

Begin, who presided over a highly divided cabinet, was far more fearful of making the wrong agreement than of having no agreement at all. Of the three men, he had the least to lose by leaving empty-handed. What terrified him was that in the heat of the moment he would be pressured into concessions that would leave him accountable by future generations for jeopardizing the security of the Jewish state. He came to Camp David more concerned with procedural matters, such as how many advisors each side could bring, and the protocol implications of his being only a head of government while the other two principals were heads of state. He seemed much less preoccupied with the substance of the negotiations. He also came with the belief that their goal was to develop principles for an ultimate agreement, with the details to be worked out later at a lower level. Carter had to disabuse him of this and insist that their purpose was to achieve a complete agreement.

During the first two days Carter spent time alone with each man discussing their opening proposals. He was initially dismayed by the harsh content of the Egyptian plan Sadat handed him, filled with hardline Arab rhetoric and demands that were patently unacceptable to Israel. Sadat then told Carter of the modifications and concessions he would accept in a final agreement, most of which, they both knew, Begin could accept. Sadat, however, implored Carter not to mention the compromises he was willing to make as it would destroy the strength of his negotiating position. Begin presented proposals to Carter that contained nothing new, repeating only the hard-worn Israeli position and offering no hint of flexibility. Knowing what Begin's initial response to Sadat's proposal would be, Carter beseeched him not to overreact.

When the three men met and Sadat delivered his proposal, Carter could sense the explosive tension mounting in Begin. Finally, he said jokingly to Begin, "If you would just accept and sign the Egyptian proposal as written, it would save us all a lot of time." The ensuing laughter broke the tension and the meeting ended on a note of civility and goodwill with Begin graciously expressing his appreciation for all of the hard work that had gone into the Egyptian document.

The Carters had worked hard to create an atmosphere of informality for the meetings, wearing casual clothes and allowing time for all the participants to take walks, play tennis, and even watch movies. Begin was accompanied by his wife, Aliza, but, because of a sick grandchild, Jihan Sadat was staying in Paris. The Carters hoped that the relaxed environment would eventually enable the principals to socialize together, build a greater level of trust, and enable them more easily to come to substantive agreement. While the Carters, especially as the hosts, were able to do this with the Begins and Sadat separately, they were never able to achieve harmony as a group. Although their staffs, including Ezer Weizman and Moshe Dayan on the Israeli side and Boutros Boutros Ghali on the Egyptian side, mingled freely, Begin and Sadat kept to themselves except for the formal sessions.

The Israelis predictably rejected the Egyptian proposal, but over the next two days, with Carter's careful orchestration, it proved the basis for defining the areas of difference and agreement. Sadat was committed to creating a framework for an overall Middle East peace, even if it meant sequential specific agreements as other Arab leaders joined the process. Within this overall context, Sadat's first priorities were to achieve the return of the Sinai to Egypt and work out an agreement on the West Bank–Palestinian problem. As Sadat had long asserted to Carter, it quickly became clear that while Begin was willing to negotiate over the return of the Sinai, despite paying lip service to international agreements to the contrary, his intent was to hold on to the West Bank for ultimate annexation by Israel. In a heated discussion, Sadat confronted Begin over what he saw as a duplicitous approach, saying forcefully, "Security, yes. Land, no!"

Putting aside the West Bank–Palestinian issue, they focused on the one area of potential progress—the Sinai. But even there they eventually deadlocked over Sadat's demand that all Israeli settlements be withdrawn. After a long meeting at the end of the third day, when it seemed further discussion was pointless, Carter moved quickly to get between the door and his two guests so as to convince them not to break off the talks and to allow him time to find some way out of the deadlock. That evening, as all the delegations attended entertainment provided by a U.S. Marine unit, there was a sense of discouragement and a belief that the talks had irretrievably broken down. Some of Sadat's aides told Carter their team was preparing to leave Camp David. To head this off, Carter and his top aides arranged to meet with the Egyptian delegation after the Marine Corps display. They talked until after midnight.

Sadat had given Carter a list of the issues on which he would not compromise. Beyond that he had authorized Carter and the American team to draft proposals that they could use as a basis for negotiation with the Israelis. Carter found Begin's staff much more flexible than Begin himself, whereas Sadat's advisors were more hardline than Sadat. At times the irreconcilable nature of some of the differences seemed so great that Carter's primary job was just to keep the parties at Camp David and not have them view the situation as hopeless.

Over the next two days, with the input of his aides, who were constantly consulting with their counterparts, Carter prepared the comprehensive proposal to be presented to the Egyptian and Israeli delegations. It was a complex document involving more than fifty intertwined issues. Carter omitted the matter of the settlements in the Sinai, knowing that if it was there, Begin would focus on that and nothing else. By leaving it out he hoped to get broad agreement on everything else and create an irresistible momentum. Late the following morning, a Sunday, and the sixth day of the talks, Carter had arranged for all of the participants to visit the nearby Gettysburg battlefields. It was a welcome break from the increasingly claustrophobic atmosphere of Camp David, but also served as a not very subtle reminder of the horrors of war that can ensue when leaders fail to settle their differences by peaceful negotiation.

By longstanding prior agreement Carter was obliged to show any proposal to the Israelis for their comments before allowing the Egyptians access to it. Beginning that afternoon and continuing late into the night, the American and Israeli teams went over Carter's plan in minute detail. Parts of the plan were acceptable, but at other points Begin seemed to be backsliding. At one point he questioned the acceptability of the wording in U.N. Resolution 242—"inadmissibility of acquisition of land by war." Together with Resolution 338, this had been the basis for all the Middle East peace discussions up to that point. To question such a fundamental premise angered Carter and made him seriously doubt whether Begin really was interested in peace. The matter was eventually resolved, but when the meeting broke up, Carter asked Dayan to walk back to his cottage with him. The two men, already exhausted, talked until dawn. Carter greatly respected Dayan, whom he saw as tough but pragmatic. He also knew him to be very close to, and trusted by, Begin. Carter shared with Dayan his feelings that Begin was being unreasonable and his doubts about whether he really was interested in peace. Dayan emphatically reassured Carter that Begin did want an agreement. The two men then spent the rest of the night discussing possible compromises on the settlement issue.

After a brief sleep, Carter was up incorporating the changes that had come out of the discussion with the Israelis into the draft proposal. He gave the new draft to both sides. The Egyptians would spend the next twenty-four hours studying it. In the meantime, Carter began working with the technical experts, using copious maps, on a parallel agreement to the overall proposal that would detail the specific terms of Israel's withdrawal from the Sinai.

That evening, the eighth day, Carter ate dinner in the dining hall with the Israeli delegation. Afterward, Begin told him that he needed to have what he described as "the most serious talk we have ever had." Again he raised the issue of Resolution 242, saying that while his government had approved it, he could accept no reference to it in their Framework for

Peace. As he did frequently, he resorted to quoting biblical texts. For Carter it reinforced what had always been Sadat's primary complaint about Begin—that he was preoccupied with a bitter inclination to look back into ancient history rather than address the present and the future. Begin finally pulled from his pocket what amounted to a draft press statement thanking the United States for inviting Egypt and Israel to Camp David, and saying that there had been some areas of agreement. He claimed that while he sincerely wished to do so, he could not sign Carter's draft proposal. Carter responded with frustration and anger. According to Carter, the heated discussion was "unpleasant and repetitive."

But Carter was not about to give up. The next morning he set out to draft a new version of the framework document. He did so with the help of Israeli Attorney General Aharon Barak, whom he knew Begin trusted, and Osama el-Baz, perhaps the most militant on the Egyptian side. For eleven hours they pored over the draft, seeking to eliminate or soften the wording that each side found objectionable. Cyrus Vance was also a key participant, bringing not only his diplomatic skills but also those of an experienced international lawyer. Most of the contentious issues were resolved, but when it came to the questions of settlements, Barak said that only Begin could address that issue. Later when Carter went to thank Begin for staying at Camp David and allowing his staff to work with him on the new draft, Begin warned him that he could not sign anything that called for Israel to remove its settlements.

On the tenth day, Carter eagerly joined Sadat for his early morning walk. Sadat's early retirement to bed the night before and their close personal friendship made Carter worry about the psychological toll that failure of the talks might have on the Egyptian president. He also knew that, whatever the outcome, Sadat would return home to face a serious threat to his physical safety. Sadat talked as they walked about how, since the visit to Gettysburg, he had come to appreciate how Carter, as a southerner, must understand the hardships of rebuilding the spirit of a nation after devastating military defeat.

Discussions during the day suggested broad agreement on the new document. Yet in the final analysis the key stumbling block remained the intractable issue of the settlements. Both sides were adamant. It was a stalemate. Carter asked Mondale to come to Camp David so that they could begin to plan how to minimize the negative fallout from the failure of the talks. Carter was under steadily growing pressure to focus his attention on other urgent matters of government business. He asked the Israelis and Egyptians to provide him with material for a joint communique and he started working on a speech he intended to make to Congress detailing both the successes and the failures of the talks.

Suddenly, Vance burst into Carter's cottage to announce that after a fruitless meeting with Dayan aimed at salvaging the talks, Sadat was packing to leave. Even Carter's careful plans to minimize the failure and have a harmonious departure were falling apart. Carter stared out of the window at the Catoctin Mountains and, for several minutes, prayed for divine intervention. Then he walked over to Sadat's cabin. Carter implored Sadat to stay, invoking what he described as their most precious possession—their personal friendship and mutual trust. Carter even told Sadat that, if he left, not only their political relationship but their personal friendship would be at an end. Sadat felt the Israelis had no real intention of signing any agreement and that they had wasted everyone's time for ten days. He had, he argued, agreed to everything in the Carter proposal. He could not, however, sign a unilateral agreement embodying all the concessions he had made if the Israelis were going to walk away having made none. Carter promised him that if either nation subsequently rejected any part of the agreement, none of the proposals would stay in effect.

After a long pause, Sadat said, "If you give me this statement, I will stick with you to the end."

Carter hurried back to his cottage to inform Rosalynn and the other U.S. negotiators that Sadat had agreed to stay.

The following morning, the twelfth day, Carter proceeded with the "failure" strategy. He made courtesy visits to Sadat and Begin, thanking them for their participation, and in the case of Sadat, promising that he and Rosalynn would accept his invitation to come to Egypt. Similar conversations were occurring among other members of the teams. Although everyone was willing to accept that the talks had failed, there was a continuing effort to find a way around the problem of the settlements. Weizman, always the most optimistic, told Sadat he believed that if the matter were submitted to the Knesset and it remained the only impediment to peace, the legislators would vote to remove the settlers. Sadat had, he later reported to Carter, expressed a willingness to consider such a compromise in the final Sinai agreement. This was not what Carter took to be Sadat's position, but still tenaciously hoping to grab success from the jaws of defeat, Carter asked the Israeli delegation to meet with him.

Reflecting long discussions that had gone on in the Israeli delegation, Begin finally promised Carter that within two weeks he would submit to the Knesset the question: "If agreement is reached on all other Sinai issues, will the settlers be withdrawn?" It was the breakthrough they had all sought. Sadat was willing to accept the compromise. Always fearful of being held ultimately accountable for an error, Begin had shown, as he would repeatedly, far greater flexibility if the responsibility could be shared or placed on others.

Later in the day, other lesser obstacles emerged. Carter wanted a joint letter on the future of Jerusalem appended to the agreements, the wording of which generated heated contention, but was finally resolved. The most lasting difficulty would arise from a commitment Begin made to end future construction of settlements on the West Bank after the signing of the framework document. Although the record is clear, Begin would later claim, after violating the agreement, that he had meant the building of settlements would be suspended for only three months.

Finally, at 10:15 P.M. on the thirteenth day, Carter, Begin, and Sadat appeared in the East Room at the White House to sign the two documents: the Framework for Peace in the Middle East and the Framework for the Conclusion of the Peace Treaty Between Egypt and Israel.

Carter received deserved accolades for the achievement. Joseph Kraft wrote in the *Washington Post* that Carter had taken "a first, big step toward realizing the promise of his presidency." The *Wall Street Journal* would note that with his "brilliant success" and "inspired leadership" he had "reestablished his presidency in fundamental terms." In a single month his standing in the polls rose more than 15 points.

Carter's extraordinary accomplishment was more a contribution to the world and the future of humankind than it was to America. It was also only the beginning, although the crucial building block, of what would be a long and tortuous path toward a comprehensive peace settlement. Twenty years later it would still not be fully achieved. The amount of Carter's time and mental energy consumed by the Camp David negotiations specifically, and the Middle East peace process generally, severely compromised his ability to achieve success in other aspects of his presidential agenda. However, Carter's personality and particularly his faith made him feel that any accomplishment that history would interpret as a legacy to humanity should take precedence over whatever accomplishments would ultimately be seen as merely domestic political triumphs.

CHAPTER 25

In the sweltering dog days of summer in Washington during nonelection years, news stories that would pass largely unnoticed at any other time take on a life and tenacity of their own. Such was the case with the so-called "Lance Affair."

Bert Lance had a symbiotic relationship with the president, his ebullience a counterpoint to Carter's shyness. For Carter, who as a child had always been concerned about his slight stature, Lance's six-foot-four frame and hulking presence made him seem like a physical as well as a political protector. Carter had little interest in spending time at Georgetown dinner parties, or engaging in informal gatherings with members of Congress or journalists—time-honored and often vital aspects of the political process in Washington. Bert and LaBelle were happy to play the role of understudies for Jimmy and Rosalynn in the social life of the city.

Carter preferred to spend what little time he had away from the Oval Office with his family. He, Rosalynn, and the boys had agreed they needed to pay special attention to Amy in order to compensate for her otherwise abnormal existence in the White House.

The Lances and the Carters shared a deep religious faith, although unlike Carter who truly believed "the real message to me from Christ is that of humility," Lance's flamboyant style suggested the opposite. Acquiring wealth had been an important goal for him. Following his failed gubernatorial bid in 1974, he had established a financial base for himself in Atlanta by buying a controlling share in the National Bank of Georgia (NBG). He and LaBelle also purchased a mansion they named "Butterfly Manna," in the most prestigious section of the city. They bought a second home in Sea Island, an exclusive enclave for the wealthy.

In accordance with Carter's directive that all appointees divest themselves of any financial holdings that might prove a conflict of interest, at the time of his appointment as OMB director, Lance agreed to place his $3.3 million worth of NBG stock in a blind trust with instructions that the entire portfolio be sold by the end of 1977. By July the value of the stock had declined to $1.7 million. Combined with the considerable drop in income Lance had experienced by joining the Carter cabinet, it became difficult to service his various personal financial obligations and put him in what he felt was a perilous financial state. After consulting with Charles Kirbo, Carter wrote a letter on Lance's behalf to Senator Abraham Ribicoff, chairman of the Senate Government Operations Committee, which had confirmed Lance, requesting an indefinite extension of the December 31 deadline for selling the stock. Lance appeared before the committee and was granted the extension.

The attention focused on Lance over the NBG stock issue unleashed a deluge of other accusations. Leaks began to emerge from the Treasury Department about earlier closed investigations done under the Ford administration concerning his management of the National Bank of Calhoun. Lance attributed these leaks in part to his conflicts with Treasury Secretary Blumenthal. With Watergate still fresh in their minds and memories of careers enhanced by toppling a president, reporters engaged in a relentless effort to inflate even the most trivial story about Lance. His close personal relationship with the president made him an irresistible target. William Safire, already antagonistic to Carter over his Middle East policy, implied that Lance had peddled his influence in obtaining a $3.4 million loan from the First National Bank of Chicago.

As Lance hung on under withering attack, comptroller of the currency John Heimann released a long-awaited 394-page report on Lance's banking practices on August 18. While the report cleared Lance of having done anything illegal, it did accuse him of "unsafe and unsound banking practices." It particularly referred to his policy as president of the National Bank of Georgia of permitting sizable overdrafts on the accounts of its officers and their relatives. It might also have mentioned, but did not, his willingness to make loans and overdrafts available to poor whites and blacks with little or no security, who could obtain credit from no other source.

The White House chose to emphasize the positive aspects of the report, ignoring the critical sections. Carter held a news conference to announce the findings in which he implied that Lance had been fully vindicated. With Lance standing next to him, he warmly assured him, "Bert, I'm proud of you."

Instead of dying away as Carter and Jordan hoped and predicted, the problem continued to escalate over the next two weeks. Hurt by his high visibility and close relationship with the president, Lance could not avoid being a stand-in for those who wished to attack Carter. He was also a victim of the promises Carter had repeatedly made to bring the very highest ethical standards to government. Lance's transgressions pale to insignificance against those of dozens of appointees by Carter's successor, Ronald Reagan, but Lance was judged by the different standard Carter had set.

With new and damaging stories leading the network news almost every night, Lance's picture on the cover of *Time* and *Newsweek*, and the pressure to resign ever mounting, the White House took on a siege mentality. There was also internal conflict. Mondale, who liked Lance, had said to him early on, "Bert, get out of here. There's no medicine to take care of this. They're after you and they won't stop until they get you." As the days wore on and Mondale remained silent, there was growing frustration with him among Carter's intimates. They believed it was Mondale's liberal friends who were leading the assault on Lance, and a clear public defense of him by the vice president, they argued, would turn the tide. Frustrated by Carter's continuing squandering of his moral leadership, Mondale told him, "When you get into personnel matters like this, it is far better to cut your losses than to keep your friends." Mondale also wanted to maintain his distance for fear of what it would do to his own credibility and political future. Carter continued to defend Lance, believing that "some things are more important than politics," even though Jordan warned Carter and Lance that the situation was inflicting huge damage on the administration.

It was finally agreed that Lance would appear on Wednesday, September 15, before Ribicoff's committee, together with his lawyer Clark Clifford, to defend himself publicly. Carter argued that Lance should have his "day in court," saying later that he believed "Bert would be permanently disgraced if he left office without having some chance to defend himself." Carter asked people to suspend their judgment until they had heard Lance's side of the story. Early that morning, Lance went to the White House, Bible in hand, and in Carter's small study next to the Oval Office the two men took turns reading scriptures to each other. Their session ended with Lance reading from Ecclesiastes: "To everything there is a season, and a time to every purpose under the heavens . . . a time to keep silent and a time to speak."

In a two-hour opening statement and under intense subsequent questioning, Lance acquitted himself impressively and there was a momentary belief that he might be able to salvage his job. However, at a meeting on Saturday morning attended by Mondale, Jordan, Powell, and Charles Kirbo, Carter accepted that Lance should step down.

Over the weekend, Senate Majority Leader Robert Byrd had told Carter that despite Lance's stellar performance, the problem would not vanish. The presidency, he warned Carter, was more important than any single individual. He met with Lance on Monday morning to congratulate him on his performance, but also to tell him that the opposition was not receding and that he should consider resigning. Lance said that before making a decision he wanted to talk to his wife and to Clark Clifford. Late in the afternoon he played tennis with Carter, Jordan, and speechwriter Jim Fallows. After the game he and Carter talked for forty-five minutes. At the end of the discussion, Lance said he intended to resign; however, he could not reconcile LaBelle to his decision, and the following morning, September 21, they met again with Carter in his study. In an agonizing conversation that was deeply painful for Carter, LaBelle accused him of betraying his best friend. The decision, nevertheless, had been made, and later in the day Lance submitted his official letter of resignation. At a news conference announcing the decision, Carter rejected the written statement Powell had prepared for him, feeling that he needed to speak extemporaneously to convey the emotion he felt and the sincerity of what he wanted to say. "Nothing," he said, "has shaken my belief in Bert's ability or his integrity."

That night Carter recorded in his diary that it had been "one of the worst days I've ever spent." Lance's departure was a profoundly significant turning point in Carter's presidency. Although he sought to conceal it, the loss not only had a shattering emotional effect on Carter, it also deprived him of someone who had been his right arm in government since his earliest days as governor. He was now more isolated than ever and, while he would turn even more to Rosalynn for emotional solace and to share in decision making, there was no one to replace Bert in his frontline operational role. Without Bert, Carter quickly abandoned tennis and took up the more solitary exercise of jogging.

Lance's resignation also took the wind out of the administration's sails. The momentum of the first seven months was halted and the resignation itself became an immense distraction, drawing public attention away from the administration's priorities and diverting the White House staff from Carter's legislative agenda. The media was emboldened by their success in getting rid of Lance. Carter was seen as vulnerable and on the defensive.

It was also a time when many of Carter's programs were beginning to run into trouble and they needed his full-time attention. In the early months the frenzy of activity and cornucopia of initiatives had created the impression of Carter seizing control of the reins of government and instituting the radical changes that he had promised. Reassuring plans, projects, legislation, and rhetoric had been promulgated to please and captivate almost every constituency group. By summer the administration was running up against the harsh realities involved in trying to fulfill what had always been exaggerated expectations, substantially created by Carter's own rhetoric.

Reluctantly, and against the advice of Stuart Eizenstat, Carter had signed the compromise bill on the water projects that still contained several expensive and environmentally unsound initiatives. Environmentalists were not happy, especially because Carter, too often a captive of his southern hyperbole, had initially posed the elimination of the projects as a clear issue of morality and fiscal responsibility. He was now compromising with the very forces of evil he had originally condemned.

Thanks to Tip O'Neill, the energy package had successfully passed the House. However, the flaws in the plan—resulting from the speed with which Carter required that it be put together—and the relentless assault it was undergoing from special interests, had it bogged down in the Senate. Having invested so much political capital in what he had told Americans was "the moral equivalent of war," his failure to drive the legislation unscathed through the Congress with the same urgency he had delivered it to them was seen by the public as a failure of presidential leadership. Carter would later say, "We had a very heavy agenda of items that I thought would be beneficial for our country. I can tell you with complete candor that we didn't assess the adverse political consequences." The public had little sympathy for the Senate, or the oil interests that had a stranglehold on key members, but they were counting on Carter, as the people's president, to overcome the opposition on their behalf. In an October 12 memo, Eizenstat told Carter, "The administration's performance in the first year will be measured in large part by the outcome of your national energy plan." "True," Carter wrote in the margin. Frustrated, he used his press conference on October 13 to attack the oil companies for perpetrating "the biggest rip-off in history," and demanded Senate action. There had been an exponential growth in the power of lobbying groups in the 1970s, which Carter later referred to as "insidious legal bribery."

In addition, what emerged after the early honeymoon months was evidence of the profound schisms in the Democratic Party. Historian Steven Gillon has stated it well:

> The central question which liberals and the Democratic Party needed to address in the mid-1970s: How does a party, whose coalition was forged during depression and sustained by decades of economic growth, face the threat posed by slower growth and rising inflation? It would be a difficult balancing act for even the most adroit politician because the party's two major factions were frequently hostile to each other's interests. Younger, independent voters tended to be economically conservative and socially liberal, with little sense of partisan feeling. They resented even the image of pandering to well-organized interests. Older voters remained wedded to the economic agenda of the New Deal and Great Society. Deeply partisan, they took pride in past accomplishments and jealously defended their organizational interests.

Carter was squarely in the first category, deeply committed to improving the quality of life for ordinary, and especially poor Americans, but at the same time strongly convinced that limiting federal spending, balancing the budget, and controlling inflation had to take precedence over the continued growth of government social programs. Carter would reminisce, "I wish . . . you . . . could have seen the stricken expression on the faces of

those Democratic leaders when I was talking about balancing the budget."
Dick Moe, Mondale's Chief of Staff, would later say:

> At this point in history . . . the Congress had all these pent-up demands. . . .
> Mondale was part of this mind set. We thought that the Nixon years were just
> an interruption of the normal—the standard way of doing things which was
> the Kennedy/Johnson years. But the world had changed, and it was going to
> change even more. But Democrats did not recognize that. That was the great
> unacknowledged fact of the Carter years. Carter, more than any other Demo-
> crat, acknowledged the fiscal realities, and congressional Democrats, Mon-
> dale included, did not.

The marriage of convenience contrived between the Carter campaign
and the majority liberal wing of the party began to break down the day he
was elected. In their eagerness to win back the White House, liberals had
been willing to suppress the ambiguity they felt toward Carter, believing
that once in the White House he would follow the traditional Democratic
policies with a return to heavy government spending. Now, eight months
into the administration, as it became clear this was not what Carter
intended to do, liberal groups became increasingly angry, claiming that
Carter had betrayed them. It could be argued that Carter had skillfully
used titillating and misleading rhetoric to get the liberal vote, but it was
equally true that liberals, so eager to recapture the White House, had
failed to discern the careful precision with which Carter had made his
promises. Despite the overwhelming role that liberal Democrats had
played in his victory, Carter felt little obligation to accommodate them
ideologically.

Shortly after the election, Carter asked HEW secretary Joseph Califano
how soon he could have a welfare reform package ready, something
promised in the campaign. "May 1," Califano replied cavalierly, not anticipating that Carter would actually hold him to it. Working with Ray Marshall,
secretary of labor and, like himself, a Lyndon Johnson liberal, Califano
began to develop a series of reform plans. Trying to protect the interests of
the constituencies served by their respective departments, Califano and
Marshall were unable to agree on a single specific plan. What they did agree
on was that any reform plan would require additional funding. They met with
Carter on March 25, both in an attempt to get the May 1 deadline moved back
and to see if they could resolve their differences. However, Carter was res-
olute. He wanted to stick to May 1 and he wanted proposals redesigned at
"current funding levels." With the two department heads unable to resolve
their differences, three zero-cost reform plans were developed. The first
featured a Labor Department jobs program for welfare recipients who
could work. The second, conceived by HEW, involved scrapping the exist-

ing nine separate programs and replacing them with the so-called negative income tax that would provide cash payments to the poor based solely on need. The third, backed by organized labor, combined a jobs program with cash payments to those who could not work.

Meeting with Carter on April 11, Califano argued that regardless of the plan, without additional funding many welfare recipients would be worse off after the reforms than they were before. Firmly convinced that a reorganization and streamlining of the existing patchwork of programs had to deliver better services more economically, Carter exploded: "Are you telling me that there is no way to improve the present welfare system except by spending billions of dollars? In that case, to hell with it! We're wasting our time."

Following the meeting, Jordan wrote Carter the following:

> As I sat in the welfare meeting today, several things were obvious to me: You don't have a clear idea yet of what kind of program you want. . . . HEW has provided at best sketchy options. . . . The critical relationship between welfare reform and tax reform has not been well defined.

He pointed out that no effort had been made to discuss the proposal and build consensus support on the Hill. He concluded, "I don't believe it is humanly possible to have a good welfare program ready by May 1 that you believe in and are comfortable with."

Califano and Marshall continued to try to resolve the deeply entrenched institutional differences between their departments, but with only limited success. On May 1, to meet his self-imposed deadline, Carter was forced to issue merely a statement of principles upon which his welfare reform plan would be based, deferring the actual legislative package until August. Carter's failure to provide specific direction, his overloaded legislative agenda, his increasing exhaustion, and his insistence on holding to unrealistically tight deadlines just compounded the more fundamental philosophical schism.

Although largely overshadowed by the conflicts with Congress and public failures, Carter did achieve some notable successes. He received authority to reorganize the executive branch. The Byrd Amendment was repealed, allowing him to reimpose an embargo on chromium importation from Rhodesia. The Tax Reduction and Simplification Act was passed. A bill was passed allowing the appointment of 148 new judgeships. Carter's judicial appointments, including many women and minorities, were widely praised. In June, he and the Congress launched what would prove an extremely successful deregulation of airline rates. He climaxed a ten-year environmental struggle, signing an anti–strip mining and reclamation bill. On October 12, he signed a $13.7 billion Housing and Community

Development Act. In December, he signed a Social Security measure that would keep the system solvent until 2030, even though Republicans attacked it as "the biggest peacetime tax increase in U.S. history."

At the same time, Carter's eroding support among traditional Democratic groups became increasingly manifest. His economic stimulus package fell well short of what labor leaders and the Congressional Black Caucus had requested. He further angered labor by denying their request for an increase in the minimum wage. Carter had benefitted during the campaign from Ford's decision to veto the 1975 emergency farm bill on the grounds that it was too expensive. Farmers, anticipating special understanding from a fellow farmer, were sorely disappointed. His initial farm program proposed support prices even lower than those that existed. Only under pressure from an inevitable veto override did Carter accept a compromise. Carter had perhaps unnecessarily aggravated his already difficult relations with Congress by threatening, on May 26, to veto "excessive" spending on farms, water projects, and HEW appropriations. Speaker O'Neill responded a week later by warning Carter not to precipitate a "veto war" with his own party.

Carter, and especially Jordan, had envisioned a role for Mondale in which he would use his relationships with Democratic constituency groups to recruit their support for the Carter agenda. In practice the reverse was often the case. Mondale became the in-house advocate for these groups, relentlessly pressing Carter to accommodate their interests, especially on budgetary matters. Mondale interpreted Carter's failure to do so as reflecting a serious lack of political savvy. Much of the problem was that they were products of their own quite different political backgrounds. As Dick Moe says, "Mondale's political experience . . . in Minnesota was of coalition building. Humphrey taught us how to do this. Put together the pieces to get a majority—labor, liberals, farmers, intellectuals, minorities, and so forth. That wasn't how you did it in Georgia. There was a strong populist tradition and Carter was heir to that." Carter saw organized constituency groups as inherently self-serving and therefore seeking to skew government budgetary decisions away from the interests of the country as a whole. "Carter's anti-political attitudes used to drive me nuts, because you couldn't get him to grapple with a political problem," the vice president would later reminisce.

Carter compounded the difficulty by becoming testy when his fundamental commitment to groups to which he felt he had demonstrated his loyalty was called into question. On July 12, 1977, he would defend cuts in abortion spending for poor women against the charge they were unfair, by saying, "There are many things in life that are not fair." In part it reflected his own psychological conflict over the issue, but it angered feminist groups. Then on July 25, at the Urban League Convention, he responded to an accusation that his administration had ignored blacks, by saying angrily that he had "no apologies to make" for his performance and argued that attacks by men like his friend, Vernon Jordan, only served to injure the "hopes and aspirations" of poor Americans.

Too often Carter thought liberal constituencies could be bought off with sympathetic rhetoric alone and his frugality often made him blind to the political benefit relatively small expenditures could achieve. After a moving trip to visit sites of urban decay in the South Bronx, he announced plans for a comprehensive urban policy and program. As with welfare reform, he believed merely reorganizing existing programs with little or no increase in expenditures would suffice. After a long delay, his proposal offered new expenditures of only $600 million. Siding with Mondale in a March 24, 1978, memo, Jordan warned, "If you propose an urban policy that only contains 600 million new federal dollars, I will predict that it will be the single biggest political mistake we have made since being elected." A substitute plan with substantially greater funding would ultimately prove one of his more important legacies.

For Carter the issue was a good deal more complex. Mondale was grasping what others already knew when he observed, "Carter thought politics was sinful," adding, "The worst thing you could say to Carter if you wanted to do something was that it was politically the best thing to do." Carter had never fully put that mental quandary to rest. He frequently made decisions that were devoid of political considerations, or that he had convinced himself were not politically arrived at. Referring to Carter's annoying refusal to pander to the various Democratic constituencies, Mondale would recall, "While Carter agreed with me in principle, when he sat down with his slide-rule, he came up with programs that had little appeal to these groups. That bothered me."

Carter valued Mondale's input, particularly because he knew his views represented the majority perspective among Democrats in Congress. Charles Schultze, chairman of the Council of Economic Advisors, on the other hand, would recall that Carter "appreciated well before Fritz did that the fifty years in which the Democratic Party made its mark by building a whole batch of new social programs was coming to an end."

Carter's personality also made him vehemently intent on being his own man. He wanted the widest possible range of advice and suggestions on an issue, but, as state senator Ford Spinks in Georgia had discovered, he did not in the final analysis want anyone trying to tell him what to do. Dick Moe recalls:

> Carter would sit in these meetings, you'd be talking about welfare reform or something and someone would make a political argument. And he would

say, particularly in the first year, "I don't want to hear any political arguments. I just want the arguments on the substance. I will make the political decisions." . . . Well it turns out you cannot divorce substance from politics. . . . It's not that we didn't have the right goals for the country. It's that we didn't always have the right political skills to achieve those goals and pursue those policies. It's a political office. *It's a political office.* It's a political process and you cannot divorce it from politics.

In Carter's mind the ideal was to make every decision purely on the basis of merit. Every time political pragmatism entered the picture, it represented a degree of betrayal of that ideal. He therefore wanted to be the only one making that compromise, and to be able to do it as parsimoniously as possible. Even when Rosalynn urged him to make more political concessions, he responded, "Would you rather I compromise and get only 5 percent of what I believe in or not compromise and get 80 percent." Discussing the issue years later, Rosalynn would say, "He's just not a politician." Mondale never fathomed this aspect of Carter's personality, leading him to reflect later, "I never understood how Carter's political mind worked," and adding, "Carter's got the coldest political nose of any politician I ever met."

Concerned about Carter's lack of political focus, Jordan prepared a long memo accurately pinpointing the problems:

> You are making major domestic policy decisions with tremendous political implications in a political vacuum. These decisions are also being made at the eleventh hour with no opportunity for political give and take. . . .
>
> We send proposals to the Congress which represent your own views and are probably correct technically, but they are not politically credible. . . .
>
> When Herman Talmadge [chairman of the Senate Agriculture Committee] calls your farm bill "a silly thing," we have made a political mistake somewhere. . . .
>
> I realize that you are trying to balance the budget and improve the economy, but these goals are not well served if your economic proposals are not even a factor in the minds of the Congress.

During the late summer of 1977, there were several stories in the press raising doubts about Mondale's clout in the White House. His apparent failure to persuade Carter to abandon Lance, and his seeming lack of success in protecting social programs dear to liberals, caused many in the media to reassess their earlier glowing promotion of his influence. Following the Lance affair, and with Carter sliding in the polls, it was an additional perception problem he did not need. "It is in your interests to keep Mondale in a strong position to take the load off your shoulders," Jody

Powell wrote to the president. "Fritz would appreciate your personal help tremendously. He is very concerned." Carter called Hedrick Smith, and his old friend Jack Nelson, Washington bureau chiefs of the *New York Times* and *Los Angeles Times,* both of whom had requested interviews with him to discuss the "Mondale situation." Carter reassured them of his reliance on Mondale and the value that he attached to his advice.

As the first anniversary of Carter's inauguration approached, public confidence in the president was declining. For Carter, who was always inclined to lead by example rather than by exhortatory rhetoric, his response was to work ever harder, putting in even longer hours reading memos and studying option papers—as much as 300 pages per night. Increasingly, however, the public interpreted his style as conveying an attitude of moral superiority. "I adopted . . . I think an attitude of piety that aggravated some people," he said. At the same time he was visibly aging, causing growing concern among his staff. His haggard look was also noted by the press and the public, adding further to the concern raised by those who were asking, as did the title of an article in the *New Republic,* "Can Carter Cope?" A nationwide poll in mid-February 1978 by NBC and the Associated Press (AP) revealed that only 34 percent of Americans thought Carter was doing an excellent or good job—a 21 percent decline in six months. Jordan had sent Carter a memo saying in part: "An even more important consideration is your own health and peace of mind. You badly need rest and the opportunity to rejuvenate. . . . You don't look good." It was only when the staff enlisted Rosalynn's active help that he was willing to listen to their entreaties.

The economy continued to dominate Carter's thinking. In the administration's early months, the transition team's projection seemed accurate that Carter could achieve a surplus of $52 billion by holding down government spending. The economy grew in the first quarter of 1977 by an encouraging 5.2 percent with a projection of 6.4 percent for the second quarter. However, the January trade gap was announced at $1.67 billion, the largest ever. By the summer there was evidence that the economy was slowing down. Charles Schultze, who earlier had dubiously called the transition team's goals "optimistic," was now being proved right. Third-quarter growth dropped substantially to around 4 percent, and inflation, a persistent legacy of Lyndon Johnson's decision to fight the Vietnam War without raising taxes, remained intractably high between 6 and 7 percent. Inflation was not a problem unique to the United States but one that was afflicting all the industrialized nations in the late seventies. Schultze warned Carter that without "additional measures to stimulate growth" his own hopeful projections for the coming year would not be met. Eizenstat shared this view and told Carter that without higher growth he would not be able to reach his dual targets of full employment and a balanced budget by 1981.

Seared by his childhood experience in the depression, Carter continued to believe his first priority had to be the health of the entire economy, before focusing on the needs of individual groups. Seeking both to control inflation and stimulate economic growth, Carter produced a budget in January 1978 that included an overall spending increase of only 2 percent, less than during the Ford years, but included a proposed tax cut of $25 billion, which increased the deficit to $60.6 billion. He also asked major corporations and labor unions to give the administration prior notice of their wage and price plans.

After leaving the White House, Eizenstat would identify three things that in retrospect should have been done differently:

> First, we should have sought wage and price control standby authority in 1977 as the president had suggested he would do in the '76 campaign. . . . Second, in not seeking wage and price control authority in 1979 and 1980 when those huge energy price increases came . . . you could have prevented those increases lapping over into the rest of the economy until there was some chance to digest them. . . . Third . . . the '78 tax cut should have been vetoed . . . but nobody knew you would have a 125 percent increase in oil costs.

Unlike the budget of the previous year that was largely a product of the departing Ford administration, the budget for fiscal 1979 was the first fully owned by the Carter administration. Scrutinized closely as an indication of the direction the president intended to follow, it was a thorough disappointment to liberals in general and Mondale in particular. It had the effect of sharply crystallizing the differences between the two men. While scrupulously loyal in public, Mondale had fought ferociously inside the administration to preserve spending on social programs. He reserved most of his effort for the final appeals meeting in the Oval Office where he was alone with Carter and James McIntyre, who had taken over at OMB after Lance's departure.

McIntyre, who had been Carter's budget director in Georgia, was a constrained introvert. He knew Carter's thinking inside out and confidently argued against the social spending Mondale sought while Carter himself sat silent. Mondale, sometimes red in the face, pleaded with Carter that he needed to "take care of our friends" and that "we made promises." The $3 billion to $5 billion that it would take to buy the continuing goodwill of these groups was nothing, he argued, in an overall budget of a trillion dollars. McIntyre, never emotional, and with a technocratic attachment to government efficiency and a balanced budget, would respond that cutting the budget by even $3 billion to $5 billion would send a clear message to the business community, the markets, and Americans generally that Carter was committed to reducing the deficit and cutting inflation.

Carter and McIntyre saw plenty of support for their position. "It is impossible to overestimate the importance of inflation to your presidency," Rafshoon wrote to Carter. A *New York Times*/CBS poll conducted during the first half of April showed that 63 percent of those surveyed cited inflation as their greatest worry. Apart from Mondale, there was no countervailing voice in the White House. Liberal cabinet officers who shared Mondale's view could not separate objective advice on the economy as a whole from what seemed like a self-serving interest in the budgets of their own departments.

Carter's firm handling of the economy won him few plaudits in the press or from the public. Liberal members of the administration, strongly opposing Carter's budget cuts and lacking loyalty either to his economic strategy or to him personally, freely shared their displeasure with others including those in the media.

Carter's economic policy was further clouded in the public mind by his preference for allowing several players to provide economic advice to him directly. In addition to Mondale and McIntyre, he consulted with Schultze, Eizenstat, Blumenthal, and Robert Strauss (whom he would later make his special counselor on inflation). Although Blumenthal chaired the administration's Economic Policy Group, he was difficult to get along with and did not have Carter's ear the way the others did. The result was that there was no disciplined process by which differences were resolved and a clear set of economic recommendations was submitted to the president. Instead, every time one of these individuals publicly stated his own viewpoint, it was interpreted as an additional conflicting signal about the administration's economic policy. In one instance, when Blumenthal gave what he thought was the president's position, he was promptly rebutted by the White House press office.

Carter was further a victim of an economy in rapid flux, undergoing an unprecedented combination of trends. There was little consensus among perplexed economists as to the appropriate course of action to follow. In a little over a year he had gone from trying to maintain stability, to seeking to stimulate an economy that seemed headed for stagnation, to attempting to control what was becoming increasingly runaway inflation. By the first few months of 1978, the GNP was growing at 7 percent while unemployment had edged slightly below 6 percent and inflation was roaring forward at 11.3 percent. The value of the dollar was falling. This uncertainty caused considerable consternation in the business community, leading to a steady decline in the stock market. In response, on October 20, Carter warned the Federal Reserve not to raise the prime interest rate. They ignored him and moved it up to 6 percent. By November 1977, the stock market had dropped to just about 800 points, having lost nearly 25 percent of its value since Carter took office. A Harris poll at that time showed only 26 percent of the public approved of the way Carter was handling the economy. The same poll showed, paradoxically, that 54 percent of the population thought the country was in a recession despite the steady growth in GNP.

Carter was confronted in September 1977 with another issue for which there was no easy solution. Alan Bakke, a thirty-seven-year-old white man and former marine, had applied in 1973 for admission to medical school at the University of California at Davis. He filed suit against the University of California Regents claiming his rights had been violated because the school had accepted several less qualified minority applicants under an affirmative action plan that reserved sixteen places for disadvantaged students. The California Supreme Court had sided with Bakke, prompting the Regents to appeal to the U.S. Supreme Court.

On the surface the case appeared an ideal opportunity to mend fences with minorities discouraged over the budget battles. Paren J. Mitchell, chairman of the Congressional Black Caucus, notified Carter and Attorney General Griffin Bell that they attached to Bakke the "same significance as the *Brown [v. Board of Education]* decision." Despite a letter from B'nai B'rith urging White House neutrality, Eizenstat told the president that he saw it as an opportunity for the administration to make a clear statement of its support for affirmative action programs. Conservatives and labor generally opposed any quota system. Carter, who seemed oblivious to angering constituency groups in his budget cutting, was deeply concerned about antagonizing them on such an important symbolic issue as this. Having appointed an unprecedented number of minorities to his administrations in Georgia and in Washington, he was clearly committed to affirmative action as a remedy for past injustices, but he told a reporter, "I hate to endorse the proposition of quotas for minority groups, for women, or for anyone else."

Griffin Bell's Justice Department had prepared the draft of an amicus curiae brief that supported Bakke and concluded the action of the medical school was unconstitutional. Bell tried to soften the impact by telling Carter that the Justice Department would still continue to take a strong position in favor of affirmative action generally. Eizenstat and Lipshutz felt the document was a disaster that left open the question of the administration's commitment to affirmative action. Jordan shared their view, writing to Carter:

> Neither you nor I have been able to understand the legalisms in this case—how can we expect illiterate and disadvantaged people to understand when they are told by their leaders and the media that "Carter has ruled against the blacks and Hispanics of the country." Judge Bell—who [sic] I love and respect—takes comfort in the fact that the original decision was

written by two blacks [Drew Days and Wade McCree], which will make our official involvement on behalf of Bakke more palatable. It will not.

Carter concurred and Mondale intervened with Griffin Bell. Both Califano and Eleanor Holmes Norton, who had been appointed chair of the Equal Employment Opportunities Commission, also weighed in with strong arguments against Bakke. The final brief filed by the Justice Department on September 19 was a ringing endorsement of affirmative action, which at the same time ignored the thorny issue of quotas. The Court did not rule until the following June, by which time the case was no longer a political issue. The administration's brief therefore took on a definitive quality. However, the generally positive reaction Carter received from the minority community was significantly undermined by leaks of internal documents by liberal opponents to Bakke in the administration. Quite unfairly, liberal critics in the media used these documents to raise the specter of Carter seeking to have it both ways on racial issues as he had done in the 1970 gubernatorial race.

By the spring of 1978, Carter was in serious political trouble. Through the budget process he had antagonized the traditional Democratic constituencies. Organized labor was discouraged by his failure to implement a program of national health insurance or raise the minimum wage; Jews, never his greatest supporters, were increasingly alarmed about his attitude toward Israel; business leaders were angry over the uncertainty of the economy; and conservatives, including many of his southern supporters, were unhappy about the Panama Canal treaties and his prodigious appointment of blacks. Even fundamentalist Christians felt betrayed that he had not imposed his Baptist beliefs firmly on the country and that he supported the Supreme Court ruling on abortion, still backed the Equal Rights Amendment, and continued to serve alcohol at White House functions, although it was no longer available in the White House Mess.

Carter's difficulties boiled down to two basic problems. First, in order to win the presidency he had not only promised widely but too often extravagantly. Americans had believed their government was not working for them anymore and they wanted to elect someone who could bring about profound change—streamlining programs, cutting out waste, and saving taxpayers' dollars. They liked the fact that Carter was not a typical politician and did not have deep ideological ties to either party.

Most had few quarrels with his program, but they were frustrated by his failure to drive his legislative agenda through Congress, sweeping aside special interests and creating the kind of government they felt he had promised. He had not warned them how difficult that would be, partly because he did not understand it himself. The word most commonly used to describe their feelings about Carter at this stage was *disappointed.* They had put their hope in him, but he was not proving to be a powerful enough leader to get the job done. For the next twenty years voters would continue to demand *change* from their national leaders. It was a theme that Reagan, Clinton, and especially another Georgian, Newt Gingrich, would ride to success.

Carter's second major problem was that he had no reliable core constituency at the national level. Alliances of convenience, not legions of ideological admirers, had won him the presidency. As these alliances crumbled away, he was left with no organized following to articulate his goals and accomplishments to the media and the American public. The pillars of the Democratic Party in the Congress—Jackson, Humphrey, Kennedy, O'Neill, among others—had little interest in publicly defending his program. Unlike most presidents who come to the job with a lifetime of political friendships in Washington to fall back on, Carter had almost none. Jody Powell, adept but preoccupied with the day-to-day handling of the media, had little time to organize a broad public relations strategy for Carter. In addition, Carter's genuine humility made him ambivalent about any initiative that smacked of transparent self-promotion. However, Gerry Rafshoon, who had remained outside the administration, was increasingly consulted for advice and would eventually join the White House staff.

Carter's lack of gregariousness and tendency toward reclusiveness, a liability in his dealing with the Georgia legislature, was proving a similar problem in Washington. He far preferred to spend time alone mulling over the details of proposals than chatting with columnists and convincing them to write favorably of their merits. Jordan, who gave Carter sound political advice most of the time, had honed his skills in the narrow adversarial world of electioneering, and had little grasp of how to shape public opinion for governance in a broader political context. Washington is made up of a number of powerful and influential individuals and groups, movers and shakers, who disproportionately influence public opinion. Among them are members of former administrations, senior journalists, the intelligence community, retired senior military officials, former ambassadors, the leaders of major international institutions such as the World Bank, the International Monetary Fund, the Pan American Health Organization, and scientific organizations, and the academic leaders at six major universities in the Washington/Baltimore area, several independent centers, and "think tanks" such as the Brookings Institution. Despite their political sophistication, most of these people were easily flattered, and an invitation to a White House event or call from a member of the president's staff seeking their advice, needed or not, could quickly make them ardent defenders of a president's policy. In addition, many had been used to such treatment by former presidents, so being ignored itself generated resentment.

Jordan never included these groups in his political calculations. Reflecting the same populist view that inhibited courting the liberal constituencies within the Democratic Party, he rejected them as self-important
elitists (as many were). Those in the White House who sought to build
bridges to these groups were anonymously denigrated in leaks to the press
as having little influence with the president, or as disloyal, by consorting
with those he considered the enemy.

In the terminal stages of a troubled marriage, Jordan compounded the
problem by his own erratic behavior. In December 1977, at a party given
by Barbara Walters, Jordan turned to the wife of Egyptian Ambassador
Ashraf Ghorbal and, staring at her ample bosom and low décolletage, commented, "I've always wanted to see the pyramids." On January 10, 1978,
Jordan and his wife Nancy announced that they were separating. On February 12 the *Washington Post* noted Jordan's presence at a state dinner in
Riyadh with his tie loose and his shirt undone. On February 19, 1977, the
same paper ran a story describing Jordan, apparently inebriated, spitting
amaretto down the front of the dress of a woman he met in a Georgetown
bar. Jordan denied the story, and a major effort by Jody Powell to refute it
called into question some of the details in the article, but served primarily
to draw further attention to the event and maintain it as active news for
days longer than necessary. A high price was paid by creating an unnecessary sea of cynicism and hostility among the so-called chattering classes in
Washington at a time when Carter was already losing the support from so
many other groups. Years later the *Washington Post* would reflect (not
entirely fairly), "When people talk about the mistakes of the Carter years,
it's shorthand for Hamilton Jordan, who created more ill will singlehand-
edly than anyone until John Sununu came along."

Despite the growing national discussion about Carter's competency at
the end of 1977 and early 1978, he had significantly impressed people with
his intellectual ability. Tip O'Neill would write about Carter:

> When it came to understanding the issues of the day, Jimmy Carter was
> the smartest public official I've ever known. The range and extent of his
> knowledge were outstanding: he could speak with authority about energy,
> the nuclear issue, space travel, the Middle East, Latin America, human
> rights, American history, and just about any other topic that came up. Time
> after time, and without using notes, he would think of the arguments on both
> sides of a question. His mind was exceptionally well developed, and it was
> open too. He was always willing to listen and learn.

Katharine Graham, publisher of the *Washington Post*, would say, "Carter
is by far the most intelligent president in my lifetime."

Reminiscing several years later, when asked, "What American president have you admired most?" icon of television news Walter Cronkite would respond,

> I think that as far as intellect goes, sheer intellect, Jimmy Carter would probably be my nominee. I think that his brain power was extraordinary He could absorb more complicated information, keep it neatly catalogued and filed, and bring it forth with the most perfect syntax organization that I have ever seen of anybody. I think that this was quite extraordinary.

Never at home in Washington, Carter was at pains to maintain his network of relationships, including both friends and adversaries, in the South and especially in Georgia. Betty Rainwater on Jordan's staff had this as her primary responsibility. Carter appointed Marvin Shoob a federal judge and made a point of inviting Ellis Arnall to a state dinner. Carter never forgot the role George Wallace had played in making it possible for him to win the White House. When Wallace notified him that he did not intend to seek a U.S. Senate seat, Carter responded to his fellow southerner,

> I would like to take this opportunity to express again my sincere appreciation for what you have meant to me . . . your friendship, your support at a critical time, sound advice, and a gentle sensitivity about some of the important political issues have all been important to me. I value your friendship.

In December 1978, the Democratic Party had scheduled another "mini-convention," this time in Memphis, Tennessee, to address remaining issues relating to its new charter and party rules. It was an event the White House did not want, but could not avoid. There was fear it would become a forum for the liberal wing of the party to lambast its own president in public. Carter was probably saved by the political skills of his newly appointed party chairman, John White.

Born in Texas, John White shared with Carter the experience of having grown up poor in the rural South, undergoing the same dramatic transformation in his early life brought about by the New Deal, the arrival of electricity, and indoor plumbing. White, however, was a career politician who, at the age of twenty-five, won the first of fourteen successful races for Texas agriculture commissioner. He mingled with and became friends of the most powerful political figures in the state—John Connally, Ralph Yarborough, Lloyd Bentsen, and Robert Strauss, among others. Yet he never forgot his roots, maintaining his ties to the rural poor—whites, blacks, and Mexican Americans. They reciprocated his friendship. Above all, he was a loyal party man. In 1952 he worked for Adlai Stevenson in a state where Dwight Eisenhower was overwhelmingly popular. He did so again in 1956 when Stevenson's cause was even more hopeless. In 1972 he was willing to cochair the McGovern campaign, working with a young campaign coordinator, Bill Clinton.

The White House had worked hard to get Carter loyalists elected as delegates, but they had had only modest success. John White skillfully engineered a 13–7 vote by the executive committee that required a majority of the delegates to be present on Sunday, the final night to pass any resolution, since he knew most of them, having to be back at work the next day, would leave early. Among others, resolutions were proposed criticizing Carter for reducing spending on social programs, and against the idea that "We can fight inflation with joblessness and the misery of inflation." One long-sought resolution that the White House did support, and which was adopted, gave 50 percent of delegate seats to women.

The forces critical of Carter were led by Douglas A. Fraser, president of the UAW, and Ted Kennedy. For them the key issue was national health insurance, yet the pragmatic Fraser was reluctant to force a public showdown as long as any potential for passage of such legislation remained. Averting a major problem for Carter, White was able to get them to accept a compromise resolution reaffirming the 1976 platform with its general commitment to national health insurance, but not setting any starting date.

On December 7, Carter had addressed a group of 200 religious and civil rights leaders on the occasion of the thirtieth anniversary of the U.N. Universal Declaration of Human Rights. "Human rights is the soul of our foreign policy," he told them. The following day he made his most critical statement, to date, of the Shah of Iran's record on human rights, adding that he thought the Shah might not survive in power. He came to Memphis with considerable self-confidence about what he believed and what he had to do as the leader of the country, even if it meant castigating friends such as the Shah. The delegates were deluding themselves, he told them, if they thought "progressive" government that seeks to help the poor could continue without first bringing inflation under control. "Inflation is robbing those we most want to help: working families, the pensioner, the widows, and the poor. It breeds a narrow politics of fear," he added. Carter invoked the names of Jefferson and Humphrey, calling them "Democrats and practical dreamers."

The *Washington Post* political correspondent, Ed Walsh, noted, "The reaction to the speech was polite, but hardly enthusiastic." Carter's greatest applause from the half-filled convention hall had come when he mentioned his continuing support for the Equal Rights Amendment and the D.C. voting rights amendments. Later, visiting with Andrew Young the site where Martin Luther King, Jr., had been killed, he stuck to his basic theme, saying, "If we don't end the ever-rising cost of living, we will be driven out of office like we were by the Vietnam War."

Carter's willingness to confront the reality of inflation found little resonance. Congressman John Conyers told a closed-door meeting of 100 black delegates that Carter's anti-inflation policies "will flatly result in his defeat in 1980." "He owes us the presidency," Conyers added. "If you like your president and want to keep him, you'd better knock some sense into his head about a program of full employment, housing, and national health insurance."

If his problems with liberals were not enough, he was also attacked by conservatives. At a news conference Carter was questioned about his decision to raise real defense spending by 3 percent, to which he responded, "As long as I am in the White House, I will keep a strong defense," adding, "We build weapons for peace and to let the world know that our nation is strong." While Carter supporter Mayor Coleman Young of Detroit, said, "It would be unconscionable to raise defense funds and put the burden on the back of the poor," Representative James Jones of Oklahoma and Ben Wattenberg of Senator Jackson's staff questioned whether a 3 percent raise was enough.

The magnitude of the problem Carter faced was apparent the following day when Senator Edward Kennedy addressed a cheering capacity audience of 2,500, telling the delegates it was time to "sail against the wind" of public opinion and reject "drastic slashes" in domestic spending. Although he dropped a paragraph directly critical of Carter, he warned the president that his planned budget cuts would divide the party as badly as the Vietnam War.

Despite the tepid sentiment for Carter among the delegates, Hamilton Jordan and Tim Kraft had put together a well-organized and disciplined floor team that included Hillary Rodham Clinton, the wife of the newly elected governor of Arkansas. This structure, combined with 150 members of the administration roaming the corridors and the consummate skill of John White, enabled the president to win all the votes and create the impression that he had commanding control of the party. It allowed John White to announce that the votes showed "the president and his party are in tune with one another." *Washington Post* columnist Joseph Kraft would write, "The Memphis convention showed that the president can easily carry the national mandate within the Democratic Party."

Viewed in historical perspective, however, the event showed how thoroughly fractured the party had become. Liberals, increasingly out of step with most Americans and seemingly unable to grasp the new economic realities, were in adamant ideological revolt against their own president. Democratic agenda leader Michael Harrington summed it up well:

It's a weird period for liberals. In many respects this is like the calm before the storm. The problem is the conventional liberal wisdom of the past doesn't work anymore. This is like 1931. Just as the conventional wisdom of the 1920s was totally shattered by the depression, the conventional wisdom of the 1960s has been shattered by inflation.

CHAPTER 26

Among Carter's earliest memories were those of his mother donating her nursing skills to the poorest residents, black and white, of Webster County. His approach to health care, shaped by this experience, was to depend on volunteerism and Christian noblesse oblige. He did not see health care as every citizen's right, which the government had an obligation to meet. He also believed, from his tenure as governor and considerable study, that government could be most helpful in addressing health needs by focusing on preventive programs such as immunization, nutrition, and housing, rather than assuming responsibility for the massive cost of health care.

As early as April 1974 he accepted, as a political necessity, the framework of a broad comprehensive national health insurance plan. During the 1976 primary campaign, when he needed the early crucial support of the UAW in Iowa and Florida, their price was his endorsement of their plan for universal coverage paid for by a combination of payroll taxes and general revenue. His first speech on the subject to the black Student National Medical Association was developed by his health-care task force, made up mostly of progressive physicians and federal health-care experts, in collaboration with Steve Schlossberg, general counsel for the UAW. Its content was meticulously negotiated with Carter, who, uncomfortable with the magnitude of the federal commitment, changed the wording of early drafts to extend the time frame for implementation and limit the scope of the coverage. The union representatives rejected several of those changes. Negotiations continued until after midnight of the evening prior to the speech. So insistent had Carter been on the precision of the language, lest he overcommit himself, that he was awakened to approve last-minute wording before the final speech was typed. Sitting up in bed in his underwear, he continued to reject overly specific language, sleepily insisting, "If I do what you're asking, I'll have George Meany knocking on the door the first day I'm in the White House making demands on me I cannot meet." Nevertheless, the day after the speech the *Washington Report on Medicine and Health* ran a headline, "Carter Becomes Fourth Candidate to Back Labor's NHI Plan."

Throughout the rest of the campaign his commitment to comprehensive national health insurance remained a vital element in securing liberal, and especially union, support. Carter never really accepted it. He preferred to talk movingly of his deep and genuine empathy for those who suffered for lack of health care, as though the depth of his compassion could be a substitute for embracing a major new and expensive government solution for the problem. The compassionate side of his personality was never so at odds with the hard-nosed, penny-pinching facet. At the same time, there was also a calculated ambiguity to his position.

At the Democratic convention in New York, the party plank on health care was presented in a speech by Mary King, who had carried out the negotiations with Schlossberg and was also viewed as one of the most liberal individuals in the Carter campaign. This reassured those still dubious about the sincerity of Carter's commitment to social programs.

During the first month in the White House when Eizenstat prepared Carter's "book of promises," national health insurance was prominently featured. Dating from the early discussions with the UAW, the statement included, however, certain key phrases such as "phasing-in *as revenues permit*," and "*eventual* universal and mandatory participation: *eventual* compensatory coverage." This allowed Carter to defer action without, in his mind, having violated his commitment. He continued to maintain his overall rhetorical support of the concept of national health insurance, but with concern for inflation and his desire to reduce government spending, he had little inclination to proceed with the sort of comprehensive program for all Americans that many people had understood him to support. He quickly indicated that he would not introduce national health-care legislation until 1978.

An added problem for Carter was that the choicest political territory for national health insurance was already staked out by the Kennedy–Corman bill (named for Senator Edward Kennedy and Congressman James Corman). Liberals wanted him to throw his wholehearted support behind that legislation, but Carter, and more especially Jordan, knew that if it even passed the primary credit would go to Kennedy, who had built his senatorial career around the health issue in the preceding decade. From the start, Carter criticized Kennedy–Corman as unrealistically expensive (even conservative estimates pegged the cost at $30 billion) and stressed the need to bring health-care costs down as a precondition to expanding coverage. Carter would not support the Kennedy–Corman plan, yet he had no viable alternative.

Union leaders, especially Douglas Fraser, felt they had been betrayed by Carter. At the UAW annual meeting on May 16, 1977, Kennedy won resounding applause when he said that the American people should not tolerate any further delay in obtaining national health insurance. When Carter appeared the following day, he too received his loudest applause when he said, "I'm committed to the phasing-in of a workable national health insurance system." (*Workable* had become a new qualifier.) He added, "And we are aiming to submit legislative proposals early next year." Then, reflecting the fiscally conservative side of his nature, he warned them:

> We must move immediately to start bringing health-care costs under control. If we don't—and I want you to listen carefully to this—if we don't bring the health-care costs, particularly hospitals, under control, no matter what kind of health-care system we have in our country, the cost will double every five years.

Neither Kennedy nor Carter wanted to attack each other directly. Kennedy knew that he needed Carter's support if anything approaching the Kennedy–Corman bill was to be passed. Carter needed Kennedy's continued support on a variety of unrelated issues and sought to keep his goodwill by making tantalizing general statements about national health insurance, yet constantly procrastinating about actually doing anything. By the fall of 1977, with Schultze warning him of a sluggish economy and rising inflation, Carter had abandoned any intention he may have had to introduce a comprehensive health program. With his own credibility on the line, especially with the unions, Kennedy tried different strategies to cajole or corner Carter into cooperating. Through the early months of 1978, he had repeated meetings with the president, Califano, Eizenstat, and other White House staff including myself. With Carter, Kennedy was initially deferential to a fault, but as he was increasingly stonewalled or outmaneuvered, he became frustrated and confrontational.*

A "summit" meeting was held in the cabinet room on April 6, 1978, that included, besides Kennedy and the president, Douglas Fraser of the UAW and George Meany, president of the AFL-CIO. With no legislation forthcoming from the administration, Kennedy suggested the formation of a working group with administration officials, labor representatives, and members of his own staff to resolve their differences and draft a bill. Carter deflected the suggestion by calling it "premature."

Carter was stuck in a difficult position. He had made many clear, repeated pledges in the campaign to the union leadership and to Kennedy that he would introduce health-care legislation. Eizenstat warned him that he could appear to have broken his word, but simultaneously argued that a new program of this magnitude would destroy his efforts to balance the

---

*On a completely different issue, Carter had gone out of his way to accommodate Kennedy's concern with northern Ireland and Kennedy had not wanted to jeopardize White House assistance to him on that matter.

budget and fight inflation. There was also a growing belief that a comprehensive plan like Kennedy–Corman had no chance of passing Congress. As with the welfare reform plan, Carter opted for issuing a statement of the principles upon which a national health-care program would be based, then sought to buy further time by saying that he would wait until the next session of Congress to submit legislation.

In July 1978, Kennedy came to the White House in a last-ditch effort to resolve the differences with Carter. In a major concession he offered to accept the president's provision to phase-in national health insurance over several years. In return he wanted Carter to agree to implement the plan regardless of other budgetary considerations or adverse turns in the economy. Carter refused. Later Kennedy would tell reporters that Carter had shown a "failure of leadership on the issue." The break between the two men was irrevocable. I had been the most active advocate in the White House of a plan along the lines of Kennedy–Corman. When I left, at about that time, there was no one on the president's staff with any interest in accommodating the Kennedy plan.

Seeking to refute the argument that he had abandoned national health insurance, Carter did subsequently submit a hospital cost-containment bill that was construed as the first necessary step in an eventual comprehensive plan. It generated fierce opposition from the health-care industry and would ultimately be killed.

Although in the interests of the party, Kennedy agreed not to make an issue of his health plan at the mini-convention in Memphis, Carter's failure to launch a major health-care initiative of his own had the effect of boosting the Massachusetts senator's role as the titular leader of the disaffected Democrats. While there were many issues over which liberals were unhappy, national health insurance had taken on special symbolic significance. Kennedy's rousing speech to the delegates in Memphis further strengthened his position.

The inflation rate at the end of 1978 had risen to 9 percent, the third highest since 1945 and 3 percentage points above the administration's predictions. In his "State of the Union" address on January 25, 1979, Carter somberly warned of the need for further fiscal restraint, with the fight against inflation continuing to be his top domestic priority. In his budget message he warned, "The spending restraint in this budget means that in some areas the government will simply not be able to do as much as it has in the past. Inevitably real sacrifices must be made if we are to overcome inflation." He held the deficit in his proposed FY 1980 budget to $29 billion, pointing out that it was the smallest of the preceding six years.

Liberals were further outraged and demands for Kennedy to enter the race against Carter in 1980 became increasingly frequent. Kennedy for

President committees began to spring up. Pat Caddell's polls for Carter showed Kennedy ahead not only among liberals but also with moderates and conservatives. Carter would lose every region of the country, the survey showed, even the South.

Notwithstanding Carter's concern about inflation from the day he entered the White House, and the unpopular countermeasures he had taken, wholesale prices increased at an annual rate of 14.1 percent during the first three months of 1979. At the same time, the economy had slowed dramatically with the GNP growing by only 0.4 percent during the first quarter.

Dramatic rises in international oil prices seriously hindered Carter's efforts to deal with inflation. After considerable debate inside the administration, he felt he had little choice but to allow domestic oil prices to rise to international levels. Since his 1974 speech at the National Press Club, where he had warned of the nation's overdependence on foreign oil, it had been a constant concern for him. Five years later, America was importing even more oil, with the Congress rejecting or watering down the measures he had proposed. Now he was the victim of the very problem he had warned against. To reduce the inevitable inflationary impact he announced that the decontrol process would be phased-in. At the same time, he proposed a plan for standby authority for gasoline rationing coupled with a windfall profits tax on what he labeled "huge and undeserved" profits that would accrue to the oil companies from decontrol. In May, Congress rejected the rationing plan. Kennedy had called the Carter initiative "seriously flawed." He urged Carter not to implement decontrol until after the windfall profits tax was in place, because he knew that once the oil industry had decontrol, Senator Russell Long would ensure for them that the tax was not enacted. By then, gasoline prices had risen over a dollar a gallon and long lines at the gas pump were angering Americans. In June, OPEC announced a further 50 percent increase in oil prices.

Many Americans blamed Carter for the country's economic problems. But he had few options open to him and was himself a victim of events over which he had little control. The other nations of the industrialized world were facing the same problems posing similar political difficulties for their leaders.

By December 1978, the Camp David accords, in which Carter was so heavily invested, were beginning to unravel. They were at best a fragile framework for peace rather than a full peace agreement. Several of the more contentious issues, such as the settlements on the West Bank and in Gaza, and the future role of the Palestinians, had been deferred. A deadline of December 17, 1978, had been set for the completion of negotiations on the final peace settlement between Israel and Egypt. Carter had also overoptimistically presumed that Jordan and Saudi Arabia would be drawn into the peace process.

Sadat, but for his affection for Carter, would never have made the concessions he agreed to at Camp David; he had returned home disappointed with Egypt's minimal gains and subject to serious domestic criticism. He remained a pariah in the Arab world, having achieved nothing that would induce other Arab leaders to join the peace process. Similarly, Menachem Begin, despite the exquisite difficulty of extracting the most modest concessions from him, clearly felt he had gone too far and was backpedaling even before he left the United States. On his return to Israel he was subjected to harsh criticism within his own Herut Party, and on his way to a party conference he was set upon by right-wing demonstrators who broke the windshield of his car and pelted it with eggs and tomatoes. Because of his own ambivalence he seemed to have difficulty articulating the accomplishments of Camp David. At the same time, the accusation that he had sold out Israel seemed to weigh heavily on him. In addition, the Palestinians felt Camp David had given them little or nothing.

Despite six days of intense shuttle diplomacy by Cyrus Vance and the efforts of his newly appointed Middle East negotiator, Sol Linowitz, the December 17 deadline for the peace agreement was not met. By the new year, the specter of Carter's greatest triumph turning to ashes was casting a long shadow over the White House. There was an atmosphere of discouragement that made it that much harder to deal with the other mounting problems. Carter invited the Israeli and Egyptian foreign ministers (the chief negotiators) back to Camp David, but they did not have sufficient authority to enable them to break the deadlock. Both urged Carter to invite Begin back for further discussions, which he did. Despite an earlier letter from Carter beseeching Begin not to add additional impediments to the peace process, Begin had announced plans in November to expand the West Bank settlements. He also said that he was contemplating moving his office to East Jerusalem. He informed an angry Carter that the actions were necessary to keep the support of the extremist wing of his party. However, it inflamed the passions of the Palestinians and cast considerable doubt among Arab leaders about his sincerity and trustworthiness.

Further dampening expectations, immediately upon his arrival at Andrews Air Force Base, Begin stated that he would not sign any "sham" document and that he had brought no new proposals. Although some saw it as merely a negotiating posture, he seemed obsessed in their first meeting with letting Carter know how much he had suffered back in Israel for the concessions he had made at Camp David. He rambled in their discussions in the Oval Office, suggesting that Israel needed more armaments. He was aggressively negative with a larger group of Carter's Middle East advisors in the cabinet room, claiming Sadat still wanted to destroy Israel. That evening after a dinner with the Israeli delegation, Carter returned to the White House and sat for a long time alone in the dark on the Truman balcony, "wondering what in the world we would do next." He was convinced the peace process was probably at an end. He worried that Americans were getting tired of his seeming obsession with an apparently futile pursuit. His biggest concern was the frightening neglect his preoccupation with the peace process had inflicted on other pressing issues, some of which were approaching crisis proportions.

Nevertheless, as a last resort Carter decided to go to the Middle East. As he later wrote, "My proposal was an act of desperation." His advisors, especially the cautious Jody Powell, worried that it could prove a humiliating embarrassment if Carter came back with nothing. Flying first to Egypt, the president and first lady were warmly received by Anwar Sadat, who was as concerned as the White House staff that Carter's trip prove fruitful. Completely isolated in the Arab world, having gambled everything on the peace process, he had even more at stake than Carter. Paradoxically this allowed him to make the additional concessions necessary for Carter to go on to Israel with a package Begin would find hard to refuse. Carter, however, had become increasingly worried that Sadat entrusted his own political welfare to him too much. Sadat said to him several times, "Brother Jimmy, I will do whatever you think is best." It bore heavily on Carter when ultimately Sadat paid with his life for making peace with Israel.

Begin seemed as recalcitrant as he had in Washington. From their earliest meetings, Carter had regularly tried to get Begin to look at the negotiations in a broad historical context, envisioning Israel five or ten years hence at peace with its neighbors. Begin did not see things in that light. He was nervously preoccupied with the immediate implications of the negotiating process, unable to resolve the anguish he felt over making further concessions. His mind was deeply colored by the Holocaust and a life devoted to a belief in the doctrine that Israel's ultimate security was tied to the acquisition of land and military might. At one moment he would convincingly tell Carter that he "wanted peace as much as anything in the world." At another, he would be racked by a fear that under the pressure of the negotiating process, or seduced by Carter, he might allow something that would grievously damage Israel's security. He had profound difficulty reconciling his lifelong construct of Israel's security with the notion that the concessions he was being asked to make for the peace process would ultimately bring Israel even greater security. He felt he carried a sacred trust and he was terrified of being held accountable for betraying it. His rigidity reflected more than anything else his insecurity.

Begin asked Carter to meet with the cabinet and with the twenty-five-member Foreign Relations Committee of the Knesset. Carter ultimately succeeded in achieving the agreement, but only after he and his delegation had brought together for Begin a sufficient consensus that he did not feel he bore the whole burden for Israel's future by himself. Carter returned briefly to Cairo to finalize the pact with Sadat.

For Carter it was an extraordinary triumph. For six months he had held the process together by sheer force of personality, by his deep understanding of the personalities of the two principals, and by a determination never to give up. He would later write, "I think if I could have one political attribute as the cause of my success, to begin with, it would be tenacity. Once I get on something, I am awfully hard to change. And that may also be a cause of my political failure."

There was an atmosphere of exhilaration and exhaustion on Air Force One flying back to Washington as Carter walked through the plane personally thanking all the participants. Robert Lipshutz, who had played an important role both in Israel and in mobilizing Jewish support in the United States, sat with a glass of Scotch and dictated a memo for the record summarizing the experience and what it had meant to him. In it he listed the characteristics Carter exemplified that had made success possible. Among them were Carter's willingness to study and thoroughly understand such a complex situation involving "so much history, emotions, geopolitical considerations," his ability to work dispassionately with so many people, both attractive and unattractive, using personal relationships in a highly constructive manner, his patience and tenacity "in the face of tremendous opposition, frustration, and discouragement." Lipshutz accurately summarized Carter's role: "I personally believe that he really has taken this on as a 'mission' not only because he is president but because of his personal feelings and concern about this entire situation."

On March 26, 1979, Carter hosted Begin and Sadat at a historic treaty-signing event on the White House lawn. It would become one of the most widely remembered events of his presidency.

Two days later a major accident occurred at the Three Mile Island nuclear reactor in Pennsylvania. As one of the few Americans with first-hand experience of a nuclear meltdown, Carter was unusually prepared to deal with the disaster and to understand its implications. In the short term it offered him the opportunity to show strong leadership. But it also put added pressure on the need to deal with the nation's energy problem, by calling into question the soundness of promoting atomic energy. On April 1, Carter visited Three Mile Island to reassure local residents and the country as a whole of the absence of any residual radiation. It was also the kind of dramatic visit that, especially as governor, he had always enjoyed making.

In the aftermath of Three Mile Island, during the first week of May, 65,000 demonstrators marched on Washington to demand a shutdown of America's nuclear plants. Carter said in a statement, "That is out of the question."

On April 30, the Senate approved Carter's proposal to create a Department of Education. In so doing he was honoring a campaign promise to the National Education Association. It did, however, reflect his own longstanding interest in education and his belief that separating out these functions from the old Department of Health, Education and Welfare would give a needed boost to one of his top priorities for the country.

In a surprise television appearance on December 15, 1978, Carter announced that as of January 1, 1979, the United States would officially recognize the People's Republic of China. He also announced that Deputy Prime Minister Deng Xiaoping of China would visit the United States in January. Although normalization was the culmination of an initiative begun by Nixon and advanced by Ford, Carter was roundly attacked by Republicans with the ever-extreme Senator Barry Goldwater terming it "one of the most cowardly acts ever performed by a president of the United States."

Normalization of relations with China was very much under the wing of Brzezinski, who saw "playing the China card" as a salutary warning against Soviet expansionism and a way of continuing to mount relentless pressure on them. He had early coined the phrase "crescent of crisis," referring to the political and social instability stretching from Somalia and Ethiopia in the south through Turkey and Iran and extending to Afghanistan and Pakistan in the north. The entire region was ripe, he argued, for takeover by regimes hostile to the United States, which the Soviets would seek to draw into their orbit. Within the White House he found ready allies in Jordan and Powell as he pushed his concern about the Soviet threat.

Despite the inauspicious beginnings, the disarmament talks with the Soviets had slowly progressed so that by the end of 1978 the SALT II agreement was near completion. The Soviets, however, responded to the U.S. initiative with China not by restraint in the "crescent of crisis" but by a surge of inflexibility on finalizing SALT. There were a number of complex technical issues to resolve including "telemetry encryption"—the electronic coding system for transmitting secret data from Soviet missiles. But in the view of Secretary of State Vance, primarily responsible for overseeing the SALT negotiations, it was Washington's new relationship with China that was the main obstacle. Matters were made worse when Deng, probably with Brzezinski's acquiescence, used his visit to the United States as an opportunity to attack Moscow. It also further strained the rocky relationship between Vance and Brzezinski.

Eventually the differences on SALT II were overcome. On June 18, at the end of a five-day summit conference in Vienna, Carter and Brezhnev signed the SALT II Treaty, limiting each nation to 2,250 strategic weapons. It was another foreign policy triumph for Carter, but it was overshadowed by growing uncertainty about the prospects for ratification in the Senate.

On April 16, CIA director Stansfield Turner had warned that loss of secret monitoring stations in Iran would make it significantly harder to verify compliance with the SALT agreement. Opponents in the Senate, both Republicans and Democrats, especially "Scoop" Jackson, accused Carter of not having cut a hard enough deal with the Soviets. Having already angered liberals by his increase in defense spending, he aggravated them further by approving construction of the MX missile system in early June. It was a significant reversal aimed at winning the support of Senate hawks.

The energy crisis and the economy still plagued Carter. In mid-May it was reported that auto sales had dropped 25 percent, an ominous portent for the future. Carter had gone from Vienna to Tokyo for the annual economic summit of the seven major industrialized nations. It was an acrimonious meeting dominated by discussion of the energy crisis at which Chancellor Schmidt asserted that a primary cause of the oil price increase was Carter's "meddling" in the Middle East, antagonizing Arab producers. Carter, however, scored a minor success when his fellow heads of government among the G-7 unanimously agreed to restrict oil imports through 1985. Simultaneously, however, OPEC announced its fourth and largest price hike in five months. And Venezuela announced it was cutting its oil exports by 7 percent, thereby putting an additional upward squeeze on oil prices.

In Carter's absence a sense of increasing despair was settling over the White House. Stuart Eizenstat, working with Mondale on the draft of yet another energy speech for the president, felt matters were getting desperate and called Carter, urging him to cancel a planned vacation in Hawaii and return right away to Washington. Over the July 4 weekend, 90 percent of the gas stations in the New York City area were closed, 80 percent in Pennsylvania, and 50 percent in Rhode Island. The public was becoming increasingly angry and blaming Carter. Jordan would later note to Carter, "People in gasoline lines were asking, 'What in the hell is Carter doing in Japan and Korea when all the problems are here at home?' "

Heeding the advice of Eizenstat and Mondale, Carter returned to Washington, but instead of remaining at the White House, he went to Camp David. For him the retreat had taken on many of the virtues of Plains. In four years he would go there sixty-seven times. In this rural ambience he felt he could better recover from adversity and gather his strength psychologically to reenter the fray. It now had the added positive association of the successful Middle East agreement.

Carter took with him a series of polls and memos from Pat Caddell. Carter did not like the drafts of the new energy speech he had been given. Eizenstat, Jordan, Rafshoon, and Schlesinger all urged slightly different approaches. On July 4, he wrote in his diary, "I had already made four speeches to the nation on energy and they had been increasingly ignored." Caddell concurred, arguing that his polls showed that people were inured to warnings about an energy crisis and for Carter to give them essentially the same message again would put them to sleep or alienate them even further. "America is a nation deep in crisis," Caddell wrote. "Psychological more than material, it is a crisis marked by a dwindling faith in the future." He argued that, "Fundamentally, Americans believe themselves exempt from the process of history." The assassinations, the Vietnam War, Watergate, and inflation had, he said, ended that myth and undermined traditional hope for the future. His prescription was for Carter to scrap the energy speech and, instead, speak to this broader crisis of confidence in the American people.

Caddell's thematic analyses had been invaluable to Carter during the election campaign. From his polls he seemed able to distill, articulate concisely, and reinforce what Carter himself was picking up as he talked to people all day long on the campaign trail. Carter placed great faith in Caddell's sweeping sociology, except that now, isolated in the presidency, he was not in a position to check it against his own reading of the public pulse.

Carter's staff, while only lukewarm, accepted Caddell's approach when they saw their boss's enthusiasm. Mondale, however, was adamantly opposed. He thought Caddell's ideas were stupid and that Carter was being seduced by half-baked psychology that had no relevance to their immediate political needs. "Everything in me told me that this was wrong. I was morose about it because I thought it would destroy Carter and me with him." Mondale wanted a bold, assertive, upbeat speech on the energy crisis with a series of concrete solutions, not criticism and blame heaped on the American people.

Mondale's uncharacteristic display of emotion disturbed Carter. "I grew quite concerned about him," Carter later wrote. "He was distraught and could not be reconciled." Carter broke off the meeting and invited Mondale to walk alone with him around the Camp David perimeter. He tried to dispell Mondale's concerns, but with little effect.

What Carter did not know was the extent to which Mondale had become generally discouraged and disillusioned in the preceding months. At the time of his selection as Carter's running mate, what seemed like large areas of shared beliefs and priorities now appeared trivial to Mondale. What was apparent was the yawning gap between their differing views on the role of the federal government, economics, unemployment, housing, health care, and most of all their approach to politics. According to Steven Gillon, Mondale shared the view of much of Washington that Carter and his staff were politically inept, incapable of understanding the inner workings of Congress, and unable to project a clear and compelling vision to the public. Mondale was by no means the only vice president to be at odds with the man in the Oval Office. The difference was that he was the first to be brought into the West Wing and given a highly touted role as a key participant in the formulation and execution of policy. As the president's policies had increasingly diverged from Mondale's recommendations, his seeming impotence was hard to hide. At the same time, as he loyally sought to sell the administration's positions, he was accused of having sold out his "liberal" friends. Indeed it was those groups at the heart of his constituency that were now the most angry with Carter. Mondale was caught between his loyalty to Carter and his commitment to traditional liberal values.

Increasingly, Mondale saw his own political future sinking with Carter. By early May 1979, he was toying with the notion of resigning. Of the various scenarios he discussed with his top staff, the most attractive was to announce at the Democratic convention that, for personal reasons, he would not seek renomination as Carter's running mate. On May 27, after a speech at the University of Wisconsin, he departed to the isolation of the woods and lakes of northern Minnesota, ostensibly for a brief fishing vacation. As he agonized over his future, he used the high-powered communications equipment of the Secret Service to talk to his wife and closest friends. On May 29, Joan, who had watched her husband slide steadily deeper into despair, and worried about the toll a second term might take, told him, "It'll be better if you quit."

Mondale did not resign. Whether it was his natural caution, his loyalty to Carter, or his belief that if he reapplied himself with new commitment he could turn things around, he decided at the end of the sojourn to remain in office. On Monday, June 3, back in Washington, he called his senior staff together for breakfast and announced to them, "I am ready to begin again."

A month later at Camp David, facing the prospect of being asked to defend a Carter speech that Mondale saw as a disaster for both of them, all of the arguments for resigning came rushing back to him, triggering the emotional outburst that so startled Carter. As they walked together, Mondale told Carter that a speech based on Caddell's ideas was political suicide and he could not defend it. It was not just the energy speech, Mondale argued, that needed to be changed, but Carter's entire approach to the presidency. Despite the frankness of their discussion and the profound political differences that had become apparent, the bond of friendship between them was strong. "When I think back, it is extraordinary the length Carter went to try to handle me with dignity. I will never forget his generosity," Mondale later reflected.

Over the next eight days Carter invited nearly 150 people to come to Camp David to talk with him. They included members of Congress, mayors, governors, businesspeople, religious leaders, economists, labor leaders, and wise men of previous administrations. Among those flown up to Camp David were Clark Clifford; John Gardner; Sol Linowitz; Lane Kirkland of the AFL-CIO; Barbara Newell, president of Wellesley; Jesse Jackson; and political consultant Bob Keefe. Charles Kirbo was also present throughout the eight days. At the end Carter made unannounced trips to meet with small groups of citizens at the homes of Mr. and Mrs. William Fisher in Carnegie, Pennsylvania, and Mr. and Mrs. Martin Porterfield in Martinsburg, West Virginia. It was an unprecedented exercise for any president. It was a reflection of Carter's remarkable openness that he was willing to undertake this activity, which largely amounted to sitting, hour upon hour, listening to people criticize him. "It's not easy for me to accept criticism and reassess my ways of doing things," he wrote in his diary on the night of July 9. In failing to meet the expectations the American people had had of him, he felt he had let them down. It was an important act of humility now to hear their grievances. "I spent 90 percent of my time listening," he later wrote.

The value of those eight days to Carter was immense. "It was one of my most productive times," he would later write. "I learned a lot." However, what it pointed up, more than anything, was that he should have been having this kind of dialogue from the start of his presidency. In the first two years he had adamantly refused to do so. Obsessed with using every moment of his time to manage the government, his legislative program, and his foreign policy initiatives, he had no time to step back and reflect on the broader aspects of his leadership, much less seek advice from those with a lifetime of experience around the presidency.

Carter carefully noted the comments he received from those he met with at Camp David. Many of Caddell's assertions were reinforced. "In the past we have controlled others' lives; now OPEC controls ours." "We've been through a series of national crises, and the country hasn't recovered." "We have a crisis of confidence." "The people are just not ready to sacrifice." Repeatedly Carter heard that "The country was waiting for stronger and clearer leadership from me." They told him to be more cautious about his promises, that some of his cabinet did not seem loyal and changes were needed, and that he should improve his relations with the press. Almost unanimously they agreed that the energy crisis was the nation's most pressing concern. But, they criticized, don't declare the "moral equivalent of war" and then "issue us BB guns." They faulted him for his failure to sufficiently exhort the nation: "Mr. President, we're in trouble. Talk to us about blood, sweat, and tears." They blamed the Congress and oil interests, but they equally blamed him for his failure to deal effectively with them.

In an extensive memo to the president, Jordan would later summarize the conclusions of the meeting:

> You have agreed to adopt a different attitude about your presidency.
>
> You have agreed to lead the country instead of manage the government.
>
> You have agreed for the need of a different structure and mechanism to accommodate this change in focus on your part.
>
> You have agreed for the need for greater discipline and accountability in the White House and the government.

Carter's eight days in seclusion mystified the American people. For a minority, his willingness to examine his shortcomings and show a degree of contrition for his failures was refreshing, but for most people, who wanted clear decisive leadership, public evidence of handwringing further confirmed in their minds that he was not up to dealing with the nation's problems. Frankness and honesty were not what they wanted. They wanted the reassurance of someone who would not burden them with the difficulties, but would appear to be thoroughly in command.

When Carter returned to the White House, he had created expectations akin to Moses's descent from Mount Sinai. He spoke to the American people on Sunday night, July 15, 1979. Initially it seemed he had listened only to Caddell. He talked of the "crisis of confidence" and said, "We've always believed in something called progress. We've always had faith that the days of our children would be better than our own," adding, "Our people are losing that faith not only in government itself but in the ability as citizens to serve as the ultimate rulers and shapers of our democracy." But then he said, "Energy will be the immediate test of our ability to unite the nation." With stirring rhetoric, as Mondale had urged, he laid out a detailed six-point plan for dealing with the energy problem.

The speech, which Carter described as "one of my best," was well received at the time, drawing plaudits from politicians, journalists, and ordinary citizens. "One of the strongest and best he has made," Speaker O'Neill allowed. The president's approval rating jumped 11 points to 37 percent.

As he did frequently in his career, Carter now allowed the euphoria in the immediate aftermath of a success to obscure his judgment and drop his guard. It led him to a misstep that would undercut a stellar accomplishment. He had received almost unanimous advice at Camp David that he should shake up the cabinet. However, by his own admission, "I handled the cabinet changes poorly." Instead of merely announcing the resignation of Blumenthal and Califano, whom he had decided to fire, and the departure of Schlesinger, who had previously decided to leave, he concluded the entire cabinet should offer to resign and he would then announce which of the resignations he would accept. He made a similar announcement with regard to the White House staff, eliciting a total of thirty-four resignations from top administration officials. He ineptly created the impression of a governmental crisis, spawning a blizzard of media stories—the first mass action of the kind since 1842, the press noted. It all but entirely obscured the positive coverage of his speech. In time the events of those two weeks would become fused together, with the speech increasingly derogated as the "malaise speech," although it was a term Carter never used.

Califano posed a particular problem. A man of considerable talent and ego, Califano knew that he was in the cabinet by virtue of his reputation as Johnson's chief of domestic policy and his close relationship with Mondale. He had never felt much loyalty to Carter, and pursued a largely independent course from the White House. He understood well the limits of influence the White House can exert over a cabinet officer. As an unabashed liberal who wanted to maintain his own favorable relationship with Democrats in Congress, he seemed to make only a halfhearted effort to sell the president's austerity measures. A reformed smoker, he launched a major anti-smoking campaign based on the health hazard of cigarettes. He did so knowing full well that Carter's political base was in tobacco-growing states. On one occasion, Jim Hunt, the governor of North Carolina, called me and said, "Tell the president that if he cannot shut up Joe Califano, he can kiss North Carolina goodbye in 1980." Yet Carter could not shut him up.

Mondale was Califano's protector. During the walk around the Camp David perimeter, Carter told Mondale he was contemplating some cabinet changes. Mondale asked that Califano not be fired without consulting him first. Carter did not do so, and Mondale, in Philadelphia when he received the news, did little to support the president's action. Liberals in Congress castigated Carter for firing Califano, with Kennedy noting, "the extraordinary irony that in a time of energy and economic crisis, the resignation of Secretary Califano was the first to be accepted."

On July 18, Carter finally announced that he was appointing Hamilton Jordan the formal chief of staff, although he had twice previously declined the position. "He was quiet, he was not forceful, he was not proud, he didn't put himself in a superior position to other people, but folks trusted his judgment," Carter later reflected on the attributes he felt Jordan brought to the job. Carter friends and critics alike were unanimous in their belief that Jordan's strange role had been the single greatest shortcoming of the Carter White House. That Jordan had no managerial experience, had lost respect on Capitol Hill where he was actively disliked by many, including the Speaker, and was a source of ridicule in the media, seemed less important than that Carter was finally coming to grips with the staff problems that had crippled his presidency.

Having spent two years fostering the conflict and compartmentalization within the White House staff, Jordan faced an impossible task in trying to build a cohesive team. When as his first act he sent out a memo announcing that henceforth he would be coordinating all staff activity, he received a terse note from Brzezinski responding that he was hired to work for the president, not for Hamilton Jordan, and he subsequently ignored Jordan's role. Reflecting his deep loyalty to his top staff, which often led him to be oblivious to glaring shortcomings, Carter later reminisced, "When any of my subordinates are criticized, I defend them." This he loyally did. As in the campaign, Carter intensely and narrowly focused on his own responsibilities. He had an aversion to facing staff problems, leading him to say, astonishingly to some, "I don't permit them to squabble among themselves."

Jordan's new role was bolstered by the appointment of a number of seasoned veterans, but it was very much a case of too little too late. Louis Martin, who had drafted John Kennedy's dramatic speech on civil rights, came in as Carter's liaison with the African-American community. Washington insider Lloyd Cutler took over as the White House counsel. Anne Wexler, the highly regarded political operative, rejected by the men around Carter at the start of the administration for being "too powerful a woman," was the community liaison. Alonzo McDonald, a corporate executive, was appointed to provide hard-nosed management. Hedley Donovan, a senior executive at *Time* magazine, became the in-house expert on media communications. Ed Sanders was hired in place of Mark Siegel, worn down trying to defend Middle East policies into which he had had no input. Sanders, a successful lawyer, had been the president of the American Israeli Political Action Committee (AIPAC). In recommending him to Carter, Jordan noted, "He has stuck with you through all the difficulties with the Jewish community . . . because he believes in you and your commitment to Israel." He added, "It would be a mistake to ask him . . . only to be our 'front man' with the Jewish community." Unlike Siegel, Sanders would be accepted as a full participant in formulating and executing policy.

Blumenthal was replaced by William Miller, chairman of the Federal Reserve Board, so Carter had the opportunity to refill that job also. Driven by the skyrocketing price of oil, the economy seemed out of control, with interest rates approaching 12 percent, wholesale prices in July at an annual rate of 13.7 percent, and minimal growth of the GNP. The commodity markets, fueled by speculators, were gyrating with the dollar declining and the price of gold steadily rising. Uncertainty, the greatest fear on Wall Street, led to the accusation that Carter did not have his hand firmly on the nation's economic tiller. "The markets are scared to death. Their fear is that

President Carter may now sacrifice economic prudence for political expediency," an anonymous administration source told the *New York Times*.

Carter assigned to Dick Moe the task of developing a list of names for the Federal Reserve job. After working over the weekend, he submitted four names to Carter: Paul Volcker, president of the New York Fed; A. W. "Tom" Clausen, president of the Bank of America; David Rockefeller, CEO of Chase Manhattan; and Bruce MacLaury, president of the Brookings Institution, whom Carter had first met through the Trilateral Commission. By Monday morning, Carter's choice was narrowing to Volcker. With misgiving about Volcker's willingness to be a "team player," Moe went to the Oval Office and suggested that Carter should at least call Clausen to see if he would be interested. Carter reached him in San Francisco having breakfast with his wife. Would he consider moving to Washington to become chairman of the Federal Reserve, Carter asked. He'd speak to his wife, Clausen said, putting the president on hold. He eventually came back on the line to say that his wife really did not want to move to Washington.

The following day, the balding, six-foot-seven Volcker met with Carter in the Oval Office. Bright, able, and conservative, he was well known in financial circles and on Wall Street, but not to the general public. They talked about the statutory independence of the Fed, with Volcker stressing to Carter that, unlike his predecessor, he would in practice as well as in law be totally independent. Carter agreed. Writer William Greider, in his authoritative book *Secrets of the Temple*, described the Volcker appointment as the "most important of Jimmy Carter's presidency." He added, "What Carter also did not grasp was that he was inadvertently launching a new era and ceding his own political power." The average American understands far less about the role of the Federal Reserve than about the CIA. Yet with an increasingly interdependent global economy, the Fed has the capacity to wield more power than any other agency of the U.S. government except the Pentagon. This was particularly true in the fluid economic circumstances of the late 1970s. In Greider's view, in the coming months and years, "Volcker and the Federal Reserve would prove to be more powerful, more effective than any element of the elected government in Washington."

Stuart Eizenstat explained Carter's choice: "Volcker was selected because he was the candidate of Wall Street. This was their price in effect. . . . What wasn't known was that he was going to impose some very drastic changes." Late in the afternoon, Bert Lance called Gerry Rafshoon and said, "I want you to tell him [Carter] something from me. He should not appoint Paul Volcker. If he appoints Volcker, he will be mortgaging his reelection to the Federal Reserve." Carter had already made up his mind.

Wall Street showed its gratitude. The next day the bond market rallied;

the Dow Jones Average jumped 10 points. The value of the dollar suddenly improved against other currencies and the price of gold fell $2.50 an ounce.

On Saturday, September 15, a hot, humid day, President Carter ran in a 10K race near Camp David. A little over halfway through, he collapsed and was forced to withdraw. Often in politics a single image has a curious way of distilling and symbolizing a series of diffuse events. Such was the case when pictures of an ashen, collapsing Carter were flashed across the nation. To many it seemed like a caricature of the state of his presidency. Like most caricatures it was a damaging exaggeration, making things seem much worse than they were. But the picture stuck irrevocably in people's minds, shaping their overall perception of his leadership in a far more forceful way than any of the positive actions he was taking.

A similar image was inadvertently created by Jody Powell. One afternoon in the spring of 1979, as he and Carter were drinking lemonade on the Truman balcony, the president, who had recently returned from Plains, recounted with amusement how, while fishing, a rabbit diseased or injured had swum, hissing and foaming at the mouth, directly toward his boat. Several months later, in casual conversation Powell mentioned the story to AP reporter Jackson Brooks. The following day the *Washington Post* ran a front-page story with the headline "President Attacked by Rabbit." It was picked up all over the country and used by the media and his opponents as a metaphor for the beleaguered state of his presidency.

The second half of 1979 was a particularly difficult time for Carter with relentless attacks in the media. Despite significantly improved management of the White House, the continuing public perception was that he was "on the ropes." Nevertheless, it was a period during which he had notable successes. A $5.7 billion welfare reform package was finally passed as well as $3.7 billion aid package for the ailing Chrysler Corporation. In addition to creating the Department of Education, he secured passage of legislation providing assistance programs for middle-income students, and a grant program for particularly impacted areas. The Elementary and Secondary Education Act, with substantial increases in funding for schools, was also passed.

Despite its savaging by special interests, after nearly three years the energy package would be passed, still yielding considerable benefits to ordinary Americans. Eizenstat summarized the accomplishment:

> He broke the Gordian knot on pricing crude oil and natural gas, leading to world prices, which will increase incentives for production of both fossil fuels and will help with conservation . . . the first series of comprehensive tax credits for conservation, for insulation . . . a series of incentives for solar

energy through tax credits and vastly expanded research and development efforts. He put coal at the center of his energy policy and . . . vastly increased its overall production.

In the most dramatic change in the relationship between government and business since the New Deal, in addition to the airlines, Carter also successfully deregulated trucking, rail, banking, and communications. The administration's program against drug abuse successfully brought drug-related deaths to what would prove to be their lowest level in the thirty-year period between 1966 and 1996.

In the second week of June 1979, Carter had responded offhandedly to a question about his low standings in the polls by saying that, if Kennedy chose to run against him for the Democratic nomination, "I'll whip his ass." It was a comment that struck many as inappropriate and demeaning to the office of the presidency. It could have been quickly rephrased by the staff to limit the damage. Instead, for the remainder of the week, when asked by incredulous members of Congress whether that really was what Carter had said, Frank Moore assured them, "Yes sir, that's exactly what he said." Kennedy was respected as a legislator even among those opposed to him, and neither Carter's stature nor his legislative agenda were helped by the incident.

By mid-September, with a Harris poll showing 70 percent of the American people believing Carter could not get reelected, the likelihood of a Kennedy candidacy seemed virtually certain. On September 20, Kennedy had lunch with the president and first lady on the terrace overlooking the Rose Garden. Rosalynn remained only briefly then left. In a cordial discussion, Kennedy told Carter that he felt America was adrift, and that for the sake of the country and the party, he planned to run against him. Carter expressed his disappointment, but was not surprised.

Carter received a letter from Dr. Benjamin Mays, the former president of Morehouse College, to say that he, Coretta Scott King, and "Daddy" King had met with Kennedy to try to dissuade him from running, because it would split black loyalties. Carter responded: "Thanks for the effort. There are no philosophical differences between me and the senator. He's just an impatiently ambitious man."

On October 13, the White House suggested it was time for Kennedy supporters in the administration to resign. At Jordan's suggestion, Carter invited Tip O'Neill to be his guest at the seventh game of the World Series between the Pittsburgh Pirates and the Baltimore Orioles. Carter used the opportunity to ask O'Neill to chair the 1980 Democratic National Convention, putting him, at least formally, in a neutral position. A straw poll in Florida in early October gave Carter a victory over Kennedy by 2 to 1. On

October 20, Carter went to Boston for the opening of the John F. Kennedy
Presidential Library. In what might have been an awkward situation,
Carter gave a moving speech reflecting his deep admiration for Jack
Kennedy, which was appreciated by the Kennedy clan.

In a speech at Faneuil Hall, on November 6, Kennedy formally
announced his candidacy.

CHAPTER 27

Crimes so great they make even
the laws themselves tremble.

—ANDREA CHENIER

On November 4, 1979, a mob of 3,000 fanatical Iranian students invaded the U.S. embassy in Tehran and seized sixty-six Americans as hostages. It was the most fateful day of the Carter presidency.

Significant U.S. involvement in Iran had begun in 1953 after the Iranian parliament had nationalized the Anglo Iranian Oil Company through which the British government had controlled all Iranian oil. A CIA initiative, code-named project Ajax, under the direction of Kermit Roosevelt, grandson of President Theodore Roosevelt, overthrew the nationalist prime minister, Muhammad Mussadegh. The young Shah Muhammad Reza Pahlavi, with covert CIA backing, was restored to a position of dictatorial power. The oil industry was taken over by an international consortium in which U.S. companies had a 40 percent share and the British portion was reduced to the same level. The *New York Times* editorialized that for "underdeveloped countries with rich resources" it was an important object lesson in what would happen to them if they "went berserk with fanatical nationalism."

Over the next twenty-five years the Shah became the guardian of U.S. interests in the Persian Gulf. Not only did U.S. companies profit magnificently from Iranian oil but the Shah guaranteed a steady supply to Israel while the Arab nations exercised a vehement boycott. Additionally the Shah was a boon to the U.S. arms industry. During the Nixon administration he was told he could purchase whatever weapons in whatever quantities he wanted. With his immense oil wealth the Shah took full advantage of the offer. That the Shah was a repressive dictator was of little concern. The United States provided not only military advisors but training for SAVAK, the Shah's notoriously brutal secret police. The CIA collaborated closely with SAVAK on intelligence matters, and a blind eye was turned to SAVAK agents operating in the United States, where they spied on and harassed dissident Iranian students. In the mid-1970s, Amnesty International had documented the existence in Iran of thousands of political prisoners imprisoned by the Shah, and the widespread use of torture.

What the Shah particularly understood was that he could buy the support of people of power and influence in the Western world. He lavishly entertained, and showered expensive gifts on prominent Americans in business, in the foreign policy establishment, in the military, and in the media. His embassies threw extravagant parties in London, Paris, and Washington, to which the powerful or potentially powerful were invited.

With innumerable other foreign policy priorities on his plate, Carter was happy to accept the conventional wisdom among his advisors that Iran was a key to stability in the Middle East, that the Shah was an unshakable ally who should be backed at all cost, and that his regime was inherently stable. While concerned about the Shah's human rights policies, Carter had deliberately tempered his criticism during the campaign. With more pressing priorities, he was induced initially to take Iran for granted without devoting to it the intense study that he had applied to other foreign policy issues.

In November 1977, the Shah was among the first foreign leaders to be invited for a state visit by Carter. A large vociferous demonstration by Iranian exiles opposed to the Shah took place in front of the White House. Tear gas used by the D.C. police wafted toward the South Lawn, disrupting the welcoming ceremonies. It led Carter to quip, "There's one thing I can say about the Shah—he knows how to draw a crowd."

After the ceremony, Carter took the Shah into his small private office next to the Oval Office and delivered a strongly worded admonition about the human rights violations by his regime. Carter, the evangelist, believed that if he had a strong personal relationship with someone, he could appeal to his better instincts and raise him up to his own idealistic point of view. The Shah, jaded by many visits to the White House and countless meetings with eight presidents, beginning with Franklin Delano Roosevelt in 1943, shrugged off Carter's demands, claiming that he was already doing as much as he could. Needing the Shah's backing for the Middle East peace process, Carter was reluctant to push any further. He did, however, find he liked the Shah.

Carter had planned a multicountry trip between Christmas and New Year's of 1977. He asked Rosalynn in which country she would like to be for New Year's Eve. In light of the pleasant personal relationship they had established with the Shah and Empress Farah, she emphatically settled on Iran. At a glittering banquet in Tehran attended also by Jordan's King Hussein, the Shah proposed a glowing toast to Carter and U.S.–Iranian relations. In the spirit of reciprocity, and with the encouragement of Brzezinski, Carter said:

Iran, because of the great leadership of the Shah, is an island of stability in one of the more troubled areas of the world. This is a great tribute to you, Your Majesty, and to your leadership and to the respect and the admiration and love your people give you.

He wanted to underscore again his concern about human rights, but the way he phrased it, "The cause of human rights is one that is shared deeply by our people and by the leaders of our two nations," left him open to considerable later criticism.

Within a month, serious rioting broke out in the holy city of Qom. As unrest intensified over the next several months, the Shah used increasingly repressive measures in an effort to crush dissent. On September 7, he declared martial law. Vance and Brzezinski agreed that Carter should call the Shah to express his support. Strikes and demonstrations spread throughout the country. Hundreds were killed by the Shah's forces. The institutional attachment to the Shah in Washington was so strong that no one wanted to accept that he could be overthrown. Eventually the Shah was forced to leave, fleeing first to Egypt, and then Morocco, from where he hoped he could orchestrate a military coup that would enable him to return to Iran. Subsequently he went to Mexico.

Although there was a brief hiatus during which a degree of normality returned to U.S.–Iranian relations, the secular leaders to whom power had been bequeathed by the Shah were gradually ousted by the fundamentalist followers of the Ayatollah Khomeini. Increasingly strident anti-American rhetoric began to come out of Iran. At the same time, it became apparent that the U.S. government was completely unprepared for the change of power. Having bet everything on the Shah, no channels of communication had been established with the new leadership. There was little or no informed understanding anywhere in the U.S. government about the political implications of Islamic fundamentalism. Gary Sick, who handled Iran on the National Security Staff under Brzezinski, recalled a meeting at which Vice President Mondale asked CIA director Stansfield Turner, "What the hell is an 'Ayatollah' anyway?" "I'm not sure I know," Turner responded.

Brzezinski had initially suggested to Carter that the Shah be invited to come to live in exile in the United States as a gesture of support for an old ally. Hopeful of establishing amicable relations with the new regime, Carter felt it better that he remain elsewhere, a view shared by Vance. Throughout the summer, Carter was bombarded by requests from friends of the Shah, including David Rockefeller and Henry Kissinger. By the end of October, there were reports the Shah was seriously ill. David Rockefeller had sent his personal physician, Dr. Keane, to Mexico; he reported that the Shah was suffering from lymphoma with an obstruction of the bile duct. If he were not admitted to the United States for treatment, he would likely die. Again the president was deluged by requests from the Shah's American friends that he be admitted on purely humanitarian grounds.

Carter remained dubious. At one meeting he asked, "Does somebody have the answer as to what we do if the diplomats in our embassy are taken hostage?" When others in the room, including Mondale, remained silent, Carter continued, "I gather not. On that day we will all sit here with long, drawn, white faces and realize we've been had."

On October 23, despite his reservations, and with assurances from the Iranian government that there would be no reprisals, Carter agreed to let the Shah come to the Sloan-Kettering Institute in New York. Although Iranian students in the United States demonstrated against the Shah, the situation remained quiescent in Tehran. On the morning of November 4, Brzezinski called Carter to inform him of the embassy seizure.

Despite the previous assurances from Tehran, the Ayatollah, grabbing the opportunity to consolidate his own support in the still very splintered and fluid situation in Iran, threatened to put the hostages on trial and to blow up the embassy compound if a military rescue attempt was made.

Carter assumed a high-profile, warning that the consequences would be "grave" if the hostages were harmed. He ordered two aircraft carrier task forces into the region and won wide international support, including that of the World Court and the United Nations Security Council. On November 12, he terminated all oil purchases from Iran (4 percent of U.S. supplies), and two days later froze all Iranian assets in the United States. Without jeopardizing the lives of the hostages, he knew his military options were limited, and it seemed inconceivable that this would be anything other than a short-term crisis. He therefore focused his primary attention on a diplomatic strategy.

The impact these events had in further driving up international oil prices posed a serious threat to Carter's efforts to control inflation. The U.S. ambassador in Beirut, John Gunther Dean, served as a clandestine communications channel with the PLO, and on November 9 he contacted Hasib Sabbagh, a wealthy Palestinian businessman with considerable influence in the region, to solicit his help. Two days later, Sabbagh flew to Saudi Arabia with two Americans of Middle Eastern background, A. Robert Abboud and Odeh Aburdene, where they met with Crown Prince Fahd. Sabbagh convinced the prince to call Yasir Arafat and, stressing the importance of the hostage issue to him personally and to Saudi Arabia, asked him to use his influence with the Ayatollah Khomeini to get the hostages released. As a result, on November 17, thirteen black and female hostages were given their freedom. The three men also conveyed Carter's plea that Saudi Arabia substantially increase its oil production to offset the shortfall from Iran and bring down oil prices from their unprecedented high of $34 per barrel. The prince agreed to do this. It would have a dramatically positive effect on the world economy, but the full effect would not be felt until Carter left office, benefitting primarily his successor, Ronald Reagan.

The nightly television pictures of Iranian students—burning the U.S. flag, parading the hostages blindfold, and shouting defiant anti-American slogans—enraged the American public. Carter's tough response captured the nation's support. Kennedy's formal announcement two days after the seizure of the embassy could not have been more unfortunately timed. His criticism of Carter under the circumstances seemed almost unpatriotic. His candidacy was further undercut by a television interview with Roger Mudd for CBS, taped earlier but shown the very night of the events in Iran. Intended as a friendly interview dramatically launching his campaign nationwide, it was a complete flop. Tentative and vague, he seemed unable to answer effectively even the most fundamental questions, such as why he wanted to be president, and how a Kennedy administration would differ from Carter's. Jordan immediately saw a crucial opportunity to exploit Carter's decisive handling of the hostage crisis against Kennedy's indecisiveness, playing directly back into Kennedy's greatest liability—Chappaquiddick. After the interview, Kennedy's lead over Carter in the polls would drop to 10 percent from a high of 30 percent only eight weeks earlier.

On December 3, Kennedy criticized Carter for letting the Shah into the United States, but the public reaction to Kennedy's comment was distinctly negative, and it further damaged his campaign. The following day, Carter officially announced his own candidacy for reelection. The polls showed Carter's approval rating to have jumped from 32 percent to 61 percent, the single greatest one-month reversal in history. Against his most probable Republican opponent, Ronald Reagan, he held a 14-point lead.

Carter had earlier promised to debate Kennedy and fellow contender Jerry Brown, in Iowa. In late December he announced that in view of the hostage crisis he was going to postpone active campaigning. "While the crisis continues I must be present to define and lead our response to an ever-changing situation of the greatest security, sensitivity, and importance." Hamilton Jordan had convinced Carter to adopt the "Rose Garden" strategy, enabling him to enhance his stature as president while avoiding getting mired in the fray of the primaries.

In mid-December, apparently taking advantage of the Carter administration's preoccupation with Iran, the Soviet Union announced that it was sending 85,000 troops into Afghanistan to support the Marxist regime of Hafizulah Amin. They arrived on Christmas Day. The ineffectual Amin was quickly overthrown and replaced by Barbrak Karmal, a pro-Moscow hard-liner who had been in exile in Czechoslovakia. In Pakistan, 20,000 Moslem demonstrators stormed the American embassy and in Saudi Arabia several hundred fanatics seized control of the Grand Mosque in Mecca. Hundreds died before Saudi forces regained control. The Soviet action, together with their earlier decision to send Cuban troops as well as their own to support the brutal dictatorship of Haile Mengistu in Ethiopia, lent credibility to Brzezinski's relentless effort to convince Carter of the intractable malevolence of Moscow.

On January 3, 1980, Carter asked the Senate to table the SALT II Treaty. It was a wrenching decision for Carter, who saw reducing the world's stockpile of nuclear weapons as a prime objective of his presidency. Hamilton Jordan says, "The failure to ratify the SALT II Treaty was the greatest disappointment of the Carter presidency, and my greatest disappointment." Although it was unratified, both sides would subsequently abide by the terms of the treaty.

Despite heated argument, especially from Mondale, even in the face of the upcoming Iowa caucuses, Carter decided to impose an embargo on U.S. grain sales to the Soviet Union. In a televised speech he announced that he would also ban the sale of high technology and other strategic items to the Soviets. He asked the International Olympic Committee to change the venue of the summer games planned for Moscow. When that did not happen, he withdrew U.S. participation.

Although Carter was having to deal with an unprecedented level of international turmoil, his handling of it enhanced his image as a strong leader. On January 21, he crushed Kennedy in the Iowa caucuses, carrying ninety-eight of ninety-nine counties.

The hostage crisis, however, which had initially led Americans to rally behind the president, was becoming a steadily greater liability. The nightly count of how many days the hostages had been held and the creation of *Nightline*, a television program devoted solely to the crisis, were relentless reminders of Carter's failure to secure their release. Concerned that failure to resolve the hostage crisis might be seen as an indication of weakness, he adopted a particularly hard line with the Soviets. He was also angry with them for having destroyed the potential for his dream of ratifying SALT II.

In his State of the Union speech on January 23, Carter took a strong aggressive stance. Responding to concern that the invasion of Aghanistan was a prelude to achieving the longstanding Russian dream of a warm-water port on the Indian Ocean and a threat to the oil-rich nations of the Persian Gulf, he enunciated what became known as the "Carter Doctrine," saying, "Any attempt by any outside force to gain control of the Persian Gulf region will be regarded as an assault on the vital interests of the United

States of America." He went on to propose a reintroduction of the registration requirement for a possible future military draft. Most significant, he announced that he was seeking five annual increases of 5 percent in real defense spending as opposed to the 3 percent he had sought since 1977. His successor, Ronald Reagan, would accuse Carter of cutting defense spending and claim credit for reinstating support for the Pentagon. In fact, it was this speech by Carter that marked the turning point that launched the defense buildup of the eighties.

In early February, Carter defeated Kennedy in the New Hampshire primary despite his overwhelming support in neighboring Massachusetts. Carter, however, faced growing problems. By April, Volcker raised the prime rate to 18.5 percent. Inflation was running around 20 percent. Housing starts plummeted, car sales continued to decline, and unemployment in Detroit was close to 25 percent. The stock market turned bullish as Carter seemed to be acting decisively on Afghanistan and with the promise of increased defense spending. Then as fear of inflation again gripped the market, the Dow Jones Average dropped more than 10 percent in a month. Uncertainty about the U.S. economy, the situation in Iran, and the impact on oil prices if America headed toward war caused wild speculation in the price of gold, which rose beyond $850 per ounce.

On March 14, Carter announced a new anti-inflation plan that reflected his continuing determination to balance the budget even if it meant giving political ammunition to Kennedy's liberal supporters. He proposed slashing $13 billion in federal spending for 1980, cutting politically sensitive programs such as CETA (Comprehensive Employment and Training Act), food stamps, and child assistance. Mondale, who was forced to loyally defend Carter's actions on the campaign trail, argued vehemently inside the administration that cutting a few billion dollars or even balancing the budget would have little effect on inflation, but a devastating impact on the campaign. Mondale urged Carter to make token expenditures or at least leave untouched those programs such as education, public works, and assistance for the poor and elderly, which were dear to the constituencies they were trying to win from Kennedy.

In private, Mondale complained Carter was "hurting the poor, raising defense to the roof, dropping SALT, alienating the Jews and even moderate liberals." Jordan, also, had long been concerned, earlier writing Carter, "I do not see how we can continue to alienate key groups of people who were responsible for your election and still maintain our political base." The cuts were harshly attacked by Kennedy as "completely intolerable," liable to harm the most vulnerable in society. Douglas Fraser called Carter's policies an outrage and accused him of reviving Herbert Hoover's economic policies.

In the first half of March, Carter and Jordan saw Kennedy as an increasingly spent force. Carter had decisively defeated Kennedy in Florida on March 11 and again in Illinois a week later. However, the deteriorating economy, the agonizing failure to secure the return of the hostages, and the inability to rebut Soviet aggression in Afghanistan created the impression of a weak president who was the victim of forces he could not control. Kennedy increasingly offered people an opportunity to register their disapproval. Mondale had hoped that the Kennedy campaign could be terminated by a decisive defeat in the New York primary on March 25. Kennedy, however, skillfully capitalized on Carter's announced budget cuts and then was dramatically helped by an administration blunder.

On March 2, the United States voted in favor of a unanimous U.N. resolution calling on Israel to dismantle the settlements in the occupied Arab territories including Jerusalem. Carter had earlier been assured that reference to Jerusalem had been removed from the resolution and, wanting to send a strong message of his opposition to the settlements, approved the vote. Strauss, who was managing the Carter campaign, angrily told him, "Either the vote is reversed or you can kiss New York goodbye." Using a technicality the vote was repeated the next day, allowing the United States to abstain. Carter issued a statement saying that there had been a communications problem over the removal of the mention of Jerusalem, but the damage was done.

When Vance, whose relations with the White House and especially with Brzezinski had become seriously strained, testified before the Senate on March 21, four days before the primary, he had a chance to redeem the situation. However, he defended the vote, saying that the United States had always opposed the settlements as being "contrary to international law and an impediment to the successful conclusion of the Middle East [peace] process." He would later confide, "The vote was the right thing to do. If it had not come right before the primary, no one would have made much fuss. But I believe that sound foreign policy comes before local politics." Vance knew that whatever Carter was being forced to do for expediency by his political operatives, he privately shared the same view. Carter sent Vance a personal note congratulating him on his testimony. In a strong display of Jewish antipathy, he lost the New York primary to Kennedy by 16 percent. Kennedy also won neighboring Connecticut. Kennedy's dual victories breathed new life into his campaign. The debacle at the United Nations further damaged Carter by adding to the impression of a presidency in disarray.

The hostage crisis continued to preoccupy Carter. Hamilton Jordan says, "There were two White Houses—one working on the hostages, the other working on everything else." Shortly after the embassy was taken, planning was initiated for a rescue mission. Aggressive military action against Iran would have won Carter wide support among the American people, but he was deeply concerned about jeopardizing the lives of the hostages. On April 7, Carter announced that he was formally terminating diplomatic relations with Iran and tightening the embargo. On April 11, he informed the members of the National Security Council that he planned to go forward with the rescue mission. The joint chiefs of staff had presented him with convincing evidence that it could succeed without unduly endangering the hostages. Mondale strongly urged military action, feeling Carter could no longer allow his seemingly passive acquiescence to America's humiliation to continue. In addition, with the Kennedy campaign revitalized, the crisis made him more vulnerable to his challenger.

The only opposition to this course of action came from Secretary of State Vance. Gradually pushed aside by the aggressive infighting of Brzezinski, Vance was becoming increasingly frustrated. With years of experience working with the Defense Department, he had serious misgivings and would tell Mondale, "I'll guarantee you something will go wrong. It never works the way they say it's going to work. There's a good chance a disaster could occur here." Vance's opposition provided him with the opportunity to tender his resignation over a matter of principle. He agreed to remain until after the mission and then leave regardless of whether it was successful or not.

Vance was vindicated when the mission proved a disastrous failure. Of the eight helicopters that departed from the aircraft carrier *Nimitz*, one suffered mechanical problems and another got lost in a sandstorm. When they rendezvoused in the desert 100 miles south of Tehran with six C-130s carrying the rescue team, they unexpectedly encountered several vehicles, including a bus, filled with Iranians. Although most of the Iranians were killed or taken prisoner, two escaped. Then one of the remaining helicopters developed a hydraulic problem, bringing the total number of operational helicopters down below the required minimum of six. Colonel Charles Beckwith, the former Green Beret in command, decided he had no alternative but to scrub the mission. As the rescue team was reboarding the C-130s in preparation for evacuating the site, one of the remaining helicopters went out of control and crashed into one of the transport planes. The wreckage burst into flames, killing eight servicemen and badly burning four others.

The following morning, Carter somberly addressed the nation, taking full responsibility as commander-in-chief for the failure of the mission. A combination of bad luck and military ineptitude, both of which were beyond Carter's control, had led to the failure, yet it compounded the impression of a president impotent in defending the nation's honor against a Third World power. He was further unjustly accused of having timed the rescue effort as a way of galvanizing public support to score a knockout blow against Kennedy in the upcoming primaries. When Vance's promised resignation became public, it further discredited Carter's judgment in launching the rescue effort, even though Senator Edmund Muskie was simultaneously announced as his replacement.

With public approval of Carter's handling of the hostage crisis dropping into the 30 percent range, Kennedy narrowly defeated him in both Pennsylvania and Michigan. However, the arithmetic of the delegate selection process was on Carter's side, and the White House had hoped Kennedy would pull out and allow Carter and Mondale to begin uniting the party for the general election. Kennedy was determined to stay in the race all the way to the convention.

Following the failure of the rescue effort, Carter's Rose Garden strategy had diminished credibility and it appeared increasingly as though he was trying to avoid facing Kennedy. Mondale, who had been carrying the main burden of campaigning for the administration, implored Carter to go out on the hustings as a way of visibly assuming leadership and showing he was in control. Carter's return to the campaign trail paid off, winning primaries during May in Indiana, Tennessee, and North Carolina. On June 3, the final day of the primary season, Kennedy carried California and New Jersey, but Carter's victory in Ohio gave him enough delegates to assure him a first-ballot victory at the convention.

On June 11, Hamilton Jordan announced that he was leaving the White House to manage the reelection campaign. With his blessing, Carter appointed Jack Watson to be his successor, a vindication that had been a long time coming.

Carter invited Kennedy to the White House in the mistaken belief that they could now heal their differences and begin uniting the party. Instead, Kennedy insisted that they have a televised debate to air those differences and declined to give any assurance that he would support the ticket even if such an event were held. On July 16, the Republicans nominated Ronald Reagan as their candidate, and despite his image as an extremist, he jumped to a 28 percent lead over Carter.

Billy Carter was the only member of the family really damaged by Jimmy's ascendancy to the presidency. Unable to handle the publicity that descended on him, his already serious drinking problem became significantly worse. In 1978, he made a highly publicized trip to Libya and subsequently hosted a Libyan delegation in Atlanta. He was hospitalized and successfully treated for his alcoholism. Short of money, he agreed to represent the Libyan government in oil sales and received a $200,000 advance against future commissions. The financial arrangement drew the attention of the media, as well as the Department of Justice, the Internal Revenue Service, and several congressional committees. Throughout July 1980,

Billy dominated the news. Eventually he appeared before a Senate committee, coming across as a plausible and sympathetic figure. There was no evidence of influence peddling as charged or anything to suggest that the president had been aware, except through the media, of what Billy had been doing. Nevertheless, at a time when he was beset by a plethora of other problems, the episode only served further to weaken Carter's standing with the public.

As the Democrats convened in August in New York, an ABC–Louis Harris poll showed Carter's approval rating to have fallen to 22 percent— lower even than Nixon's during Watergate. While the Republicans had consolidated around their nominee, Ronald Reagan, the Democrats remained seriously divided. Kennedy made a last-ditch effort to secure a resolution freeing delegates from their obligation to individual candidates in the hope that he could lure Carter delegates to his side. The measure was handily defeated. On Tuesday night, August 12, Kennedy gave a rousing speech extolling the virtue of traditional liberal values. Kennedy, whose near total absence at the two previous Democratic conventions had divided the party, now sought to do so with his presence. It was only later that night that he formally withdrew from the fight.

Unable to resolve the rifts within their party, both Carter and Mondale sought instead to achieve unity by focusing their attacks outwardly on Ronald Reagan. Mondale warned that, if elected, Reagan would "repeal what Roosevelt and Truman and Kennedy and Johnson, and two generations of Americans have done to build a more just and hopeful society." Striking a similar theme, Carter said Reagan would "launch an all-out nuclear arms race" and start "an attack on everything that we've done in the achievement of social justice and decency in the last fifty years." The choice, Carter warned, was between a Democratic future of "security and justice and peace" and the Reagan future of "despair, surrender, and risk." The press particularly credited Mondale with defining effectively Reagan's shortcomings, but legitimately remarked that in attacking Reagan they implied that the administration's record of the last four years was insufficient to run on for reelection.

The Democratic cause was further damaged during the closing minutes of the convention. Kennedy was on the podium with Carter and Mondale sharing the wild applause; he deliberately and very visibly circled away from Carter to avoid joining him in the traditional symbol of party unity— clasped hands held high.

Reagan and Carter not only offered the voters differing personalities, parties, and ideologies, they also represented two quite distinct thematic streams in American history and political culture. In the tradition of those who had come to America primarily for religious freedom, Carter was the inheritor of a philosophy in which concerns for matters of conscience and a sense of community dominated. Reagan represented a later wave of immigrants from religious and cultural backgrounds that differed substantially from those of men like Madison and Jefferson. The newcomers saw America differently, as a land of unlimited economic opportunity where unfettered competition enabled the most ambitious, the most industrious, the fit, and the fortunate to excel to the limit of their abilities and claim their just rewards.

If Carter was John Walton, Reagan was a character from the works of Louis L'Amour, the prolific writer of action-packed, pulp fiction novels about the American frontier where right and wrong were never in doubt and the gun was the final arbiter of any dispute. Reagan was a voracious reader of L'Amour's more than 100 books and as president would award him the Presidential Medal of Freedom, the nation's highest civilian honor. While Carter seemed often to agonize in public over the many complex decisions he had to make, Reagan emanated an appealing certainty, never in doubt, no matter how simplistic or unrealistic his solutions.

Reagan had adamantly opposed the civil rights legislation of the sixties and understood that the future of the Republican Party lay in appealing to disaffected white voters, especially in the South. Meeting with groups of southern convention delegates in both 1976 and 1980, he left them in no doubt that he would do more to halt, or turn back, the progress made by blacks in the region than any of his Republican opponents. He chose to speak early in the campaign in the tiny Mississippi town of Philadelphia, which had come to international prominence as the site where three civil rights workers had been brutally murdered by local whites including members of the Ku Klux Klan. Making no mention of the martyred young men, Reagan declared, "I believe in states rights," code words of Goldwater vintage that had replaced the traditional racial epithets. To whites across the South the message was clear that his sympathies lay not with the victims but with the perpetrators of the crime.

Carter also needed to attract that same constituency, which had formed the base of his support in 1976. On September 1, he launched his general election campaign in Tuscumbia, Alabama, with a speech appealing to the better nature of his fellow white southerners, stressing racial harmony. Hooded members of the Ku Klux Klan were present carrying "Reagan for President" signs. The next day, Reagan perversely sought to imply that their presence showed Carter was seeking to appeal to racists. Realizing the absurdity of his comments, Reagan quickly reversed himself, saying, "I shouldn't have said it, because the minute after I said it, I knew this was what would be remembered."

Reelection campaigns are inevitably referenda on the incumbent's performance. Carter had no experience running for reelection except for his second state senate race when he was unopposed. Rather than extolling his accomplishments and promoting his vision for a second term, he chose to make his thrust an attack on Reagan's lack of qualifications to be president. Focusing on his opponent rather than himself was a formula that had worked well for Carter in his race with Carl Sanders and to a lesser extent against Gerald Ford. While such an approach was enhancing for a populist outsider, it seemed demeaning for a head of state.

In a speech before a black audience in Atlanta, Carter attacked Reagan, implying that he was a racist. Significant visible advances for blacks under Carter, combined with growing economic insecurity, had created a strong white backlash—and not just in the South. With a substantial segment of the electorate sharing Reagan's views, Carter found little sympathy. Instead he was seen as mean and spiteful. "The president seems bent on discarding his last ace, his reputation as a decent and compassionate man," commented the *Boston Globe*. Carter shifted his attack to foreign policy, where polls indicated the public saw Reagan as weak. Adopting a less strident tone, Carter criticized Reagan's announcement that he would scrap the still-unratified SALT II agreement and launch a new arms race. Carter was still heavily faulted for suggesting that Reagan would lead the nation into war.

In a lengthy June 25 memo, on the assumption that Reagan would be the Republican nominee, Jordan had laid out for Carter a detailed strategy for the fall campaign that called for both the attack on Reagan and a need to spell out where he would lead the country in the next four years. Concerned about the "meanness" issue that Reagan was turning to his advantage, Carter's advisors urged him to be careful about his stridency. They were joined by Mondale, who still believed that the surest route to reelection was to reconstitute the alliance of traditional Democratic constituency groups.

Carter found it difficult to accept their advice. He was appalled that on so many complex issues of major consequence to the country, such as the energy policy, Reagan appeared to have only the most superficial under-standing, seemed to mind little about making statements that were wildly inaccurate, and showed no comprehension of the often catastrophic impli-cations of the simpleminded positions he was offering. What was particu-larly frustrating was that the voters did not seem to know the difference.

On October 7, at Carter's request, Eizenstat provided him with a list of extreme Reagan quotes, including: "What needs to be done is to repeal the energy legislation and turn the industry loose." "Urban aid is one of the biggest phonies . . . that we have had for a number of years." "There is no health-care crisis in America." Speaking of the unemployed and welfare recipients, "freeloaders wanting a prepaid vacation plan." "The minimum wage has caused more misery and unemployment than anything since the

Great Depression." "The anti–nuclear power people . . . behind the scenes they are being manipulated by forces sympathetic to the Soviet Union." "I just don't think it [nuclear nonproliferation] is any of our business." "Fascism was the real basis for the New Deal." Even Reagan's own handlers became concerned about his past assertions that Social Security be made voluntary, that the Vietnam War was a "noble cause," and his claim—while his running mate, George Bush, was touring China—that he would restore diplomatic relations with Taiwan. They made sure that, from then on, he was always accompanied by a senior staff member, spoke only from prepared texts, and had little opportunity for impromptu answers to questions.*

While Carter would make some headway in creating doubts about Reagan's competency, many voters liked his affable avuncular style. Part of Carter's problem derived from the special nature of the American political system combining the roles of head of state and head of government. Carter was attacking Reagan primarily for his lack of qualifications to be head of government, while Reagan was mainly selling himself to the electorate on the basis of the inspirational skills he would bring to the role of head of state. As the "great communicator," he offered a clear if flawed vision, an ethnocentric love of country, reinflamed fear of communism, and scorn for government. He promised to make people feel good about themselves and about America. He did not pretend to know about the details of policy and the operations of government; indeed he made it evident that he viewed government as the enemy. Carter's criticisms of Reagan in that context seemed petty and unreasonable to many people.

In 1976, Carter had captured the support of an electorate cynical about the size of government and its ability to respond to their needs by promising to bring to it competency and efficient management. Seemingly overwhelmed by the deluge of events that had descended on him in the previous year—mostly not of his own making—by attacking Reagan's competency, Carter also caused people to question his own. At the same time, Carter could offer no competing ideologically derived vision. As one observer noted, "The American people wanted simple, short, black-and-white answers. Carter's honesty compelled him to ambivalence and gray areas . . . he acknowledged the complexity of modern life and Reagan didn't."

Carter's problems were compounded by the independent candidacy of liberal Republican John Anderson. Kennedy's challenge and his lukewarm

---

*Reagan would ultimately be diagnosed with Alzheimer's disease, a condition of insidious onset, symptoms of which, including prosopagnosia—the inability to recall familiar faces—were in retrospect present at least as early as his first term. What was then interpreted as dissembling for political advantage now appears to have been, at times, confabulation in which the brain, to cover memory deficits, instantaneously fabricates information that the sufferer does not consciously know is untrue.

backing of the ticket left many of his supporters either unenthusiastic about working for Carter's reelection or siphoned off by Anderson. No one better embodied the problems Carter faced than Patrick Lucey, the former governor of Wisconsin. Despite Lucey's having been a dubious backer from the start, as part of his effort to bring all segments of the party into his administration Carter had appointed him ambassador to Mexico. He left the administration to support the Kennedy challenge and then joined Anderson in the general election. Mondale sought gamely to return liberals to the fold, but with only modest success.

By doing what he believed was right without much regard for the political consequences, Carter had alienated to some degree all of the constituencies that had supported him in 1976. His commitment to fiscal conservatism, and especially a balanced budget, had lost him the liberals. Despite the triumph of Camp David and the removal of Egypt as the greatest military threat facing Israel, Jews showed a little gratitude and would desert him, failing to give the majority of their votes to the Democratic nominee for the first time in recent history. As Rafshoon points out, it was not so much that they were unhappy about Camp David as much as they feared what concessions an overzealous desire for peace might make him wring from Israel in a second term. What business backing he had enjoyed he lost because of the gyrations of the economy, high inflation, and interest rates. Conservatives abandoned him for his active promotion of blacks and women, as well as his concern for Third World nations—including an unprecedented trip to Africa—his emphasis on human rights, his early cuts in defense systems he deemed unneeded, and a posture in foreign affairs they saw as insufficiently belligerent. Ironically, despite Jordan's disparagement of Watson as a "policy person not a political person," Carter's most significant remaining constituency was the nation's Democratic mayors and governors. As their contact point in the White House, Watson had gone to considerable length to nurture their loyalty and remind them not only how well Carter had served their interests but how much they stood to lose if a Republican were elected.

One group that Carter's advisors had taken for granted was the born-again Christians. There was a sense that "The religious [Christian] community belonged to Carter," but as Bert Lance notes, "They were the first to abandon him." While Carter was an evangelical, believing it his responsibility to spread the word of God, he was not a fundamentalist. He saw the Bible as the ultimate authoritative guide to be studied and followed in leading a truly Christian life, but not, as fundamentalists considered it, the literal word of God. The more than 40 percent of Americans who considered themselves "born again" were by no means a monolithic group; they were mainly, but not exclusively, Baptists. Most fundamentalists and evangelicals were Baptists, but they existed in significant numbers in other denominations. Most evangelicals, especially the Baptists, were fundamentalists, although the minority, generally the more worldly and educated, like Carter, were not.

Many Christians, especially fundamentalists, felt betrayed by Carter: he served alcohol in the White House; he supported the Equal Rights Amendment; while personally opposed to abortion, he had not taken a sufficiently activist position against it; he did not speak out for prayer in the schools; he allowed homosexuals to work in the White House; and he had not, as they claimed he had promised, hired evangelicals for his staff. "He surrounded himself with Godless people," they claimed. Hostility was particularly focused on Anne Wexler, a powerful and competent woman they labeled a "pro-abortion feminist," and Sarah Weddington, who had argued the *Roe v. Wade* case before the Supreme Court.

As early as May 1978, when Carter spoke to the Brotherhood Commission of the Southern Baptist Convention, he encountered deep hostility from the leadership. Later in 1979, Carter invited Adrian Rogers, the first of a string of conservatives elected president of the Southern Baptist Convention, to visit him in the Oval Office. At the end of an otherwise cordial meeting, Rogers accused Carter of abandoning his religious roots and said, "I hope you will give up your secular humanism and return back to Christianity."

Finally, Reverend Robert Maddox, a Baptist preacher who at one time had been Jody Powell's pastor in Vienna, Georgia, was hired through Rosalynn's intercession to reverse the Christian tide against the president. "He was in deep trouble with the religious community," Maddox says. James Dunn of the Cooperative Baptist Fellowship would later go further, saying, "The fundamentalist faction in the southern Baptist convention had a lot to do with his defeat." After generations of turning their backs on politics, conservative Christians had been awakened, at least in part by Carter's 1976 campaign, to play a more activist role. Sensing their disillusionment with Carter, the political right had quickly sought to link up with the religious right, creating most significantly the "Moral Majority." According to Maddox, the issue of race was exploited in that appeal;

> The president got in trouble in the campaign when he suggested racism was there. But it is—right beneath the surface. The same kind of mentality that cranked out the anti-nigger stuff in the fifties, cranked out this anti-Carter stuff in the eighties.

What was astonishing, even to sophisticated Baptist preachers like James Dunn, was that Reagan could become the choice of Christian conservatives over Carter.

One of the real puzzles . . . was how Mr. Reagan could capture the affections of these people. He was a Hollywood libertine . . . had a child conceived out of wedlock before he and Nancy married, admitted to drug use during his Hollywood years, and according to Henry Steele Commager, was the least religious president in American history.

However, as Maddox points out, the conservative religious movement "tends to be Republican so it becomes difficult for them to separate their Republican leanings from their religious leanings." Conservative Christians had taken over religious radio and television stations playing the tapes that Reagan had been churning out as a commentator during the previous four years and painting him as the "Christian candidate." In addition, Robert Billings, executive director of the Moral Majority, who along with Falwell had mastered the skill of exploiting negative issues, especially for fund-raising, became the religious advisor for the Reagan campaign.

The League of Women Voters had again organized a presidential debate, but insisted that as long as Anderson was above 15 percent in the polls, he be included with Carter and Reagan. Reagan similarly refused to participate without Anderson. Fearful of having Carter simultaneously attacked by two opponents, Rafshoon and Jordan advised him not to participate. Unlike his refusal to debate Carl Sanders in 1970, Carter's absence would hurt him, although mildly, in this instance.

However, by the beginning of October the situation was looking better for Carter. A rise in the GNP was predicted for the fourth quarter, housing starts were up, and the recession seemed to be bottoming out. A *Newsweek* poll showed Reagan leading by only 4 percent compared to the 28 percent lead he had held on July 16, the day of his nomination. Despite the election, Carter's primary preoccupation remained with the hostages. His seeming impotence in the face of the nightly television count of how many days had elapsed since the hostages were captured played directly into Reagan's bare-knuckles approach to foreign policy. Although he had announced that he would not speak directly about the hostage situation, Reagan was still able to imply that if he were president, America would never again be subjected to such humiliation.

Early in September, the Iranian government communicated through the German ambassador that they were willing to begin discussing the release of the hostages. A five-person delegation, headed by Deputy Secretary of State Warren Christopher, flew to Bonn for discussion with a representative of the Iranian government, Sadegh Tabatabai. The discussions were relatively fruitful, but due to the outbreak of the Iran–Iraq war, several weeks elapsed before Tabatabai could return from Tehran with an official response.

News of these developments leaked out, further strengthening Carter in polls and giving him a few points' lead over Reagan in some crucial states. It caused panic in the Republican camp, where they began talking of an "October surprise" in which the release of the hostages would cost them, by their own polls, as much as 10 percentage points. As early as late July, a senior Reagan advisor had flown to Lebanon, where he met with Bassam Abu Sharif, a top lieutenant of PLO leader Yasir Arafat. Fearful of going to the PLO headquarters, he persuaded Abu Sharif to have Arafat come to a nighttime meating at his apratment. Sharif says the Reagan representative asked that Arafat stop trying to get hostages freed and instead use his influence in Tehran to delay the release until after the election. According to Sharif the result he promised was that "the PLO would be given recognition as the legitimate representatives of the Palestinian people and the White House door would be open for us."

Reagan's campaign manager, William Casey, a man with a penchant for intrigue and long involved with the Central Intelligence Agency, had established his own channels to Tehran through relationships in the French intelligence community. As Gary Sick, a Carter, and later a Reagan National Security Council staffer has documented, Casey and others met at Madrid's Ritz Hotel in late July and early August with Iranian representatives led by cleric Mehdi Karrubi, and offered to help them obtain the arms they were seeking in return for stalling negotiations with Carter. This meeting would result in the hostages being kept imprisoned at least until after the election. At a subsequent meeting on August 12, Karrubi reported that the Ayatollah Khomeini had approved the deal. They wanted Iranian financial and military assets unfrozen, something Casey responded could not be done while the Republicans were still out of power. They could perhaps broker an arms deal through a third country.

There is little doubt that Carter, had he been willing, could have cut a similar deal to trade arms for the hostages. He refused to do so, however, as a matter of principle. When Begin visited Washington on April 13, he had told Carter that the Israelis had contacts in Iran that might be helpful in securing the release of the hostages, but it would require the United States to authorize Israel to sell arms covertly to Iran. Carter rejected the offer, and asked Begin to adhere strictly to the arms embargo. Returning to Israel, Begin admonished the chief of staff of the Israeli Defense Forces to stick to the letter of the law. But, ten days later when the rescue mission failed, he noted to a visiting American, "Jimmy Carter is finished." On that assumption, Begin seemed subsequently willing to cover Israel's bets surreptitiously with the Republicans. Israel's decision to help arm Iran was also significantly influenced by increasing fear of an Iraqi victory in the recently launched Iran–Iraq conflict. In the four months following the

August 12 Madrid meeting, a 5,000-ton ship of Greek origin would make four separate arms deliveries from Eilat in Israel to the Iranian port of Bandar Abbas in direct breach of the U.S.-imposed embargo.

Concerned that the Iranians might still negotiate a deal with Carter, Casey and other members of the Reagan team held urgent meetings with Israeli and Iranian representatives at the Waldorf Florida and Raphael hotels in Paris between October 15 and 20. The scope of the arms deal was expanded in return not only for assurances that the hostages would be held through the election, but in order to maximize Carter's humiliation, they would not be released until Reagan was inaugurated.

Considered even by his friends to have long flirted with the wrong side of the law, to accomplish the strategy with Iran Casey had drawn on a lifetime of relationships with individuals currently or previously associated with the intelligence community. They were professional operatives who not only had the necessary international contacts and were coldbloodedly involved in breaking of governments through clandestine deals and furtive manipulation, they were also people who could keep secrets even if it meant perjuring themselves. As part of their trade, they knew how to cover their tracks. They had a deep dislike for Carter and his administration. Stansfield Turner had infuriated the intelligence fraternity by initiating an overdue shift in emphasis away from the use of human agents toward technology, and especially satellites, as the primary source of intelligence gathering. Carter's populism and advocacy of open government conflicted with the unaccountable, secretive, elitist view of many in the agency. Carter was widely disliked while Casey and Reagan's vice-presidential nominee, George Bush, were considered members of the club. "Reagan/Bush '80" bumper stickers with the Reagan portion cut off began appearing at the agency's headquarters during the campaign.

Casey's espionage ethos pervaded the Reagan camp. A coordinated network of Reagan sympathizers infiltrated the administration, including the White House, passing information—much of it sensitive, some classified—to campaign operatives. An organized network of retired military officers monitored air force bases for any sign of unusual activity that might suggest the administration had achieved a breakthrough with Iran. The Reagan camp declined repeated offers by the administration to brief them on the hostage situation.

With their own polls on October 14 showing Carter leading 41 percent to 39 percent, the Reagan staff reconsidered their earlier refusal to debate Carter without Anderson, a decision made easier by the fact that Anderson had now dropped below 15 percent in the polls. Although Caddell in particular expressed some trepidation about a head-to-head confrontation, there was no way Carter could refuse.

The debate took place on October 28 in Cleveland. What Carter did not know was that a copy of his secret briefing book on foreign policy and national defense had made its way into the hands of the Reagan–Bush team. Well prepared, knowledgeable, with a thorough grasp of complex issues, Carter seemed intellectually poised to devastate Reagan. What he was not prepared for was the challenger's consummate skills as a performer honed during his many years as an actor. Familiarity with the contents of the president's briefing books gave Reagan an added aura of relaxed self-confidence. Trying to seem down-to-earth, Carter related that he had asked Amy what she regarded as the most important issue of the day. "Nuclear weaponry and the control of nuclear arms," she had replied. It left the impression that he was trivializing the issue and detracted from his greatest asset—the stature of his office. Even Rafshoon groaned as he listened to Carter.

In contrast to the respectful awe with which Carter had viewed the office of the presidency in his debate with Ford in 1976, Reagan skillfully treated Carter with kindly condescension. "There you go again," Reagan said in a deflating rebuke to Carter's attempts to criticize his lack of qualifications. Most devastating were Reagan's comments at the end of the debate when he asked the audience, "Are you better off than you were four years ago? . . . Is America as respected throughout the world as it was? Do you feel our security is safe, that we're as strong as we were four years ago?" Opinion polls showed the public perceived Reagan as the winner.

Carter was hopeful that agreement might still be reached leading to the release of the hostages. But on November 2, the Iranian Majlis issued a statement which, while offering useful conditions for future negotiations, signaled the certainty that it would not happen before the election. It was a great disappointment for Carter, who returned hurriedly from campaigning in Chicago. The Republicans had repeatedly warned that Carter might pull a last-minute surprise. In an attempt to counter those artificial expectations, and in response to Jordan's advice that it would show he was still on top of the hostage issue, he made a televised address to the nation. If anything, it had the opposite of its intended effect, reminding people of the stalemate and Carter's seeming impotence in dealing with it. Over the weekend, Caddell's polls showed a dramatic shift of the 25 percent undecided to Reagan. Carter called Rosalynn, who was campaigning in Texas, and told her to cancel the remainder of her itinerary and return to Washington.

Reagan defeated Carter by 51 percent to Carter's 41 percent, with Anderson receiving 7 percent. Reagan received 489 Electoral College votes to Carter's 49 (Rhode Island, West Virginia, Georgia, Minnesota, Maryland, and the District of Columbia). Carter was hurt by a low turnout—only 52 percent of registered voters. Exit polls showed that among those who cast their vote for Reagan, roughly half said they were voting against Carter rather than for the challenger, suggesting that Reagan had won with the positive vote of under 15 percent of the eligible electorate. Yet Carter was injured most by the sense that he had become the victim of events rather than their master. He had been elected on the promise that he would bring managerial efficiency to government, which implied being in control. Yet many voters perceived that the economy and foreign policy matters were out of control.

In the absence of a clearly articulated vision for Carter's second term, he seemed to offer only more of the same. He had ministered to the American psyche traumatized by Vietnam and Watergate. Now, having recovered, people were ready again to start feeling good about themselves and America. Jimmy Carter might never lie to them, but they were not sure they wanted the unvarnished truth anymore. For all his obvious shortcomings, Reagan offered reassuring national boosterism and a sense that he would be thoroughly in charge. Reagan's chauvinistic appeal tinged with racism attracted many white blue-collar Democrats. Perhaps most crucial for Carter were not so much the votes that went to Reagan but his failure to inspire the support of traditional Democratic constituencies who preferred to stay home rather than vote for either man.

The blow of defeat fell far more heavily on Rosalynn. While a lame duck, the responsibilities of the presidency continued to keep Carter busy. On November 20, Carter invited Reagan to the White House for a private meeting in the Oval Office. Carter had prepared a list of the most important and sensitive issues that the incoming president would face. For an hour, Carter went down the list as Reagan sat without comment or question. When Carter offered Reagan a pad so that he could take notes, Reagan declined. It was apparent that Reagan had little grasp of, or interest in, the subjects, but as the meeting ended Reagan asked Carter for a copy of his notes for his staff.

Unlike the orderly transition that occurred between the Ford and Carter administrations, Reagan's appointees almost universally declined to meet with their departing counterparts, creating serious continuity problems especially for America's allies. As Carter's foreign policy team was struggling to pressure leaders in Central America to protect the human rights of their people, young Reagan acolytes traveled to the region, assuring them the days of U.S. concern for such issues were over, triggering a bloodbath by right-wing death squads. Charles Schultze told Carter with dismay that Reagan's economic proposal for massive tax cuts and increased military spending was a prescription for a crippling increase in the national debt.

The hostages, however, remained Carter's primary preoccupation. Gratified by Carter's defeat, the Ayatollah Khomeini instructed the militants holding the hostages to turn them over to the Tehran government. A commission was appointed to work out the condition of their release using the government of Algeria as an intermediary. A complex web of frozen assets, loans, and fluctuating exchange rates had to be unscrambled to everyone's satisfaction by an army of lawyers, accountants, bankers, and diplomats.

Meanwhile, Carter put aside the disappointment of his defeat by monitoring, moment to moment, the status of the negotiations and by a determined effort to complete his unfinished business with the Congress. During November he achieved two of his most important victories: the passage of a bill creating a $1.6 billion toxic waste superfund to clean up chemical dump sites, and the Alaska Land Bill. Ending a two-year battle against oil, gas, mineral, and timber interests, the law more than doubled the size of the country's national parks, and almost tripled the amount of land designated as wilderness. Carter viewed it as one of the three or four accomplishments of his presidency of which he was most proud.

In the waning days of the administration the focus was entirely on securing the release of the hostages before Carter left office. A round-the-clock vigil was maintained in the Oval Office, with Cutler, Jordan, Gary Sick, Mondale, and Carter almost continuously on the phone with Deputy Secretary of State Warren Christopher heading the negotiations in Algiers. Phil Wise, the appointments secretary, had calculated that Carter would have to leave no later than 2 P.M. on Monday, January 19, to greet the hostages in Germany and still be back in time for the inauguration. The deadline passed and the continuing procrastination of the Iranians over the final details seemed incomprehensible. At 6:18 A.M. on inauguration morning, Christopher signed the final agreement. At 7 A.M. Carter called Reagan to brief him, but was told Reagan was asleep and was not to be disturbed. The hostages, after further agonizing delay, were put in a plane in Tehran, but it was held on the runway until the moment of Reagan's swearing-in. After attending the inauguration, Carter was with his staff on the plane to Georgia when he finally got the message that the hostages were out of Iranian airspace. One of Carter's greatest wishes had been achieved. Every single hostage had been released alive and well.

Within days the Reagan administration began shipping a long laundry list of military equipment to Iran.

CHAPTER 28

Jimmy Carter used the presidency as a stepping stone to what
he really wanted to do in life.

—STAN CLOUD, *Time* magazine

Jimmy and Rosalynn were greeted by Maxine Reese and the people of
Plains, who had organized a covered-plate dinner on Main Street to welcome them home. Hundreds of other friends and supporters had come
from around the country. However, as Maxine Reese recalled, "Everything
that had ever happened here—every outside gathering, every fund-raiser,
anything that we ever had—the weather was good. . . . But when Jimmy
came home to stay, it rained." The downpour did not dampen the enthusiasm of the reception, and Jimmy and Rosalynn were received as returning
heroes. Jimmy, however, remained only a matter of hours and then left for
Germany to welcome the returning hostages.

Finally returning exhausted to Plains, the former president slept for
close to twenty-four hours, awaking to what he described as "an altogether
new, unwanted, and potentially empty life." The demands of the presidency, and especially the ongoing hostage crisis, had left little time to deal
emotionally with his defeat while still in the White House. "Although my
disappointment was great, I kept it bottled up for a long time." Now in the
solitude of Plains, his traditional place of healing, it was time to let it all
come out. When alone he would ruminate about the events of the previous six months and whether there was anything he could have done
differently.

The natural depression began to dissipate rapidly, particularly after
Carter convinced himself that he had done his best, and he could have
done nothing more to change the outcome. He relied on his well-honed
ability to put setbacks behind him and focus only on the future. Following
the election he had received a letter from Admiral Hyman Rickover, which
said in part, "As long as a man is trying as hard as he can to do what he
thinks to be right, he is a success regardless of outcome." Among the many
letters of thanks he wrote in those first few weeks was a response to Rick-

over in which he wrote, "As I leave office, my realizations of your great contributions are matched only by my thanks for your personal kindness and
consideration. I've never gone wrong by following your advice."

The house on Woodland Drive had hardly been lived in for ten years
and the necessary fixing up became useful therapy. Together, and without
help, Jimmy and Rosalynn installed a new tongue-and-groove floor in the
attic to provide much-needed storage space.

In addition to the trauma of the electoral defeat and the letdown of
returning to the mundane life of private citizens, Jimmy and Rosalynn
found, to their horror, that the warehouse business they had placed in a
blind trust was now more than $1 million in debt. They still owned approx-
imately 4,000 acres of farmland, but in terms of cash they were near bankruptcy. In the weeks before they left Washington they had both been
approached by publishers about writing their memoirs. In light of their
finances, writing now provided a way to earn an income and begin to pay
off their debts. Jimmy started writing as a form of therapy even before an
actual contract was signed. Fortunately they were soon able to sell the
warehouse business to the Archer-Daniel-Midland Company, headed by
longtime Democratic Party supporter Dwayne Andreas.

For Rosalynn the election had exacted a more profound and lasting toll.
"There was no way I could understand our defeat. It didn't seem fair that
everything we had hoped for, all our plans and dreams for the country,
could have gone when the votes were counted on election day," she later
reminisced. Although she had immediately given vent to her feelings, her
grieving process proved long and arduous. After several months she began
to develop joint and muscle pain, which she initially attributed to long
hours at the word processor. An extensive workup at Emory University
Hospital revealed a mild thyroid deficiency, but no satisfactory diagnosis
for many of her symptoms other than the possibility that they were psycho-
somatic. As she progressively lost flexibility, Rosalynn vowed that she
would "wear the disease out" and launched into a regular exercise program, using the Jane Fonda workout tapes. Eventually she found her body
returning to normal.

For months they labored steadily on their memoirs. Jimmy had, as president, dictated his thoughts at the end of every day on a small handheld
recorder. Susan Clough transcribed the recordings and, with a Watergate-
induced phobia for any kind of tapes, they were then erased. The tran-
scriptions filled eighteen large black volumes—6,000 pages from which to
work. They both sought advice from presidential scholars and biographers,
but insisted on writing and typing every word themselves. As a farewell gift
from his staff and the cabinet, Jimmy had received a complete set of tools
and machinery for a woodworking shop. Applying skills he had learned in

high school and perfected in the navy, he took respites from his writing to build pieces of high-quality furniture. Although his teaching and the publication of his memoirs drew considerable attention, mentioning this activity to reporters allowed an erroneous image to be created in the public mind, which persisted for several years, that one of the major things he was doing in retirement was woodwork.

One unexpected problem was the constant interruptions from visiting friends and dignitaries. The Carters missed the isolation of Camp David. While they sought assiduously to protect their privacy, the constant stream of tourists who came to Plains felt they were entitled to some personal contact with the Carters. This was partially solved by opening his weekly Sunday school class at the Maranatha Baptist Church to anyone who wished to attend. Then John and Betty Pope convinced them to invest jointly in building a cabin on a 20-acre lot on a trout stream in the North Georgia mountains. Jimmy made all the furniture and one of his paintings decorated the wall. It served as a convenient retreat.

In addition to the small staff office that had been set up in Miss Lillian's house in Plains, for formal business activities Carter had the use of an office in the Russell Federal Building on Spring Street in Atlanta. The demands on the Carters' time were considerable; nearly 68,000 pieces of mail were received in the first three months out of office. Included were countless speaking invitations, virtually all of which were declined.

However, in early May 1981, Carter went to Independence, Missouri, to receive the eighth annual Harry S Truman Award. His speech was mainly lighthearted and included several jokes provided by Jack Kaplan. On May 17, he gave his first substantive speech dealing with the Camp David accords and the future of the Middle East peace process to the 100th anniversary celebration of the New York Board of Rabbis.

Relations with the new president were not good. Reagan extended to Carter the bare minimum of courtesies to which he was entitled by law as a former president. The White House simultaneously orchestrated a concerted public relations campaign that seemed to be aimed at discrediting Carter policies, erasing his legacy of programs, and ridiculing him personally. While Carter, in 1977, had chosen Notre Dame for his major foreign policy speech calling for peace and disarmament, Reagan pointedly selected the same venue to call for an escalation in weapons of all kinds. Unlike most former presidents, especially Kennedy and later Reagan, there was no body of Carter advocates in the capital to enshrine his accomplishments, or even to correct the distortions coming from the Reagan admirers.

Outside the United States, however, still perceived primarily as the champion of human rights, social justice, and concern for the poor and oppressed, Carter maintained a considerable and growing following. Typical was a story in June in which a young man in the African nation of Malawi, when asked his view of Reagan, responded to a reporter from the *Chicago Sun-Times,* "What about Carter? Carter understood us. He cared about our lives. He started us on a road toward real friendship with your country. But now President Reagan has changed the course to a track that takes you away from Africa. Why?" On August 9, President Anwar Sadat, following formal meetings with the new administration in Washington, insisted on traveling to Plains to visit Carter. Within a matter of months, the head of state with whom Carter had established the closest friendship would be assassinated. In a historic tribute to Sadat, who paid with his life for making peace between his country and Israel, Reagan sent three former presidents—Carter, Ford, and Nixon—to the funeral in Cairo.

The Chinese leadership still revered Carter as the president who had restored diplomatic relations with their nation and severed formal ties with Taiwan. Stopping for a family vacation in Yellowstone National Park en route, Jimmy and Rosalynn went to China at the invitation of Deng Xiaoping in August 1981. They were received with elaborate fanfare as though he was still a sitting head of state, providing Carter a needed psychological boost. It also suggested that, even out of office, a former U.S. president carried considerable weight in the world. They also stopped in Japan to visit their old friend Tadeo Yoshida, president of the YKK Zipper Company. Carter used the Global 2000 report—an influential study on the future of the world environment he had commissioned as president—as the basis of a major speech in Japan. He said the willingness of the international community to deal with the increasingly critical issues of declining global resources, the environment, and population would determine human survival, and, rather than armaments, was really what national defense was ultimately about.

Buoyed with renewed self-confidence after the successful trip, Carter warned in a September 24 interview with the *Atlanta Constitution* that increased defense spending by Reagan would inevitably result in record deficits. "It's easy for the rich and secure to stigmatize those who accept handouts," he said, "and easy to forget for a while the fine returns we have already received from the beneficial human investments." In a newsletter to former White House staff and cabinet officers, he was even more forthright. "There is always a latent tinge of prejudice among some powerful political leaders against less fortunate fellow citizens who may be partially dependent on the government for student loans, medical care, school lunches, welfare, food stamps, a job, legal protection, or decent housing. . . . This prejudice took form in the budget decisions this year." The reaction from the Reagan administration was predictably hostile.

Carter still had detractors in Washington. On October 5, 1981, the *Washington Post,* in its "Ear" column, said:

    Y'ALL COME . . . well. Quite a little ripple among White Housers new
and old. That tired old tale about Nancy dying for the Carters to blow out of
the White House as swiftly as possible is doing a re-run—with a hot new
twist. (Remember the uproar? Nancy supposedly moaned that she wished
Rosalynn and Jimmy would skip out *before* the Inauguration, so she could
pitch into her decor.) Now, word's around among Rosalynn's close pals,
about exactly why the Carters were so sure Nancy wanted them out. They're
saying that Blair House, where Nancy was lodging—and chatting up First
Decorator Ted Graber—was *bugged.* And at least one tattler in the Carter
tribe has described listening in to the Tape Itself. Now the whole story has
been carried back to the present White House inhabitants, by another tattler. Ear is absolutely appalled. Stay tuned, uh, whoever's listening.

Jimmy and Rosalynn were outraged. Not only was the story completely
untrue but it was clearly an attempt to undermine the area in which he most
enjoyed the public's continuing respect, his honesty and integrity. He
would tell the *New York Times* that after leaving the presidency he was not
wealthy and had "just some privacy and my reputation. It really hurts me in
this country and throughout the world to say I would stoop so low as to
eavesdrop on the conversations of my successor." Jody Powell called the
paper's editor, Ben Bradlee, to complain and seek a retraction. Bradlee
stuck by the story and promised to get back to Powell after checking their
sources. According to Terry Adamson, Carter's longtime friend and attorney,
he never did. Three days later Adamson wrote to the chairman of the board
of the Washington Post Company, Katharine Graham, stating, "The article is
false, defamatory, libelous per se, injurious to the reputation of President and
Mrs. Carter, and was published with actual malice." A libel suit was
planned. An editorial in the *Post* on October 14 lamely argued that the original piece had never said Carter bugged Blair House, and of course, it
claimed, everyone knows that someone of Carter's character would never do
something like that. They were, the editorial professed, merely reporting a
rumor circulating that he had done so. When *New York Times* reporter Phil
Gailey suggested to Bradlee that admitting he knew the rumor was false did
not sound like much of an apology, Bradlee responded, "How do you make
a public apology—run up and down Pennsylvania Avenue bare bottom
shouting, 'I'm sorry'?"

Carter, who had been in Washington for a brief meeting with Reagan and
to solicit Senate support for the sale of AWACs to Saudi Arabia, told
reporters as he departed for several days of fly fishing in Pennsylvania with
Wayne Harpstra that he would be spending the time deciding whether to file
his libel suit. The *Washington Post* was deluged with editorial criticism
around the country. The *Richmond* (Kentucky) *Register* was typical in

pointing out that "The job of a responsible newspaper is to find out the truth and dispel rumors and misinformation," not, it added, to lend them legitimacy. After the *Washington Post* successfully forced the resignation of Richard Nixon, Bradlee seemed to many to be less concerned with the news than using the paper as a personal instrument of power. The *Post* was already under scrutiny for factual inaccuracies and breach of journalistic ethics, and many critics believed that Bradlee's dislike of Carter had led him to turn a blind eye to distortions and innuendos in stories about the president and members of his administration. His wife, Sally Quinn, had been forced to retract a story erroneously reporting that Zbigniew Brzezinski had made improper advances to women.

What turned so many of his fellow journalists against Bradlee was his arrogance and hubris in dealing with a former president. Over the next several days, as Carter decided to move ahead with a million-dollar libel suit, the pressure on Bradlee grew. Finally, on October 24, a comprehensive apology came in the form of a letter to Carter from publisher Donald E. Graham. It was accompanied by a front-page story about the apology and retraction. Carter dropped the planned libel suit.

The *Post* exacted retribution by treating Carter subsequently as a "nonperson." Although there has been some change in recent years, his extensive public activities and utterances were largely ignored while those, often quite trivial, of his fellow former presidents received regular notice.

Even before he left the White House, Carter had been approached by several major universities with job offers. He chose to become a "distinguished professor" at Emory in Atlanta, teaching in the university's various schools. He was provided with an office in the special collections section of the Woodruff Library, where he and historian Steve Hochman, beginning September 1, 1982, were also able to continue the work on his memoirs.

A primary concern was the desire to raise $25 million for a presidential library—an onerous task. An ideal 30-acre site had been identified on a hill overlooking Atlanta from which Union generals had watched the city burn. It was also just a short drive from Emory. Several architects had offered drawings of towering edifices, one with a spire seen from different perspectives as a cross, a Star of David, and a Moslem crescent. Carter liked none of them and said disconsolately, "I'm not going to have a library."

Part of the discouragement Carter felt was because he could not summon up much enthusiasm for building a mausoleum for his presidency, where dusty tomes and aging, yellowing memos would be stored, when he and Rosalynn were seeking a new and dynamic role. Even before leaving the White House, he had the idea of creating an institutional base for his continuing role in public life. One night Rosalynn woke to find Jimmy, normally a sound sleeper, sitting upright in bed. "I know what we can do with the library," he said. "We can develop a place to help people resolve disputes." Instead of just the traditional presidential library, he envisioned a center, he said, that would serve as the archive for his presidency, but would also be an active institution where, under his leadership, academic and activist experts could work with parties in conflict to resolve their differences. There was no forum, even the United Nations, where opposing sides— either countries or factions within a country—could come together to resolve their differences as had been accomplished at Camp David. As they talked through the concept over the next few weeks, it was broadened to incorporate many of their longstanding interests: peace and nuclear arms control; human rights, including the alleviation of hunger and suffering among the world's poor; health care and adequate services for the mentally afflicted. It was a concept that ultimately would transform the nation's thinking about the post-presidency in America.

At about the same time, Chris Hemmeter, a real estate developer from Hawaii, arrived in Plains with a new set of artist's drawings of the proposed library.* They depicted a structure of interlocking and overlapping pie-shaped buildings that blended naturally into the hillside surrounded by elegantly landscaped gardens and a lake. The low profile of the design, as opposed to the skyscraper depicted in previous proposals, implied a degree of humility that immediately appealed to both of the Carters. The idea of a Carter presidential center housed in this structure suddenly infused their lives with new meaning and direction. Immediately the task of raising money seemed less daunting.

Unwilling to wait for the structure to be built, Carter established the Carter Center out of his office in the library, but quickly moved it to a house on North Decatur Road near the Emory campus in September 1982, with Jim Waits, dean of the Emory Divinity School, serving as the director half-time.

In December 1981, Carter had called 100 major donors to his presidential race, seeking funds for the center, but with little success. The only significant contribution he had received was $50,000 from the Rockefeller Brothers Fund. He had asked Tom Watson, Jr., former president of IBM, who had served as ambassador to Moscow in his administration, to serve as chairman of the board of the new institution. Watson had declined. Carter asked a young Tennessean, Jim Brasher, whom he had met in connection with fund-raising activities for the United Negro College Fund, to assist

---

*Carter had met Hemmeter on a trip to Hawaii and explained to him his dissatisfaction with the earlier architectural drawings. Hemmeter would become a major backer of the Center and representative of a whole new group of individuals who became involved with Carter only during the postpresidency.

him. He told Brasher, "I never faced anything with greater trepidation than this." Hamilton Jordan, who remained in an advisory role, told Carter to throw away his political contributors list, telling Brasher, "They were only people who used Carter and just wanted what they could get."

Brasher designed a campaign that was geared primarily toward foundations and corporations plus a few exceptionally wealthy individual donors. Carter still found it hard to relate comfortably to corporate leaders. At a gathering of potential business contributors at Atlanta's Capitol City Club, Carter said to Brasher as they arrived, "It's your job to protect me from these people."

Early on, foreign business leaders were among his largest contributors, including Tadeo Yoshida; philanthropist Ryoichi Sasakawa; Aga Hassen Abedi, president of the Bank of Credit and Commerce International; and Hasib Sabbagh, head of CCC, the largest construction company in the Middle East, who as a champion of the peace process had quietly helped Carter in the region. While the association of Abedi and Sasakawa with the center would later cause controversy when information about their past political and financial dealings emerged, Carter's attitude was that as long as these people were giving their money for the center's humanitarian programs with no strings attached, he was happy to receive it.

In January 1983, Carter and Brasher went on a nationwide trip, stopping in Houston, Dallas, Aspen, and Los Angeles, where supporters had been asked to host dinners at which the guests would be invited to be founders of the Carter Center. The trip and its follow-up letters and phone calls raised $10 million.

The Carter Presidential Center, to establish its academic credibility and to attract scholars of stature, needed to affiliate with an existing institution. Emory was the obvious choice, so it became the "Carter Center of Emory University." Another justification was that the corporate supporters of Emory were also likely to be the corporate supporters of the Center. The relationship, however, was at times a stormy one. Carter believed that Emory president James Laney had agreed to take the lead to raise funds and, when that did not happen, that the university had reneged on their commitment. Laney, on the other hand, saw fund-raising for the center as competing with the university's broader effort. There was also concern on the part of the school's board of trustees that the center's international programs in agriculture and health were outside the institution's valid interests, and that Carter was generating a wide range of programs that the university would be financially responsible for after he was gone.

The directorship of the center was taken over by Middle Eastern scholar Ken Stein, and a series of program areas was established, each area headed by a distinguished scholar. These included human rights, arms control, health, conflict resolution, and the Middle East. The administrative structure of the center repeated the "spokes-of-the-wheel" approach that Carter had used in the White House and over time the same management shortcomings would become manifest, but it remained Carter's preferred way of operating. In November 1983, the center hosted its first conference on the topic of the Middle East, cochaired by President Carter and President Ford. Freed from the political constraints of holding public office, they were able to invite representatives of all major parties to the conflict, including several distinguished Palestinians. The approach reflected Carter's philosophy that conflict resolution through reconciliation must involve both the participation and the trust of all parties to a dispute.

In September 1980, the Carters had invited their neighbors from Plains, Ralph and Jane Gnann, to visit them in the White House. The Gnanns were about to leave for two years as volunteers to build houses in Zaire. They were going to Africa with an organization called Habitat for Humanity. Its founder, Millard Fuller, had been a partner in the mail-order business in Montgomery of Carter's presidential campaign fund-raiser, Morris Dees. Fuller had become wealthy, but during the late sixties he had faced both a crisis of conscience and difficulties in his personal life. These troubles eventually led Fuller, a deeply religious man, to Koinonia, where he fell under the influence of Clarence Jordan. He decided to give away his money, and with his wife, Linda, to commit their lives, as a manifestation of their faith, to providing shelter for impoverished people throughout the world. After spending three years themselves in Zaire, where they built 162 houses in the city of Mbandaka, they returned to Americus and in 1976 founded Habitat for Humanity.

After Jimmy and Rosalynn returned to Plains, they became increasingly familiar with the work of Habitat. At the annual board of directors meeting on October 16, 1982, Jimmy spoke about his concern for the poor and refugees in Indochina, Haiti, and elsewhere, his admiration for the work of Habitat, and also about the legacy of Clarence Jordan. "I think I will be a better Christian because of Clarence Jordan, Koinonia, and Habitat," he said. Subsequently he and Rosalynn made a generous contribution to Habitat.

In February 1984, Carter agreed to take on a substantial role in promoting the organization in the media, assisting it in raising funds and serving as a member of its board of directors. He and Rosalynn also decided to make Habitat, apart from the Carter Center, the only organization for which they would allow their names to be used for fund-raising purposes.

A month later, responding to a request from Millard Fuller, Carter arrived at a Habitat site in Americus to contribute a day's labor. After ten minutes of devotion he spent the next eight hours putting up the framing of a new house for Dorothy and Willie Solomon. That spring, while in New

York, Carter agreed to visit a Habitat rehabilitation site at 742 East Sixth Street. It was a derelict building filled with trash and debris that had become a haven for drug addicts and the homeless. Many of the ceiling joists were rotted or burned through. As Carter stood with project director Rob DeRocker on the top of the building, he said, "I can see you've got a lot of work ahead of you here, Rob. Let Millard know if there's anything I can do to help."

"Why don't you come back with a group from your church for a week of work?" DeRocker replied.

"We'll think about it," Carter responded.

Carter thought only briefly before deciding to organize a work crew of volunteers from the Maranatha Baptist Church and other friends from around Georgia. They chartered a Trailways bus, and on September 1 left on the twenty-five-hour drive to New York. The idea of a former president riding a bus and spending a week working with his hands generated considerable media attention—the most intense since Carter left office. With another presidential election only weeks away, there was a particular interest in what he was doing. Several journalists, including *New York Times* reporter Esther Fein rode with the thirty-six-person group from Atlanta. They stayed at the Metro Baptist Church on Fortieth Street. Everyone, including Jimmy and Rosalynn, slept in bunk beds—men on the third floor, women on the fourth. Almost the entire interior of the East Sixth Street building had to be replaced. For five days, taking only brief breaks to accommodate the ever-present media, wearing jeans and T-shirts, they laid floors, nailed Sheetrock, and framed doors and windows with the rest of the group.

The Carters would return again to the building on the Lower East Side for further work in July 1985, and again in the fall for its official opening. This experience led them to set aside a week every June to work on Habitat projects either in the United States or overseas. Jimmy was already a skilled carpenter, but Rosalynn also rapidly acquired a high degree of proficiency. Although Carter never explicitly drew attention to it, their initial involvement with Habitat was lent added poignancy by the fact that it coincided with massive cuts by Reagan—in federal support for public housing, a surge in homelessness, and the emergence of thousands of desperate people, begging in the affluent downtown areas of American cities for the first time since the depression. But it was the spiritual aspects of Habitat that held the greatest attraction for Carter. As someone who sought so hard to model his life on that of Christ, working as a carpenter inevitably carried special significance. At a subsequent Habitat meeting he would say:

> I've had many experiences in my life and in Christian work, in business, government, and politics. I've traveled almost everywhere in the world, and

I do not know of anything I've ever seen that more vividly illustrates love in action than Habitat for Humanity.

He felt we should be ashamed of the suffering we allowed in society. He went on to describe one of his trips to New York when he had gone out jogging early in the morning and seen the homeless on the streets, adding:

> A lot of them only have a towel or a coat or a newspaper between their human face and a filthy sidewalk. And some of them are older women, without any place to sleep at night except on the streets. That's in the richest city in the richest nation on earth.

In 1990, addressing a ballroom of civic dignitaries and Habitat contributors in Baltimore, he described growing up with the injustice of racial segregation, then went on to say, "but the greatest discrimination in the world is between the rich and the poor. Most of us in this room, including me, are rich, so we have a special obligation to see that discrimination is ended." It was something he would say repeatedly to audiences, often causing listeners to squirm in their seats.

The involvement of the Carters with Habitat helped to boost the organization to national prominence. Carter assisted Millard Fuller in mounting a campaign to raise $10 million by the end of 1986 and the publicity he generated led thousands to volunteer their services. By the end of 1986, Habitat was in 171 U.S. communities and 17 foreign nations. The global nature of Habitat and its commitment to build at least one house overseas for each it constructed in the United States had special appeal to the Carters.

Carter had received repeated invitations from different Latin American leaders to visit their countries. In mid-1984, he asked Dr. Robert Pastor, who had been in charge of Latin America and the Caribbean on his National Security Council staff in the White House, to organize a trip to Brazil, Argentina, and Peru.

While in Peru, Bob Pastor received a message from the U.S. embassy in Argentina that in effect said "[President] Alfonsin and the government do not want you to come" because, they claimed, President Carter was so disliked by the military in Argentina that his visit might well precipitate a coup against the recently elected Alfonsin. The message concluded on a sarcastic note: Wouldn't it be ironic if the president, who had spoken so much about human rights, would unwittingly contribute to the destruction of a new democracy?

Pastor was annoyed by the tone of the cable, but he was especially concerned because he believed that some action by the Argentine army was possible, particularly if someone in the U.S. embassy winked at some important Argentine generals. The Secret Service checked on the security implications. When the party arrived in Brazil, Pastor asked Lionel Brizola, the governor of Rio de Janeiro and a close friend of President Alfonsin and Argentinian foreign minister Dante Caputo, if he would phone the Argentines to determine whether the U.S. embassy's report was correct. Brizola was pleased to do it. On Carter's arrival, Brizola was at the airport and told reporters that Carter's human-rights policy had saved his life and let him go into exile in the States.

Brizola learned that the U.S. embassy report was without any substance and that the Carters' visit was eagerly awaited by Alfonsin, a point that he personally conveyed. U.S. ambassador Frank Ortiz left the country rather than host Carter's visit.

The Carters arrived in Buenos Aires to be greeted by thousands of cheering people, and to find he was viewed as a national hero for having spoken out on human rights as president, and specifically for his willingness to criticize the military dictatorship for its brutal supression of democracy. Day and night throughout their visit, an adoring crowd remained outside the residence hoping to catch a glimpse of the Carters. Rosalynn recalled that they even had to be careful about walking past windows because it would immediately trigger sustained cheering.

In Peru, where Rosalynn had previously come as first lady, they enjoyed a similar reception. While there, they visited their first overseas Habitat project in Puno on a bluff overlooking the city.

Carter and Pastor believed strongly that the future political stability and economic development of Latin America was dependent on establishing democracy. Free elections were at the heart of the process. However, in many countries the political parties were so distrustful of each other that fair elections and the peaceful transfer of power was all but impossible. The answer, Carter believed, was the creation of teams of international observers who would monitor the voting process to deter fraud or abuse. If the monitors were to be accepted, being scrupulously careful to be nonpartisan was essential to maintain the trust of all parties.

In the summer of 1986, the Carters made a longer trip through Latin America, visiting Venezuela, Costa Rica, Nicaragua, El Salvador, and Mexico. The primary purpose of the trip was to discuss inter-American relations with leaders throughout the hemisphere in advance of two conferences on the debt crisis and democracy that were being planned for the Carter Center. At the latter meeting twelve current and former heads of state established an organization of "Freely Elected Heads of Government," which became one of the primary vehicles for monitoring elections. At their final stop in Mexico, they encountered another hostile Reagan ambassador, former movie actor John Gavin, who canceled a reception at the embassy for the Carters after learning he could not sit in on Carter's meeting with the Mexican president. Gavin's subordinates insisted that the reason for the cancellation was that his mother was ill. In a note written before his departure, Carter extended his sympathy and expressed the hope that Gavin's mother would have a swift recovery. Without shame, Gavin wrote back that his mother had not been ill.

On October 1, 1986, the Carter Center was officially opened. A few weeks later, Carter convened the first major meeting in the new facility, a conference on "Democracy in the Americas." He cochaired the event, which was attended by twelve current or former heads of state, with President Andres Perez of Venezuela. The meeting launched what would become a highly successful program to promote democracy in the hemisphere through the independent participation of monitors in the election process as Carter had envisioned.

Health, especially preventive health-care programs, remained a primary concern for the Carters. As governor, Carter had launched a program called "Cripplers and Killers," which identified and sought to prevent the primary causes of death and disability among Georgians. Under Carter's presidency, Surgeon General Julius Richmond had, in 1979, published a comparable report, "Healthy People," looking at similar issues on a national scale. Together with Rosalynn, he had pushed an ambitious national immunization program that included the goal of immunizing 90 percent of children against measles by 1979. After he left office the program had been largely abandoned, as had other preventive health programs.

Painful matters were also part of their lives. On September 26, 1983, Ruth died at age 54. A month later, on October 30, Carter also lost his mother. Billy would die in September 1988 at age 51 and Gloria in March 1990 at age 64. Losing his mother and all of his siblings at relatively young ages within a seven-year period was a difficult emotional burden to bear. In addition, his father, Ruth, Gloria, and Billy all died of cancer of the pancreas, suggesting some environmental factor to which the entire family might have been exposed. Doctors at Emory and the federal Centers for Disease Control (CDC) looked for some common cause, but except for the fact that, apart from Jimmy, all had been heavy smokers, no single causative factor was identified. Nevertheless, it led Jimmy and Rosalynn to take particular interest in preventive health in general and their own in particular. Exercise and adherence to a healthy diet, excluding red meat except when socially unavoidable, became very important to them.

As an outgrowth of all of these factors, the Carter Center sponsored a conference in October 1984 entitled "Closing the Gap." It was organized by Dr. William Foege, the director of the Atlanta-based Centers for Disease

Control, who had joined the Carter Center full-time when the meeting took place.

With many of the nation's top public health specialists in attendance, the Carters approached the meeting not as conveners of just another medical meeting but as eager pupils presented with an enormous learning opportunity for themselves. They would later write:

> We felt like students facing an amazing array of teachers. . . . Much of what we learned was disturbing and some of it shocked us, but there was also a great deal that was encouraging. The heartbreaking part was to realize how much mental and physical suffering there still is, how many American lives are lost prematurely because we do not use widely and wisely what we already know about health.

At this early stage Jimmy and Rosalynn were just beginning to discern and explore the parameters of the hitherto unrealized potential to be a force for good that a former president has at his disposal. Public health officials could talk endlessly about lengthening and improving the quality of life through proper nutrition, exercise, not smoking, and drinking alcohol only in moderation, but it would have little impact. Carter realized that he could steep himself in a topic like health, becoming enough of an expert to speak authoritatively, then use his stature and position to command public attention. The result was that he had the capacity to influence public attitudes and behavior in a way that none of his predecessors had either appreciated or attempted.

The initial conference on domestic health was followed in May 1986 by a conference on international health issues. During the Carter presidency, smallpox was eradicated worldwide. With a considerable interest in alleviating health problems in the Third World, Carter had asked me as his health advisor whether there were other diseases that might similarly lend themselves to a global eradication campaign that he could lead. I and a member of my staff, Dr. Don Hopkins, who had been involved in the smallpox campaign, concluded that guinea worm, a parasitic disease transmitted in contaminated drinking water and afflicting more than 10 million individuals in India, Pakistan, and the middle of Africa, was the most promising candidate. The problem was that this disease, posing no threat to Americans, was not something on which we could reasonably use up presidential capital.

Subsequently as an assistant secretary general with the United Nations, I was responsible for a program, the International Water Decade, aimed at providing clean drinking water for people worldwide. Don Hopkins, by then with the Centers for Disease Control, and now thoroughly committed to eradicating guinea worm, asked me if I would make it a specific goal of the U.N. program. I agreed, and over the next six years we worked with modest success toward achieving the eradication goal, although it was hard to persuade health ministers of Third World governments to give the campaign the priority it really needed. Despite the U.N. leadership, it was clear that without some dramatic new impetus we could not alone achieve the goal of total eradication.

At the Carter Center conference I spoke about the importance of providing clean drinking water as a way of protecting people from many diseases such as cholera, typhoid, and the several causes of infant diarrhea. I particularly focused on guinea worm—the only disease exclusively transmitted by contaminated drinking water—partly because of the horrific nature of the affliction, but more to stress the simple measures by which it could be eliminated: merely by drilling a well, filtering the water, or providing some other clean drinking source.

"If it's that simple, why has it not been eradicated everywhere?" Carter asked.

I explained that it was almost impossible to get national leaders to assign sufficient priority or adequate resources to guinea worm when it affected only poor people in rural areas. It was easy to get rid of, but it required political will.

In a month I again raised the issue of guinea worm with Carter, stressing that if someone such as he, a former president, took it on, it might be given the visibility and attention to make eradication possible. With the encouragement of Bill Foege, Carter decided to make ridding the world of guinea worm one of the primary activities of the Carter Center. Suddenly the initiative had an irresistible momentum and the leaders of the affected countries were willing to pay attention. Able to go directly to heads of state, which others generally could not do, he educated them about the disease, and made a personal plea to them to become involved, arguing that it was an accomplishable goal that would lead to overwhelming gratitude from their people. He went with Jerry Rawlings, the president of Ghana, into affected villages, where the horrific sight of infected abscesses on people's limbs made a previously reluctant Rawlings the most outspoken advocate for eradication in his country.

For nearly ten years, whenever Carter went to Africa he relentlessly promoted guinea worm eradication. He made a major speech to the Organization of African Unity on the subject, never wasted an opportunity at a press conference to promote the campaign, always raised it when he met with officials from an affected country, and personally attended all the major conferences on the topic. He convinced the Norwegian and U.S. governments to contribute money as well as several foundations and wealthy individuals. He also assumed control of the entire campaign by hiring Don Hopkins to work for him.

On December 4, 1995, Carter hosted an event at the State Department celebrating the eradication of guinea worm. Technically the disease was still not totally eliminated, but the goal was near enough. Carter had demonstrated the enormous power for good that lay at the disposal of someone in his position. The blow he dealt to guinea worm arguably resulted in the saving of more lives and certainly the prevention of more suffering than anything he had done as president.

In articulating the mission of the Carter Center, the former president stressed two things. First, he was not interested in duplicating what others were doing, in the U.S. government, in the U.N. agencies, in foundations, or at academic institutions. Second, it was not to be a think tank in the traditional sense, turning out position papers or learned treatises. It was to be an action center, where its direct intervention would influence events. Several distinguished academic experts were hired on the staff, receiving faculty appointments at Emory, but their role primarily was to serve in a staff support capacity to Carter rather than to foster their own independent ambitions. Certainly they were not expected to engage in any independent activist role themselves. Over time this would periodically rise as a source of conflict at the center. Carter, however, demonstrated in an unprecedented way how with the right support he could take an issue out of the academic realm and, using his tenacity and prestige, accomplish a goal such as eradicating guinea worm that no one else could achieve.

CHAPTER 29

Carter is the American Gandhi.

—DR. M. S. SWAMINATHAN

While in the White House, Carter had initiated a Presidential Commission on World Hunger and Malnutrition, taking a strong personal interest in the findings and recommendations. Asked what he would do after he left the presidency, he had, at different times, replied that he might become a missionary or that he might devote himself to trying to end world hunger. In late 1985, in response to the famine of that year and the precarious overall decline in agricultural production in sub-Saharan Africa, Carter met with Japanese philanthropist Ryoichi Sasakawa, and Nobel Prize–winning agriculturist Norman Borlaug. Borlaug had been an architect of India's so-called "green revolution" that led to a massive increase in rice production in the 1960s and 1970s. In January 1986, the three men went to Africa, where they discussed with national leaders the prospects for establishing action-oriented projects to improve food production. In response to the strong interest their proposition elicited, it was agreed that two experimental projects would be commenced that year in Ghana and the Sudan. Borrowing from the title of the environmental study Carter initiated as president, the project was named Global 2000. Later in the year, Zambia would be added to the list of project countries, with Tanzania included in 1989. Related development projects, including the guinea worm eradication campaign and a reforestation program, were placed under the Global 2000 management umbrella.

While Sasakawa provided the funding and Borlaug the expertise, Carter offered the ability to acquire the indispensable backing and personal interest of African heads of state. This derived partly by virtue of his being a former president of the United States, but equally because of the personal relationships he had with these men and the genuine concern he evidenced regarding the problems of their people. In Ghana, the very public involvement of President Jerry Rawlings was crucial in promoting the project and facilitating the timely distribution of fertilizer and seeds as well

490

as setting up small-scale credit systems. The Global 2000 strategy involved the use of high-yielding strains of corn or sorghum, moderate amounts of chemical fertilizer, and trained agricultural extension workers to teach farmers improved cultivation techniques, especially planting methods and weed control. Beginning with a handful of farmers in two districts in Ghana, it had expanded within three years to all eleven districts, involving more than 100,000 individuals and a two- to threefold increase in production. These farmers were also asked to teach their neighbors the techniques they had learned, so that eventually most of the country had adopted them.

The success of Global 2000 not only led several other African presidents to ask Carter to initiate similar projects in their countries but also to the creation of a new Carter Center program labeled Project Africa. Directed by Jeffrey Clark, based on the assumptions from the Global 2000 experience that food security largely depended on the adoption of low-cost crop production techniques managed at the village level, its aim was to assist countries in developing long-range strategic plans for food self-sufficiency. In July 1989, Carter chaired a meeting in Harare, Zimbabwe, at which African leaders and representatives of international organizations and funding agencies came together to begin charting such a course. He also established at the Carter Center the African Governance Program to promote democracy in the least-developed region of the world.

Carter's attraction to Africa and his empathy for its people was a natural outgrowth of his childhood relationships with African Americans and the central role that their struggle for social justice had played throughout his political career. It was also an opportunity for him to apply his own considerable knowledge and experience as a farmer and his longstanding interest in public health. In a way he was doing for an entire continent what he and his mother, each in their own way, had done for the residents of Sumter and Webster Counties.

The central theme of the Carter Center and Carter's greatest personal investment remained in the issue of conflict resolution. For nearly thirty years, Eritrea had been involved in a brutal war of secession against Ethiopia. Tens of thousands had died on both sides. Following a meeting in Addis Ababa with Ethiopia's Marxist president, Mengistu Haile Mariam, Carter invited representatives of both sides to come to the Carter Center, where under his mediation they sought an end to their civil war. He convened subsequent meetings in Nairobi and Atlanta. Although a peaceful settlement was not achieved under the auspices of the Carter Center, the negotiations he initiated became the basis for the eventual independence of Eritrea and the resignation of Mengistu achieved by the Bush administration.

Over several years Carter also served as the mediator between the warring factions in Sudan. He had the trust of both President Omar Bashir and John Garang, leader of the secessionist Sudanese Liberation Army (SLA), enabling him to achieve a series of cease-fires. Because of his success in placing human rights at the forefront of the international agenda, Carter carried increasing moral authority worldwide. When the dictatorial ruler of Somalia, Siad Barre, sentenced to death more than two dozen intellectuals and professionals, he received pleas for clemency from the Reagan administration, Senator Ted Kennedy, human rights groups, and national leaders from around the world. He ignored them all. It was only when Carter personally interceded with him that he agreed to commute their sentences. In gratitude, respected exile leader and businessman Abdullahi Omaar became a significant contributor to the Carter Center.

Carter's most enduring interest remained the Middle East. Perhaps his greatest regret in not being reelected was that it prevented him from completing a comprehensive peace agreement. In 1983, he made a month-long trip to the region. Among those with whom he met was Hafez al-Assad, president of Syria. Despite his reputation for sponsoring terrorism and his hostility to the Camp David accords, Assad was a man of intellectual depth who held the key to a comprehensive peace settlement. Carter had known him for ten years and saw him as a shrewd and tough negotiator who impressed him as a man of his word. In 1985, Carter published *The Blood of Abraham,* which combined a brief history of the Middle East conflict, his insights into the thinking of the leaders of the region, and what amounted to the strategy for a permanent peace that he would have pursued in a second term.

Carter would return for long meetings with Assad again in 1987. His ensuing complimentary statements about Assad were not well received by the Reagan administration, bent on demonizing and isolating the Syrian leader. Carter also began a dialogue, through intermediary Mary King, with Yasir Arafat, using his influence to induce the Palestinian leader to make the concessions necessary to enter the peace process. Seen as impartial and concerned only with advancing a Middle East settlement, Carter was trusted and listened to while Washington still refused any official contact with the PLO. The two men finally met face-to-face at the Hotel de Crillon in Paris on April 4, 1990, where they discussed Middle East politics at length, and then, at Carter's suggestion, the two leaders and Rosalynn prayed together for peace.

Carter sought Arafat's assistance on a personal matter. He had had little contact with David Rabhan since leaving the governorship. The entrepreneurial Rabhan had been involved in different business ventures in the intervening years, including establishing a factory in Iran to produce soy-based infant formula. He had remained in Tehran throughout the hostage crisis and, despite repeated warnings, stayed on after it ended. Eventually he was seized, charged with being a spy, and incarcerated in the notorious Evin prison. Carter relentlessly pressed for Rabhan's release and succeeded after nearly a decade, with the help of leaders in the region, including Arafat, in convincing the Iranians to let Rabhan go.

Under the auspices of the Freely Elected Heads of Government, the National Democratic Institute, and the International Republican Institute for International Affairs, Carter and Ford co-led a team of monitors to the elections on May 9, 1989, in Panama. The Council had sent a team to assess the electoral procedures several months before, and it was already clear that General Manuel Noriega was putting up obstacles in the path of a genuinely free and fair election. Finally, less than one month before the election, he denied visas to the election monitors, and Carter sent Pastor to Panama to persuade Noriega to modify his decision. Noriega finally agreed, recognizing that he could not say "no" to the author of the Canal Treaties.

The Bush administration was certain that Noriega would not allow fair elections and would steal the vote from the opposition. Some in the administration thought Carter would cover up any fraud, fearful that it could harm the Canal Treaties. The State Department sent a congressional delegation to Fort Howard in the Canal Zone that announced a fraud even before the election. Carter's team did the opposite; they encouraged the people to vote, and Panamanians did so in great numbers. A "quick count"—a random sample of the election returns—permitted Carter to know that the opposition led by Guillermo Endara had won the election overwhelmingly, and when Noriega tried to manipulate the returns, Carter denounced him in the strongest terms. Pictures flashed around the globe of opposition vice-presidential candidate Guillermo (Billy) Ford dripping blood from his head after a beating by Noriega henchmen dramatized Carter's condemnation.

The U.S. media, which up until then had substantially ignored Carter's post-presidential international activities, gave his role considerable coverage. In many respects it was a turning point. The American public became aware that Carter was doing worthwhile things other than building houses.

Carter had first visited Nicaragua in 1986 for talks with the government and the opposition and to help build a house under the auspices of Habitat for Humanity. While the Reagan administration was funding the Contra guerillas in an attempt to overthrow the Sandinista government, Carter was more concerned with reconciliation among Nicaraguans and between the two countries. On his return he was quoted as saying, "We've got a lot of friends in Nicaragua. We want folks down there to know that some American Christians love them and we don't all hate them." The following year, when President Daniel Ortega visited the United States, Carter invited him to visit the Habitat project on Manhattan's Lower East Side. Following the elections in Panama, Ortega invited Carter to head a monitoring team for the elections next year. "If the count is fair, will you accept the results?" Carter asked on the eve of the elections. Ortega agreed that he would. Over the next several months Carter and Pastor made six trips to Nicaragua to help prepare for the election.

On election day, quick counts done in randomly selected precincts showed the Sandinistas were headed for defeat. Between 11 P.M. and midnight, Carter went to Ortega to deliver the bad news. Ortega was incredulous, saying, "No, it's impossible."

"I can tell you from my own experience that losing is not the end of the world," Carter reassured him.

"I thought it was the end of the world!" Rosalynn interjected.

"Your greatest accomplishment as president," Carter advised him, "will be if you lead a peaceful transition of power."

Ortega told Carter he needed time to deal with his enthusiastic supporters who were preparing a victory celebration. Jimmy and Rosalynn went to the headquarters of Ortega's opponent, Violetta Chamorro. They asked her not to make a triumphal victory speech and delay until the morning any formal statement. She agreed. Carter also persuaded her to call for national reconciliation provided Ortega officially conceded his loss. Shuttling back and forth between the campaign headquarters, they negotiated these agreements and also arranged for the voting results to be released so that the Sandinista loss would not be evident until dawn. By the time Ortega had been able to convince his followers to accept defeat gracefully, they were exhausted and ready to go home. At 4 A.M., Carter called Secretary James Baker and asked him to issue a statement later in the day in which there would be no Ortega bashing and calling for the Contras to be disbanded. A Nicaraguan diplomat at the United Nations would later say to me, "Jimmy Carter saved my country from civil war."

The Carter Center would subsequently send similar election monitoring teams to Haiti (1987, 1990), the Dominican Republic (1990), Surinam (1991), Guyana (1990–92), Zambia (1993), Paraguay (1993), Mexico (1992–94), and for the Palestinian elections (1996). In both Guyana and the Dominican Republic, where he was involved only at the end, his presence was responsible for preventing rioting in the streets by the losers.

While the Reagan administration had used every opportunity to undercut and discredit Carter, the Bush administration took a more temperate view. Secretary Baker shared Carter's Christian belief in the power of moral suasion in diplomacy and worked collaboratively with him. Carter viewed Baker with respect and admiration as someone, like himself, willing to take the time to study and learn the intricate details of an international conflict, and was more interested in healing and forgiveness than retribution and bloodshed. They were more concerned with results than posturing. Often when nations, after years of distrusting the intentions of the U.S. government, refused to allow official delegations to monitor their elections, they would accept Carter because his reputation for impartiality was above reproach. At the same time, Baker knew U.S. interests would be served because Carter would not hesitate to expose any irregularities if they occurred. In Togo, in August 1993, Carter left the country before the polling day, announcing to the international media that there was no way a fair election could be held. His judgment was enough to force the cancellation of the vote. Through three administrations Carter always consulted Washington and provided detailed written reports of his trips.

Carter's global reputation continued to grow partly because of his successes, partly because of his scrupulous neutrality in approaching a dispute, assiduously favoring neither side, even if meant being at odds with his own government. His skills were innate, but he had also carefully studied the techniques being articulated by the leading figures in the emerging science of conflict resolution. Ken Stein, who participated with Carter in several negotiations, was struck by his ability to consciously divorce himself from any judgment about the parties in a dispute. "He temporarily suspends what he feels about any particular ideology, philosophy, or the background of the person he is dealing with. . . . His goal is to achieve an accommodation of the two sides. For him the objective is of greater or higher importance than his personal feelings." Stein points out that Carter's strategic objectives were often more far-reaching than the short-term policies to which the U.S. government was inevitably limited. He knew where those policies ultimately had to go. "Yet," says Stein, "he was often five years ahead of his time."

Whatever conscious overlays Carter may have added to his negotiating style, at heart remained his commitment to the Christian doctrine of love, or agape. Agape does not distinguish between the worthy and the unworthy, or between friends and enemies, but seeks only to achieve redemptive goodwill. The attack is directed against the forces of evil rather than against the persons who happen to be doing the evil. Combined with the concept of nonviolence, it had formed the basis for Gandhian philosophy (although his notion equivalent to agape was derived more from non-Christian roots). Gandhi believed his goal should be "to liquidate the antagonisms, not the antagonists themselves." Martin Luther King, Jr., had shown in the civil rights movement how effective the Gandhian approach, merged with southern black Christian beliefs, could be. It was something of which Carter was very much aware. Carter, Gandhi, and King all believed that to meet hate with retaliatory hate would only intensify the presence of evil in the universe. Hate begets hate, violence begets violence, bloodshed begets bloodshed. Meeting the forces of hate with love was ultimately the way of the strong man. Resorting to violence was not only an admission of failure but it represented cowardice. Contact and dialogue had to be maintained at all cost.

Carter also understood that when he, as a former president, met with a leader considered a pariah in the international community—an Assad, an Aideed, an Arafat, or a Mengistu—his very presence bestowed on them a mantle of legitimacy in return for which there was an implied expectation that they would address and make concessions on the issues he brought to them. Rather than seeing the loan of his credibility as something lost to an adversary, Carter viewed it in opposite terms—as a negotiating chip to extract something from them. He knew the leaders would exploit their meetings to try to enhance their own stature and that he would be subjected to criticism by traditionalists in the United States who believed you should never talk with your enemies. But Carter was tough and thick skinned, willing to endure the criticism if it meant a peace agreement was made or deaths avoided.

Invitations to speak or participate in events exceeded a thousand a month and his schedule was booked a year in advance. He and Rosalynn traveled for much of each year. They visited more than a hundred countries. Their ability to maintain such a hectic pace was in large part due to a loyal personal staff willing to work slavish hours—his personal assistant Faye Dill; Nancy Konigsmark, who has worked for the Carters longer than any other person; and Rosalynn's assistant, Melissa Montgomery. Because of the amount of preparatory work he insisted on if he was to participate in an election, he eventually had to curtail the number of new countries with which he could become involved. Yet his participation in the monitoring process had become for many Third World nations the sine qua non for the legitimacy of their elections. In early 1993, Yemen had held the most democratic elections in the Arab world to that point. Carter could not be present for the election itself, but after repeated invitations from the president, he and Rosalynn went there three months later so the Yemenis could proudly show him what they had accomplished.

Most of Carter's trips received little coverage in the U.S. media. But he refused to go to a country merely as a tourist and insisted that there be a concrete purpose for his visit. His little-noticed accomplishments were often of considerable significance. The government of Albania had drafted a law to protect religious freedom, but it had addressed only the concerns of the three major religious groups: Catholics, Greek Orthodox, and Moslems. Carter was contacted by Albanian Baptists through two missionaries from Georgia, Bert and Debbie Ayers, asking for his help in assuring that the law be changed to guarantee that their rights would also be protected. After an exchange of letters with President Sali Berisha, Carter was assured that if he came to Albania the law would be changed. In a meeting with religious leaders, at the beginning of September 1993, he told them, "Each of you would like his religion to expand, but this must be restrained. The U.S. Constitution says, 'Congress shall pass no law regarding the establishment of religion'—very brief. I hope all of you realize that your attempts to restrict others may end up inhibiting you." He then offered to take up with Berisha a list of complaints from all of the religious leaders, which he did. As a result of his meeting with Berisha, the law was changed to assure full religious freedom.

At a news conference before he left Tirana, Carter was asked what he felt about Moslem fundamentalism. He answered, "Religious fundamentalism is always a threat to human rights, and to democracy and freedom." He added, "I feel a threat in my own church from Baptist fundamentalists." It was an issue that had been very much on his mind in the preceding months. The election of Tennessee preacher Adrian Rogers as president of the Southern Baptist Convention had marked a profound shift in the traditional theology of the denomination. Carter had been shocked and angered when Rogers accused him as president of abandoning his Christian beliefs in favor of "secular humanism." Carter felt that over the intervening fourteen years the Southern Baptist Convention had turned its back on the central doctrine of the faith, which had played such a vital role in shaping American political values, the separation of church and state, and especially the primacy of the individual and his right to find his own relationship with God. Convinced that his own "deep beliefs were different from those being mandated" by the leadership of the Southern Baptist Convention, he would say that for several years, "Rosalynn and I have been in a quandary about what to do."

In mid-May 1993, more than 5,000 moderate Baptists came together in Birmingham, Alabama, to adopt a constitution and pass bylaws for the Cooperative Baptist Fellowship, an alternative to the Southern Baptist Convention. Addressing the meeting, Carter said, "In the Cooperative Baptist Fellowship my wife and I have found a home," prompting a lengthy ovation. "I pray that as Rosalynn and I cast our lot with this fellowship for the rest of our lives, we can be part of a transcendent movement." He praised the fellowship for upholding the Baptist principles in which he believed—the autonomy of the local church, total separation of church and state, and the priesthood of believers. Repeatedly during the meetings he said that Baptists should not impose uniformity of belief on others. In a direct slap at the efforts of the Southern Baptist Convention to impose a uniform doctrine with strong partisan political overtones on all its members, Carter said, "When there is a definition of what is a proper person, a proper Baptist, a proper American, we are violating the basic principles of what we believe. . . . When we enforce uniformity on other people it saps their freedom."

Hunting and fishing had always been an important part of Carter's life. As governor he had been invited one Saturday by Jack Crockford, head of the Georgia Game and Fish Department, to go hunting woodcock. The following Wednesday, Carter called and said he wanted to go again that afternoon. "I was supposed to be the expert," says Crockford, "but between Saturday and Wednesday he had read the final-word book on woodcock. He knew more about woodcock than I did." Crockford accurately notes, "He was not real good at playing . . . but he found out I knew how to play better than most folks." Crockford attributed what became a long, close friendship in large part to the fact that he carefully avoided ever bringing up political issues during their many hours in the woods or on the riverbanks. Together they took up fly fishing, a skill that Rosalynn also learned.

Subsequently, in the White House, Jimmy and Rosalynn continued to squeeze fly fishing into the interstices of presidential life. He set up a fly-tying vise and other paraphernalia next to their bedroom. On one weekend they invited a dozen of the most accomplished fly fishermen on the East Coast to visit them at Camp David. They took every opportunity to sneak in a few hours of fishing, especially at Spruce Creek after they met Wayne Harpster.

After leaving the White House, fishing, and to a lesser extent hunting, became an increasingly important part of their lives. Still the perfectionist, Jimmy had studied with experts and read countless books. He fished with grandson Jason for steelhead in Alaska, with Rosalynn in Nova Scotia for Atlantic salmon—filmed by an ABC camera crew for the TV program *American Sportsman*—and for bonefish with Jack Crockford in the British Virgin Islands. During the ten years after leaving the White House, Jimmy and Rosalynn fished the great trout streams of the world in Montana, New Zealand, Switzerland, Wales, on Mount Fuji in Japan, and in the classic chalk streams of the Test and Itchen in England.

Former presidents have limitless opportunities for recreation thrust upon them. Jimmy and Rosalynn chose those involving some degree of challenge. They learned to ski and made a week in Vail, Colorado, an annual event. They went to Nepal and trekked in the foothills of Everest to a height of around 20,000 feet. And as a family project they climbed Mount Kilimanjaro on the Kenyan–Tanzanian border.

In 1988, Jimmy published *An Outdoor Journal,* recounting his lifelong experiences as a hunter and fisherman. In 1992, he published *Turning Point*, an account of his first election to the Georgia Senate. Since his days as a pupil of Julia Coleman, he had enjoyed poetry—an interest enhanced by his exposure to Dylan Thomas—and over the years he had written poems for his own amusement. Following the success of his earlier books, he eventually convinced his skeptical publisher to put out *Always a Reckoning*, a collection of his poetry that surprised everyone by appearing on the *New York Times* best-seller list. He was a regular contributor to the *New York Times* op-ed page, but regularly published in other periodicals as well. He wrote about foreign policy and he reiterated the central concerns he had throughout his public life: "American society is steadily becoming more racially and economically polarized. Many poor and minority Americans are convinced, with good reason, that the basic system of justice and law enforcement is not fair." He wrote passionately seeking forgiveness for baseball player Pete Rose, who gambled on games and was convicted of tax evasion, making him ineligible for election to the Hall of Fame. For both Jimmy and Rosalynn, who had authored *Care Givers*, writing would become their primary source of income. Although he received countless awards, many of which carried a monetary component, and often honoraria when he spoke, he gave a significant portion to the Carter Center. In 1989, when Ronald Reagan, fresh from the White House, accepted a $2 million personal honorarium for an appearance in Japan, the sharp contrast with the selfless Jimmy Carter boosted his public stature as much as it damaged Reagan's.

The Carter Center had expanded dramatically during its first five years of operation. With success, funding began to flow from foundations and corporate sources. It became one of the most sought-after sites for conferences and meetings, especially if the Carters were willing to participate. Dr. William Foege had taken over as the director, helping in particular to build the health component of the overall program.* He would be succeeded by Dr. John Hardman, whose grandfather, Lamartine, as governor in the 1930s had developed the reorganization plan that inspired Carter's own reorganization initiative. The Child Survival Program, in collaboration with UNICEF and the World Health Organization, set as its goal the immunization of all the world's children. In collaboration with Betty Bumpers, wife of U.S. Senator Dale Bumpers, Rosalynn set up "Every Child by Two" to immunize children within the United States. She also established the Carter Center Mental Health Task Force to focus especially

---

*Foege enjoys an internatonal reputation and is a man of extraordinary ability with a deep, religiously rooted commitment to improving the quality of health of people worldwide. He was the ideal partner for the Carters because of his extensive technical knowledge.

on the issue of stigma. She was also appointed a distinguished professor at Georgia Southwestern College. Thanks to former White House aide Anne Wexler who served on its board, the pharmaceutical giant Merck joined with the center in a campaign to control river blindness, a leading cause of vision loss in Africa. Merck donated 29 million tablets of Mectizan, a single dose of which will cure the disease and prevent blindness. The Carter Center established a protocol to monitor the distribution of the drug in order to prevent it from being siphoned off into the lucrative veterinary market.

In 1990, Carter and Mikhail Gorbachev, former president of the Soviet Union, established and cochaired a commission on radio and television aimed at developing models of fair media coverage in nations with newly won media freedom. In the old Soviet Union there had been only two television channels. By Carter's estimate in 1993, there were more than 100 separate television outlets in Russia and the Commonwealth of Independent States. Carter's personal efforts at peacemaking were formalized under the International Negotiating Network that he cochaired with former U.N. Secretary General Javier Perez de Cuellar. Meetings of the group brought world leaders in politics and the media to the Carter Center on a regular basis.

Together with Dallas-based philanthropist Dominique de Menil, Carter created the Carter–de Menil Human Rights Award, given annually for several years to those in the forefront of the worldwide struggle.

The relationship between the Carter Center and Emory University had always been an uneasy one. Anytime there was a bureaucratic or other obstruction to implementing a program under the center, Carter would impatiently move ahead, setting up the initiative independently. In addition, because so many of the programs were overseas, Emory became increasingly concerned about the university's ability to sustain them after Carter was gone. "I have long felt uncomfortable with the fact that we are dealing with such a heavy emphasis on overseas problems," Carter conceded. Finally, Emory president James Laney urged Carter to use his prestige to focus on local domestic problems as well. Carter noted, "I have wanted to get more deeply involved in domestic affairs, but I didn't have a concept about where to do it, where do you start."

In October 1991, Jimmy Carter announced the creation of the Atlanta Project. "Rosalynn and I have decided to mount a major effort to prove that in at least one troubled city something can be done about the problem of teenage pregnancy, drug addiction and crack babies, juvenile delinquency, school dropouts, homelessness, and unemployment." Gearing the effort to the city's pride in hosting the Olympic Games nearly five years hence, he gave a moving speech to Central Atlanta Progress. "The former president electrified business, political and civic leaders during the annual meeting of . . . the powerful Downtown business group," the *Atlanta Journal* reported. Carter told the initially skeptical audience, "The disparities between those who make decisions and those who suffer . . . are so great that we have in effect two cities." Urging their backing for the initiative, he said, "Rich and poor can work together. Black and white can work together in Atlanta," adding with the certainty of a Southern Baptist who believed that with God all things are possible, "If we want it to work, it will work." One of those at the meeting, Gerald L. Bartels, recalled, "If you didn't go away from there feeling that you, personally, must do something, then you're pretty hardhearted."

The design of the project reflected a recapitulation of the characteristics that Carter had brought to community problem solving from Plains to the White House. He began like a politician mobilizing support, but also like a scientist gathering information and statistics, talking to experts on urban problems around the country, and, with total immersion, laboriously analyzing the situation in Atlanta. With a team led by Dan Sweat, a seasoned veteran of city and county government, Carter identified twenty "cluster communities" representing those census tracts that had the highest infant mortality rates, the highest unemployment and school dropouts, the highest crime, the largest number of single-parent families and teenage mothers. He then enlisted one or more corporations, including such giants as Delta Airlines, IBM, UPS, AT&T, Coca-Cola, and Turner Broadcasting, to take responsibility for each "cluster community," contributing financial largesse, detailing staff, and providing volunteers. He also persuaded congregations from the churches and synagogues of Atlanta's more affluent areas to adopt these deprived communities. Volunteers were at the heart of Carter's vision and more than 100,000 signed on and $20 million was raised.

Using the high school in each "cluster community" as the administrative focus, the Atlanta Project staff helped the local residents identify their own priorities, possible funding sources, and the technical help they needed. Carter continued to believe that the failure of government to meet people's needs was significantly a product of poor coordination, duplication, and the overgrowth of federal laws and regulations. He made a well-publicized trip to Washington where he met with a receptive President Bush and congressional leaders to get the collaboration from the federal bureaucracy he felt the project needed.

The Atlanta Project was not without problems. The quintessential Carter message of reconciliation had focused on bringing together, with a sense of community responsibility, the overwhelmingly white affluent Atlanta with the predominantly black poor Atlanta. Most of those in leadership positions and 90 percent of the volunteers were white. Paradoxical accusations of "racial arrogance" or even racism were raised. A 1995 report accused the program of having little to show for its three-and-a-half-year multimillion-dollar investment. Built on the inspirational leadership of the Carters, it was at its best when they were out personally immunizing children, leading community meetings, or bringing figures to town to promote the program, like pop singer Michael Jackson. In between, petty administrative problems frequently got in the way of the higher purpose of the project. Jane Smith, who joined as the project director following the critical report, has worked hard to turn the image around. At the end of five years, despite whatever specific shortcomings the project might still have, its greatest impact had been in achieving a massive commitment by the Atlanta community as a whole to deal with its social problems.

For the average American, little concerned with foreign policy, the Atlanta Project brought Carter's post-presidency role more directly to their attention. He now enjoyed the highest approval rating (74 percent) of any living former president. His willingness to take a brave stab at dealing with the perplexing problems of the inner city attracted civic leaders from around the country. Corporate executives liked the emphasis on finding nongovernmental solutions to the problems. Congressman Newt Gingrich became an enthusiastic backer. The Atlanta Project not only generated strong corporate financial backing for its own needs but also spawned interest in the center's other initiatives. In 1994, the center raised $42 million. John Moores, a Texas businessman and owner of the San Diego Padres, subsequently pledged $25 million to support the river blindness and guinea worm programs.

Carter was scheduled to be in Africa at the time of the inauguration of the Reagan library. Lod Cook, president of the Atlantic Richfield Corporation and organizer of the ceremonies, agreed to send his corporate jet to enable Carter to make the event. The two men subsequently got along so well that Cook became a fervent supporter of Carter's programs, lending him the plane for international travel on a regular basis.

Since leaving the White House, Carter had vehemently eschewed any interest in elective office. He had similarly stayed away from involvement with partisan politics. In 1992, he did announce that he had voted for Governor Bill Clinton, as a fellow southerner, in the Georgia primary. Clinton consulted occasionally with Carter during the campaign and transition but, following his inauguration, the discourse declined. From time to time, Clinton did consult with Carter on such issues as Haiti, NAFTA, Cuba, and Bosnia. Preferring to identify himself publicly with Republican Reagan, Clinton seemed to fear it would adversely affect the image of his administration if it was too closely associated with that of his only living Democratic predecessor. Warren Christopher, Clinton's low-key secretary of state, with some legitimacy, reportedly feared that Carter, because of his extensive international experience and his global moral stature, would potentially overshadow himself and the young new president in the area where he was weakest—foreign policy. Ironically, at the time of his appointment, Warren Christopher was the chairman of the board of directors of the Carter Center. As deputy secretary of state at the time of the Iran hostage crisis, he was referred to by Carter as "the best public servant I have ever known." There had been speculation that Carter might be appointed by Clinton as a special negotiator for the Middle East, an appointment Carter would have accepted, and which would have been widely applauded in the region.

The Clinton administration inherited a difficult situation in Somalia where U.N. troops had become bogged down in a misguided effort to capture faction leader General Mohammed Farah Aideed. With a seeming stalemate in which U.S. troops were embarrassingly and unnecessarily dying, Aideed appealed to Carter, who had followed the complex situation in the country for some time, to act as mediator. Taking advantage of his neutral role, Carter invited a delegation representing Aideed to the Carter Center. He convinced the Clinton administration to seek a political rather than a military settlement. His credibility with Aideed was such that during a hurried trip to East Africa, working through the regional heads of state, Carter was able to get him to accept an arrangement that would eventually allow the safe evacuation of all U.S. troops.

Korea had long held a special attraction for Carter. Ending one of the world's most unyielding and contentious feuds through reconciliation and reunification of the North and South was something Carter had long sought. The success of American missionaries in the South had sowed the seeds of Christian forgiveness, and a reunified Korea would mean an open door to preach the gospel throughout the peninsula. With Carter's encouragement, Christopher selected James Laney, who had spent seven years in Korea as a Methodist missionary and spoke the language, to be the administration's ambassador in Seoul. Interestingly both the leader of Korea's ruling party and of the opposition were Emory graduates. Before he left, Laney and Carter discussed their shared dream of reunification and agreed to look for opportunities to work together toward that goal.

During the early months of 1994, the United States became concerned about the North Korean potential for building nuclear weapons. Relations headed toward confrontation when the Koreans removed 8,000 spent fuel rods, capable of reprocessing grade plutonium into weapons, from their nuclear reactor at Yongbyon. They refused either to clarify the ultimate disposition of the rods or to allow international inspection of their facilities. Washington announced its intention to seek gradually escalating sanctions, steps that the Koreans announced they would consider acts of war. Amid increasingly belligerent rhetoric from both sides, the United States prepared a series of military options including massive air attacks on the nuclear facilities. Warmongering escalated in Washington with Senator Daniel Patrick Moynihan saying that he would favor air attacks even if it resulted in nuclear contamination of the entire Korean peninsula.

Carter had received an open invitation from North Korean President Kim Il Sung in 1991, but the Bush administration had discouraged him from accepting. Alarmed by what seemed an inevitable slide toward war, the Carters left with Clinton's aquiescence for Pyongyang in mid-June 1994. With Carter's stature as a former president, his years of diplomatic negotiation and training as a nuclear engineer, including his experience with the Chalk River reactor, it is hard to imagine that anyone could have brought better qualifications to the mission. Carter persuaded Kim Il Sung to allow the international inspection teams to resume their work and to freeze the North Korean nuclear program, provided the United States entered into high-level negotiations. Kim also agreed to shift the program from existing graphite-moderated reactors to light-water reactors if he received U.S. financial and technical help. The move would end the production of enriched plutonium and the possibility of building nuclear weapons. As a goodwill gesture, Kim also agreed to return the bodies of 3,000 Americans who had died in the Korean War.

Leaving North Korea, Carter carried a message from President Kim Il Sung to South Korean President Kim Young-Sam requesting a summit meeting to begin discussions on reunification. Strongly encouraged by Jim Laney, Sam accepted the invitation, setting the meeting for July 25.

Carter returned, having neutralized a confrontation that could have led to war, possibly nuclear war. He had negotiated an agreement that offered the basis for North Korea to end its military nuclear program, and he had launched a dialogue with the potential to end in reunification of the two Koreas. While he was a hero to many Americans, Carter's remarkable success engendered widespread jealousy and resentment in many quarters at the State Department, which declined his offer to immediately brief them. Initially the White House also was uncertain how to respond, focusing on disagreements with the minutiae of Carter's negotiations and his appearance on CNN discussing the deal, rather than the historic consequence of the overall accomplishment. Eventually it became apparent that it was politically more advantageous to share the credit for Carter's achievement than continue to take potshots at it in the media. At a press briefing on June 22, Clinton said, "I would like to thank President Carter for the important role he played in helping to achieve this step." Sadly, Kim Il Sung died three weeks later, on July 8, aborting the planned reunification talks. Out of the glare of publicity, Carter and his staff subsequently worked well with Assistant Secretary of State Robert Gallucci to turn the understanding he had worked out with Kim into a successful long-term agreement.

Three months later, Carter was again thrust into the limelight. He had been involved in Haiti with both the aborted poll of 1987 and as the leader of the monitoring team for the successful election that had brought Father Jean-Bertrand Aristide to power in December 1990. During that time, Carter had made nine trips to the country. Following his ouster by a military junta led by General Raoul Cedras in early September 1991, Aristide had been a frequent visitor to the Carter Center. The former president felt a personal responsibility to see this champion of the poor, who still enjoyed overwhelming public support, restored to his legitimate position. Carter strongly supported the Bush and Clinton efforts to remove the new regime. With the backing of the United Nations and the Organization of American States, and under increasing pressure from TransAfrica's Randall Robinson and other liberal groups, by early September, Clinton was pushing toward a showdown with the junta. However, with ambivalent support in the Congress, concern about the number of lives that might be lost on both sides, and intimations from the ruling generals that they sought a negotiated way out, Clinton announced that the invasion would take place and that all diplomatic initiatives had been exhausted.

Because of his lengthy involvement with Haiti and his earlier acquaintance with General Cedras, Carter had offered his services as a mediator to the administration during the preceding weeks. He had been rebuffed. Returning from a two-week trip to Africa and Russia on September 11, he found a letter forwarded to him by the Reverend Dr. Robert Westcott, head of the Caribbean Latin American Foundation for Peace, from Charles David, the de facto foreign minister of Haiti, saying that the regime would respond favorably to a fact-finding team headed by Carter. Westcott had also given Carter's phone number to Mrs. Yannick Cedras, urging her to get her husband to call Carter. Later in the day, the two men talked. After discussing the situation with President Clinton, Carter consulted Senator Sam Nunn, who spoke with General Colin Powell. Nunn and Powell said they would only consider joining Carter on a mission if the president approved it. With opposition from Warren Christopher and support from Vice President Albert Gore, Clinton authorized the mission.

Early on Saturday, September 17, the three men, together with Carter's Haiti expert Robert Pastor, flew on an air force jet to Port-au-Prince. With U.S. warships waiting over the horizon, the team began an all-out blitz to cut a deal that would force the junta to relinquish power and allow Aristide to return. They met with business leaders, parliamentarians, a retired general who was one of Carter's earlier contacts, and with Emil Jonassaint, the provisional president. Jonassaint had been written off in Washington as an inconsequential, senile figurehead. From Saturday afternoon until 2 A.M. on Sunday, and again for most of the day on Sunday, Cedras and the general staff met with the team of negotiators in the ornate National Military Command Headquarters. The Haitian leaders were consistently resistant to what they saw as surrender. However, they admired Powell's military credentials and his Jamaican heritage, which enabled him to convince them that they could preserve their honor by stepping down in a formal ceremony rather than appearing to have been ignominiously ousted. Nunn and Carter also convinced them that the invasion would occur if agreement was not reached. "If you cannot accept the agreement," Carter told Cedras, "I can assure you that there is no way to stop the invasion. If you accept the agreement, that will be an honorable decision, and I assure you that I will be at your side and will express my gratitude and admiration for your decision." Before Carter left, Rosalynn urged him to talk with Yannick Cedras to get her to persuade her husband to accept a settlement. The discussion with her proved curcial.

Clinton had told the team that they needed to be out of Haiti by noon, but had then extended the deadline to 3 P.M. Tenacious and unwilling to fail, Carter pleaded for extra time. A Haitian intelligence report saying that the U.S. planes had taken off almost derailed the talks, making it impossibe for Cedras to sign the agreement. It was the discounted eighty-two-year-old President Jonassaint who finally proved the key player signing on behalf of Haiti. Notifying the White House that agreement had been reached for the generals to step down, the invasion force was turned around in midair. Subsequently, a U.S. peacekeeping force arrived to oversee the implementation of the accord, the departure of Cedras with the promised military ceremonies, and the restoration of Aristide to power.

Despite a lack of appreciation by the Clinton administration, Carter was feeling increasingly gratified by what he had been able to accomplish in the international arena and the stature he enjoyed globally. Both the natural aging process and the sense of vindication he felt as a result of the worldwide acclaim for his post-presidency accomplishments had led to an increasing mellowness in his character. He was less driven and intense, taking a sincere personal interest in the lives of those who worked for him, in a way he had never done during his political years.

As a family, the Carters had drawn closer than at any time since Jimmy won the governor's mansion. Both Chip and Jack had been divorced, but were happily remarried. Jack, who for years had felt an emotional distance from his father, worked through a rapprochement that reestablished a bond they had not had in years. While a student at Brown University, Amy had drawn the attention of the press and the public support of her father when she demonstrated against the excesses of the CIA. She had received a bachelor of fine arts degree from Memphis College of Art, and then moved to New Orleans to pursue a master's degree in art history. She had provided the illustrations for a children's book, *The Little Baby Snoogle-Fleejer*, that she coauthored with her father. She remained the apple of her parents' eye. Jimmy and Rosalynn also devoted increasing time to their grandchildren, including setting aside several weeks a year to take them on cruises or other vacation trips.

When James Laney resigned as president of Emory to become ambassador to Korea, he was succeeded by William Chace, with whom Carter seemed able to work in a more comfortable collaborative relationship. At their monthly meetings they increasingly focused on the long-term future of the Carter Center. The building of a substantial endowment fund, and the attraction of figures with national or global reputations as full- or part-time fellows, became the top priority rather than the launching of further new initiatives identified exclusively with the Carters.

On October 1, 1994, his seventieth birthday, Jimmy Carter was told by his staff and Rosalynn that a group of Atlanta's top chefs were coming to the Carter Center that night so he could sample their fare for an upcoming fund-raising event. When he arrived he found the lobby filled with his children and grandchildren shouting birthday greetings. He assumed they had planned a surprise family party for him. They led him toward the darkened auditorium. As he entered, the lights went up and more than 500 people from every stage of his life rose to sing "Happy Birthday." They included the citizens of Plains who had known him all his life, John Pope, Edna Langford, Betty Talmadge, Terry Adamson, John Girardeau, Jack Nelson, Cloyd Hall, John White, Bert Lance, Robert Lipshutz, Dot Padgett, David Rabhan, Jack Crockford, Jody Powell, and Frank Moore. Even Sam Donaldson was present. In a moving hour-and-a-half, emceed by actor Kirk Douglas, Carter was lionized. A video retold his life story and the Morehouse College Glee Club entertained. When Carter rose to respond, he was almost speechless. The formal proceedings were followed by a reception at which he cut a giant birthday cake, and the evening of deep affection and nostalgia ended with a spectacular fireworks display.

It has become a cliché to say that Jimmy Carter is the best ex-president in American history. While few would argue with this, it generally implies a comparison with his performance as president. Certainly, if the sole criterion is the capacity to get elected to a second term, then he failed. However, had it not been for the unique circumstances of the hostage crisis and the impact on the economy of the unprecedented rise in oil prices, he would almost certainly have been reelected. In addition, Carter was unusual for someone holding high political office in the extent to which he viewed politics as merely a means to an end. As a result, adherence to principle throughout his career regularly jeopardized political accomplishment.

His entire career in politics lasted only eighteen years, a remarkably short period of time for someone who won the presidency. Always viewing himself as more a spiritual and moral figure than a politician, and by nature leading by example rather than oratory, he saw a natural continuity in his life that did not lend itself to being artificially divided between the presidency and the post-presidency. In particular, his faith led him to strive for the same objectives by whatever means were at hand while he was in Georgia, as president, and after he left office. Throughout his career, Carter was guided by a consistent set of values and beliefs. Perhaps nothing better sums up the philosophy of his public life than his oft-repeated quote from Reinhold Niebuhr that, "The sad job of politics is to bring justice to a sinful world."

NOTES

The author was a participant in many of the events described in this book. In some parts, it is a firsthand account based on the author's recollections as well as informal conversations with friends and colleagues at the time and since. Incomparable information was gleaned in informal, sometimes chance discussions with Jimmy and Rosalynn Carter over more than twenty-five years. Undocumented at the time and long before this book was conceived, these conversations formed part of the fund of knowledge the author brought to the project. Formal taped interviews with dozens of individuals and extensive research through government archives and the existing literature were subsequently used to elaborate, document, and detail in a more methodical way the extensive material the author already had.

CHAPTER 1

9. *The Carters of King's Langley,* R. Humphrey provides an account of the most likely location and earliest documented roots of the Carter family. The village of Aldenham has been suggested as a possible alternative place of origin for the Carter family (interview with Mary Tisdale, local historian in King's Langley, December 11, 1992). The author feels the balance of the evidence, however, favors King's Langley. Noel Currer-Briggs's *The Carters of Virginia* details the early years of the family in the New World. Additional material was obtained in an interview (July 10, 1992) with Kenneth H. Thomas, Jr., historical researcher at the Georgia Department of Natural Resources, and the leading authority on the genealogy of the Carter family in North Carolina and Georgia. His articles are: "Georgia Family Lines: Carter-Gordy," *Georgia Life,* Winter 1976, and "Georgia Family Lines: Carter-Gordy—An Update," *Georgia Life,* Spring 1980.
9. The early European settlement of Georgia and the impact of the development of the cotton gin is described in detail in Kenneth Coleman's *History of Georgia* and Numan Bartley's *Jimmy Carter and the New South.*
9. The expulsion of the Creek Indians from Southwest Georgia is detailed by Coleman and in William Williford's *Americus Through the Years.*
9. The allocation of land to members of the Carter family is recorded in *The Georgia Land Lottery Papers 1805–1914* compiled by Robert Davis and Silas Lucas and *The Third 1820 Land Lottery of Georgia* compiled by Davis.
10. Accounts of the life of Wiley Carter and his three sons are drawn from the National Archives oral history interviews with Donnel Carter and Hugh A. Carter, Sr., Carter Library, and *Cousin Beadie and Cousin Hot* by Hugh A. Carter, Sr.
10. Billy married Nina Pratt: National Archives oral history interview with Helen Pratt, Carter Library.
11. The death of Billy Carter: Interview with Carter Ray, December 2, 1993; H. Carter, *Cousin Beedie and Cousin Hot,* National Archives oral history interview with Jeanette Carter Lowery and Betty Jennings Carter, Carter Library.
12. Calvin Jeremiah became like a second father: Interview with Carter Ray.
12. Plains had changed dramatically: *History of Plains, Georgia 1885–1985* by Beth M. Walters.
13. When Earl was twenty-five: National Archives oral history interview with Lillian Carter, Carter Library.
13. The family history of the Gordys: National Archives oral history interview with Emily Gordy Dolvin (Sissy), Carter Library.
14. Thomas Edward Watson was born near Thomson: "The Sage of Hickory Hill," *Atlanta Journal,* January 15, 1965, and *Thomas Watson: Agrarian Rebel* by Comer V. Woodward. Several letters from Watson to Jim Jack Gordy are in the Special Collections Department of the Robert E. Woodruff Library of Emory University.

16. The description of Jim Jack Gordy and his family are drawn from National Archives oral history interviews with Mary Elizabeth Gordy Braunstein, Lillian Carter, and Emily Gordy Dolvin (Sissy.)

17. "That's where I got it into my head that blacks were people": National Archives oral history interview with Lillian Carter.

18. The account of the courtship and marriage of Earl and Lillian Carter is from the interviews with Lillian Carter and Emily Gordy Dolvin (Sissy.)

CHAPTER 2

20. James Earl Carter, Jr.: National Archives oral history interview with Lillian Carter.
20. Plains was a bustling boomtown: Interview with Jeanette Carter Lowery and Betty Jennings Carter; and Walters, *History of Plains, Georgia, 1885–1985.*
21. "I am more like my father": Interview with Lillian Carter.
22. The description of Carter's childhood home and life in Archery is drawn in part from National Park Service interview with Gloria Carter Spann and *Why Not the Best?* by Jimmy Carter.
23. "Daddy never worked in the fields": Interview with Gloria Carter Spann.
24. "We sold overalls": J. Carter, *Why Not the Best?*, p. 19.
24. "No rent was charged": Ibid., p. 21.
26. "They're going to open the movie": Interview with Gloria Carter Spann.
27. "My father was a very firm": J. Carter, *Why Not the Best?*, p. 14.
27. "One reason I never thought": Ibid., p. 16.
27. "He was a stern disciplinarian": Ibid.
27. "He hated a liar": Interview with Lillian Carter.
27. On one of the first occasions: *Jimmy Carter, in Search of the Great White House* by Betty Glad, p. 35.
27. "My father loved me very much": National Park Service interview with Jimmy and Rosalynn Carter, Carter Library.
27. "He was always my best friend": Ibid.
28. "Let her out": Interview with Gloria Carter Spann.
29. "The strong memory": National Park Service interview with Jimmy and Rosalynn Carter.
29. "Queenlike": Interview with Jimmy Carter.
29. Such was her stature: Interview with Gloria Carter Spann.
30. "A wise guy": J. Carter, *Why Not the Best?*, p. 25.
32. With the start of the depression: Walters, *History of Plains, Georgia, 1885–1995.*

CHAPTER 3

33. "Any boy": Statement regularly made by Julia Coleman to her students.
33. "He was a very bright boy": National Park Service interview with Eleanor Forrest, Carter Library.
33. At the lunch break: National Archives oral history interview with Willard Slappey, Carter Library.
34. Earl was in a position: *Jimmy Carter, in Search of the Great White House* by Betty Glad, p. 33.
34. "the single most important": National Park Service interview with Jimmy and Rosalynn Carter, Carter Library.
37. Jimmy Carter says: Interview with Jimmy Carter, May 5, 1993.
37. The role of FDR in the Georgia Senate race is described by L. H. Zeigler, Jr., in the *Georgia Historical Quarterly,* December 1959, p. 333.
37. Background on Julia Coleman was provided by her niece Ann McGarrah Moss in an interview, February 20, 1993.
38. "She was nothing like": National Archives oral history interview with Allie Smith, Carter Library.
38. "I have never known": National Park Service interview with Jimmy and Rosalynn Carter.
38. When Jimmy's cousin Don: Interview with Donnel Carter, May 20, 1993.
38. In the late 1920s: Interview with Ann McGarrah Moss.
40. Jimmy's cousin Hugh: National Archives oral history interview with Hugh A. Carter, Sr., Carter Library.
40. "I don't think": National Park Service interview with Jimmy and Rosalynn Carter.
41. "If I speak": I Corinthians, Chapter 13, King James Version of the Bible.

41. "to show that the course": *Why Not the Best?* by Jimmy Carter, p. 33.
42. His first love was: Interview with Jimmy Carter, May 5, 1993.
43. As graduation neared: Glad, *Jimmy Carter, in Search of the Great White House,* p. 46.
43. During May 1941: *Americus Times-Recorder,* May 15, 1941.

CHAPTER 4

44. Jimmy Carter has said: *Why Not the Best?* by Jimmy Carter, p. 41.
44. Tom sent Jimmy: National Archives oral history interview with Fannie Gordy, widow of Tom Watson Gordy.
45. "Some of the physical requirements": J. Carter, *Why Not the Best?,* p. 42.
45. "It was," he says, "the driving force": National Park Service interview with Jimmy and Rosalynn Carter.
45. The gathering clouds of war: *Americus Through the Years* by William B. Williford.
46. Jimmy, one of his friends noted: Interview with Dr. Beverly Forester, October 7, 1993.
46. Jimmy astonished the others: *Americus Times-Recorder,* May 16, 1993.
46. Jimmy continued to date: Interview with Jimmy Carter, May 5, 1993.
47. Georgia Tech: *Jimmy Carter, in Search of the Great White House* by Betty Glad, p. 48.
47. "Tech was the most": Letter from President Jimmy Carter, *Georgia Tech Alumni Magazine,* Fall 1977, p. 23.
47. "My biggest adjustment": James L. Townsend, "Jimmy Carter: Definitely Not Peanuts," *Georgia Tech Alumni Magazine,* November 1975, p. 14.
47. Ormsby launched him: Carter letter to *Georgia Tech Alumni Magazine,* Fall 1977.
47. On June 26: Jimmy Carter's Annapolis diary, Carter Library.
47. According to Rachel Clark: National Archives oral history interview with Rachel Clark, Carter Library.
48. That night he wrote: Letter dated June 28, 1943, from Jimmy Carter to his parents, Carter Library.
48. Jimmy was originally assigned: Jimmy Carter's Annapolis diary.
48. Life was entirely regimented: Glad, *Jimmy Carter, in Search of the Great White House,* p. 50.
48. "We never ate a peaceful meal": J. Carter, *Why Not the Best?,* p. 43.
48. An upperclassman: Jimmy Carter's Annapolis diary.
49. One of his classmates: *Jimmy Carter: A Character Portrait* by Bruce Mazlish and Edwin Diamond, p. 97.
50. On weekends Jimmy: Jimmy Carter's Annapolis diary.
50. A classmate, Dr. Francis Hertzog: Mazlish and Diamond, *Jimmy Carter,* p. 100.
50. In a letter home: Ibid., p. 99.
51. "From the way": Interview with classmate Al Rusher, March 15, 1994.
51. The second and third years: J. Carter, *Why Not the Best?,* p. 45–47.
52. Jimmy's sister Ruth had a friend: *First Lady from Plains* by Rosalynn Carter, pp. 20–22.
52. When Jimmy got home: National Archives oral history interview with Lillian Carter.
52. The next night: Interview with Jimmy Carter, May 5, 1993.
53. On Christmas morning: R. Carter, *First Lady from Plains,* p. 23.
54. Jimmy and Rosalynn were married: *Americus Times-Recorder,* July 8, 1946.
55. After the ceremony: Interview with Emily Gordy Dolvin (Aunt Sissy), February 15, 1993.

CHAPTER 5

56. The history of the Smith and Murray families is drawn from oral history interviews with Allie Smith (Rosalynn Carter's mother), Elder Fulford Smith (brother of Rosalynn Carter's father), Jerrold Smith and Murray Lee Smith (brothers of Rosalynn Carter), Carter Library, and an interview by the author with Rosalynn Carter, October 5, 1993.
57. "God was a real presence": *First Lady from Plains* by Rosalynn Carter, p. 9.
58. When Rosalynn was eight: Interview with Rosalynn Carter.
60. When Rosalynn was in the ninth grade: R. Carter *First Lady from Plains,* 19.
61. The perfection of Rosalynn's: Ibid., p. 17.
62. Assignments for the new Annapolis graduates: *Why Not the Best?* by Jimmy Carter, p. 48.
62. The Carters had rented: Interview with Rosalynn Carter.
63. His former roommate: Interview with Al Rusher.

63. At the same time: *Living Faith* by Jimmy Carter, p. 40.
63. "Despite our love": Ibid.
63. "Tears, I had learned": R. Carter, *First Lady from Plains*, p. 26.
63. "I don't know": Interview with Rosalynn Carter.
64. "The postwar navy": J. Carter, *Why Not the Best?*, p. 48.
64. "I got to the final screening": *Jimmy Carter: A Character Profile* by Bruce Mazlish and Edwin Diamond, p. 102.
64. "That comes natural": Interview with Jimmy Carter, May 5, 1993.
64. For the first time: R. Carter, *First Lady from Paris*, p. 27.
65. Their next-door neighbors: Interview with Rosalynn Carter.
65. The Truman/Dewey presidential race: *Turning Point* by Jimmy Carter, p. 55, and J. Carter, *Living Faith*, p. 92, offer two slightly different versions of this event.
65. Jimmy and Rosalynn: Interview with Rosalynn Carter.
66. "He had a helluva time": *Jimmy Carter, in Search of the Great White House* by Betty Glad, p. 60.
67. "We were there to operate": Interview with Jimmy Carter, May 5, 1993.
67. Each evening on the *Pomfret*: Glad, *Jimmy Carter, in Search of the Great White House*, p. 60.
67. Says Sam Colston: *Washington Post*, November 27, 1976.
67. At the end of the cruise: Letter from Rosalynn Carter to the author, November 30, 1993.
68. Rosalynn says: R. Carter, *First Lady from Plains*, p. 29.
68. Their social life: Interview with Joy Colegrove, October 1, 1994.
68. Their circle of friends: Letter from Rosalynn Carter to the author, November 30, 1993.
68. "I would go": Interview with Jimmy Carter, May 5, 1993.
68. James Earl Carter III: Interview with Joy Colegrove.
68. Jimmy and Rosalynn: R. Carter *First Lady from Plains*, p. 29.
68. They stayed in Los Angeles: Interview with Rosalynn Carter.
69. Housing was scarce: Ibid.
69. Spending their meager cash: Interview with Al and Betty Rusher.
69. Jimmy had consistently impressed: *Washington Post*, November 27, 1976.
70. "We would stay submerged": J. Carter, *Why Not the Best?*, p. 52.
70. William Lalor: Glad, *Jimmy Carter, in Search of the Great White House*, p. 62.
70. Lt. Commander Frank Andrews: *Washington Post*, November 27, 1976.
70. It was primarily Rosalynn: Interview with Rosalynn Carter.
71. On one cruise: J. Carter, *Why Not the Best?*, p. 37.
71. Rosalynn was happy: Letter from Rosalynn Carter to the author, November 30, 1993.
71. They experienced heavy snow: R. Carter, *First Lady from Plains*, p. 31.

CHAPTER 6

72. "And you, my father": "Do Not Go Gentle into that Good Night" by Dylan Thomas.
73. "Very carefully": *Why Not the Best?* by Jimmy Carter, p. 59.
73. Jimmy returned despondent: *First Lady from Plains* by Rosalynn Carter, p. 32.
74. Early in 1952: J. Carter, *Why Not the Best?*, p. 56. This incident is also described by Orvill E. Goedeke in his letter to the editor, *Galesburg Register Mail*, September 28, 1991, Galesburg, Illinois.
75. In Schenectedy they attended: Interview with Rosalynn Carter.
75. "Admiral Rickover": J. Carter, *Why Not the Best?*, p. 57.
76. Carter's naval records, Carter Library.
76. "It was a long": J. Carter, *Why Not the Best?*, p. 57.
77. Rickover's critics: Admiral Elmo Zumwalt, cited in *Jimmy Carter, in Search of the Great White House* by Betty Glad, p. 65.
78. He saw the compassionate side: Interview with Jimmy Carter, August 19, 1976.
78. Miss Lillian minced no words: *Jimmy Carter: A Character Portrait* by Bruce Mazlish and Edwin Diamond, p. 121.
78. Footnote-The comparison of Carter and Martin Luther was earlier made by Mazlish and Diamond.
79. "I remember it clearly": Mazlish and Diamond, *Jimmy Carter*, p. 120.
79. "It was almost like": Glad, *Jimmy Carter, in Search of the Great White House*, p. 67.
79. "I was having": Interview with Rosalynn Carter.
79. "I had three little babies": Ibid.
80. "That made a great impression": Ibid.

80. "God did not intend": Interview with Jimmy Carter, August 19, 1976.
81. "She almost quit me": Interview with Jimmy Carter, May 5, 1993.
81. As Jimmy appeared: Interview with Rosalynn Carter.
82. The following day: Interview with Jimmy Carter, May 5, 1993.
82. As Rosalynn says: Interview with Rosalynn Carter.
82. "I became more and more": R. Carter, *First Lady from Plains,* p. 34.

CHAPTER 7

83. Jimmy and Rosalynn: Interview with Rosalynn Carter.
83. "It's good to be home": *First Lady from Plains* by Rosalynn Carter, p. 36.
83. Meanwhile, Jimmy: *Jimmy Carter, in Search of the Great White House* by Betty Glad, p. 69.
84. "No matter what": National Park Service interview with Rosalynn and Jimmy Carter.
84. He did, however: Interview with Jimmy Carter, May 5, 1993.
85. One day: R. Carter, *First Lady from Plains,* p. 37.
86. "It was almost preordained": *Billy* by Billy Carter, p. 50.
86. Billy was more blunt: Ibid., p. 49.
86. "Finally, I decided": Ibid., p. 51.
86. Years before, Gloria had: *Jimmy Carter: A Character Portrait* by Bruce Mazlish and Edwin Diamond, pp. 58–60.
87. "Uncle Buddy": Ibid., p. 47.
88. Eventually, after two years: Interview with Lillian Carter, March 15, 1976.
88. There was one other matter: National Archives oral history interviews with Emily Gordy Dolvin (Sissy) and with Fannie Gordy, Carter Library.
88. "We wanted": National Park Service interview with Jimmy and Rosalynn Carter.
88. "If any customer's daughter": Ibid.
89. "He kind of had a way": Interview with John Pope, December 5, 1992.
90. Working with the mayor of Plains: National Park Service interview Jimmy and Rosalynn Carter.
90. "He was always the leader": Interview with John Pope, December 5, 1992.
90. By 1959: R. Carter, *First Lady from Plains,* p. 44.
91. On several occasions: Interview with John Pope, December 5, 1992.
92. During the building of: Ibid.
92. On one occasion: R. Carter, *First Lady from Plains,* p. 41.
92. John's wife: Interview with Rosalynn Carter.
93. "Growing up": Interview with Frank Myers, October 8, 1993.
93. "Growing up in Americus": Interview with Griffin Bell, May 7, 1993.
93. "The South was divided": Ibid.
93. "I remember being at a table": Interview with Warren Fortson, February 10, 1993.
94. The history of Clarence Jordan and Koinonia is described in *The Cotton Patch Evidence* by Dallas Lee.
95. "I don't know": R. Carter, *First Lady from Plains,* p. 42.
96. "Plans were outlined": *Atlanta Journal,* June 9, 1954.
96. Jimmy Carter has described the efforts to get him to join the White Citizens Council in several places including in an interview with the author (August 26, 1976) and in *Why Not the Best?,* p. 66.
97. "I was told": Interview with Chip Carter, February 10, 1995.
97. After years of relative tolerance: *Americus Through the Years* by William Williford, p. 334.
98. Jack Singletary: Mazlish and Diamond, *Jimmy Carter,* p. 138.
98. Florence Jordan: Glad, *Jimmy Carter, in Search of the Great White House,* p. 84.
98. "I went there several times": Interview with Jimmy Carter, May 5, 1993.
98. "Our little boy finally died": Mazlish and Diamond, *Jimmy Carter,* p. 136.
99. "He said he reckoned": Ibid., p. 137.
99. "You just knew where Jimmy stood": Interview with Warren Fortson.
99. "One day a black farmer": R. Carter, *First Lady from Plains,* p. 43.
100. "We came out here": Williford, *Americus Through the Years,* p. 337.
100. Years later, Frank Myers: Interview with Frank Myers.
100. The visiting preacher: Interview with Jimmy Carter, May 5, 1993.
101. When Tommie Jones left: *The Church that Produced a President* by James Hefley and Marti Hefley, p. 195.

CHAPTER 8

104. One was Frank Myers: Interview with Frank Myers.
105. Frank Myers believes: Ibid.
105. In the early fall of 1961: Interview with Warren Fortson.
106. "I despised his [Forrester's] attitude": Letter to the author, February 10, 1993.
106. Jimmy, who had carefully studied: *First Lady from Plains* by Rosalynn Carter, p. 45.
107. "I sat there": Ibid., p. 46.
108. "a stinging disappointment": *Why Not the Best?* by Jimmy Carter, p. 79.
108. Following a Board of Regents meeting: Conversation with the author, May 10, 1975.
108. "It was this 1868 document": *Turning Point* by Jimmy Carter, p. 9.
111. Griffin Bell was made chairman: Interview with Griffin Bell.
112. Byrd's doctor: Interview with Beverly Forrester.
112. "Governor-nominee Sanders": J. Carter, *Turning Point*, p. 50.
113. "It wasn't a structured discussion": *The Church that Produced a President* by James Hefley and Marti Hefley, p. 198.
113. "If you want to be of service": J. Carter, *Why Not the Best?*, p. 79.
114. "He got up on his birthday": Interview with Rosalynn Carter, September 25, 1976.
114. There were fifteen days: Jimmy Carter recounts the details of this campaign in *Turning Point*.
115. Some of Carter's friends joked: Interview with Warren Fortson.
115. "It seems hard to believe now": J. Carter, *Why Not the Best?*, p. 66.
115. "integration back then": Interview with Warren Fortson.
116. "Jimmy Carter has shown": *Americus Times-Recorder*, October 15, 1962.
118. When John Pope entered the courthouse: Interview with John Pope and a written summary of the events of that day he prepared for the author.
120. "Warren, Jimmy is so naive": Interview with Warren Fortson.

CHAPTER 9

121. Jimmy hated to lose: Interview with Rosalynn Carter, September 25, 1976.
121. "Carter Considers Contesting Race": *Americus Times-Recorder*, October 17, 1962.
121. "Moore Wins": *Columbus Ledger*, October 17, 1962.
122. "was not willing": *Turning Point* by Jimmy Carter, p. 104.
122. "I don't remember": Ibid.
122. Warren Fortson, knowledgeable: Interview with Warren Fortson.
123. "every election law": *Atlanta Journal*, October 22, 1962.
124. "I could tell Jimmy": Interview with Charles Kirbo, October 6, 1976.
124. "Nevertheless," he says: J. Carter *Turning Point*, p. 116.
124. The account of Carter's struggle to overturn the fraud and secure the election victory are drawn, in significant part, from Jimmy Carter's own description in *Turning Point*.
128. Jimmy had received some help: Interview with Brooks Pennington, October 4, 1993.
132. "I was totally disillusioned": *First Lady from Plains* by Rosalynn Carter, p. 49.

CHAPTER 10

133. "I made what later": Interview with Jimmy Carter, August 19, 1976.
134. He did cosponsor a bill: *Jimmy Carter, in Search of the Great White House* by Betty Glad, p. 94.
134. However, early in 1963: Interview with Jean Wheeler Smith, October 20, 1994.
134. In April: *Freedom Song* by Mary E. King, p. 159.
135. Early in August: *Americus Through the Years* by William Williford, p. 354.
135. On August 8: King, *Freedom Song*, p. 159.
135. "The guards took away": Ibid., p. 160.
135. The city council: Williford, *Americus Through the Years*, p. 355.
136. "I hope they will get": Ibid., p. 356.
136. "an amalgamation": Ibid.
136. Footnote-In *The Church that Produced a President*, James Hefley and Marti Hefley detail the commitment of the early American Baptists to human rights and their strong opposition to slavery. They show how the lure of quick wealth led them to reverse that position.

137. There were a few brave individuals: *Newsweek,* September 20, 1963. This article focused in particular on Warren Fortson's heroic struggle, generating further local hostility toward him.
137. "Jimmy was not part": Interview with Warren Fortson.
137. "Only in the battle": *The Struggle for Black Equality, 1954–1980* by Harvard Sitkoff, p. 83.
137. "They could no longer": Ibid.
138. By mid-1963: The process leading up to Kennedy's speech is described in detail in *President Kennedy: Profile of Power* by Richard Reeves.
140. "We felt such sorrow": R. Carter, *First Lady from Plains,* p. 51.
140. Chip, who had been the Kennedy youth coordinator: Interview with Chip Carter.
140. He and Carter were asked: Interview with Marvin Shoob, September 28, 1993.
141. Over the next year: Interview with Betty Gail Gunter, April 10, 1993.
141. "I recall him as being": Interview with Don Carter.
141. "He saw I needed some education": Interview with Jimmy Carter, May 5, 1994.
142. "Sheer racism": Interview with Rosalynn Carter, October 5, 1993.
142. "black menace": Williford, *Americus Through the Years,* p. 375.
142. Warren Fortson became: Interview with Warren Fortson.
142. Chip bravely wore: Interview with Chip Carter.
143. Jimmy began to focus: Interview with Frank Moore, February 11, 1994. See also *Why Not the Best?* by Jimmy Carter, p. 99, and Glad, *Jimmy Carter, in Search of the Great White House,* p. 98.
143. With a group of friends: Interview with Frank Myers.
144. "I spoke in that chamber": Interview with Jimmy Carter, August 19, 1976.
145. Jimmy was increasingly viewing: Ibid.
145. In May 1965: Glad, *Jimmy Carter, in Search of the Great White House,* p. 82.
145. On July 20, 1965: Williford, *Americus Through the Years,* p. 362.
146. On August 1, a mixed group: Ibid., p. 364.
146. Warren Fortson, a member of the church: Interview with Warren Fortson.
146. Pastor Robert Harris: Hefley and Hefley, *The Church that Produced a President,* p. 158.
146. There were more than 200 people: Interview with Jimmy Carter, August 19, 1996.
147. Finally, on August 13: Williford, *Americus Through the Years,* p. 366.
147. "The thing that distinguishes Jimmy": Interview with Warren Fortson.
147. Early in September: Williford, *Americus Through the Years,* p. 371.
148. Jimmy suggested to Shoob: Interview with Marvin Shoob.

CHAPTER 11

149. On the last day of the legislative session: Interview with Hal Gulliver, September 29, 1993.
149. Each day Jimmy: *Why Not the Best?* by Jimmy Carter, p. 99.
149. He and Rosalynn thought up: Interview with Jimmy Carter, May 5, 1993.
150. Ernest Vandiver, announced: *Atlanta Constitution,* May 19, 1966.
150. Talmadge announced: *Atlanta Constitution,* May 23, 1966.
150. He and Jimmy had: Interview with Betty Gail Gunter.
151. He went with Hal Gulliver: Interview with Hal Gulliver.
151. At lunch with Gulliver: Ibid.
151. "I told him it was a big gamble": Interview with Charles Kirbo, October 6, 1976.
151. On the night of June 1: Interview with Hal Gulliver.
152. "like Kennedy": Interview with Brooks Pennington, October 4, 1993.
152. "Draft Carter Movement": *Atlanta Constitution,* June 3, 1966.
152. "Jimmy Carter Thinks He Could Be Elected Governor": *Atlanta Constitution,* June 7, 1966.
152. The following day: *Atlanta Constitution,* June 8, 1966.
152. Bill Gunter was energetically calling: Interview with Hal Gulliver.
153. He had first called: Interview with David Gambrell, February 15, 1993.
153. According to Alston's wife: Interview with Elkin Alston, May 20, 1993.
153. On the morning of June 12: "Senator Carter Qualifies and Reveals Aims," *Atlanta Constitution,* June 13, 1966.
153. One such individual was John Girardeau: Interview with John Girardeau, December 1, 1992.
154. Jimmy called Marvin Shoob: Interview with Marvin Shoob.
154. Jimmy convinced Brooks Pennington: Interview with Brooks Pennington.
154. In late June: Interview with Elkin Alston.
155. "They do not want": *Community Power Structure* by Floyd Hunter, p. 153.
155. Shortly after the campaign began: Interview with Robert Lipshutz, September 1993.

155. A campaign trip to the mountains: Interview with Bert Lance, October 8, 1992.
156. "There was a lot I admired": Interview with John Girardeau.
156. "It is hard to meet": *Atlanta Constitution,* July 2, 1996.
157. "to let people know": *Jimmy Carter, in Search of the Big White House* by Betty Glad, p. 104.
157. In a speech on July 14: *Atlanta Constitution,* July 15, 1996.
158. Arnall well ahead of Callaway: *Atlanta Constitution,* June 23, 1966.
158. He castigated Arnall: *Atlanta Constitution,* July 13, 1966.
158. He described Arnall: "Carter, Gray Leap on Arnall," *Atlanta Constitution,* June 22, 1966.
158. Byrd announced that Lyndon Johnson: *Atlanta Constitution,* August 13, 1966.
158. "There's no difference": *Atlanta Constitution,* July 22, 1966.
158. "Ellis Arnall's image": *Atlanta Constitution,* August 24, 1966.
159. "He would seek people out": Interview with John Girardeau.
159. "I was riding along in the car": Interview with Gerald Rafshoon, October 15, 1976.
160. "Here I was a struggling advertising man": Ibid.
160. "girls too young to vote": *Atlanta Constitution,* August 28, 1966.
160. One night Girardeau: Interview with John Girardeau.
161. "a life-changing experience": Ibid.
161. Finally, David Gambrell: Interview with David Gambrell.
161. Brooks Pennington had managed: Interview with Brooks Pennington.
162. As one of his fellow campaigners: Interview with John Girardeau.
162. The campaign did its best: *Atlanta Constitution,* August 30, 1966.
163. In the August 25 document: Document in the files of Brooks Pennington.
163. "I think responsible Georgians": *Atlanta Constitution,* August 31, 1966.
163. He championed the term "black power": *Atlanta Constitution,* September 8, 1966.
163. endorsed Ellis Arnall: *Atlanta Constitution,* September 7, 1966.
163. endorsement from William Bowdoin: *Atlanta Constitution,* September 13, 1966.
163. interview with Hyman Rickover: *Rosalynn: Friend and First Lady* by Edna Langford and Linda Maddox, p. 68.
164. "A funeral-like pall": Ibid., p. 70.
164. Despite the loss: *Atlanta Constitution,* September 16, 1966.
165. "John, there is no need": Letter in the files of John Girardeau.

CHAPTER 12

166. As he has written: *Why Not the Best?* by Jimmy Carter, p. 98.
167. "The prospects of my winning": Interview with Jimmy Carter, August 19, 1976.
167. "Ruth suggested": Ibid.
167. In Ruth's book, *The Gift of Inner Healing,* she describes her life and religious awakening.
169. He reminded the congregation: *The Church that Produced a President* by James Hefley and Marti Hefley, p. 59.
170. "The teachings of God": *The Spiritual Journey of Jimmy Carter* by Wesley Pippert, p. 174.
170. "did more to democratize the world": Interview with Griffin Bell.
170. The "American Creed": *American Exceptionalism* by Seymour Martin Lipset, p. 19.
171. "the most amazing thing": *Yankee from Georgia* by William Lee Miller, p. 214.
171. "He contributed to my private education": Letter to Ursula Niebuhr, August 1, 1976, PR 11, Box PR-47, WHCF-Subject File, Carter Library. Carter received Ursula Niebuhr and her son Christopher at the White House on July 18, 1979.
171. "Theology and politics are not": *Reinhold Niebuhr on Politics* edited by Harry R. Davis and Robert C. Good, p. vii.
172. "a contrite recognition": Ibid., p. 277.
172. As Burns Stanfield has written: *Faith and Politics in the Presidency of Jimmy Carter* by Burns F. Stanfield, Master of Divinity senior paper, Divinity School, Harvard University, May 2, 1988.
172. Historian Arthur Schlesinger: "Jimmy Carter, an Original," *New York Times,* Book Review, June 5, 1977, p. 38.
173. One day in the spring: Interview with Lillian Carter.
173. "I didn't dream": *Away from Home* by Lillian Carter and Gloria Carter Spann, p. 100.
174. "If he told one of the boys": Ibid., p. 44.
174. When Chip was in the eighth grade: Interview with Chip Carter.
174. During the 1966 campaign: Interview with Frank Moore.
175. During October 1967: Hefley and Hefley, *The Church that Produced a President,* p. 61.

176. "Jimmy and I": Ibid., p. 62.
176. On the drive back to Atlanta: *Jimmy Carter, in Search of the Great White House* by Betty Glad, p. 111.
176. Shortly before Thanksgiving 1968: Ibid., p. 63.
177. "How can a man": J. Carter, *Why Not the Best?*, p. 131.
178. "I was . . . overwhelmed": *Living Faith* by Jimmy Carter, p. 217.
179. He was not: Interview with Bebe Bahnson, December 7, 1993.

CHAPTER 13

180. The day after Carter lost: Interview with David Rabhan, October 10, 1992.
180. Shoob describes the Rabhans: Interview with Marvin Shoob.
181. "packed his [father's] head": Interview with Chip Carter.
181. Footnote-The elements: Interview with Terry Adamson, July 10, 1992.
182. "I'm not going to him": Interview with David Rabhan.
182. "David Rabhan knew": Interview with Jimmy Carter.
183. On the other hand: *Atlanta Constitution*, August 17, 1963.
183. Yet at the Southern Governors Conference: *Atlanta Constitution*, August 20, 1963.
183. Sanders testified before: *Atlanta Constitution*, August 20, 1963.
183. When Charlayne Hunter: *Atlanta Constitution*, September 3, 1963. See also *In My Place* by Charlayne Hunter-Gault.
184. "It was nigger, nigger, nigger": *Atlanta Constitution*, June 3, 1963.
184. "There is only one issue": Ibid., June 4, 1963.
184. In 1968: *Jimmy Carter, in Search of the Great White House* by Betty Glad, p. 127.
184. "one of the best job ratings": Randy Sanders, "The Sad Duty of Politics: Jimmy Carter and the Issue of Race in His 1970 Gubernatorial Campaign," *Georgia Historical Quarterly* 76, no. 3 (Fall 1992): 615.
187. "I was fascinated with him": Interview with Jack Watson, October 8, 1992.
187. Paul and Carol Muldawer: Telephone interview with Carol Muldawer, October 20, 1994.
188. "He could charm": Interview with Max Cleland, February 10, 1993.
188. "Sanders had alienated": Interview with Jimmy Carter, May 5, 1994.
188. "More important": "Electing a Governor in the Seventies" by James Clodfelter and William R. Hamilton in *American Governors in Behavioral Perspective* edited by Thad Beyle and J. Oliver Williams, p. 34.
189. "One of the standard speeches": *Jimmy Carter: A Character Portrait* by Bruce Mazlish and Edwin Diamond, p. 180.
189. "No one ever heard": Interview with Jimmy Carter, May 5, 1994.
190. "Cufflinks Carl": *Atlanta Constitution*, June 8, 1970.
190. "He pictured me": Sanders, "The Sad Duty of Politics," p. 622.
190. "Georgians never again want": *Atlanta Constitution*, April 4, 1970.
190. He repeatedly returned: *Atlanta Constitution*, June 14, 1970.
190. "Looks like Carl Sanders's basement": *Atlanta Journal*, April 11, 1970.
191. Carter presented to the press: *Atlanta Constitution*, August 27, 1970.
192. "overpromised and underdelivered": *Macon Telegraph*, August 28, 1970.
192. "a classic example": Editorial in the *Macon News*, reprinted in the *Atlanta Constitution*, September 3, 1970.
192. "I never criticized": Interview with Jimmy Carter, May 5, 1993.
192. "And another sheet of paper": *Atlanta Constitution*, June 14, 1970.
192. Several sources: Stephen Brill, "Jimmy Carter's Pathetic Lies," *Harpers*, March 1976, pp. 79–80; Sanders, "The Sad Duty of Politics," p. 627; Robert Coram and Remer Tyson, "The Loser Who Won," *Atlanta Magazine*, November 1970, pp. 41–49.
193. "nigger campaign": *Washington Post*, March 7, 1976.
193. "I think Sanders": Interview with Jimmy Carter, May 5, 1994.
195. "I used to dread to see": Mazlish and Diamond, *Jimmy Carter: A Character Portrait*, p. 145.
195. "Reg Murphy was fanatic": Interview with Jimmy Carter, May 5, 1994.
195. Already by June 16: *Atlanta Constitution*, June 16, 1970.
196. "The last time Carter": *Atlanta Constitution*, September 12, 1970.
196. "I don't think": *Atlanta Constitution*, September 13, 1970.
196. "Some folks say": *Atlanta Constitution*, September 23, 1970.
197. "I can win": *Atlanta Constitution*, September 14, 1970.

197. Years later: Interview with Jimmy Carter, May 5, 1993.
197. "Jimmy beat him": comment by J. B. Fuqua to the author, April 10, 1996.
199. "He [Carter] is going": *Atlanta Constitution*, January 7, 1971.
199. During the flight: Interview with David Rabhan. Carter confirms Rabhan's account.

CHAPTER 14

200. "It is a long way": *Addresses of Jimmy Carter, governor of Georgia, 1971–1975*, p. 79.
201. J. Paul Austin: Comments to the author by Andrew Young, May 14, 1994.
201. Carter denies: Interview with Jimmy Carter, West Georgia College, Georgia Political History Project, May 4, 1993.
201. Carter's friend, State Senator Lamar Plunkett: Interview with Connie Plunkett, February 9, 1995.
201. Kirbo declined: Interview with Charles Kirbo, October 12, 1976.
202. "Reorganization": *Atlanta Journal*, November 16, 1970.
203. "I was": Interview with Cloyd Hall, February 11, 1995.
203. "Sanders still had many friends": *Prelude to the Presidency* by Gary Fink, p. 24. Fink provides a detailed and comprehensive account of Carter's reorganization initiative.
204. "He has brought a standard": *Atlanta Constitution*, October 29, 1970.
204. Maddox had warned: *Atlanta Journal* and *Atlanta Constitution*, October 8, 1970.
204. "He's *really* mad": *Atlanta Journal* and *Atlanta Constitution*, November 8, 1970.
205. "Persons who engender": *Atlanta Constitution*, February 8, 1971.
206. "He doesn't understand": Interview with Hamilton Jordan, October 3, 1976.
206. "His personal curiosity": Interview with Bert Lance.
206. "He wasn't big": Interview with Cloyd Hall.
206. Finally, his friend Senator Ford Spinks: Interview with Bert Lance.
206. Early in the session: Interview with Max Cleland.
207. Carter read an article: Note to the author, October 6, 1994.
208. "with the people": Interview with Cloyd Hall.
208. "that experience": *First Lady from Plains* by Rosalynn Carter, p. 89.
209. In 1968, Carter had attended: *The Church that Produced a President* by James Hefley and Marti Hefley, p. 207.
210. "I finally got him": Interview with Bert Lance.
210. On one occasion: Interview with Cloyd Hall.
211. The account of events in Hancock County are taken from the author's interview with Cloyd Hall and stories in the *Atlanta Constitution* and the *Atlanta Journal* between September 1 and October 3, 1971.
212. In August 1973: Interview with Conley Ingram, September 30, 1993.
212. They differed, however, over the death penalty: Interview with Betty Gail Gunter. She retains a copy of the letter in her files.
212. "I do not know": Interview with Jimmy Carter, May 5, 1993.
213. On one occasion Jordan: The author was present during this interchange.
214. He called a press conference: *Atlanta Constitution*, April 3, 1971.
214. "I have no intention": Fink, *Prelude to the Presidency*, p. 56.
216. After Warren Fortson complained: Interview with Richard Harden, October 2, 1993.
216. "The Speaker is a horse trader": *Atlanta Constitution*, March 13, 1971.
217. He told newsmen: *Atlanta Constitution*, August 21, 1971.
217. "Unless he [Carter]: *Atlanta Constitution*, September 23, 1971.
218. "The choice we have": "State of the State," *Addresses of Jimmy Carter*, p. 119.
218. "Don't pay any attention to that smile": *Atlanta Constitution*, December 14, 1971.

CHAPTER 15

223. "At the time Jimmy and I discussed it": Interview with Charles Kirbo, October 12, 1976.
224. Running the McGovern campaign: Interview with Bebe Bahnson Smith, December 7, 1993.
225. Morris Dees: Dees and Carter had met several years earlier when they served together on a panel for the Jaycees to pick the "Outstanding Young Men in Georgia."
225. Wallace claimed: *George Wallace: American Populist* by Stephen Lesher, p. 490. Lesher suggests that Wallace felt Carter had not only agreed to nominate him but that if he stayed out of Georgia

during the primary season, Carter would ultimately commit his delegates to him. Both Carter and Powell concur on their airplane conversation.

226. "I encouraged it": Statement to the author, October 8, 1976.
228. "Carter's speech is interesting": *Jimmy Who?* by Leslie Wheeler, p. 95.
228. "I . . . asked Andy Young": Ibid., p. 97.
228. Morris Dees, an Alabaman: McGovern asked each of his top staff members to submit to him their three top choices for the vice presidential slot. Dees listed Jimmy Carter, Jimmy Carter, Jimmy Carter, but to no avail.
229. The headline: *Atlanta Journal,* July 12, 1972.
231. The same day, Carter invited: Interview with Julian Bond, September 26, 1994.
231. I prepared a ten-page memo: This document is on file at the Carter Library.
232. "Great presidents like Washington": *Why Not the Best?* by Jimmy Carter, p. 137.
232. "Jimmy knew a lot more": Interview with Rosalynn Carter, September 25, 1976.
235. Finally Carter asked Hamilton Jordan: Document on file at the Carter Library.
235. "Senator Talamdge met me there": Interview with Jimmy Carter, August 19, 1976.

CHAPTER 16

237. Rusk said: Interview with Jimmy Carter, August 19, 1976.
237. He used the opportunity: National Press Club, February 9, 1973, *Addresses of Jimmy Carter, governor of Georgia, 1971–1975.*
238. "I'll be damned": After writing on his place card, Andrew Young passed it to the author.
239. In Bonn, Carter met: Interview with Jimmy Carter, August 19, 1976.
240. "We had a remarkable visit": Ibid.
240. On April 13, 1973: This account was provided in a telephone interview with George Franklin, November 15, 1992.
241. Carter has often been accused: This account was provided to the author by Richard Holbrooke in April 1976.
241. "Everyone thought he": Interview with Jimmy Carter, May 5, 1994.
242. "Things that really concerned me": Ibid.
242. One of those in Kennedy's entourage: Hunter Thompson, "Jimmy Carter and the Great Leap of Faith," *Rolling Stone,* June 31, 1976, p. 52.
243. "He [Strauss] and I": Interview with Jimmy Carter, August 19, 1976.
243. "I did not intend": Ibid.
243. Jordan told friends: Interviews with Hamilton Jordan, October 10, 1976. Jordan had initially sought a job as a teaching assistant at Georgia State University.
244. "We asked every group": Interview with Jimmy Carter, August 19, 1976.
244. "Later we had a series": Ibid.
248. "Lester Maddox . . . as the last notable champion": *Washington Star,* September 19, 1974.
249. "Governor Carter is something new": *Richmond News Leader,* November 2, 1974.
251. In late 1973: Interview with Barbara Blum, July 10, 1992.
251. When invited to: Interview with Marvin Shoob.
251. In another meeting: Interview with Warren Fortson.
252. Robert Kuttner: *Washington Post,* November 18, 1974.

CHAPTER 17

254. A story in: *Kansas City Star,* December 7, 1974.
254. The creation of the Charter and Delegate: A detailed account of the efforts to democratize the party after the debacle of the 1968 convention is provided in *Jimmy Carter and the Politics of Frustration* by Garland Haas, pp. 11–15.
256. "It would convey": Memo from Charles Rafshoon to Jimmy Carter, September 1974.
256. In his speech: National Press Club, December 12, 1974, *Addresses of Jimmy Carter,* p. 286.
258. "I am planning to run for president": Ibid., p. 293.
258. How was he going to beat?: *San Francisco Examiner,* December 20, 1974.
260. "lack of success": Interview with Jimmy Carter, August 19, 1976.
260. "more of an outsider": Interview with Bert Lance.
261. Landon Butler had: Interview with Landon Butler, June 6, 1995.
261. "Again and again": *San Francisco Chronicle,* January 26, 1975.

262. "Democratic hopefuls gather": *San Francisco Chronicle,* January 28, 1975.
262. "He doesn't need California": Ibid.
262. "Edna and I just drove": Interview with Rosalynn Carter, September 25, 1976.
264. "I was embarrassed": Interview with Jimmy Carter, August 19, 1976.
265. "The [two] thing[s]": Interview with Pat Caddell, October 2, 1976.
266. Richard Harden, who had distinguished: Interview with Richard Harden.
267. The next morning: *Los Angeles Times,* May 25, 1975.

CHAPTER 18

272. according to Moore: Interview with Frank Moore.
273. Phil Walden, president of Capricorn Records: Interview with Cloyd Hall and Ellen Metsky interview with Tom Beard, October 2, 1976.
274. The other significant development: A detailed summary of his role in fund-raising for the Carter campaign was prepared for the author by Morris Dees in August 1976.
274. "one of the few bona fide geniuses": *Right from the Start* by Gary Hart, p. 42.
275. "Watson is absolutely": Interview with Morris Dees, July 25, 1976.
276. "Stuart Eizenstat is upset": Peter Bourne to Hamilton Jordan, September 10, 1975.
276. "He could have cared less": Interview with Bert Lance.
277. "On my first trip": Interview with Rosalynn Carter, September 25, 1976.
278. The turning point: *New York Times,* October 25, 1975.
279. He had written the foreword to a book: *Women in Need* by Jimmy Trussell and Bob Hatcher. He wrote: "Each chapter concludes with a series of suggestions for the reader who wants to accept a more active role in making sex education, contraceptives, abortion, and sterlization more available in our society. This book makes a plea to our citizens." Carter was clearly identifying himself with that plea.
279. He had given private encouragement: *Liberty and Sexuality* by David Garrow, pp. 422–431, describes the circumstances of the Georgia case.
281. "He [Carter] is": *Washington Star,* January 21, 1976.
281. "He was very happy": Interview with Greg Schneiders, June 10, 1976.
281. Ken Dean, president of WLBT-TV: Interview with Ken Dean, March 15, 1994.
282. While Carter's campaigning: Interview with Ken Hays, June 15, 1976.
283. "I know, but I hate to lose anything": Interview with Greg Schneiders.
283. The Oklahoma caucuses: Interview with Ken Hays.

CHAPTER 19

287. He stayed at Lucille's house: Interview with Lucille Kelly, July 10, 1976.
287. Chip and Caron, a teacher, moved to New Hampshire: Interview with Chip Carter.
288. Thus, the "Peanut Brigade" was born: *Jimmy Carter's Peanut Brigade* by Harold Isaacs and *Into the Jaws of Politics* by Genelle Jennings recount the adventures of these Georgians.
288. "Just wing it": Interview with John Pope.
289. "We were never behind": Interview with Landon Butler.
293. "I cannot let": Interview with Greg Schneiders.
294. "He wasn't angry": Interview with Pat Caddell.
294. "I think he was unhappier": Interview with Greg Schneiders.
294. Rosalynn's early trips: Interview with Connie Plunkett.
294. Because name recognition: Interview with Gerald Rafshoon.
296. proviso that if Nelson Rockefeller: *How Jimmy Won* by Kandy Stroud, p. 173.
297. "Religion is about life": Ibid.
299. "I remember we were": Interview with Pat Caddell.
300. "It's hard to believe": Ellen Metsky memo to Peter Bourne, July 6, 1976.
300. A *Washington Post* survey: *Washington Post,* March 11, 1976.
301. "James Earl Carter, Jr.": *Time,* March 16, 1976.
301. Joseph Kraft: *Washington Post,* March 11, 1976.
302. Plains remained his refuge: *Marathon* by Jules Witcover, p. 261.
302. "Almost everyone there": Comment to the author later that night.

CHAPTER 20

303. Wall warned Carter: Telephone interview with James Wall, October 16, 1995.
305. Because of the potentially explosive: Jules Witcover, "Profound Event," *Washington Post*, March 21, 1976.
305. "I was out on a back terrace": Interview with Jimmy Carter, August 19, 1976.
306. "Our politicians are expected": *The Culture of Disbelief* by Stephen Carter, p. 21.
306. "When I": Interview with Jimmy Carter, May 5, 1994.
306. "Relax, Eastern Establishment": *Washington Post*, March 28, 1976.
307. "The people in North Carolina": *Running for President* by Martin Schram, p. 113.
307. "The people have a right": Ibid.
307. "This party will deny us": Pat Caddell memo to Governor, Hamilton, Jody, Bob, Charles, Jerry, and Rick, March 24, 1976.
309. "Carter Upset by Udall": *Milwaukee Sentinel*, April 7, 1976.
311. "Candidates who make an attack": *Marathon*, by Julies Witcover, p. 293.
311. "I was primarily talking": Ibid., p. 294.
311. "Can a black central city": *New York Daily News*, April 4, 1976.
312. Schneiders handed Carter a note: Interview with Greg Schneiders.
312. "So what?": Witcover, *Marathon*, p. 305.
313 "Either he'll be repentant": Ibid.
314. Some people argued: Julian Bond, making clear that he had never been a Carter supporter, said that they were "remarks I'm accustomed to hear from Adolf Hitler."
314. Andrew Young said: Comments to the author by Andrew Young, May 14, 1994.
314. "If we destroy": *Washington Post*, April 11, 1976.
315. warehouse full of watermelons: Comment by Jordan to the author and others.
315. Even the venerated White House: *How Jimmy Won* by Kandy Stroud, p. 179.
315. "The trouble with you": Ibid., p. 180.
317. The following Thursday: *Washington Post*, April 30, 1976. Humphrey's dilemma in the campaign is well described in Robert Sam Anson, "The Very Last Hurrah of Hubert Horatio Humphrey," *New York Times Magazine*, March/April 1976.
318. "We noted two disturbing notes": Pat Caddell memo to Governor Carter, April 8, 1976.
318. Shrum's involvement: Witcover, *Marathon*, pp. 321–326.
319. It was a campaign: Interview with Dr. James Dunn, December 2, 1993.
321. Brown had sought: Witcover, *Marathon*, p. 333.
322. His assistant: Interview with Caroline Wellons, November 8, 1992.
322. "I made": Schram, *Running for President*, p. 172.
327. He had not deviated: Richard Reeves, "Is Jimmy Carter Good for the Jews," *New York* magazine, May 24, 1976.
327. "I'm going to tell you": Schram, *Running for President*, p. 215.
327. "This man Carter has fought": Witcover, *Marathon*, p. 349.

CHAPTER 21

329. "When you belong somewhere": Lucilla Lady Noble quoted in Sue Carpenter, "When Loss iIs Definitely More," *The Field Magazine*, June 1996, p. 57.
329. "There is no way": Interview with Jimmy Carter, August 29, 1976.
332. "I thought he was": *Keeping Faith* by Jimmy Carter, p. 37.
333. The following morning: *How Jimmy Won* by Kandy Stroud, p. 316.
334. "I consider this": Ibid., p. 326.
334. "This is": Ibid.
334. "I couldn't wait": *First Lady from Plains* by Rosalynn Carter, p. 130.
334. At 8:26 A.M.: Interview with Richard Moe, June 30, 1995.
335. "Call bright young people": *Electing Jimmy Carter* by Patrick Anderson, p. 45.
335. "I got hot at him": Interview with Gerald Rafshoon.
337. "Why did this smart": Anderson, *Electing Jimmy Carter*, p. 68.
338. "It was clash of cultures": Interview with Richard Moe.
340. "If we make a mistake": Anderson, *Electing Jimmy Carter*, p. 90.
341. "He went through": Interview with Max Cleland.
345. "She has always had": Interview with Jimmy Carter, October 8, 1976.
345. heated confrontation: Interview with Connie Plunkett.

346. "Committing adultery": "Jimmy, We Hardly Know Y'All," *Playboy*, November 1976, p. 136.
347. "The thing that is": Ibid.
348. "I am highly offended": *The Church that Produced a President* by James Hefley and Marti Hefley, p. 160.
348. "I had a million-and-a-half-dollar": Ibid., p. 208.
348. "The Republican Party was divided": Interview with Jimmy Carter, October 8, 1976.
350. "The only thing that ever": Ibid.
351. "I'll tell you why you can't": John Dean and Ralph Steadman, "Rituals of the Herd," *Rolling Stone*, October 7, 1976, p. 38.
353. "During our recent debate": Press conference, Albuquerque, New Mexico, October 7, 1976.
353. "President Ford's campaign aides": Transcript of Jack Anderson's statement, October 11, 1976.
354. "Well, you know my friends": Conversation with Jim Free, October 10, 1995.
355. "We owe him a lot": Ibid.

CHAPTER 22

357. "Preparing for the Presidency": Jack Watson memo to Charles Kirbo, May 11, 1976, Carter Library.
357. "I said to myself": Interview with Jack Watson.
359. On election night: Interview with Landon Butler.
359. "I went along": Interview with Jack Watson.
360. "I never have wanted": Interview with Jimmy Carter, White Burkett Miller Center, Jimmy Carter Project, Carter Library.
360. President Kennedy had preferred: *President Kennedy: Profile of Power* by Richard Reeves, p. 52.
361. "You would have had": Interview with Griffin Bell.
361. "They went on to cite": National Archives oral history interview with Frank Moore, Carter Library.
361. "I don't think": Interview with Jack Watson.
362. "He did not want": Interview with Bert Lance.
362. "Here I was from South Georgia": National Archives oral history, White Burkett Miller Center, Jimmy Carter Project, Carter Library.
362. "I felt completely free": Ibid.
363. "If I went into": Ibid.
364. "I can't underline": Interview with Esther Peterson, June 18, 1996.
365. He assigned him an office: Interview with Dick Moe.
366. "Senator Cranston asked me": Interview with Max Cleland.
366. "90 percent of the calls": National Archives exiting interview with Janet Pleasant, Carter Library.
366. "I think he [Carter] would": Interview with Griffin Bell.
366. "If Cyrus Vance": Robert Scheer, *Playboy*, November, 1976.
367. "We almost tried": Miller Center interview with Vernon Jordan.
367. On December 28: Interview with Jim Bishop, May 20, 1993.
368. several elder statesmen: When it was suggested to Carter that he meet with Clark Clifford he instead sent Kirbo to talk with him.
369. "Carter was not": Miller Center interview with Vernon Jordan.
369. However, his confirmation: Telephone interview with Ted Sorensen, October 12, 1996.
370. "His dealings with the legislature": Interview with Bert Lance.
370. "You don't mean to tell me": *Man of the House* by Thomas O'Neill, p. 360.
371. "As a matter of preference": Interview with Bert Lance.
372. "jealousy, sheer jealousy": Interview with Charles Kirbo, October 9, 1993.
373. "One that I still regret": *Keeping Faith* by Jimmy Carter, p. 79.
374. "In the presidency": Interview with Susan Clough, April 10, 1994.
374. He cut back on aid: *The Presidency of James Earl Carter* by Burton I. Kaufman, p. 29.
375. "There was never": J. Carter, *Keeping Faith*, p. 91.
376. "Our decision about energy": *Public Papers of President Jimmy Carter*, Book 1 (Washington, D.C.: U.S. Government Printing Office), p. 656.
378. "I'm completely satisfied": *The Church that Produced a President* by James Hefley and Marti Hefley, p. 267.

CHAPTER 23

382. Brzezinski would say: *Power and Principle* by Zbigniew Brzezinski, p. 156.
382. "Rosalynn and I": J. Carter, *Keeping Faith*, p. 273.
384. "I want to see our country": *Public Papers*, p. 382.
385. On May 22, 1977: Ibid., p. 954.
387. "One interesting element": Brown University Seminar on U.S./Soviet policy in the Carter Administration, Musgrove Plantation, Georgia, May 8, 1994.
387. "The most important issue": Ibid.
388. "It was always obvious": J. Carter, *Keeping Faith*, p. 212.
389. "The new proposal": Brown University seminar.
390. "Americans should recall": *The Cold War: A History* by Martin Walker, p. 45.
393. "I'll show point by G. d. point": Letter from John Wayne to Ronald Reagan, Box F.O. 3-1/Panama Canal, 10/13/77–10/27/77, Box F.O. 17, Carter Library.
393. Facing what seemed like: The successful campaign to ratify the treaties is described in the *Limits of Victory* by George Moffett, a participant in the process.
394. "So, very shortly after": Interview with Olaf Njolstad, October 20, 1993.
394. Despite his high rank: *Inside the League* by Scott Anderson and Jon Lee Anderson, pp. 150–158.
395. "I was convinced": J. Carter, *Keeping Faith*, p. 81.
395. "I felt I was confronted": Interview with Olaf Njolstad.
398. poet's corner at Westminster Abbey: Comments to the author, August 8, 1995.
398. "I never was": Interview with with Olaf Njolstad.

CHAPTER 24

401. "I would compare": Hamilton Jordan memo to the president, June 1977, Jordan Papers, Box 36, Carter Library.
402. The first Mark Siegel knew" Mark Siegel interview, June 15, 1995.
405. Mondale returned: *The Democrats' Dilemma* by Steven M. Gillon, p. 233.
406. Carter had to disabuse him: *Keeping Faith* by Jimmy Carter, p. 330.
406. The Carters had worked hard: Ibid., pp. 317–407, provides Carter's account of the negotiations and provides a unique account of the personal interactions among the three major players.
410. Carter even told Sadat: Comments by William Quandt to the author, September 27, 1996.

CHAPTER 25

414. "Bert, get out of here": *The Democrats' Dilemma* by Steven M. Gillon, p. 195.
414. Early that morning: *The Truth of the Matter* by Bert Lance, p. 138.
415. That night: *Keeping Faith* by Jimmy Carter, p. 135.
416. "We had a very heavy agenda": Interview with Jimmy Carter, Miller Center.
416. "insidious legal bribery": Ibid.
416. "The central question": Gillon, *The Democrats' Dilemma*, p. 191.
416. "I wish . . . you . . .": Interview with Jimmy Carter, Miller Center.
417. "At this point in history": Interview with Dick Moe.
417. Califano began to develop: *Governing America* by Joseph Califano, p. 89.
418. "As I sat in": Hamilton Jordan memo to the president, Jordan Papers, Box 34, Carter Library.
419. "Mondale's political experience": Interview with Dick Moe.
420. "If you propose": Hamilton Jordan memo to the president, (no date), Jordan Papers, Box 36, Carter Library.
420. "Carter thought": Gillon, *The Democrats' Dilemma*, p. 201.
420. "The worst thing you could say": Ibid.
420. "While Carter agreed with me": Ibid., p. 190.
420. "appreciated well before Fritz": Ibid., p. 199.
420. "Carter would sit in those meetings": Interview with Dick Moe.
421. "Would you rather": Comments by Rosalynn Carter to the author, August 1995.
421. "I never understood": Gillon, *The Democrats' Dilemma*, p. 192.
421. "You are making major": Hamilton Jordan memo to the president, (no date), Jordan Papers, Box 37, Carter Library.

421. "It is in your interests": Jody Powell memo to the president, September 28, 1977, Powell Papers, Box 39, Carter Library.

422. "I adopted": Interview with Jimmy Carter, Miller Center.

422. "An even more important consideration": Hamilton Jordan memo to the president, (no date), Jordan Papers, Box 37, Carter Library.

422. It was only when: In my own notes, dated October 19, 1977, I wrote: "Meeting with Carter and Jim McIntyre—Carter terribly tired and haggard—I was horrified and could not take my eyes off him." I was among those who talked to Rosalynn.

423. "First, we should have sought": Interview with Stu Eizenstat, Miller Center.

424. "It is impossible": Gerry Rafshoon memo to the president, September 1, 1978, Powell Papers, Box 50, Carter Library.

425. "Neither you nor I": Hamilton Jordan memo to the president, September 1977, Jordan Papers, Box 33, Carter Library.

428. In December 1977: *Washington Post,* December 18, 1977.

428. On February 12: *Washington Post,* February 12, 1978.

428. On February 19: *Washington Post,* February 19, 1978.

428. "When people talk": *Washington Post,* November 15, 1992.

428. "When it came to understanding": *Man of the House* by Thomas O'Neill, p. 355.

428. "Carter is by far": Comments by Katherine Graham to the author, June 1977.

429. "I think as far as intellect goes": Interview on the "Charlie Rose Show," June 10, 1994.

429. "I would like to take": President Jimmy Carter to Governor George Wallace, May 17, 1978, Susan Clough Papers, Carter Library.

430. "The reaction to the speech": *Washington Post,* December 10, 1978.

431. "It's a weird period for liberals": *Washington Post,* December 11, 1978.

CHAPTER 26

434. "We must move immediately": Address to the UAW Convention, May 17, 1977, Presidential Papers, Washington, D.C., Government Printing Office, vol. i, p. 887.

434. Eizenstat warned him: Stuart Eizenstat memo to the president, June 13, 1978, Eizenstat Papers, Box 242, Carter Library.

437. He rambled: *Keeping Faith* by Jimmy Carter, p. 414.

438. "My proposal was an act": Ibid., p. 416.

439. In it he listed: Memorandum to the file from Robert Lipshutz, March 13, 1979, Lipshutz Papers, Carter Library.

440. In a surprise television: *Power and Principle* by Zbigniew Brzezinski, p. 202–208.

442. Carter took with him: Pat Caddell, "Of Crisis and Opportunity," April 23, 1979, Powell Papers, Box 40, Carter Library.

442. "Everything in me": *The Democrats' Dilemma* by Steven Gillon, p. 261.

442. "I grew quite concerned": J. Carter, *Keeping Faith,* p. 115.

443. On May 27: Gillon, *The Democrats' Dilemma,* p. 259.

443. On May 29: According to Gillon, Mondale had contemplated several options, including telling Carter he did not want to run for a second term, allowing himself to be renominated then publicly declining, and even resigning the job as vice president as an act of principle.

443. "When I think back": Gillon, *The Democrats' Dilemma,* p. 263.

444. Over the next eight days: Elizabeth Drew, "A Reporter at Large," *New Yorker,* August 27, 1979, pp. 45–73, offers the most comprehensive account of the events at Camp David.

444. The value of those eight days: J. Carter, *Keeping Faith,* p. 118.

445. In an extensive memo: Hamilton Jordan memo to the president, July 15, 1979, Jordan Papers, Box 37, Carter Library. Reflecting Carter's continuing preoccupation with the energy problem, Jordan also noted, "if in the present atmosphere you can finally focus the attention of the American people on the root causes for the problem and point to the way out, you will have established a foundation on which we can build in the weeks and months ahead."

446. "He was quiet": Interview with Jimmy Carter, Miller Center.

447. he received a terse note from Brzezinski: Interview with Zbigniew Brzezinski.

447. "He has stuck with you": Hamilton Jordan memo to the president, (no date), Jordan Papers, Box 37, Carter Library.

448. Carter assigned Dick Moe: Interview with Dick Moe.

448. "most important of Jimmy Carter's presidency": *Secrets of the Temple* by William Greider, pp. 46–47.

449. A similar image: *The Other Side of the Story* by Jody Powell, pp. 104–105.
449. "He broke the Gordian knot": Interview with Stuart Eizenstat, Miller Center.
450. Carter received a letter: Letter to the president from Dr. Benjamin Mays, October 25, 1979, Susan Clough Papers, Carter Library.

CHAPTER 27

454. "Iran, because of the great": Presidential Papers, December 31, 1977, vol. ii, p. 2218, Carter Library.
455. "Does somebody have": *Democrats' Dilemma* by Steven Gillon, p. 271.
455. The U.S. ambassador: Conversations at different times with John Gunther Dean, Odeh Aburdene, and A. Robert Abboud.
455. As a result: Interview with Yasir Arafat, July 16, 1992.
457. "The failure to ratify": Interview with Hamilton Jordan, Miller Center.
458. In private, Mondale: Gillon, *Democrats' Dilemma*, p. 212.
459. "There were two White Houses": Interview with Hamilton Jordan, Miller Center.
460. "I'll guarantee you": Gillon, *Democrats' Dilemma*, p. 280.
463. Meeting with groups: Conversations with former *Time* correspondent Arlie Schardt.
464. Eizenstat provided him: Stuart Eizenstat memo to the president, attachment, October 7, 1980, Eizenstat Papers, Carter Library.
466. "The religious [Christian] community": Interview with Bert Lance.
467. "I hope you will give up": Interview with James Dunn.
467. "The president got in trouble": National Archives oral history interview with Robert Maddox, Carter Library.
468. "One of the real puzzles": Interview with James Dunn.
469. As early as late July: Interview with Bassam Abu Sharif, July 10, 1992, July 22, 1995, and October 30, 1996. Also interview with Yasir Arafat.
469. As Gary Sick: *The October Surprise* by Gary Sick provides meticulously detailed documentation of William Casey's elaborate scheme to prevent the release of the hostages by Iran. A congressional hearing subsequently failed to endorse Sick's conclusions, in part because they could not obtain testimony from the non-U.S. citizens involved, in part because of reluctance after several years to implicate individuals in a crime of such immense magnitude without definitive evidence, and, according to Sick and Brzezinski, because further investigation would potentially reveal far greater involvement of Israel than had already come to light.
469. "Jimmy Carter is finished": Sick, *The October Surprise*, p. 72.
473. In the waning days: *Crisis* by Hamilton Jordan describes the final year of the Carter administration and especially the handling of the hostage situation.

CHAPTER 28

474. "Everything that had ever": National Park Service oral history interview with Maxine Reese.
474. "As long as a man is trying": Letter to President Jimmy Carter from Admiral Hyman Rickover, December 10, 1980, Susan Clough Papers, Carter Library.
475. "As I leave office": Letter to Admiral Hyman Rickover from President Jimmy Carter, January 15, 1981, Susan Clough Papers. Carter Library.
475. "There was no way": *Everything to Gain* by Jimmy Carter and Rosalynn Carter, p. 9.
477. "What about Carter?": *Chicago Sun Times*, August 13, 1981.
477. "It's easy for the rich": *Atlanta Constitution,* September 24, 1981.
477. Carter still had detractors: *Washington Post,* October 5, 1981.
478. An editorial: *Washington Post,* October 14, 1981.
478. "How do you make": *New York Times,* October 9, 1981.
479. "The job of a responsible": *Richmond* (Kentucky) *Register,* October 15, 1981.
479. Finally: *Washington Post,* October 24, 1981.
479. "I know what we can do": J. Carter and R. Carter, *Everything to Gain,* p. 31.
481. "I never faced": Interview with James Brasher, November 30, 1993.
482. After Jimmy and Rosalynn: The Carters' involvement with Habitat for Humanity is described by Millard Fuller in his book *No More Shacks* as well as in J. Carter and R. Carter, *Everything to Gain,* pp. 98–103.

484. While in Peru, Bob Pastor: Interview with Robert Pastor, October 12, 1995, and letter to the author, November 21, 1996.
487. "We felt like students": J. Carter and R. Carter, *Everything to Gain*, p. 37.

CHAPTER 29

492. at Carter's suggestion: Interview with Yasir Arafat.
493. He had remained in Tehran: Interview with David Rabhan.
493. Under the auspices of: Interview with Robert Pastor.
494. "I can tell you": Conversation with Jimmy and Rosalynn Carter, August 1995.
495. "He temporarily suspends": Telephone interview with Ken Stein, June 15, 1996.
498. "I was supposed to be": Interview with Jack Crockford, February 13, 1995.
499. Although he received: The royalties from Jimmy Carter's children's book, *Talking Peace, A Vision for the Next Generation,* go to the Carter Center.
500. "Rosalynn and I": *New York Times,* October 26, 1991.
500. "The former president": *Atlanta Journal,* October 25, 1991.
501. "If you didn't go away": Ibid.
501. The Atlanta Project: *Atlanta Journal* and *Atlanta Constitution,* April 27, 1995.
504. At a press briefing: *Washington Post,* June 23, 1994.
505. Early on Saturday: Interview with Robert Pastor.

BIBLIOGRAPHY

Addresses of Jimmy Carter, governor of Georgia, 1971–1975, Atlanta, Georgia, Georgia Department of Archives and History, 1975.

Adler, Bill. *The Wit and Wisdom of Jimmy Carter.* Secaucus, N.J.: Citadel Press, 1977.

Agee, James. *Let Us Now Praise Famous Men.* Boston: Houghton Mifflin, 1941.

Anderson, Patrick. *Electing Jimmy Carter: The Campaign of 1976.* Baton Rouge: Louisiana State University Press, 1994.

Anderson, Scott, and Jon Lee Anderson. *Inside the League.* New York: Dodd Mead, 1986.

Baker, James T. *A Southern Baptist in the White House.* Philadelphia: Westminster Press, 1977.

Barber, James. *Presidential Character.* Englewoods Cliffs, N.J.: Prentice-Hall, 1992.

Barnette, Henlee H. *Clarence Jordan: Turning Dreams into Deeds.* Macon, Ga.: Smyth and Helwys, 1992.

Bartley, Numan V. *Jimmy Carter and the Politics of the New South.* St. Louis: Forum Press, 1979.

———. *The Creation of Modern Georgia.* Athens: University of Georgia Press, 1983.

———. *The New South, 1945–1980.* Baton Rouge: Louisiana State University Press, 1995.

Bass, Jack, and Walter DeVries. *The Transformation of Southern Politics.* New York: Basic Books, 1976.

Beyle, Thad L., and J. Oliver Williams, eds. *The American Governors in Behavioral Perspective.* New York: Harper and Row, 1972.

Bingham, June. *Courage to Change: An Introduction to the Life and Thought of Reinhold Niebuhr.* Lanham, Md.: University Press of America, 1973.

Boehme, Ron, and Rus Walton. *What About Jimmy Carter?* Washington, D.C.: Third Century Publishers, 1976.

Brzezinski, Zbigniew K., *Power and Principle: Memoirs of the National Security Advisor.* New York: Farrar, Straus, Giroux, 1985.

Burke, Richard E. *The Senator: My Ten Years with Ted Kennedy.* New York: St. Martin's Press, 1992.

Caldwell, Dan. *The Dynamics of Domestic Politics and Arms Control.* Columbia: University of South Carolina Press, 1991.

Califano, Joseph A. *Governing America.* New York: Simon and Schuster, 1981.

Callaghan, Dorothy. *Jimmy, the Story of the Young Jimmy Carter.* Garden City, N.Y.: Doubleday, 1979.

Carter, Billy, and Sybil Carter. *Billy.* Newport, R.I.: Edgehill Publications, 1989.

Carter, Hugh A., Sr. *Cousin Beedie and Cousin Hot.* Englewood Cliffs, N.J.: Prentice-Hall, 1978.

Carter, Jimmy. *Why Not the Best?* Nashville: Broadman Press, 1975.

———. *A Government as Good as Its People.* New York: Simon and Schuster, 1978.

———. *Keeping the Faith: Memoirs of a President.* New York: Bantam Books, 1982.

———. *The Blood of Abraham.* Boston: Houghton Mifflin, 1986.

———. *An Outdoor Journal.* New York: Bantam Books, 1988.

———. *Turning Point.* New York: Times Books, 1992.

———. *Talking Peace: A Vision for the Next Generation.* New York: Dutton Children's Books. 1993.

———. *Always a Reckoning and Other Poems.* New York: Times Books, 1995.

———. *Living Faith.* New York: Times Books, 1996.

Carter, Jimmy, and Amy Carter. *The Little Baby Snoogle-Fleejer.* New York: Times Books, 1996.

Carter, Jimmy, and Rosalynn Carter. *Everything to Gain.* New York: Random House, 1987.

Carter, Lillian, and Gloria Carter Spann. *Away from Home.* New York: Simon and Schuster, 1977.

Carter, Rosalynn S. *First Lady from Plains.* New York: Ballantine Books, 1984.

Carter, Stephen L. *The Culture of Disbelief.* New York: Basic Books, 1993.

Cleland, Max. *Strong at the Broken Places.* Marietta, Ga.: Cherokee Publishing Company, 1980.

Coleman, Kenneth. *A History of Georgia.* Athens: University of Georgia, 1991.

Corcoran, John H., Jr. *True Grits.* New York: Dell Publishing, 1977.

Currer-Briggs, N. *The Carters of Virginia.* Chichester, Engl.: Phillimore, 1979.

Davis, Harry R., and Robert C. Good. *Reinhold Niebuhr on Politics*. New York: Scribners, 1960.

Davis, Robert I. *The Third 1820 Land Lottery of Georgia*. Easley, S.C.: Southern Historical Press, 1979.

Davis, Robert I., and Silas E. Lucas. *The Georgia Land Lottery Papers 1805–1914*. Easley, S.C.: Southern Historical Press, 1979.

deMause, Lloyd, and Henry Ebel, eds. *Jimmy Carter and American Fantasy: Psychohistorical Explorations*. New York: Two Continents, 1977.

Fallows, James M. *A Capitol and a New President*. Bloomington: Indiana University Press, 1979.

Fink, Gary M. *Prelude to the Presidency*. Westport, Conn.: Greenwood Press, 1980.

Fischer, David H. *Albion's Seed*. New York: Oxford University Press, 1989.

Fuller, Millard. *No More Shacks: The Daring Vision of Habitat for Humanity*. Waco, Tex.: Word Books, 1986.

Garrow, David. *Liberty and Sexuality*. New York: Macmillan, 1994.

Gates, Robert. *From the Shadows: The Ultimate Insider's Story of Five Presidents and How They Won the Cold War*. New York: Simon and Schuster, 1996.

Gaver, Jessyca R. *The Faith of Jimmy Carter*. New York: Manor Books, 1977.

Germond, Jack, and Jules Witcover. *Blue Smoke and Mirrors*. New York: Viking, 1981.

Gillon, Steven, M. *The Democrats' Dilemma: Walter F. Mondale and the Liberal Legacy*. New York: Columbia University Press, 1992.

Glad, Betty. *Jimmy Carter, in Search of the Great White House*. New York: Norton, 1980.

Greider, William. *Secrets of the Temple*. New York: Simon and Schuster, 1987.

Grover, William F. *The President as Prisoner*. Albany: State University of New York, 1989.

Gulliver, Hal. *A Friendly Tongue*. Macon, Ga.: Mercer University Press, 1984.

Haas, Garland A. *Jimmy Carter and the Politics of Frustration*. Jefferson, N.C.: McFarland and Co., 1992.

Hargrove, Erwin C. *Jimmy Carter as President: Leadership and the Politics of the Public Good*. Baton Rouge: Louisiana State University Press, 1988.

Hart, Gary. *Right from the Start*. New York: Quadrangle, 1973.

Hefley, James, and Marti Hefley. *The Church that Produced a President*. New York: Wyden Books, 1977.

Hertsgaard, Mark. *On Bended Knee*. New York: Farrar, Straus, Giroux, 1988.

Hodgson, Godfrey. *All Things to All Men*. New York: Simon and Schuster, 1980.

Humphrey, R. *The Carters of King's Langley*. King's Langley, England: John Bourne, 1978.

Hunter, Floyd. *Community Power Structure*. Chapel Hill: University of North Carolina Press, 1953.

Hunter-Gault, Charlayne. *In My Place*. New York: Farrar, Straus, Giroux, 1992.

Hyatt, Richard. *The Carters of Plains*. Huntsville, Ala.: Strode Publishers, 1977.

Isaacs, Harold. *Jimmy Carter's Peanut Brigade*. Dallas, Tex.: Taylor Publishing Company, 1977.

Jennings, Genelle. *Into the Jaws of Politics: The Charge of the Peanut Brigade*. Huntsville, Ala.: Strode Publishers, 1979.

Johnson, Haynes B. *In the Absence of Power*. New York: Viking Press, 1980.

Jones, Charles O. *The Trusteeship Presidency*. Baton Rouge: University of Louisiana Press, 1988.

Jordan, Hamilton. *Crisis: The Last Year of the Carter Presidency*. New York: G. P. Putnam's Sons, 1982.

Karp, Walter. *Liberty Under Siege*. New York: Franklin Square Press, 1993.

Kaufman, Burton I. *The Presidency of James Earl Carter*. Lawrence: University Press of Kansas, 1993.

Key, V. O. *Southern Politics in State and Nation*. New York: Knopf, 1949.

King, Mary E. *Freedom Song*. New York: Morrow, 1987.

Kraus, S., ed. *The Great Debates: Carter vs Ford*. Bloomington: University of Indiana Press, 1979.

Kucharsky, David. *The Man from Plains*. New York: Harper and Row, 1976.

Lake, Anthony. *Third World Radical Regimes: U.S. Policy Under Carter and Reagan*. New York: Foreign Policy Association, 1985.

Lance, Bert. *The Truth of the Matter*. New York: Summit Books, 1991.

Lance, LaBelle. *This, Too, Shall Pass*. Chappaqua, N.Y.: Christian Herald Books, 1978.

Langford, Edna, and Linda Maddox. *Rosalynn: Friend and First Lady*. Old Tappan, N.J.: Fleming H. Revell Company, 1980.

Lankevich, George J., ed. *Jimmy Carter, 1924– : Chronology, Documents, Bibliographic Aids*. Dobbs Ferry, N.Y.: Oceana, 1981.

Lasky, Victor. *Jimmy Carter, the Man and the Myth*. New York: R. Marek, 1979.

Lee, Dallas. *The Cotton Patch Evidence*. New York: Harper and Row, 1971.

Lesher, Stephen. *George Wallace: American Populist*. New York: Addison-Wesley, 1993.

Lewinson, Paul. *Race, Class and Poverty*. New York: The Universal Library, Grosset and Dunlap, 1965.

Lewis, Finlay. *Mondale: Portrait of an American Politician*. New York: Harper and Row, 1984.

Linowitz, Sol. *The Making of a Public Man*. Boston: Little, Brown, 1985.

Lipset, Seymour Martin. *American Exceptionalism*. New York: Norton, 1996.

Lynn, Laurence E., and David deF. Whitman. *The President as Policy Maker: Jimmy Carter and Welfare Reform*. Philadelphia: Temple University Press, 1981.

Maddox, Robert L. *Preacher at the White House*. Nashville: Broadman Press, 1984.

Mazlish, Bruce, and Edwin Diamond. *Jimmy Carter: A Character Portrait*. New York: Simon and Schuster, 1979.

McLaurin, Melton A. *Separate Pasts: Growing Up White in the Segregated South*. Athens: Brown Thrasher Books, University of Georgia Press, 1987.

McMorrow, Fred. *Jimmy: The Candidacy of Carter*. New York: Strawberry Hill, Whirlwind Book Co., 1976.

Miller, William L. *Yankee from Georgia: The Emergence of Jimmy Carter*. New York: Times Books, 1978.

Moens, Alexander. *Foreign Policy under Carter*. Boulder, Colo.: Westview Press, 1990.

Moffett, George D. *The Limits of Victory*. Ithaca: Cornell University Press, 1985.

Mollenhoff, Clark R. *The President Who Failed*. New York: Macmillan, 1980.

Muravchik, Joshua. *The Uncertain Crusade: Jimmy Carter and the Dilemmas of Human Rights*. Lanham, Md.: Hamilton Press, 1986.

Neyland, James. *The Carter Family Scrapbook*. New York: Grosset and Dunlap, 1977.

Niebuhr, Reinhold. *Justice and Mercy*, edited by Ursula Niebuhr. New York: Harper and Row, 1974.

Nielsen, Niels C. *The Religion of President Carter*. Nashville: T. Nelson, 1977.

Norton, Howard. *Rosalynn*. Plainfield, N.J.: Logos International, 1977.

Norton, Howard, and Bob Slosser. *The Miracle of Jimmy Carter*. Plainfield, N.J.: Logos International, 1976.

O'Neill, Thomas P., Jr. *Man of the House*. New York: St. Martin's Press, 1988.

Orman, John. *Comparing Presidential Behavior*. New York: Greenwood Press, 1987.

Pippert, Wesley, G. *The Spiritual Journey of Jimmy Carter*. New York: Macmillan, 1978.

Pomerantz, Gary M. *Where Peachtree Meets Sweet Auburn*. New York: Scribner, 1996.

Powell, Jody. *The Other Side of the Story*. New York: Morrow, 1984.

Raines, Howell. *Fly Fishing Through the Midlife Crisis*. New York: Morrow, 1993.

Reeves, Richard. *President Kennedy: Profile of Power*. New York: Simon and Schuster, 1993.

Rozell, Mark J. *The Press and the Carter Presidency*. Boulder, Colo.: Westview Press, 1989.

Schram, Martin. *Running for President*. New York: Pocket Books, 1976.

Shogan, Robert. *Promises to Keep: Carter's First Hundred Days*. New York: Crowell, 1977.

———. *The Riddle of Power: Presidential Leadership from Truman to Bush*. New York: Dutton, 1991.

Shoup, Laurence H. *The Carter Presidency and Beyond*. Palo Alto, Calif.: Ramparts Press, 1980.

Sick, Gary. *The October Surprise: America's Hostages in Iran and the Election of Ronald Reagan*. New York: Times Books, 1991.

Simmons, Dawn L. *Rosalynn Carter: Her Life Story*. New York: F. Fell, 1979.

Sitkoff, Harvard. *The Struggle for Black Equality, 1954–1980*. New York: Hill and Wang, 1993.

Smith, Gaddis. *Morality, Reason, and Power*. New York: Hill and Wang, 1986.

Spencer, Donald S. *The Carter Implosion*. New York: Praeger, 1988.

St. John, Jeffrey. *Jimmy Carter's Betrayal of the South*. Ottawa, Ill.: Green Hill Publishers, 1976.

Stapleton, Ruth Carter. *The Gift of Inner Healing*. Waco, Tex.: Word Books, 1976.

———. *Brother Billy*. New York: Harper and Row, 1978.

Stroud, Kandy. *How Jimmy Won*. New York: Morrow, 1977.

Thomas, Dylan. *Collected Poems 1934–1953*. London: Everyman, J. M. Dent, 1993.

Thomas, Sunny. *Jimmy Carter: From Peanuts to Presidency*. Cornwall, Ont.: Vesta, 1978.

Thompson, Kenneth W., ed. *The Carter Presidency*. Miller Center, Charlottesville: University of Virginia Press, 1990.

Thornton, Richard C. *The Carter Years: Toward a New Global Order*. New York: Paragon House Publishers, 1991.

Tindall, George B. *The Disruption of the Solid South*. Athens: University of Georgia Press, 1972.

Trussell, James, and Robert Hatcher. *Women in Need*. New York: Macmillan, 1972.

Turner, Robert, W. *"I'll Never Lie to You" Jimmy Carter in His Own Words*. New York: Ballantine Books, 1976.

Turner, Stansfield. *Secrecy and Democracy: The CIA in Transition*. Boston: Houghton Mifflin, 1985.

Vance, Cyrus R. *Hard Choices*. New York: Simon and Schuster, 1983.

Veale, Frank H. *Carter, a Son of Georgia*. Cairo, Ga.: Veale, 1977.

Walker, Barbara. *The Picture Life of Jimmy Carter*. New York: Watts, 1977.

Walker, Martin. *The Cold War: A History*. New York: Henry Holt, 1996.

Walters, Beth M. *History of Plains, Georgia, 1885–1985*. Americus, Ga.: Gammage Print Shop, 1985.

Walton, Hanes. *The Native Son Presidential Candidate.* New York: Praeger, 1992.

Wheeler, Leslie. *Jimmy Who?: An Examination of Presidential Candidate Jimmy Carter.* Woodbury, N.Y.: Barron's Educational Series Inc., 1976.

Williford, William B. *Americus Through the Years.* Atlanta: Cherokee Publishing Co., 1975.

Wills, Gary. *Under God: Religion and American Politics.* New York: Simon and Schuster, 1990.

Witcover, Jules. *Marathon.* New York: Simon and Schuster, 1977.

Woodward, Comer V. *Tom Watson: Agrarian Rebel.* Savannah, Ga.: Beehive, 1973.

Wooten, James. *Dasher: The Roots and the Rising of Jimmy Carter.* New York: Summit Books, 1978.

Young, Andrew. *A Way Out of No Way.* Nashville: T. Nelson, 1994.

INDEX